W9-BGA-622

THE PACIFIC PROVINCE

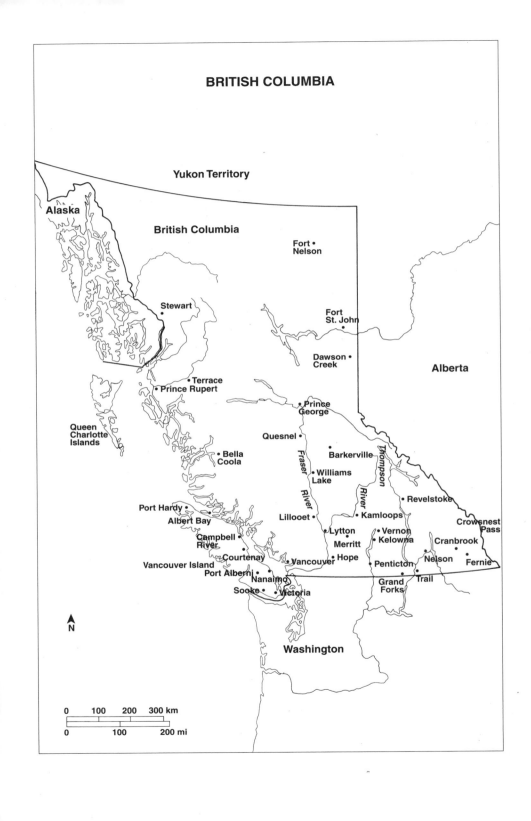

BRITISH COLUMBIA

Yukon Territory

Alaska

British Columbia

Fort
Nelson

Stewart

Fort
St. John

Dawson
Creek

Alberta

Terrace
Prince Rupert

Prince
George

Queen
Charlotte
Islands

Quesnel

Bella
Coola

Barkerville

Williams
Lake

Fraser River

Thompson River

Revelstoke

Port Hardy

Albert Bay

Lillooet

Kamloops

Crowsnest
Pass

Campbell
River

Lytton

Merritt

Vernon
Kelowna

Cranbrook

Courtenay

Hope

Nelson

Fernie

Vancouver Island

Port Alberni

Vancouver

Penticton

Nanaimo

Sooke

Victoria

Grand
Forks

Trail

N

Washington

0   100   200   300 km

0   100   200 mi

THE PACIFIC PROVINCE

A HISTORY OF BRITISH COLUMBIA

HUGH J. M. JOHNSTON
GENERAL EDITOR

Douglas & McIntyre
Vancouver/Toronto

96 97 98 99 00 5 4 3 2 1

Douglas & McIntyre
1615 Venables Street
Vancouver, British Columbia
V5L 2H1

Canadian Cataloguing in Publication Data

Main entry under title:

The Pacific province

ISBN 1-55054-193-5

1. British Columbia—History. I. Johnston, H. J. M. (Hugh J. M.), 1939–
FC3811.P32 1996   971.1   C95-911223-5
F1088.P32 1996

Editing by Margaret Campbell
Cover photograph by Graham Osborne
Cover design by Peggy Heath
Text design and typesetting by Fiona MacGregor
Index by Annette Lorek
Printed and bound in Canada by Friesens
Printed on acid-free paper

The publisher gratefully acknowledges the assistance of the Canada Council and of the British Columbia Ministry of Tourism, Small Business and Culture for its publishing programs.

Financially assisted by the Province of British Columbia through the British Columbia Heritage Trust.

CONTENTS

PREFACE

This examination of British Columbia's past, drawing on the recent explosion of specialized articles and books on the subject as well as on older studies and on archival and census materials, is the work of current and former faculty and graduate students from Simon Fraser University. It has been a team project in the sense that, while the authorship of each chapter belongs to one or two people, the contributors as a group determined the general framework—a thematic approach within broad periods—and discussed, critiqued and suggested changes to each other's drafts. What we were seeking was the best of two worlds—individuality and teamwork. We wanted to give reasonably free reign to chapter authors, taking advantage of their focus and expertise without losing the direction and balance of the whole. The project started under the leadership of Robin Fisher, who guided us through a successful application for funding from Simon Fraser University, and then nudged contributors along until nearly everyone had completed a first or second draft. After he left to become the first Chair of the Department of History and then Acting Dean of Arts and Science at the University of Northern British Columbia, the task of chasing down the last chapters and editing the manuscript fell to me. The final result, however, remains true to the original conception.

Each chapter reflects the perspective, style and concerns of its author and each author stands behind his or her contribution. Throughout the process of research and writing, we pushed each other to see the book as a totality and to make changes for the sake of coverage and consistency. Nonetheless, this is not history by committee or according to a predetermined formula and it contains differences in emphasis from one chapter to another. For example, in discussing critical junctures in the history of Native people or the importance of resource-based industries, contributors have not all underscored the same points. One can still see that they are dealing with a common history within a shared framework.

As a team, we set ourselves the challenge of illustrating the particular features of a province that finds itself at a Canadian extremity, socially and culturally as well as geographically. Despite the antiquity of its Native culture, British Columbia has the perpetual appearance of a very new place. The explanation lies in the long isolation of the North Pacific region, followed by rapid industrial and technological advance. For Europeans, the northwest coast of North America lay at the end of the world. It was—as Professor Barry Gough has observed—the last temperate coastline that Europeans mapped. They did so at the dawn of the industrial age and British Columbia has developed subsequently as the expression of the industrial world's capacity to invade and exploit raw nature. This history has given the province a modern society with a frontier outlook and setting.

In eastern Canada many towns and villages achieved a staid and rooted look within a couple of generations, but that does not seem to have happened to British Columbia: the population has been too transient, the influx of immigrants too continuous, and the racial and ethnic mix too diverse. From the moment in the eighteenth century when outsiders first saw possibilities here, British Columbia has attracted a restless population of opportunists. This population has thrived in a speculative atmosphere encouraged by the promise of continuing economic expansion in a comparatively unregulated environment. Inevitably, the cultural point of reference for many British Columbians has been located outside the province. And, because people came by many routes from many parts of the globe, their common sense of themselves has not developed very far.

In the post-Confederation era, the absence of a single dominant industry—such as farming—has distinguished British Columbia from much of the rest of the country. British Columbia's extractive industries, which have required large-scale enterprise and the close co-operation of government and business, have afforded few openings for small, independent operators—and fewer as time has passed. As a consequence, the lines between capital and labour have been clearly drawn, though the industrial complexity of the province has distributed employment across several major economic sectors and tended to fragment the working class.

Although British Columbia's industrial diversity has given it a generally buoyant economy that has attracted heavy immigration for more than a century with few extended interruptions, economic growth has depended on immigrant labour in lower-paying jobs. The benefits of growth have not been evenly distributed and because employers persistently recruited unskilled labour from specific ethnic and racial groups, the province took shape as a society in which ethnic background and socio-economic status were closely associated—a "vertical mosaic" as Professor Porter has called it. Porter, of course, applied his term to all of Canada, but we can see British Columbia as a prime illustration—a province in which this aspect of Canadian social development has been most evident.

The province's relationship to the rest of the country has waxed and waned over time. The sharp contrast that long ago existed among Native people, between the cultures of the coast and those of the Interior, has perpetuated itself in the modern province in the alternating pull of the continent and the Pacific. Over the past two hundred years, the main impetus for change has come from the Atlantic world—from Britain, eastern Canada, and the eastern United States. In the late eighteenth and through much of the nineteenth century, this still meant a Pacific orientation for European enterprise on the northwest coast because the main connection back to the North Atlantic was by ocean routes. In the railway age, the overland route became primary. And with the railway the Canadianization of British Columbia began—a process that has proceeded unevenly but unmistakably until recently.

In January of 1922, when British Columbians began to drive on the right-hand side of the road instead of the left, they were giving up one of the last eccentricities of a British outpost on the Pacific and recognizing their physical attachment to Canada and the rest of the continent. Now, more than seventy years later, the pendulum is moving in the other direction. As the twentieth century draws to a close, the Pacific looms larger in the minds of British Columbians who are more conscious than ever before of opportunities in Asia.

Any account of British Columbia's past must pull us in many directions. Archaeological evidence takes the human story back thousands of years. The historical period, on the other hand, is short, and the diverse and frontier character of the province has left an uneven record that makes the historian's task difficult. This book could not have been completed without the insights, enterprise and skills of the following researchers: Robin Anderson, William Burrill, Ira Chaikin, Paul Claremont, Douglas Cruikshank, Steve Hicks, Siân Johnston, Mary Ellen Kelm, Ross Mackenzie, Kevin O'Donnell, Peter Parker, and David Roth. They were all vital participants in the project and share credit for the best features of the result.

I must also say that a book in which many people have had a hand can present challenges to the editor, and in this respect I wish to acknowledge the invaluable work of Margaret Campbell in the final editing of the manuscript.

H. J.

PART I

Prehistory

Chapter 1
THE FIRST BRITISH COLUMBIANS
R. L. Carlson

There was a time when no one could have lived in what is now British Columbia. Mile-thick glaciers covered the land, and icebergs spawned by seacliffs of glacial ice rendered the coast both uninhabitable and impassable.[1] Between 15,000 and 14,000 years ago the glaciers began to melt, and by 12,000 years ago peoples migrating from Alaska could have followed the coast to the Strait of Juan de Fuca and beyond, or reached the Peace River country in the northeastern interior by traveling south from ice-free regions in the Yukon. What was required was an Arctic survival kit and a reason for moving into new and unfamiliar territory. The Americas were far removed from the early centres of human biological and cultural evolution in Africa and Asia, and were reached by immigrants from Siberia only after social and technological skills had advanced to the point that livelihood could be wrested from the cold Arctic environment. Even though this point was reached in northeast Asia sometime between 40,000 and 25,000 years ago, there is still no good evidence for human presence in the Americas before 12,000 to 14,000 years ago. Claims of tools and human bones dating to earlier periods have been shown to be based on the identification of naturally fractured stones or bones as artifacts, on invalid dating or experimental dating techniques, or on erroneous assumptions regarding the age of genuine tools. Fanciful models of early voyages across the Atlantic have been made, but are insupportable until the time of the Vikings in the tenth century A.D., long after the entire New World was inhabited. Trans-Pacific voyages have also been postulated, but have no archaeological support until the Edo Period (A.D. 1604-1868) when policies of Japan's government were causative factors in the drifting of Japanese junks to the Pacific coast.[2] The only feasible route by which people could have reached North and South America before the invention of large sea-going ships is from Siberia through Alaska and Canada and thence south. The genetic similarity between New World aborigines and the native peoples of northeast Asia is clear evidence of the close biological relationship between these peoples.[3]

In Beringia, the region on both sides of Bering Strait between Alaska and Siberia including the Bering platform (which is now under water), glaciers did not form because there was too little precipitation to permit the build up of large masses of ice. In addition, the remoteness and the cold, harsh environment of Beringia served as a filter that permitted only a few successful Arctic hunters to pass through. Nonetheless, by 14,500 years ago, there is meagre evidence of hunters at Bluefish Cave in the Yukon, north of the glaciated regions, and by 11,000 years ago, people had reached the southern tip of South America.[4] In the interval between these two dates, glaciers had begun to melt and passages to open.

There are two feasible routes by which early peoples could have come south from Beringia: one passes along the eastern flanks of the Rocky Mountains above the morass of glacial meltwater lakes that filled the lowlands, and thence out onto the prairies and south, and a second follows the coast of Alaska and British Columbia. Advocates of the interior route argue that both the Siberian peoples of about 15,000 years ago and the earliest known peoples in North America were not fisher folk but hunters of the large ice-age mammals, particularly mammoth, who were funneled south through an ice-free corridor that joined the unglaciated parts of the Yukon with the plains of Alberta. Advocates of the coastal route argue that food was more plentiful along the coast and that peoples who had adapted to the coastal margins of Beringia and who had knowledge of skin-covered boats and marine subsistence could easily have moved south along the coast.

There is much logic in favour of both routes, but for several good reasons, little evidence. Initial populations would have necessarily been very small in order to sustain themselves in the resource-limited, ice-free but frigid refuges of eastern Beringia prior to deglaciation, and archaeological evidence of small groups of migratory hunters and gatherers is difficult to discover. On the coast, erosion of the shoreline and the changing land and sea levels offer even greater barriers to discovery. The sea level rose as glacial meltwater flooded ice-age shorelines, but when relieved of the ponderous weight of glacial ice, like a jack-in-the-box the land also rose. These events were neither synchronous nor of equal magnitude. Most of the coastline exposed earlier than 10,000 years ago is now under water.[5]

There is no written record of the indigenous cultures of British Columbia before the time of European contact. Evidence of their occupation is contained in the archaeological record of sites and artifacts found throughout the province. The archaeological evidence to date indicates that this pre-contact period can be conceptualized as a time in which a number of cultures or cultural traditions were growing, changing, and influencing each other over a 10,500-year time span subdivided into three periods: Early, Middle, and Late.

"Culture" and "cultural tradition" both refer to the customary behaviour of different peoples. There are indeed some cultural universals, but it is the differences that permit archaeologists to define separate cultures and cultural traditions on the basis of archaeological data. The two terms are similar in meaning:

the term "culture" implies a localized and temporally shorter expression of a more enduring and geographically widespread "cultural tradition." Pre-contact cultures and cultural traditions are defined on the basis of first, the way of life indicated by the environment and by subsistence remains found in archaeological sites, and second, by the uniqueness of particular types and styles of artifacts. Assemblages that contain the same or similar types of artifacts are considered to belong to the same culture or cultural tradition providing they are found in a continuous distribution in time and space and other aspects of the assemblages are not radically different. The closer the similarities in forms and fabrication techniques of the tools and the propinquity of the assemblages in time and space, the greater the probability of ethnic congruity of the people who made them.

The model of growth and change in the cultures of the first British Columbians that is presented in this chapter is based on inferences drawn from many archaeological and paleoenvironmental facts as well as from what is known of the processes and events in the development of human culture throughout the world. A map showing the locations of important archaeological sites in British Columbia is shown in Map 1.

THE EARLY PERIOD: 10,500 TO 5,000 YEARS AGO

In spite of the fact that migrant peoples from Beringia could have reached British Columbia 14,000 to 12,000 years ago, archaeological remains of this period have not yet been found. The first traces of human culture begin 10,500 years ago. By 10,000 years ago there is evidence for human presence along both interior and coastal routes. By 9,000 years ago, different styles of stone spear points and other stone tools have made their appearance in different regions of the province. These tools are similar in that they were all made by flaking stone, an ancient technique going back to the very beginnings of human technology, but differ in some of the specific flaking techniques as well as in the shapes and sizes of artifacts, particularly of the stone points made to tip spears. Customs in stone-tool making differed in the different regions of the province and it is these regional clusters of similar stone tools that form the basis for the definition of the cultural traditions of the Early Period.

In the period between 10,500 and 8,500 years ago, there is evidence for five cultural traditions in British Columbia: the Fluted Point Tradition, the Plano Tradition, the Intermontane Stemmed Point Tradition, the Pebble Tool Tradition, and the Microblade Tradition. The term "point" used as part of the names of two of these traditions means "projectile point," whereas "microblade" and "pebble tool" refer to other kinds of stone tools. Some of these projectile points served as the tips of spears used with the spear thrower, a weapon for extending the arm and vastly improving the penetrating power of the spear, which had previously been invented in the Old World. Others may have been used to tip thrusting spears or as knives. The bow and arrow is unknown until the Late Period. Although the difference between cultural traditions is indicated by differences in the forms of stone tools, it is probable that there were also other differences.[6]

The Fluted Point Tradition

A distinctive style of spear point called a "fluted point" has been found in sites in the northeast corner of British Columbia, east of the Rocky Mountains in what was part of the ice-free corridor. This type of artifact is typical of the Fluted Point Tradition, the most widespread early cultural tradition in the entire New World. Its hallmark is a large chipped-stone spear point with a distinctive attribute: its concave base has been thinned by a process known as fluting, which consists of the removal of one or more vertical channel flakes from both faces of the point. The purpose of fluting was to facilitate attaching—or hafting—the point to the end of the spear shaft. The Fluted Point Tradition ranges in age from at least 11,500 to 10,000 years ago. Its earliest expression is a culture called Clovis, which has been dated between 11,200 and 10,800 years ago at sites in the plains and southwest regions of the United States. Several Clovis sites are "kill sites" where fluted points have been found in direct association with the bones of the ice-age elephant, the mammoth. At many more Clovis sites, there are finds of single points. During the time span of this tradition, a number of temporal and regional varieties of fluted points were made. In museum collections there are several points from the Princeton-Kelowna region that are similar to fluted points, which may be late derivatives of this tradition.

Several fluted points have been found in the Peace River district. These points are a late variant and the one found at Charlie Lake Cave has been dated by radiocarbon to 10,500 years ago. Charlie Lake is just north of Fort St. John and is a small remnant of a much larger lake that existed at the end of the Ice Age. The cave is near the shoreline of this ancient lake and the deposits in front of the cave show a sequence of sporadic human occupation from 10,500 years ago to late pre-contact times. The earliest occupation zone contained a fluted point, a large slug-shaped stone scraper, a single stone bead, and the bones of bison and small animals. The remains indicate that this was a hunting camp and that bison were a main source of food. Peoples who rely on bison for food must follow the herds and gear their culture to such nomadism. Similar fluted points have been found in farmers' fields and other disturbed sites in the same general region and at a number of sites on the prairies of Alberta and Saskatchewan. These points are too late in time to belong to the people who first moved south through the ice-free corridor. Instead they probably indicate a late northward movement of their descendants, possibly trying to continue a way of life doomed by changing climatic conditions and the extinction of the Ice Age animals.

The Plano Tradition

Sometime after 10,500 years ago, fluted spear points were replaced in the Peace River region by types of large spear points known as Alberta and Scottsbluff points whose main area of distribution is the grasslands east of the Rocky Mountains. These points differ from the earlier fluted points in that they were not prepared for hafting by fluting, but by indenting the edges of the proximal end of the point to form a stem. All of the finds in British Columbia are isolated, undated surface finds. On the prairies, points of the Plano Tradition are known to be between 10,000 and 7,000 years old. The peoples bearing these types of spear points were also hunters and relied mostly on bison. Lanceolate spear points very similar to one of the Plano types called an "Agate Basin point" have recently been found to be widespread in Alaska and to date between 10,200 and 9,700 years ago. It is probable that some of the peoples making Plano types of points were descendants of the earlier peoples of the Fluted Point Tradition, although the Agate Basin type may represent an incursion of new peoples from the north.[7]

The Intermontane Stemmed Point Tradition

Large, stemmed, non-fluted spear points different in style from those of the Plano Tradition of the prairies are typical of the intermontane region between the Rocky Mountains on the east and the Coast-Cascade-Cordilleran range on the west between approximately 10,500 and 8,000 years ago. This tradition has many regional names: in the Kootenays it is known as the Goatfell Complex, in eastern Washington as the Lind Coulee culture or Windust Phase, in eastern Oregon as the Western Pluvial Lakes Tradition, and further south in Nevada as the Lake Mojave Complex. Stemming a point must be a more efficient hafting method than fluting, since various types of stemmed points replaced fluted points throughout the New World. There are no dated occurrences of this tradition in British Columbia. The closest date is at Crowsnest Pass in Alberta where big horn sheep and bison remains associated with a large, stemmed point were dated at 8,550 years ago. Other remains dated about 1,500 years earlier are known from sites near Banff. The peoples bearing this culture clearly relied on hunting, and from sites in Washington there is direct evidence for the spear thrower.[8]

The Goatfell Complex in the Kootenays is a local expression of this tradition on its northern periphery. The Goatfell Complex is found high on the shorelines of ancient glacial lakes and consists of stemmed points, large side-scrapers, discoidal unifaces, and flake tools made of black siltstone from the Goatfell quarry on the divide between the Moyie and Goat River drainages. The points are large and some of them exceed 10 cm. in length. They have not been discovered in a datable context, but are so similar to points dated elsewhere between 10,500 and 8,500 years ago that they must be of that age. The earliest dated archaeological remains from the Thompson River region might belong to the Intermontane Stemmed Point Tradition, but since no artifacts were found, it is impossible to be certain. At Gore Creek, a tributary of the Thompson River near Kamloops, the skeleton of a young male buried by a mud slide has been dated to 8,250 years ago. Isotopic analysis of his bones demonstrated that the protein in his diet came almost entirely from terrestrial sources, which is an indication that hunting was the main subsistence activity in that region at this time period. However, a small proportion of his diet probably did come from marine sources, which indicates that some salmon were making their way up the Fraser and Thompson Rivers and were taken for food.[9]

The Intermontane Stemmed Point Tradition is probably a derivative of the Fluted Point Tradition. The earliest assemblages are found in eastern Oregon and Nevada, and it is probable that the hafting technique of stemming evolved in that region from fluting, and then spread among related peoples northward throughout the Columbia River drainage area.

The Pebble Tool Tradition

Whereas the three cultural traditions summarized so far are centred in interior parts of the continent, the fourth early cultural tradition found in British Columbia centres on the coast.[10] The area encompassed by the Pebble Tool Tradition stretches from the Queen Charlotte Islands south through the Strait of Georgia and the lower Fraser Valley across the international boundary into the Puget Sound area and on to the lower Columbia River region and the Oregon coast. The typical stone points are simple leaf-shaped forms without flutes or stems. Some may be knives. Also found are numerous choppers and scrapers made from large pebbles or cobbles, which give this tradition its name. The sites are in locations that indicate that fishing and sea-mammal hunting rather than the hunting of land animals were the most important subsistence activities. The pebble choppers and large scrapers may well have served many purposes, but were probably mostly wood-working tools for constructing shelters, canoes, fish traps, and other necessities of life.

The most important sites are the Milliken and South Yale sites near the mouth of the Fraser Canyon, the Glenrose Cannery site on the south arm of the Fraser River in Surrey where the uplands begin, the Bear Cove site on Hardy Bay on northern Vancouver Island, Namu near the mouth of Burke Channel on the central coast, and Skoglund's Landing on Massett Inlet in the Queen Charlotte Islands. Pebble tools occur as isolated finds in many other coastal locations and have been reported on the high terraces above the Skeena and the Bella Coola Rivers.

Not all pebble tools are early; they continued in use on some parts of the coast as expedient tools until at least 2,000 years ago. The earliest radiocarbon dates are 9,700 years ago at Namu, 9,000 at Milliken, and 8,000 at both Glenrose and Bear Cove. The small assemblage at Skoglund's Landing, which contains pebble choppers but no projectile points, occurs in an ancient, raised beach deposit of unknown age, but could pre-date these other occurrences. At other sites in the Queen Charlotte Islands, recent research has uncovered bifacial points that have been Carbon-14 dated at earlier than 9,300 years ago, and other simple flaked stone tools.

The coastal distribution of the Pebble Tool Tradition indicates that its bearers must have had efficient watercraft and the technical knowledge for taking fish and sea mammals, and that they spread down the coast 10,000 years ago or earlier and settled into the river valleys. The location of the Milliken site in the steep canyon of the Fraser River strongly indicates that the people were there to take advantage of the salmon runs 9,000 years ago even though no salmon or any other bones have been preserved in the acid soils. Charred chokecherry pits from hearths of this early occupation indicate people were there when this fruit ripens, which is the time of the fish runs.[11]

At Namu, even though the earliest occupation begins close to 10,000 years ago, animal bones were not preserved until about 6,500 years ago when the deposits yield remains of almost all local land and sea species and mollusc shells.[12] Salmon are the most common species found throughout the Namu deposits, but are not quite as frequent in this period as they are later. Sea mammals are more common relative to other species at this time than in later periods. Artifacts used for fishing by the Native peoples of the historic period are mostly of bone, wood, and fiber and did not survive in the acid soil of the earliest deposits at Namu. The only possible fishing implement in the earliest deposits is a small grooved pebble from a layer dated 9,000 years ago, which could have been a line or net weight, but could also have been a bolas stone. Small bone barbs for fish hooks are found beginning between 6,500 and 5,000 years ago in the earliest layers containing clam shells whose alkaline content aids in preserving tools made of bone. Small bone harpoon heads for sea mammal hunting are first found at this same time, but were probably in use much earlier.

The Namu data strongly support salmon as the single most important resource, and what was true at Namu by 6,500 years ago should also have been true up and down the coast. Not all coastal sites of this early period yield abundant salmon bones, however, and there is disagreement among archaeologists as to the meaning of this fact.[13] At Bear Cove, for example, there are a great many sea mammal remains found in layers dated about 5,000 years ago, and also considerable numbers of fish, though few of the latter are salmon. Of course, unlike Namu, Bear Cove is not at the mouth of a salmon stream, so a high incidence of salmon bones would not be expected there. At the Glenrose site on the Fraser River a different situation prevails; there, elk and deer were most important judging from the quantities of edible meat inferred from the remains, even though the Fraser is a major salmon stream. One can speculate that even when salmon become the most important subsistence commodity everywhere on the coast, variations in bone frequencies would occur in sites and probably reflect differences in local resources, season of occupation, and use and disposal of bones. The faunal remains also indicate that techniques for taking other animal species were also known and that resource-specific locations were exploited in what was probably a scheduled seasonal round of subsistence activities.

As a basis for promoting culture growth, salmon must be considered as the most important resource. They occur at predictable times in massive quantities during very short time intervals, which promotes the scheduling of activities, the storage and preservation of the surplus, and leads to sedentism and to social mechanisms involving redistribution of goods and services. If salmon had become the most important subsistence item, as is suggested by the data from Namu, then people must have developed a place to preserve it and store it. As peoples of the Pebble Tool Tradition spread down the coast of British Columbia and up the river valleys, it is probable that, as salmon became the most important food resource, there was a shift in settlement pattern from nomadism and short-term encampments to permanent winter villages and resource-specific seasonal camps. Population growth would have been a concomitant part of this change.

Evidence for aspects of culture other than subsistence and tool technology is largely indirect, however. Obsidian, a black volcanic glass used for making flaked stone tools, has been found at Namu in deposits dating between 10,000 and 9,000 years ago, and has been traced back to the Rainbow Mountains in the Coast Range at the head of the Bella Coola Valley. Obsidian from an unknown source in Oregon has been found at the Milliken site in the Fraser Canyon in layers dating between 9,000 and 8,000 years ago. Whereas the existence of trade may be inferred from these facts, there is no comparable direct evidence for other social institutions.

The Microblade Tradition

The Microblade Tradition appears earliest in the northwestern part of the province. The sites of this tradition are characterized by assemblages containing small, parallel-sided, stone flakes called microblades and the nodules of stone from which these small blades had been expertly detached, which are called microcores. Judging from examples found elsewhere in the world, microblades were inset into the ends or sides of bone or wooden points and hafts to form the cutting edges. This method of making a projectile point or knife differs radically from that used by the other early traditions in which the projectile point or knife was made from a single piece of stone shaped and flaked on both faces. Except for this different method of making stone tools, the way of life of the peoples of this tradition was probably little different from that of peoples of the Pebble Tool Tradition.

Microblade technology appears much earlier in northern China, Siberia and Alaska than in northern British Columbia. It is present in sites in central

Alaska at 10,500 years ago, in northeastern British Columbia at Charlie Lake Cave at 9,500 years ago, in the Alaska Panhandle and the Queen Charlotte Islands by 9,000 years ago, at Namu between 9,000 and at 8,500 years ago, at the Landels site in the Thompson River region about 8,400 years ago, and further south at Kettle Falls on the Columbia River below a layer of volcanic ash deposited by the eruption of Mt. Mazama about 6,800 years ago. In the Alaska Panhandle, shellfish remains and bones of sea mammals have been found in early assemblages of this tradition.[14]

The evidence indicates the spread of microblade technology from Alaska and the Yukon as far south as the lower Columbia River between 9,500 and 7,000 years ago. The question is, how did this spread take place? Was it through the migration of a distinct people or through cultural borrowing, that is, the diffusion of techniques or ideas from one group to another? This type of question is much debated in archaeology, and conclusive answers are difficult to come by. What is clear is that in North America, microblade technology is centred in the area occupied by Native peoples speaking languages belonging to the Na-Dene language group: the Haida of the Queen Charlotte Islands, the Tlingit of the Alaska Panhandle, the Eyak of the Copper River in Alaska, and the Athapascan speakers who occupy the interior of Alaska and the Yukon and the entire northern interior and part of the Fraser River drainage in central British Columbia.[15] The most economical answer, then, is that the Microblade Tradition probably represents the culture of the ancestors of these peoples, and from them microblade technology spread to their neighbours.

Cultural Transitions

Within the Early Period, archaeological remains that date between 10,500 and 7,000 years ago can be grouped with considerable justification into the five cultural traditions just described. However, remains that date slightly later, between 7,000 and 5,000 years ago, are less easily categorized. For example, tool assemblages on the southern coast begin to contain microblades as well as pebble tools and leaf-shaped points, and assemblages from the interior contain pebble tools, leaf-shaped points, stemmed points, and microblades. Several reasons for these changes may be inferred. The favourable climate of the post-glacial period combined with the growth in food resources would have led to growth of the human population, and as human populations grew they would expand geographically and come into closer contact with neighbouring peoples. Useful innovations would quickly spread from one group to another, and people who were originally somewhat different in culture would through time become more and more similar. Thus both adaptation to the more abundant resources of the post-glacial and the borrowing of existing ideas and technology changed the appearance of the archaeological record and reduced some of the differences in technology present at the beginning of the Early Period. This later part of the Early Period should be considered a time of acculturation and adaptation. Significant growth in the complexity of culture is not evident, however, until the Middle Period.

THE MIDDLE PERIOD: 5,000 TO 2,000 YEARS AGO

In the Middle Period, it is possible to move away from culture history couched mostly in terms of subsistence and types of stone tools. Additional data become available on art, religion, and the nature of society as a result of having more known and excavated sites and vastly improved preservation of bone in the many coastal shell middens in which the dead were normally buried along with some of their belongings. Information on culture growth attributable to adaptations and innovations, to population expansion and to outside influences is available. Unfortunately, the archaeological record is never complete, nor do all archaeological sites of the same time period and cultural affiliation yield information on the same aspects of culture, so it is still necessary to generalize from the small samples of archaeological material actually recovered as to the customs and beliefs of entire populations. Since much archaeological data do represent shared, habitual behaviour of bygone peoples, these generalizations should have considerable validity even though they must be considered to be probability statements.

Some cultural differences similar in kind to those noted for the Early Period continued to exist in the Middle Period, particularly between the coast and the interior, though they were overridden to some extent by the continued spread of ideas and technology through trade and probably other forms of social interaction. Environmental differences helped keep the coast and interior from becoming identical in culture so these areas will be considered separately.

Middle Period Coastal Cultures

The most significant assemblages dating to the early part of this period come from the sites of Namu on the central coast, BlueJackets Creek in the Queen Charlotte Islands, and Pender Canal in the Gulf Islands. Data for the later part come from Yuquot at Friendly Cove on Vancouver Island, and from sites around Prince Rupert Harbour and near the mouth of the Fraser River, though there is some information from all parts of the coast.[16] Stone-tool technology shifted from one based on the flaking of stone to one based on grinding, polishing and sawing of stone, though both technologies were used throughout the period. Microblade industries disappear on the central and northern coasts, but continue on the Strait of Georgia.

Certain steps necessary to the elaboration of culture during the Middle Period had already taken place during the Early Period. The most important of these was the development of salmon-based subsistence. Salmon had begun their colonization of the river systems following the retreat of glacial ice. Knowledge of fishing had undoubtedly been brought by the earliest peoples in their movements down the coast, though the particular techniques used at that time can only be guessed at. The 6,500- to 5,000-year-old bone barbs for composite fish hooks from Namu have already been mentioned as well as the frequencies of salmon bones, which indicate the considerable importance of this resource from the earliest time that bones have been preserved.

The careful quantitative assessment of the relative frequencies of the different animal and fish bones from the stratified site at Namu indicates that, in the deposits dating between 5,000 and 4,200 years ago, salmon outnumbered all other species combined and reached their highest relative frequency. This situation persisted throughout the Middle Period deposits at that site.[17] Few investigators would argue against the idea that if salmon were ascending the small Namu River they were also established in the other minor and major rivers and streams of the coast, and that if the inhabitants of Namu were harvesting them in abundance at this time, so were the other coastal peoples. Finding evidence is more difficult, however. Part of the problem is discovery and excavation of sites where salmon were actually processed and the bones left behind rather than thrown into the river or disposed of in some other manner. Carbon isotope studies of a large sample of human skeletons from the coast spanning the last 5,000 years have demonstrated that, with minor exceptions, 90 per cent or more of the protein in the diet was derived from the sea.[18] Although dietary protein from salmon has not been differentiated from that of sea mammals and shellfish in this type of analysis, the Namu data on relative bone frequency argue that the marine protein signature is based heavily on salmon.

Catching and eating salmon only when available would not have been enough to change the way of life of peoples who at the time of migration to the coast must have been organized as small bands of nomadic fishers and hunters. A stable food surplus, on the other hand, would facilitate a change. The need to preserve and store food for use during the lean months would encourage development of a permanent home base, and that in turn would allow the accumulation of a surplus of goods beyond the necessities of day-to-day subsistence. The establishment of a settlement pattern of permanent winter villages and seasonal resource camps must be envisioned by 6,500 years ago, even though direct evidence is lacking. Surpluses in food and material goods also require someone to manage them and an exchange or trade system for their distribution. The step following mastery of preservation and storage was in all probability the development of specialists, individuals who did not have to spend all or most of their time participating in the food quest.[19] Such individuals would then be free to put their energy into politics, religion, war, arts and crafts, or whatever was dictated as important by the society of which they were a part. There is evidence that this development did take place during the Middle Period.

At some time in the Middle Period the cedar plank house, which served as a permanent locus for storage of food surpluses as well as a natural smokehouse for preserving fish hanging from its ceiling, must have developed. This event is not well documented in the archaeological record: remains of the earliest houses have not yet been found. There is evidence for an increase in quantity and quality of specialized woodworking tools—splitting wedges made of antler, and adzes and chisel blades of bone and ground stone—in the millennium between 4,000 and 3,000 years ago, and it seems probable that the plank house was part of this development. The record of tree pollen preserved in stratigraphic sequence in bogs indicates that climax forests of cedar, the single most important natural resource for houses, utensils and clothing of the ethnographic coastal peoples, were available from 5,000 years ago onward. At Kitselas Canyon on the Skeena River, there is evidence of a permanent village of two rows of plank houses dating between 3,200 and 2,700 years ago. At the Pender Canal site, holes for large house posts and stone slab boxes for storage occur 2,500 years ago, but were probably preceded in time by earlier examples no longer present because of rising sea levels around the Gulf Islands. Eventually the plank house became the standard coastal dwelling from Alaska to northern California.[20]

Food surpluses alone do not lead to the better things in life. For benefits to accrue, such surpluses must be concentrated in the hands of a leader or management specialist with the authority to dispose of them in a productive manner. It is probable that the male head of an extended family or clan filled this role during the Middle Period and maximized surpluses for the benefit of his kin group with, of course, himself as chief. Two models of this development have been proposed, one in which the rich get richer as wealth becomes increasingly concentrated in the hands of fewer and fewer people, and the other in which the role of the chief at the top is to see that wealth, at least in the form of surplus food, is redistributed for the benefit of all relatives.[21] Whichever model one prefers—and both may have been operative on different parts of the coast—the concentration of wealth or power or both leads to the development of social hierarchies and of symbols of social rank.

How can knowledge of surpluses, craft specialization and social differentiation be obtained from the archaeological record? The presence of luxury goods is indicative of a surplus, and the goods themselves are sometimes clues to craft specialization and social rank. Social differentiation can sometimes be inferred from differential wealth in grave goods (that is, the objects accompanying burials), though since blankets and wood carvings and similar luxuries normally perish in the coastal climate, such inferences are somewhat equivocal. Particular kinds of graves and grave goods can also indicate individual status. Cross-cultural studies have shown that complexity of design of art objects is an indicator of social structure: the greater the number and degree of interlocking figures portrayed on an art object, and the less the amount of open space, the greater the probability that the art object was a product of a ranked, non-egalitarian society in which important people were differentiated from others.[22]

The archaeological assemblage from the Main Midden deposit at the Pender Canal site in the Gulf Islands, which spans the period between 4,000 and 2,500 years ago, clearly indicates the presence of a society with luxuy goods, craft specialists and a social hierarchy. Adult burials range from simple interments of individuals placed on their sides with their knees drawn up and no accompanying wealth objects to the same type of interment with wealth objects, to individuals who were seated in stone slab tombs or cists and ritually fed with elaborate, carved-antler spoons or clamshell dishes. Some of the spoons are well carved, indicating the work of a master craftsman, and some are so similar in style that they were probably the work of an individual who specialized in their manufacture. The carvings on the spoon handles are composed of two to four human and animal figures carved three-dimensionally with little open space, not unlike totem poles and house posts of the late eighteenth and early nineteenth centuries when the historical record begins. A range of simple to complex soapstone lip ornaments or labrets and different sizes of ear spools were found scattered throughout the burial area as were numerous other types of standardized soapstone ornaments. The range in labret types suggests that these ornaments were not simple luxuries, but necessities for marking differences in social rank.[23]

Evidence of labrets first appears near the beginning of the Middle Period at three sites—Pender Canal, BlueJackets Creek and Namu. Labrets at this time were worn by some men and some women who would, by inference, have been of higher rank than individuals who did not wear labrets. Other data from the latter two sites suggest that the males were sea-mammal hunters, which suggests further that the female wearers may have been their wives. If these speculations are correct, it may be further inferred that they constituted the top echelon of society. Although salmon were probably the most important food resource, the hunting of sea mammals may well have been the most prestigious occupation. The earliest labrets dated between 5,000 and 4,000 years ago are small, simple, one-piece ornaments, whereas later forms are larger and some are elaborate composite affairs. Large ear spools, which probably filled the same social function as labrets, are also found in the Gulf Islands and on the adjacent mainland between 3,000 and 2,500 years ago and mark the climax in this region of what is probably a system of indicating social rank by the size and elaboration of identifier objects worn in the lip or ear. The sequence of labret types probably marks the evolution of a progressively more rigid and precise system of social ranking during the Middle Period. If so, this system continued on the northern coast until historic times where among Haida women, for example, the larger the labret the higher the social rank of the wearer. On the southern and central coasts, labrets went out of use towards the end of the Middle Period, and were replaced by artificial head deformation as a visible mark of high status.

Craft specialization may be inferred from the uniformity of products found over a continuous geographic area and from the presence of high-quality, well-designed artifacts of any sort. The spoons from the Pender Canal site have already been mentioned. The uniformity of nephrite adze blades throughout the Strait of Georgia and along the lower Fraser River beginning about 2,500 years ago strongly suggests that they were made by specialists. It is probable that they were also used by specialists. The technical requirements of dugout canoe manufacture, for example, are such that it seems unlikely that each person made his own. Full-time craft specialists may well have been few. Salmon-based subsistence allows periods of available time during the winter months after the food supplies have been preserved and stored, and it seems probable that this was the time craftspeople produced their wares. During the historic period, this season was also the time of ceremonies, and there is considerable inferential evidence for this to have been the case during the Middle Period also.

Potlatches were the most widespread ceremonies of the historic period. They took many forms and were undertaken for various reasons, but their common features were feasting and the distribution of property. They were the basis of the legal system, and their main function was the public validation of rights and privileges. The most widespread type of potlatch was the memorial potlatch, a feast for the dead that took place after an interval of mourning. The earliest glimmerings of this institution are found at the BlueJackets Creek site where three burials dating between 5,000 and 4,000 years ago show the dead in a seated position. This suggests the beginning of the custom of seating the important dead as part of their memorial services. At the Pender Canal site between 4,000 and 3,000 years ago not only were some of the dead found in a seated position, but they also had either a spoon placed at the mouth or a large clamshell bowl in the hand or near the body. Why feed the dead? Rituals in which the dead are fed probably reflect the social importance of giving gifts of food to the living, which is in turn one of the basic ingredients of the potlatch. Some of the carvings on the handles of the spoons depict masks similar to those used in potlatches during the historic period. All of these facts indicate potlatching-type behaviour and suggest that the memorial potlatch, if not other types, developed between 4,000 and 3,500 years ago.

The earliest evidence for a religious specialist, the shaman, also dates from this time, though the nearly worldwide occurrence of this specialized role indicates that it has great antiquity and was probably already present in the Early Period. During the historic period human and animal masks were used by some coastal peoples not only in potlatches, but also in spirit dances, secret society performances and shamanic rituals, all divergent aspects of a religious system based on a belief in spirits both as helpers and as a source of illness. Masks indicate transformation beliefs. The shaman or "medicine man" had the ability to diagnose illness and to cure it, though the theatrical theme that pervades shamanism may in some cases have been more important than curing.

Evidence of shamanism appears in Middle Period assemblages with carvings of miniature masks of long-beaked birds, wolves, mountain goats and humanoids as well as representations of owls, serpents, salamanders, and other creatures who were probably spirit helpers. Some of these creatures exhibit joint marks, ribs and backbones, indicators of the shamanic power of re-birth from bones.[24] Certainly shamanism and the belief in animal spirit helpers and the custom of representing them in art were present early in the Middle Period. Whether spirits and art had yet been brought into the service of the elite—as they were among the peoples of the northern and central coast during the historic period with their totem poles, family crest ownership, and secret societies—cannot be determined, but certainly the ingredients for this evolution were there.

Whereas the potlatch may have begun to function as a means of redistribution of goods on the local level, long-distance trading was also taking place. Analysis shows that almost all the obsidian found on southern Vancouver Island and in the Gulf Islands came from eastern Oregon, though a small percentage came from a source centred on or near northern Vancouver Island and an even smaller amount from Mt. Garibaldi near Squamish. At Namu and at adjacent sites on the central coast almost all obsidian came from the same sources as in the Early Period—Anahim Peak and the Rainbow Mountains up Burke Channel and along the Mackenzie Trail to the east—but lesser amounts found their way from eastern Oregon, northern Vancouver Island, and Mt. Edziza on the headwaters of the Stikine. Anahim obsidian also reached Prince Rupert Harbour from points east, as did Edziza obsidian from the north; the latter is also found across Hecate Strait at the BlueJackets Creek site on Graham Island. Seashells found in interior sites presumably constituted part of the goods moving in the opposite direction. Obsidian and shells must have been only a small part of much larger trading networks.[25]

Raiding was an integral part of historic period coastal culture since it brought in slaves to help produce the wealth necessary for the potlatch and the maintenance of high status. Hand-to-hand fighting and the taking of trophy skulls were part of the system. Warrior weapons are known earliest from BlueJackets Creek where two fancy bone daggers with geometric designs were found buried with an adult male dated at 4,900 years ago. At Namu an adult male dated to 4,400 years ago had been buried with his dagger and sea-hunting equipment of walrus ivory; the blade of a bone dagger or spear head was found wedged in his backbone. Skeletons from Prince Rupert Harbour and Pender Canal show healed parry fractures—fractures of the lower forearm presumably the result of hand-to-hand fighting. Stone war clubs of elaborate design from the Queen Charlotte Islands and the Skeena River area testify to the social importance of warfare and to the integration of spirit beliefs with the war complex. Isolated skulls have been found at many sites and could be war trophies. A cache of warrior weapons including copper-wrapped rod armour dating to 2,500 years ago was excavated from a site in Prince Rupert Harbour. The many large, lanceolate ground slate points from Strait of Georgia sites dating to about 2,500 years ago may actually be daggers. At Tsawwassen near Vancouver two skeletons buried away from other people bear cut marks clearly related to scalping. The hilltop fortresses—of which many have been found, but few excavated—begin near the end of the Middle Period but belong mostly to the Late Period, according to the few dates available. All in all, there is considerable evidence for warfare.[26]

Were slaves taken? Slavery is associated with societies that have a strong sense of social rank and a propensity for raiding. The likelihood that the historic period cultural system in which slavery was integrated with warfare, with the creation of wealth and the potlatch, and with the production of craft and food surpluses evolved during the Middle Period suggests that, in spite of the lack of direct evidence, slavery was probably part of it.

At Namu, at Prince Rupert Harbour, and at Yuquot at Friendly Cove on Vancouver Island, culture continued with little change from the late Middle Period to historic times, whereas on the lower Fraser River and around the Strait of Georgia several sequent phases of culture are present. This change in the archaeological record has led some researchers to postulate population replacement and the movement of peoples out of the interior region. Since these prehistoric phases were spread over the same geographic region as was occupied by the central Coast Salish people during historic times, it seems more probable that these phases mark poorly understood changes in the archaeological record of the resident population rather than major population replacements.

Although the overall social and subsistence system of the Middle Period seems largely self-generated, there is some evidence of external influences. Labrets and bilaterally barbed styles of harpoon heads occur earlier than 5,000 years ago on Kodiak Island to the north, and much earlier in the Siberian Maritime district and on the Kamchatka Peninsula in Asia. Ground slate daggers have much the same distribution, but are a thousand years later. Spoons and animal masks and the rib-and-socket or x-ray style of shamanic art also show a general north Pacific continuity, and the copper-wrapped rod armour found at Prince Rupert Harbour is Asiatic in style. These distributions indicate that coastal British Columbia was receiving cultural influences from Asia via the Aleutian Islands and Alaska throughout the Middle Period. Although these external influences are discernible, evolution of the social system of which they became a part could not have taken place without the sedentism permitted by the winter village and stored surpluses.

The following model of the events of the Middle Period on the coast emerges from the data at hand. Cultural elaboration took place based on the surplus wealth derived from the organization of society around the procurement, preservation and storage of salmon, though other food resources obtained through a seasonal round were also important. By the end of the

Middle Period at 2,000 years ago there is evidence for salmon-based subsistence and the seasonal round, symbols of rank and status based presumably on wealth, cedar technology including the plank house, the memorial potlatch if not other types, sculptural art related to shamanism and a belief in spirits, and warfare with attendant slavery. These socio-cultural complexes formed an integrated system that persisted with little modification until the time of European contact. Evidence of trade and cultural similarities indicates that a shared system of culture existed throughout the coastal area, though local differences were also present. Although the basic cultural system had already crystallized, the Late Period on the coast probably witnessed increased warfare and a shift to the use of art motifs as symbols of social status.

Interior Cultures of the Middle Period

The interior region is a much larger area than the coast and is usually divided into a northern or Cordilleran portion including the upper Fraser River drainage area north of Quesnel, and a southern or plateau portion consisting of the drainage areas of the middle Fraser and Thompson Rivers, the Arrow Lakes, and the upper Columbia River. During the historic period, Athapascan-speaking peoples centred in the Cordilleran area and Salishan-speaking peoples centred in the plateau area. With a few exceptions the peoples of the Pacific drainage area had access to salmon, whereas those in the Arctic drainage area did not, and relied mostly on hunting. Unlike the coast, chipped stone artifacts continued to be important markers of various cultures and time periods. Much less is known about the Middle Period in the northern than in the southern interior region.

Assemblages from the Middle Period of the northern interior are known from the Callison site almost on the Yukon border, Charlie Lake Cave and the Farrell Creek site near Fort St. John, Mt. Edziza, Natalkuz Lake in Tweedsmuir Park at the headwaters of the Nechako River, several sites including Punchaw Lake on the Mackenzie Trail between the Fraser River and Mackenzie Pass, and from miscellaneous finds of Middle Period types of artifacts.[27] Technologies originating from different cultural traditions are found in these sites, but it is not always clear whether they are contemporaneous or sequent, and if the latter, the correct chronological order. Charlie Lake Cave is the only excavated, well-stratified site in the region and not all periods and cultures are represented in the sequence there. Fluted points are unknown after the Early Period, and are followed about 6,000 years ago by both lanceolate and large, side-notched points. These types of points continue throughout the sequence until they are replaced by arrow points in the Late Period. At Charlie Lake Cave a single microblade was found in deposits dated to 4,800 years ago. At Mt. Edziza microblade industries are present by 4,900 years ago; younger assemblages there at about 4,000 years ago have large lanceolate and expanding-stem or "fishtail" points that may be belated derivatives of the Plano

Tradition. Similar weapon points occur in the Yukon, the Peace River district east of the Rockies, on the upper Skeena River, and in Alberta. The interfingering in time and space of three technologies—microblades from the north and west, lanceolate points that are vaguely derivative of the Plano culture from the east, and large, notched points from the south—seems to be characteristic of the northern interior between 6,000 and 4,000 years ago. In cultural-historical terms these distributions could indicate either amalgamation of various groups, interaction or shifting boundary areas between groups, or periodic movement into the area by hunting peoples of diverse ancestry. The northern interior with its long cold winters was never an area in which it was easy to make a living.

In the upper Fraser River area between 4,000 and 3,000 years ago, villages indicating a shift from a nomadic to a semi-sedentary way of life began to be established along rivers and lakeshores. At Tezli on the Blackwater River the earliest date on a circular pit house is 3,850 years ago; at Nakwantlun near Anahim Lake the earliest date on such a house is 3,500 years ago; at Punchaw Lake the earliest occupation from below the floor of a surface dwelling is dated at 3,980; at Natalkuz Lake a Carbon-14 date of 2,415 years ago was obtained on charcoal from the central hearth of a surface dwelling with a microblade industry and a corner notched point. All of these sites also have more extensive Late Period occupations. At no Middle Period site in the northern interior is there evidence for the development of sizeable populations or of any of those institutions dependent on the accumulation of a surplus.

The southern interior as far east as the Arrow Lakes is better known archaeologically in the Middle Period than is the northern interior.[28] At about 7,000 years ago the culture of the southern region looks like an amalgamation of earlier biface and microblade technologies based around a nomadic lifestyle. The bearers of this culture were primarily hunters of deer and elk, although some salmon remains are found. Between 7,000 and 5,000 years ago, flaked stone artifacts similar to those of the Pebble Tool Tradition of the coast with its leaf-shaped points and pebble choppers begin to show up in sites on the middle Fraser and Thompson Rivers. These artifacts seem to mark the up-river movement of coastal peoples following the salmon as these fish developed spawning runs farther and farther up the river systems. This change is actually better documented for the Columbia River system. At Kettle Falls, just over the border in Washington, the earliest assemblage pre-dates 6,800 years ago and contains notched sinkers for nets and salmon bones as well as stone tool types originating with various early cultural traditions—pebble tools, a microblade industry, and projectile points of leaf-shaped and stemmed types.[29] By 4,000 years ago winter villages of circular pit houses made their appearance along both the Fraser and upper Columbia River drainages.

The earliest evidence for increased salmon consumption in the interior comes from two skeletons excavated near Clinton and dated 4,950 years ago. Isotopic analysis indicated 37 to 38 per cent marine protein in their diet. Later skeletons show even higher values of 40 to 60 per cent. Notched pebbles probably used as net sinkers are the earliest evidence of fishing technology. River molluscs were extensively used. Evidence of storage pits is not present until 4,000 years ago.[30]

Eighteen sites in the region between Williams Lake in the north, the Arrow Lakes on the east, Lillooet on the west, and the Okanagan River in the south have revealed evidence of Middle Period occupations between 4,000 and 2,400 years ago. Twelve of these sites are pit-house villages and the rest are surface scatters of flaked stone tools. Use of the pit house begins just after the advent of a phase of cooler and wetter weather. This climatic change may have been responsible not only for a presumed shift to warmer winter dwellings, but also for an increased presence of salmon in the Fraser River system, which in turn would have contributed to surpluses, to the development of winter villages with storage facilities, and to the subsequent general elaboration of culture. The pit houses tend to be large—7.6 to 16 metres in diameter—with internal storage pits and hearths; their size indicates they were multi-family dwellings. Fishing implements including harpoons, and wood-working tools including wedges and nephrite chisels or adze blades occur. Luxury goods are not common, though bone bracelets, pendants and beads have been found in limited numbers. Art work is present in limited amounts. For example, the end of a pecked stone maul or pestle shaped into the form of a bear's head was discovered. Shamanism is indicated by depiction of the backbone on figurines. Trade with the coast is shown by a dentalium shell and another marine shell ornament found at a site at Kamloops. Obsidian is surprisingly rare; its near absence is possibly an indicator of hostile relationships with peoples just to the north who straddled the region between the middle Fraser River area and the obsidian sources of the Rainbow Mountains. The cultural complexes of this period are all more elaborate in the Late Period and are known from many more excavated sites.[31]

The Kootenay region remained somewhat distinct from the rest of the southern interior during the Middle Period. Sites are generally unstratified thin scatters of debris and flaked stone tools, suggesting that hunting remained the primary subsistence activity. The chronology there is based partly on changes in the preferred type of stone for tools. Between 3,000 and 5,000 years ago large spear points with expanding stems made of Kootenay argillite are characteristic. Archaeological sites are situated adjacent to present-day water systems. Notched pebbles for fish nets are also present. A site near the confluence of the Wildhorse and Kootenay Rivers yielded a Carbon-14 date of nearly 4,000 years for the middle of the period in which the producers of these artifacts occupied this area. Top-of-the-World chert—from high altitudes—was preferred for tool making from 3,000 years ago onward.[32]

In some ways the development of Middle Period culture in the Pacific drainage region must have paralleled that of the coast, though it is difficult to envision the large winter villages (of which Keatley Creek near Lillooet with its more than 100 pit houses is only one such site) as being viable without a salmon-based storage economy and all it entails.[33] Evidence for some social stratification in the Pacific drainage area is suggested by houses of different sizes containing different artifactual and subsistence contents, though symbols of social rank such as labrets and ear spools and evidence for potlatch-type feasting have not been found.

THE LATE PERIOD:
2,000 YEARS AGO TO EUROPEAN CONTACT

Whereas the archaeology of the first five millennia of culture history documents the settlement of the province by people who survived by fishing and hunting, and that of the next three sees the growth of sedentism and cultural complexity, few major changes are revealed by the archaeology of the final two millennia. The cultures just described anchor the beginning of the Late Period; the end of this period belongs to the various Native peoples whose language and culture are known from the written historical record and to whom it is possible to attach real names.

There were only an estimated 75,000 Native people in all of British Columbia at the time of European contact two centuries ago. This estimate is low, but even if it were doubled or tripled as suggested by some demographic modeling, that is still not very many people. There is some archival evidence of a smallpox epidemic in the Alaska Panhandle in the 1770s, and it is quite possible that the entire population of the Pacific Northwest was greatly reduced in number at that time.[34] The culture of all the peoples of the province at the time of European contact was similar in that metal working (other than grinding and cold-hammering copper and possibly iron from shipwrecks), ceramic making, and the growing of food crops, which were widespread elsewhere in the world, were unknown. Everyone relied on combinations of fishing, hunting, and collecting wild vegetal foods and molluscs for subsistence. There is abundant pre-contact evidence of harvesting and processing wild roots in the Hat Creek locality of the southern interior region, and some historic accounts of tending cinquefoil and clover and of burning fields to promote plant growth on the coast.[35]

Food preservation techniques—drying, smoking, and preservation in oil—were known everywhere and were essential in some regions to actual survival during the lean winter months. Cache pits for storing food were common throughout the interior region. In 1952, over 2,000 such pits were counted on the ridge behind the village of Chinlac on the Stuart River, and many are known elsewhere. Fishing was highly developed throughout the province. Hunting of land mammals with the bow and arrow was more important in the interior areas than on the coast where sea hunting with the harpoon was widely practised. Peoples of the west coast of Vancouver Island actually pursued whales into the near reaches of the Pacific Ocean, harpooned them, and towed them to shore.

Stone, bone, shell and wood were still the raw materials for tools, weapons, ornaments and other implements, though some native copper had been used since the late Middle Period. On the coast, clothing was of shredded and woven cedar bark, dog and mountain-goat wool, and sometimes tanned skins as in the interior. Other industries included the weaving of baskets and blankets, hide preparation and the tanning of skins, use of traps and deadfalls, and many other activities that required both knowledge and skill. Wood-working techniques were highly developed. The pit house remained the standard dwelling in the southern interior region, though rectangular wooden houses apparently modeled on coastal types were used in part of the northern interior. Both pit houses and wooden plank houses were used on the lower Fraser River, though the multi-family plank house was used everywhere else on the coast.

Complex socio-political organizations such as kingdoms, states and even tribes in the political sense were absent in the late eighteenth century at the beginning of the contact period. Instead, those regions with abundant, storable food had autonomous villages, whereas other regions supported semi-nomadic bands. Peoples were united through ties of kinship and intermarriage into sophisticated networks of multi-village or multi-band units whose members recognized the similarities in language and culture that bound them loosely together and differentiated them from their neighbours. Today such groups refer to themselves as "First Nations," though there is no exact congruity with earlier networks. The coastal regions, including the lower reaches of the river systems, had the highest populations and the greatest elaboration in social institutions. The complexity of their arts and industries was correspondingly high. Wealth and rank were of great importance, and raiding for slaves was endemic. The southern interior area had fewer people and less complex cultures. The northern interior area with its long winters and short summers had an even smaller population density.

Because of the absence of complex political units such as named tribes or states that could serve as meaningful units whose culture history could be investigated, archaeologists instead tend to use language to designate groups of related peoples (see Map 1). The Native peoples of British Columbia as they are identified in written records spoke about fifty-four mutually unintelligible languages, but many of these languages were related to each other, meaning that over a period of time they had diverged from a common mother language. People speaking related languages must obviously have either descended from the same ancestral group or borrowed the language from their neighbours. In view of the tenacity with which people retain their language, the first alternative is more common except where a neighbour is more powerful or prestigious in which case either the borrowed language might prevail or a hybrid language

Map 1: Major Native Ethno-Linguistic Groups, and Locations of Archaeological Sites

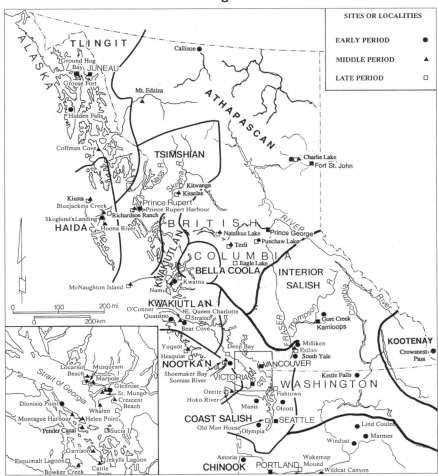

The sites shown here are only a small portion of excavated sites in the province.

could result. In some historic villages on the borders of language areas several languages were commonly spoken, and this contributed to the borrowing of language features by peoples of diverse linguistic origins. With these exceptions, however, peoples speaking related languages may be considered maximum units of historic relationship. As populations expanded and segmented into distant socio-geographic groups, the mother language would have diverged into dialects and eventually, depending on the degree and length of separation, into mutually unintelligible separate languages. Cultures would have diverged similarly. Common ancestry should be reflected in the archaeological record, though the internecine borrowing of technology and adaptation to similar environments by diverse peoples makes common ancestry difficult to demonstrate archaeologically.

The language families of British Columbia in descending order of estimated numbers of aboriginal speakers at 1775 A.D. are Salish or Salishan, Athapascan or Dene, Waskashan, Haida, Tsimshian, and Kootenay. The following paragraphs briefly summarize Late Period archaeology by language family and indicate probable cultural antecedents.

Salish Prehistory

Languages belonging to the Salish family were spoken by about 32,500 people, about half of whom were in the southern interior and the other half in the lower Fraser River area, on the Gulf Islands, on southern Vancouver Island and on both shores of the Strait of Georgia. There was also an isolated group of 2,000 in the Bella Coola Valley. The presence of words for coastal plants and animals in reconstructed forms of the ancient Salish language indicates the origin of this language family on the coast rather than in the interior.[36]

Interior Salish. The archaeology of the Salish territory in the southern interior shows clear continuity in culture from 4,000 years ago to contact. Changes were few, and were far outweighed by the continuation of the same customs in subsistence, housing and basic technology. Projectile points became smaller through time, were rather consistently notched for hafting, and divide the Late Period into sequential horizons. The reduction in size is related first to changes in the size and weight of the spear and later to the introduction of the bow and arrow about the time of Christ. Hunting tactics would have changed, too, since the bow and arrow can be used in wooded terrain whereas the spear thrower requires more open country. The effect of this change on patterns of warfare is so far undetermined. There seems to have been an increase in the amount of decorative art, though this trend may be illusory, accounted for merely by the increase in the number of excavated sites. The numerous panels of rock art and small anthropomorphic and zoomorphic figurines probably relate to a belief in spirit power, though some may document war exploits. The variations in the sizes and forms of pit houses may indicate periodic shifts in kin group organization.

Coast Salish. Cultural continuity in the territory of the Coast Salish is not as clear cut as in the interior region because of poorly understood breaks in cultural sequences between 2,500 and 1,500 years ago. These breaks may have been caused by environmental factors. For example, modern fisheries research suggests that periods of El Nino warm the sea water, which causes the sockeye salmon bound for the Fraser River to change their migration path, coming through Johnson Strait instead of the Strait of Juan de Fuca, and therefore missing the Gulf Islands. Although most archaeological knowledge of the Middle

Period comes from village sites in the Gulf Islands, Late Period sites there appear to have been occupied only seasonally, though so few have been excavated that it is impossible to generalize. If El Nino occurred prehistorically, it could have caused this shift in population centres within Coast Salish territory.

Another factor is the tilt of the Juan de Fuca plate, which has raised the outer edge of Vancouver Island and lowered the Gulf Islands and the Fraser River delta.[37] Any Middle Period sites at high tide level 2,200 years ago or earlier are now under water. Only deposits left by activities at higher elevations have survived. It is little wonder, then, that the archaeological records of the Middle and Late Periods in the Coast Salish area look different.

Some changes, however, do not have direct environmental links: labrets disappeared and were replaced by frontal head deformation, the obsidian trade from Oregon declined drastically, chipped stone including microblades went out of use almost entirely, tubular pipes for smoking tobacco came into use, a shamanic cult using stone bowls carved to represent a seated human figure embellished with snakes and other reptiles became prominent, and the practice of placing the dead in rock shelters or grave houses rather than burying them in middens became common. There is some evidence of large (ca. ten metres in diameter) burial mounds on southern Vancouver Island and along the lower Fraser River containing single interments and wealth objects of native copper. Such mounds indicate the importance of powerful individuals, but all too little is known about them.

By A.D. 1200, the archaeological record shows direct continuity with historic Coast Salish culture.

Bella Coola. The people of the Bella Coola Valley call themselves the Nuxalk. Excavation at the village of Nusqualst, visited by Alexander Mackenzie in 1793, has uncovered both historic and late pre-contact deposits, and provided evidence that the Bella Coola Valley was one source of the greenstone adze and chisel blades found throughout the central coast during the Late Period.[38] Middle Period sites have yet to be found and excavated, but pebble tools and some large obsidian spear points of generalized form that must belong to the Early Period have been found on old river terraces.

The Pebble Tool Tradition is the earliest culture in the territories of Salish speakers, and it is probable that their ancestors were the bearers of this tradition, which first spread down the coast 10,000 or more years ago and then up the Fraser and Columbia Rivers about 7,000 years ago, displacing or absorbing interior peoples of the earlier Intermontane Stemmed Point Tradition.

Athapascan Prehistory

Athapascan was the only language family present in the northern interior region at contact and was spoken by an estimated 15,000 people. The most southerly group in British Columbia were the Stuwihamuk or "people of the high country," an isolated, almost legendary band of Athapascan speakers in the Nicola Valley who were absorbed by their Salish neighbours early in the historic period. Other scattered bands of Athapascan speakers are found on the coast from Washington to northern California. The Tlingit language of the Alaska Panhandle and the Haida language of the Queen Charlotte Islands are usually considered to be remotely related to Athapascan, though Haida is so different that some linguists consider it to be totally unrelated.

The Athapascan inhabitants of the headwaters of the rivers flowing into the Pacific borrowed many coastal customs during the late prehistoric or early historic periods. Rectangular wooden houses are found at sites such as Chinlac on the Stuart River. The Babine or "labret Indians" borrowed many coastal customs including that which gives them their name. The Taku took over many social customs including the Tlingit language from their high-class neighbours. The peoples of the Arctic drainage area, on the other hand, continued a way of life little different from that found earlier except for use of the bow and arrow.[39]

Much of the Late Period archaeological research in the border areas between Athapascan speakers and Salish speakers has been aimed at determining which of these peoples first occupied the middle and upper Fraser River areas. The largest numbers of Athapascan bands are in the interior of Alaska and the Yukon, and on distribution grounds alone it looks as though they spilled over into the Fraser River drainage area and moved even farther south at some time in the past. A possible causative event was a major volcanic eruption and fall of ash at White River in the southern Yukon at A.D. 700. Traditions of the Athapascan-speaking Chilcotin indicate only that their original settlement was above the confluence of the Chilcotin and Chilko and perhaps upper Nazco Rivers and in their move to the main Chilcotin River they displaced a pit-house-dwelling, salmon-using people. Archaeological research at Eagle Lake supports the likelihood of a late southward movement of Athapascans whereas research at sites on the Blackwater River does not.[40]

Microblades are still found in Late Period sites near Anahim Lake, and unless intrusive from earlier periods, indicate the strong persistence of this technology. Within most of the territory occupied by the Athapascan-Tlingit-Haida speakers, the earliest prehistoric culture is the Microblade Tradition and it seems probable that the ancestors of peoples speaking these languages introduced microblade technology, which then persisted with some descendants, died out with others, and spread to unrelated peoples.

Wakashan Prehistory

The Wakashan language group includes both the Nootkan languages spoken by about 6,000 Nuu-chah-nulth of the west coast of Vancouver Island, and the Kwakiutlan languages spoken by about the same number of people on northern Vancouver Island and the adjacent mainland north to Kitimat. A locality called Kwatna on the border between the Bella Coola and Kwakiutlan language areas has provided the most information on the late prehistory of this region.[41] Occupation began there about 2,000 years ago at village sites whose names are still known, and lasted until 1840 when the inhabitants were massacred by Native raiders. Kwatna is at the mouth of a salmon river and was a winter village site; it is mentioned in traditional accounts of both the Nuxalk (Bella Coola) and Heiltsuk (Bella Bella). Excavations have uncovered a wealth of wood-working tools—chiefly fragments of greenstone adze blades—and many fish-hook barbs, harpoon parts, stone hammers, and some art work. Evidence of two large rectangular houses was also found. A waterlogged deposit at the mouth of the Kwatna River yielded many items—wooden wedges, cedar-bark rope, basketry hats, matting, bentwood and composite fish hooks, and fragments of bentwood boxes. Two small, chipped-stone arrow points and obsidian indicate trade from the interior. Other sites near Namu and along Queen Charlotte Strait in the core areas inhabited by Kwakiutlan speakers exhibit much the same technology and a way of life based on salmon. These sites show continuity over the last 2,000 years.[42]

In Nuu-chah-nulth territory the longest archaeological sequence is at the village of Yuquot on the outer coast, and continuity in culture there can be traced back 4,200 years.[43] Specific whaling equipment is found only after A.D. 800, but other sea-mammal hunting and fishing equipment is found throughout the sequence. No obsidian or chipped-stone projectile points were found even in Middle Period deposits. Other types of artifacts for fishing and wood-working are found throughout the sequence and nearby at Hesquiat. The artifacts for fishing and sea-mammal hunting from these excavations are generally similar to those found to the north at Namu and other sites.

The Pebble Tool Tradition is the earliest cultural tradition found in the territory occupied by Wakashan speakers, so it seems probable that their ancestors as well as those of the Salish belonged to that cultural tradition. Namu is actually in the territory of the Heiltsuk who speak a northern Kwakiutlan language. It is tempting to equate the earliest assemblage at Namu with the ancestors of the Salishan speakers who moved down the coast and settled in the river valleys, and the later components—beginning 9,000 to 8,500 years ago—in which there are microblades as well as points and choppers, with the ancestors of the Wakashan speakers who settled the outer coast, but such an equation is highly speculative. Somewhat later the ancestors of the Nuu-chah-nulth would have diverged from the Kwakiutlan speakers and continued the southward spread along the west coast of Vancouver Island. Place name studies have shown that Nootkan speakers did spread southward across the Strait of Juan de Fuca displacing earlier peoples in northwest Washington.[44] The Nootkan language also spread eastward absorbing Salish speakers at the head of Alberni Inlet in the late pre-contact or early historic period. On Quatsino Sound just beyond the north edge of Nootkan territory, the pebble tools and leaf-shaped points of the Pebble Tool Tradition have been found in undated contexts on the beaches. At the east end of Nootkan territory at the head of Alberni Inlet, leaf-shaped points, pebble tools, and microblades and cores have been found in deposits on ancient river terraces along the Somass River.[45] These deposits are undated but certainly long pre-date the founding of the village at Yuquot. Overall, the best available hypothesis is that the Wakashan ancestors reached parts of their present territory from the north by 8,500 years ago, and that the divergence between Nootkan and Kwakiutlan speakers took place sometime between then and 4,200 years ago.

Haida Prehistory

Ethnographically, the Queen Charlotte Islands or Haida Gwaii, as the islands are called by the Haida, were home to a resident population of about 8,400 speakers of a single language, Haida. A group of Haida is also resident just to the north at Hydaburg in Alaska where according to tradition their ancestors moved several hundred years ago. The similarities in the ethnographic period cultures of the Haida, the Tlingit of the Alaska Panhandle, and the Tsimshian of the Nass and Skeena regions, and the similarities in the archaeology in the territories of all three groups indicate a great amount of cultural interchange and assimilation in spite of differences in language. Salmon were important to Haida subsistence, though in some localities halibut and cod may have been more important. Whale bone found in Late Period sites on Moresby Island suggests that whaling may have been undertaken. Two sites, the Richardson Ranch on the east side and Kiusta on the far northwest tip of Graham Island, have yielded archaeological assemblages belonging to the early historic period. Excavation reports on Kiusta, near where the Spaniards first glimpsed the Haida, provide evidence of deep pre-contact deposits as well as data on the effect of the fur trade such as the incorporation of American designs from Sandwich glass into native handicrafts. The BlueJackets Creek site is the most important Middle Period site so far excavated.

The evidence is not entirely clear cut, but assemblages of the Pebble Tool Tradition with leaf-shaped points and pebble choppers seem to pre-date assemblages of the Microblade Tradition in the Queen Charlotte Islands. The latter persists to the beginning of the Middle Period, about 5,000 years ago. Cultural continuity from the Early Period into the Middle Period and from there into the Late Period remains to be demonstrated by further work.[46]

Tsimshian Prehistory

At the time of contact an estimated 7,000 speakers of the several Tsimshian languages occupied the valleys of the Nass and the Skeena Rivers downriver from the Bulkley, and the adjacent coastline south to Milbanke Sound. The Tsimshian languages are different from the languages of their neighbours, and speculation concerning linguistic relationships has always pointed to the south, to the Penutian language superfamily of eastern Washington, Oregon and

California. There have been extensive excavations in sites around Prince Rupert Harbour and in a few in the Skeena River area, but surveys of the Nass River area have found few pre-contact sites.

The fortress at Kitwanga on the Skeena River has been extensively excavated, and shows both late pre-contact and early historic period components.[47] The site is situated on top of an isolated hillock, and the historic component consists of five rectangular houses with features such as hidden cachement areas. The fortress provides physical evidence of the traditional role of the site as the stronghold of a famous warrior named Nekt. Kitwanga was one of a string of five forts situated near the junctions of trails linking the headwaters of the Iskut, Nass, and Skeena Rivers. How far backward in time this system of fortresses goes is unknown. Warriors were certainly important people by 2,500 years ago, the date of a cache of warrior weapons at Prince Rupert Harbour, and the pattern of raiding, which was widespread on the coast ethnographically and is attested to by unexcavated fort sites in all coastal regions, could well date to at least that time.

Both archaeology and traditional history indicate that Tsimshian culture is a fusion of elements from many sources. The Prince Rupert Harbour sequence indicates cultural continuity from about 5,000 years ago. The archaeology of the Skeena River area at Kitselas Canyon and Hagwilget shows the constant interplay between cultures of the coast and the interior. The first known occupants there were armed with coastal microblade and pebble tool technologies whereas in the subsequent period, between 3,600 and 3,200 years ago, projectile points and scrapers that resemble those of belated Plano peoples in the northern interior make their appearance.[48] Cultural influence and intermarriage or even a migration of peoples from that region might account for the Tsimshian language becoming grafted onto an existing salt-water tradition. Myths place the origin of some Tsimshian speakers at Temlahem or "Prairie Town" upriver on the Skeena, though there is debate as to whether this is a real place or whether it is a metaphor perhaps analogous to the Garden of Eden. If the suggested link between the Penutian language family and the Tsimshian languages is ever clearly demonstrated, then further support for the idea of partial derivation of Tsimshian ancestry from the Plano Tradition would be provided.

Kootenay Prehistory

The final aboriginal language of British Columbia is Kootenay, which at contact was spoken by only about 1,200 people whose territory covered the Kootenay River basin and extended south into Idaho and Montana. About half of these people lived in the southeast corner of the province. The Kootenay language is different from its neighbours and its larger affiliations, if any, are uncertain. The Kootenay exploited the mosaic of accessible forests, grasslands, lakes and rivers within and adjacent to their mountainous habitat, and not only fished in the rivers and lakes, but hunted sheep in the high mountains and crossed the Rockies to hunt bison. Salmon were not important to their subsistence. Their settlements lacked the permanence of the pit-house villages situated along the salmon-bearing rivers elsewhere in the interior region.

In British Columbia, seventeen sites in the Kootenay region have been tested, but most have only shallow cultural deposits. Therefore, much of the local chronology must still be inferred from sequences established in adjacent parts of the United States and Alberta.[49] The clearest evidence of cultural continuity is the use of Top-of-the-World chert over the last 3,000 years preceding contact. The Intermontane Stemmed Point Tradition is the earliest cultural tradition found in the Kootenay area and it is possible that the ancestors of the Kootenay belonged to this much earlier tradition.

Cultural Stability

Although archaeological, ethnological and linguistic facts provide evidence of the history of peoples and cultures, such facts must be integrated into a cultural/historical framework if the past is to be both explained and understood. The method employed in this chapter has been to assess these facts and from them develop a model of the events that culminated in Native culture at the time of European contact in the late 1700s. The model developed is that between 10,500 and 9,000 years ago the province was colonized by peoples bearing five different cultural traditions who are the ancestors of the peoples living in British Columbia at the time of contact. These original inhabitants were organized as small nomadic bands who brought with them the knowledge of flaked stone tools and of hunting and fishing, small-boat building, and hide working—all ingredients of an Arctic survival kit—and probably shamanism to deal with the spirit world. Implicit in this model is that the earliest people differed in language as well as in the technology that serves to differentiate them from each other archaeologically, and that with the types of exceptions mentioned, core linguistic differences were maintained throughout prehistory.

The following hypotheses about the relationships between the pre-contact archaeological cultures and ethno-linguistic groups of the historic period are part of this model: the Kootenay and the Tsimshian are descended in part from the Intermontane Stemmed Point and Plano Traditions respectively; the ancestry of the Salish- and Wakashan-speaking peoples lies in the Pebble Tool Tradition; the ancestors of the Tlingit, Haida and Athapascan peoples brought in the Microblade Tradition and introduced microblade technology to neighbouring peoples. None of these hypothesized relationships have necessarily been proven, and all are subject to testing through further research, though all are based on the most economical explanation of presently available facts.

Following the period of initial settlement in which expanding populations segmented into separate socio-geographic groups as they spread throughout the province, cultural fusion—the melding of cultural differences—took place through the spread of ideas and technologies from one group to another, so that by the time of European contact a sameness in culture (except for language) prevailed among adjacent peoples occupying similar habitats and relying on the same kinds of resources. Such acculturative influences are indicated by the trade in obsidian and by the widespread dissemination of several technologies, which eventually reached all regions of the province. Microblade technology, new hafting techniques such as stemming and later notching of projectile heads, ground stone wood-working tools, and the bow and arrow are all examples of such technologies.

The Middle Period was primarily a time of cultural growth. By 3,500 years ago in the Gulf Islands, Prince Rupert Harbour, Namu and the Queen Charlotte Islands there is evidence for the beginning of cultural complexes in technology, art, ceremonialism and elitism similar to those that typify the coast ethnographically. Some of the culture content of the Middle Period stems from influences spreading around the north Pacific rim: ground slate, labrets, types of harpoon heads, sawn adze blades, and ideas and beliefs expressed in masked animal dancers and shamanic motifs. However, the primary achievement of this period was the indigenous development of the elaboration of culture organized around salmon-based subsistence in which these external influences played their parts. Once the food supply had become stable and those social mechanisms for controlling and expending the surplus had evolved, population would grow until such time as either the carrying capacity of the environment was reached or other mechanisms such as warfare and slave raiding became widespread. Warfare and slave raiding probably evolved late in the Middle Period, though the evidence for the latter is not as full as is desirable.

The Late Period is primarily a continuation of the Middle Period. There are changes in the archaeological record in the region of the Strait of Georgia towards the beginning of this period, but many of these are probably a result of divergent samples of materials related to differential preservation of special purpose sites or parts of sites as a result of sea-level changes. Another problem related to sampling is the change in burial patterns in that those kinds of artifacts found with burials in the Middle Period are no longer found in the Late Period coastal sites because the dead were no longer buried in shell middens. There were other kinds of changes such as the introduction of the bow and arrow (its potential effect on warfare, land hunting and ecology has yet to be assessed), and of the tubular tobacco pipe, which spread through the southern interior and along the coast as far as southern Vancouver Island and indicates contact with the rest of North America. However, as far as is known, these introductions had little effect on the cultural systems that had already been long in place. The archaeological data indicate that the cultural systems of the ethnographic period were fully evolved by 2,000 years ago and except for localized changes remained relatively stable until European contact.

NOTES

1. See R. C. Harris, ed., *Historical Atlas of Canada*, Vol. 1 (Toronto: University of Toronto Press, 1987), for the most recent reconstructions of glacial and early post-glacial conditions and the article by Josenhans *et al.* in Note 5.

2. See K. Plummer, "Circumstances in Japan that Led Up to Sea Drifting in the Edo Era," in *The North Pacific To 1600, Proceedings of the Great Ocean Conference* (Portland: Oregon Historical Society Press, 1991) I: 311-326. For a fuller account, see *The Shogun's Reluctant Ambassadors—Sea Drifters* (Tokyo: Lotus Press, 1985).

3. Recent conclusions regarding biological relationships between New and Old World human populations are based on comparisons of the genetic attributes of teeth. For the most recent analyses, see C. G. Turner II, "New World Origins: New Research from the Americas and the Soviet Union," in D. Stanford and J. Day, eds., *Ice Age Hunters of the Rockies* (Boulder: Denver Museum of Natural History and University Press of Colorado, 1992): 7-48.

4. See C. Ochsenius and R. Gruhn, *Taima Taima: a late Pleistocene PaleoIndian Kill Site in Northernmost South America* (Coro, Venezuela: Monografias Cientifica, Universidad Francisco de Miranda, 1984); J. Cinque-Mars, "La Place des grottes du Poisson-Bleu dan la prehistoire berengienne," in *Revista de Arqueologia Americana* (1990) 1: 9-32; and J. B. Bird, "The Archaeology of Patagonia," in J. Steward, ed., *Handbook of South American Indians* (Washington: Bureau of American Ethnology, Bulletin 143, 1946) 1: 17-24.

5. For the most current information on Clovis see R. Bonnichsen and K. Turnmire, eds., *Clovis Origins and Adaptations* (Corvallis: Center for the Study of the First Americans, Oregon State University, 1991); and for the meagre information on fluted points in south central British Columbia see A. Stryd and M. Rousseau, "The Early Prehistory of the Thompson River Area" [chapter 17 in R. L. Carlson and L. Dalla Bona, eds., *Early Human Occupation in British Columbia* (Vancouver: University of British Columbia Press, 1995)]. For the latest on late Pleistocene sea levels on the B.C. coast, see H. W. Josenhans *et al.*, "Surficial geology of the Queen Charlotte Basin: evidence of submerged proglacial lakes at 170 m on the continental shelf of western Canada," *Current Research, Part A, Geological Survey of Canada Paper* 93-1A (1993): 119-127.

6. For a detailed description of the archaeological evidence of these five early period cultural traditions, see Carlson and Dalla Bona, eds., *Early Human Occupation in British Columbia*.

7. The Plano Tradition contains a number of complexes based on slightly different styles of lanceolate projectile points. See J. D. Jennings, *Ancient North Americans* (San Francisco: W. H. Freeman, 1983). The most recent data from Alaska are in M. L. Kunz and R. E. Reanier, "Paleoindians from Beringia: Evidence from Arctic Alaska," *Science* 25 (1994): 660-662; and in the *Abstracts of the 45th Arctic Science Conference* (Anchorage and Vladivostok, 1994). Lanceolate points from the sub-Arctic area that do not closely resemble named Plano types, and are younger in time, are frequently referred to as "Northern Plano."

8. See the following: R. L. Carlson, "The Far West" in R. Shutler Jr., ed., *Early Man in the New World* (Beverly Hills: Sage, 1983): 73-96; J. C. Driver, "Early Prehistoric Killing of Bighorn Sheep in the Southeastern Canadian Rockies," *Plains Anthropologist* 27 (1982): 265-272; Choquette, "Early Post-Glacial Habitation of the Upper Columbia Region," in R. L. Carlson and L. Dalla Bona, eds., *Early Human Occupation in British Columbia* (Vancouver: University of British Columbia Press, 1995).

9. See J. S. Cybulski *et al.*, "An Early Human Skeleton from south-central British Columbia: dating and bioarchaeological inference," *Canadian Journal of Archaeology* 5 (1981): 49-59, and B. S. Chisholm, *Reconstruction of Prehistoric Diet in British Columbia using Stable-Carbon Isotopic Analysis* (Ph.D. thesis, Simon Fraser University, 1986).

10. For definition of these cultural traditions see R. L. Carlson, "Cultural Antecedents" in W. Suttles, ed., *Handbook of North American Indians Northwest Coast*, Vol. 7 (Washington: Smithsonian, 1990): 60-69. This volume contains full coverage and an extensive bibliography of all Native peoples of the coast.

11. For data on the Milliken site see C. E. Borden, "Origins and Development of Early Northwest Coast cultures to about 3000 B.C.," *Mercury Series Archaeological Survey Papers* 45 (Ottawa: National Museum of Man, 1975). For Skoglund's Landing, see K. Fladmark, "Possible Early Human Occupation of the Queen Charlotte Islands, British Columbia," *Canadian Journal of Archaeology* 14 (1990): 183-221. For recent discoveries in the Queen Charlotte Islands, see D. W. Fedje *et al.*, "Early Period Archaeology in Gwaii Haanas" (chapter 13 in Carlson and Dalla Bona, eds., *Early Human Occupation in British Columbia*).

12. The analysis of the Namu fauna and the site chronology is contained in A. Cannon, *The Economic Prehistory of Namu* (Burnaby: Archaeology Press, Simon Fraser University, 1991).

13. For Bear Cove see C. Carlson, "The Early Component at Bear Cove," *Canadian Journal of Archaeology* 3 (1979): 177-194. For the Glenrose Cannery site see R. G. Matson, "The Glenrose Cannery Site," *Mercury Series Archaeological Survey Papers* 52 (Ottawa: National Museum of Man, 1976).

14. See R. E. Ackerman *et al.*, *Archaeology of Heceta Island: A Survey of 16 Timber Harvest Units in the Tongass National Forest, S. E. Alaska, Project Report Number 3* (Pullman: Center for Northwest Anthropology, Washington State University, 1985); and A. Stryd and M. Rousseau, "The Early Prehistory of the Mid Fraser-Thompson River Area" (chapter 17 in Carlson and Dalla Bona, eds., *Early Human Occupation in British Columbia*).

15. The renowned linguist E. Sapir originally grouped the Tlingit, Haida, and Athapascan languages together as having a common ancestry. Haida was later removed and considered an isolated language, unrelated to any other. Greenberg has recently reviewed the evidence and re-grouped Haida with the other two. See J. H. Greenberg "Language in the Americas," *Current Anthropology* 28 (1987): 647-667, for a discussion of the controversy. The Navajo and Apache are also Athapascan speakers, but their movement to the American southwest was long after microblade technology went out of use almost everywhere.

16. For Namu data see Cannon reference in Note 12; J. Curtin, *Human Skeletal Remains from Namu.* (M.A. thesis, Simon Fraser University, 1984); J. Hester and S. Nelson, eds., *Studies in Bella Bella Prehistory* (Burnaby: Department of Archaeology Simon Fraser University Publication 5, 1978); and R. L. Carlson, "The Early Period on the Central Coast of British Columbia," *Canadian Journal of Archaeology* 3 (1979): 211-228; and "Early Namu" in Carlson and Dalla Bona, eds., *Early Human Occupation in British Columbia*. For BlueJackets, see P. Severs, "Archaeological Investigations at BlueJackets Creek FlUa 4 1973," *Canadian Archaeological Association Bulletin* 6 (1974): 163-205; and J. S. Murray, "Prehistoric Skeletons from Blue Jackets Creek (FlUa 4), Queen Charlotte Islands, British Columbia," in J. S. Cybulski, ed., *Contributions to Physical Anthropology, 1978-1980 Mercury Series Archaeological Survey Papers* 106 (Ottawa: National Museum of Man, 1981): 127-175. For Yuquot, see J. Dewhirst, "The Indigenous Archaeology of Yuquot, a Nootkan Outside Village," in W. J Folan and J. Dewhirst, eds., *The*

Yuquot Project I (Ottawa: National Historic Parks and Sites Branch, History and Archaeology 39, 1980). The fullest account of the Prince Rupert harbour materials is G. MacDonald, "Prehistoric Art of the Northern Northwest Coast," in R. L. Carlson, ed., *Indian Art Traditions of the Northwest Coast* (Burnaby: Archaeology Press, Simon Fraser University, 1983): 99-121.

17 .See Cannon, *Economic Prehistory of Namu.*

18. See Chisholm, *Reconstruction of Prehistoric Diet in British Columbia.*

19. For evolutionary theory, see C. Coon, *A Reader in General Anthropology* (New York, Chicago, San Francisco: Holt, Rinehart, and Winston, 1948): 612-613; and V. G. Childe, "Early Forms of Society," in C. Singer, E. J. Holmyard and A. R. Hall, eds., *A History of Technology* (New York and London: Oxford University Press, 1954) 1: 38-57.

20. See R. J. Hebda and R. W. Mathewes, "Holocene History of Cedar and Native Indian Cultures of the North American Pacific Coast," *Science* 225 (1984): 711-713; and G. C. Coupland, *Prehistoric Cultural Change at Kitselas Canyon.* (Ph.D. thesis, University of British Columbia, 1985).

21. For one view of the potlatch, see W. Suttles, "Coping with Abundance: Subsistence on the Northwest Coast," in R. B. Lee and I. DeVore, eds., *Man the Hunter* (Chicago: Aldine, 1968): 56-68; and for another see G. C. Coupland, "Prehistoric Economic and Social Change in the Tsimshian Area," in B. L. Isaac, ed., *Prehistoric Economies of the Pacific Northwest Coast, Research in Economic Anthropology Supplement* 3 (London: JAI Press, 1988): 211-244.

22. For relationships between art styles and social complexity, see J. L. Fisher, "Art Styles as Cultural Cognitive Maps," *American Anthropologist* 63 (1961): 79-93. See also A. E. Pickford, "Prehistoric Cairns and Mounds in British Columbia: with a report on the Duncan Burial Mound," *British Columbia Historical Quarterly* 11 (1947): 237-263; and for the most recent data on burial mounds, M. Blake, G. Coupland and B. Thom, "Dating the Scowlitz Site," *The Midden* 25-1 (1993): 7-9.

23. See the following: G. R. Keddie, "The Use and Distribution of Labrets on the North Pacific Rim," *Syesis* 14 (1981): 59-80; R. L. Carlson and P. M. Hobler, "The Pender Canal Excavations and the Development of Coast Salish Culture," *B.C. Studies* 99 (1993): 25-52; I. R. Dahm, "Cultural and Social Dimensions of the Prehistoric Gulf Islands Soapstone Industry." (M.A. thesis in Archaeology, Simon Fraser University, 1994).

24. See M. Eliade, *Shamanism: Archaic Techniques of Ecstasy* (New York: Pantheon Books, 1964) for symbolism connected to shamanism.

25. For detailed evidence of the obsidian trade, see R. L. Carlson, "Trade and Exchange in Prehistoric British Columbia," chapter 11 in T. G. Baugh and J. E. Ericson, eds., *Prehistoric Exchange Systems in North America* (New York: Plenum Press, 1994). See also Figure 1:4 in R. L. Carlson, "Prehistory of the Northwest Coast" in Carlson, ed., *Indian Art Traditions of the Northwest Coast.*

26. See J. J. Hester and S. M. Nelson, *Studies in Bella Bella Prehistory*, 32-33, and J. Curtin, *Human Skeletal Remains from Namu*, 16 for data on burial FS4.H. For historic period slavery, see L. Donald, "The Slave Trade on the Northwest Coast of North America," *Research in Economic Anthropology* 6 (1984): 121-158 (Greenwich and London: JAI Press). Dates on fortified sites are given in M. L. Moss and J. M. Erlandson, "Forts, Refuge Rocks, and Defensive Sites: the Antiquity of Warfare along the North Pacific Coast of North America," *Arctic Anthropology* 29 (2): 73-90.

27. See D. W. Clark, "Prehistory of the Western Subarctic," in J. Helm, ed., *Handbook of North American Indians Subarctic* (Washington: Smithsonian, 1981) 6: 107-129. Clark gives a summary of and references to archaeology of the northern interior of British Columbia.

28. See the following for detailed coverage of prehistory of the past 4,000 years in the southern interior: T. H. Richards and M. K. Rousseau, *Late Prehistoric Cultural Horizons on the Canadian Plateau* (Burnaby: Department of Archaeology, Simon Fraser University Publication 16, 1987).

29. The archaeology of Kettle Falls in described in D. H. Chance and J. V. Chance, *Kettle Falls: 1978* (Moscow: University of Idaho Anthropological Reports No. 84, 1985).30.See Chisholm, *Reconstruction of Prehistoric Diet in British Columbia*, Note 9.

31. See Richards and Rousseau, *Late Prehistoric Cultural Horizons*, Note 28.

32. See W. Choquette, "A proposed cultural chronology for the Kootenai region," in S. Gough, ed., *Cultural Resource Investigations of the Bonneville Power Administration's Libby Integration Project, Northern Idaho and Northwestern Montana* (Cheney: Archaeological and Historical Services, Eastern Washington University Reports in Archaeology and History, 1984): 100-129.

33. B. Hayden and J. Spafford, "The Keatley Creek Site and Corporate Archaeology," *B.C. Studies* 99 (Autumn 1993): 106-139.

34. Population figures are those of C. E. Borden, "Distribution, Culture, and Origin of the Indigenous Population of British Columbia." *Transactions of the 7th B.C. Natural Resources Conference* (1954): 196-196. Similar figures may be found in A. L. Kroeber, *Cultural and Natural Areas of Native North America*, Vol. 38 (Berkeley: University of California Publications in American Archaeology and Ethnology, 1939). R. T. Boyd, *The Introduction of Infectious Diseases among the Indians of the Pacific Northwest, 1774-1874* (Ph.D. thesis, University of Washington, Seattle, 1985) would increase this figure by about 33 per cent based on an estimated 33 per cent loss from the first smallpox epidemic in 1775.

35. See D. L. Pokotylo and P. D. Froese, "Archaeological evidence for prehistoric root gathering on the southern Interior Plateau of British Columbia: A case study from Upper Hat Creek Valley," *Canadian Journal of Archaeology* 7 (1983): 127-157.

36. See M. D. Kinkade, "Prehistory of the Native Languages of the Northwest Coast," in *The North Pacific to 1600, Proceedings of the Great Ocean Conference* (Portland: Oregon Historical Society Press, 1991) 1: 137-158; and W. Suttles, *Coast Salish Essays* (Vancouver: Talon Books, 1987). Also see Note 10.

37. See H. F. L. Williams and M. C. Roberts, "Holocene sea-level change and delta growth: Fraser River delta, British Columbia," *Canadian Journal of Earth Science* 26 (1989): 1657-1666.

38. Recent unpublished work by Philip Hobler in the Bella Coola Valley.

39. See ethnographic chapters in J. Helm, ed., *Handbook of North American Indians Subarctic*, Vol. 6 (Washington: Smithsonian, 1981).

40. Compare P. F. Donahue, "Concerning Athapaskan prehistory in British Columbia," *Western Canadian Journal of Anthropology* 5 (1975): 21-63, with M. Magne and R. G. Matson, "Identification of 'Salish' and 'Athapascan' side-notched projectile points from the Interior Plateau of British Columbia," in M. Hanna and B. Kooyman, eds., *Approaches to Algonquin Archaeology* (Calgary: University of Calgary Archaeological Association, 1982): 57-59.

41. See P. M. Hobler, "Prehistory of the Central Coast of British Columbia," in W. Suttles, ed., *Handbook of North American Indians Northwest Coast* (Washington: Smithsonian, 1990) 7: 298-305.

42. See D. Mitchell, "Prehistory of the Coasts of Southern British Columbia and Northwestern Washington," 340-358.

43. See J. Dewhirst, *The Indigenous Archaeology of Yuquot: A Nootkan Outside Village*, in W. J. Folan and J. Dewhirst, eds., *The Yuquot Project*, Vol. 1 (Ottawa: National

Historic Parks and Sites Branch, History and Archaeology 30, 1980), and A. McMillan, "Since Kwatyat Lived on Earth: An Examination of Nuu-chah-nulth Culture History." (Ph.D. thesis in Archaeology, Simon Fraser University, 1996.)

44. For place name evidence of the southern spread of the Nootkan language, see M. D. Kinkade and J. V. Powell, "Language and the Prehistory of North America," *World Archaeology* 8 (1976): 83-100.

45. See A. D. McMillan and D. E. St. Claire, *Alberni Prehistory: Archaeological and Ethnographic Investigations on Western Vancouver Island* (Penticton and Port Alberni: Theytus Books and Alberni Valley Museum, 1982).

46. See the following: K. R. Fladmark, K. M. Ames, and P. D. Sutherland, "Prehistory of the Northern Coast of British Columbia" in W. Suttles, ed., *Handbook of North American Indians Northwest Coast* 7 (Washington: Smithsonian, 1990): 229-239; and D. W. Fedje *et al.*, "Early Period Archaeology in Gwaii Haanas: Results of the 1993 Field Programme" in Carlson and Dalla Bona, eds., *Early Human Occupation in British Columbia.*

47. See G. F. MacDonald, *Kitwanga Fort National Historic Site Skeena River, British Columbia, Historical Research and Analysis of Structural Remains* (Ottawa: Parks Canada Manuscript Report Number 341, 1979).

48. See G. Coupland, *Prehistoric Cultural Change at Kitselas Canyon.* (Ph.D. thesis, University of British Columbia, 1985), and R. Inglis and G. MacDonald, eds., *Skeena River Prehistory* (Ottawa: Museum of Man Mercury Series, Archaeological Survey of Canada Paper No. 87, 1979).

49. See Note 32.

PART II

Fur Trade and Colonization
1774–1871

Chapter 2
CONTACT AND TRADE, 1774–1849
Robin Fisher

When Europeans began to visit British Columbia late in the eighteenth
century, they encountered indigenous populations whose traditions
were strong and whose cultures were rich and diverse. Each group had developed distinctive patterns in exploiting the region's abundance and in surviving
its scarcity. Although they were not always constant, the boundaries between
groups were well defined and rights to exploit valued resource-gathering locations were clearly understood. In summer the people scattered over their land
to hunt and gather food; in winter they congregated in larger villages and celebrated the spiritual side of life with ritual and ceremonial. Social patterns based
on kinship and lineage were deeply ingrained. The extended family was the
basic unit of social organization. Particularly on the coast, the societies were
hierarchical and individuals knew their place in the order. Birth, wealth and
ability were the attributes of leadership, and yet leaders had a mutual relationship with their people and also led by consent. Geography tended to isolate
Native groups, but there were trading connections over considerable distances
and cultures developed partly through contact with one another.

Beyond those that are obvious, however, generalizations about the indigenous cultures of British Columbia are difficult and dubious.[1] Linguistic divisions were compounded by economic and geographical differences. The
greater part of the Native population was concentrated on the coast, which is
often described as a single cultural area, yet even there the similarities should
not obscure the important distinctions between the groups. On the northern
coast, the cultures of the Haida and the Tsimshian were similar but not the
same, and there were considerable differences between the Haida and the
Coast Salish in the south. Both the Haida and the Tsimshian had matrilineal
kinship structures and in both societies the local group was divided into exoga-
mous clans. At the same time, Haida villages were split into two clans—Eagle
and Raven—while Tsimshian groups had three or even four clans—Eagle,
Raven, Wolf and Killer Whale. Or, to take another example, Haida and
Tsimshian art shared common characteristics, but the bold austerity of the figures on Haida poles also contrasted sharply with the crowded, fussy groupings

on many Tsimshian poles. Among the Coast Salish, social divisions were not as clearly defined as they were in the northern groups. Kinship tended to be determined patrilineally, and clans did not exist. Coast Salish art was quite different from that of the northern coast. In the eyes of many European beholders, it was also less impressive than Haida art.

If there were cultural variations up and down the coast, there was a quite fundamental distinction between peoples of the coast and those of the Interior. On the coast Native people lived off a seasonally abundant maritime environment and had evolved a complex social structure, elaborate and opulent ceremonies, and a highly stylized art form. East of the coast mountains the natural environment was less prolific and the population was much smaller. In order to gather the resources of the land these people had to be more mobile. Partly as a consequence of their mobility, the social organization of the Interior people was looser and, in comparison with those on the coast, their ritual and material culture appeared less elaborate.

The basic distinction between coast and Interior should not obscure the great cultural variety among inland groups. Those Interior people who were in contact with the coast absorbed some features of the coastal cultures. The Chilcotin, for example, had a version of the potlatch ceremony that was typical of the coastal groups. In the far southeast, by contrast, many aspects of the Kootenay culture were similar to features of the cultures of the Native people of the plains, with whom they made contact during the annual buffalo hunts east of the Rockies.

No culture is static and, from the Kootenay in the southeast to the Haida in the northwest, the Native cultures were evolving at the time of European contact. This change was a source of strength. Far from being vulnerable and brittle, the various Native cultures were flexible and adaptive during the early years of contact. Native people met the newcomers on their own terms and molded the European presence to suit their own needs and priorities. Ethnohistorians writing about the early history of other parts of Canada have referred to the dominant Indian cultures, and it is just as appropriate to use the phrase to describe the period of contact and trade in the area that was to become British Columbia. The first Europeans who came among Native people were looking for new worlds to explore and exploit. What they found was an old world where the cultures were vigorous and the people were confident in their own tradition.

EARLY CONTACT

When Europeans first came to the northwest coast they were stretched to the limit as they grasped at the outer reaches of imperial expansion. Whether they came by sea or by land, their approach to the coastline was tentative and uncertain. The mythology of the coast speaks of drift voyages from China or Japan, and Russian explorers had reached the area north of 54° 40' in earlier years, but the first recorded contact with the people of British Columbia was in 1774 when the Spanish voyager, Juan Pérez, met a group of Haida off the northwest point of Langara Island.

Although the initial encounter was fleeting, it was a harbinger of things to come. The Haida paddled around the Spanish vessel throwing feathers on the water. They could not be convinced to go aboard, but when their desire to trade overcame their fear of the strangers, the exchange of goods began. The Spanish offered clothes, beads and knives, and in return the Haida traded some sea-otter furs and a variety of handmade articles including mats, hats, plates, spoons, ornately carved wooden boxes, and what appear to have been chilcat blankets.[2] Pérez and the crew of the *Santiago* spent two days in the area and they left without setting foot on land. The Spanish expedition later made contact with another group of Native people in the vicinity of Nootka Sound, but again no one landed and Pérez was vague about the exact location of the meeting.

European contact with the coast between latitudes 49° and 54° 40' was not renewed until the spring of 1778 when the greatest navigator of them all, Captain James Cook, arrived at Nootka Sound and spent a month refitting his vessels. Cook was the first European to set foot in British Columbia and, more importantly, his was the first extended encounter with the Native people of the northwest coast. Cook and his men established contact with the people who lived at the summer village of Yuquot, or Friendly Cove as it would later be known by Europeans. Relations between the British sailors and the Nootka people were amicable and based on a good deal of mutual respect. Trade was a daily occurrence and the crew members were impressed with the astuteness of the Native people involved. It was immediately clear to Cook that his Yuquot hosts had assumed the role of intermediaries and were controlling the trade at the vessels, particularly when other groups of Native people wanted access to the new source of wealth. A variety of items changed hands. Although they did not know it at the time, the most valuable article that the seamen traded from the Native people was the pelt of the sea otter. Cook and the members of his crew recorded a great deal of accurate and valuable information about the Nootka people and their way of life, but the discovery that was to have the greatest impact on the history of the coast was of the prices that the sea-otter furs fetched when the expedition stopped at Canton on the return voyage.[3]

The appearance, in 1784, of the published account of Cook's third voyage triggered the first round of commercial development on the northwest coast. Lieutenant James King drew attention to the profits to be made on furs in China and gave some specific advice on how to organize a fur-trading expedition to the northwest coast.[4] When the fur trading vessel named *Sea Otter*, under the command of James Hanna, arrived at Nootka Sound the following year, the rush for furs was on. By the early 1790s as many as twenty-one vessels would be on the coast during the summer trading season.

The development of the fur trade in the early years was facilitated by the continued exploration of the coastline. Cook's visit had been a reconnaissance, and others followed to complete the work. Captain George Vancouver, who as a midshipman under Cook on *Resolution* had learned his navigation from the master mariner, returned to the coast in 1792 to complete the work that Cook had begun. Over three successive summers, Vancouver surveyed the intricate coastline from Puget Sound in the south to Cook Inlet in Alaska. He charted an accurate delineation of the foreshore "through all the various turnings and windings"[5] and in the process revealed that which did exist as well as that which did not. He established major points of geography such as the insularity of Vancouver Island and, although his critics would still quibble, he virtually eliminated the possibility of a navigable northwest passage connecting Europe with the Orient.

What Vancouver was unable to find from the sea, others would discover by land. In the summer of 1793, in a tiny notch in Dean Channel called Elcho Harbour, there was what one scholar has called an historic "near miss."[6] On the night of 4 June Vancouver's boat crew rested near the mouth of Elcho Harbour. The next day they examined the small inlet before proceeding down Dean Channel, leaving the spot that another explorer, coming from the opposite direction, would reach a few weeks later. The North West Company explorer, Alexander Mackenzie, had left Fort Chipewyan in the Athapasca country in October 1792, wintered over at the junction of the Peace and Smoky Rivers, and set out in May 1793 on a journey towards the Pacific Ocean. Mackenzie drove his men hard and travelled fast. He reached tidewater at Bentinck Arm on 20 July and two days later, on 22 July 1793, he wrote the terse inscription "from Canada, by land," on a rock on the eastern side of the entrance to Elcho Harbour. He was standing where Vancouver had been just six weeks earlier. Native people described to Mackenzie how Vancouver had left his ship off to the southwest and come to their village in a small boat. The two Europeans had missed each other, but for the Native people, although they did not yet know the significance of these events, the connection had been made.

THE TRADE IN FURS

Vancouver and Mackenzie represented the two lines of development in the fur trade west of the Rockies. The maritime fur traders were engaged in a triangular trade that brought them from the home port to the northwest coast with goods to trade to the Native people for sea-otter pelts that were taken to China to exchange for tea, spices and silk. This commerce was initially dominated by British vessels, but by the early 1790s most of the trading captains were Americans out of Boston. By the turn of the nineteenth century, the peak years of the maritime fur trade had passed as the North West Company was following up on Mackenzie's transcontinental exploration. Another Northwester, Simon Fraser, established the first permanent fur-trading post west of the Rockies at

McLeod Lake in 1805. After founding other forts in the north, Fraser followed the river that now bears his name to the sea. It proved to be neither the Columbia as he had expected, nor a satisfactory route to the sea as he had hoped, and it was not until after the amalgamation of the North West Company and the Hudson's Bay Company in 1821 that the fur resources of the area were systematically exploited. Under the general direction of Governor George Simpson, the Hudson's Bay Company's enterprise west of the Rockies was managed by John McLoughlin from his headquarters at Fort Vancouver. A chain of forts was established both on the coast and in the Interior and later in the 1830s the Company ran vessels up and down the coast as it continued its efforts to eliminate competitors.

There were important differences between the early maritime fur trade and the later land-based trade. The trading captains who came from the Pacific were transitory visitors. They came to the coast to do business and when the transactions were complete they left as soon as they could. Individually, their influence was as fleeting as their presence. Hudson's Bay Company men stayed for longer periods, built permanent forts, and established more sustained relations with Native people. Yet they were few in number and, isolated in their little enclaves, their influence was much more limited than they were willing to admit. And, although the logistics at the European end of the maritime and land-based fur trade may have differed, the role of the Native people in each phase was much the same.

Some of the first maritime fur traders, whose objectives were primarily commercial, still cloaked themselves in the mantle of Cook by expressing an interest in discovery.[7] But it was the search for profit that sent the traders to the farthest reaches of the Pacific. At first the prospects looked good. When James Hanna took 560 sea-otter furs to Canton in 1785 and sold them for twenty thousand Spanish dollars other merchants quickly calculated the wide differential between outlay and income.[8] This initial enthusiasm was short lived, however, as the margins in the supercargoes' account books became tighter and tighter. The backers of maritime fur-trading expeditions soon found that the Canton market, where sea-otter pelts were a luxury item, was easily saturated and prices fell accordingly. Even more disconcerting was the rapid increase in the price that had to be paid for furs on the northwest coast. Contrary to the expectations of some early traders who had not read Cook carefully enough, Native people were not simple-minded savages who would part with dozens of furs for a few trinkets. Rather they were experienced, astute traders who knew all about margins of profit and how to drive a hard bargain. Trade was not new to Native people who had well-defined patterns of commerce between themselves long before the Europeans arrived.[9] As one maritime fur trader put it, "we found to our cost . . ." that the Native people of the northwest coast "possessed all the cunning necessary to gains of mercantile life."[10]

The first traders to arrive on some parts of the coast found that Native people were exuberant and unrestrained sellers. On 2 July 1787 Captain George Dixon arrived at a bay on the northern Queen Charlotte Islands that would later be known as Cloak Bay. Once the Haida had overcome their initial reticence there followed a scene "which absolutely beggars all description." The crew was "so overjoyed, that we could scarcely believe the evidence of our senses," because Native people were falling over themselves to trade their cloaks and furs: "they fairly quarrelled with each other about which should sell his cloak first; and some actually threw their furs on board if nobody was at hand to receive them." In half an hour Dixon obtained three hundred furs.[11] But, alas for those who followed, such scenes were seldom repeated. The fur trade quickly settled down into a regular pattern, and it was a pattern of trade over which Native people exercised a great deal of control. Whatever the preconceptions and intentions of European traders, once they got to the coast it was the demands of Native people that had to be met before furs changed hands.

Europeans had to modify their trading methods to suit the Native people. Captains quickly realized that the initial practice of coasting down the shoreline and expecting Native people to paddle out to a moving vessel to trade would have to be abandoned. They had to anchor at their villages and, subject to their notions of time, spend longer and longer negotiating deals. For Native people, ceremonies—singing, dancing, and the display of wealth—were usually a part of trading encounters and often irritated captains anxious to be on their way. But it was necessary to spend more time on the coast to get enough furs to make the trip to China profitable. Despite their preference for the Hawaiian climate, fur traders eventually found it necessary to winter over on the northwest coast. Even the land-based fur traders, for whom the pressure of time was less immediate, had quotas to meet. They too expressed frustration when Native people devoted more time to winter dancing than to hunting for furs. At the same time they recognized that their ability to change such customs was very limited.[12]

Nor did Native people merely control the formalities of the trade. Although ritual was important to Native people and integral to trading relations, they were also concerned with profits. Maritime fur traders who came back to the coast for a second or third time found that the prices demanded by Native people had doubled or tripled since their first visit. Particularly in the early 1790s, as more and more traders came to the coast, the Native people pressed for higher and higher prices and European traders realized that the quick profits of the early years were no longer attainable.[13] When the Hudson's Bay Company began its trading on the coast after 1821 its officers intended to impose their prices as quickly as possible. But the Native people of the northwest coast knew as much about "oeconomy" as George Simpson. Company traders thought that Native people demanded extravagant prices and Simpson described them as "tiresome in their bargaining."[14] It did not take Company men long to realize that the high prices on the coast also affected the cost of furs along the chains of inter-tribal trade into the Interior. The "Columbia enterprise," as the Company referred to its operations west of the Rockies, was one that involved astute traders of two cultures and it was not until towards the end of the fur-trade period, in the 1840s, that the Hudson Bay Company was able to establish even the semblance of control over the fur market.

Native traders were exacting not only about price, but also about the nature and quality of goods that they took in return for furs. As they proved to be in other parts of Canada, Native people were discriminating consumers.[15] Although the demands of Native people changed over time they were not whimsical or inconsistent as some have argued.[16] The hottest item in the early years of the maritime fur trade was "toes," or rough iron chisels. As is typical at the beginning of an inter-cultural trading relationship, these were goods that had an equivalent in the recipient society and were relatively scarce. Northwest coast Native people could immediately see both the use and the value of metal cutting tools. But still they were not indiscriminate consumers. Iron that was brittle, flawed and could not sustain a cutting edge was usually rejected as unsatisfactory by Native traders. Nor did the demand for iron chisels last forever. As hundreds poured in, the market quickly became saturated and they lost their value: Native traders began to demand other items in return for furs. European captains, and later Hudson Bay Company officers, had to keep up with changing demands or they would leave empty handed. When the demand for metal declined, cloth, clothing and blankets became important trade items. The demand for blankets particularly remained fairly constant and they became a staple in the trade. Native people also acquired other tastes. A liking for rum, smoking tobacco and molasses developed, and firearms began to change hands. But the acceptance of all goods remained subject to quality. Even the famous Hudson's Bay Company blanket was rejected when it was not heavy enough.

The old stereotype of European traders getting a stack of furs for a few beads and trinkets was never true of the fur trade on the west coast. There were fads, but, as in all economies, they were usually short lived. Native people would also accept items as presents that were not a part of the actual trading deal. These baubles were offered to sweeten relations as part of the negotiations that preceded trade. When it came to a trading transaction, however, Native people were tough-minded dealers: they knew what they wanted and were determined to get it.

Native people were able to assert and maintain control over the fur-trade economy largely because of their ability to manipulate competition. From the early 1790s through to the 1840s no European had a monopoly over the fur trade, so when Native people did not get a satisfactory offer from one fur trader they could usually turn to another. Competition was always a factor on the coast and when the fur trade moved into the Interior, Native people there could trade with coastal groups when the price offered locally was not high enough. During the peak years of the maritime fur trade, when activity was concentrated at a few locations and there were several vessels on the coast at once, Native people could move from one trader to another comparing prices and bargaining to force them upwards. As one captain put it, "the Indians are sufficiently cunning to derive all possibly advantage from competition, and will go from one vessel to another, and back again, with assertions of offers made to them, which have no foundation in truth, and showing themselves to be well versed in the tricks of the trade as the greatest adepts."[17] Richard Cleveland's barely concealed annoyance was shared by many European traders who paid the price of dealing in a competitive market.

Hudson's Bay Company managers, following their policy in other areas after 1821, intended to establish a monopoly west of the Rockies, but they were thwarted by the competition that persisted through the 1820s and 1830s. Prices at all the company's coastal forts were affected by American fur-trading vessels and the Russian American Company to the north provided Native people with a second alternative market. The Hudson's Bay Company's most important coastal operation north of Fort Vancouver was Fort Simpson, which was established on the Nass River in 1831 and moved to a site on the Tsimshian Peninsula a few years later. Throughout the 1830s Company traders constantly complained in the fort journal about Native people holding out for higher prices because they expected the American vessels would soon be in the area or because they knew that they could do better at the Russian forts.[18] Rather than lowering prices west of the Rockies as he had hoped, John McLoughlin had to maintain three different prices levels: one in the Interior, another on the coast, and a third on the coast when competitors were in the area.[19] By the early 1840s the company was able to reduce this competition somewhat. An 1839 agreement with the Russians removed them as a source of opposition, and by contracting to provide the Russian forts with supplies the Hudson's Bay Company also took an important source of revenue away from American captains. Fewer vessels came to the coast but they did not disappear entirely. As long as there was any alternative market the Native people of the coast would bargain for higher prices and the effects of their trading acumen was felt as far west as the Rocky Mountains.

SOCIAL AND CULTURAL CONSEQUENCES OF THE FUR TRADE

Some groups of Native people and their leaders were particularly well placed to manage the fur trade. Often because of the location of their villages, these people became experienced intermediaries. They discouraged Europeans from trading with other groups and made sure that outlying people brought furs to them rather than trading directly with the vessels or forts. In this way they ensured that as many furs as possible went through their hands so that they could control the price and, of course, add their own mark-up. That is not to say that for Native people the fur trade was simply a matter of making higher profits. At least as much as in European society, making a good deal was a source of prestige as well as profit. Indeed among the Native people of the northwest coast there was a very close association between wealth and prestige and power. Native groups and leaders who were dealers in furs did not just increase their wealth, they also became much more powerful.

The best known of these leaders during the maritime fur-trading period was Maquinna of Nootka Sound. Maquinna was the name of the ranking leader among the Moachat people who had one of their summer villages at Friendly Cove. As the village became a major port of call for European traders it was clear that Maquinna and his people controlled access by other groups on the west coast of Vancouver Island and also managed a trading network with the Native people who lived near the mouth of the Nimpkish River on the east coast of the island.[20] Though he was well known to trading captains, Maquinna's position was by no means unique. Wickanninish, at Clayoquot Sound, exercised similar control over the trade in that area as did the Haida leaders Cunneah and Kow on the northern Queen Charlotte Islands.

Although the principles were the same, the pattern was slightly different during the land-based fur trade. Once a fort was built a group of local people would set up their village close by and assert themselves as intermediaries. These Native people were known as "home guards" by Company traders who looked upon them with mixed feelings because of the impact that they had on prices at the fort. At Fort Simpson, for example, several Tsimshian groups moved their village to the fort and under a series of leaders named Legaic established control over the trade. Legaic maintained a tight monopoly over the Gitksan people of the upper Skeena River, which he backed up with armed force when necessary. Controlling the powerful Haida was less easy, but often they too had to trade through the Tsimshian rather than directly with the fort. Legaic's trading rights were a rich privilege that enabled him to enhance his prestige within his own group and his power over others. The traditions record at least one occasion when he was able to defeat a threat to his life by humiliating his rivals with his great wealth.[21]

The assertiveness of Native people was also evident at a more personal level in the marriages between their women and Company traders. The first European visitors to the coast, particularly in the north, commented on the power and authority of Native women. When fur traders became more permanent residents, as happened elsewhere in western Canada, Native women sought marriage alliances with them. And they did so for their own good reasons.[22] It made economic sense for a Native women to establish a kinship relationship with a Company trader and they often assumed important roles as mediators between the two races. The marriage of John Kennedy, a senior trader at Fort Simpson, to a daughter of Legaic was one these mutually beneficial alliances. The marriage was part of a pattern whereby Legaic married his daughters to the leaders of Native groups with whom he traded. Now he was bringing the leader of a new and particularly wealthy tribe into his family. From the Company's point of view it was only logical, as Legaic rose to preeminence, to forge a close personal connection with him. Such marriages were clearly good business, but often they were also based on strong affection and many were lasting relationships rather than temporary liaisons. The children of such marriages formed a mixed-blood society that was smaller but no less significant than the Metis society of Red River in what is now Manitoba. Thus fur-trade marriages and the families that resulted were another measure of the reciprocity of race relations.

Partly because they were a controlling influence over the fur trade, Native people also remained in control of their cultures through this early contact period. Within their own world, they continued to be confident of themselves and their way of life. If there was dependence during the fur-trade phase, then it was mutual dependence. Native people began to rely on some European goods, but Europeans relied on Native people to provide the furs that were essential to their economic success. Often European traders were dependent on Native people for their very survival. Some maritime expeditions and, on occasions, the inhabitants of Company forts would have starved without Native people to supply food. "Reciprocity" would therefore seem to be a better word than "dependence" to describe the nature of Native-European relations prior to the late 1840s.

Certainly the Native people cannot be said to have been conquered. Maritime fur traders were transient visitors who came to the coast in small numbers in little vessels and land-based traders were isolated and vulnerable in forts that could easily be destroyed. Although later, in the context of litigation on the land question, some would make the case that by setting up forts the fur traders had conquered Native people, the argument had more to do with politics than history.[23] In fact, both sides in the fur-trading relationship realized that killing potential customers was not a good way to do business. As John McLoughlin so clearly put it in 1843, "Is it not self-evident we will manage our business with more economy by being on good terms with the Indians than if at variance."[24] Although the possibility of inter-racial misunderstanding was great, both sides were interested in keeping hostility to a minimum. There were individual acts of violence and a few attacks on fur-trading vessels, but they were the exception rather than the rule. F. W. Howay argued that attacks on trading vessels were common, but in the end he could only provide a few concrete examples.[25] After the establishment of the land-based fur trade there were virtually no major attacks by Native people on forts west of the Rockies. And Native people accepted the existence of trading posts out of self-interest rather than because they were overawed with the power of Europeans.

All of this is not to say that Native cultures were unchanged by the end of the fur-trade period. There was cultural evolution after the coming of Europeans, just as there had been before, but much of the post-contact change occurred along pre-existing lines. Although there was obviously some innovation, the overwhelming impression during this period is of cultural continuity. Traditions that had existed for thousands of years were not suddenly wiped out because some small groups of newcomers who made limited economic demands had arrived on the scene.

Some anthropologists have argued that, on the contrary, Native cultures were stimulated by the fur trade and that the "golden age" of northwest coast Native culture came after European contact. They point to the fact that the new wealth injected into Native cultures by the fur trade led to increased artistic and ceremonial life.[26] More efficient metal tools made wood carving easier and Native leaders who controlled more wealth could "commission" more artists to work for them. The ethnographer Marius Barbeau once claimed that the totem pole actually originated out of the stimulation of the fur trade.[27] Barbeau was wrong on that point, as the accounts of early visitors to the coast make it clear that totem poles stood in front of Native houses at the time of contact.[28] But clearly poles were carved more frequently and became more elaborate during the fur-trade period. The forests of tall, free-standing totem poles in front of Haida houses in the photographs taken in the late nineteenth century are indicative of many changes brought by the fur trade.[29] The florescence of carving was a change that involved the elaboration of pre-existing forms rather than disruptive innovation.

The potlatch provides a similar and related example, both of the nature of change and of disagreement among scholars. In northwest coast cultures the potlatch was a ceremony in which wealth was distributed to guests in order to celebrate the power of the hosts or to signify a rite of passage.[30] Although some writers have raised doubts on the matter, the potlatch, like the totem pole, did exist at the time of contact, at least among some groups.[31] The ceremonies became more numerous, more elaborate and probably more widespread when the fur trade brought new wealth to Native societies.[32] Beyond making the point that increased wealth led to more potlatches, however, anthropologists differ widely on the question of why they became more frequent. Few would now agree with Ruth Benedict's notion that this development reflected the megalomaniac tendencies in Kwakiutl culture.[33] Helen Codere is more convincing when she suggests that the potlatch became a substitute for warfare as a means of expressing the competitive drive within some Native cultures.[34] Here again, an existing cultural element took on new significance, rather than being replaced with a completely new form.

Obviously the profits of the fur trade were not evenly distributed among Native groups. Patterns of wealth and power ebbed and flowed through the period, as some groups and some individuals benefited more than others. The Moachat of Nootka Sound were important traders in the last two decades of the eighteenth century but gradually their supply of furs dried up. The trade passed them by as captains preferred to go to Nawitti on the northeast coast of Vancouver Island where pelts were more plentiful. Although the Native people of Nootka Sound fell into relative obscurity as traders, the Haida offset their declining wealth with other sources of income. During the height of the sea-otter trade they had been among the most wealthy Natives on the coast. With the depletion of the fur-bearing animals traders moved on to other places, but the Haida began to cultivate potatoes, which they sold in large quantities. Haida artists produced "curiosities" made of wood or argillite to sell to visiting sailors, a precursor of the tourist trade in Native artifacts. The Haida also began to make canoes for export. In these ways they were able to regain some of the lost income of the fur trade.

Some groups rose and fell, whereas others expanded by pushing weaker people aside. The extension of the Kwakiutl as far south as Cape Mudge was in part made possible by the acquisition of new wealth from the fur trade.[35] The trade could also lead to jockeying for position within Native groups. When the nine Tsimshian tribes relocated at Fort Simpson, they were all living at the same place for the first time, so an acceptable order of rank, both of phratries and of individuals, had to be established. Disparities in wealth were not new and nor were shifts in the inter-tribal balance of power, yet it is equally clear that the fur trade did not simply inject new wealth into Native societies, it also produced greater inequities. Maquinna and Legaic both became more powerful than they would have prior to European contact because of their role as fur traders, but at the same time they both had traditional claims to positions of leadership. Lines of continuity with the indigenous past persisted even through this time of social change.

Not all of the changes that occurred within Native cultures through contact and trade were merely a matter of degree. There were also changes of kind. The European newcomers, even if they did so inadvertently, brought cultural items that the Natives could not control quite so easily. Firearms, disease, and the consequent depopulation were all indicative of the down side of European contact. And yet their impact should not be over emphasized. The precise effect of each innovation has to be looked at carefully and their combined influence must be seen in the context of the overall process of change. Some earlier writers, who subscribed to the "fatal impact" view of Pacific history, tended to exaggerate the negative consequences of European contact.[36] Even F. W. Howay, who was probably the most meticulous student of the maritime fur trade, writing in 1942, argued that the trade was disastrous because it "seriously dislocated the finely balanced economic and social fabric of the Indians."[37] Nowadays we are entitled to take a somewhat more balanced view.

CONFLICT AND DISEASE

On the west coast, as in other parts of the Pacific, European weapons were a good deal less powerful than voyagers assumed at the time and some historians have thought since.[38] In and of themselves, firearms did not necessarily confer a great advantage on European fur traders or on those Native groups that acquired them. The smoothbore, flintlock musket, the weapon that Europeans most relied upon and also traded to Native people, was not a very efficient, reliable or accurate gun. Even a good quality musket under ideal conditions was slow to load, awkward to control, and revealed one's presence with the first shot. Trade muskets, however, were poor quality guns and the damp climate of the northwest coast was hardly ideally suited to their use. The Native people already possessed projectile weapons of their own, but most of their fighting was done hand to hand. When in came to fighting at close quarters the Native people were more experienced and better armed. On the rare occasions when there was concerted hostility between Native people and fur traders, Native people also had the advantages of greater numbers and knowledge of the territory. Firearms were not a major counterweight that tipped the balance of power away from the Native people.

Nor was there a significant increase in the level of warfare, either between the races or between tribes, during the fur-trade period. The reciprocity of the trade outweighed the potential for inter-racial misunderstanding that is inherent in any contact situation. There was little to be gained by Europeans in turning their big guns on Native villages and Native people knew the risks they ran if they destroyed a vessel or fort. When Maquinna and his men attacked the *Boston* and killed almost the entire crew in 1803 the lesson was clear enough. Trading captains avoided the area, the Yuquot people faced a declining economy and Maquinna found it less easy to sustain his leadership.[39] Although disparities in wealth increased, the fur trade did not bring new incentives for intertribal conflict as economic motives had also been powerful in indigenous warfare. Rivalries developed over rights to exploit the trade with Europeans, but at the same time energy expended in warfare could not be devoted to hunting and trading. In short, there is no evidence to suggest that there was a massive increase in warfare after contact, or that larger numbers of Native people died violent deaths.

The level of warfare was something that the Native people could govern, but they had little control over the introduction of disease by Europeans. Venereal disease and smallpox were probably the most prevalent and tuberculosis along with various respiratory illnesses were also present. Many of the first crews to come to the northwest coast were infected with venereal disease, though not necessarily with its most virulent forms. Nor can anyone be absolutely sure that venereal disease was not already present on the coast by 1774. Smallpox probably was introduced by Europeans and, unlike venereal disease where the means of transmission was specific, it was an extremely contagious epidemic disease. But, like venereal disease, smallpox came in a variety of forms of differing potency, and not all Native people who contracted smallpox died from it. What is beyond dispute, however, is the fact that disease caused significant fluctuations in the Native populations.

Estimating the demographic impact of disease in the early contact period has become a kind of numbers game based on very pliable evidence. In large part, the issue turns on the size of the point-of-contact Native population, which scholars are prone to revising up or down according to their notion of the impact of disease. The first visitors to the coast provide wildly differing estimates of the population of even a single village. When Cook was at Nootka Sound estimates by crew members of the population of Yuquot ranged from 500 to 2,000.[40] Subsequent scholars who reckon the pre-contact population of the northwest coast to have been, say, 200,000 are making what are, at best, well-informed guesses.[41] Evidence on the impact of disease is also spotty and impressionistic. Both syphilis and smallpox result in nasty symptoms and often agonizing deaths and so reactions to even the possibility of their existence among a population were, not unnaturally, more hysterical than scientific. Contemporary observers often took deserted villages to be evidence of population decline rather than seasonal mobility. Accounts in the journals of explorers and fur traders are usually of outbreaks in particular localities, which scholars then extrapolate to the whole west coast. Scholarly writing on the subject is therefore littered with words like "probably" and "very likely," as authors build up worst case scenarios. The geographer James Gibson, for example, tells us, on the one hand, that disease was "rampant" on the northwest coast at the beginning of the nineteenth century, but, on the other hand, that the Tlingit were particularly hard hit by smallpox in the late 1830s because the last epidemic had been in either 1779 or 1795 and the new generation had no inbuilt immunity.[42] The literature continues to be overwhelmingly concerned with death rates and there is little discussion of birth rates and the extent to which populations regenerate after an epidemic.[43] The question of how quickly immunity is built up after people are hit with a disease for the first time needs to be looked at, as does the nature and impact of medical practice both among Native people and fur traders. What effect did the Hudson's Bay Company's program of inoculating Native people against smallpox beginning in the 1830s have on the death rate? No doubt the Native population declined during the fur-trade period, but there is room for a good deal more caution in assessing the precise extent of that decline.

The impact of so-called "virgin soil" diseases was not, of course, confined to demographics.[44] There was both a social and a psychological impact that was not necessarily commensurate with the level of mortality. It has been argued that one consequence of introduced disease was that individuals were elevated to social positions that they would not otherwise have attained. Vacancies in the higher social ranks as a result of epidemics were filled by people from the lower orders.[45] Of course, if the death rate from disease was lower than commonly thought, then the rate of social mobility would be slower. It is also tempting to conclude that, when Native groups face devastating new diseases that do not appear to be amenable to old beliefs and practices, they are likely to reject those traditional ideas. They "apostatize," as one ethnohistorian has forcefully argued happened among some Native groups in eastern Canada.[46] The critics of this view have pointed out that other groups reacted in exactly the opposite way. They responded to the threat of disease by reaffirming the power of traditional spirits who, it seemed, had sent these visitations upon the people because they were offended.[47] Blanket explanations of the effect of new diseases on indigenous people will always be unsatisfactory because they obscure the variations and nuances, whether they be between or within groups.

The impact of disease is representative of the culture contact situation generally. The response of Native people to contact and trade was complex rather than straightforward, and therefore it is better to avoid words like "positive" and "negative" and the moral judgments that they imply. At the end of each trading season captains or Company officers could do some simple addition to see whether they had come out ahead. The effect of their presence among Native people is less easy to calculate. Certainly the fur trade brought cultural profits and losses along with the economic ones. By the end of the period the Native people were in some ways better off and in some ways worse off. But then change is always that way. So the question is not whether the Native cultures had changed, rather it is whether Native people were able to cope with the change or were they devastated and demoralized?

FUR TRADE AND SETTLEMENT

The fur trade may have been a mixed blessing, but it certainly was not an unmitigated disaster. Just as the Native people exercised a good deal of control over the economics of the trade they also kept a grip on their own cultures. To start with fur traders were merely transitory visitors and even when they established permanent posts they were a tiny minority living among an overwhelming Native population. Representatives of a different culture, if they are determined and aggressive enough, can have an influence out of all proportion to their numbers, but fur traders made very limited demands on Native people. Hudson's Bay Company traders clearly understood that, even if they had wanted to, they were not in a position to eradicate, or even modify, deeply ingrained customs of Native people.[48] They simply lacked the power to force change. Traders came to do business and not to acquire territory, so land was not an issue. It is also significant that missionaries met with little success in converting Native people, either spiritually or culturally, during the fur-trade period.[49] Native people were still free to pick and choose from among the cultural elements brought by Europeans and they chose not to accept Christianity. The first seventy years of European contact was a period of non-directed cultural change for the Native people.

By the end of the fur-trade era, however, new developments were pending that would eventually bring much more drastic change to the Native people of British Columbia. When settlers replaced fur traders, Native people would have less autonomy. The vanguard was the American pioneers who came to Oregon in the mid-1840s, though initially their presence affected the operations of the Hudson's Bay Company in the south more than the Native cultures to the north. The settlers received some assistance from the Company when they first arrived, but they soon raised noisy objections to the existence of a British, monopoly company in what they saw as American territory. Seeing the writing on the wall, the Company established Fort Victoria as a potential new site for its western headquarters in 1843. Then in 1846 its worst fears were realized when the old fur-trading preserve was divided in half by the Oregon Treaty, which established the international boundary at the 49th parallel. The more perceptive of the Company's managers on the west coast saw the implications of these developments even before they had happened. James Douglas, who was then a rising star at Fort Vancouver, observed as early as 1838 that the interests of settlement and the fur trade "will never harmonize." A settlement colony, he wrote, could only flourish "by establishing a new order of things, while the fur trade must suffer by each innovation."[50] Because he foresaw the extent of the upheavals that would follow, Douglas referred to the agreement between Britain and the United States on the boundary west of the Rockies as a "monstrous treaty."[51]

The fur trade, the Native people and the Hudson's Bay Company all had a respite in the area north of latitude 49, but it could only be brief. With the establishment of the British colony of Vancouver Island in 1849 farming settlers began to arrive there too. While their numbers were small and their influence limited prior to the gold rush on the mainland in 1858, as in the Williamette Valley a decade earlier, their coming heralded changes for the Native people unlike anything they had known during the fur-trade era. In the face of the settler onslaught, the Native people would lose their land, their wealth and their power as the pace of cultural change quickly outstripped their capacity to control it. Although the process was underway by 1849, its consequences lay in the future for most Native people in what was soon to become British Columbia. Yet it may well be that, having become used to dealing with Europeans who made limited demands within the co-operative relationship of the fur trade, the Native people were ill-prepared to cope with the upheavals brought by the settlement frontier.

There was, perhaps, some inevitability about the way in which the fur trade led to settlement on the west coast, but we should not be seduced into making ahistorical judgments by attributing the consequences of settlement to the earlier era. Prior to 1849 the Native people had a controlling interest in the fur-trade economy. Their demands had to be met by European fur traders and, in many ways, the trade was carried on according to usages that were well established before the newcomers came to the area. The various cultures were strong and vibrant in 1774 and the Native people remained confident during this early contact and fur-trading period. The trade enriched the traditional cultures and change tended to run along pre-existing lines. The greatest impact that the Europeans had on the Native people was the diseases that they brought with them. There can be little doubt that the Native population had declined by 1849, but the effect of disease should not be exaggerated. In the short run, European contact was not a disaster for the Native people. On the contrary, they played a decisive role in the early history of British Columbia.

NOTES

1. The general literature on the Indian cultures of British Columbia reflects the overwhelming scholarly interest in the northwest coast. The best introduction is still Philip Drucker, *Cultures of the North Pacific Coast* (San Francisco: Chandler Publishing, 1965). There is no equivalent book on the cultures of the Interior.

2. Tomás de la Peña and Juan Crespi, diaries, 20 and 21 July 1774, in Donald C. Cutter, ed., *The California Coast: A Bilingual Edition of Documents from the Sutro Collection* (Norman: University of Oklahoma Press): 159-161, 229.

3. For an account of Cook's visit to Nootka Sound, see Robin Fisher, "Cook and the Nootka" in Robin Fisher and Hugh Johnston, eds., *Captain James Cook and His Times* (Vancouver: Douglas & McIntyre, 1979): 81-98.

4. James Cook and James King, *A Voyage to the Pacific Ocean . . . Performed under the Direction of Captains Cook, Clerke, and Gore, in His Majesty's Ships the Resolution and Discovery. In the Years 1776, 1777, 1778, 1779 and 1780* (London: G. Nichol and T. Cadell, 1784) 3: 438-440.

5. George Vancouver, *A Voyage of Discovery to the North Pacific Ocean and Round the World 1791-1795*, W. Kaye Lamb, ed. (London: The Hakluyt Society, 1984) 1: 182.

6. *Ibid.*, 3: 931; see also Alexander Mackenzie, *The Journals and Letters of Sir Alexander Mackenzie*, W. Kaye Lamb, ed. (Cambridge: The Hakluyt Society, 1970): 375-376.

7. David Mackay, *In the Wake of Cook: Exploration, Science and Empire, 1780-1801* (London: Croom Helm, 1985): 65.

8. *Ibid.*

9. Knut R. Fladmark, *British Columbia Prehistory* (Ottawa: National Museum of Man, 1986): 138-139; R. Cole Harris, ed., *Historical Atlas of Canada: Vol. 1, From the Beginnings to 1800* (Toronto: University of Toronto Press, 1987): plate 14.

10. John Meares, *Voyages Made in the Years 1788 and 1789, from China to the North West Coast of America* (London: J. Walter, 1790): 141-142.

11. George Dixon, *A Voyage Round the World; but more Particularly to the North West Coast of America: Performed in 1785, 1786, 1787 and 1788 in the "King George" and "Queen Charlotte"* (London: G. Goulding, 1789): 199-201.

12. See, for example, James Douglas to governor, deputy governor and committee, 18 October 1838, in E. E. Rich, ed., *The Letters of John McLoughlin from Fort Vancouver to the Governor and Committee, First Series, 1825-1838* (London: Hudson's Bay Record Society, 1941): 238. The general point is developed more fully in Robin Fisher, *Contact and Conflict: Indian-European relations in British Columbia, 1774-1890* (Vancouver: University of British Columbia Press, 1977): 42-44.

13. Vancouver, *Voyage of Discovery*, 2: 627; John Boit, journal, 9 June 1795, "Journal of a Voyage Round the Globe, 1795 and 1796 [in the *Union*]," University of British Columbia Library; Cecil Jane, trans., *A Spanish Voyage to Vancouver and the North-West Coast of America being the Narrative of a Voyage Made in the Year 1792 by the Schooners "Sutil" and "Mexicana" to Explore the Strait of Fuca* (London: Argonaut Press, 1930): 90; Alessandro Malaspina, "Politico-Scientific Voyages Around the World . . . from 1789-1794," trans. Carl Robinson, University of British Columbia Library.

14. Sir George Simpson, *Narrative of a Journey Around the World during the Years 1841 and 1842* (London: H. Colburn, 1847) 2:192; and see also Fisher, *Contact and Conflict*: 26-33.

15. See, for example, Arthur J. Ray, "Indians as Consumers in the Eighteenth Century," in Carol M. Judd and Arthur J. Ray, eds., *Old Trails and New Directions: Papers of the Third North American Fur Trade Conference* (Toronto: University of Toronto Press, 1980): 255-271.

16. Particularly F. W. Howay, "An Outline Sketch of the Maritime Fur Trade," *Report* (Canadian Historical Association, 1932): 14; and also Hubert Howe Bancroft, *History of the Northwest Coast* (San Francisco: A. L. Bancroft and Co., 1884) 1: 370-371.

17. Richard J. Cleveland, *Voyages and Commercial Enterprises of the Sons of New England* (New York: Leavitt and Allan, 1865): 94.

18. John Work, *Journal* of 23 February 1835, in *Journals, 1823-1851*, Provincial Archives of British Columbia (hereafter PABC); Fort Simpson, *Journal* of 5 August 1839 [Hudson's Bay Company Archives, Provincial Archives of Manitoba (hereafter HBCA), B-201/a].

19. J. S. Galbraith, *The Hudson's Bay Company as an Imperial Factor 1821-1869* (Berkeley and Los Angeles: University of California Press, 1957): 138-139.

20. See Yvonne Marshall, "Dangerous Liaisons: Maquinna, Quadra and Vancouver in Nootka Sound, 1790-95" in Robin Fisher and Hugh Johnston, eds., *From Maps to Metaphors: The Pacific World of George Vancouver* (Vancouver: University of British Columbia Press, 1993): 160-175.

21. Fisher, *Contact and Conflict*: 46.

22. This argument has been developed in detail in books that focus on the Prairies but also cite some examples from west of the Rockies. See Sylvia Van Kirk, *Many Tender Ties: Women in Fur Trade Society in Western Canada, 1670-1870* (Winnipeg: Watson and Dwyer, 1980); and Jennifer S. H. Brown, *Strangers in Blood: Fur Trade Company Families in Indian Country* (Vancouver: University of British Columbia Press, 1980).

23. Canada, Parliament, Senate, *Journals*, 16th Parl., 1st sess., 1926-27, Appendix to the Journals of the Senate . . . Special Joint Committee of the Senate and House of Commons Appointed to Inquire into the Claims of the Allied Indian Tribes of British Columbia . . . , *Report and Evidence* (Ottawa: F. A. Acland, King's Printer, 1929): vii.

24. John McLoughlin to the governor, deputy governor and committee, 15 November 1843, in E. E. Rich, ed., *The Letters of John McLoughlin from Fort Vancouver to the Governor and Committee, Second Series, 1839-1844* (London: Hudson's Bay Record Society, 1943): 118.

25. F. W. Howay, "Indian Attacks upon Maritime Fur Traders of the North West Coast, 1785-1805," *Canadian Historical Review* 6 (1925): 287-309, lists only fifteen examples that could possibly be described as Indian attacks on trading vessels. At least five examples are highly doubtful ones and many others are based on second- or third-hand evidence.

26. The point seems to have been first made by Phillip Drucker, "Archaeological Survey on the Northwest Coast," *Bulletin 133, Archaeological Paper no. 20,* Bureau of American Ethnology, Smithsonian Institiution: 27; but also by J. A. Wike, "The Effect of the Maritime Fur Trade on Northwest Coast Indian Society" (Ph.D. dissertation, Columbia University, 1951): 92; and Wilson Duff, *The Indian History of British Columbia: Vol. 1, The Impact of the White Man*, Anthropology in British Columbia Memoir no. 5 (Victoria: Provincial Museum, 1964): 57-58.

27. Marius Barbeau, "Totem Poles: A By Product of the Fur Trade," *Scientific Monthly* (December 1942): 507-514.

28. Wilson Duff, "Contributions of Marius Barbeau to West Coast Ethnography," *Anthropologica* 6 (1964): 63-96; and Phillip Drucker, "The Antiquity of the Northwest Coast Totem Pole," *Journal of the Washington Academy of Sciences* 38 (1948): 389-397.

29. Examples of such photographs are to be found in *Marius Barbeau, Totem Poles: Vol. 2, Totem Poles According to Location*, Bulletin no. 119 (Ottawa: National Museum of Man, 1950).

30. One sentence cannot begin to explain the complexities of the potlatch, about which there is a vast literature. The best general introduction to the subject is H. G. Barnett, "The Nature of the Potlatch," in Tom McFeat ed., *Indians of the North Pacific Coast* (Toronto: McClelland and Stewart, 1966): 81-91.

31. Lewis O. Saum, *The Fur Trader and the Indian* (Seattle and London: University of Washington Press, 1965): 11; for an early and detailed account of a potlatch see [Bernard Magee], Log of the *Jefferson*, 9 July 1794 (University of British Columbia Library); and also Jose Mariño Moziño, *Noticias de Nutka: An Account of Nootka Sound in 1792* (Toronto and Montreal: McClelland and Stewart, 1970): 33; and John R. Jewitt, *A Journal Kept at Nootka Sound . . .* (Boston: J. Jewitt, 1807): 12.

32. Helen Codere, *Fighting with Property: A Study of Kwakiutl Potlatching and Warfare 1792-1930*, Monographs of the American Ethnological Society, no. 18 (Seattle and London: University of Washington Press, 1966): 89-97.

33. Ruth Benedict, *Patterns of Culture*.

34. Codere, *Fighting with Property*, 89-97.

35. Herbert C. Taylor Jr., and Wilson Duff, "A Post Contact Southward Movement of the Kwakiutl," *Research Studies of the State College of Washington* 24 (1956): passim.

36. The classic statement of the fatal impact idea for the wider Pacfic is Alan Morehead, *The Fatal Impact: An Account of the Invasion of the South Pacfic 1767-1840* (Harmondsworth: Penguin Books, 1968).

37. F. W. Howay, W. N. Sage, and H. F. Angus, *British Columbia and the United States: The North Pacific Slope from Fur Trade to Aviation* (Toronto: Ryerson, 1942).

38. The argument in the paragraph is developed in more detail in Robin Fisher, "Arms and Men on the Northwest Coast," *B.C. Studies* 29 (Spring 1976): 3-18; for other parts of the Pacific, see Dorothy Shineberg, "Guns and Men in Melanesia," *The*

Journal of Pacific History 6 (1971): 61-82; and K. R. Howe, "Firearms and Indigenous Warfare: A Case Study," *The Journal of Pacific History* 9 (1974): 21-38.

39. These developments are apparent from the journal of John Jewitt who was a captive of the Moachat for two years following the attack on the *Boston*. See Jewitt, *Journal*, passim.

40. Public Record Office, London, Adm. 51/4528, James Burney, journal, 22 April 1778.

41. Robert T. Boyd, "Demographic History, 1774-1874," in Wayne Suttles, ed., *Northwest Coast: Handbook of North American Indians*, volume 7 (Washington: Smithsonian, 1990): 135.

42. James R. Gibson, "Smallpox on the Northwest Coast, 1835-1838," *B.C. Studies* 56 (Winter 1982-1983): 61, 66.

43. This point is made for parts of the south Pacific by Norma McArthur, *Island Populations of the Pacific* (Canberra: Australian National University Press, 1967): 347 and passim.

44. The idea of virgin soil diseases, meaning those against which there is no built up immunity, is developed by Alfred Crosby, "Virgin Soil Epidemics as a Factor in the Aboriginal Depopulation in America," *William and Mary Quarterly*, 3rd series, 33 (April 1976): 289-299.

45. See, for example, Wayne Suttles, "Post-Contact Culture Change Among the Lummi Indians," *British Columbia Historical Quarterly* 18 (1954): 45.

46. Calvin Martin, *Keepers of the Game: Indian-Animal Relationships and the Fur Trade* (Berkeley and Los Angeles: University of California Press, 1978): 53.

47. Bruce Trigger, "Ontario Native People and the Epidemics of 1634-1640," in Shepard Krech ed., *Indians, Animals, and the Fur Trade: A Critique of Keepers of the Game* (Athens: University of Georgia Press, 1981): 29-32.

48. Fisher, *Contact and Conflict*, 42-43.

49. *Ibid.*, 118-123.

50. Douglas to governor, deputy governor and committee, 18 October 1838, Rich, *McLoughlin's Letters, First Series*, 242. On the career of James Douglas, see Margaret Ormsby, "Sir James Douglas," *Dictionary of Canadian Biography* (Toronto: University of Toronto Press, 1972) 10: 238-249.

51. Hudson's Bay Company Archives, A-11/72, London, Inward Correspondence from HBC Posts, Victoria, 1845-1869, Douglas and John Work to governor and committee, 7 December 1846.

Chapter 3
THE FOUNDATIONS OF GOVERNMENT
J. I. Little

The British government was losing interest in its North America empire at the very time it established a colony on Vancouver Island. This explains the tentative way in which it proceeded. In the past, Britain had valued colonies in North America for three reasons: as reliable sources of grain and timber, as markets for manufactured goods, and as checks on the rival development of the United States.[1] When Britain moved to free trade in the 1840s, the possession of protected markets and secure sources of raw materials ceased to matter, but concern about the United States remained. Only when the British government felt reasonably confident that colonials were loyal to the empire was it prepared to grant them control over their own internal affairs,[2] which is why the people of Nova Scotia and the United Province of Canada had to wait until 1848 before being granted responsible government. This development might have signalled the end of British imperialism in North America if, less than a year later, Britain had not chartered the new colony of Vancouver Island and put it under the control of a merchant monopoly.

Colonizing Vancouver Island was a strategic move. The Americans had taken sole possession of Oregon in 1846, ending a period of joint jurisdiction with Britain. Since the United States had taken California from Mexico in 1848, it was clear that, if the British wished to keep their access to the Pacific and the Orient from a base in North America, they would have to act. In this respect, the British government was still thinking in a traditional way, despite the onset of free trade. This did not mean it was prepared to spend public money to colonize Vancouver Island. As an economical solution, the government made the Hudson's Bay Company the "true and absolute lords and proprietors" of the new colony in spite of the objections of strict free traders to any kind of chartered monopoly.[3] The main conditions imposed on the Company were to establish "a settlement or settlements of resident colonists" from the United Kingdom or its other "dominions" by the end of 1854, and to devote 90 per cent of the revenues from land sales to the establishment of an economic infrastructure.[4] During the following few years the territory under civil government on the west coast expanded in a piecemeal fashion after gold discoveries brought successive influxes of miners into British territory from California. In a series of reactions to the threat of American annexation, the authority of Governor James Douglas was extended to the Queen Charlotte Islands in 1852, the colony of British Columbia was created in 1858, and its boundaries were expanded northward to the 60th parallel and eastward to the 120th meridian in 1863.[5]

Britain also maintained a visible naval presence in the region after 1853. The outbreak of war with Russia in 1854 intensified concerns about the security of the British position on Vancouver Island and in British Columbia, but a more serious concern was the rapid expansion of American settlement into Washington Territory after its Native population was crushed in 1859. In the same year American soldiers occupied the strategically important San Juan Island, which the British continued to claim according to their interpretation of the Oregon Treaty.[6] The British would not risk war over the matter, but American aggressiveness in the region and the large American contingent in the gold rush population made the Colonial Office unwilling to listen to the demands of settlers for a more effective voice in government.

At the same time, the Colonial Office expected the colonies to be financially self-supporting. This meant that the colony of British Columbia carried the cost of the roads built to extend British authority into the rugged Interior during the gold rush. From settlers came the complaint that an arbitrary government had burdened them with excessive debt, which they did not have the resources to meet. Not until after the Colonial Office had engineered British Columbia's entry into Confederation in 1871 would its settlers finally acquire the political rights that their counterparts in the eastern colonies had enjoyed for a generation.

CONSTITUTIONAL AND POLITICAL DEVELOPMENT

The British government granted the Hudson's Bay Company property rights over Vancouver Island in 1849, and attempted to appease critics by insisting on the appointment of an outsider as governor. The Company's choice fell on an inexperienced thirty-two-year-old barrister, Richard Blanshard, whose principal qualification was a willingness to forego an immediate salary. The Company promised to pay all civil and military expenses and Blanshard expected to receive land in lieu of salary in the initial period until settlement began to produce revenues. Unfortunately, he discovered that the situation provided him with no resources—no residence, no staff or officials, and no income—and the land he anticipated as a private grant was, the Company insisted, attached to his official position.[7] Indeed, Blanshard had almost no one to govern since all but a few individuals were Company employees, and therefore answerable in most matters to the imposing chief agent, James Douglas. Plagued as well by serious illness, Blanshard asked to be recalled within nine months of his arrival, and Douglas became governor, over the objections of the few independent settlers, in the spring of 1851.

Douglas had difficulty promoting colonization on an island that held little attraction for agricultural settlers and the Hudson's Bay Company, working within Colonial Office guidelines, increased his difficulty by adopting a restrictive settlement policy. Land sales failed to generate enough revenue for all the public works needed in a new colony, yet no import duties could be imposed on the sole authority of the councillors whom Blanshard had appointed to serve until the population was large enough to elect an Assembly. Douglas nevertheless managed to circumvent the constitutional requirement for popular consent to taxation by pushing a liquor licensing bill through his rather reluctant council. The new governor justified this bill on the basis of his authority to keep the peace, and the large quantities of alcohol consumed by the small community produced sufficient revenue to begin construction in 1854 of a high road running west from Victoria to the disgruntled settlers in Sooke.[8]

Although Douglas believed that "the best form of government, if attainable, is that of a wise and good despotism," the constitutional authorities in London declared in 1855 that to be legal the colony's legislation would have to be ratified by an elected General Assembly.[9] A restrictive franchise of twenty acres freehold limited the vote to forty-three individuals distributed over seven districts. Nanaimo had no qualified electors aside from the Company's representative, and only Victoria had enough interested qualified residents to require a contested election.[10] As a result, five of the seven members were or had been linked to the Hudson's Bay Company, but the Assembly did remain independent enough to prevent the government from solving its revenue problems. The representatives simply refused to sanction customs duties, or any other form of supplementary taxation, on the grounds that the colony's charter stated that the Company was obligated to "defray the entire expense of any civil and military establishments" from land sales and royalty payments.[11]

The situation became critical in 1858 when the Fraser River gold rush dramatically increased demand for public works and government services even though the mainland had become a separate colony. The following year, when the Company's grant expired and the Island became a Crown colony, the Assembly was left with little choice but to raise funds independently through taxes and whatever additional revenues it could command. This produced a confrontation between the Assembly and the governor's council over the control of Crown revenues, which the governor's council possessed and the Assembly wanted. A little more than two decades earlier, in Upper and Lower Canada (Ontario and Quebec), this issue had sparked popular rebellion. On Vancouver Island, as in the eastern colonies, the Assembly would not agree to a permanent civil list (guaranteeing high salaries for the principal government officers) in exchange for control over Crown land revenues. In this matter the governor and the Assembly remained deadlocked for the life of the Colony of

Vancouver Island. The Assembly also insisted that the governor's council be exclusively an executive body, with no right to amend money bills. In this case the Assembly enjoyed success because, in 1863, shortly before Douglas stepped down as governor, the Colonial Office finally authorized separate Executive and Legislative Councils in line with the practice elsewhere in British North America.[12]

Early in his career as governor on the Island, Douglas faced opposition from the small number of British gentry who had arrived as settlers and who considered him to be too tied to the fur-trading monopoly and too unaccustomed to "civilized" society. However, the growing pressure for responsible government came essentially from the rising business class in Victoria, which resented being governed by the "family-Company compact" of former Company officials and Douglas family members. The two most prominent examples of the so-called compact were the governor's brother-in-law, David Cameron, and his son-in-law, Dr. John Sebastian Helmcken. The former was appointed to the Supreme Court and Legislative Council, while the latter served as the Company physician and first Speaker of the Assembly.[13] Two contemporary historians have noted that this group, like its namesake in Upper Canada, "believed in a hierarchical social order, to be maintained through government support for an established church, a landed gentry, and a private, denominational system of education."[14] However, social, cultural and economic conditions on the west coast made such a blueprint even less appropriate here than it had been in the eastern colony.

The chief spokesman for the opposition in Victoria after 1858 was the colourful newspaper publisher, Amor De Cosmos ("Lover of the Universe"), who had been born in Nova Scotia with the more prosaic name of William Smith. He had improved his fortunes and changed his moniker in California before migrating northward to establish the *British Colonist* and speculate in real estate. Drawing on the ideas of his former mentor, Joseph Howe, De Cosmos argued that government should be run "according to the well understood wishes of the people."[15] But whereas Howe felt that Nova Scotia's future would be most secure within an imperial federation, De Cosmos was a strong supporter of Confederation and critic of the imperial connection. He argued that it simply imposed an extravagant system of government while forcing the colony to be self-supporting financially on an open international market.

De Cosmos, who became a member of Vancouver Island's General Assembly in 1863, realized that the first step towards joining a British North American union would have to be union with the mainland colony of British Columbia. In 1858, with the onset of the gold rush, the British government had created a separate colony on the mainland—without an Assembly—because it had simply not been prepared to extend Vancouver Island's electoral system to an area whose non-Native population was largely composed of transients from California and Oregon. Victoria nevertheless dominated the mainland because

Douglas governed there as well with the power to legislate by proclamation. The new colony's secretary and attorney general also remained in Victoria despite Colonial Office instructions to move to New Westminster. As a heavy investor in Victoria real estate, Douglas proceeded to ensure that town's hegemony over the gold fields by imposing a revenue tariff of 10 per cent *ad valorem* on the mainland, while Victoria enjoyed free-port status.

As early as 1859 the mainland colonists established a Reform League to demand resident officials and a popular voice in government.[16] As far as popular representation was concerned, the most that Douglas was initially willing to concede was a municipal council for New Westminster in 1860. Victoria's merchants were too beholden to Douglas to press for the same privilege, which was granted only in 1862 under the condition that all by-laws were subject to the governor's veto.[17] As for New Westminster, even though the election of its five councillors was subject to Douglas's approval, they did not hesitate to demand wide-sweeping reforms.[18] Furthermore, when grand juries were called they seized the opportunity to raise local complaints, in the manner of the grand jury foreman in 1861 who addressed Judge Matthew Baillie Begbie: "It may appear to Your Honour that in introducing some of the topics adverted to above, we have exceeded our duty as Grand Jurors, but the total absence of a more legitimate medium through which the people might express their views, and make known their wants, is our only, and we think sufficient, apology."[19]

In an attempt to exert more effective pressure, residents of New Westminster organized a province-wide convention of elected delegates in the fall of 1860. All five would-be delegates who ran on the "Government Ticket" in New Westminster were defeated. In addition to drafting the customary demands for a government entirely unconnected with Vancouver Island, and the establishment of representative institutions, the convention protested against high taxes, the profligate public works policy, faulty administration of Crown lands, and the favouritism shown to Victoria in foreign trade and in awarding ship-building contracts. Douglas declined to recognize the convention delegates "as representatives of the inhabitants of British Columbia," but did meet them "as a deputation of Her Majesty's subjects from Douglas, Hope, and New Westminster." He clearly felt that there was little danger of civil unrest, for he associated the convention with a "public exhibition got up for the amusement of the people."[20] When the Colonial Office ignored their memorial, the convention delegates met again in the fall at Hope. This time Douglas was less dismissive, though still disinclined to accept any of the demands:

> I have no desire to accuse the authors of this memorial of entertaining any malevolent designs, the majority of them being known as quiet, well meaning tradesmen, sincerely attached, I believe, to the Institutions of the Colony, but at the same time have not disposed to overlook the fact that they may become for seditious purposes, the dupes of artful men. I have therefore charged the Magistrates

to keep an eye over their movements and not to interfere with their proceedings so long as they commit no violation of the law.[21]

Presumably one of the "artful men" referred to by Douglas was the New Westminster newspaper editor, John Robson, who had been influenced by the political reform movement of his native Upper Canada. In May 1861 Robson declared in his *British Columbian*: "We are in a state of veriest serfdom . . . and the result will be one universal burst of long pent-up indignation, which will appal [sic] the Imperial, and shatter the Colonial Government."[22] As spokesman for the Royal City's commercial aspirations, Robson went so far as to suggest a retaliatory tariff to discriminate against ships first stopping at Victoria.[23]

In 1863, when the mainland colony was five years old, the Colonial Office finally concluded that the British element was strong enough to allow the appointment of a chamber with a "popular" element, based on Ceylon as model. The Legislative Council was to be composed of fifteen members, one-third of whom would be colonial officials, one-third magistrates and one-third selected by the people. The ratio of popularly chosen members would increase over time, but the manner of their selection and their formal appointment remained in the hands of the governor. Douglas proceeded to divide the colony into five districts, and to invite residents in each "to select a person of good character and approved loyalty" to represent them in the legislature.[24] The Colonial Office foresaw the day when British Columbia and Vancouver Island would be united, but the mainland was still not judged to be ready for representation in a Legislative Assembly. In fact the two colonies became completely distinct entities in 1863 when Douglas was replaced by Arthur Edward Kennedy on the Island, and British Columbia finally gained its own governor, Frederick Seymour.

Paradoxically, the creation of separate mainland and Island executives each with its own governor actually hastened the union of the colonies because it ended the mainland's subsidy to Vancouver Island for its civil establishment. Islanders had vainly attempted to salvage some sort of executive union while holding onto their representative institutions as well as Victoria's status as capital and free port, but mainlanders had nothing to gain from these arrangements. In the absence of any financial support from the mainland, the Executive and Assembly of Vancouver Island quickly reached an impasse. This happened during the deepening economic recession in 1865. Not only did the Vancouver Island Assembly—in its campaign to gain control over the Crown land revenue—refuse to vote the monies needed for the continued business of government, but the principal bank in Victoria, the British-owned Bank of British Columbia, rejected further loans to a colonial government that was already heavily in debt.[25]

Under these conditions the Assembly accepted De Cosmos's motion that the two colonies be united "under such constitution as her Majesty's Government may be pleased to grant." Two Victoria seats were vacated as a test of public opinion, and pro-union advocates won both. Union was also supported in the economically declining Cariboo area where the local newspaper complained that the needs of miners who paid nine-tenths of the taxes were ignored, while "esplanades, leading avenues and useless roads are constructed at the public expense at New Westminster. Cariboo in the eyes of officialdom must just pay the fiddle for New Westminster to dance."[26] The settlers of the Lower Mainland and British Columbia's governor, Seymour, favoured the status quo, but he was summoned to England to be firmly reminded that the Colonial Secretary was determined to unite the two colonies. Seymour was able to ensure, however, that British Columbia's constitution was retained while that of Vancouver Island was abolished, that New Westminster was confirmed as the capital, and that Victoria lost her free-port status. Thus the mainland effectively annexed the Island in the spring of 1866.[27]

The residents of Vancouver Island were shocked to learn that they had lost the right to elect Assembly members. Instead, the Legislative Council was expanded from fifteen members to twenty-three, with the mainland keeping its five districts and the Island being granted only four. Victoria's *Colonist and Chronicle* lamented:

> By our own deliberate act we have flown to other ills we dreamed not of. We relinquished our right of selfgovernment, sacrificed a liberal constitution, and transferred the seat of government, for what? in order to become the annexure to a *Crown Colony* under a hostile and unpopular Governor. We have abandoned our Free Port and for what? for the privilege of adding ten per cent. to the cost of living, and the blessings of being taxed to pay for a heavy debt we neither incurred nor were benefitted by.[28]

At more than $1 million, the debt of the mainland was indeed three-and-a-half times that of the Island. Victoria was nevertheless placated to some extent when, with support from the councillors from the interior of the province, it recaptured the status of capital in 1868.

In itself, the union was a justifiable move, for, as students of the event have stated, "neither the social, economic, legal, nor military requirements admitted the necessity of two independent entities."[29] But the failure to provide for an elected Assembly was certainly a harsh measure that reflected the Colonial Office's exasperation with the Vancouver Island Assembly as much as its fears of American influence on the mainland. By 1868 the popularly selected members in the Legislative Council were a majority of one, but their choice still had to be ratified by the governor. Seymour died the following year without completing his plan to have them become truly elected representatives. Finally, with the last session of the Legislative Council in 1871, the system was changed so that nine of fifteen members would be "formally and legally elected" by the people,[30] but the Colonial Office resisted responsible government for fear that it would interfere with the rapid movement towards Confederation with Canada.[31] These developments will be examined in the last section of this chapter.

DEVELOPMENT POLICY

The British government's colonial development strategy for Vancouver Island and British Columbia was profoundly influenced by its primary aim of discouraging American penetration of this last stronghold on the Pacific. Aliens were not permitted to purchase Crown lands prior to 1858. Then, when the gold rush brought a sudden and massive influx from California, no expense was spared to build a system of roads that would guarantee British commercial and military control of the mountainous Interior. The fact that the colonists bore much of the economic burden of the restrictive settlement policy, as well as the profligate roads policy, goes far to explaining the demands noted above for more political power.

Roads

Given the coastal location of its settlements, major road construction projects were not a priority on Vancouver Island. The situation was entirely different in the mainland colony. Prior to the Fraser-Thompson gold rush, the only non-indigenous people in the Interior were fur traders who relied largely on pack trains and canoes to transport their goods. To reach the mouth of the Fraser River they had to resort to trails that were blocked by snow in the higher passes for eight months of the year. In 1858, however, steamboats penetrated more than one hundred miles up the Fraser River to Yale, from where a mule trail was cut to Lytton at the mouth of the Thompson River. Partly in order to remove from Victoria the disorderly miners who were waiting out the spring run-off, Douglas arranged for five hundred of them to work on an alternate route from the head of Harrison Lake to Lillooet. Although these men received no pay, the construction costs were nevertheless more than £12,000, far more than anticipated. Furthermore, the British authorities could hardly rely upon foreign miners to build the colony's transportation network.[32]

As a result, during the summer of 1858, the Colonial Office dispatched a corps of Royal Engineers to perform the double duty of public works development and defence. Among the 172 men were carpenters, masons, bricklayers, smiths, miners, architects and photographers. They were commanded by Colonel Richard Clement Moody, who was also appointed British Columbia's commissioner of lands and works, surveyor-general, and lieutenant governor. After a brief period, the troops were to be financed entirely by the colony, but Moody initially set his own military priorities ahead of Douglas's desire to improve the transportation links to the gold fields. Furthermore, although

Douglas had begun preparations for a capital at Old Fort Langley, Moody objected that this site was too vulnerable to American attack. As a result, in 1859 the Royal Engineers spent most of their efforts preparing a site for the capital at New Westminster on the thickly forested, steep-sloped north bank of the Fraser River. They also extended the North Road from New Westminster to Burrard Inlet.[33] Thereafter, Douglas appears generally to have had his way. Even though the municipal council representing local residents was denied the promised revenue from the sale of Crown lots or rental of water frontage within the town limits, it was left with the responsibility of clearing land and grading streets in the new capital.[34]

In 1860 the Royal Engineers, greatly assisted by private contractors, transformed the Douglas-Lillooet route into a four-metre-wide wagon road, but freight on this route had to be transferred from steamer to wagon, and wagon to steamer, at least eight times, with each transfer bringing a substantial increase in shipping costs.[35] As a result, in 1862 the Royal Engineers began construction on the 600-kilometre Cariboo Road from Yale to the centre of the new gold rush at Barkerville. However, the military proved not to be the most economical tool for supervising public works, and Douglas requested that the "costly ornament" be withdrawn the following year.

In addition to the tonnage duty imposed to raise revenue for the roads, Douglas borrowed £50,000 ($200,000) a year in 1861 and 1862, allowing the colonial government to budget close to $400,000 annually for roads during the following three years. As a result, by 1865 the entire length of the Cariboo Road could be negotiated by stage coach during the summer season. A return journey previously requiring two months by mule train had been reduced to eight days.

By this time, however, Cariboo gold production had already passed its zenith, the centre of activity having shifted to Wild Horse Creek in the Kootenay district. All the mining supplies for the thousand men working in the Kootenay mines in 1864 and 1865 were provided from the American side of the border, but before the Hope-Similkameen Trail had been extended the full 466 kilometres to the Kootenays, the focus had shifted once again, this time to the more accessible Big Bend area. Yet another lengthy road was built by the government, this one stretching from Cache Creek along the Thompson River to Kamloops Lake, from where steam navigation extended to the end of Shuswap Lake, but the rush was already over by 1866.

Furthermore, with the Cariboo and Kootenay miners able to evade the gold export tax imposed in 1864, the $500,000 loan of that year was exhausted by the end of the next. The roads budget for 1866 was slashed to $125,500 and earmarked for repairs only, but it was too late to escape the effects of the recession that lay just around the corner. Because of the crippling debt, only $26,844 was spent on the entire mainland road system in 1867. Expenditures increased thereafter, but the amounts remained barely sufficient to keep the main routes open.[36] The need for additional roads, and the poor condition of the Cariboo Road, became constant themes in the *Cariboo Sentinel*. It pointed out in 1868, for example, that the pack trains had not reached Barkerville until 3 May with passage still not possible for wagons on 8 June.[37] Yet the retrenchment in public works expenditures made little impression on the debt, which had reached $1,267,160 by 1867. Clearly, then, ongoing colonial autonomy was becoming less and less viable.

Land

Land sales offered little relief from the debt burden, for as late as 1870 they contributed only one-fortieth of the colony's total revenue.[38] Douglas had recommended in 1848 that the first settlers receive free grants of two hundred acres or more as a "powerful motive to attach them to the country,"[39] but Edward Gibbon Wakefield's theory that access to colonial land should be restricted to those with capital held sway in the Hudson's Bay Company headquarters. Douglas was informed by the Company secretary:

> . . . some of the worst evils that afflict the Colonies have arisen from the admission of persons of all descriptions; no regard being had to the character, means or views of the immigrants. They [the committee] have therefore established such conditions for the disposal of lands, as they trust will have the effect of introducing a just proportion of labour and capital, and also of preventing the ingress of squatters, paupers and land Speculators. The Principle of Selection, without the invidiousness of its direct application, is thus indirectly adopted.[40]

Under the conditions referred to, colonists would have to bring to Vancouver Island five single men or three married couples for every hundred acres purchased, though Douglas succeeded in having this conditions removed by 1850. One could expect a fur-trading company evolving into a general resource company with a need for cheap labour to promote a restrictive settlement policy. What was less predictable was that the Colonial Office should be in complete agreement. It recommended that Crown land should not be sold for less than £1 ($4) an acre. Between 1851 and 1858 only 180 individuals purchased land on the Island, and they nearly all had links to the Company. Over half of them acquired town or suburban lots, which Douglas was able to price competitively with those south of the border.

Even if land policy had been more liberal, the quality of the soil represented a serious impediment to agricultural settlement on Vancouver Island. When the high prices for food at the gold diggings brought a sizeable influx of stockmen and farmers to the mainland, Douglas proceeded to facilitate access to land title despite his instructions to continue the Wakefieldian sales policy in the new mainland colony. First, he sanctioned the sale of land to aliens who had taken the oath of allegiance; then, in 1859, he cut the upset price of unsurveyed land almost in half to ten shillings four pence (slightly more than $2) an acre. Two years later, the price was reduced again to below the American level at four shillings two pence ($1) per acre. Furthermore, the slow pace of surveying by the Royal Engineers led Douglas to authorize the pre-emptive occupation of 160-acre lots. An occupant who improved a claim to the value of ten shillings ($2) per acre would receive a certificate of improvement making the land eligible for sale or mortgaging.[42] Full payment did not have to be made until after a survey of the land had been completed, but, because many disputed land claims awaited resolution, the slow progress of the survey work caused great inconvenience.

Douglas's land policy also failed to prevent speculation by those with capital, for individuals could purchase large tracts of unsurveyed land with a 50 per cent down payment, and—prior to a change in regulations in 1861—without having to fulfill settlement conditions. The pre-emption system had clearly outlived its original purpose in the New Westminster district by 1868, for only 27,797 acres of the 83,440 acres surveyed there had been claimed. Furthermore, much of this surveyed land was acquired for speculation, since there was no limit set on the amount of land an individual could purchase at auction, and no residence requirement. As of 1868, a mere 250 acres of the land purchased in the New Westminster district had been brought into cultivation. One solitary settler on the south side of the Fraser wrote in 1862 that "not a week passes without one or two parties visiting this side of the river looking for land to pre-empt, and when they find out that all this wilderness around me is taken up and secured by gentlemen of ease and position, their curses are loud and long."[43] Colonel Moody himself acquired 3,750 acres, chiefly on the North Road and around Burnaby Lake.[44]

The policy of pre-emptions and land sales at one dollar per acre was extended to much of Vancouver Island in 1861,[45] but the problem of the Hudson's Bay Company's pre-colonial claim to a reserve of 3,084 acres in Victoria remained. Between February 1859 and January 1862, while the Company's legal claim to the land remained in dispute, it sold the choicest of Victoria's remaining lots, largely to a few speculators, for a net profit of $300,000. On the grounds that lengthy judicial proceedings would hold the town's development in limbo, the government proposed a compromise whereby the Company would keep about half the acreage it claimed. A committee of the Assembly attacked the "indenture of 1862," but to no avail. When the law officers of the Crown eventually upheld the Company's claim to this land, the *Colonist* did not mince words:

> Was there ever such an instance of gross injustice perpetrated by even the Khan of Tartary? We hope Vancouver Island will never forget how its patrimony was jealously guarded by its trustees—and how the English Colonial Office consented to measures which left the Island a pauper—a disinherited heir . . . . Do our Imperial authorities really desire to drive us out of the British connection or are

they simply carrying out one of their paternal schemes for testing our loyalty?"[46]

Major modifications in land policy were still more necessary for the mainland Interior where a ranching community sprang up to serve the large market for beef created by the gold rush. Although ranchers could not purchase enough land for grazing purposes, the government hesitated to offer pastoral leases because drovers who were bringing in American cattle to feed the miners wanted free passage and pasture for their animals. In 1865, however, with the mining boom drawing to a close and bunch grass being replaced by sage in the Cariboo due to the pressure of over-grazing, legislation was passed that enabled land-holders to take out pastoral leases in their immediate vicinity.

The rent and the number of livestock allowed on each leasehold would be determined by the local stipendiary magistrate. In most cases the maximum was one head for every ten acres, with $75 being the average cost for a holding of one thousand acres. Records show leases of five thousand acres and six thousand acres in the Similkameen and Hat Creek districts, respectively.[47] To prevent ranchers from discouraging settlement, all leased land was liable to preemption or purchase without compensation, and all leases were limited to seven years with no right to renewal. This legislation was developed and implemented without much consultation with either the ranching population of the Interior or their political representatives. Yet even though the small number of government agents could not be expected to enforce regulations in the sparsely settled territory stretching from Quesnel to Osoyoos, a specialized study of British Columbia's ranching frontier indicates that the ranchers were generally "conscientious about fulfilling pre-emption claims, certificates of improvement, and other legal and administrative details."[48]

If the government was not entirely successful in looking after the land requirements of the ranchers, it was much less so in considering the rights of the indigenous population. Aboriginal title was recognized in the fourteen purchase agreements Douglas signed with Vancouver Island tribes between 1850 and 1854, but no more "treaties" were negotiated thereafter. The chief reason was that Douglas disagreed with the Colonial Office about whether London or Victoria should provide the necessary funds, but it also appears that by the time Douglas was governor of the mainland he no longer supported the principle of aboriginal title. Instead, he laid out reserves in areas that settlers were beginning to move into, with the aim of encouraging the indigenous population to follow a European-style, village-agrarian economy. The ultimate goal was to have the Natives become fully integrated into settler society by offering them equal rights in the pre-emption of unsurveyed land off the reserves. Reserve deeds therefore remained in the hands of the Crown, leaving the way clear for their future reduction.[49]

The general attitude, as expressed by the *British Colonist* in 1861, was that "the Indians must give way in order to make room for a race more enlightened, and by nature and habits better fitted to perform the tasks of converting what is now a wilderness into productive fields and happy homes."[50] The reduction process began soon after Douglas's resignation, for his successors effectively left Native land policy in the hands of Joseph William Trutch, the surveyor and engineer who served as commissioner of Crown lands between 1864 and 1871. Trutch's consistent policy was simply to move the Natives out of the way so that European settlement could progress.

The first step was taken in 1866 when the forty-mile stretch along the Thompson River that had been set aside for the Kamloops and Shuswap bands was reduced to holdings of six thousand acres and five thousand acres, respectively. The following year approximately forty thousand acres were reclaimed in the lower Fraser Valley, again without compensation. Not only were Native village sites and cultivated fields intruded upon under Trutch, but their residents could no longer pre-empt land as individuals, and reserves were henceforth limited to ten acres per family. The Natives of British Columbia were stuck in limbo for they were neither given special status as aboriginal peoples nor encouraged to become full-fledged participants in the settler economy. Unfortunately for them, they were too dispersed and culturally diverse to take effective action during the period in which they still held the numerical upper hand.[51]

LAW AND AUTHORITY

It should not be surprising that the governments of Vancouver Island and British Columbia took their military and policing functions very seriously. In the imperial game plan the principal role of these colonies was to prevent the expansion of a rival power; and the gold rush frontier after 1858 created an environment that threatened stability and invited American intervention. Furthermore, one of the chief tasks of the governing authorities in Vancouver Island and British Columbia was to ensure that the indigenous majority was kept in check by forcing it to adhere to British laws in its contacts with settlers and miners. Indeed, the leading historian of the British navy on the northwest coast claims that "a desire to eradicate slavery and slave-trading, piracy, murder, theft, cannibalism, and intertribal warfare" motivated British imperial authorities and contributed to the general concern about law and order.[52] It was fortunate for the British that the involvement of Native people in the fur trade helped cushion the shock of contact between the two cultures, particularly during the Douglas era.

The heavy-handed manner with which Blanshard handled the Nawitti, at the northern tip of Vancouver Island makes the subsequent appointment of Douglas appear wise. Blanshard had ordered the destruction of the Nawitti village by naval gun boats in 1850, and again in 1851, after the killing of three British sailors who had deserted their ship. Blanshard held the whole tribe of the Nawitti responsible but the situation was complicated by the fact that

Company officials had asked the Nawitti for help in capturing the sailors and the Nawitti may have regarded these men as slaves, with no human rights. Douglas argued that "it is inexpedient and unjust to hold tribes responsible for the acts of individuals,"[53] and he also pointed out that, had the village residents attempted to defend themselves, violence might have escalated into a war with disastrous consequences for the infant colony. When a Company employee was killed by Natives in the Cowichan Valley in 1852, Douglas was able to capture the individuals involved without punishing their tribes, and without loss of life.[54]

Douglas effectively had a free rein in dealing with the indigenous population, and increasingly he had to exercise quick judgment as settlement on the Island spread into isolated unprotected areas. In addition to requests for protection against imagined invasions by Natives, he had to respond to Natives who resented the infringement of coal miners on an important source of their income.[55] Indeed, indentured white labourers were themselves a troublesome concern, for they bitterly resented the Hudson's Bay Company's low-wage policy at a time when the California gold rush was promising quick riches to the south.[56] Blanshard had appointed Dr. Helmcken as magistrate on a short-term basis to deal with the miners at Fort Rupert, but they had simply refused to recognize his authority.[57] Subsequently, Douglas administered the law himself during the first two years of his governorship. Finally, in the spring of 1853, he appointed as justices of the peace the Company's three farm managers, as well as the manager of a nearby privately owned farm. A court of petty sessions, composed of one or more of the justices, was to be held once a month, and a general quarter session every four months.[58]

The inexperience of these four justices of the peace quickly led to problems in cases in which large sums of money were involved. As a solution, Douglas established the Supreme Court of Civil Justice for cases of more than £50 ($200) and appointed his brother-in-law, David Cameron, as the first chief justice despite the fact that he had no legal training. The aggrieved justices of the peace consequently agitated against Douglas and the Hudson's Bay Company, which only encouraged the governor to limit their jurisdiction further in 1857 by establishing an Inferior Court of Civil Justice, which would also be presided over by Judge Cameron.[59]

The major threat to civil order at Victoria did not come from the settlers, but from the several thousand Haida, Tsimshian and other northern Natives who began to visit the post yearly in the mid-fifties. Large quantities of illegal alcohol exacerbated inter-tribal tensions and contributed to disintegrating social behaviour, with increasing levels of theft, prostitution, assaults and murder. The first full-time constable was appointed in 1854, and a local militia was instituted two years later. Nevertheless, to instill "a respect and fear of the law in the minds of the Native population," Douglas continued to rely heavily on the presence of the navy.[60] Naval vessels expelled visiting Natives who had outlived their welcome, but Douglas did resist local demands for removal of the Songhees from their reserve across Victoria's inner harbour. When small-pox broke out among the Songhees in 1862, however, their houses were razed. This pushed them into more immediate contact with other Natives encamped in the vicinity and contributed to the spread of the disease up the coast and into the Interior as members of the northern nations fled for home.[61]

Meanwhile, the gold rush in 1858 had brought to Victoria "large numbers of professional crooks, gamblers and confidence men," in addition to rowdy miners during the winter months.[62] To help maintain order, the government established a regular police force under the authority of Augustus Pemberton, and appointed a stipendiary magistrate for the city. By 1863 there were five magistrates on the Island, including two naval officers who could carry out summary punishments wherever their ships happened to be located.[63] In 1860 alone 755 charges were laid for misdemeanours such as assault, larceny, felony, desertion and selling liquor to the Natives. That same year the chief justice was given jurisdiction over criminal affairs. Cameron's new duties were clearly con-sidered to be rather burdensome, for his salary was increased from £100 ($400) to the level of the governor's at £800 ($3,200) per annum.[64] Governor Kennedy did his best to increase the size of the police force and to eradicate corruption by raising salaries, but the Assembly's refusal to pass his estimates in 1866 resulted in a reduction in the number of positions. The consequence, accord-ing to Kennedy, was "a great danger to the fabric of British legal, moral and social tenets."[65]

Relations between settlers and the indigenous nations on the Gulf of Georgia remained strained during the 1860s,[66] but it was in the mainland Interior that the most severe tensions developed, as the symbiotic relationship of the fur trade was replaced by one of competition for gold. In 1856 and 1857 the Natives of the Thompson River managed to protect their gold monopoly and salmon-spawning beds by forcing American miners to retreat, but there was no turning back the rush of 25,000 individuals in 1858.[67] Supported by the pres-ence of three naval vessels and the Hudson's Bay Company steamer, *Beaver*, Douglas did not wait to receive official jurisdiction over the mainland before appointing salaried officials at Fort Langley, Fort Yale and Lytton. Their assign-ment was to enforce not only the purchase of mining licences, a mechanism based on British practice in Australia, but also the payment of royalties and the posting of £2,000 ($8,000) bonds on claims. Douglas aimed to impress the supremacy of the Crown, finance the costs of administration and police, and achieve economic stability by discouraging individual miners.[68]

He also managed to prevent bloodshed near Yale in June by appointing Native and white magistrates to keep the peace within their respective groups. The governor wished to impress Native people with "the great point that the law will protect the Indians equally with the white man."[69] Unfortunately, this desire was not enough to stop a serious conflict from developing in August, when miners moved into the territory of the Thompson bands who tried to prevent them from working. The well-armed miners destroyed several villages and fought a full-pitched battle with the Thompson Natives, forcing them to stop obstructing mining activities. To demonstrate his intolerance of such violence, Douglas brought in a force of thirty-five men from a naval vessel, and then conducted a tour of the gold-mining centres where he appointed local officials.[70]

These officials played a unique multi-faceted role. In the absence of British gentlemen-settlers to serve as justices of the peace, they acted as salaried magistrates charged with settling all mining disputes, minor criminal cases and civil disputes involving sums under £50 ($200). They also served as civil officers who collected the miners' licences, registered all mining claims, supervised the work of local mining boards, acted as Crown land agents, electoral officers and Indian agents, and appointed special constables to assist in enforcing the law.[71] To fill these positions, Douglas selected young men, mostly of the Anglo-Irish gentry, who had arrived in Victoria carrying letters of introduction from the colonial secretary. Perhaps because they were willing to settle disputes by somewhat unorthodox methods, the judicial officials—variously known as assistant gold commissioners, justices of the peace, or stipendiary magistrates—were generally successful in maintaining law and order. The major exception was Peter Brunton Whannell, an Australian infantry deserter, who attempted in 1858 to close down all the saloons and gambling halls at the Fraser River mining community of Hill's Bar. In response, the notorious Ned McGowan and his gang simply usurped local authority, compelling Douglas to dispatch a military force to the area.[72] British Columbia's six stipendiary magistrates held their offices until 1880, when they were replaced by professional lawyers.[73]

Presumably because it relied on bringing in military personnel whenever necessary, the government felt little need for a strong police force. In 1859 it appointed Chartres Brew as Chief Inspector for a projected force to be modelled on the Irish Constabulary, but then it rejected his repeated requests for 150 men. At the height of gold production, there were no more than eighteen constables in regular employment. The power to appoint constables lay with the assistant gold commissioners until 1864, when the murder of eighteen workers and settlers by Natives in the Chilcotin district caused Governor Seymour to centralize the police force under his own control.[74]

Initially, in the absence of any alternative means of regulation, Douglas had to permit miners to establish their own mining codes at the various river bars, as they had in California. Yet he made it clear from the start that the government would not sanction the molesting of Natives, the exclusion of Chinese from mining, or the impromptu justice of lynch law. By 1859 Douglas had designed a system of local mining boards under government supervision. These bodies were to consist of six to twelve members who would be elected by no less than 101 local miners before being approved by the governor. They were empowered to establish regulations relating to mining methods and claims, though the

Gold Fields Act of 1859 did set fundamental rules governing the frontage of a river claim (7.5 metres), the length of time one could be absent from a claim before losing it (three days), and so on. Furthermore, their decisions could be overturned by the assistant gold commissioners.[75]

Perhaps it is not surprising that the Cariboo miners were rather apathetic about the value of such a board until they began to search for political tools to combat economic decline. In 1866, when they finally did elect a board, it did not concern itself with mining regulations at its first meeting, but demanded reforms to the mining disputes adjudication process, as well as government subsidies for three projects: the Cariboo hospital, an extended network of trails and a proposed quartz mining project.[76] The mining board was clearly acting as a surrogate municipal council, but its members' enthusiasm soon waned when they discovered that they did not have the legal authority to enforce such fundamental decisions as the construction of a bulkhead to control the course of the river.[77]

On the mainland, the legal system was effectively controlled by the Cambridge-educated Matthew Baillie Begbie who acted as Douglas's legal advisor. Begbie's Supreme Court of Civil Justice exercised jurisdiction in all cases, criminal as well as civil. As the only judge on the mainland for more than a decade, Begbie spent the summer months on circuit, thereby ensuring that prisoners from outside New Westminster would not have to be tried far from their peers.[78] Begbie had the reputation of being severe—even harsh—in his judgments, but his presence in the mining camps was generally viewed as an effective antidote to frontier lawlessness.

Begbie himself wrote to the colonial secretary in 1866:

Crimes of violence are extremely rare; highway robberies almost unknown; I think only 4 or 5 cases by white men since my first circuit in 1859. The express has for years travelled constantly over 500 miles of road, chiefly through mountainous or forest country. It carries from $50,000 to $200,000—protected I believe by two armed men—I don't think it has ever once been attacked. Stabbing and pistoling, so common in the adjacent territories are almost unheard of on the British side of the line: although the population is composed of the same ingredients.[79]

The judge might have added that the government's gold escort was losing money because private express companies offered greater security to the miners.[80] However, his general claim that law and order prevailed was supported by the grand jury in 1866, which commented on "the total absence of crime" among the district's white population.[81] The *Cariboo Sentinel* also boasted about the lack of local crime, even while reporting robbery from sluice boxes and incidents of fights and rowdyism as evidence that police protection was needed in Barkerville. A certain measure of violence was clearly tolerated in the interests of business, for closing down the "gamblers and the hurdies" would "send a hundred men down the country to spend the winter and their money."[82] The *Sentinel* assumed an air of wounded pride in 1867 when the Victoria *Colonist* suggested a show of armed force to make the Canadian Company of Grouse Creek submit to the authority of the Cariboo district's Mining Court. In the words of the Cariboo paper:

> What need would there be for an armed force; the moral force of this community would have been amply sufficient to check any attempt to invade the majesty of the law. We claim to be just as loyal and patriotic subjects as our fellow citizens in Victoria, and if required, would as readily lend our aid and assistance to suppress anything like an approach to mob law.[83]

As for the Lower Mainland, the records of New Westminster's "House of Correction" include charges of assault, stabbing and murder, as well as felony, larceny, horse stealing and selling spirits to the Natives.[84] The homicide rate in colonial British Columbia was much higher than that of Victorian England where public concern was paradoxically much greater. Colonists appear to have associated violent crime essentially with the indigenous population, which they considered to be naturally depraved.[85] Begbie's biographer claims that he was sympathetic to the plight of the Natives, "urging their claim for aboriginal land rights, protecting their fishing rights, advocating trials by their own tribunals for some offences, [and] many times urging reprieves for men convicted of murder (never for a white man)."[86] The fact remains, however, that a Native person's word was given subordinate status in court, and Native people represented four-fifths of the twenty-seven individuals hanged for murder in the colonial period.[87]

As the Grouse Creek affair illustrated, it was in the realm of civil law that the greatest challenges to constituted authority presented themselves. A recent study of law and authority in colonial British Columbia argues that this was a particularly litigious society because the law enabled residents to solve problems that in more settled communities might have been resolved outside formal institutions.[88] It was Begbie's arbitrary and authoritarian style of handling mine-related cases in particular that created the local demand for decentralization of authority in the interests of "efficiency, predictability and standardization."[89] A mass meeting held at Richfield in June 1866 collected £800 ($3,200) to send emissaries to New Westminster in order to demand that appeals of the gold commissioners' decisions be heard in a local court, and not by Begbie in Chancery where rules and procedures of equity rather than common law were applied. In response to a widespread campaign to this effect, the government amended the Gold Fields Act in 1867 to limit appeals from the mining court to questions of law only.[90] In addition, county courts had already been established in 1866 with jurisdiction in all civil actions up to £100 ($400), or double that of local courts prior to that time.[91]

The act that united British Columbia and Vancouver Island in 1866 made no reference to the administration of justice. This provoked a clash between the two chief justices. Judge Joseph Needham of Vancouver Island argued that the status quo remained in effect, while Begbie insisted that the Act of Union had simply eliminated the old colony of Vancouver Island and all its legal institutions. Governor Seymour tended to side with Begbie, but in 1869 he agreed to the provisional establishment of separate Supreme Courts for the Island and the mainland. The following year Governor Musgrave settled the thorny problem of concurrent jurisdiction and two different sets of laws when he secured the chief justiceship of Trinidad for Needham, clearing the path for a merger under Begbie who remained chief justice for another twenty-four years. In this way, the decentralized system of the mainland—necessitated by a dispersed population—was extended to the Island. The imperial authorities were able to countenance decentralization because public participation in the legal process through juries was simultaneously reduced.[92] The same attitude caused the Colonial Office to withhold responsible government until after the colony became a province of Canada.

CONFEDERATION

The political sacrifice that the residents of Vancouver Island made in joining the mainland colony did little to solve the government's financial problems during a lengthy recession. By 1867, when the British treasury contributed only £1,295 ($5,180) for naval charges and miscellaneous assistance, nearly one-third of British Columbia's revenue went to pay interest on the debt.[93] Disgruntled businesspeople in Victoria began to advocate political union with the United States. Annexation appeared increasingly inevitable after the American purchase of Alaska from Russia in 1867, which the United States secretary of state, William H. Seward, saw as a crucial step towards the acquisition of British Columbia. He was demanding the colony as compensation for the damage done to American shipping by British-built Confederate raiders during the Civil War. The Fenian threat was another element in the situation. In 1866 Fenian activity among Irish-Americans in San Francisco prompted New Westminster to establish a militia artillery company, as well as a second infantry unit, and to encourage the Royal Navy to keep its only ironclad vessel in the Pacific at Esquimalt for nearly two years.[94] But the victory of the North in the Civil War had convinced Britain that the American preponderance of power on the continent was unchallengeable. Rather than making further military commitments in North America, Britain encouraged the extension of the Canadian Confederation westward, expecting the new Dominion to be responsible for its own defence. The first step in this process was the extinction of the Hudson's Bay Company claim in Rupert's Land.[95]

The officials who dominated the Legislative Council in British Columbia realized that their privileged positions would not be protected under a new constitutional arrangement. One of their strongest opponents was Amor De

Cosmos who began to stir up popular enthusiasm for joining the eastern province. Early in May 1868 he and his allies established the Confederation League in Victoria, and then enlisted support for it in New Westminster, Yale, Lytton, Clinton and Barkerville. In September, the League's convention of twenty-six delegates at Yale demanded immediate union with Canada, the institution of responsible government, retrenchment of public expenditures, and reciprocity with the United States.[96] The campaign suffered a serious setback, however, when De Cosmos and all the other pro-confederationists on Vancouver Island were defeated in the election for a new Legislative Council. Seymour had helped determine the outcome by widening the franchise from British subjects only to all males except Natives and Chinese. Although all Council members elected on the mainland supported Confederation, this did not prevent the official majority from passing a resolution declaring that union with Canada was "undesirable, even if practicable."[97]

Neither the Canadians nor the British exerted any direct pressure on British Columbia until 1869 when the incorporation of the North-Western Territories into the Dominion of Canada was settled. With the convenient death of the increasingly ineffectual Governor Seymour in the spring of that year, Prime Minister John A. Macdonald recommended the appointment of the experienced and dedicated Anthony Musgrave, then retiring as governor of Newfoundland. Newfoundland's last-minute decision not to enter into Confederation only increased Musgrave's resolve to bring in British Columbia, even at the cost of neglecting all other aspects of his mandate.[98] The task appeared to be a daunting one, for the governor's inaugural tour of the colony left him thinking that it was "by no means clear" that the majority favoured union with Canada. Nor did he relish the motives of the leading Confederationists, observing pessimistically that, "The more prominent Agitators for Confederation are a small knot of Canadians who hope that it may be possible to make fuller representative institutions and Responsible Government part of the new arrangements, and that they may so place themselves in positions of influence and emolument.[99] Musgrave would have received a different impression in the Cariboo, where there was little support for responsible government, yet such strong expectation of the economic benefits of an overland route that citizens began to celebrate Dominion Day as early as 1868.[100]

Looking at the economic prospects, British investors in British Columbia argued that Canada could not offer the two chief requisites for development: population and capital. Union with the United States, however, was not an option that they could consider, which left them with little choice but to focus on attaining the best deal possible from Confederation.[101] Support for annexation to the United States was confined largely to the American inhabitants, whose general inactivity suggests that they realized the hopelessness of their cause. Indeed, the governor's hand was strengthened by reaction to the initiative of the German and Jewish merchants of Victoria who sent a pro-annexation petition with forty-three signatures to President Grant.[102] Opinion began to shift in Victoria and De Cosmos emerged victorious in a by-election held in late 1869 on the clear-cut issue of Confederation. As for the obstacle presented by the officials in the Legislative Council, Musgrave's solution was simply to promise pensions for those forced into retirement by the new regime.[103]

The terms of union became the chief concern of the pro-Confederation reformers, for they feared that without popular input the needs of the colony would be sacrificed to imperial interests. The appointment to the Executive Council of two popular Legislative Councillors, Doctors J. S. Helmcken and R. W. W. Carrall, did little to allay those concerns, but it was hard to find fault with the demands ultimately presented by the executive. These included the assumption of all debts and liabilities by the Dominion, a request for federal grants based on a highly inflated population figure initially set at 120,000, a coach road from Manitoba's Fort Garry, plus an annual investment of $1 million in the construction of a rail link to commence from British Columbia within three years, and a minimum of four Senators and eight Members of Parliament. The proposals were passed by the Legislative Council with only minor modifications, including a clause calling for the protection of agriculture, though a heated and prolonged debate did take place concerning the failure to provide for responsible government.[104]

The three delegates chosen to negotiate with Ottawa represented the dominant sectional and economic interests of the colony. Dr. Carrall was spokesman for the Canadian investors in the Cariboo; Joseph Trutch represented the commercial and transportation interests of the Lower Mainland; and the unenthusiastic Dr. Helmcken was the agent for the British element in Victoria. Musgrave had been careful not to select a proponent of responsible government, but Robson and the proprietor of the Victoria *Colonist* nevertheless sent a "People's delegate" to lobby for their cause.[105] In Ottawa, British Columbia's draft terms were accepted with little modification by the Canadian negotiating team, led by George-Étienne Cartier. The fictional population base was halved to 60,000 (still six times the European total) and federal representation reduced from four Senators and eight members of the House of Commons to three and six, respectively, but the $1,045,000 debt would be absorbed, ten years' interest on a loan of up to £100,000 ($400,000) would be guaranteed for a dry dock at Esquimalt, and construction of a transcontinental rail link would begin within two years, to be completed within ten, thereby obviating the need for a wagon road. British Columbia would help finance the railway project by contributing a twenty-mile belt of land on each side of the track, but it would be compensated by an annual grant of $100,000 in perpetuity.

Musgrave had informed the Canadian government that "it would be necessary, if Union is to be real and entered upon cordially, that present visible advantages and local improvements should spring from the measures."[106]

However, the chief reason for the Canadian government's willingness to improve upon British Columbia's transportation demands appears to have been its prior determination to begin rapid construction of a rail link to the rebellious Red River settlement. From there it would be relatively easy to proceed through the Prairies and the lower northern passes of the Rockies. To placate British Columbia's farmers, the Confederation deal left the new province free to retain its own higher tariff schedule until the completion of the railway. Finally, responsibility for Native people was transferred to the federal government. However, the hypocritical provision that the federal government "shall be as liberal as British Columbia . . . formerly was" ensured that future reserve grants would continue to be limited to ten acres per family.[107]

The Canadian government obviously was not anxious to interfere in the internal politics of British Columbia. The terms of the Confederation agreement simply stated that the province would be free to introduce responsible government when it wished. In order to amend its own constitution by accepting the terms of Confederation, however, the Legislative Council had to become a more representative body.[108] Musgrave therefore removed the nine magistrates and declared that nine of the fifteen remaining positions would be elective. The November 1870 election resulted in the return of a complete slate of Confederation supporters, but responsible government and the timing of its introduction had been the dominant question in the election campaign.[109] Still smarting from the experience of his previous posting, Musgrave was adamant that reform be delayed until after the union was consummated. During the election he had written to Macdonald:

> Notwithstanding all the boasted eagerness of the Community for Confederation the only men I can depend on are the officials. De Cosmos and the leading Demagogues like their fellows in Newfoundland would throw Confederation to the winds tomorrow if without it they could obtain Responsible Government which with them does not mean rational self government as in a larger community, but official plunder and possession of the public offices . . . ; if I were weak enough to yield this point we might whistle to no purpose for Confederation for years to come.[110]

Yield he did, however, promising a bill to provide for the introduction of responsible government if the Legislative Council adopted the terms of union.[111] Those terms were subsequently accepted with little debate in January 1871, after which Musgrave presented a bill to provide for the replacement of the Legislative Council by a Legislative Assembly consisting of twenty-five members to be elected for four-year terms. The governor would then select five of these members to form an Executive Council,[112] but whether or not he would be bound by the advice of political leaders would have to be settled in the new regime.

The only remaining obstacle to British Columbia's entry into Confederation was the rising fear in the east that the transcontinental construction schedule would bankrupt the young country. Five hundred and fifty residents of Victoria had petitioned late in 1870 for a branch line from Nanaimo to Esquimalt, but Musgrave warned: "If we attempt to add a ryder [sic] to the terms, they may be defeated."[113] Instead, the visiting Joseph Trutch was pressured by his hosts in Ottawa to give an unauthorized promise in April 1871 that his province would not insist upon a literal interpretation of the agreement's terms. Those terms were then quickly passed by Parliament, and the date for becoming a part of Canada was set for July 20. British Columbia's decision had been based essentially upon pragmatic considerations, but the fact that union with the United States was never seriously considered suggests that, in the final analysis, "loyalty to a set of values loomed larger than mere economic advantage."[114]

AN ACCEPTABLE PRICE FOR CHANGE

In the issue of 19 July 1871, the editor of the Victoria *Colonist* wrote: "Today is the last in the life of British Columbia as a distinct colony of the British crown. . . . For more than a decade it has been governed from Downing Street, governed by men pitch-forked into office by the periodic revolution of the political wheel of home administration."[115] Perhaps the most striking feature of British Columbia's political history in the pre-Confederation period was the degree of control exercised by the governors. They were officially responsible only to the British government, and their great distance from the Colonial Office left them with a good deal of discretionary power. Musgrave, for example, was sent directly from Newfoundland to the west coast where, as a student of his administration puts it, "he was left to his own resources, the colonial records, and the memory of the present and former officials on the spot to discover the basic legal, financial, procedural, and social facts."[116] Under such conditions, the local officials inevitably became an influential elite, but it appears that British Columbia was too young, too underpopulated, and too geographically divided for its equivalent of Upper Canada's Family Compact to take deep root. Certainly, Musgrave had little difficulty in neutralizing the Victoria officials who saw union with Canada as a threat to their handsome salaries and naturally opposed it.

It was not easy to organize an effective political movement among members of the general white population when they were denied truly representative institutions, and when they were mostly transient males of various national backgrounds. As residents of an isolated frontier, threatened by American expansionism and a justifiably disgruntled indigenous population, British Columbia's colonists had little choice but to tolerate a form of government that had long become anachronistic in Britain's other settlement colonies. The rising middle class nevertheless laid the foundations for self-rule in its attempts to fashion effective instruments of local government and political protest. To this group, the sacrifice of colonial autonomy in 1871 was an acceptable price for responsible government and the promise of economic security.

NOTES

I wish to thank Wendie Nelson for her painstaking research assistance, as well as Tina Loo, Bob McDonald, Richard Mackie, Keith Ralston, and my co-authors for their useful critiques of earlier drafts.

1. Phillip Goldring, "Province and Nation: Problems of Imperial Rule in Lower Canada, 1820 to 1841," *Journal of Imperial and Commonwealth History* IX (1980): 40-42.

2. Phillip A. Buckner, *The Transition to Responsible Government: British Policy in British North America, 1815-1850* (Westport, Conn.: Greenwood Press, 1985): 335.

3. J. S. Galbraith, "Bulwer-Lytton's Ultimatum," *Beaver*, Outfit 268 (Spring 1958): 21.

4. Richard Mackie, "The Company Transformed: The New Fur Trade on the West Coast, 1821-1858." (Unpublished paper presented to the fifth B.C. Studies Conference, 1988): 18-22.

5. Barry M. Gough, " 'Turbulent Frontiers' and British Expansion: Governor James Douglas, the Royal Navy, and the British Columbia Gold Rushes," *Pacific Historical Review* XLI (1972): 16-17.

6. Barry M. Gough, *The Royal Navy and the Northwest Coast of North America, 1810-1914: A Study of Maritime Ascendancy* (Vancouver: University of British Columbia Press, 1971): 95, 150-168; Jean Barman, *The West Beyond the West: A History of British Columbia* (Toronto: University of Toronto Press, 1991): 75.

7. Margaret A. Ormsby, *British Columbia: A History* (Macmillan of Canada, 1958): 99.

8. Ormsby, *British Columbia*, 114-121.

9. Quoted in Margaret A. Ormsby, "Sir James Douglas," *Dictionary of Canadian Biography [DCB]* X: 244.

10. Lionel H. Laing, "The Family-Company-Compact," *Washington Historical Quarterly* XXII (1931): 123; Barman, *The West Beyond the West*, 60.

11. Quoted in James E. Hendrickson, "The Constitutional Development of Colonial Vancouver Island and British Columbia," in W. Peter Ward and Robert A. J. McDonald, eds., *British Columbia: Historical Readings* (Vancouver: Douglas & McIntyre, 1981): 245.

12. Hendrickson, "Constitutional Development," 252-256.

13. Ormsby, *British Columbia*, 119, 122-123.

14. Robert A. J. McDonald and Keith Ralston, "Amor De Cosmos," *DCB* XII: 238.

15. Quoted in McDonald and Ralston, "Amor De Cosmos," 238.

16. James E. Hendrickson and Robert L. Smith, "The Union of Vancouver Island and British Columbia, 1866." (Unpublished paper presented to the annual meeting of the Canadian Historical Association, 1975): 2, 6-7.

17. Peter A. Baskerville, *Beyond the Island: An Illustrated History of Victoria* (Burlington, Ontario: Windsor Publications, 1986): 26-27.

18. Margaret Lillooet McDonald, "New Westminster, 1859-1871." (M.A. thesis, University of British Columbia, 1947): 75-76, 133-134, 202-204.

19. *British Columbian*, 5 December 1861. Quoted in Clive Fairholm, "John Robson and Confederation," in W. George Shelton, ed., *British Columbia & Confederation* (Victoria: Morriss Printing Company Ltd., 1967): 106.

20. Douglas to Newcastle, 22 April 1861. Quoted in McDonald, "New Westminster," 139. See also H. Keith Ralston, "Leonard McLure," *DCB* IX: 478-479.

21. Douglas to Newcastle, 8 October 1861. Quoted in McDonald, "New Westminster," 142.

22. *British Columbian*, 2 May 1861. Quoted in McDonald, "New Westminster," 143.

23. Hendrickson and Smith, "The Union," 7.

24. Quoted in Hendrikson, "Constitutional Development," 265.

25. Hendrickson, "Constitutional Development," 258; Ormsby, *British Columbia*, 216.

26. *Cariboo Sentinel*, 12 June 1865.

27. Hendrickson and Smith, "The Union," 14-19.

28. 28 Sept 1866. Quoted in Hendrickson and Smith, "The Union," 23.

29. Hendrickson and Smith, "The Union," 25.

30. Musgrave to Granville, 23 February 1870. Quoted in Hendrickson, "Constitutional Development," 270.

31. Isobel Bescoby, "A Colonial Administration: An Analysis of Administration in British Columbia, 1869-1871," *Canadian Public Administation* X, 1 (1967): 53.

32. R. Cole Harris and John Warkentin, *Canada Before Confederation* (Toronto: Oxford University Press, 1974): 300-304; Helen Ferguson, "The Development of Communications in Colonial British Columbia." (M.A. thesis, University of British Columbia, 1939): 55-57; Ormsby, *British Columbia*, 159-160.

33. Margaret A. Ormsby, "Richard Clement Moody," *DCB* XI: 605; Clarence G. Karr, "James Douglas: The Gold Governor in the Context of His Times," in E. Blanche Norcross, ed., *The Company on the Coast* (Nanaimo: Nanaimo Historical Society, 1983): 70-71; Frances M. Woodward, "The Influence of the Royal Engineers on the Development of British Columbia," *B.C. Studies* 24 (Winter 1974-74): 3-51.

34. See McDonald, "New Westminster," chapter 3.

35. Art Downs, *Wagon Road North* (Surrey, B.C.: Foremost Publishing Company Limited, 1969): 23.

36. Ormsby, *British Columbia*, 183, 187, 212-213; Harris and Warkentin, *Canada*, 304; Ferguson, "The Development of Communications," 39-79, 91-118; Angus MacLeod Gunn, "Gold and the Early Settlement of British Columbia, 1858-1885." (M.A. thesis, University of British Columbia, 1965): 31-35, 39-40, 45-49.

37. *Cariboo Sentinel*, 5 May 1868, 4 June 1868, 8 June 1868.

38. Phyllis Mikkelson, "Land Settlement Policy on the Mainland of British Columbia, 1858-1874." (M.A. thesis, University of British Columbia, 1950): 162-163.

39. James Douglas to Sir John Henry Pelly, Fort Victoria, 5 December 1848. Quoted in Hartwell Bowsfield, ed., *Fort Victoria Letters, 1846-1851* (Winnipeg, Hudson's Bay Record Society, 1979): 34.

40. Archibald Barclay to Douglas, 17 December 1849. Quoted in Margaret Ormsby's Introduction to *Fort Victoria Letters*, liii.

41. W. Kaye Lamb, "The Governorship of Richard Blanshard." *British Columbia Historical Quarterly* XIV (1950): 18-19; Bescoby, "A Colonial Administration," 50; Baskerville, *Beyond the Island*, 19-20; Richard Mackie, "Finding Home: British

Settlement on the West Coast Before 1858." (Unpublished paper presented to the annual meeting of the Canadian Historical Association, 1990): 12-18.

42. *Cariboo Sentinel*, 8 October 1866.

43. *British Columbian*, 11 October 1862. Quoted in Mikkelson, "Land Settlement Policy," 146.

44. McDonald, "New Westminster," 109-111. The foregoing summary of land policy on the mainland is essentially from Robert E. Cail, *Land, Man, and the Law: The Disposal of Crown Lands in British Columbia, 1871-1913* (Vancouver: University of British Columbia, 1974): 8-14; and Mikkelson, "Land Settlement," chapter 3: 78-102, 144.

45. See Cail, *Land, Man, and the Law*, 15-16; and Leonard A. Wrinch, "Land Policy of the Colony of Vancouver Island, 1846-1866." (M.A. thesis, University of British Columbia, 1932), chapter 9.

46. *British Colonist*, 30 November 1865. Quoted in Wrinch, "Land Policy," 120. Details on this issue can be found in Wrinch's chapter 5, and in Baskerville, *Beyond the Island*, 28-29.

47. Mikkelson, "Land Settlement Policy," 122-131.

48. Gregory, E. G. Thomas, "The British Columbia Ranching Frontier: 1858-1896." (M.A. thesis, University of British Columbia, 1976): 80. See also 40-41, 54.

49. Paul Tennant, *Aboriginal People and Politics: The Indian Land Question in British Columbia, 1849-1989* (Vancouver: University of British Columbia Press, 1990): 18-38; Robin Fisher, *Contact and Conflict: Indian-European Relations in British Columbia, 1774-1890* (Vancouver: University of British Columbia Press, 1977): 151-154. Fisher places less emphasis on the assimilative goal behind Douglas's policies.

50. *British Colonist*, 19 February 1861. Quoted in Fisher, *Contact and Conflict*, 95.

51. Fisher, *Contact and Conflict*, 116-117, 156-165; Tennant, *Aboriginal Peoples*, 39-43; Thomas, "Ranching Frontier," 64.

52. Barry M. Gough, *Gunboat Frontier: British Maritime Authority and Northwest Coast Indians, 1846-1990* (Vancouver: University of British Columbia Press, 1984): 17.

53. Quoted in Fisher, *Contact and Conflict*, 53. For details see also 50-52; Lamb, "The Governorship," 12-17; and Gough, *Gunboat Frontier*, chapter 3.

54. Fisher, *Contact and Conflict*, 54-55; Gough, *Gunboat Frontier*, 51-56.

55. See Fisher, *Contact and Conflict*, 62-63; William S. Thackray, "Keeping the Peace on Vancouver Island: The Colonial Police and the Royal Navy, 1850-1866." (M.A. thesis, University of Victoria, 1981), chapter 2; and Patricia Elizabeth Vaughan, "Co-operation and Resistance: Indian-European Relations on the Mining Frontier in British Columbia, 1835-1858." (M.A. thesis, University of British Columbia, 1978), chapters 1 and 2.

56. See William J. Burrill, "Pioneers and Proletarians: The Development of a Free Labour Market on Colonial Vancouver Island, 1848-1858." (Unpublished paper presented to the B.C. Studies Conference, 1989). On the broader context of the company's relations with its labourers, see Tina Merrill Loo, *Making Law, Order, and Authority in British Columbia, 1821-1871* (Toronto: University of Toronto Press, 1994), chapter 1.

57. Loo, *Making Law*, 36-37.

58. David M. L. Farr, "The Organization of the Judicial System in the Colonies of Vancouver Island and British Columbia, 1849-1871," *The U.B.C. Law Review* III, 1 (1967): 3-4.

59. Provision was made for several more of these small claims courts in 1866. For details, see Ormsby, *British Columbia*, 119-121; and Loo, *Making Law*, chapter 3.

60. Thackray, "Keeping the Peace," 48, 82.

61. Fisher, *Contact and Conflict*, 63-65, 111-115; Gough, *Gunboat Frontier*, 68-72.

62. S. D. Clark, "Mining Society in British Columbia and the Yukon," in Ward and McDonald, eds., *British Columbia*, 219.

63. Thackray, "Keeping the Peace," 150-152.

64. Farr, "The Organization," 5-12.

65. Quoted in Thackray, "Keeping the Peace," 195. See also Baskerville, *Beyond the Island*, 41-44.

66. See Gough, *Gunboat Frontier*, chapter 9.

67. Vaughan, "Co-operation and Resistance," 45-46.

68. The mining licences stipulated that at least twenty persons must be employed on the claim within six months. David Ricardo Williams, "The Administration of Criminal and Civil Justice in the Mining Camps and Frontier Communities of British Columbia," in Louis A. Knafla, ed., *Law and Justice in a New Land: Essays in Western Canadian Legal History* (Toronto, Calgary, Vancouver: Carswell, 1986): 219-220; Karr, "James Douglas," 61-62, 66; Gough, "Turbulent Frontiers," 19-23; Gough, *The Royal Navy*, 134-141.

69. Douglas to Lytton, 11 October 1858. Quoted in Fisher, *Contact and Conflict*, 147.

70. Vaughan, "Co-operation and Resistance," 50-53; Farr, "The Organization," 15.

71. Farr, "The Organization," 13-14, 21, 34; Ormsby, *British Columbia*, 180. The magistrates actually presided over a dual system of courts, the County or Small Debts Courts, and the Mining or Gold Commissioners Court. Loo, *Making Law*, 61.

72. Margaret Ormsby, "Some Irish Figures in Colonial Days," *British Columbia Historical Quarterly* XIV (January-April 1950): 63-73; Farr, "The Organization," 22; Loo, *Making Law*, 54-55.

73. Susan Dickinson Scott, "The Attitude of the Colonial Governors and Officials towards Confederation," in Shelton, ed., *British Columbia & Confederation*, 102.

74. Margaret A. Ormsby, "Chartres Brew," *DBC* IX; Edward Sleigh Hewlett, "Klatsassin," *DBC* IX.

75. Barry M. Gough, "Keeping British Columbia British: The Law-and-Order Question on a Gold Mining Frontier," *Huntingdon Library Quarterly* XXXVIII, 3 (1975): 275; Williams, "Administration" 220-223; Loo, *Making Law*, 61.

76. *Cariboo Sentinel*, 13 August 1866.

77. *Cariboo Sentinel*, 27 September 1865, 1 October 1865, 22 October 1865, 30 November 1866, 8 August 1867.

78. Farr, "The Organization," 16-18.

79. Quoted in Farr, "The Organization," 18.

80. Gunn, "Gold and Early Settlement," 40.

81. *Cariboo Sentinel*, 14 June 1866.

82. *Cariboo Sentinel*, 2 October 1868. See also 28 November 1868.

83. *Cariboo Sentinel*, 24 October 1867. For details on this case, see Loo, *Making Law*, 118-122.

84. McDonald, "New Westminster," 207-208.

85. Loo, *Making Law*, 143-148.

86. David R. Williams, "Sir Matthew Baillie Begbie," *Pacific Northwest Quarterly* LXXI, 3 (1980): 105.

87. Loo, "Law and Authority in British Columbia, 1821-1871." (Ph.D. thesis, University of British Columbia, 1990): 280-287.

88. Loo, "Law and Authority," 135.

89. Loo, "Law and Authority," 177.

90. *Cariboo Sentinel*, 25 June 1866, 28 June 1866; Loo, *Making Law*, 115-117.

91. Farr, "The Organization," 21-22; Hon. David R. Verchere, *A Progression of Judges: A History of the Supreme Court of British Columbia* (Vancouver: University of British Columbia Press, 1988): 39-40; Loo, "Law and Authority," 120-121, 230, 242.

92. Farr, "The Organization," 24-26; Williams, "Sir Matthew Baillie Begbie," 103; Loo, "Law and Authority," 231-235, 247; Kent MacLean Haworth, "Governor Anthony Musgrave, Confederation, and the Challenge of Responsible Government." (M.A. thesis, University of Victoria, 1975): 47-51.

93. Bescoby, "A Colonial Administration," 58; Ormsby, *British Columbia*, 225.

94. Ormsby, *British Columbia*, 235-236; David E. Shi, "Seward's Attempt to Annex British Columbia, 1865-1869," *Pacific Historical Review* XLVII (1978): 220-223; Woodward, "The Influence of the Royal Engineers," 29; Moogk, *Vancouver Defended*, 13-15; Gough, *The Royal Navy*, 210-214.

95. David Joseph Mitchell, "The American Purchase of Alaska and Canadian Expansion to the Pacific." (M.A. thesis, Simon Fraser University, 1976): 74-75; Glynn Barratt, *Russian Shadows on the British Northwest Coast of North America, 1810-1890* (Vancouver: University of British Columbia Press, 1983): 62-63, 68-70; Kenneth Bourne, *Britain and the Balance of Power in North America, 1815-1908* (Berkeley and Los Angeles: University of California Press, 1967): 301-304; Gough, *The Royal Navy*, 215-216.

96. Ormsby, *British Columbia*, 226; H. Robert Kendrick, "Amor De Cosmos and Confederation," in Shelton, ed., *British Columbia & Confederation*, 82-85.

97. Susan Dickinson Scott, "The Attitude of the Colonial Governors and Officials towards Confederation," in Shelton, ed., *British Columbia & Confederation*, 147.

98. Kent M. Haworth, "Sir Anthony Musgrave," *DCB* XI: 634-635; Bescoby, "A Colonial Administration," 79-80, 82-84.

99. Musgrave to Earl Granville, 30 October 1869. Quoted in Ormsby, *British Columbia*, 242. On Cariboo attitudes towards responsible government, see *Cariboo Sentinel*, 23 April 1870, 21 May 1870, 17 September 1870, 24 December 1870.

100. *Cariboo Sentinel*, 2 July 1868, 6 July 1868, 3 July 1869, 2 July 1870.

101. Bescoby, "A Colonial Administration," 86-91.

102. Willard E. Ireland, "British Columbia's American Heritage," in J. Friesen and H. K. Ralston, ed., *Historical Essays on British Columbia* (Toronto: McClelland and Stewart Limited, 1976): 19-20; Ormsby, *British Columbia*, 243-244.

103. Kendrick, "Armor De Cosmos," 85-86; Scott, "The Attitude," 148-149, 155-156; Gordon R. Elliott, "Henry P. Pellew Crease: Confederation or No Confederation," *B.C. Studies* 12 (1971-2): 63-74.

104. Fairholm, "John Robson and Confederation," 116; Derek Pethick, "The Confederation Debate of 1870," in Shelton, ed., *British Columbia & Confederation*, 179-192.

105. Brian Smith, "The Confederation Delegation," in Shelton, ed., *British Columbia & Confederation*, 195-199; Haworth, "Governor Anthony Musgrave," 61, 70, 78-80.

106. Dispatch 11, Victoria to Ottawa, 20 February 1870. Quoted in Truesdell, "From Sea to Sea," 137.

107. Bescoby, "A Colonial Administration," 68, 72, 92; Truesdell, "From Sea to Sea,"

135, 139-140; W. L. Morton, *The Critical Years: The Union of British North America, 1857-1873* (Toronto: McClelland and Stewart Limited, 1964): 247; Ormsby, *British Columbia*, 248; Tennant, *Aboriginal Peoples*, 43-45.

108.Hendrickson, "Constitutional Development," 270.

109.Haworth, "Sir Anthony Musgrave," 636.

110.Musgrave to Macdonald, 24 November 1870. Quoted in Bescoby, "A Colonial Administration," 74.

111.Haworth, "Sir Anthony Musgrave," 636; McDonald and Ralston, "De Cosmos," 11-12.

112.Truesdell, "From Sea to Sea," 139.

113.*B.C. Sessional Paper* 18, p. 18.

114.Introduction to Shelton, ed., *British Columbia & Confederation*, 15.

115.Quoted in Bescoby, "A Colonial Administration," 103.

116.Bescoby, "A Colonial Administration," 64. The cross-Panama connection did, however, reduce return correspondence between London and the Pacific Northwest from up to a year to three or four months. Karr, "James Douglas," 69.

Chapter 4
COLONIAL SOCIETY AND ECONOMY
Sharon Meen

In March 1850, when Governor Blanshard first reached Vancouver Island, his ship anchored before a barricaded cluster of rude wooden buildings adjacent to a patch of snow-covered ploughed land spotted with tree stumps. This was Fort Victoria. The only other European habitation on the Island was at the northern end, at Fort Rupert where coal had been discovered. At these forts the personnel were all Hudson's Bay Company people. Otherwise, Blanshard's colony had no colonists. On the mainland as well, the only Europeans were Company employees. Thirty miles from the mouth of the Fraser River, at its major depot of Fort Langley, the Company ran a 240-acre farm. Far to the north near the mouths of the Skeena and the Nass rivers they maintained two trading posts—Essington and Simpson—which were supplied by the steamship *Beaver*. In the Interior, on the Fraser, Peace and Skeena River systems they staffed another dozen posts. The oldest, Fort McLeod in the northern Interior, dated back to 1805. The newest, Fort Hope on the lower Fraser, had just been built. Most of these posts had been in business for more than a quarter of a century and a number of them for more than forty years. In a territory that was four times the size of Britain and still barely mapped, these posts and the Company's trails along the Fraser and through the Okanagan were all that spoke of a European presence (see Map 2).

Twenty-one years later, when British Columbia entered Confederation, ten thousand Europeans lived on the Island and mainland. Their various activities pushed the Company operation into the background. Sawmills, mines and farms had spread along the coast and up the rivers; rustic encampments had become towns. Native people, though they still outnumbered the Europeans, no longer controlled the most profitable resource. In comparison with the more gradual changes of the preceding era, the transformation of the 1850s and 1860s was astounding; and the process was not gentle. A catastrophic smallpox epidemic in 1862 cut the Native population by one-third, and the European population had fluctuated dramatically with the coming and going of gold miners.

Seven-and-a-half years after Blanshard arrived—six years after he left—the white population still numbered less than 1,000. Radical transformation began

Map 2: Trails to the Upper Fraser in 1859

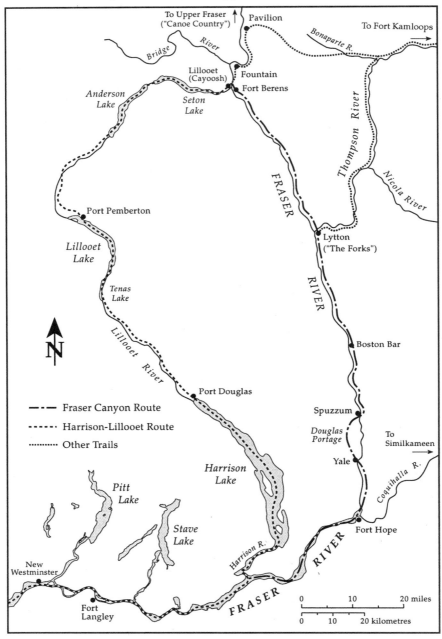

in 1858 with the first gold rush. Gold brought an extraordinarily diverse influx of people from nearly every corner of the world, and this influx completely overwhelmed the tiny settler population built up over the previous few years. Many who came for gold left soon after they arrived, but at the end of the 1860s, when successive rushes had passed by, the immigrant population was ten times greater than it had been in 1857. Most of these new inhabitants were men, but there were enough women to establish settlements that would outlast the lure of gold. Most of the new people were white, but the Chinese and the blacks who came prefigured the multi-racial and multi-cultural pattern that characterizes British Columbia today. The new population and the new economy pushed Native people towards the economic and social margin. Power became concentrated in the hands of the immigrants. Within the immigrant community, however, the centre of power did not shift: a white, British, masculine elite had run the Hudson's Bay Company; a similar elite would dominate the colony and the province.

The gold soon petered out, leaving a disgruntled populace to face a load of debt. This was the first example of the boom-and-bust economy that was to plague the province for years to come. On the eve of British Columbia's entrance into the Dominion, participants in the new economy and society found themselves in a state of uncertainty. Gold or furs, or small, isolated ventures such as family farms did not produce the sums required to finance the state and provide the services expected by the settlers. The creation of wealth in this rugged and remote land was going to require large-scale enterprise. The possibilities for such enterprise were evident because the foundation of a new industrial edifice had been laid by the Company and the gold rush colony. As the newcomers scrambled for places in the mines, hacked down the trees along Burrard Inlet, or set their nets in the rivers, thinking all the time of getting rich or merely staying alive, the fecund coastal wilderness that had supported the Native cultures suffered the first blows of an assault that would continue to the present day.

ECONOMIC DEVELOPMENT

Throughout the colonial period, the Hudson's Bay Company attempted to broaden its range of economic activities. The fur trade continued and the Company's successes in its new endeavours were uneven, but the pattern of diversification was clear well before the discovery of gold. The Company had begun to diversify from furs into coal, timber, fisheries and farming before moving its main base north from American territory to Vancouver Island. This early diversification served Company objectives in cutting costs and developing new exports. Supplies for the posts were bulky, requiring more space than furs: if the posts could provide for themselves, fewer shipments would be necessary; if they could produce for export, shipping space would not be wasted on the return trips. Food was the first concern and prompted efforts at farming and fishing. Timber was an obvious choice: a sawmill was operating at Fort Vancouver in the 1830s.

In 1837, the Company, seeking to renew its licence to the exclusive trade of the Pacific coast, expressed its intention to expand cultivation and to develop an export trade in wool, tallow and hides. George Simpson, the Company's general superintendent in North America, regarded these schemes as subsidiary, but he clearly saw their usefulness. When he toured the region in 1841, he recommended Fort Victoria as the site for a new post, not with furs in mind—it was a poor fur area—but because it was a promising location for lumber, salmon fishing, farming, and trading with the Russians at Sitka.[1] From the time the Company moved its main base north to Fort Victoria in 1849, diversification picked up speed. For strategic reasons, the British government now expected the Company to act as a colonizing agent, drawing new population to the coast. Chief Factor Douglas found himself in charge, not only of a trading post, but of agricultural and mining settlements. The discovery of coal on Vancouver Island, the construction of sawmills, and the development of an export trade in salmon, shingles and other items extended his responsibilities. The Company imported labourers for its farms and mines; and a trickle of independent settlers and merchants established a foothold on the Island. After the discovery of gold on the mainland, a wild scramble for quick returns obscured all other activities, but when the dust settled, diversification had appreciably advanced through the activities of the new population. These developments reduced the economic importance of furs, and changed British Columbia from a fur preserve to a colony.

As long as furs remained the chief European interest west of the Rockies, the number of Europeans in the region was minimal. Native people gained enough from the trade to want it to continue, and their relations with the fur traders were generally harmonious. The Hudson's Bay Company and the Americans in the Oregon Territory jockeyed for position until 1846, when Treaty of Washington divided British from American interests with a line through the mountains and river valleys at the 49th parallel. The creation of a border meant that the Company had to pay American tariffs if they continued to use the old mainland trail through the Okanagan from New Caledonia to the Columbia River. The Company's answer was to cut a new, more difficult trail from the lower Fraser River to the Thompson (see Map 3). This trail was in use by 1850, and furs then travelled via the Fraser to Fort Victoria. By this time, the Company no longer enjoyed exclusive trading rights on Vancouver Island. The creation of a colony on the Island in 1849 meant competition, except in coal and possibly furs. On the mainland, the Company kept its exclusive rights until 1858, when the gold rush brought forth a new colony there.

By the time the gold rush began, the fur trade had already reached its limits. Hunters and trappers had exhausted animal populations in one area after

Map 3: Forts and Travel Routes of the Fur Trade

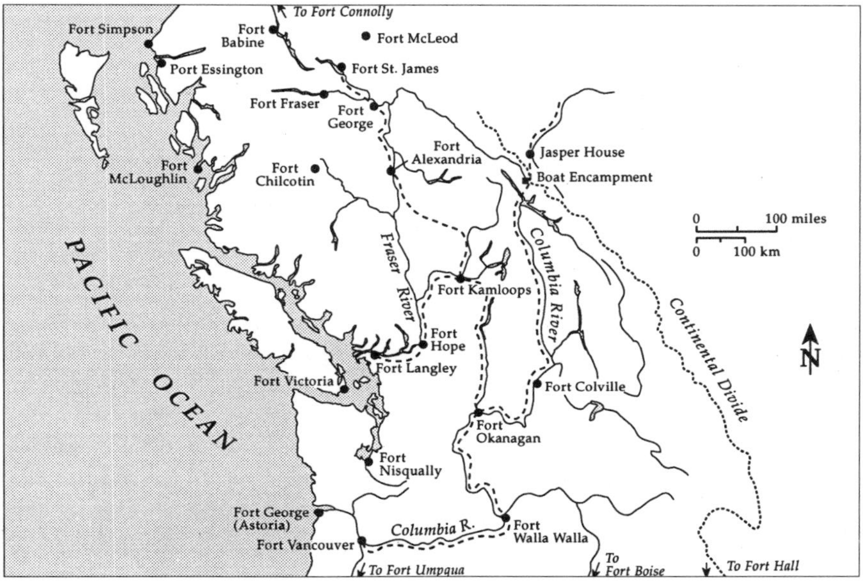

another until there were no new regions to exploit. The sea otter, once abundant, had been trapped out. In the 1790s, 100,000 pelts were collected by American and British ships, creating a glut that caused prices in China to plummet. But the slaughter—a joint endeavour of European and Native people—continued until the sea otter was nearly extinct. Supplies of marten pelts, newly fashionable in the European market, dwindled in turn. As early as 1839, William Tolmie at Fort Vancouver attributed a decrease in Company profits to "the exterminating system of hunting pursued, which if not checked, will speedily eventuate in the destruction of the more valuable fur-bearing animals."[2] At the southern coastal posts, in the decade preceding the gold rush, the value of other exports, particularly salmon, often exceeded the value of furs. In the northern Interior, which was better country for furs, a steady trade carried on, and furs figured in British Columbia's exports long after Confederation, but their place in the economy became less and less significant. By 1870, furs accounted for only 13 per cent of the colony's exports.[3] The fur trade occupied a small place in the colonial world because it could not provide an economic base for a settler society: it employed few people and depended on the control of vast, undeveloped territories.

Diversification, for the Company, began with agriculture. From the earliest days, fur traders at isolated posts planted gardens for their own use. Farming of

101

a more ambitious kind began at Fort Vancouver on the Columbia River and at Fort Langley on the Fraser. As early as 1828, Simpson, on his second visit to Fort Vancouver, observed that the farming operations there were "of vital importance to the whole of the business on this side of the continent."[4] Company employees at Langley planted fields of potatoes that same year, and wheat, barley and peas the following spring.[5] In 1839, the Company agreed to provide the Russian posts on the northern coast with food and manufactured goods from England. The agreement nearly removed the competition from American ships, which had been selling supplies to the Russians while trading in furs along the coast. It also obliged the Company to expand its food production beyond the acreages at Forts Vancouver and Langley. For this purpose, the Puget's Sound Agricultural Company started farms at Cowlitz and Nisqually on Puget Sound. This agricultural company was a subsidiary of the Hudson's Bay Company, though it was given an independent structure on paper to circumvent criticism. After ten years on Puget Sound, it became the Hudson's Bay Company's colonization vehicle on Vancouver Island.

Farming on Vancouver Island was harder than it had been on the banks of the Columbia. There was little grassland for grazing, and the pockets of good soil were densely forested. Nevertheless, the Company's directors in London were determined to develop agriculture on the Island. They wanted farmers not only to raise grain, potatoes and livestock for local needs, but also to produce for the export market, including supplies of salt beef and pork for the increasing number of ships visiting the region.[6] A grist mill was constructed in 1850. By the spring of 1852, the Puget's Sound Agricultural Company had acquired 2,500 acres of the best land, divided into four farms, all in the immediate vicinity of Fort Victoria. Walter Grant, the first independent settler to come to the colony, scorned the men employed by the Puget's Sound Agricultural Company as miserable farmers who ruined the land;[7] however, when a good market for their produce appeared, they were able to profit from it. In 1856, the farms supplied the Royal Navy at Esquimalt with one thousand pounds of meat and four hundred pounds of vegetables per day.[8] Simultaneously, farming at Fort Langley prospered. The 240-acre farm there supplied Interior posts and exported to the Sandwich Islands (Hawaii) and San Francisco. The post also obtained cranberries from Native people and exported them in kegs to California.[9]

Before the gold rush, "independent" settlers—those who financed themselves, rather than being shipped out as Company employees—were thin on the ground. The region was far from Britain or from the heavily settled parts of North America; it was not a natural agricultural area; and the strictures of the Hudson's Bay Company did not promote the freewheeling settler activity that characterized the American frontier. Most of the immigrant population of the early 1850s consisted of male labourers brought out by the Puget's Sound Agricultural Company. In 1853, for example, some eighty men and only two or three women arrived in the barque *Norman Morison.*[10] The labourers received £17 per year (equivalent to $68 at the time), and were to be rewarded with twenty acres of land after five years of faithful service. Many found the conditions onerous and some escaped to Oregon, where land was free, or to the gold fields of California. Independent settlers did not find the terms easy, either. Land cost £1 ($4) per acre, with a minimum purchase of twenty acres. For each one hundred acres, the purchaser was bound to bring out a labour force. Not surprisingly, only three settlers bought parcels of over one hundred acres during the Company's tenure. Nor did many clamour for the privilege of obtaining twenty acres. In 1856, only forty-three "settlers" owned the twenty acres necessary to vote in colonial elections, and most of these were or had been in the employ of the Company. Company ranks also supplied most of the approximately two dozen independent entrepreneurs in lumbering and trade.[11]

The gold rush created a hungry and lucrative market for Langley produce; with potatoes selling for $90 per hundred pounds, and eggs for $8 per dozen, independent farmers were also encouraged to try their luck. Although agriculture expanded to meet the needs of the gold miners who arrived in numbers in 1858, this new market did not last. Nevertheless that year, the first application was made for a farm on the mainland.[12] From 1859, farming spread through the logged valleys on the Island and supplied the market in Victoria. Settlers took up land on the Gulf Islands, ranching cattle and hogs at Miners Bay on Mayne Island as early as 1861. The Puget's Sound Agricultural Company had grazed cattle on San Juan Island much earlier, and ranching also began on the mainland. The herd at Fort Vancouver had increased from a meagre 17 in 1824 to 450 by 1833. From Fort Vancouver, cattle were driven up the fur brigade trails to Interior posts, and the region around Kamloops was found to be good grazing country. Five to six thousand head pastured there in 1848.[13] By this time, the herds in Oregon were seven or eight times that number, and they continued to multiply. Consequently, when gold miners flowed north, cattle from Oregon followed close behind.

More than seven thousand cattle crossed the border in the first four years of the gold rush.[14] A number of American drovers took up land in British Columbia and stayed on and prospered. The best-known of these were the Harper brothers who amassed thousands of acres, including, eventually, the famous Gang Ranch in the Chilcotin district. But the ranchers were not all Americans: the gold rush attracted them from all over the world. And the land policy of the new colony was better designed to encourage settlers than the old Company policy on Vancouver Island. Nonetheless, British Columbia did not become a land of farmers. Only a scattered 5 per cent of the land was arable, and not much of that was first-class farmland.[15]

The Cariboo gold rush that began in 1860 provided the greatest impetus to farming and ranching. Settlers in Chilliwack, for example, sold butter to the miners for $1 a pound. Others made a living by opening inns along the Cariboo trail, by wintering transport animals, by cutting wood for steamers, and by selling hay, grain and stock.[16] When the party was over, many farms were abandoned. Ultimately, neither the settler population nor the Hudson's Bay Company had much success in agriculture. The land was not easy to work, and the Company managers were not conspicuously talented farmers.[17] For the Company, the results were not enough to satisfy the expectations of its directors.

Coal offered more potential than agriculture. The Company developed the first coal mines in British Columbia, but it sold its interests too early to reap the vast returns of the future. As early as 1835, the Company knew that deposits existed on Vancouver Island. Kwakiutl trading at Fort McLoughlin provided the information, which was verified the next year when the steamer *Beaver* stopped to investigate the surface outcroppings at what later became Fort Rupert.[18] The coal deposits were of small interest to the Company at first, but the increasing use of steam power in the Pacific, coupled with the expense of importing steam coal from Britain, prompted Simpson to recommend the establishment of a post and the exploitation of the coal. Native people were already working the surface seams, exchanging the coal for trade goods, but, in 1848, the Company signed a contract to supply coal to the Pacific Mail Steamship Company, and decided to bring Scottish coal miners to Fort Rupert. The tiny group of colliers and their families arrived in the autumn of 1849. Seven months later, they were on strike, and in the summer of 1850 most of them left for California. A second crew of miners was recruited, including Robert Dunsmuir, who was to be one of the first men to make a fortune out of the industrialization of British Columbia. As it turned out, there was not enough good coal at the site to satisfy the new demand. Moreover, the methods used for its extraction and transport to waiting ships were extraordinarily inefficient. The tools provided for both colliers and Native people were few and poor, and the coal was carried five miles in baskets and canoes before it was taken on board; loading a steamship took a month.[19]

At the end of 1849, Company officers at Victoria received the first news of coal deposits at what is now Nanaimo. A Cowichan from Nanaimo Bay, taking an interest in the coal fire in a blacksmith's shop in Victoria, reported that coal was abundant where he lived. Requested by a Company trader to bring some, he returned in the spring of 1850 with a canoeload, for which he received a bottle of rum and the free repair of his gun. The Company promptly moved to establish possession of the coalfield. The Crown obtained title to the land from the Cowichans living at Nanaimo, and the Company purchased the land from the Crown: six thousand acres at £1 sterling per acre. By 1852, Native people were labouring in the coalfields in exchange for trade goods such as powder and shot, gunflints, tobacco, cotton, molasses and blankets.[20] Throughout the Company era, Native men continued to collect surface coal and to work as hauliers and longshoremen. Native women were hired to carry brick and clay to the mines and move coal in canoes. The work of hewing the coal face was reserved for white men. In the autumn of 1852, the Company abandoned its mining project at Fort Rupert and the colliers imported by the Company moved to Nanaimo. Their numbers included some miners from the first group who had returned from California to work for the Company again. In September, their first shipment went out. In 1853, a steam engine was used to pump water from the first shaft sunk by the miners: the industrial revolution had begun in British Columbia.

What was peculiar about the Company directors' behaviour was that, although they brought skilled labourers from Britain, they did not put anyone in charge who knew the first thing about coal mining. For two years, there was no one in Nanaimo able to plan the diggings. Labour shortages, desertions and discontent also impeded the operations. Most miners were paid according to the amount of coal they sent to the surface each day, so they were unwilling to waste their time performing other tasks. For men who came from an industry in which work was highly specialized, to be treated as general labourers was to lose status.[21] But the primitive conditions on Vancouver Island, coupled with the Company's cheese-paring ways and its ignorance of mining practices, constantly forced the miners off the coal face where they felt they belonged.

Although profits were there to be made in the coalfields, the demands of heavy industry were greater than the Company wanted to meet. The amount of capital outlay required to exploit the coalfields efficiently was excessive by Company standards; trading for furs had not prepared the Company for the expenses of industrial development. After James Douglas resigned as chief factor to become governor of British Columbia, his successor, Alexander Grant Dallas, counselled the Company to sell. The Vancouver Coal Mining and Land Company paid £40,000 ($160,000) and took over in 1862; colonial production rose, dipped and then peaked in 1868 at 44,000 tons.[22]

The Hudson's Bay Company was not slow to see the possibilities of British Columbia's greatest resource—its trees. The Company began milling lumber as early as the 1830s. Later, logging and lumbering provided some of the first opportunities for independent entrepreneurs. The immense forests that rose from the rocky shores and marched over the mountains to the grasslands beyond the Great Divide appeared to the European newcomers to be infinite. Some were awed; some were appalled; and some saw money to be made, sizing up forests as so many spars, so many shingles, so many barrels and planks. The trees, some of them six centuries old, reached enormous size in the damp climate of the coast. Among them were Douglas firs hundreds of feet tall and as much as twenty-five feet thick at the base. They dwarfed the wooden ships and forts that huddled at the waterside.

Native people made canoes, dwellings and magnificent totem poles out of the big trees, but their use did not change the landscape. The Europeans, however, were interested in exploitation on a large scale. Ten years after Captain Cook's hefty bundle of sea-otter pelts attracted attention to the region, spars and timber were being exported to China from Nootka Sound. Captain John Meares imported Chinese labourers (captured and later released by the Spanish) long before coal and railway magnates did the same.

The Hudson's Bay Company built the first water-powered sawmill in the northwest at Fort Vancouver, but it was on Vancouver Island that lumbering began in earnest. In 1848 at the head of Esquimalt Harbour a Company sawmill began producing for local needs, and it was soon exporting to California, where the flood of gold seekers created a sudden demand for lumber. Shipments also went to Hawaii, where the market expanded with the sugar industry.[23] In 1853, another mill was built at Nanaimo. Native people supplied most of the logs, in exchange for blankets. At Fort Rupert, Nisqually and Victoria, Native people manufactured shingles for the export trade.

Lumbering offered opportunities for smaller entrepreneurs. Two of the early efforts were unsuccessful: Captain Grant, the first settler, who seems not to have extracted much profit from any of his endeavours, started a mill but soon abandoned it. James Douglas and several other Company employees established a steam mill in 1851; they were under-capitalized and had to sell in 1857. On the other hand, two of the Muirs, who had been among the colliers brought to Fort Rupert, established a mill at Sooke and did not go back to mining. They exported spars and lumber to London, China and South America, and opened a lumber yard in Victoria.[24] Partners James Cooper and Thomas Blinkhorn traded coal, potatoes and cranberries, and bought piles, spars and squared timbers at Sooke to sell in California.

The California gold rush reached its height in 1853. British Columbia's timbermen could make fine profits, in spite of the 20 per cent duty levied by the Americans. Skippers paid eight cents a foot for heavy beams or piles delivered alongside the vessel, and sold them in San Francisco for $1 a foot. According to Douglas, a good axeman could make from $4 to $6 a day—"highly remunerative" employment, which added to the scarcity and price of labour on the Island.[25] In 1855, the Muirs could charge £12 (about $48 at that time) for an eight-foot spar; however, attempts to export as good or better spars from Fort Rupert met with no success, owing to the distance from the market. When the California economy slumped and prices fell, the American duty became a larger factor in the Island's export trade. The nearby Puget Sound mills were able to satisfy much of the California market as well as exporting to British Columbia. The result was a depression of the timber and lumber business on the Island.

Later in the decade, a new market appeared with the gold rush in British Columbia. It was supplied by the American mills in Puget Sound and, within a few years, by mills on the mainland and therefore did not produce an instant rash of large new mills on the Island. One opened in 1858 and then moved to New Westminster, and two small ones were built in 1859 and 1860 by Fort Langley's former chief trader. Throughout the 1860s, new mills, logging camps and lumber yards, locally owned, appeared here and there—at Cowichan, Chemainus and Alberni. In 1866, there were six mills on the Island.[26] On the mainland, the first mill was built at Burrard Inlet in 1862.[27] Small mills were later built in the Interior to service the demands of the gold industry for housing and sluice boxes.

By then, the Alberni mill had closed. The new steam sawmill had been opened by Captain Edward Stamp on behalf of a London syndicate. Workmen and machinery were brought from England in 1860, and £20 ($80) in goods paid to the Sheshat people in return for a townsite. A cluster of white people arrived, and in the summer of 1861, the mill was cutting 14,000 feet per day. A farm and a fishing station were in operation as well. Lumbering at Alberni expanded with enormous rapidity for three years and then abruptly collapsed. In those few years, the mill had cut down every big tree within reach. In the 1860s, there were only two ways to bring logs to the mill: float them downstream or drag them with oxen. The broken country, the small streams, the nature of forest growth—which produced the best trees in inconvenient, sheltered pockets—meant difficulty in supplying the logging camps, and much worse difficulty in moving logs to the mill. More extensive logging in the great forests would have to wait for new industrial developments: steam donkeys and railways.[28]

Like the forests, the fishery could not be exploited on a large scale without new technology. The Company did what could be done before canning was invented, and its early export trade in salmon stimulated the search for improved methods of preservation. Every year, at the end of the summer, salmon appeared in the coastal waters and rushed in silver torrents up the rivers and streams. An obvious source of food and trade, they were salted and exported by the Company from the early days at Fort Langley. Native people brought salmon in trade, and the Company shipped the salmon in barrels made by a local cooper. In 1840, four hundred barrels left Langley.[29] A decade later, production had risen to two thousand barrels, and salmon had surpassed furs in the Fort Langley books. The main market was Hawaii, where the value per barrel was about $14 U.S. This advantageous trade continued to thrive until the end of the Company era.[30] Dried salmon also supplied the Company's posts in the Interior, as well as the gold miners of California and British Columbia. Salmon fishing for export did not, however, become an important industry until the techniques for preservation improved. In the wake of the prosperity built on gold, farmers in the Fraser Valley were catching and selling salmon, and even experimenting with canning.[31] The first exports of salmon in tin boxes went out in 1870.[32] In this form, salmon could travel all the way to Europe and arrive in palatable condition. Cheaper and tastier than canned meat, it found a ready market in industrial Britain.

The curing and packing of salmon added two satellite businesses to the Company's range: the production of salt and barrels. Barrels—like other wood products (squared timbers, spars, assorted boards for construction, shingles and firewood)—found both domestic and export markets. In addition, Native people brought the Company small quantities of isinglass (a gelatin from the air bladders of fish) as well as whale oil and dogfish oil, which sold in London and San Francisco.[33] The whale fishery's importance only increased the new hunting technology at the end of the 1860s. Subsequently, like the more famous whale fishery of the Atlantic ports, so many whales were killed that the industry rapidly extinguished itself.

Every one of British Columbia's major industries originated with the Company. When the discovery of gold wrenched the region's economy away from the old emphasis on furs, these industries were in their infancy. Their development depended on new markets, new technologies, transportation, injections of capital and a larger labour force. At this point, the Company turned away from industrial development, and found a path to success in a new age through canny management of its large real estate holdings and by transforming its old trading posts into a service network for the expanding settler population.

Diversification would have continued with or without the discovery of gold, but gold was a stimulant like no other. Gold fever came to British Columbia in 1858. It was a minor event compared with the big California discovery and the migration of "forty-niners." The series of gold strikes that began with California continued through the second half of the nineteenth century, ranging as far afield as Australia and ending with the Klondike. They were made possible by mass communications and mass mobility. The telegraph, the newspaper and the steamboat spread the news, and thousands booked passage to the goldfields. What drew people, above all, was the accessibility of placer gold to amateur miners. Hardrock gold deposits cannot be mined without skill and expensive equipment. Placer or alluvial gold deposits, in which gold has been washed from the bearing rock and settled in stream beds, can be scooped up by any person lucky enough to find it first. It was this possibility that lured miners to the goldfields, where a few made their fortunes, and fewer still kept them. It was a dream of sudden riches and, by some accounts, a dream of escape from the drudgery of the new industrial era.

The phenomenon of the "rush" was by its nature short-lived. The rumour of a strike would attract an instant crowd, who would stake claims and quickly scratch up what they could with cheap and primitive equipment. Before long, the surface deposits would be exhausted, and the miners would move on to the next find. Alternatively, some would form small companies and invest in more complex equipment in order to exploit deeper deposits. They would sink shafts in the bars and banks, and sift the gravely muck with sluices. The deeper the deposit, the more labour and machinery required, until the obligatory level of investment shut out the hopeful adventurer with no capital. Each rush, then, had its lifespan after which the goldfield was abandoned or left to a few well-financed companies. The extreme expansions and contractions of the population that accompanied each gold rush took local economies and societies on a wild ride; many besides the miners won and lost riches as unpredictably as if they had staked their livelihoods at the gambling table.

Reports of gold on the Queen Charlotte Islands and in the Thompson River area had come to the Company early in the 1850s, prompting Douglas to institute miners' licences as a method of control. In 1856, Salish on the Thompson River were extracting gold using shovels, picks and pans provided by the Company. The Thompson River Salish intended to exploit this resource themselves, an aspiration that Douglas supported, since he feared the consequences for the Company if a large and rowdy crowd of miners from California were to appear on Company territory. The Native people were also clear-sighted about the environmental consequences of a free-for-all. They resisted attempts to work gold in tributaries of the Thompson, having well-founded fears of disturbing the salmon runs—their principal source of food.[34] Douglas was anxious to keep the Americans out, but ironically it was he who precipitated the rush by despatching eight hundred ounces of gold to the mint in San Francisco, thus giving substance to the rumours circulating there.

Within months, in the spring of 1858, the miners began to arrive. The first boatload disgorged 450 at Victoria, doubling the population in a morning. Two more ships jammed with miners docked that month. A tent city rose around the fort, and then a wooden one. That year, 25,000 to 30,000 people arrived in Victoria. Although not a few died crossing the Georgia Strait on homemade rafts, some 10,000 were scrabbling in the sand bars of the Fraser in August. Many others had remained in Victoria to open businesses that served the new population. The "gold colony" of British Columbia was proclaimed in November 1858 with Douglas as governor, cutting short the Company's trading monopoly on the mainland. The first strike was downstream from Yale, about 150 miles inland. Beyond Yale, the raging rapids of the Fraser River Canyon kept small boats at bay, so the miners swarmed over the lower valley. Tent towns sprang up at Langley, Hope and Yale. Miners also trekked upriver to Lytton and then to Lillooet, searching for the mother lode. Harrison Lake acquired a steamer. Many thousands of ounces of gold were taken out that first year.[35] Despite the frenzy, thousands of miners had no luck. Many found life miserably uncomfortable and supplies intolerably expensive. Some left the country but others, broke and at loose ends, were a worry to Douglas, and he employed several hundred of them building trails to the Upper Fraser. In Douglas's view, the best course for the state, once the miners had come, was to open up routes to the goldfields and share in the profits. Otherwise, the miners would come and go through American territory—and so would the money. The mule trail to Lillooet, poor though it was, cost his administration £14,000 ($56,000),[36] and Douglas would spend many times that sum on roads before the gold rush was over. After the first big strike in the Cariboo, in 1859, hopes ran very high, many supposing that these new fields would equal or surpass California's.

The most prominent manifestation of the region's new status was the arrival of a corps of Royal Engineers, who made concrete the authority of the Crown, who laid out the townsites, including the capital at New Westminster (named, like the colony, by the unimaginative Queen), and who undertook the great labour of building roads to the goldfields. Under their direction, the Harrison-Lillooet route became a wagon road; they built the Dewdney Trail to Rock Creek (later extended to the Kootenays), and they surveyed the route for the Cariboo wagon road.

As the waters of the Fraser rose after the spring runoff, and the gold-bearing sand bars were drowned, many disappointed miners left the country, but others looked upstream, expecting larger deposits and found them near Quesnel and in massive amounts in Antler Creek and Williams Creek. News of the Cariboo strikes brought a second wave of miners. The newcomers were fewer in number than those who came in 1858, and frequently less experienced. They came from Canada, the eastern United States, Wales, Scotland and Australia. Many turned back without staking a claim, defeated by the cost of food and the appalling conditions. The trail was terrible. "By the roadside lay the dead bodies of horses and mules, some standing as they had died, still stuck fast in the deep, tenacious mud. We passed a score of them in one day in full view. . . ."[37] Men on foot slogged 350 miles over the mountains, meeting every day other men who were returning penniless. The long, rough trail raised the cost of living, even in the most primitive conditions. Without a substantial amount of cash in hand—£100 ($400) in the estimate of a would-be miner from Wales—few could remain in the Cariboo long enough to find a good claim.[38] During this second phase of the gold rush, the Cariboo Road was built to Barkerville at a cost of over $1 million. The road was intended to improve the situation. When it was completed in 1865, prices in the Cariboo tumbled, easing life for the miners but snatching the props from beneath a multitude of other businesses. Stores closed and farms failed. Moreover, the rush had dissipated by this time, since no more large surface deposits were discovered. Smaller groups of miners and companies remained to clean out their claims, but the value of the gold coming out of the Cariboo dwindled rapidly and did not pay off the debt contracted by the government to build the road. This was the situation when federation with Canada was proposed.

Brief though the bonanza was, it had lasting effects. By bringing to British Columbia a large population requiring not only basic food and shelter but clothing, equipment, transportation and many services, from banking to laundry, gold fostered the rapid development of a complex economy. From 1858 to 1865, after which gold production dropped off, gold valued at more than $18,500,000 was exported.[39] As the gold flowed out, imports flowed in. The colony could not feed itself, despite the expanding acreage under cultivation, and continued to import flour, beef and rice from the United States, as well as spirits from Britain. Victoria, the centre of import-export activity, grew with the gold rush. Inflated property values, mud streets and the stench of over-crowded graveyards characterized Victoria's boomtown days. Wells Fargo came to town and opened a bank. Affiliating with local couriers who shuttled between the Interior and the coast, Wells Fargo took gold dust to San Francisco and carried the mail. In the mid-1860s, four banks were operating in Victoria: the Bank of British Columbia, the Bank of British North America, McDonald and Company, and Wells Fargo. Hotels, saloons and boarding houses served the transient population. Merchants, profiting from Victoria's status as a free port, outfitted the miners. Ships thronged the harbour, increasing the market for coal. Two hundred miners were employed at Nanaimo and the settlement, including the surrounding farms, numbered seven hundred. A small manufacturing base was established in and around Victoria, including tanneries, sash mills, a foundry, a soap factory, a shipyard and a gas works.[40] This last provided Victoria with its first street lights in 1873.[41]

Urbanization proceeded more slowly on the mainland. New Westminster, no more than a stump field at the onset of the gold rush, could not compete with the free port at Victoria in the warehousing trade, and the Interior settlements remained small. Lumber and flour mills served local needs at the mines but did not export. Breweries appeared in the Cariboo with the availability of grain, but by 1870 the brewing and distilling industries were concentrated around Victoria.[42] The gold towns themselves, particularly Barkerville, afforded unusual possibilities for individual enterprise. The miners had urgent needs and a dearth of competition allowed prices to climb. There were few women in the Cariboo but those who were there seized this unusual opportunity, running hotels, restaurants, saloons and laundries. In 1869, twelve were listed as businesswomen in their own right.[43]

Managing the gold rush presented the embryo government with new problems, and like governments before and since, it conjured up a new bureaucracy to deal with them. The administration expanded—absorbing in the process some excess sons exported by Britain's privileged classes—until falling revenues from licences, land sales, tolls and customs duties forced a reduction in expenses. The solution in 1866 was to join the two separate colonies of Vancouver Island and British Columbia under one administration with the capital at Victoria, the largest settlement.

The second half of the 1860s was a transitional period for British Columbia. Gold was in decline, and the non-Native population of British Columbia fluctuated, falling and then rising to the same level in 1870 as it had been at in 1865. In these five years, the labour pattern, as listed in the Blue Books, had shifted. In 1865, 72 per cent of a labour force of nearly six thousand was concentrated in the mining industry; in 1870, 61 per cent worked in other occupations, about half of them in agriculture.[44] Gold was still the dominant export, acounting for 75 per cent of the value of the colony's exports, while furs accounted for 13 per cent, but these sources of revenue were clearly insufficient if the colony was to progress and gold was dwindling. Canada's offer to relieve the colony of its debt, pay part of its administration costs, and build a railway that would tie British Columbia to eastern Canadian markets—as San Francisco was tied to the markets of the eastern states—was compellingly attractive. Without gold, federation with Canada in 1871 would have been unlikely. Gold, or rather the population and development that came with it, made the continental project feasible. On the other hand, gold—like furs—would not continue to support a settler society. Those who wanted British Columbia to grow—and pioneer societies are very sure that growth is good—were looking towards a new economy based on timber, coal and fish, the very industries started by the Hudson's Bay Company a generation before the first gold nugget turned up at a trading post.

THE COLONIAL POPULATION

The colonial society that developed on Vancouver Island and the mainland was shaped not only by the resources of the region, but by the kinds of people who came to gather the spoils. British Columbia's population in the colonial period was a remarkable mixture of races and ethnic groups and striking for the predominance of males. These demographic characteristics were as influential in the creation of British Columbia as were furs, gold and forests.

The sources for determining the demography of British Columbia before the twentieth century are fragmentary. Early efforts at population counts attempted accurate enumeration of the white population but guessed at the numbers of Native people. The counts of white persons were sometimes unreliable, particularly during the gold rush. In 1859 and 1860, no census was possible because the gold miners moved about incessantly. Efforts to elaborate beyond a simple head count—to distinguish persons by sex, age, race and geographical origin—were erratic and often confused.

Nevertheless, the broad characteristics and trends of the period between 1849 and 1871 can be discerned. The Native population, already in decline owing to the effects of contact with Europeans during the fur-trade era, continued to decrease, both as a percentage of the whole population and in absolute numbers. Although Native people still accounted for over 70 per cent of the population in 1870, their absolute numbers had probably dropped by a third or a half since 1858. According to the census of 1870, there were 36,247 people in British Columbia, including fewer than 26,000 Native people. The immigrant population, on the other hand, swelled. In 1849, a handful of white men had dug themselves in at the southern end of Vancouver Island, and a second handful were scattered through the mainland Interior. In 1870, nearly 30 per cent of the inhabitants of British Columbia—over 10,000 people—were newcomers.

The vast majority of these were white.[45] This white population would be the nucleus of future settlement.

The figures at the two ends of the period, however, obscure the significant demographic event that occurred in the middle: the gold rush, during which thousands of temporary immigrants flooded Victoria and penetrated the mainland, with pronounced effects on the environment, economy and geology of British Columbia. During the gold rush, the population was astonishingly diverse, including hundreds of black Americans and thousands of Chinese, as well as Jews from California and Europe, Canadians (both French- and English-speaking), Kanakas (Hawaiians) and West Indians. With the dwindling of profits from the goldfields in the mid-1860s, most of this population ebbed away, leaving a largely white residue to build the new extractive economy. This was the settler population that joined Confederation and waited for the railway to bring another boom.[46]

The gold rush produced a social atmosphere not found in other British North American colonies where agriculture played a much more significant part. People who came to farm intended to stay, even though some failed and moved on. On the other hand, most of the immigrants to British Columbia and especially those who came during the gold rush—many of whom remained for only a few months—came to wrest wealth from the earth and leave again. They were largely a population of sojourners: men in their working years who did not bring families. The scarcity of women (and children) in the white and Chinese communities was constantly remarked upon by contemporary observers. This imbalance persisted for decades, though the trend, as more women arrived and children were born, was towards a correction.[47]

Nothing affected the future of the province more than the crash of the Native population. Attempts to describe what happened to this population in the 1850s and 1860s are hampered by a severe shortage of data. Impressionistic accounts of travellers and officials, supplemented by isolated enumerations of uncertain reliability, are no substitute for the modern census. It is known that the Native population of the coast was denser and richer than that of the Interior; and that death took a terrible toll on Native people, in particular during the smallpox epidemic of 1862. Compared to the number of inhabitants in pre-contact days, there were few Native people in British Columbia by the end of the gold rush. This depopulation facilitated white settlement and numerical domination. Within a couple of decades there would be more white people than Native people.

There were possibly twice as many Native people in the region on the eve of the gold rush as there were in 1870 when they were estimated to number 25,000.[48] The pre-gold rush population already represented a decline attributable to diseases and weapons brought by European traders, though the extent of this decline, as well as the further decrease up to 1870, is debated by historians. No one doubts that large numbers of Native people died. Possibly the mortality rate was so devastating that during the fur-trade period the Native population was cut in half, and perhaps in half again in the brief colonial era.[49] But the impact of disease may have been exaggerated: for example, the deserted villages seen by voyagers might indicate Native mobility rather than mortality.[50]

The worst sufferings were caused by smallpox. There were three epidemics, the last occurring in 1862. It began in Victoria, in the spring, brought by a white visitor from San Francisco. The white population, largely immune through vaccination or previous exposure, was little affected but the disease quickly spread among Native people, especially the Haida and Bella Bella traders from farther up the coast who were camped in Victoria. Some residual immunity was doubtless present in those who had lived through the epidemic of 1835-1838, but since the Hudson's Bay Company had made little effort to vaccinate Native people, most of them were vulnerable when the disease returned.[51] As more Natives sickened, the town authorities drove them out, sending the northerners home and thus hastening the spread of smallpox up the coast. Whites and Native people alike were ignorant of the etiology of the disease, and the white residents were frightened by its appalling effects on Native people, so Native people were sent away and their huts were burned. This policy was repeated in further outbreaks, despite the knowledge that those departing would take the disease with them. A few thousand Native people were vaccinated, but the devastation spread up the coast and into the Interior where, for example, one-half to two-thirds of the Chilcotin may have died.[52] During the colonial period, other contributors to Native mortality were alcohol, tobacco, venereal disease and such illnesses as tuberculosis, but it is not possible to quantify their effects.

The composition of the Native population has generally been assumed to be "normal," this is, equally divided between males and females but it is possible that the number of males decreased more rapidly, owing to their more frequent contact with the immigrants and their participation in warfare. In the epidemic of 1835-1838, many more men than women died at Fort Simpson; this distribution may have been typical and repeated in 1862. Old people were also disproportionately affected in the earlier epidemic,[53] but residual immunity may have countered that tendency in 1862. In any case, as in most communities where life is hard and hygiene deficient, the numbers of old people were not large. Likewise, infant and maternal mortality was probably high. To these common afflictions, European addictions and diseases added a burden that the Native population could not sustain.

The history of the white population is one of erratic expansion in response to economic opportunity. In 1849 the little trading post of Fort Victoria stood alone in the wilderness, and a few fur traders lived on the mainland. Then, as the Hudson's Bay Company pursued its efforts to diversify, it imported miners and farm labourers, and the number of whites slowly grew. Between 1848 and 1852, the Company brought out at its own expense 435 people, nearly two-thirds of them men.[54] In 1854, there were 744 whites on Vancouver Island, including 232 in Victoria, 154 on nearby Company farms and 151 at the Nanaimo coalfields. There were three times as many men as women, but those women who were present were busily adjusting the balance: almost half the population was children, equally divided between the sexes. Most of these early white immigrants were from the labouring classes, and possessed no capital to invest in the new land. They hoped for land and for opportunity, which some of them soon sought in the goldfields of California. A much smaller group—including the bailiffs hired to run the Company farms and John Sebastian Helmcken, the Company doctor—was better off.

The price of land on Vancouver Island was high, and deliberately so. The Company, subscribing to the theory that successful colonies were built by respectable landowners rather than penniless riff-raff, intended to sell land to buyers who could afford to bring workers with them and who would reproduce the hierarchy that was so pronounced a feature of life in Britain.[55] However, not many who filled the bill cared to come. Vancouver Island was far away and lacked glamour. On the eve of the gold rush, the white population of British Columbia was still about eight hundred, though interest in the settlement was picking up. Land sales around Victoria in 1857 were three times those of 1856.[56]

In 1858, the town of Victoria and the mainland were inundated by wave upon wave of gold miners. The gold in the Fraser River brought over 25,000 people to British Columbia within four months. Most came from the goldfields and towns of California and most, disappointed, left by the end of the summer, calling the Fraser strike a humbug. Some stayed on, however, swelling the population of Victoria to several thousand and throwing up instant towns along the river at Fort Langley, Hope, Lillooet and Yale. Some set to work with pans and rocker cradles, and others established themselves as merchants and suppliers. Many of these early arrivals were able to profit by their experience in California.

The gold miners were nearly all men and mostly white, though certainly ethnically diverse. Ships crammed to the gunwales with illegal numbers of passengers sailed forth from San Francisco. Of the 450 men who arrived in the first shipload, startling the Victorians who were just coming out of church, only 60 were British subjects.[57] Other miners, often ignorant of the distances and difficult terrain ahead, tried to make their way overland. In the eyes of some Victorians, the newcomers were a motley crew of opportunists. On the other hand, the newcomers did not admire the tight little British hierarchy on Vancouver Island. "The business portion here," Alfred Waddington remarked at the time, "is generally owned by old fogies, who are destitute of Yankee enterprise."[58] The flash flood of immigration that Victoria experienced in 1858 never recurred, even at the height of the Cariboo strike in 1862, but many more people came to British Columbia during the next few years as the miners moved upriver and then hit the big gold deposits of William's Creek. These immigrants arrived by boat around the Horn and across the Pacific and on foot across the continent.

Women came but their numbers remained small. In the towns of Lillooet and Lytton, for example, the census for 1862-1866 gives the following numbers for white women and men:[59]

Figure I:
White Women and Men in Lillooet and Lytton, 1862–1866

	1862		1863		1864		1865		1866	
	F	M	F	M	F	M	F	M	F	M
Lillooet	23	431	29	240	29	240	18	222	18	256
Lytton	6	94	26	175	26	175	7	550	70	214

There were few women indeed in the most remote mining camps, but there were on average in these years 260 women in the town of New Westminster. This represented a quarter of the male population at the outset and a third at the end, as more men than women left when the profits from the goldfields dwindled. But even in Victoria, where women were relatively numerous, the surplus of males was so striking that one observer thought they outnumbered the women 100:1.[60] Attempts were made to remedy the situation, for not all the inhabitants were transient, and the desire for permanent settlement could not be realized without women.[61] The Anglican Church sponsored two "brides' ships" in 1862 and 1863 in a scheme to solve two problems at once by exporting single British women who would otherwise have been charity cases. In this way, nearly 100 white women were added to the colony. Their status as a commodity—like other shipments of supplies from Britain—is apparent in a contemporary description of the second group as "an invoice of 60 young ladies destined for the colonial and matrimonial market."[62]

In early British Columbia, women were expected to produce children and perform the back-breaking domestic work of pioneer life: both functions were indispensable to the survival of the settlement. Most women fulfilled these roles. Many also contributed to the economy in other ways that have seldom been recognized. Although the evidence is scanty, it is plain that, as in other pioneering societies, women did every kind of farm work, including the heavy labour of clearing land. Family farms not only needed women to cook, nurse, run the dairy and the henhouse, raise vegetables, make clothes and join in the work of the harvest, but often depended on the income women made from selling their butter and eggs, and sometimes on country businesses, such as a store or trading post, staffed by women. In the towns, women ran hotels, restaurants, laundries and schools. Women's skills could be the key to family survival. When coal-mining families left Fort Rupert for the goldfields of California, the women supported them by doing laundry for the other passengers on the ship. In 1864, when Thomas Glennie deserted his family, his step-daughter, Susan Allison, took in sewing and embroidery to help her mother make ends meet and later the two women opened a school in Hope.[63]

Among the array of ethnic groups coming and going during the gold rush, the Jews were a small but distinctive element. The evidence suggests that many—perhaps most—of them came with the intention of staying. The first recorded arrivals, in July 1858, were a couple with a baby who settled in Victoria, and a bachelor who went to the goldfields but later moved to Victoria and married. More Jews immigrated during the next few years. There were approximately one hundred in Victoria in 1861 and sufficient numbers to build and consecrate a synagogue in 1863. A study of this Jewish community, which traces the activities of about thirty-five men in Victoria and another fifteen in Nanaimo, New Westminster and the Cariboo, shows that nearly half of them became permanent residents of British Columbia. Wives and children are mentioned in about a third of the accounts and implied in others.[64]

Some Jews came from England and Australia but most came from California. They came not as refugees but as pioneering merchants, some with education and capital and many with knowledge of the gold economy developed during the California rush. This knowledge and their family connections to established businesses elsewhere helped them thrive in their new enterprises. Few were miners. By the early 1860s, a number of Jewish firms worth thousands of pounds were engaged in businesses as various as lumber, tobacco, clothing and groceries. They shipped supplies to the Cariboo, opened shops there and built part of the Cariboo wagon road.[65]

The diminishing returns from the goldfields had two effects on the white population: it shrank and it became more urban. In 1863, Victoria was a town of 6,000, while another 7,000 went to the mushrooming camps of the Cariboo. But by 1870, when gold fever had died away, fewer than 1,000 white people remained in the Cariboo. The centres of population were Victoria, with a rump of 3,000 plus another 800 or so in the surrounding district; the Fraser River area with over 700 in Hope, Yale and Lytton; New Westminster with about 1,300; and Nanaimo with 600. In all, 8,500 to 9,000 white people remained in British Columbia.[66] Although most of the transient miners and most of the long-term settlers were white, both populations were multi-racial. Thousands of Chinese and hundreds of black people, some of whom stayed on to weave their lives into the fabric of the new province, responded to the opportunities offered by the gold rush.

Chinese merchants and miners from California were among the earliest arrivals. The first, Ah Hong, an agent for a company in San Francisco, arrived in mid-May 1858 and his favourable report drew a contingent of three hundred in June. More boats carrying Chinese people followed. In addition, Chinese miners came overland to New Westminster. In California, the Chinese suffered from abuse and discrimination; they hoped for better treatment in British Columbia.[67] In the first summer of the gold rush, Chinese people bought land in Victoria and Esquimalt, opened businesses, and hunted for gold along the Fraser. By August, there were thirty-seven Chinese miners at Port Douglas. In Victoria, a Chinese laundry was established and Lee Chong, a merchant from San Francisco, opened a successful importing business. He was the first Chinese immigrant to bring his family to Victoria.[68]

The second year of the gold rush brought immigrants from Hong Kong and a Chinatown took shape in Victoria. At the beginning of 1860, there were about 1,200 Chinese optimists in the goldfields. As the gold rush spread upriver, many Chinese miners worked over the placer deposits of the lower Fraser River that had been abandoned by white miners. Others collected jade or moved on to the Cariboo where they mined, provided services such as laundries and restaurants, or sold firewood and fresh vegetables.[69] By 1863, there were perhaps 4,000 in the Cariboo. Several thousand lived in Barkerville where in 1862 alone sixteen Chinese businesses opened. Estimates of the total Chinese population of British Columbia in the most prosperous years of the gold rush reach 6,000 to 7,000. At this time, there was no head tax—a measure introduced in 1884 to induce unwanted Chinese railway workers to leave—and in fact there were no immigration controls of any kind. But as the rush ran its course, the number of Chinese people rapidly dwindled again. In 1871, the census counted only 1,548.[70]

The Chinese who came to British Columbia in this period were almost all men. The proportion of women in the Chinese community was even lower than among the whites. Although the first Chinese baby was born at Port Douglas as early as 1861, there were very few others. In 1871, the census counted only fifty-three women in the province.[71] Both economic and cultural conditions led to the absence of women. Most of the Chinese immigrants came from the rural poor of southeastern China who could not afford the luxury of importing their families. They were expected to send money home, and to return themselves when they had achieved their financial goals. They were sojourners who remained attached to their place of origin, rather than rooting themselves in the new country. Moreover, there were deep prejudices in Chinese society against female emigration. The role of the wife was to care for her family, particularly her aging parents-in-law, and that meant staying at home. The Chinese were also targets of hostile and sometimes thuggish behaviour in British Columbia; however, comparative studies of rural Chinese who moved to Southeast Asia and even to cities in China itself indicate many reasons for them to return home whatever reception they were given abroad.[72] In this concession, it bears stating that most immigrant groups "sojourned" in British Columbia during the gold rush.

Most of the Chinese who came were labourers but there was also a small elite of merchants and a number of lesser businessmen. The labourers worked in the goldfields, on the Cariboo wagon road, in restaurants, laundries and, from 1864, in domestic service. In the absence of European wives and maids, the Chinese provided single white men with the services that were usually "women's work." Only twenty or thirty worked in the coal mines during the latter half of the 1860s, though many more would do so in the following decade.[73] Victoria's Chinatown throve. Eleven businesses paid tax under a new Trade Licence Ordinance in 1862; Lee Chong's company, Kwong Lee, was worth £6,500, second only to the Hudson's Bay Company.[74] Chinese merchants in the Interior towns supplied food and often acted as bankers, offering credit and sending money to families in China.[75] In the wake of the gold rush, some Chinese companies were able to extract profitable amounts of gold but many Chinese people left the region, and those who stayed gathered in the towns.

The gold rush also brought black immigrants from California to Vancouver Island and the colony of British Columbia. Like the Chinese, blacks had faced discrimination in California and they cherished hopes of encountering a less hostile society in British territory. These hopes were to some extent realized. In California they had been menaced by laws pertaining to fugitive slaves and could not vote, while "under the British lion" they were equal before the law. Nevertheless, the prejudices of the white population found a number of unpleasant outlets. In 1865, when economic opportunities dwindled in British Columbia and the threat of slavery ceased with the close of the Civil War, most of the black people returned to the United States. They had found that equality would have to be fought for wherever they were.[76]

Also like the Chinese, they immigrated in response to encouraging reports from the first arrivals in the spring of 1858. Thirty-five black people disembarked on 25 April and formed a "Pioneer Committee." They were followed by several hundred immigrants that same season.[77] In Victoria, the black population at its height in the early 1860s numbered five hundred to six hundred people. Several hundred more went to the mainland. Some established mining companies in the Cariboo; one was a dentist in Barkerville. The number of black people in the region is not known but the distribution of a black newspaper published in San Francisco—*The Elevator*—and the presence of a correspondent in the Cariboo suggest a population of some size.[78] Another contingent left Victoria for Saltspring Island in the spring of 1859. Saltspring had been uninhabited, though it received regular seasonal visits from the Cowichan, and settlers were permitted to pre-empt unsurveyed land. The black settlers joined a varied group of early settlers, including Australians, Americans, English and Germans. Many of the white settlers left after the first winter; and, for a short time, as the black men brought their families, they dominated the island's population. In 1861, seventeen of twenty-one houses in Ganges were occupied by black settlers. They were soon outnumbered, however.[79]

The black immigrants who came from California were not runaway slaves. Some were ex-slaves from the southern United States; some were freeborn northerners; some were illiterate, but a number were well-educated and had capital to invest. Many members of the Pioneer Committee bought land in Victoria immediately, while others hired on at the farms of white settlers. The best-known black entrepreneur was Mifflin Gibbs, who established the firm of Lester and Gibbs. He had come north with miners' supplies; these were snatched up in the frenzy of 1858, and he was able to buy a $3,000 house and open his business. Other blacks opened clothing stores, barber shops, restaurants, and worked as lawyers, carpenters and, briefly, policemen.[80]

The history of the black community in British Columbia presents a record of family migration that contrasts with the masculine character of most other groups. Although the Pioneer Committee seems to have been exclusively male, most black immigrants came with intention of staying, and therefore brought their women and children when they could. Many black children were born— sometimes eight, ten or twelve in a family—compensating to some extent for the numbers of black people who left after 1865. Mifflin Gibbs's wife, Maria, bore five children in Victoria and references can be found to at least two more women of the Gibbs family in the Cariboo. The best-documented of the Saltspring pioneers, the Estes and Stark settlers, came north from California as a family of three generations, including small children.[81]

SOCIAL STRUCTURE, MOBILITY AND CONFLICT

Before the gold rush, the immigrant community was largely composed of Hudson's Bay Company employees, from Chief Factor (and then Governor) James Douglas, who ruled the roost, down to the British farm labourers and Kanaka packers. The Company traditions were authoritarian, relying upon a masculine chain of command, standards of discipline and social distinctions not dissimilar to those of the Royal Navy. These traditions set the tone of early Victorian society and set the stage for early conflict with the coal miners. Throughout the colonial period, new groups of immigrants would challenge the old structure, set up their own communities, and attempt, with varying success, to find a satisfying place in the new land. The Native people straddled two worlds, labouring in the fishing, mining and lumbering economy that was coming into being, and maintaining their traditional social links and means of livelihood.

The most advantageous sort of person to be—before or after the gold rush—was a white middle- or upper-class British male, who would be welcomed into the inner circle of Company officers, invited to attend balls and theatricals, to ride, and to enjoy the shining silver and ironed linen at the Douglas dinner table. Should such a person arrive during the gold rush destitute of funds and reluctant to face the suddenly real hardships of the bush, he would be given a job in the administration. He could expect to marry a daughter of the local elite and play his part in the creation of a new old-boy network.

If he had a little capital, he could buy land and set himself up as a country squire, the dream of many of the socially ambitious.[82] He would stand at the top of the social pyramid, and at the centre of the circle of political and economic power. Before there were many independent newcomers, two classes of people populated the colony—Company officers and Company "servants," and the social gulf was great. Those in the servant class were housed and fed separately from the officers. Their children went to different schools, and they were not included in the officers' dances and teas. The Kanakas in Victoria, for example, lived in Kanaka Row, an early formulation of the racial separations that would characterize the immigrant society.[83]

Although the gold rush spelled the end of Hudson's Bay Company rule, the same people retained their position in government, business and social life. In 1869, for example, the official posts in the Legislative Council were still filled by Englishmen, as was the rest of the civil service. A man who personified the dominant social class at the time was Alexander Grant Dallas. He not only succeeded James Douglas as the head of the Company's Western Department, he also married Douglas's daughter, Jane. When the Company sold the Nanaimo coal mines to a group of British investors, he arranged the sale and at the same time acquired shares in the new Vancouver Coal Mining and Land Company. Like most men in the upper echelons of colonial society, he chose a partner who would preserve or enhance his status, thus maintaining the tightly woven social fabric of the elite. Although some white women did not marry and some managed their own enterprises, the place of a white woman in the social structure was usually determined by her husband.

The gold rush years expanded the merchant class. Americans, European Jews, black, Chinese and British merchants multiplied and prospered in Victoria and in smaller numbers at New Westminster and elsewhere on the mainland. But merchants, however prosperous, were not always accepted as equals by the British landowners, some of whom cherished old prejudices against those in "trade." British traders could take advantage of old connections with the Company,[86] but others often encountered racial or ethnic prejudice as well as snobbery. Within the merchant class, the Jews seem to have mixed easily with other whites, but the black people, who made vigorous efforts to participate in society as equals, were often rudely rejected, while the Chinese were socially isolated. The different racial groups rarely if ever intermarried.[87]

The rough-and-tumble society of the gold frontier was undoubtedly more egalitarian than Victoria. The hardships, the dirt and the risks were shared by everyone, and the compelling dream of riches to be swiftly gained through individual luck and labour ran counter to rigid social divisions. However, this freemasonry of wealth-seekers did not readily welcome all comers. Black people who went to the goldfields were sometimes accepted, but the more numerous Chinese were regarded as an economic threat. As for the Native people, the first gold miners in British Columbia, they occupied a marginal position once the flood of newcomers arrived. Where they were able to retain their claims, they continued to mine, using the more efficient techniques and equipment brought by the immigrants. Some worked as wage labour—packers and miners—for white mining operations along the Fraser River and in the Cariboo; there was a Native shack town on the outskirts of Barkerville. But Native people did not mine independently in the Cariboo or participate in the wild scramble for the best claims.[88]

In the socio-economic structure established by the immigrants, Native people were at a disadvantage, but they did take part in the new economy. In response to the economic change, they diversified, seeking wage labour in the resource economy, undertaking commercial crop production and commercial fishing, and pursuing subsistence agriculture as well as hunting and fishing for their own consumption. They participated in all the new economic sectors: agriculture, mining, logging and fishing.[89] The Haida, for example, were selling canoeloads of potatoes to the Hudson's Bay Company posts as early as the 1830s; Native people mined coal at both Fort Rupert and Nanaimo and were employed in sawmills. But they were constrained by the racism that conferred privilege on white people. They were regarded as cheap labour to be paid less than white men for similar work, and they were excluded from the most skilled and best-paid jobs, such as that of hewer in the coal mines.[90] Nor did they mingle in white society. They lived on reserves defined by the government or in squalid temporary quarters on the outskirts of towns. They were not welcome, for example, at the Royal Theatre in Victoria, which promised that no seats would be offered to them.[91] Native men did not marry immigrant women, and although Native women married white men in the days of the fur trade, and also in some isolated regions of settlement like Saltspring Island,[92] such partnerships were regarded with increasing disfavour by white settler society. At the same time, the social structures of Native people were under attack from several quarters: loss of land that supported traditional subsistence living, diseases, cheap alcohol, prostitution, and missionaries bent on changing their religious beliefs.

Colonial society in British Columbia was therefore neither fluid nor democratic from most points of view. However, it did provide unusual opportunities for social and economic mobility—for some people. Middle-class British professionals, like the Company doctor, and the sons of impecunious minor gentry could occupy a place at the apex of society; it was a position they could not approach at home. These immigrants imagined themselves among "the few very few upper ten" in a social hierarchy modelled on Britain.[93] The Cornwall brothers, sons of gentry with Cambridge degrees, became cattle ranchers near the Thompson River and eventually, with financial help from home, acquired almost 6,500 acres of land. As they prospered, they reproduced the life of the landed aristocracy as best they could: they built a race track and imported thoroughbreds, and they rode to hounds—chasing coyotes, not foxes.[94] Immigrants with fewer initial advantages also improved their lot. Land-hungry labourers acquired land in return for service to the Company, and canny or lucky miners struck it rich. It was not necessary to find gold; perhaps the most spectacular rise was that of Robert Dunsmuir, who was hired by the Hudson's Bay Company to work in the mines at Fort Rupert and who in 1869 discovered the Wellington seam. He became the richest man in British Columbia and built Victoria's Craighdarroch Castle.

In a society with an excess of men, women could marry to advantage. Susan Allison's sister Jane, of a "good" but penniless family, married Edgar Dewdney, later lieutenant-governor of the province.[95] Some Indian or part-Indian women married into the fur-trade elite. James Douglas's wife, Amelia, herself the daughter of a Cree mother and an Irish-Canadian chief factor, found herself at the formal centre of colonial society—not always a comfortable place to be, given the attitudes of settlers towards Native people and their growing intolerance towards mixed marriages. Some women, like Joan Dunsmuir who immigrated with Robert, rose to prominence with their husbands. A few were able to take advantage of the unusual opportunities of the gold frontier to turn domestic services into profitable businesses. Nonetheless, the possibilities for women were more limited than those for men.

Did women protest the limits of their condition? Gender conflict has often been expressed individually and in private. Such conflict is less easy to document than public and collective actions such as strikes. The evidence, if it is to be found, is still buried in legal documents and in private diaries and letters. A few indications have been noted; some wives charged their husbands with assault, for example.[96] But studies like Constance Backhouse's work on women and the law in British North America are needed before it will be possible to analyze women's attitudes and actions in colonial British Columbia. Certainly a public forum for women's issues was emerging in North America during British Columbia's colonial period. In 1848, American feminists in Seneca Falls, New York, passed a resolution demanding the right to vote. This action launched the women's suffrage movement, and through the following decades it received much publicity. Even in the remote Cariboo, women were aware of it; a surprising number of references to the women's rights movement were printed in the *Sentinel*. Susan B. Anthony, the American suffragist, gave a series of lectures in Victoria in 1871. She was received with enthusiasm, and the following year a bill supporting the provincial vote for women was introduced in the legislature. It failed, but in British Columbia women property holders, married and unmarried, received the municipal franchise in 1873—a first for Canada.[97]

Whites habitually excluded blacks, Chinese and Native people from all but strictly economic relationships. For the black people who came to British Columbia, the barriers they faced were a bitter disappointment. They struggled hard to become part of the local community: they were not prepared to accept a "niggers' corner" in the church or the worst seats in the theatre—Victoria's version of the back of the bus. What they sought was "to enjoy those common social rights that civilized, enlightened, and well regulated communities guarantee to all their members."[98]

Unlike Native people or the Chinese, the blacks fully shared the values, customs and religious beliefs of white settlers. They were English speaking, Christian, often literate and well versed in the skills required by the gold rush economy. Nor could their numbers present a threat to white predominance in the colony. Nonetheless, their ambitions were hindered by attitudes towards the black skin. Attempts were made to exclude them from churches or restrict their seating, they were at times refused service in hotels and bars, and in 1860 riots broke out in the Colonial Theatre when blacks insisted on their right to good seats. A similar incident occurred a year later when Gibbs and his family refused to move from seats they had paid for. Appeals to Governors Douglas and Kennedy to put a stop to this kind of overt racism were received with sympathy but inaction.[99]

Black people were also denied membership in community organizations. Unwanted by the fire brigade, they formed their own Pioneer Rifle Corps, which was then not allowed to march in a welcoming parade for Governor Kennedy because it would have been at the head of the procession. On the other hand, they were not denied the franchise, as they were in the United States, and they were treated with warmth and respect by some white Victorians, such as Reverend Cridge who welcomed them at his Anglican church services. They fought for admission to Victoria's congregations and schoolrooms, and were partially successful. Racial tensions declined after 1865, when the American Civil War ended and many Americans left the colony; Mifflin Gibbs was elected to city council in 1866 and 1868, chaired the finance committee and served as acting mayor.[100] While the crudest expressions of racism can perhaps be attributed to Americans, British attitudes combined class discrimination, which placed a prosperous merchant like Gibbs higher on the social ladder than a white labourer, with a quiet racism that excluded black people from private social occasions and formal ceremonies. These forms of prejudice, it has been suggested, gave the British a sense of superiority over the vulgar intolerance of the Americans.[101]

In the Cariboo, blacks appear to have participated as equals with more ease. Blacks and whites shared accommodations, made up mixed companies of miners, and drank together. Amor De Cosmos's racist sentiments, frequently aired in the Victoria papers, did not appear in the *Cariboo Sentinel*. White miners protested in support of black miners against a legal decision by Judge Matthew Baillie Begbie that favoured a white mining company.[102]

The Chinese people encountered race prejudice compounded by cultural differences and fears inspired by their numbers. Unlike the blacks, they did not make strenuous efforts to integrate into white society, but their economic mobility was impeded by discriminatory treatment. The Customs Amendment

Ordinance of 1865 set a different—higher—tariff on goods imported by Chinese miners; according to the Trade Licence Ordinance of 1866, Chinese gardeners had to buy monthly licences for the use of Crown land and trading licences in order to engage in retail trade.[103] They were paid lower wages than white men in the coal mines. They were not permitted to exercise the franchise; in 1863, when they voted in the first election for representatives to the Legislative Council of British Columbia, the returning officer at Quesnelmouth struck out their votes; in 1872 they were explicitly disfranchised by act of the provincial legislature. Partially as a result of white hostility towards economic competition from the Chinese, Chinese workers were concentrated in low-status occupations, such as laundering and domestic service, which then reinforced white beliefs in white superiority.

Social boundaries were manifested in most aspects of the social structure. Intermarriage was rare; residential segregation—Chinatowns, Indian reserves—was common; the division of labour was race related. The various groups had their own institutions: religious, political, educational and philanthropic.[104] The Chinese freemasons in Victoria and Barkerville and the locality associations representing specific homeland communities were examples of social organizations restricted to Chinese members.[105] The whites had their fire brigades, rifle corps, and a multitude of churches, schools and commercial associations. These exemplified class and ethnic divisions within the white community. Already in 1849, the Anglican minister and his wife taught school to Protestant children, and a French priest taught the Catholic French Canadians. Separate schools were established for labourers' children in Victoria (1852), at Craigflower (1855), and in Nanaimo. The latter two were coeducational, but for some years the Victoria school admitted only boys, and girls were not sent to school unless their parents could afford the school for "young ladies" at Colwood.[106]

Among the wide variety of institutions, the only ones to make an active effort to bridge the racial divisions were some churches and missionary organizations. Schools for Native children were among early efforts of these organizations; the Methodists started one in Nanaimo in 1857, and the Anglicans opened a school on the Songhee Reserve near Victoria in 1860. On the mainland, the only school that preceded the gold rush was begun by the Anglican missionary William Duncan at Fort Simpson in 1857. Children attended during the day and adults at night. New Westminster's first school, a Methodist mission school, accepted a Chinese pupil along with its white children.[107]

The racism that was so evident in the white population had a cultural basis independent of economic issues. The primary cause of overt conflict, however, was usually economic. Violence and the threat of violence were used on the gold frontier by white gold miners who regarded Chinese miners as a threat to their own chances. In Victoria, early Chinese arrivals merely amused spectators or were regarded as new customers, but in Hope, a mob of white miners tried to prevent a steamer carrying Chinese miners from landing. This was only one of many instances of attempted intimidation. Chinese miners were driven off new goldfields, their claims were jumped and some of them were murdered. Begbie commented on the inability of the law to protect them.[108] When they retreated from confrontation and worked abandoned claims they were accused of exhausting the placer mines; when they moved to new areas they were accused of taking over. In this early period, few Chinese miners worked in the coal mines but white miners were instantly hostile, threatening with violence "the first Chinaman who forgets his Celestial origin so far as to descend" into the mines. The lower pay offered the Chinese workers was seen as a menace to the jobs of white colliers. Protests, a lockout and a strike ensued.[109]

Conflict between whites and Native people also resulted from competition for mineral resources. In Fort Rupert, the Kwakiutl threatened the imported coal miners when they began to sink a shaft, jeopardizing the trade that Native people enjoyed in surface coal. The Haida forced out American miners who sought gold in the Queen Charlottes. And the considerable Native resistance to immigrant miners on the Fraser and Thompson Rivers was based on the wish of Native people to profit from the gold themselves as well as to protect their salmon fisheries.[110]

The most insistent record of conflict concerns relations between white and white: coal miners and mine owners. From the arrival of the first contingent of Scottish miners to the strikes and stoppages at Nanaimo in the 1860s, the history of early coal mining in British Columbia is a story of strife.[111] Coal miners were highly specialized workers, proud of their skills. The undeveloped coal industry in British Columbia, the availability of cheap labour and the eagerness of their employers to pay as little as possible threatened their hard-won advantages. They resisted unskilled labour, and again and again they went on strike against poor working conditions, poor pay, and a range of devices designed by the companies to increase their profits at the miners' expense. When it seemed possible, they left to seek gold or better jobs across the border. Relations between the colliers and the mine owners in these early years gave a foretaste of the bitter struggles to come in the following decades.

THE COLONIAL LEGACY

Between 1849 and 1871, a new population and a new economy were planted in British Columbia. In these years of rapid change, Native people lost numbers while a community of miners and settlers fluctuated wildly in size as perceptions of opportunity shifted. The newcomers were mostly male, a demographic predominance that would persist far into the new century. The gold rush's boom-and-bust cycle established a pattern that would be repeated in the major industries of the provincial economy, as indeed would the unreflective greed with which the land's resources were extracted.

By the end of the period, the outlines of a new and diverse economy had emerged, and the authority of the Hudson's Bay Company had been replaced by colonial institutions. The future, however, was uncertain. The colony was in debt, and far from the markets needed by its new industries. Native people and immigrant labourers alike were struggling to make a living in the doldrums that followed the gold rush. Many Chinese and black people had left; the remaining settler population was overwhelmingly white. The great variety of people who had found their way into British Columbia had not discovered an open society, but one built on economic and racial inequalities. When the decision was made to join the Dominion of Canada, only a minority of the population had a political voice.

NOTES

1. Simpson wrote: "It has been said that Farming is no branch of the Fur Trade but I consider that every pursuit tending to lighten the Expense of Trade is a Branch thereof." Frederick Merk, ed., *Fur Trade and Empire: George Simpson's Journal, 1824-1825* (Cambridge, Mass.: Harvard University Press, 1931): 50. Quoted in Richard Mackie, "The Company Transformed: The New Trade on the West Coast, 1821-1858." (A paper presented to the fifth B.C. Studies Conference, November, 1988).

2. William Tolmie, quoted in James R. Gibson, *Farming the Frontier: The Agricultural Opening of the Oregon Country, 1786-1846* (Vancouver: University of British Columbia Press, 1985): 199.

3. Paul Phillips, "Confederation and the Economy of British Columbia," in G. Shelton, ed., *British Columbia and Confederation* (Victoria: Morriss Printing, 1967): 58.

4. "It has been said that Farming is no branch of the Fur Trade but I consider that every pursuit tending to lighten the Expense of Trade is a Branch thereof." Merk, *Fur Trade and Empire*, 50. Quoted in Richard Mackie, "The Company Transformed: The New Trade on the West Coast, 1821-1858." (A paper presented to the fifth B.C. Studies Conference, November 1988): 11.

5. James R. Gibson, *Farming the Frontier: The Agricultural Opening of the Oregon Country 1786-1846* (Vancouver: University of British Columbia Press, 1985): 49.

6. Barry M. Gough, "Corporate Farming on Vancouver Island: The Puget's Sound Agricultural Company, 1846-1857," in D. Akenson, ed., *Papers in Canadian Rural History* IV (Gananoque, Ontario: Lagdale Press, 1984): 77.

7. James E. Hendrickson, "Two Letters from Walter Colquhoun Grant," *B.C. Studies* 26 (Summer 1975): 11.

8. Gough, "Corporate Farming," n. 22.

9. Mackie, "The Company Transformed," 32, 35.

10. "Diary of Robert Melrose, 1854," *B.C. Historical Quarterly* VII (1943): 206, and passim. A. N. Mouat, "Notes on the 'Norman Morison,' " *British Columbia Historical Quarterly* III (July 1939): 205. A schoolmaster arrived in this vessel as well.

11. Jean Barman, *British Columbia, A History*. [Unpublished manuscript subsequently

published as *The West Beyond the West* (Toronto: University of Toronto Press, 1991)]: 117. The Company accepted colonization without enthusiasm, but with the recognition that American expansion could no longer be stopped by trading posts, and that if there were to be colonization, the Company's interest would be better served by its own management than by that of another organization. Should colonization fail, and the colony revert to the Crown, then the Company would still have secured five more years to mop up the last profits of the fur trade. To what extent the Company encouraged or discouraged settlement is a matter still debated by historians.

12. Margaret A. Ormsby, "Agricultual Development in British Columbia," *Agricultural History* 19, no. 1 (1945): 12.

13. Marie Anne Elliott, "A History of Mayne Island" (M.A. thesis, University of Victoria, 1982): 11; James R. Gibson, *Farming the Frontier*, 197.

14. F. W. Laing, "Some Pioneers of the Cattle Industry," *British Columbia Historical Quarterly* VI (October 1942): 259.

15. *Ibid.*, 335.

16. John Edgar Gibbard, "Early History of the Fraser Valley 1808-1885." (M.A. thesis, University of British Columbia, 1937): 193.

17. Brian C. Coyle, "Problems of the Puget's Sound Agricultural Company on Vancouver Island 1847-1857" (M.A. thesis, Simon Fraser University, 1978).

18. Lynne Bowen, "Independent Colliers at Fort Rupert: Labour Unrest on the West Coast, 1849," *Beaver* 69, no. 2 (1989): 25.

19. Lynne Bowen, *Three Dollar Dreams* (Lantzville, B.C.: Oolichan Books, 1987): 29.

20. Barbara Standard and T. D. Sale, "Joseph William McKay, 1829-1900," *B.C. Historical News* 19, no. 1 (1985): 6; Bowen, *Three Dollar Dreams*: 50-51.

21. John Belshaw, "Mining Technique and Social Division of Vancouver Island, 1848-1900," *British Journal of Canadian Studies* 1, no. 1 (June 1986): 50-51.

22. Bowen, *Three Dollar Dreams*, 98. Keith Ralston, "Miners and Managers: The Organization of Coal Production on Vancouver Island by the Hudson's Bay Company, 1848-1862," in E. Blanche Norcross, ed., *The Company on the Coast* (Nanaimo: Nanaimo Historical Society, 1983): 53-55; Phillips, "Confederation and the Economy of British Columbia": 51.

23. W. Kaye Lamb, "Early Lumbering on Vancouver Island, Part I: 1844-1855," *British Columbia Historical Quarterly* II (April 1938): 39.

24. Lamb, *ibid.*, 50-51, 95. Sixteen thousand feet of spars went to Chile in a shipment of January 1853.

25. *Ibid.*, 49, 52.

26. W. Kaye Lamb, "Early Lumbering on Vancouver Island, Part II: 1855-1866," *British Columbia Historical Quarterly* II (April 1938): 111-116.

27. F. W. Howay, "Early Shipping in Burrard Inlet: 1863-1870," *British Columbia Historical Quarterly* I (January 1937): 4. In 1869, when Anthony Musgrave, the new governor, toured the colony, there were mills operating at Hastings and Moodyville, and a logging camp at Jerry's Cove (Jericho). Lumber and spars were loaded for a wide-ranging Pacific trade, including Australia, South America, China, Mexico, California and Hawaii. Farmers in the Fraser Valley, their business shrinking with the post-gold rush population, supplemented their income by selling shakes. Margaret Ormsby, *British Columbia: A History* (Toronto: Macmillan of Canada, 1964): 237-238.

28. For an illustrated history of logging tools and techniques, see Mary Shakespeare and

Rodney H. Pain, *West Coast Logging 1840-1910*, National Museum of Man Mercury Series, History Division, Paper No. 22 (Ottawa: National Museums of Canada, 1977). The size of the trees in British Columbia required many innovations.

29. Robie Reid. "Early Days at Old Fort Langley," *British Columbia Historical Quarterly* 1 (April 1937): 71-84.

30. Mackie, "The Company Transformed," 36.

31. Ormsby, *British Columbia: A History*, 238.

32. Paul Phillips, "Confederation and the Economy of British Columbia."

33. Mackie, "The Company Transformed," 38-39.

34. Douglas to Labourchè, 15 July 1857, C.O. 305/8; Robin Fisher, *Contact and Conflict* (Vancouver: University of British Columbia Press, 1977): 101. Mercury was used in separating the gold dust from crust rock. Whether or not the Native people knew how poisonous mercury was, they would have been aware of the erosion, turbidity and destruction of plant life that were caused by placer gold mining.

35. Estimates of its value vary from $500,000 to $700,000. Douglas Fetherling, in *The Gold Crusades: A Social History of Gold Rushes 1849-1929* (Toronto: MacMillan of Canada, 1988): 79, says 100,000 ounces were mined, but at $16 to the ounce, this works out to be $1.6 million.

36. Ormsby, *British Columbia: A History*, 160.

37. Dr. Cheadle, travelling the Cariboo trail in 1863. Quoted in Richard Wright, *Barkerville* (Vancouver: Special Interest Publications, 1984): 17.

38. Alan Conway, "Welsh Goldminers in British Columbia during the 1860s," *British Columbia Historical Quarterly* XXI, nos. 1-4 (1957-58): 58-59.

39. Phillips, "Confederation and the Economy," 46.

40. *Ibid.*, 57.

41. Patricia Roy, "The Illumination of Victoria: Late Nineteenth-Century Technology and Municipal Enterprise," *B.C. Studies* 32 (Winter 1976-77): 83.

42. Phillips, "Confederation and the Economy," 50.

43. Sylvia Van Kirk, "Women in the Cariboo Gold Rush, 1862-1875, or 'Preliminary Diggings Yield Unexpected Nuggets.' " (Unpublished paper, 1988): 15.

44. Extrapolated from table in Phillips, "Confederation and the Economy," 58. Many jobs, in particular those most often done by women, were not listed in the labour statistics.

45. R. Cole Harris and John Warkentin, *Canada Before Confederation: A Study in Historical Geography* (New York: Oxford University Press, 1974): 299; James R. Gibson, "Smallpox on the Northwest Coast, 1835-1838," *B.C. Studies* 56 (Winter 1982-1983): 65. Guesses at the number of Native people at the onset of the gold rush range from 36,000 to over 50,000.

46. Peter W. Ward, "Population Growth in Western Canada, 1901-71," in John E. Foster, *The Developing West: Essays on Canadian History in Honour of Lewis N. Thomas* (Edmonton: University of Alberta Press, 1983): 160.

47. Ward, *ibid.*, 163-168. But note that the imbalance among the Chinese grew worse in the 1880s, when some 17,000 Chinese men were imported to work on the railroad. There were fewer than 160 Chinese women in the province in 1885. Edward Wickberg, ed., *From China to Canada: A History of the Chinese Communities in Canada* (Toronto: McClelland and Stewart Ltd., 1982): 26.

48. Robin Fisher, *Contact and Conflict*, 20-22.

49. Harris and Warkentin, *Canada Before Confederation*, 294.

50. Gibson, "Smallpox," 65, 81; Harris and Warkentin, *Canada Before Confederation*, 299.

51. Gibson, "Smallpox," 63. Zaffaroni, 100. Dr. Helmcken, who immigrated in 1850, vaccinated a number of the local Songhes. See Wilson Duff, "The Fort Victoria Treaties," *B.C. Studies* 3 (Autumn 1969): 42.

52. Duff, "Treaties," 42; Edward Sleigh Hewlett, "The Chilcotin Uprising of 1864," *B.C. Studies* 19 (Autumn 1973): 63; Peter A. Baskerville, *Beyond the Island: An Illustrated History of Victoria* (Burlington, Ontario: Windsor Publications Ltd., 1986): 44.

53. Gibson, "Smallpox," 73. When Douglas counted four local groups of Native people in 1850, including 700 Songhees, he found more women than men in each group. The numbers of children were nearly double those of the adults. See the census in Duff, "Treaties," 23. In 1871, there were three Indian females for every two males in the Victoria census. Zaffaroni, 202.

54. W. Kaye Lamb, "The Census of Vancouver Island, 1855," 52; Mouat, "Notes on the 'Norman Morison,' " 204.

55. For a discussion of the Wakefield theory of colonization, see Ormsby, *British Columbia: A History*, 100-101.

56. Baskerville, *Beyond the Island*, 22.

57. Alfred Waddington, *The Fraser Mines Vindicated* (Victoria: De Garro, 1858, reprinted Vancouver: Robie Reid, 1949): 30.

58. Crawford Kilian, *Go Do Some Great Thing: The Black Pioneers in British Columbia* (Vancouver: Douglas & McIntyre, 1978): 42. The labourers were not exclusively British; many were Kanakas and French Canadians.

59. B.C. Government Blue Books, 1862-1866. Though some errors must be assumed, the general picture is consistent.

60. Baskerville, *Beyond the Island*, 42.

61. Alliances with Indian women were not smiled on by the Christian churches, as will be discussed below.

62. Barman, *British Columbia: A History*, 156.

63. Gwen Szychter, "Early Agricultural Development." (Unpublished paper submitted to A. Seager, Simon Fraser University, 1989): 7, 12; Lynne Bowen, *Three Dollar Dreams*, 42; *A Pioneer Gentlewoman in British Columbia . . .* , reviewed in *B.C. Studies*, 35 (August 1977): 61-62. Susan Allison later married, ran a ranch and a trading post and had fourteen children—not an outlandish number then.

64. Cyril Edel Leonoff, "Pioneer Jewish Merchants of Vancouver Island and British Columbia," *Canadian Jewish Historical Society Journal* 8, no. 1 (1984): passim; Martin Levin, "The Founding and Restoration of Canada's Oldest Surviving Synagogue: A Different Jewish History," *Canadian Jewish Historical Society Journal* 8, no. 1 (1984): 1-11.

65. Leonoff, *ibid.*

66. B.C. Government Blue Book, 1870.

67. Wickberg, *From China to Canada*, 13-16; Gillian Marie, "Attitudes Toward Chinese Immigrants to British Columbia, 1858-1885." (M.A. thesis, Simon Fraser University, 1976): 8.

68. Wickberg, *ibid.*, 14.

69. Jin Tan and Patricia E. Roy, *The Chinese in Canada* (Ottawa: Canadian Historical Association, Ethnic Booklet No. 9, 1985): 7.

70. Wickberg, *From China to Canada*, 14-17, 19. The 1871 figure may well be an

underestimate; the 1874 census counted nearly twice as many.

71. Yuen-fong Woon, "The Voluntary Sojourner among the Overseas Chinese: Myth or Reality?" *Pacific Affairs* 56 (1983-84): 679; Tan and Roy, *The Chinese in Canada*, 4-5.

72. For a careful discussion of the issue, see Woon, *ibid.*

73. Bowen, *Three Dollar Dreams*, 125.

74. Marie, "Attitudes Toward Chinese Immigrants," 38; Wickberg, *From China to Canada*, 16.

75. Tan and Roy, *The Chinese in Canada*, 5.

76. Kilian, *Go Do Some Great Thing*, 60. By 1868, the census counted only 127 black adults in Victoria. *Ibid.*, 142. Not all the blacks were American; some came from the West Indies.

77. Kilian, *ibid.*, 36; H. Keith Ralston, "John Sullivan Deas: A Black Entrepreneur in British Columbia Salmon Canning," *B.C. Studies* 32 (Winter 1976-77): 65.

78. Kilian, *ibid.*, 90. He estimates the total black population of the British Northwest reached 800 to 1,000; this number dropped to 439 (including many children) in 1871. *Ibid.*, 147. The 1871 census lists 127 black males in Victoria and 90 females, but does not distinguish adults from children. Zaffaroni, 202.

79. Kilian, *ibid.*, 103.

80. Kilian, *ibid.*, 45-46. He paid $100 down on the house, another $1,400 within two weeks, and the balance in six months.

81. On blacks in British Columbia, see also Robin Winks, *The Blacks in Canada, A History* (New Haven: Yale University Press, 1971): 272-287.

82. See for example *A Pioneer Gentlewoman in British Columbia* reviewed in *B.C. Studies* 35 (August 1977): 61. Douglas's gold commissioners were chosen from the young men who arrived with letters of introduction; they were frequently members of the Anglo-Irish gentry. Ormsby, *British Columbia: A History*, 180-181.

82. Baskerville, *Beyond the Island*, 21; Ormsby, *British Columbia: A History*, 112-115, 125-126.

84. Ormsby, *British Columbia: A History*, 230-241.

85. Bowen, *Three Dollar Dreams*, 98.

86. For detailed example of the network of connections and intermarriages that supported the continued success of company men, see J. M. S. Careless, "The Lowe Brothers, 1852-70: A Study in Business Relations on the North Pacific Coast," in W. Peter Ward and R. A. J. McDonald, eds., *British Columbia: Historical Readings* (Vancouver: Douglas & McIntyre, 1981): 277-295.

87. For detailed explorations of race relations see Kilian, *Go Do Some Great Thing*, passim; Zaffaroni, chapter 4; Leonoff, "Pioneer Jewish Merchants," passim; Levin, "The Founding and Restoration," passim.

88. Rolf Knight, *Indians at Work: An Informal History of Native Indian Labour in British Columbia, 1858-1930* (Vancouver: New Star Books, 1978): 132.

89. See Rolf Knight, *ibid.*, and Reuben Ware's review of same in *B.C. Studies* 46 (Summer 1980). Numerous other articles document Native participation in the coal industry.

90. Zaffaroni, 92-93; John Douglas Belshaw, "Mining Techniques and Social Division on Vancouver Island, 1848-1900," *British Journal of Canadian Studies* I, no. 1 (June 1986): 54.

91. Baskerville, *Beyond the Island*, 37.

92. Marie Anne Elliott, "A History of Mayne Island," 17.

93. Baskerville, *Beyond the Island*, 21.

94. Edward Philip Johnson, "The Early Years of Ashcroft Manor," *B.C. Studies* 5 (Summer 1970).

95. *A Pioneer Gentlewoman* . . . reviewed in *B.C. Studies* 35, 62. During his term of office they lived in "Cary Castle," a name redolent of immigrant dreams.

96. Van Kirk, "Women in the Cariboo," 23.

97. Alison Prentice *et al., Canadian Women: A History* (Toronto: Harcourt Brace Janovich, 1988): 175. Some women property holders in Quebec had voted earlier in the century, as the law had not specifically forbidden it, but in 1849, probably in response to the Seneca Falls resolution of the previous year and the fear that more women would become politically active, the Quebec parliamentarians explicitly denied women the right to vote by inserting the word "male" into the Franchise Act. Women voted in B.C. despite jibes and catcalls. Prentice, *ibid.*

98. Reverend J. J. Moore, quoted in Kilian, *Go Do Some Great Thing*, 51.

99. Zaffaroni, 116-134.

100. Kilian, *Go Do Some Great Thing*, 136, 140.

101. Kilian, *ibid.*, 50; Zaffaroni, 143. Blacks were not invited to church sewing circles, for example, or to the farewell dinner for Governor Douglas.

102. Kilian, *ibid.*, 95-99.

103. Marie, "Attitudes," 23, 31.

104. Peter Ward, "Race and Class in British Columbia: A Reply," *B.C. Studies* 50 (Summer 1981): 593.

105. W .E. Eillmott, "Approaches to the Study of the Chinese in British Columbia," *B.C. Studies* 4 (Spring 1970): 44-46.

106. F. Henry Johnson, *A History of Public Education in British Columbia* (Vancouver: University of British Columbia Press, 1964): chapter 1.

107. *Ibid.*, 23.

108. Marie, "Attitudes," 2-10, 17-19.

109. Bowen, *Three Dollar Dreams*, 126.

110. For a persuasive study, see Patricia Vaughan, "Co-operation and Resistance: Indian-European Relations on the Mining Frontier in B.C., 1835-1838." (M.A. thesis, University of British Columbia, 1978).

111. Studies of early coal mining in B.C. include those by Belshaw, Bowen, Burrill, Phillips and Ralston.

PART III

From Confederation to the First World War

Chapter 5
PROVINCIAL POLITICS, 1871–1916
John Douglas Belshaw

After Confederation, British Columbia's old political elite faced democratic change reluctantly—seeing useful and even admirable qualities in the old colonial system and wishing to preserve as much of that system as they could. Moreover, they retained sufficient influence to affect the evolving structure of government, the progress of electoral law and attitudes to Confederation itself. Typically the situation set reform-minded politicians against autocratic lieutenant-governors, though it manifested itself in other ways, too. This chapter provides a sketch of the conflicts of these years and the ways in which they were played out, but the emphasis is on the structure and culture of British Columbia politics. Conflicts arose over disparate issues, but an analysis of them reveals a connecting theme: the province's political elites invariably sought to resolve conflicts so that broader economic and political goals could be achieved in a setting of relative stability.

CONFEDERATION AND "CANADIANIZATION"

Resistance to Confederation was strongest among the old colonial civil servants, particularly those officials who had gained their status in the Douglas period. Justices Matthew Baillie Begbie and Henry Pellew Crease were prime examples. After Confederation they retained a suspicion of the Dominion government that was not softened by John A. Macdonald's practice of rewarding Conservatives from the east with patronage posts in the west.[1] Insecurity produced acts of opposition and defiance. Confederation brought unmistakable change in the style of government in British Columbia and in the divisions of power within provincial society. Confederation held out the promise of greater democracy through a broader franchise, responsible government instead of the old colonial oligarchy, the retirement of the lieutenant-governor from policy making to take on the mantle of the Queen's disinterested representative, and provincially (rather than imperially) controlled courts. In short, a far greater share of authority was to be vested in the hands of popular representatives than had been the case before 1871. With the forces of reform ascendant elsewhere in Canada and Britain, these were principles that British Columbians acquired fully formed—or at least pre-packaged. The enemies of these principles, however, did not desert their posts in this conflict immediately after 1871.

The most outstanding critic of responsible government was the first lieutenant-governor, Joseph Trutch. An office holder from pre-Confederation days, Trutch resisted democratizing forces as best he could and continued to sit in on Executive Council meetings during the initial administration headed by John F. McCreight.[2] This was a red rag to reform-minded members of the Legislative Assembly (MLAs) like Amor De Cosmos, but Trutch had important allies among the judiciary and the province's Members of Parliament (MPs). In 1879, Senators Clement F. Cornwall and W. J. Macdonald joined with Edgar Dewdney, then an MP for British Columbia, to criticize the changes in the constitutional framework of the province. "Unfortunately for British Columbia," they wrote to the Prime Minister in Ottawa, "what is known as universal suffrage is in force in the Province. The lower classes, those having no stake in the country, consequently control the elections, and the representation of the Province in the Legislative Assembly is, to say the least of it, most unfortunate. The present Legislative Assembly is perhaps taken together as inferior a body of the sort as could well be imagined; and if the Province is to be unmistakebly [sic] given up to their tender mercies without the interposition of experienced guidance and to some extent *repression* from Ottawa, no thoughtful mind can view the picture without the gravest apprehension."[3] Justice Henry Pellew Crease recoiled from the personalities who found their way into British Columbia politics, claiming there was not one member of the De Cosmos administration whom he "would care to have for a friend, or to ask to [his] house."[4] Crease claimed "no sympathy with the iconoclastic tendency of this age" and his hostility towards the "unreasoning and leveling tendencies of *universal suffrage*" remained vociferous through the 1870s.[5]

The democracy decried by these members of the province's old oligarchy was, in fact, very limited. The franchise did not include all men and excluded women entirely until the end of the Great War. Yet, so far as the anti-reformers were concerned, too many people had the vote. The proposition that the franchise be extended and that voters be given a secret ballot (required in Dominion elections by an act of 1874) struck right at the heart of privilege in British Columbia. The principle of responsible government—Assembly control over the executive—was anathema to the old elite. Any move to broaden the democratic base of the Assembly made them even more apprehensive.

Premiers walked a difficult tightrope in these years and that tended to confirm the old elite in their opposition to reform. They did not like the political turmoil and the frequent turnovers of government. In 1871 the "cabinet" consisted of no more than five individuals or, rather, five portfolios. British Columbia, a "poor, struggling, bankrupt colony off on the edge of things," could barely afford this many.[6] In an Assembly without disciplined parties, a government was vulnerable because it could not depend on many votes. With only four or five executive positions in a legislature of twenty-five members, a government required the continuing support of at least eight additional MLAs.[7] Maintaining this support and avoiding votes of confidence involved negotiating legislation with independent members of the Assembly. This meant that the Assembly exercised considerable power over the executive.

In the early twentieth century, the British Columbia Legislative Assembly—and the Dominion Parliament—still followed the British parliamentary tradition that required new ministerial appointees to resign their seats and stand again in by-elections. In these circumstances, cabinet members were often returned by acclamation. Their absence during by-elections, however, could be critical, allowing independent members to flex their muscles and encouraging the assertiveness of the Assembly. The uncertain status of the premier created further confusion. So far as the 1871 Constitution Act was concerned, no such creature as a premier existed. The position developed because one member of the Executive Council had to play the role of the chairman. Often it was the provincial secretary who took on the responsibility and "Premier" was a courtesy title, not a legal description.[8] Only in 1921 did the office of the premier achieve *de jure* recognition in the provincial constitution. This is not to suggest that pre-1916 premiers behaved in a manner completely at odds with their post-war successors. Even today the role of premier is defined largely by convention and the convention has not changed much over time.[9] In the early years, however, the position of the premier in relation to both the Assembly and the lieutenant-governor was much weaker than it has become.

From 1871 to 1914 the political culture of British Columbia, while remaining in many ways distinct, grew closer to the political culture of eastern Canada. The 1894 Legislative Assembly was the first in which there were more native-born Canadians than English immigrants; even so, with the addition of Scots and Irish, the British contingent remained dominant a decade after the Canadian Pacific Railway (CPR) reached the coast. Federally the pattern was similar: in 1879 only one of the province's MPs was born in British North America; the 1883 Dominion general election returned four Canadians—two of United Empire Loyalist descent—and only two British candidates (from Victoria, of course).[10]

While Confederation may have stimulated eastern Canadian interest in the Pacific territory and while it may have encouraged migration to the west, British immigrants remained influential. "British" Columbia held a special attraction for British emigrants, which meant that their numbers remained proportionately higher than in most of the rest of Canada and connections with the Old Country were refreshed in each generation.[11] Whatever eastern Canadians might have thought of their possession by the western sea, for many in England it was still a discrete part of the Empire. *The Times* of London (which carried exaggerated descriptions of life on the gold frontier) remarked in an 1898 editorial that: "to the average untraveled man, sitting perhaps at home in comfort either retired from business on a comfortable income or still trying to attain that end, little is known with any geographical exactitude of such portions of our great Empire as British Columbia. Even the better informed seem to have an idea that British Columbia is still a separate colony and not a part of the Dominion of Canada."[12] This is not to infer that everyone in Victoria felt more British than Canadian; but, generally, the psychological bonds between the Far West and the British Isles remained strong while emotional ties with the Canadian confederacy were slow to develop.

During the Confederation debates, John Helmcken identified two possible sources of a future loyalty to Canada. One was fiscal and the other filial.[13] For a long time, the force of filial loyalty was muted. British Columbia's population grew much more from immigration than from natural increase. The adult immigrant population with loyalties and traditions drawn from elsewhere, over-whelmed—in numbers—the Canada-loving children of the province. It is impossible to say accurately when the sense of belonging to Canada became greater in British Columbia than the sense of autonomy. Important economic links continued to be forged with Asia, Britain and, most critically, California. The British Columbian business cycle reflected Californian oscillations very clearly in the early twentieth century and even the Bank of British Columbia had its head office in San Francisco.[14] Annexationist rhetoric offered a measure of un-Canadian feeling in the province but by the 1890s this was a force that was largely spent. Secessionism (not always with the prospect of linking up with the United States) was threatened by De Cosmos in the 1870s and by successive premiers who were after better terms from Confederation. By the turn of the century, however, these poses were transparent. The political culture of British Columbia—more so than her economy—had become securely fastened to the shirt-tails of the CPR and the Dominion.

POLITICIANS AND POLITICAL PARTIES

Until 1903, provincial politicians in British Columbia avoided party labels. In Dominion elections after 1896, the chief contestants were Liberals and Tories (or Conservatives).[15] But in the Assembly in Victoria the Speaker still presided over a shifting collection of "loose fish," cliques, cabals and coalitions rather than disciplined party groups. The character of the Assembly metamorphosed around the turn of the century when party lines were introduced. At this point, British Columbia politics became much more like the Canadian norm. The change seemed to produce more stability in government. In the previous twenty-two years, the province had seen fourteen different premiers. During the next thirteen years, from 1903 to 1916, one man—Richard McBride—held the position.

Before the McBride era, politics revolved around alliances of individuals, so much so that it is possible to speak of a succession of "dynasties." In some instances it could be argued that the dynasties themselves were held together by the glue of shared policy objectives, ideology, religion, social status, and common (often venal) interests. These alliances—decried by contemporary commentators as a source of instability—had organizing principles. McBride's achievement in 1903 was not so much the *creation* of party politics as the translation of existing bonds into recognizably partisan arrangements.

Figure 1: Premiers of British Columbia, 1871–1916

Name	Dates	Dynasty/Party
McCREIGHT, John F.	1871–1872	Walkem/Trutch
DE COSMOS, Amor	1872–1874	Walkem/Liberal
WALKEM, George A.	1874–1876	Walkem/Non-Partisan
ELLIOTT, A. C.	1876–1878	Smithe
WALKEM, George A.	1878–1882	Walkem/Non-Partisan
BEAVEN, Robert	1882–1883	Walkem/De Cosmos
SMITHE, William	1883–1887	Smithe
DAVIE, A. E. B.	1887–1889	Smithe/Dunsmuir
ROBSON, John	1889–1892	Smithe
DAVIE, Theodore	1892–1895	Smithe/Dunsmuir
TURNER, John H.	1895–1898	Smithe
SEMLIN, Charles A.	1898–1900	Non-Partisan/Tory
MARTIN, Joseph	1900–1900	Non-Partisan/Liberal
DUNSMUIR, James	1900–1902	Non-Partisan/Tory
PRIOR, Edward Gawley	1902–1903	Non-Partisan/Tory
McBRIDE, (Sir) Richard	1903–1915	Conservative
BOWSER, William J.	1915–1916	Conservative

John Foster McCreight, Q.C.—a political neophyte—headed the province's first administration. He was chosen in 1871 from the freshly elected Members of the Legislative Assembly (MLAs) by the newly appointed lieutenant-governor, Joseph Trutch, for reasons that remain unclear. Some have argued that McCreight was selected because, like Trutch, he was suspicious of democratic reform.[16] Others have emphasized McCreight's apparently lacklustre personality, which might have made him an easy instrument for a strong-willed lieutenant-governor.[17] Certainly Trutch sought to exercise the broadest prerogative in the Executive Council and for that reason alone would have considered the more demagogic MLAs inappropriate for the premiership.

In its twelve months the McCreight ministry was able to accomplish much of importance. The legislation necessary to the running of the Assembly, the creation and payment of a civil service independent of Westminster, the establishment of a judicial framework—these were all part of the McCreight record.[18] His government also eliminated tariffs on the Cariboo Road (a nod to the economy of the hard-pressed mainland), and introduced the secret ballot as well as the province's first education bill.

Whatever its merits, McCreight's administration never enjoyed great popularity in the Assembly or in the province. The lieutenant-governor's conspicuous involvement in the Executive Council was one factor. The personality of the premier may have been another, though that is less easy to assess. Contemporaries described him as "nervous fidgety queer tempered"; one biographer regarded him as "cold and withdrawn"; and there is the suggestion that he was malleable in the hands of the more forceful Trutch.[19] He was treated roughly in the newspapers, though issues rather than character may have been the leading reason. John Robson—editor of the Victoria *Colonist* at the time, a reformer and a future premier—contended that McCreight's greatest shortcoming was his hostility towards responsible government and democratic reforms. McCreight's history in British Columbia, said Robson, was "chiefly remarkable for the uniformity of his shrinking from every public movement and the morbid antipathy with which he regarded those liberal institutions he was thus so strangely called upon to work."[20]

McCreight was defeated narrowly on a vote of non-confidence in December 1872 following the speech from the throne. He was defeated at the first opportunity after the province's formative legislation was in place by an Assembly that was more reform minded than he. In resigning he made a parting contribution to British Columbian politics. A vote of non-confidence then did not automatically produce the dissolution of a government, so technically McCreight could have soldiered on, introducing a new budget in the hope that more votes could be mustered in his favour. If no credible majority emerged to replace him such a strategy might have succeeded. Without the support of a caucus whip along the backbench, however, the prospects were dim. McCreight chose to resign and this became the accepted practice in British Columbia politics following non-confidence defeats.

McCreight was succeeded by Amor De Cosmos, *the* outstanding political personality in British Columbia at the time—alternately a Father of Confederation and a British Columbian separatist. Perhaps bitter at being passed over by Trutch as leader of the first government, De Cosmos had gone to Ottawa in 1872 as the Member of Parliament for Victoria. He was also a member of the provincial legislature, and it was shortly after he went to Ottawa that he was called on to form the second provincial administration in British Columbia. During his short term as premier, he spent almost as much time in Ottawa and London, and in transit, as he did in Victoria.[21] His lengthy absences found little sympathy in the provincial legislature and ex-premier McCreight introduced a bill to bar politicians from sitting in both parliaments. In 1874 De Cosmos decided to resign his provincial seat and the premiership so that he could concentrate on federal politics.

Despite his often provocative pose before 1871, De Cosmos pursued a rather cautious tack as premier. His single monumental achievement—the removal of the lieutenant-governor from the Executive Council—was a milestone on the road to responsible government in British Columbia. Yet his contemporaries were exceptionally uncharitable to him during his brief administration, and during his tenure as an MP, and even in later years when he experienced personal misfortunes. As a politician, he was accused of financial misbehaviour and corruption regarding mines and railways. Edgar Dewdney alleged that in 1873 De Cosmos tried to persuade the province's federal MPs to "combine and inform the then Government, that we would oppose them, unless they allowed us $75 or $80,000 of Pacific Railroad stock."[22] Accusations like this contributed to a growing sense that De Cosmos compromised Island interests. When he died in 1897, Dr. Helmcken—no great friend—reported with sadness the funeral of the one-time firebrand and radical: "A few hacks, a score of men at the residence, the foot[f]all of a dozen men sounding from the sidewalks, three-score men and a few women in the church, no sepulchral tones from the organ, no singing of sacred, hopeful hymns, a short reading of the burial service—all dead, dead, as cold and lifeless as the corpse in the dismal coffin. . . . That such a man should have come to this—alas, poor Yorick! Such a funeral is neither worth living, nor dying for."[23] In a province where everything—including the political realm—was changing dramatically, the political prophet of an age quickly became simply yesterday's man.

The premiers who followed in the 1870s—Walkem (1874–1876), Elliott (1876–1878) and Walkem again (1878–1882)—were neither as attractive nor as repellent as De Cosmos. But their prominence denoted an emerging pattern in British Columbia's politics. Walkem had been a member of both McCreight's cabinet and that of De Cosmos. When he shifted allegiance from an anti-reform to a pro-reform premier, he demonstrated that ideological flexibility was quite acceptable in the British Columbia legislature. Indeed, such flexibility seems to have been essential. Yet, in the absence of rigid party affiliations, certain combinations were coalescing. Elliott, who was one of the casualties of cutbacks in the colonial administration during the transition to Confederation, had served very briefly behind William Smithe on the opposition side during Walkem's regime. When Elliott formed an administration in 1876 and brought in Smithe as minister of finance and agriculture, he began the most successful dynasty of the period, the Smithe line—so called subsequently because it started with Smithe's leadership in opposition. The Smithe dynasty included six premiers who held power for seventeen of twenty-two years between 1876 and 1898.

The odds that British Columbia's provincial politicians would choose to affiliate with Canada's national parties seem to have worsened in the mid-1870s. When the Liberals took power in Ottawa in 1873, they sought to renegotiate the terms of union with British Columbia, terms that Prime Minister Alexander Mackenzie viewed as unrealistic and overly generous.[24] Mackenzie made a plea for an additional ten years to complete the line and, more seriously, he sought to extricate his government from a commitment Macdonald had made to bring the railway to Vancouver Island via Bute Inlet. Islanders saw this commitment as one of the vital terms of the Confederation agreement. Edgar Dewdney, the surveyor and now MP, responded with the cry "The Terms, the Whole Terms and Nothing but the Terms" but, to the horror of most Vancouver Islanders, mainland politicians showed signs of capitulating.[25] Increasingly discussion focused on a Fraser River terminus for the CPR. This option meant that the Bute Inlet route would be bypassed altogether and Islanders' hopes of a direct link with Canada would be dashed. The differences between the mainland and the Island were sharply drawn.[26] A full-blown rupture was averted but it is clear that public feeling on the future of the province — especially among rival business elites — was far from united. Islanders saw the spokesmen for the small and struggling settlements at New Westminster, Yale, Kamloops and elsewhere in the Interior as loose cannons in the struggle with Ottawa.[27] Mainlanders still saw Victoria as the seat of oligarchic power, a nest of effete bureaucrats whose main concerns were patronage, an impractical railway along Bute Inlet and a hugely expensive fixed-link across the Strait.[28] But mainlanders shared the exasperation of Islanders with the Canadian government over the fulfillment of the terms of union. A special correspondent for the Toronto *Globe*, travelling with Governor General Lord Dufferin on a vice-regal tour of British Columbia in the summer of 1876, immediately grasped the division, anxiety and anger that the railway issue and union were provoking in the province. But he was inclined to dismiss the excitement as small town politics: "It always happens," he wrote, "that the local contentions and animosities are in inverse ratio to the size of the community, and in Victoria the isolation of the country has an intensifying rather than a mitigating effect."[29]

The railway issue involved alternative visions of economic development in British Columbia. It began with the first discussion of the CPR and continued long after the transcontinental line was complete. As one author put it, by the mid-1880s "British Columbia and railways had become inseparable."[30] The question was always provocative because the future of communities across the province depended on the success of one projected route or line over another. Under the premierships of Walkem, Robert Beaven (1882–1883) and William Smithe (1883–1887) the development of railway lines within the province became a principal concern of economic policy. Dominating the debate was the Islanders' desperate attempt to bind the CPR to a Victoria terminus. Under the terms of an agreement negotiated by Governor General Lord Carnarvon in 1874, the Dominion was supposed to build a railway on the Island from the Royal Navy base at Esquimalt to the coal town of Nanaimo.[31] This was construed as compensation for the Dominion government's failure to complete the transcontinental railway on time. But the agreement—an "egregious compromise . . . a travesty of the original terms of union"—was not well received in British Columbia, and it ran into difficulty in Ottawa. Negotiations went badly during the premiership of George A. Walkem. After Walkem stepped down—accepting John A. Macdonald's offer of an appointment to the Supreme Court of British Columbia—the new administration under Beaven gave the federal government fresh reason to delay by rescinding earlier legislation transferring railway lands on the Island to the federal government. Beaven was forced out of office in January 1883, but he remained a popular figure on the Island for years and successfully switched to civic politics in Victoria. The new Smithe government was more accommodating, and construction on the Esquimalt and Nanaimo Railway finally began in 1884 when the federal government handed the project to Robert Dunsmuir, the owner of the Wellington coal mine near Nanaimo. The federal government's deal with Dunsmuir involved a subsidy of $750,000 (an average of $10,000 per mile) and a grant of two million acres along the railway right-of-way.

The Smithe government provided something of the continuity that had been lacking to that point in British Columbian politics. Smithe was able to hold on to office for four years but, more significantly, he secured a body of supporters in the legislature who functioned much like a party, though not exactly. Smithe and his heirs—A. E. B. Davie (1887–1889), John Robson (1889–1892), Theodore Davie (1892–1895), and John H. Turner (1895–1898)—achieved a record fifteen years of relative political stability. (Dunsmuir was also connected to this group. From 1882 he represented Nanaimo in the Legislative Assembly and during the Davie administration he was president of the Executive Council.) The rapid turnover of premiers during the years of the Smithe dynasty was due to the fact that Smithe, A. E. B. Davie and Robson all died in office. This meant that several times the government had to survive during the absences of leaders who were suffering from serious or terminal illnesses. In an Assembly dominated by independent—loose-fish—members, the Smithe dynasty proved itself able to fend off challenges.

Ideologically Smithe's successors were mostly conservative. John Robson was a qualified exception. During the Confederation debates he had been a vigorous advocate of constitutional change to end the old oligarchic control.[32] But he was just as interested in the spoils of government as any of his contemporaries. He was a minister in the Smithe administration that had encouraged the CPR to move its transcontinental terminus from Port Moody to Vancouver with a grant of six thousand acres, and he had profited personally as the owner of land in the vicinity of the new terminus. As premier, he was hardly distinguishable from his "dynastic" colleagues. The reformer in him was evident chiefly in the sweeping changes in education that he legislated in 1891. This initiative was not altogether surprising coming from a newspaper publisher dependent on a literate public.

Theodore Davie was the premier who replaced the old colonial "birdcages" with the present Parliament Buildings. More than just a public works project, the new legislature confirmed Victoria as the capital. This was something to which many mainlanders were opposed—with good reason because as mainland politicians moved house to Victoria they became increasingly sympathetic to the Island agenda.[33] Davie continued the established tradition of previous governments, managing the Assembly without recognizing a clear distinction along party lines. He was conscious of the danger to this system of the socialistic or radical elements of the labour movement and sought to keep workers in the political mainstream. His approach, according to a contemporary observer, was to warn working-class voters that "to antagonize the investing class and to drive away capital . . . was unwise, unpatriotic and suicidal." He urged them "not to be led away by the specious appeals to class prejudice and the theoretical dogmas of agitators inexperienced in governing, who appreciated neither the responsibility attaching to it nor the practical application of their own doctrines therewith."[34] As long as he remained in politics, ideological differences in the Assembly were muted, and another decade passed before candidates in provincial elections were identified as Socialists, Liberals and Conservatives.

When Davie resigned in 1895 to become chief justice of British Columbia, the nature of British Columbia politics began to change. His successor, John H. Turner, began his administration with one great liability. While he had been minister of finance under Davie, the provincial debt had quadrupled, a development that won him stinging criticism in the Assembly and in the press. A new political climate emerged as the quietly Liberal members of the opposition found encouragement in the Dominion successes of Wilfrid Laurier's Liberal party in 1896. They portrayed Turner as a Conservative lame duck and suggested that his fate was linked to that of the federal Tories who were now in opposition after eighteen years in power.

As a dispenser of spoils, Turner was without equal: under his administration, more provincial railway charters were issued to railway promoters than under any other before McBride's.[35] During his first term as premier, Turner lost supporters: some were lured away by the call of Party, others were incensed at alleged gerrymandering before the 1898 provincial election.[36] Viewed less and less as an heir to the respectable Smithe mantle and increasingly as the originator of a dubious and ineffectual political style nicknamed, unkindly, "Turnerism," the premier expected a rough ride from the electorate. In fact he was narrowly victorious in 1898. The absence of a strong party tradition helped him because many of his supporters ran ambiguously under the guise of "Independents."

By 1898 British Columbia had seen eleven premiers—a new government, on average, every three years.[37] The 1898 election initiated five turbulent years with five changes in the premiership (including one administration that lasted fewer than four months) and a prolonged constitutional crisis involving the executive, the Assembly and the lieutenant-governor. This period of confusion began with a decision by the lieutenant-governor, Senator Thomas R. McInnes, not to call upon Turner to form a government but to invite former premier and defeated candidate Robert Beaven instead.[38] McInnes was encouraged to intervene in this way by the election protests filed in twenty-nine ridings (out of thirty-eight) and the likelihood that Turner's slim majority would disappear in the recounts. He also reacted to evidence of Turner's unpopularity on the mainland. Beaven, however, proved to be the wrong choice, and four days later McInnes turned to Charles Semlin, a long-serving provincial parliamentarian, a Conservative and the leader of the opposition during the Turner years.

It was not long before Semlin's cabinet was damaged by increasingly public disagreements between his attorney general, Joseph Martin, and the minister of finance, Francis Carter-Cotton. Martin had enjoyed an illustrious—not to say tempestuous—career in Manitoban politics before moving to Vancouver. A Liberal, an advocate of alien exclusion legislation, the author of the Manitoba Schools Act, and a supporter of the eight-hour day for labour, Martin was in every respect provocative so far as arch-Tories like Carter-Cotton were concerned.[39] Obliged to cut loose one of two liabilities, Semlin settled on Martin as the greater problem. Once in the opposition ranks, Martin launched swinging attacks on his former colleagues. In February 1900, with Martin leading the opposition, the government failed to pass a redistribution bill. Semlin wanted an opportunity to face a formal vote of confidence, but McInnes dismissed him and called Martin to form a new government. Members of the Assembly saw this as a coup d'etat by the lieutenant-governor. The only one who approved was Martin and the Assembly greeted him with an immediate twenty-eight to one vote of non-confidence. McInnes dissolved the Assembly and Martin assumed the premiership stripped of any moral authority.

The Martin regime lasted from the dissolution of the Assembly in February until an election in June. "Fighting Joe" was hard pressed to find anyone who would sit with him in his cabinet; he was obliged to recruit a group of novices who had never been members of the Assembly and who did very little in the brief time they were in office. Despite running a fairly successful populist-style campaign in the June 1900 election, Martin did not secure a majority. He had the financial backing of the railway baron J. J. Hill, but when he looked for political support from the federal Liberals, it was not forthcoming. Martin's attempt to fight the election as the leader of a provincial Liberal party didn't wash with a great many Liberals, and a few days after the election results were in, Martin resigned. McInnes—whose own credibility depended on Martin's success—was forced out of office a week later.[40] An inveterate politician, Martin was subsequently active on the opposition benches, then moved to England where, in 1910, he became the Member of Parliament for St. Pancras East.[41] During the First World War he returned for a spell to British Columbia where he sought the mayor's office in Vancouver. On that occasion, as at the polls in 1900, Martin's luck failed him.

In the summer of 1900, the premiership was assumed by James Dunsmuir, the son of Robert Dunsmuir, the coal mining and railway magnate. With Semlin gone there was no one else from the opposition side who could attempt to form a government: Dunsmuir won the responsibility by default. A Conservative, Dunsmuir was the only prominent member of the provincial economic elite to play a leading role in politics in this period. Following in his father's footsteps, James had acquired a reputation as an uncompromising capitalist, a mine owner who would brook no interference from unions. Like his father, the younger Dunsmuir opposed anti-Chinese legislation because his Vancouver Island collieries hungered for cheap Asian labour. In this respect, as in others, Dunsmuir demonstrated the gulf that existed between the province's economic leaders and most of the politicians.

Dunsmuir had supported Turner and, not surprisingly, favoured business throughout his political career. And he favoured his friends: Turner was made minister of finance in Dunsmuir's administration. Additionally, Dunsmuir introduced to cabinet politics a young New Westminster lawyer, Richard McBride, whom he made minister of mines. However, Dunsmuir showed no pleasure in politics, something for which he displayed few natural skills.[42] He stumbled into an avoidable crisis by filling a vacant cabinet post with a veteran of the discredited Martin administration, a manoeuvre that provoked McBride's resignation. When Dunsmuir decided to step down in 1902, the Conservatives in the B.C. legislature were divided between those who supported the government and those on the other side of the house—like McBride, who was now leader of the opposition.

Edward Gawley Prior, McBride's replacement as minister of mines, rapidly emerged as the man to succeed Dunsmuir. In 1902 Prior's opportunity came, but it was quickly squandered. His administration was notoriously corrupt and in less than a year the lieutenant-governor demanded his resignation. To form a new government, the lieutenant-governor summoned Richard McBride, who promptly called an election. The 1903 campaign was the first to be fought under party labels and it finished in a near dead heat. McBride's Tories had only one seat to spare. They survived as a government through party discipline, a practice that was soon picked up by an increasingly Liberal opposition. In this way, by creating a whippable government backbench, McBride also created an organized opposition, the yin to his yang.

McBride held power for twelve years and through four elections—longer than any British Columbian premier up to the time of W. A. C. Bennett. Following his first election, McBride took dramatic steps to ensure his administration's survival. He recruited the support of two socialist MLAs; he alienated large chunks of Crown lands in resource giveaways; and he supported a vast program of railway construction to secure votes in the Interior—an issue that could be regularly pumped. The Grand Trunk Pacific project was to generate enormous problems, despite the political advantages it offered.[43] The announcement of a line into the central Interior was made on the eve of the

1909 provincial general election and, although it was followed by two resignations from cabinet, the overall reception was immensely favourable, producing a huge majority for the Conservatives. In the years that followed, however, it became increasingly clear that the political implications of railway projects were many-sided. The Pacific Great Eastern Railway—a line intended to join Vancouver to Fort George and to the Peace River country beyond—soon began to experience difficulties, provoking dissent within McBride's cabinet.[44] As well, the Premier's connection with the railway interests of Mann and Mackenzie was to become a source of embarrassment when, on the eve of the war, provincial militia units were sent to Nanaimo to put down a strike by miners against the railway-and-mine-owning consortium.

Knighted in 1912, shortly after securing yet another big majority in a general election, Sir Richard displayed some outstanding qualities that insulated him from too much criticism. It took considerable panache to obtain, as McBride did on the eve of the First World War, two submarines for the use of the Canadian navy. Nonetheless, towards the end of his regime he appeared to be out of touch with the social issues and concerns that were coming to the forefront in the early twentieth century. His policies aroused considerable suspicion in some circles. In April 1915, a church leaders' association, the Ministerial Union of the Lower Mainland, gained public attention with *The Crisis in British Columbia: An Appeal for Investigation*, a publication that attacked McBride's spending practices, his dispersal of public resources, and the alleged corruption of his government.[46] In declining health and perhaps concerned that he had run his political course, McBride resigned in 1915, leaving the party and the government in the hands of his attorney general, William Bowser. Bowser was an easier target for the Liberals, to be sure, but his dramatic failure at the polls in 1916 undoubtedly reflected discontent with McBride's regime in its last few years.

SOCIETY AND POLITICS

By the mid-1880s the cry of "Fight Ottawa" had lost much of its resonance in British Columbia. With the completion of the railway to Vancouver and the dry dock at Esquimalt as well as the resolution of associated financial issues, the focus of attention shifted. Islanders might—and did—complain that they had received no national railway, but mainlanders—whose numbers were increasing rapidly—were mostly satisfied. Other concerns were emerging.

The most notable of these were the economic and social consequences of resource alienations in the 1880s and 1890s.[47] Settlement on the Prairies over the last three decades of the century was geared to developing a farming economy, but west of the Rockies the economic priorities were much more industrial. British Columbia, with its limited agricultural potential, could not depend on the offer of homesteads to bring in people, so provincial administrations concentrated on attracting heavily capitalized enterprises. Nonetheless, land was still the main asset the province possessed and land grants were used to encourage private capital to develop the region's resources.[48] At the same time, industrial enterprises required a mobile workforce with varying degrees of skill and paid relatively high wages, which attracted immigrant labourers. To some extent, these immigrant labourers were also drawn into the province by the possibility of obtaining cheap—if not free—land in the future.[49]

The political landscape of nineteenth century British Columbia—with its non-partisan tradition provincially, and stunted bipartisan approach federally—contained many disparate parts. These included: a reform movement that would have been at home in Upper Canada in the 1830s or 1840s; an endangered political establishment with intellectual roots in early nineteenth century Tory Britain; independent producers throughout the mining districts of the Interior and the farming regions of the Lower Mainland and Vancouver Island; and a working class that introduced a leaven of socialism to the political dough. This last element first made itself heard on the issue of Asian exclusion.

The province's commercial and industrial interests had so much influence in Victoria that successive governments could not readily deal with labour's demands for legislation covering the length of the working day and conditions in the province's mines. Bills brought forward to the Assembly for first reading thereafter saw little of the light of day. An alternative means of placating militant labour in the towns, the canneries and the mining districts was to meet its demands for exclusion legislation.[50] The legislature in Victoria passed a series of anti-Asian bills only to have them disallowed by the Dominion government.[51] By 1885, the anti-Chinese lobby had brought enough pressure to bear on Ottawa to obtain action in the form of a Dominion "head tax," which was introduced as means of discouraging further Oriental immigration. It was soon apparent that the head tax was a lucrative source of revenue, drawing more than $4 million for Ottawa from 1885 through 1908, by which time the levy had increased from $50 to $500 per person.[52] Immigration from China fell drastically, though whether this would have happened without the tax—as a consequence of the economic uncertainties of the 1890s—is difficult to say. Nevertheless, Asian immigration remained a source of division in British Columbia between the representatives of capital and those of white labour. James Dunsmuir, a major employer of Asian workers, became lieutenant-governor in 1906 as the immigrant issue heated up because of a sharp increase in immigration from Japan and India. During the economic downturn of 1907-1908, the agitation of white labour prompted the Dominion government to take measures to stop immigration from India and to reduce the immigration of Japanese labourers to four hundred a year.[53]

From the 1880s the complexion of the political elite changed noticeably. Professor Martin Robin, author of a lengthy study of British Columbia's political history, calls the first generation of provincial leaders part of a "shopocracy" comprised of small merchants. This generalization should not be taken in too literal a fashion: the premiers were most often barristers or newspapermen and the attorney general's office was usually held by a lawyer, sometimes drafted from outside the Assembly. Robin's description is more applicable after 1886. To an extent not witnessed in any other province, the men who governed British Columbia before the Great War came from outside the economic elite. The economic sectors that created the greatest fortunes—timber, fisheries, shipping and land speculation—produced few successful politicians. The same was true for the professions. A thorough and extensive study of Vancouver elites indicates that only one family, the Dunsmuirs, crossed the apparent divide between economic and political spheres. Even this example, however, was largely unsuccessful.[54]

What, then, were the roots of the political elite in pre-war British Columbia? First, strong Canadian connections helped, especially from the 1890s on. Former Maritimers and Ontarians were, ironically, the most vituperative of Ottawa-bashers. Second, a friendship or relationship with local captains of industry was advantageous.[55] During the 1891 Wellington coal mine strike, for example, the major participants in the political arena included James Dunsmuir (mine owner, future premier and future lieutenant-governor), C. E. Pooley (Dunsmuir's lawyer and soon-to-be member of cabinet), Attorney General Theodore Davie (close friend of both Dunsmuir and Pooley, brother to former premier A. E. B. Davie and premier himself a year later) and Dunsmuir's brother-in-law, Henry Croft, MLA, who chaired one of two Select Committees on the dispute. (Dunsmuir's other brother-in-law, John Bryden, had served earlier as the local MLA.) Despite their direct forays into politics, Robert and James Dunsmuir preferred to work through political proxies and this seems to have been the strategy pursued by many other leading economic figures as well. Finally, membership in the Masonic Lodge connected a number of early British Columbian politicians. McCreight and De Cosmos were Masons and George Walkem had been active in his Toronto Lodge before transferring to Kamloops and establishing new connections. Other premiers may also have been affiliated with the order. Evidently the Masonic Lodge provided a means of networking for newly arrived aspirants in both business and politics; membership in the Lodge was at the least a sign of respectability and, perhaps more importantly, acceptability. Nonetheless, while associational ties helped build support in one direction, the inherent competitiveness of business interests in the Assembly generated division.

INTERESTS AND PARTIES

Drawing together such diverse interests into partisan structures proved difficult. The non-party system had advantages and it enjoyed a degree of legitimacy. Arguably, this system smoothed relations with Ottawa by avoiding confrontation between rival parties in power at the federal and provincial levels. The absence of parties before 1903 hid the fact that there were alliances in place based not on ideology but on pragmatic mutual advantage. It was not uncommon to see members who were equally far to the right in the political spectrum sitting on opposite sides of the house. A large portion of the Assembly at any time in these years appears to have been chiefly concerned with obtaining railway charters for themselves or for interests they represented, for example.

From 1883 to 1903, 116 railway charters were granted in British Columbia, each of which involved considerable lobbying within the legislature. The track records of many turn-of-the-century MLAs suggest that they sought election specifically to obtain charters, and in a number of cases, these charters were for bogus railways. For example, the owner and founder of the Crowsnest and Kootenay Lake (CN & KL) Railway Company, Colonel James Baker (MLA 1886–1900), was chairman of the Select Committee on Railways when he obtained his charter. The Railway Aid Act of 1890 was passed with Baker voting in favour, the result being a windfall 20,000 acre per mile land subsidy to the CN & KL Railway.[56] John H. Turner lost out on an early bid to obtain the Esquimalt and Nanaimo Railway but, after being elected to Victoria in 1886, he received from Ottawa a charter for his Shuswap and Okanagan Railway (S&O). His partners included MPs and provincial cabinet ministers when the legislature in Victoria voted to guarantee $1,250,000 in bonds of the same S&O at 4 per cent for twenty-five years.[57] If this kind of personal enrichment was the main purpose of a political career then it is no wonder that the competition for gain inhibited the establishment of party lines.

The personality of Richard McBride played a part in changing the complexion and vocabulary of provincial politics. His background inclined him towards social consensus on many issues: he was the son of an Irish Catholic mother and an Ulster Protestant father and felt at home in the religious communities of both parents.[58] He was the first British Columbia-born candidate for the premiership and that equipped him with a fresh perspective. Having said that, it must also be observed that McBride embraced the same politics of resource exploitation and railway patronage that typified his predecessors.[59] From 1903 to 1915, for example, his government issued charters for fifty-two railways. None of this, however, ensured that he should be instrumental in the development of the party system. Contemporary events were critical.

McBride arrived in provincial politics in 1898, in the thick of the McInnes affair and he saw five years of political instability before emerging as premier. His transformation of the existing parliamentary order in Victoria was no mean feat, an unexpected initiative from a Conservative. Reformism was the more dynamic and expansive movement at the turn of the century. The problem for reformers or the liberal-left was that they encompassed everyone from free-trade Liberals to farm-labour candidates. In 1903, the possibility of negotiating some kind of coalition between reciprocity-minded Granville Grits from Vancouver and parliamentary socialists from Nanaimo appeared slight. Yet the Conservative establishment found building the core of an official party even more daunting. At Revelstoke in 1902, when the Conservative Party of British Columbia passed a resolution in favour of introducing party lines to provincial politics, McBride was not among the party powerbrokers. He had recently abandoned the Dunsmuir government and was by that stage leading the Official (largely Liberal) Opposition. Instead of trying to take over the incipient Conservative party organization in the province, McBride turned to the options open to him in the Assembly. In June 1903, following Dunsmuir's retirement and the collapse of Prior's short-lived administration, McBride agreed to form the government. As premier, McBride took the opportunity to declare himself Conservative and extended the label to all who stood by him in his government.

McBride was betting that party lines would produce a victory and would frustrate the flitting of loose fish. He was also assuming that the "Conservative" brand name enjoyed wider popularity than that of the "Liberals." Moreover, McBride's bold strategy undercut the previously dominant Conservatives, those attached to the Prior-Dunsmuir camp. Their leader, Charles Wilson, might claim to speak as the chief Conservative but McBride was the one who had power. The Conservative old guard was predictably livid. Charles H. Tupper, a wealthy Vancouver barrister and a prominent British Columbian Tory from a famous Maritime political family, snarled in 1903: "I firmly believe our Party will do well to spew the McBride government out of its mouth."[60] But the thirty-three-year-old McBride had deftly appropriated the party while its venerable leaders slept. Despite a continuous barrage of criticism from the party executive, McBride could not be expelled from a party that he quickly came to embody in the eyes of the electorate.[61]

Was McBride a populist in 1903 and during his subsequent tenure as premier? Populism is "a notoriously ambiguous concept" and that its place in British Columbia's politics has not been fully assessed.[62] However, populism can be taken to mean a kind of politics that seeks and secures spontaneous mass support; asserts the primacy of local popular culture over ideology; promotes the notion that too much power has been concentrated in too few hands through a network of political and economic institutions; and seeks to return power to the "people."[63] In British Columbia, the idea that the well-being of the community was threatened by an external authority established itself early on when De Cosmos, Walkem and many others made careers of lambasting Ottawa. McBride kept after this whipping horse. As well, McBride harped on the dangers that organized labour and socialist ideology posed in an economy dependent on natural resource exploitation and railway development. As a local boy McBride had an appeal that was denied carpetbaggers like Tupper. British Columbia was still a parochial electoral environment; politicians like McBride who knew the province well could play this to their advantage.[64]

Willing and able to defuse the threat from the left and unbowed before the whole Conservative party establishment, McBride was able to weld together a "party" that answered the need for a right-wing consensus with a loose adherence to political ideology. Moreover, McBride was steadfast against the religious sectionalism that in other parts of Canada pitted Protestants against Catholics.[65] The brief and thankless premierships of arch-Protestants Joseph Martin and William Bowser testify to the voters' desire to be free from sectarian schisms and their authors. Although "partisanship" suggests division, it also implies the recognition of shared interests on which a disciplined organization can be built. It was in constructing a party of consensus—however limited—that McBride secured his long hold on power.

THE ELECTORATE

The character of politics on the Pacific coast after Confederation clearly changed as the electorate evolved. Not only was the population growing rapidly after 1871, but the extent (and intent) of the franchise was also in flux. Moreover, the mobility of a male population shifting between resource extraction communities compounded the problem of maintaining an up-to-date voters' list. Any assessment of British Columbia's political culture in the pre-war period should address the basis of this emergent democracy: the voters.

Following Confederation the population grew at a phenomenal rate. Doubling every decade until 1911 (and only narrowly failing to do so again to 1921), British Columbia held about 400,000 people on the eve of the First World War. At the same time the proportion of the population born in British Columbia declined. This was a society that was being swamped by newcomers, one in which a homegrown political culture would have to contend with freshly imported prejudices.[66] Moreover, demographic instability probably made the introduction of party politics more difficult: there was no political elite sufficiently well-established to organize political cadres even if it wanted to do so. Likewise, there was no "family compact" against which reformers could collectively rail.

The size of the provincial electorate expanded more rapidly than the population as a whole during this period (see Figure 2). Again, the primary force driving this growth was migration and immigration, not natural increase (Figure 3). The preponderance of single males on the Pacific slope—though seldom so great as was recorded south of the 49th parallel—gave democracy a peculiar character in British Columbia. More of the adult population could vote because a greater share was male. Specifically, more of the voters were young males in their prime working years.

Although the population as a whole grew by nearly 400 per cent between 1881 and the turn of the century, the number of registered voters in 1900 was almost *ten times* greater than it had been in 1881 (see Figure 2). Moreover, the increases occurred unevenly: urbanization inflated Vancouver and Victoria while draining other areas; the labour demands of various resource extraction industries were critical factors too; the economic impact on British Columbia of Prairie settlement and rising wheat exports from the Prairie region also had implications for the distribution and size of the electorate.

Figure 2: Voters and MPPs/MLAs in British Columbia, 1871–1914
(Selected Years)

Year	Population	Voters	MLAs	MLAs *per* 1000 *voters*
1871	36,247	N/A	N/A	N/A
1874	—	2,858	25	8.7
1878	—	4,394	25	5.7
1881	49,459	4,766	25	5.3
1885/6	—	7,239	27	3.7
1891	98,173	N/A	N/A	N/A
1895	—	23,268	33	1.4
1898	—	34,369	38	1.1
1900	—	44,069	38	0.9
1901	178,657	N/A	N/A	N/A
1903	—	39,296	42	1.1
1906	—	49,443	42	0.9
1909	—	3,606	42	0.6
1911	392,480	79,765	42	0.5

Source: Canada, *Census of Canada, 1931* (Ottawa) vol. 2, p. 106; British Columbia, *Electoral History of British Columbia, 1871-1986* (Victoria 1988), pp. 462-472.

Figure 3: Sources of Population Growth, 1881–1911

Decade	Natural Increase	Canadian Migration	Immigration: British	Other
1881–1891	2,882	17,158	14,712	12,318
(% share)	(5.9)	(35.2)	(30.2)	(25.3)
1891–1901	21,244	20,277	11,273	26,046
(% share)	(26.4)	(25.2)	(14.0)	(32.4)
1901–1911	33,676	45,388	84,388	58,987
(% share)	(15.8)	(21.8)	(39.5)	(27.6)

Source: Canada, *Census of Canada 1881* (Ottawa, 1882) vol. I, pp. 396-397; *Census 1891* (Ottawa 1892) vol. I, pp. 332-333, vol. IV, p. 294; *Census 1901* (Ottawa 1902) vol. I, p. 418; *Census 1911* (Ottawa 1911) vol. II, pp. 342-343.

One consequence was a wildly irregular distribution of votes and seats. For example, the Kootenay constituency in 1874 held only 1.2 per cent of the electorate but was served by two of twenty-five provincial legislators. In the 1890s, the expansion of hard-rock mining in the area attracted a collection of industrialists and speculators who recruited an army of wage labourers. When residence qualifications were shortened at the end of the century these towns could have been a noticeable factor in provincial politics—if there had been a better distribution of seats in the legislature. By 1894 there were three Kootenay constituencies, which together accounted for 9.1 per cent of the provincial voters' list. In 1900 this remote corner of the province—which lay within the economic hinterland of Spokane in eastern Washington State—possessed more than a quarter of the province's voters yet elected fewer than one-sixth of her MLAs. Peculiarities could be found elsewhere: 115 Comox electors had as great a voice in 1878 as 535 voters in Nanaimo. In the same year, despite rough parity in the number of voters, Nanaimo elected one representative in Victoria while the Cariboo elected three. Similarly, Vancouver City in 1909 held 26.1 per cent of the provincial votes but had only five of forty-two seats in the Assembly.[67] Cures for electoral inequities were regularly prescribed but the combination of topography, a fluid immigrant population and the self-interest of successive governments meant that inequities continued.[68]

The existence of multiple-member ridings makes it difficult to measure voter behaviour or to calculate turnouts on election day during these years. In the constituency of Victoria City, for example, 12,795 ballots were cast in the 1903 general election; the voters' list, however, contained only 4,496 names. Because the riding was served by four Assembly members, each Victorian voter could cast four ballots. Having said that, if the total number of ballots cast in 1903 is divided by four the result is 3,297.25, indicating that at least one voter plumped on his ballot. It is, therefore, possible that every last voter in Victoria participated in the election although not all cast the four votes to which they were entitled.

An analysis of single-member ridings shows a much better turnout of voters in some ridings than in others. In the 1903 election, 98 per cent of the registered voters in "The Islands" cast ballots; in Skeena it was only 66 per cent and in Richmond 69 per cent. Among the causes for the lower percentages in the last two ridings was the transience of part of the population: potential voters disenfranchised themselves by moving around. The election law in fact worked against many groups. First, the compilation of voters' lists was conducted by patronage appointees: there is some likelihood that individuals were omitted from the list on purpose by their political enemies. Second, electoral laws after 1871 restricted the vote to males twenty-one years of age or older who were resident at least six months in the province and demonstrably literate.[69] In 1875 the residence requirements were changed but only for the two main cities, where otherwise eligible voters found themselves unable to cast ballots if they had not lived in New Westminster or Victoria (as the case may be) for at least twelve months. As well as keeping names off new lists, others were struck from the existing rolls. The longer residence requirement was applied to the whole of the province in 1876.[70] Twelve months in British Columbia, however, now had to be matched with two months in the constituency. Without carefully analyzing the voters' lists of smaller resource-based towns in the Interior and on Vancouver Island it is possible only to suggest that the fraction of the workforce that was itinerant suffered from this amendment.[71] In 1899 the residence requirement dropped to six months in the province and one month in the constituency. By the turn of the century, then, the voters' list could include a greater proportion of the fluid provincial population.

Over the years, the legislature took several important steps to narrow the franchise. In 1878 most federal employees were struck from the voters' list, as were teachers (as provincial employees). In 1883 these exclusions were reversed. From 1902 to 1916 a peculiar amendment to the register of voters debarred any prospective elector unwilling or unable to make a declaration of maleness. Race became a qualification almost immediately after Confederation. In 1874 aboriginal and Chinese males lost the vote, as did the Japanese in 1895 and the "Hindus" in 1907. Tomey Homma, a Canadian of Japanese ancestry, challenged this legislation in 1900 and won his case in the lower court, but lost when the Crown appealed to the Judicial Committee of the British Privy Council. The Chinese and East Indians also launched petitions and protests but none of the Asian groups found much support in the general British Columbian community.[72]

The gender issue created still more controversy. White women, campaigning for the vote, had resources and advantages that Asians lacked. One vehicle for suffrage protest was the Women's Christian Temperance Union (WCTU).[73] Utilizing basic lobby techniques, the WCTU in British Columbia struggled for an immediate victory while recognizing part of what they were doing was laying the groundwork for success through education and proselytization. They put forward their first petition in 1885, and followed it with four more in the 1890s. Sympathetic private members' bills failed miserably but at least the issue was kept more or less on the agenda. And this was not solely a women's campaign. During the 1891 miners' strike at Wellington the men, resolutely supported throughout the conflict by women in the community, added to their list of goals the immediate extension of the franchise.[74]

Women in British Columbia did enjoy some democratic privileges throughout this period. From 1873 they could vote in municipal elections. In the 1880s, women with property gained the vote in school district elections. Complications arose in the 1890s when a legislative redefinition of the municipal electorate clumsily dropped women from the eligible list altogether. Whether this was intentional or not is difficult to say but contradictory bills in the decade suggest a measure of support in the legislature for women's suffrage at the local level. Such suffrage was, after all, well established in other parts of Canada. Some municipal councils, however, were reactionary. Victoria City Council, for example, entertained a move against female electors in 1898, but did not carry it through. Municipal voting rights for women expanded and contracted for years. In 1906 all adult women gained the municipal franchise. This change, however, was introduced accidentally and the provincial Municipal Elections Act of 1908 restricted the female vote once again, notwithstanding Premier McBride's assurances of sympathy with the suffragettes' cause.[75]

The second decade of the twentieth century began on a promising note for women. Political Equality Leagues, offspring of the Councils of Women established twenty years earlier, appeared in Vancouver and the capital city. Overlap with the WCTU was obvious and inevitable but the Leagues had more clearly defined political targets. For the Temperance Union, prohibition was the primary objective and suffrage the means; for the Leagues the vote was the high ground from which all other objectives would be secured. The campaign through to 1917 was made more difficult by growing rifts within the movement on the matter of tactics. The personality of Attorney General William Bowser was a factor. Where Premier McBride might at least speak softly to the women's campaign, Bowser had the directness of a big stick.[76] The conflicts between the Tory administration and a vital British Columbian women's suffrage movement were only resolved in 1915 in a private member's bill introduced by a socialist MLA. This bill set the stage for referenda on suffrage and prohibition during the provincial election called by Bowser—now premier—in 1916. By holding referenda at this time on these two contentious issues, Bowser sought to divorce them from the election campaign itself. Moreover, the tactic promised to defuse both issues, whatever happened. If prohibition failed and female suffrage succeeded, it would be difficult for newly enfranchised women to challenge the result in the short term. If prohibition succeeded, men might lose their beer but it would be a male electorate that was responsible.

On voting day, the WCTU achieved their secondary objective, but not their primary one. They succeeded by more than two votes to one on the suffrage issue but lost on prohibition.[77] Both the civilian and soldier polls came back in favour of extending to women in British Columbia the same electoral rights enjoyed by women elsewhere in western Canada. Although the soldiers' vote was close, the only civilian poll that ran contrary to the suffrage was in Fernie. The results of the prohibition referendum were less clear cut and the government shelved its legislation. The poll revealed dramatic differences of opinion across the province. Many constituencies—Kamloops in particular but also the main urban centres—were highly supportive of prohibition. Alberni, Esquimalt, the Cariboo and Lillooet were leaders among the few strongly opposed. More important, however, was the result of the soldiers' poll, which showed overwhelming hostility to prohibition among British Columbian servicemen: 12,719 voted for tipple, only 2,893 against. Unambiguous civilian support for prohibition—39,490 for, 27,217 against—had to be disregarded as the opposition of soldiers serving at home and abroad narrowly carried the day. For the time being at least the pro-temperance suffragettes had to be satisfied with the proverbial half-a-loaf.

LABOUR AND POLITICS

British Columbian politics involved labour-oriented parties and left-wing ideologues from a relatively early date. In 1886 a "Labour" candidate ran for provincial office in Nanaimo, and in the 1890s working-class politicians with the help of agrarian allies broke into the ranks of federal and provincial legislators. Early in the twentieth century, the labour-left exercised a balance of power in Victoria, despite holding only three seats. In 1912, with the Liberals completely routed, the tiny Socialist caucus formed the official opposition. Labour/socialist politicians like Thomas Keith, James Hawthornthwaite and Parker Williams figured prominently in Victoria until the First World War, and through careful politicking had an influence well beyond their numbers.[78]

The presence of a few left-wing/labour-oriented politicians in the Assembly at the turn of the century may well have forced the partisan lines that appeared under McBride in 1903.[79] In this sense, the later polarization between left and right in British Columbia had its roots in this period.[80] Martin Robin has argued repeatedly that the resource-extraction base of the economy produced a vibrant labour movement "intent on checking the powers of the employing class in a company-dominated province," and that "the growth of a radical and articulate labour movement . . . necessitated the introduction of a system of disciplined parties campaigning under familiar and standardized labels."[81] According to this interpretation, the instability that McBride sought to remedy stemmed not from political factionalism but from the growing presence of labour in politics. And if the answer to Labour and socialism was the introduction of Liberal and Conservative parties to provincial affairs then "the strategy must be judged a success."[82]

Among the earliest labour organizations active in politics was the Knights of Labor. American in origin, the Knights enjoyed sufficient support in British Columbia to survive after assemblies south of the border had declined and disappeared.[83] The Knights encompassed both skilled and unskilled workers and advocated an extensive shopping list of industrial and political reforms, some attainable, others visionary. The movement collapsed in the United States in 1886 after a violent episode in Chicago for which the Knights were blamed, although not responsible. The Knights continued in British Columbia essentially as an organization for labour aristocrats—skilled workers—who placed respectability at their masthead and sought to demonstrate the reasonableness and legitimacy of workers in politics.[84] In 1886 Nanaimo-area Knights established the Working Man's Party with an eye to reforming the legislative environment for industrial relations. Their party enjoyed only patchy success: the coal-miner candidate in Nanaimo in 1886 was beaten badly by Robert Dunsmuir, taking only 30 votes to the mine owner's 366.[85] Although the Knights did not assume such a direct role again, they continued to influence the left-labour groups who followed in the 1890s.

The mining districts of the Kootenays and Vancouver Island continued to provide much of the leadership for labour's political arm around the turn of the century. Faced by intransigent mine owners, murderous working conditions, and fluctuating market demand levels, miners hoped to improve their situation through legislation. In 1890 a two-man farm/labour ticket ran successfully at Nanaimo and shortly thereafter Ralph Smith, a miner and veteran of Lib-Lab campaigns in Northumberland, began his rise to prominence in working-class, provincial and federal politics. Elected president of the Trades and Labour Congress of Canada in 1897, the following year Smith won the provincial South Nanaimo riding convincingly with 78 per cent of the ballots cast.[86] Despite the presence in the Assembly of adamantly hostile mine owners and managers, Smith registered modest successes in the pre-party era. He was able to use the Assembly's inherent instability to secure a Coal Mines Regulation Act, which, among other things, satisfied the white colliers' demand for exclusion of Asian labourers from underground work. Smith also played an important role in obtaining the eight-hour day for British Columbia's hard-rock miners.[87]

These were landmark victories. Provincial politicians had plenty of British precedents from which to work but, from 1871 to the 1890s, they had ignored requests that labour legislation be brought up to par with that of the Old Country. The infusion of labour-left politicians tipped the balance. Labour-left politics still lacked a broad enough appeal to guarantee election in any single riding, however. In 1894 Thomas Keith (elected in 1890 with the support of the Miners' and Mine Labourers' Protective Association in Nanaimo) failed to win re-election, despite the additional endorsation of the Nanaimo Reform Club. The then-president of the miners' union also failed, his campaign for female suffrage collapsing with him. Another casualty in the same election was Labourite Tully Boyce. Both fell to an explicitly anti-union slate led by a mine manager.[88] Even when Ralph Smith was returned in June 1900, he was accompanied from his dual-seat riding by arch-Conservative James Dunsmuir. In short, labour's progress in the coalfields was not unimpeded.

In 1900 the first "socialist" candidate in British Columbia ran, unsuccessfully, in Vancouver with the backing of the Vancouver Trades and Labour Council. Three years later the Socialist Party of British Columbia—the first socialist party in Canada—put forward nominees in eight of thirty-four constituencies, concentrating their efforts in the Kootenays and on Vancouver Island. James Hawthornthwaite, a colliery clerk at Nanaimo and an incumbent MLA, was joined by another miners' representative, Parker Williams of nearby Newcastle. As well, Slocan elected a Labour candidate, William Davidson.

The combined labour-left vote in this general election reached a new high-water mark of 15.79 per cent, enough to elect the three MLAs and sufficient to frighten the establishment.

The socialist and labour movements in British Columbia produced an abundance of organizations.[89] Unfortunately for labour, these groups were competing more against one another than against the right. The Marxism of the Socialist Party of British Columbia no doubt alienated many Lib-Lab voters recently arrived from Britain. More extreme organizations such as the Industrial Workers of the World rejected electoral politics and recommended revolutionary change through non-parliamentary means.[90] At the other end of the spectrum, the American Federation of Labor, with considerable clout in the province's resource extraction sector, sought influence through acceptance by powerful politicians as a respectable organization. The locals of unions affiliated with the American Federation of Labor followed Samuel Gomper's dictum: reward our friends, punish our enemies. They encouraged members to use their vote as a carrot or stick for centre/right politicians and not to waste it on specifically "labour"-oriented parties.

As a challenge to the establishment, the political efforts of the labour-left groups were mostly toothless. In 1903, the first-past-the-post electoral system translated a labour-left popular vote of 15 per cent into only 8 per cent of the seats. It had been shown labour-left candidates—even incumbents—could be beaten at the polls by capitalists in ridings dominated by working-class voters. Moreover, 1903 was the best result that the labour-left obtained until after the First World War. In the McBride years, labour-left made no gains. The entry of the Conservative and Liberal parties into provincial politics was a factor, cutting into the Socialist Party of British Columbia's natural constituency. The arrival of large numbers of apolitical or moderate-voting immigrants also had an effect. The growth of anti-party forces like the American Federation of Labor or the Industrial Workers of the World played a part as well.

Although class formed an evident division in industrial British Columbian society, class lines were blurred by issues like race and self-improvement. William Stocker, an American immigrant and in 1900 the President of the Miners' and Mine Labourers' Protective Association at Nanaimo indicated the focus of many British Columbians when he described the social benefits that would follow from an improvement in miners' wages: "I consider the more money I am able to make the better member of the community I will be and would be able to do better by my family in the way of giving my little girl education and in affording my wife more luxuries—all-round living better and spending more in the community, yet still saving and making a little home for myself and settling down as a good citizen of the country."[91] With labourers moving into farming, shopkeeping, "penny capitalism," and even into management in considerable numbers, it is hardly surprising that the workers' perception of class conflict was, even in 1903, far from crystal clear.

A NEW ERA

The transition from non-partisan to partisan politics announced the end of an era. When politicians adopted party labels they were responding to emerging social realities. The conflict between labour and monopoly capital in British Columbia at the turn of the century was obviously one of the most important sources of change in the political and social environment. More profound changes in the direction of the economy—from frontier resource extraction to modest urbanization with an evolving metropolitan-hinterland relationship—played a critical role in setting the agenda of the legislature. Lobbying for the prizes of the railway era, conducted at a fevered pitch in the late nineteenth century, had absorbed the attention of a succession of ministries, but now moved off centre stage. In its place, the rise of Vancouver as a manufacturing, shipping, financial and political centre increasingly concentrated demands for favours and support from government in one urban area. As the centre of gravity in the provincial economy changed, MLAs from venerable ridings such as Yale and Nanaimo lost influence. In the past, premiers had been obliged by the distribution of population and economic activity to construct cabinets along geographic lines: as outlying areas lost political weight, parties emerged.

McBride's success in building a Tory machine has to be set against the cold shoulder he got from the old-school (largely Vancouver-based) Conservatives: he also perpetuated—indeed worsened—the rift between the political and the economic realms. From McBride's time on, the economic elites overlapped very little with the political elites.[92] Instead, politics became a way of life, a primary occupation for many politicians. A clearer appreciation of the eccentricities in B.C.'s political culture might best begin from this observation.

NOTES

1. Susan Dickinson Scott, "The Attitude of the Colonial Governors to Confederation," W. George Shelton, ed., *British Columbia and Confederation* (Victoria: Morriss Printing Company Ltd., 1967): 160; Gordon T. Stewart, "Political Patronage under Macdonald and Laurier, 1878-1911," J. M. Bumsted, ed., *Interpreting Canada's Past* (Toronto: Oxford University Press, 1986): 29-50; R. C. MacLeod, "Canadianizing the West: The North-West Mounted Police as Agents of the National Policy, 1873-1905," Lewis H. Thomas, ed., *Essays on Western History* (Edmonton: University of Alberta Press, 1976): 101-110.

2. For Trutch's attempts to divert power from the legislature to the office of the lieutenant-governor see Robin Fisher, "Joseph Trutch and Indian Land Policy," W. Peter Ward and R. A. J. McDonald, eds., *British Columbia: Historical Readings* (Vancouver: Douglas & McIntyre, 1981): 170-171.

3. British Columbia Archives and Records Service, Add Mss 54, folder 11/59, Draft of a memorandum from Cornwall, Macdonald and Dewdney to Sir John A. Macdonald, sent 7 May 1879, quoted in Hamar Foster, "The Struggle for the Supreme Court: Law and Politics in British Columbia, 1871-1885," Lou Knafla,

ed., *Law and Justice in a New Land: Essays in Western Canadian Legal History* (Calgary: Carswell Legal Publications, 1986): 168. Emphasis in original.

4. George Woodcock, *De Cosmos: Journalist and Reformer* (Toronto: Oxford University Press, 1975): 72.

5. British Columbia Archives and Records Service, Add Mss 54, folder 12/66, Crease to Deputy Minister of Justice A. A. Lash, 9 September 1878, quoted in Foster, 170-183.

6. F. W. Howay, W. N. Sage, H. F. Angus, *British Columbia and the United States: The North Pacific Slope from the Fur Trade to Aviation* (New York 1970): 183.

7. It also meant that the premier might take on two or three portfolios himself. Premier Elliott, for example, made himself both attorney general and provincial secretary—a one-man cabinet quorum—and thus acquired two salaries too. S. W. Jackman, *Portraits of the Premiers: An Informal History of British Columbia* (Sidney, B.C.: Gray's Publishing, 1969): 45.

8. Campbell Sharman, "The Strange Case of a Provincial Constitution: The British Columbia Constitution Act," *Canadian Journal of Political Science* XVII, no. 1 (March 1984): 103.

9. Neil Swainson, "Governing Amid Division: The Premiership in British Columbia," Leslie A. Pal and David Taras, eds., *Prime Ministers and Premiers: Political Leadership and Public Policy in Canada* (Scarborough 1988): 192-207.

10. *The Canadian Parliamentary Guide* (Ottawa), various editions.

11. Patrick Dunae, *Gentlemen Emigrants: From the British Public Schools to the Canadian Frontier* (Vancouver: Douglas & McIntyre, 1981): 63, 67.

12. *The Times* (London), 22 August 1898, 6.

13. Walter N. Sage, "British Columbia Becomes Canadian, 1871-1901," *Queen's Quarterly* LII (1945): 168.

14. J. M. S. Careless, "The Lowe Brothers, 1852-1870: A Study in Business Relations on the North Pacific Coast," *B.C. Studies* 2 (Summer 1969): 1-18; idem., "The Business Community in the Early Development of Victoria, British Columbia," D. Macmillan, ed., *Canadian Business History* (Toronto: McClelland and Stewart, 1972): 104-123.

15. Following a Canadian practice dating back to 1854, Tories called themselves Liberal Conservatives but it is simpler to use the term Conservative. See Edith Dobie, "Some Aspects of Party History in British Columbia, 1873-1903," J. Friesen and H. K. Ralston, ed., *Historical Essays on British Columbia* (Toronto: McClelland and Stewart, 1976): 79.

16. Derek Pethick, "The Confederation Debate of 1870," Shelton, ed., *British Columbia and Confederation*, 187.

17. George Woodcock, *British Columbia, A History of the Province* (Vancouver: Douglas & McIntyre, 1990): 145; W. N. Sage, "The Position of the Lieutenant-Governors in British Columbia in the Years Following Confederation," R. Flenley, ed., *Essays in Canadian History* (Toronto: Macmillan, 1935): 203.

18. F. W. Howay, "The Settlement and Progress of British Columbia, 1871-1914," *Historical Essays on British Columbia*, 24.

19. Margaret Ormsby, *British Columbia: A History* (Vancouver: Macmillan, 1971): 252; Jackman, *Portraits*, 14.

20. Quoted in Jackman, *Portraits*, 9; Peter Murray, *From Amor to Zalm: A Primer on B.C. Politics and its Wacky Premiers* (Victoria: Orca, 1989): 22-23.

21. I am grateful to Dan Marshall for his generous insights and suggestions on this and other aspects of this period. See Daniel Patrick Marshall, "Mapping the Political

World of British Columbia, 1871-1883." (M.A. thesis, University of Victoria, 1991).

22. Glenbow Archives, Edgar Dewdney Papers.

23. Quoted in H. Robert Kendrick, "Amor De Cosmos and Confederation," Shelton, ed., *British Columbia and Confederation*, 89.

24. J. Arthur Lower, *Canada on the Pacific Rim* (New York: Toronto: McGraw-Hill, 1975): 83.

25. Glenbow Archives, Edgar Dewdney Papers, f 15.

26. As late as 1882 Princess Louise was offered the post of "Queen of Vancouver Island" by the very short-lived administration led by Robert Beaven, an offer that signified continuing frustration with both mainlanders and Canadians. A description of the hapless Beaven administration can be found in Eleanor Mercer, "Political Groups in British Columbia, 1883-1898." (Ph.D. thesis, University of British Columbia, 1937): 5-7.

27. For the distribution of population in British Columbia in 1881 see Robert Galois and Cole Harris, "Recalibrating Society: The Population Geography of British Columbia in 1881," *The Canadian Geographer* 38, no.1 (1994): 37-53.

28. A critical assessment of the so-called Mainland-Island Split in B.C. politics by Daniel P. Marshall was given at the 1988 annual conference of B.C.'s university history departments in an unpublished paper titled "Politics Before the Age of Party: The British Columbia Legislature."

29. Molyneux St. John, *The Sea of Mountains: An Account of Lord Dufferin's Tour Through British Columbia in 1876* (London: Hurst and Blackett, 1877), I: 156.

30. Barrie Sanford, *The Pictorial History of Railroading in British Columbia* (Vancouver: Whitecap Books, 1981): 13.

31. George Woodcock, *British Columbia*, 147.

32. Biographical details can be found in John Antak, "John Robson: British Columbian." (M.A. thesis, University of Victoria, 1972).

33. R. A. J. McDonald, "Victoria, Vancouver and the Economic Development of British Columbia, 1886-1914," Alan Artibise, ed., *Town and City: Aspects of Western Canadian Urban Development* (Regina: Canadian Plains Research, 1981): 36.

34. R. E. Gosnell, "The Moral of the British Columbia Elections," *The Canadian Magazine* III (September 1894): 477.

35. British Columbia, *Sessional Papers, 1883-1915*, passim.

36. British Columbia, *Electoral History of British Columbia, 1871-1986* (Victoria: Elections B.C., 1988): 522.

37. This kind of turnover was comparable to what occurred between Legislative Union and Confederation in the Canadas or in Britain from 1902-1924. In the second half of the present century there have been provincial general elections once every three or four years so the potential turnover has been comparable, despite an apparent Social Credit stranglehold. It is important to note, as does Dr. Ged Martin, that there is no "scientific law that frequent changes of ministry are in themselves undesirable." Ged Martin, "History as Science or Literature: Explaining Canadian Confederation, 1858-1867," *Canada House Lecture Series*, no. 41 (Pamphlet, 1989): 13.

38. For an analysis of the McInnes Affair see George F. G. Stanley, "A Constitutional Crisis in British Columbia," *The Canadian Journal of Economics and Political Science* XXI, no. 3 (August 1955): 281-292; John Saywell, "The McInnes Incident in British Columbia, 1897-1900." (M.A. thesis, University of British Columbia, 1950).

39. "The one [Martin] is a Liberal with ideas almost radical and the other [Carter-Cotton] is a Conservative of the strongest conviction." T. L. Grahame, "British

Columbia Politics," *The Canadian Magazine* XV (May-October 1900): 13.

40. Peter Jeffrey Brock, "Fighting Joe Martin in British Columbia." (M.A. thesis, Simon Fraser University, 1976): 37-

56; S. W. Jackman, *The Men at Cary Castle: A Series of Portrait Sketches of the Lieutenant-Governors of British Columbia from 1871-1971* (Victoria: Morriss Printing Co., 1972): 65-73.

41. F. W. Howay and E. O. S. Scholefield, *British Columbia from the Earliest Times to the Present* (Toronto 1894) VIII: 341-342.

42. Howay, "Settlement and Progress of British Columbia," 33.

43. An overlooked aspect of the railway's progress is examined in Frank Leonard, "An Obscure Issue: The Grand Trunk Pacific Railway Company's Quest for Indian Lands in British Columbia." (Unpublished paper presented at the sixth B.C. Studies Conference, November 1990).

44. Patricia E. Roy, "Progress, Prosperity and Politics: The Railway Policies of Richard McBride," *B.C. Studies* 47 (Autumn 1980): 25.

45. J. M. S. Careless, "Submarines, Princes and Hollywood Commandos, or At Sea in B.C.," *B.C. Studies* 45 (Spring 1980): 3-7.

46. Robert K. Burkinshaw, "Conservative Protestantism and the Modernist Challenge in Vancouver, 1917-1927," *B.C. Studies* 85 (Spring 1990): 31-32.

47. John Davies Malcolmson, "Resource Development and the State in Early British Columbia." (M.A. thesis, Simon Fraser University, 1980): 66-67.

48. McDonald, "Victoria, Vancouver and the Economic Development of British Columbia," in Ward and McDonald, *British Columbia Historical Readings*, 373-377.

49. John Douglas Belshaw, "The Standard of Living of British Miners on Vancouver Island, 1848-1900," *B.C. Studies* 84 (Winter 1989-90): 37-64.

50. For the role of First Nations peoples in the fishing industry in British Columbia, see Dianne Newell, *Tangled Webs of History: Indians and the Law in Canada's Pacific Coast Fisheries* (Toronto: University of Toronto Press, 1993).

51. See Harry Con *et al.*, *From China to Canada: A History of the Chinese Communities in Canada* (Toronto: McClelland and Stewart, 1982): 45-51.

52. Anthony B. Chan, *Gold Mountain: The Chinese in the New World* (Vancouver: New Star Books, 1983): 129-130. See also Patricia E. Roy, *A White Man's Province: British Columbian Politicians and Chinese and Japanese Immigrants, 1858-1914* (Vancouver: University of British Columbia Press, 1989) especially chapter 5; W. Peter Ward, *White Canada Forever: Popular Attitudes and Public Policy Toward Orientals in British Columbia* (Montreal: McGill-Queen's, 1978): chapter 3; Gillian Creese, "Class, Ethnicity, and Conflict: The Case of Chinese and Japanese Immigrants, 1880-1923," Rennie Warburton and David Coburn, eds., *Workers, Capital, and the State in British Columbia: Selected Papers*, (Vancouver: University of British Columbia Press, 1988): 55-85.

53. Howard Hiroshi Sugimoto, *Japanese Immigration, the Vancouver Riots, and Canadian Diplomacy* (New York: Arno Press, 1978): 180-250.

54. R. A. J. McDonald, "Vancouver's 'Four Hundred': The Quest for Wealth and Status in Canada's Urban West, 1886-1914," *Journal of Canadian Studies* 25, no. 3 (Fall 1990): 55-73.

55. For an example of the ways in which railway entrepreneurs attempted to influence federal and provincial policymakers see Phyllis Veazey, "John Hendry and the Vancouver, Westminster and Yukon Railway: 'It Would Put Us on Easy Street,' " *B.C. Studies* 59 (Autumn 1983): 51, 56.

56. Robert E. Cail, *Land, Man and the Law: The Disposal of Crown Lands in British Columbia, 1871-1913* (Vancouver: University of British Columbia Press, 1974): 155-162; Barrie Sanford, *McCulloch's Wonder: The Story of the Kettle Valley Railway* (West Vancouver 1977): 18.

57. *Ibid.*, 163.

58. Martin Robin, *The Company Province: The Rush For Spoils, 1871-1933* (Toronto: McClelland and Stewart, 1971): 88.

59. For a discussion of McBride's policies and the development of the lumber industry see R. Peter Gillis and Thomas R. Roach, "A Touch of Pinchotism: Forestry in British Columbia, 1912-1913," Patricia E. Roy, ed., *A History of British Columbia: Selected Readings* (Toronto: Copp Clark Pitman, 1989): 76-99.

60. Quoted in Jackman, *Portraits*, 159.

61. For McBride's relationship with the party see Brian Ray Douglas Smith, "Sir Richard McBride: A Study of the Conservative Party of British Columbia, 1903-1916." (M.A. thesis, Queen's University, 1959).

62. David Laycock, *Populism and Democratic Thought in the Canadian Prairies, 1910 to 1945* (Toronto: University of Toronto Press, 1990): 15.

63. John Richards, "Populism: A Qualified Defense," *Studies in Political Economy*, no. 5 (Spring 1981): 5-6.

64. R. Jeremy Wilson, "The Impact of Communications Development on British Columbia Electoral Patterns, 1903-1975," *Canadian Journal of Political Science* XIII, no. 3 (September 1980): 512.

65. It is worth noting in this respect that McCreight and both of the Davie brothers were converts to Catholicism, the former having been a prominent member of Victoria's High Anglican community.

66. Canada, *Census of Canada 1881* (Ottawa, 1882), I: 396-397; *Census 1891* (Ottawa 1892), I: 332-333; *Census 1901* (Ottawa 1902), I: 418; *Census 1911* (Ottawa 1911), II: 342-343.

67. British Columbia, *Electoral History*, 462-471.

68. Norman Ruff, "The Cat and Mouse Politics of Redistribution: Fair and Effective Redistribution in British Columbia," *B.C. Studies* 87 (Autumn 1990): 50-52.

69. British Columbia, *Electoral History*, 510-511.

70. In the same year exclusions affecting officers of the electoral branch, police, magistrates and judges were partially lifted.

71. It is known for certain that despite expanding numbers overall, of the voters registered in the Nanaimo area in 1881 only 58 per cent remained in 1890, an attrition rate of about 5.5 per cent per annum. John Douglas Belshaw, "British Coalminers on Vancouver Island, 1848-1900: A Social History." (Ph.D. dissertation, University of London, 1987): 254.

72. Con *et al.*, 83, 119; Vancouver City Archives, Add. Mss. RG 2, A1, Vol. 26, G. D. Kumar, Secretary of the *Hindustanee* to H. H. Stevens, alderman, Vancouver, 6 December 1910.

73. The complexities of the social reform movements in Canada at this time are considered in Mariana Valverde, *The Age of Light, Soap and Water: Moral Reform in English Canada, 1885-1925* (Toronto: McClelland and Stewart, 1991).

74. Jeremy Mouat, "The Politics of Coal: A Study of the Wellington miners' Strike of 1890-1991," *B.C. Studies* 77 (Spring 1988): 23. See also Thomas Robert Loosmore, "The British Columbia Labor Movement and Political Action, 1879-1906." (M.A. thesis, University of British Columbia, 1954): appendix xi.

75. Doreen Madge Weppler, "Early Forms of Political Activity among White Women of British Columbia, 1880-1925." (M.A. thesis, Simon Fraser University, 1971): 63.

76. *Ibid.*, 95-97.

77. British Columbia, *Electoral History*, 413-416.

78. For the political careers of miners' MLAs and MPs see Alan John Wargo, "The Great Coal Strike: The Vancouver Island Miners' Strike, 1912-1914." (B.A. essay, University of British Columbia, 1962): 28-30.

79. See, for example, John Malcolmson, "Politics and the State in the Nineteenth Century," in Warburton and Coburn, eds., *Workers, Capital, and the State*, 19-20.

80. Alan C. Cairns and Daniel Wong, "Socialism, Federalism and the B.C. Party Systems, 1933-1983," Hugh Thorburn, ed., *Party Politics in Canada*. 5th ed. (Toronto: Prentice Hall, 1985): 283-302.

81. Martin Robin, "British Columbia: The Company Province," *Canadian Provincial Politics: The Party Systems of the Ten Provinces*. 2nd ed. (Toronto: 1978), reprinted in Eli Mandel and David Taras, eds., *A Passion for Identity: An Introduction to Canadian Studies* (Toronto: Methuen, 1987): 378; idem., Robin, *Rush For Spoils*, 86.

82. Donald Blake, *Two Political Worlds: Parties and Voting in British Columbia* (Vancouver: University of British Columbia Press, 1985): 14.

83. Paul Phillips, *No Power Greater: A Century of Labour in B.C.* (Vancouver: B.C. Federation of Labour, 1967): 12-17; Carlos A. Schwantes, *Radical Heritage: Labor, Socialism, and Reform in Washington and British Columbia, 1885-1917* (Seattle: University of Washington Press, 1979): 25-35.

84. Some conservative elements in early British Columbian labour militance are considered in John Douglas Belshaw, "The British Collier in British Columbia: Another Archetype Reconsidered," *Labour/Le Travail* 34 (Summer 1994).

85. Harold Griffen, *British Columbia: The People's Early Story* (Vancouver: Tribune Publishing Co., 1958): 68; Belshaw, "British Coalminers on Vancouver Island," 330.

86. British Columbia, *Electoral History*, 72.

87. Jeremy Mouat, "The Genesis of Exceptionalism: British Columbia's Hard-Rock Miners, 1895-1903," *Canadian Historical Review* LXXI, no. 3 (September 1990): 327-328.

88. See also J. A. Gemmill, *The Canadian Parliamentary Companion, 1897* (Ottawa 1897): 380.

89. See David Jay Bercuson, "Labour Radicalism and the Western Industrial Frontier: 1897-1919," *Canadian Historical Review* LVIII, no. 2 (June 1977): 154-175; Desmond Morton with Terry Copp, *Working People: An Illustrated History of Canadian Labour* (Ottawa: Deneau, 1980): 50-56, 93-96; Craig Heron, *The Canadian Labour Movement* (Toronto 1989): 40-41; Mouat, "Genesis of Exceptionalism," 317-345.

90. See R. A. J. McDonald, "Labourism in the 1890s," *Working Lives: Vancouver 1886-1986* (Vancouver: New Star Books, 1985): 159.

91. Canada, Sessional Papers, 1902, *Report of the Royal Commission on Chinese and Japanese Immigration* (Ottawa 1902): 87.

92. For evidence and assessment of the two elites at mid-century see John Addie, Allan Czepil and Fred Rumsey, "The Power Elite of B.C.," Paul Knox and Philip Resnick, eds., *Essays in B.C. Political Economy* (Vancouver: New Star Books, 1974): 25-32.

Chapter 6
NATIVE PEOPLE, SETTLERS AND SOJOURNERS, 1871–1916
Hugh Johnston

British Columbia entered Confederation as the second smallest province by population and the only province in which Native people constituted a majority. Over the next forty years it grew faster than the rest of Canada, except for the prairie west.[1] Immigration produced this growth; and in these years immigration brought a diverse national, racial and ethnic mix to North America. The speed, economy and safety of travel by steamship and train put North America within reach of once-remote areas of Europe and Asia; people crossed continents and oceans in both directions in unprecedented numbers. Immigrants were able to journey halfway around the world in search of work without committing themselves to staying once they arrived. British Columbia, with its resource-based economy, attracted more than its share of such mobile people. As a consequence, it manifested a number of exceptional demographic features. In the census of 1911, no other region—Ontario, Quebec, the Prairies or the Maritimes—had as large a part of its population in the workforce and as small a part in school. No region had as high a ratio of males to females or as high a proportion of people between the ages of fourteen and forty-five. And no region of the country had a greater percentage of foreign-born.

A contemporary writer described British Columbia as the most cosmopolitan province in Canada and, considering only the varied origins of its residents, the description fits. British Columbia was not cosmopolitan in the sense that it was free from prejudice or open to various cultural influences, however. By 1891, a majority of its people were white and English speaking. Their numerical, political and economic dominance made it easy for them to take a narrow view of what their community was and who belonged to it. In this narrow view, they saw Asian and continental European immigrants and even Native people as outsiders—the inhabitants of the camp and caravan on the periphery of their local world. The relative sizes of these outsider groups changed as First Nations' bands declined and immigrants increased. Altogether, however, continental Europeans, Asians and Native people made up a sizable proportion of British Columbia's population. As a pool of cheap labour, they were vital economically; as outsiders, they had no voice in government. Within Canada,

British Columbia was remarkable in having so many residents without citizenship whose opportunities were circumscribed by race and origin. In the competition for economic benefits, these people had severe disadvantages. Like members of the Anglo majority, they were active participants in change, seizing whatever openings the provincial economy afforded them. This did not bring them into the mainstream, however. As they adapted to changing demands and circumstances, they generally did so within their own framework of values and objectives.

THE CHANGING SITUATION FOR NATIVE PEOPLE

At Confederation, Native people occupied a central position in the life of the province. In 1871, according to one estimate, the duty on goods imported for Native people provided at least 25 per cent of the revenue received by the government in Victoria.[2] Native people were the principal population in most sections of the province. Beyond the southern coastal region and the Cariboo gold fields, they generated most of the trade and they made a significant contribution to the provincial economy. Despite the changes that had come with the gold rush, the commerce involving Native people had continued to expand. In the southeastern interior, for example, the Kootenays, who numbered five or six hundred, were spending $50 ($600 in today's currency) per person per year on flour and provisions purchased from white suppliers.[3] The fur trade, in which Native people were essential partners, had lost its place as the main source of exports from the Pacific coast, yet it remained vigorous. Although it was overshadowed by other economic activities, it was producing more annual income after Confederation than it had before the gold rush.[4] Moreover, during the time when fur was dominant, Native people had been employed not only as hunters and trappers, but also as hired labour on Hudson's Bay Company farms and at Company posts, and as crewmen, packers and freighters along the Company's transportation routes. In this respect, the fur trade provided an apprenticeship for the opportunities that came with white settlers and miners. By the 1870s, Native people were involved, to some degree, in all the major export industries—mining, lumbering and fishing as well as fur.

As a result, Native people throughout the province depended on cash income, though the degree of dependence varied from region to region. Subsistence fishing and hunting were the primary occupations of the Native people on the west coast of Vancouver Island, on the northwest coast of the mainland, and in the northern Interior—generally the areas farthest from white settlement. But these Natives also sold furs, hides and (on the coast) fish oil and purchased flour, biscuits, rice, sugar and other items. In 1872, the export trade in furs and fish oil generated by the Nootka alone was worth perhaps as much as $75,000.[5] In the central and southern Interior, the lower Fraser Valley, and in the Gulf of Georgia area, the cash economy was more important, though subsistence activities included agriculture and stock keeping as well as hunting and fishing.

None of the Native people of British Columbia had been agriculturalists before first contact with Europeans, but they had readily adopted what they found useful. By 1870, in many parts of the province, Native people had been growing potatoes and other garden crops for more than forty years. They had been keeping cattle and pigs from the 1820s when the Hudson's Bay Company first began bringing cattle and other livestock into the region. Their experience with horses went back even further; the horse culture had spread north from Mexico through the inter-mountain plateau system to reach the southern Interior of British Columbia by the early eighteenth century. As a consequence, the Kootenay, Okanagan and Shuswap peoples had possessed horses long before they first saw white people on their territory. Typically, the Native people of the Interior raised large numbers of horses and fewer cattle because horses had greater utility and survived with less care.[6] In the lower Fraser Valley and in the Gulf of Georgia area, where range land was limited, most bands kept some pigs and a few cattle and horses. Stock keeping as well as agriculture was well established among these people by the time British Columbia entered Confederation.

The pattern was one of a great range of activities, within as well as outside the cash economy. For bands that were close to white settlements this was especially true. In the country north and east of Hope, in the Yale and Cariboo districts, Native people worked for money chiefly on boats and as packers, though some were taking $15,000 or $20,000 in gold annually from the Fraser and Thompson Rivers.[7] In the vicinity of Victoria, New Westminster, Hope and Yale, bands found markets for fresh produce and crafts. By 1871, many Native people from the Gulf of Georgia area and the lower Fraser River area were working seasonally in the logging camps and sawmills of the Gulf Islands, Burrard Inlet and Puget Sound. And when whites in the towns and outlying areas required outdoor or indoor labour, Native men and women generally supplied it. There was no pool of white labour and, although there were fifteen hundred Chinese workers in the province, most of them were employed in the mining districts of the Cariboo.

Over the next forty years, the Native people of British Columbia became a small minority within a greatly expanded provincial population. They were roughly half the population in 1881, one-quarter in 1891, one-seventh in 1901 and one-eighteenth in 1911. By the turn of the century, they had become invisible to most of the non-Natives concentrated in and around New Westminster, Vancouver and Victoria. But the change was relative: Native people did not fall out of the market economy. On the contrary, they were drawn more and more into it, and they managed to increase their consumption of market goods and provisions without an appreciable loss of self-sufficiency. They certainly did not depend on government relief, which was insignificant throughout this period.

As late as 1910-1911, annual expenditure on relief for Native people was only $10,300.43, or less than 50¢ a person.[8] In the early years of the twentieth century, however, Native people were being pressed into greater dependency as they ran up against the limits of their situation.

Until the early 1880s, Native people were the main source of labour in the province, and even after that, they were the main source in much of the Interior and the north.[9] As a rule, they were paid as much as white men and more than Asians for labouring jobs.[10] Native people were good workers, but Asians were as well. The only satisfactory explanation for the difference in what they were paid is that Native people would not accept wages that barely covered expenses as long as they had the option of living off the land. This meant that, in the labour market, they were vulnerable to Asian competition. In an expanding economy, their participation in the wage labour force did increase, but they remained seasonal and casual workers who incorporated wage labour into an annual pattern of subsistence activity.

These observations can be illustrated with a review of the role that Native people played in the canning industry. The growth of the canning industry, which in the south began in 1871 on the Fraser River, and in the north in 1880 on the Skeena River, came to affect nearly every village on the coast.[11] In the late spring and summer, from late June through August, the canneries provided employment for both sexes and all ages. The men would fish for the cannery while the women and children worked inside, cutting and cleaning the fish and cleaning and filling the cans in preparation for canning. At peak times, old people would be called in as well. In the 1870s, this work became the main source of income for the Salish people of the lower Fraser River area. By the early 1880s, entire bands from all nations along the coast were migrating, in some cases for hundreds of miles, to either the canneries on the Fraser or those on the Skeena. In the summer of 1885, three thousand Native people could be found camped in the vicinity of the Fraser River canneries in the forty kilometres between Port Coquitlam and the sea.

By 1885, cannery owners had begun to employ Chinese men to do some of the work that Native women had done. In the Fraser River canneries, the Chinese became the core workforce, hired by the season and paid by the month, whereas Native women continued to be hired as casual workers paid by the hour. In the 1890s Japanese fishermen entered the scene in competition with Native men. These developments, however, were associated with a tremendous expansion of the salmon-canning industry, from nine canneries in 1885 to thirty-two in 1890 and sixty-five in 1900.[12] This expansion created a generally increasing demand for Native labour in the fishing industry in the 1880s and 1890s, especially in the central and northern coastal areas. At the turn of the century, the Kwakiutl, Bella Bella, Tsimshian and Haida people all depended on canneries for wage income, as did many bands of the Salish in the lower Fraser Valley and on Vancouver Island. The Nootka also came to the

Fraser River canneries as an alternative to sealing, which was the main activity of most of their men from April to October. After 1900, the Japanese monopolized more and more of the industry. By 1913, they had nearly half of the salmon-fishing licenses, while Native people had less than a fifth.[13]

When the salmon-canning season was over, Native people of all ages and both sexes worked in the crop fields of the lower Fraser Valley and Puget Sound.[14] Some families stayed on in Puget Sound for the winter to dig clams. Some men worked in logging camps and sawmills, or on the railways, or worked as guides or packers for sportsmen or prospectors or timber cruisers, or fished or hunted, not just for subsistence but to supply local markets. Women manufactured curios to sell in British Columbia and Washington. On the northern coast of the mainland and the Queen Charlotte Islands, fur trapping was still an important secondary source of cash income. This seasonal cycle of activities brought Native people from many coastal bands and nations together at the canneries and in the crop fields every summer and dispersed them every fall. It mobilized them for the demands of a major industry while returning them to their own small and isolated coastal settlements and traditional fishing and hunting grounds for most of the year. It incorporated them into the wage economy without breaking them away from their own roots and their own past.

In 1910, Native people on the coast made up about half of British Columbia's Native population, though this proportion was changing. Aside from the Coastal Salish, none of them did much farming or gardening—the west coast terrain was too uncompromising and the returns of the sea too lucrative. Nor was agriculture much attempted in the northern Interior, among the Tsimshian on the upper parts of the Skeena and Nass watersheds, or the Dene peoples scattered across the vast interior territory north of the 55th parallel. Here fishing, hunting and trapping were almost as important in 1910 as they had been fifty years earlier.[15]

It was in the central and southern Interior, among the Interior Salish, the Kootenay and some of the southern Dene that farming was a mainstay. These people had added agriculture and stock keeping to their traditional pursuits long before 1870, and as they increased their herds and extended their crops they simply followed an evolutionary process that carried on until the early twentieth century. The forty or fifty families of the Spallumcheen band, for example, kept 88 horses and cattle in 1877, 139 in 1882 and 400 in 1916. They cultivated fifty acres in 1892 and two thousand in 1916.[16] Even so, Native farming people generally were unable, at any time, to support themselves by farming alone. The six bands of the Kootenay were an exception, but they were able to sell produce to a growing population of forest workers and miners without much local competition from white farmers until the first decade of the twentieth century.

In the prime ranching and farming country of the Okanagan and Kamloops areas, where white settlers had large acreages, Native bands depended less on their own agricultural production than on other sources of income. They made more money working for white settlers, especially at harvest time or as cattle drivers, or by doing other wage work, than they did from their own land. To the north, in the more thinly settled Cariboo region, there was not as much demand for the labour of Native people, but enough to employ some men from nearly every band as farmhands, cowboys, guides or packers. Band members survived as occasional farmers and occasional labourers while pursing a great variety of other activities, including hunting and fishing. People who lived this way had to be resourceful and adaptable.

In the late eighteenth and early nineteenth centuries, the decline of the Native population was essentially a decline of the coastal people. In the central and southern Interior, the population increased from at least the mid-1880s; and in the northern Interior, it increased steadily after 1890, and possibly was on the rise for some time before that. There is little reliable information on what was happening in all parts of the province until 1890. The first Dominion census in 1881 enumerated the Native people of the coast and those of the southern Interior, but did not attempt a canvass of the bands in the whole Interior region from the Cariboo north. In 1883, the Department of Indian Affairs began to do an annual census in the southern region of the province, but did not cover all of British Columbia until 1890, and even then, some bands in the extreme north and on the central coast were missed.

The Indian agents who did the counting had difficulty in getting around to all of the bands every year, or trouble in getting around in the season when most of the bands would be in their villages. Double counting inflated some of the early censuses: band members would give the names of relatives who had married into other bands or who lived on other reserves. Some of the downward trend in the numbers that these agents reported was simply the result of more accurate counting.[17] By the mid-1890s, however, there is a reasonably accurate record of births, deaths and age structure for all but a small part of the population. This record shows a birth rate that was roughly equivalent to that of the general Canadian population, but a death rate that was much higher. From 1903-1914, annual births averaged 30 per 1,000 and deaths 34 per 1,000.[18] Among adults, the annual death rate was high, but among children of all ages it was extreme.

The situation was worse on the coast than in the Interior, and worst in the fishing villages of the more removed and inaccessible coastal areas. Only in the northern Interior did school-aged children enjoy the health and life expectancy that the white population took for granted. In much of the province, most Native children did not survive to become adults. This tragic situation was a result of contact with Europeans, but it had little to do with the intensity of that contact or with proximity to European settlements. The immediate factors were living conditions and housing. Smallpox, influenza, measles and whooping cough all contributed to the high rate of Native mortality. There was an outbreak of one or more of these diseases in one region or another nearly every year, and these epidemics were most frequent among Native people from the least accessible coastal areas. Temporary encampments at the hop fields and canneries, where coastal Natives gathered in the summers, were breeding grounds for disease. To compound the problem, when infected Native people returned to their villages, they generally removed themselves from easy access to medical care and attention.

From the 1870s on, smallpox was not the scourge it had been; vaccination contained it quite well and outbreaks were infrequent and localized. Measles and influenza, however, swept the coast and parts of the Interior many times, sometimes for several years in succession. In a healthy population, these diseases should not be fatal, except in rare cases, but among the Native people of British Columbia in the late nineteenth century, they were very dangerous. The explanation was in part the prevalence of tuberculosis, which was serious enough among Europeans, but inescapable in many Native bands by the 1870s. This disease was present in both its more typical consumptive or pulmonary form and as scrofula or chronic tubercular inflammation.[19]

Scrofula, which characteristically leaves its victims susceptible to persistent open sores, was so common among the Kwakiutl by the late 1870s that vaccinating them was a problem: they generally developed ulcers at the site of the injection and these ulcers took a long time to heal.[20] For carriers of tuberculosis, especially children, an attack of measles could be fatal. Other infections as well could turn chronic tuberculosis into an acute and deadly disease.

The traditional houses of the coastal people, accommodating forty or fifty individuals under one roof, were extremely unhealthy once a disease like tuberculosis became entrenched. The people who suffered the greatest decline in numbers were those who maintained their traditional housing the longest. By the early 1880s, most of the Native people of the lower Fraser Valley had erected European-style frame houses or cottages and by the mid-1890s this was true of all Native people of the coast with the exception of the southern Kwakiutl and the Nootka.[21] In the Interior, where the old life had been nomadic, Native people associated sickness with living in houses: permanent settlement meant increased exposure to tuberculosis. Nonetheless they did not suffer from it as much as the coastal people who continued to live in longhouses.

Venereal disease and alcohol were factors in undermining the health of some bands, but they were not such universal afflictions as tuberculosis, and by no means as devastating in their impact on the whole population.[22] Coastal people were exposed to venereal disease through prostitution, especially in the 1860s and 1870s when the greatest number of young women or girls were going to Puget Sound every summer for that purpose. In the beginning, these women attached no shame to what they were doing, but that changed as they assimilated the values of Christian missionaries. Moreover, as they began to find employment in the canneries, they stopped spending their summers in

Victoria. Prostitution continued longest among the Kwakiutl, but, by the end of the 1880s, they too were abandoning it.[23] After that, although venereal disease must have persisted, it is not much mentioned by Indian agents. Alcohol in these years was less of a problem than it became later. It was controlled fairly well by the law, which proscribed the sale of spirits to Native people, and by the self-policing of the Native people themselves. With the exception of some bands near major settlements or Europeans camps with a supply of liquor, most of the population was free of serious alcohol abuse until the twentieth century.[24]

Identifying tuberculosis as the main problem undermines the notion that disease was the product of demoralization or psychological distress among the Native people of the coast. The prevalence of alcoholism or venereal disease might support a theory of social breakdown, but the prevalence of tuberculosis does not. Once people understood how tuberculosis spread and adopted the right hygiene, it could be controlled. The pace of change was not so great in these years as to overwhelm Native society, and Native people welcomed and adopted as their own much that was new. Economic and cultural assimilation proceeded unevenly in various parts of the province, but always by means of incorporating the new with the old. Above all, band structures remained intact. Native people worked to accommodate change without losing their communities or their sense of connection with the land.

In British Columbia, in contrast to much of North America, the government made no attempt to force Native people onto a few major reserves. Instead, it left them where they were, with their village and camping sites, burial grounds, fishing stations and some fields and pastures protected from pre-emptions by white settlers. The total amount of land reserved for Native people was small and broken into many pieces: not just reserves for each of the many bands scattered across the province, but, typically, several minute reserves for each band. It took nearly half a century, beginning in the 1860s, for the government to allocate and survey each and every reserve. This work began in the south before Confederation. It reached the central and northern areas in the 1880s and continued in the northern Interior into the twentieth century. In the central and northern coastal areas, where there were few settlers, the actual staking out of reserves made little immediate difference to the way Native people lived. Even in regions with the greatest potential for settlement, the real rush for land began in the 1880s and 1890s, and only then did Native people become hedged in by the properties of white neighbours.

Reserves varied in size from region to region. The largest were in the farming and ranching country of the Okanagan and the smallest on Vancouver Island, on the principle that fishing people required little land. In the colonial period, the original reserves had been quite large. Between 1868 and 1871, the commissioner of lands and works cut off thousands of acres (as much as nine-tenths of the existing reserves) to open up prime land for white settlers. These reductions threatened the livelihood of every agricultural band, and the protest and agitation that swept through the southern Interior reached such alarming proportions by 1875 and 1876 that the provincial government, fearing insurrection, restored some of the acreage that had been taken away.[25] (At that time, there were only a few thousand whites in the inland region beyond Hope; Native people had a great advantage in numbers.) That still left bands with less land per capita than settlers could obtain by pre-emption. Moreover, these reserves included land that was of no agricultural value. But Native people had enough land to maintain and expand their crops and herds until the turn of the century, after which time the small size of their reserves became a severe limitation.

In the decades following Confederation, the Department of Indian Affairs exercised little control over British Columbia's Native people except by means of persuasion. Its budget was small and it had few officials in the province. The Department's operation began in 1872 with a single administrator, a superintendent resident in Victoria. In 1876, the Department appointed a second superintendent who maintained an office in New Westminster but who rarely ventured far from it. In 1882, the Department put six Indian agents in the field with territories covering most of the southern half of the province. By 1889, it had ten agents for the entire province. These men depended on the good will and co-operation of Native bands to be effective. When the Tsimshian of the northwest coast refused to have an agent, there was nothing the Department could do except to wait for them to change their minds. That took five years.[26] Even then, an agent could have only an modest impact working in such a large territory with such limited resources.

Missionaries arrived earlier and played a more consequential role, but their success depended upon the encouragement and support of the leadership of individual bands. By the turn of the century, 90 per cent of the Native people in the province were Christians; a majority were Roman Catholics and most of the rest were either Anglican or Methodist, though there were some members of the Salvation Army and some Presbyterians. Nearly every village had a church at its centre, except in the more remote coastal areas among the Nootka, Kwakiutl and Bella Bella, or in the far north among a few of the Dene. This was the result of sixty years of missionary work, beginning in the 1840s with the travelling missions of Roman Catholic priests who worked along the southern coast and into the Interior as far as Babine Lake, and continuing in the 1850s and 1860s with the arrival of the first Anglican and Methodist missionaries and the establishment of permanent Catholic missions on the mainland, at Okanagan Lake and at St. Mary's Mission on the Fraser River.

Catholic missionaries consolidated their position throughout most of the Fraser Valley and in the Interior, whereas the Methodists and Anglicans became entrenched on the central and northern coasts. The number of missionaries employed in this work was small and the territories they covered were immense. (As late as 1900, there were seven missionaries for twenty-four bands on the northwest coast, just one for nineteen bands in the northern Interior, two for six bands in the Kootenays, and so on.) In the whole province by 1900, there were scarcely thirty bands out of 231 with permanent missions in their villages.[27] The rest saw missionaries regularly, occasionally or infrequently, and in their absence maintained their churches and conducted their own services. Some bands did not attend church very often, perhaps only at Christmas and Easter, but most worshipped regularly with the chief or someone else of good standing officiating.

The promotion of Christianity involved a good deal of initiative on the part of Native chiefs. They invited missionaries to visit their villages in the first place and supported their efforts subsequently. They did so for the medical aid and practical help that a missionary could supply, for the prestige that they came to associate with the possession of a good-looking church building, and for the enjoyment of the ritual, ceremony and hymn singing of a Sunday service. Some chiefs sought the aid of a missionary as a conscious effort to reform their bands and to break them away from practices such as the potlatch. But many bands accepted Christianity without any sense that they were making a choice that required them to abandon old ways of thinking, and the churches that they built helped maintain band unity and vitality in a changing world by providing a focus for their communities.

When Native bands did not want change, there was little that missionaries or Indian agents could do to force the issue. A ban on the potlatch festivities and winter dancing, enacted in 1884 by the Dominion Parliament, had little effect on the Native people of the coast who had some of their largest potlatches in the years that followed.[28] The federal government introduced this legislation primarily at the urging of missionaries, but also on the advice of agents and administrators in the Department of Indian Affairs who believed that potlatching stood in the way of progress, that it was "heathenish" and "demoralizing" and that great potlatch gatherings were the main source of disease and contagion on the coast. But the law had no muscle, and when important chiefs gave every indication that they would defy it, the Department backed down and let the matter rest. In time, most Indian agents came to see the potlatch itself as fairly harmless and, for the sake of peace, in the face of strong feeling among Native people, they thought it better to proceed cautiously, or to leave well enough alone. The agent for the southern Kwakiutl did attempt to prosecute a case in 1889 (only to have it thrown out in the Supreme Court of British Columbia). And, in 1896, the Fraser River agent charged and convicted a man after he had given away everything he owned and more during a three-day potlatch. But these were the only cases that the Department of Indian Affairs brought to trial before 1914.[29]

By 1900, there was a strong anti-potlatch lobby among the Native people themselves, particularly among the Tsimshian and Nishga, and potlatching was in decline along the coast except among the Gitksan, Kwakiutl and Nootka.

This trend developed as Native people became Christians (and paid attention to what the missionaries were saying). It also followed naturally on the heels of economic integration and the acquisition of the material values of white society. Some Native people adopted Christianity to escape the potlatch system; some adopted Christianity and continued to potlatch; some adopted Christianity, but brought aspects of the potlatch to their celebration of Christian festivals.[30] If the law against potlatching had an impact, it was not decisive. Whether they potlatched or not, Native people mostly followed their own inclinations.

Assimilation could only go so far without access to the same kind of schooling that white children received. Very few Native people attended school or obtained any kind of formal education before 1900.[31] Native people in the Interior had no access to schools until the 1890s, when the Roman Catholics opened industrial boarding schools at Kamloops, in the Kootenay area, and at Williams Lake. Even then, the number of children that these schools took in was small. As late as 1902-1903, their total enrollment was only 144 (83 boys and 69 girls) out of a school-age population of about 1,000 in the southern and central Interior regions.[32] On the coast, and particularly on the northern coast where Native communities were larger and more concentrated, there were more schools and they appeared earlier. Here, day schools were more feasible, simply because the number of children within a given community was likely to be greater. From the early 1870s, the Anglicans and Methodists were able to maintain day schools with more than 30 Native students in attendance at Metlakatla and Port Simpson. The Roman Catholic residential school at St. Mary's Mission in the lower Fraser Valley was the only other school for Native children that operated continuously from that period.

By 1900, 90 per cent of the Native children on the northern coast lived within the vicinity of either a day school or, at least, a church where bible classes were held.[33] In the rest of the province, most Native children had to go to boarding schools if they were to receive any formal education. In the Fraser District in 1900, for example, there were only three schools for Native children, and all three were residential—one Roman Catholic, one Anglican, and one Methodist. Only about one-third of the Native children in the district attended these schools. Many Native parents refused to send their children because they did not want to be separated from them or to see them divorced completely from their own culture and language.[34] Some Native children did attend public schools, but this was uncommon. Under Canadian law, Native people were wards of the federal government and their education was a federal responsibility. The Department of Indian Affairs discharged this responsibility with grants to missionary schools, but the school system so created was underfunded and inadequate. As a consequence, as late as 1921, one-third of the Native people in the province spoke no English, and, among Native children over ten years of age, 40 per cent could neither read nor write.[35]

175

Through education and the acquisition of a common language in English, Native people did develop a stronger sense of their own shared identity and interests. In the past, except for a brief moment in the 1870s when the Interior Salish had begun to pull together in protest against reserve allocations, the federal government had been able to deal with individual bands in isolation. As I. W. Powell, the Indian Superintendent, put it in 1873, "If there has not been an Indian war, it is not because there has been no injustice to the Indians, but because the Indians have not been sufficiently united."[36] It required a degree of western education for Native people across the province to understand and articulate their situation in terms of European law and values and to act together. It was no coincidence that the long and unresolved fight for recognition of Native land title began on the north coast among the Nishga and Tsimshian, who had earlier access to schools. By the 1880s, they had people in their midst who understood that there was a principle under British law that defended their claim to the land and that the Canadian government had negotiated treaties to extinguish title in other parts of the country, but had not done so with them.[37] Nishga efforts to put forward a land claims case led, in 1909, to the formation of the Indian Tribes of British Columbia, an organization of the Native people of the northern coast. In 1916, Native leaders from the coast and the Interior formed a province-wide organization, the Allied Tribes of British Columbia.

These developments among Native people were evidence of a new consciousness of common interests that was, itself, the product of assimilation and education. There were also less positive signs. In the Okanagan, despite a willingness to adjust, Native bands had reached the limits of what they could do as farmers or stock keepers without access to capital and a more favourable regulatory environment or more land. They also faced increased competition in the labour market.[38] The files of the police and of the Department of Indian Affairs indicate a rise in alcohol consumption among bands in the Okanagan after 1900. For Native people across the province, lack of opportunity became an increasingly apparent reality as the twentieth century progressed.

THE ENGLISH-SPEAKING SETTLER SOCIETY

In 1871, it would have been difficult to have lived and worked in British Columbia without some contact with Native people. By the first decade of the twentieth century, their domain lay well outside the normal experience of a great many British Columbians. Settlers had come from various corners of the English-speaking world to concentrate in the urban and rural areas of the Lower Mainland and Vancouver Island. They brought many perspectives and styles, depending on class, origin and experience, but they integrated themselves into cohesive communities. Social and cultural gaps among them tended to lose meaning in an environment that promised material success for the enterprising whatever their background.[39] The boundary between wage work and small-scale business enterprise was especially fluid and the ability of white wage earners to purchase homes and enjoy good incomes with security encouraged a conservative outlook that undercut class solidarity. Martin Allerdale Grainger, working in British Columbia at the turn of the century, was aware that his educated English accent raised hackles because North Americans associated it with a patronizing attitude.[40] It was not an insurmountable problem for him, however, either when he worked as a logger or later when he was employed as the province's chief forester. A generation earlier, when the official and business elite of the province were mostly British-born, the differences cut deeper.

From the perspective of the white population living there in 1871, British Columbia was a British outpost on the edge of an American frontier, and so it remained for some time. More than a decade passed before the political connection with Canada had much impact. Until the 1890s, the port of Victoria dominated the economy, and Victoria's merchants did most of their business through San Francisco and London.[41] In these years, British Columbia's small industries were mostly locally owned, but the main bank and the main source of financing was the British-controlled Bank of British Columbia. Similarly, most of the insurance agents in the province represented British insurance companies. Investors from California, on the other hand, briefly controlled about 30 per cent of the British Columbia salmon industry; Americans acquired an early position in the lumber industry; and, beginning in 1887, American money developed the East Kootenay mining frontier as an extension of mining activity around Spokane, Washington. These economic ties revealed themselves in the movement of people. The relationship was most obvious in the migration of merchants and entrepreneurs, but was present in the growth and development of the whole settler population.

In the 1890s, as the province came more and more within the Montreal/Toronto orbit, the pattern of in-migration changed. The Canadian Pacific Railway (CPR) was the instrument of this development, which was slow at first, but picked up after 1895. The CPR organization itself, with its head offices in eastern Canada, had a powerful impact as a new and major employer and as a large landholder. British and Canadian capital replaced American in the mining districts of the southeastern Interior, though Americans continued to hold a dominant position in the lumber industry. Between 1895 and 1900, banks from eastern Canada entered the province in force, and by 1900, banking in British Columbia was entirely in eastern Canadian hands.[42] After 1890, the economy of British Columbia was, primarily, continental, rather than maritime, and it was as part of a continental Canadian system that the province subsequently attracted mass immigration from Britain and Europe and from other regions of North America.

Distances shrank even more radically in that era than they have in the present, but never enough to make British Columbia an easy destination for poor immigrants. In the 1840s, it took four to six months for Hudson's Bay Company personnel to get to the northwest coast, whether they sailed into Hudson Bay and followed the overland route from York or came by sea all the way around Cape Horn.[43] In the early 1860s, miners and settlers who came directly by steamer from San Francisco could reach Victoria in a few days. Those who set out from Britain or from eastern Canada and the United States, by the pre-ferred route, would take a steamship from New York or Liverpool to Panama, cross the forty-seven and a half miles from Atlantic to Pacific by rail, and pro-ceed north by steamer to San Francisco and Victoria. Alternatively, they took the American railway system as far as it ran, to St. Joseph, Missouri, or Atchison, Kansas, and then the stage coach for two thousand bone-jolting miles to California, and from there by steamer to Victoria.[44] Going coast to coast across the United States at that time took twenty-four days, and the trip from San Francisco to Victoria added three or four days more. British emigrants still had the cheaper option of sailing around Cape Horn; and, in those years, two groups of Canadians did come overland from Fort Garry.

In the way people thought of it, British Columbia was practically as far from eastern Canada as it was from Great Britain. With ideal connections, one could travel from Toronto to Victoria via the United States in about a month; from Liverpool it would take another ten or twelve days. The cost was substan-tial in either case. The railway, stagecoach and steamer fares, without meals and other expenses, equalled five months' salary for an Ontario headmaster and more than a year's salary for female teachers.[45] It would have taken an English labourer thirty weeks to have earned, let alone saved, the £30 (or $120) needed to go by steerage around Cape Horn. Under these circumstances, British Columbia was beyond the reach of any immigrant who did not have more than average means or resolve.

In the spring of 1869, the completion of a transcontinental railway across American territory cut times appreciably. In the early years of Confederation, with good connections, the journey from Ontario or Quebec to British Columbia took two and a half weeks, even though the routing was through San Francisco and the last leg of the journey was the steamer up to Victoria. Travelling second class from England via Halifax and San Francisco to Victoria still took £40 or $200.[46] The routing across the continent became more direct after 1883 when the Northern Pacific Railway reached Portland, Oregon. Even so, it still took ten days to reach Victoria from Montreal, with changes at Chicago and St. Paul and further rail and steamer transfers between Portland and Victoria; and the third-class fare for the full route was a steep $70.50. In July 1886, the first transcontinental CPR passenger train from Montreal rolled into Port Moody on schedule, after crossing the country in six days. This was a service that catered to first- and second-class passengers only and it did nothing to make British Columbia more accessible for the majority. In 1893, the Northern Pacific completed a line to Tacoma on Puget

Sound, and most immigrants from the east continued to come through the United States.[47]

The journey to British Columbia was long and expensive, but the wages paid there were high. In the outpost economy of Vancouver Island in the 1860s, daily wages were three or more times higher than in England; and one and a half or two times higher than in Ontario and Quebec.[48] These, however, were wages paid in a colonial economy in which the demand for labour was limited and seasonal, and in which, as a consequence, the pool of skilled labour was small. British Columbia was also an extremely expensive place. Basic food items such as beef, mutton, pork, sugar and vegetables cost three or four times as much on Vancouver Island as in the towns of eastern Canada. Rent and hotel accommodation were costly, and any kind of service or trade, such as tailoring, were exorbitant. In the Interior, the whole scale of wages and prices was further exaggerated by 25, 50 or 100 per cent.

As British Columbia became more settled, the wage difference with eastern Canada declined but remained substantial, whereas the difference in price for some consumer items largely disappeared. On Vancouver Island in 1888, the daily wages of common labourers were as much as 40 per cent higher than in eastern Canada. With artisans, the gap was generally greater than that. Bricklayers in Victoria at that time were paid $5.00 a day while bricklayers in eastern Canada were getting between $2.25 and $3.00.[49] These higher wages did amount to a sizeable advantage in real income. Dry goods, clothes, and some food items—meat, rice, and potatoes—did not cost much more on the west coast than in the east, though milk, butter, sugar, tea and tobacco were very expensive. With most of these items, prices continued to improve with time, and by 1901 or 1902, a stroll through the farmers' market in New Westminster would have presented few shocks or surprises to a newcomer from Ontario or Manitoba.

Of course, it is impossible to speak of a single wage and price structure for all of British Columbia. In the early years of the century, white labourers could get $2.50 or $3.00 a day for harvest work on the northwest coast of the mainland or in the Kootenays, but only $1.50 in the neighbourhood of Victoria.[50] For white labour, $1.50 was the bottom of the scale. In the coal mines, which employed a mostly white workforce, white labourers averaged $2.73 a day underground and $2.34 on the surface. Chinese and Japanese labourers were paid half as much. In the metalliferous or hard-rock mines of the Nelson, Slocan and Rossland districts, where there were no Orientals, labourers received between $2.00 and $2.50 a day. For miners, daily wages averaged $4.30 in the coal mines and $3.50 in the metalliferous mines. In the sawmills of the lower Fraser Valley and Vancouver Island, unskilled white labour received between $1.50 and $2.00 a day, while skilled workers got up to $5.00.

The manufacturing industry offers a glimpse of the relative levels of British Columbia wages at the turn of the century. In 1901, the average British

Columbia manufacturing plant—with thirty employees—was somewhat larger and more heavily capitalized than the average plant in other provinces. Profit margins were greater and seasonal shutdowns not as common: about 60 per cent of British Columbia's manufacturing plants worked year round. The average daily wage of $2.12 for male workers in the manufacturing industries of British Columbia was one-third higher than in Ontario, and higher than in any other part of the country.[51]

By 1901, manufacturing was a major source of jobs. Mining put British Columbia on the map, and mining was the province's leading industry throughout this period; but, after the initial boom and bust of the gold rush, most British and Canadian immigrants had alternatives to mining. By 1870, about half of the miners in the gold fields were Chinese; whites were concentrated in agriculture and commerce.[52] Ten years later, the province supported several hundred small manufacturing enterprises in which whites monopolized the better jobs. Gold and coal accounted for three-quarters of the value of British Columbia's exports in the 1870s; and in 1903, after nearly thirty years of growth and diversification, gold and coal, along with copper, lead, silver and other mineral products, still produced 60 per cent of the value of British Columbia exports.[53] By that time, however, the province had developed a complex economic infrastructure with more employment in the manufacturing and service sectors than in primary industry.

This evolution can be illustrated with census figures. In 1869, miners (half of them Chinese) made up 40 per cent of British Columbia's small workforce. As the workforce grew, that percentage dropped: to 18 per cent in 1881 and 7.6 per cent in 1911.[54] The agricultural, commercial (including trade and transport), and domestic and personal service sectors all absorbed more people than mining, and the manufacturing sector accommodated more than any other, though, at the moment of Confederation, that sector had been miniscule. According to an 1870 census, only 406 people or 10 per cent of the paid workforce in British Columbia were employed in manufacturing. In the 1911 census, the total—with managers, clerical staff, skilled workers and labourers—was 35,000, or 17 per cent of the paid workforce.[55] These figures are approximate because they include both seasonal and year-round workers and are based on census categories that are not perfectly consistent.

Until the 1890s, most industrial manufacturing was for the local market, though the canning, saw milling and shingle industries produced for export. In 1891, the province had 770 industrial establishments, including sawmills, canneries, foundries, bakeries, breweries, brick and tile makers, cigar factories. The vast majority of these establishments employed one or two, a dozen, or, at the most, a few score workers.[56] Aside from the canning industry, which furnished employment for a short season only, manufacturing attracted white male labour. In 1900, for example, saw milling employed 1,800 white, 240 Chinese and 452 Japanese workers, with skilled and semi-skilled jobs reserved for whites and paying from two to five times as much as the jobs performed by the Chinese and Japanese workers.[57] In 1891, two-thirds of the manufacturing establishments in the provinces were concentrated in and around New Westminster, Victoria and Vancouver; and 85 per cent of the wages disbursed to manufacturing workers in the province were paid in the districts containing these three towns.[58] Subsequent development followed this pattern: most of the steady, secure, year-round work was to be found in or near the principal towns. For immigrants from eastern Canada and Great Britain, these towns were the main destination.

As communication with the outside world improved, especially with the completion of the CPR, the British Columbia market, both for goods and for labour, became more competitive. The old British Columbia had been open to the adventurer and the individual who could turn a hand to anything: the new British Columbia became, increasingly, adapted to the specialized producer or tradesperson. The changing pattern of employment in agriculture illustrates this process of adaptation. By 1881, there were more than two thousand farmers in the province, 60 per cent of them on Vancouver Island and the lower Fraser Valley, and 40 per cent in the Yale and Cariboo regions. Most of these people had entered the province as miners, or in the wake of the gold rush, and had turned to farming subsequently. Many were casual farmers, sitting on the land primarily as a speculation for the future. They did quite well in the early 1880s when they had a captive local market and a large population of CPR construction workers to feed; but the depression that followed, and competition from agricultural produce brought in by rail from the east, drove many of them out of farming altogether. In the next quarter century, British Columbia's agricultural production multiplied many times, but did not keep pace with population growth. The farmers of the province struggled to supply half of the demand of the local market, and the rest was supplied from outside.[59] In this situation, there was little room for inefficiency. Only the experienced farmer with knowledge in a particular branch of agriculture—dairying, stock keeping, poultry, orchards or field crops—could survive. The people who entered agriculture in British Columbia after 1885, as a rule, came from farming backgrounds. Generally, in all occupations, experience and qualifications became more important as British Columbia became less isolated.

In 1881, there were about 2.3 white men in British Columbia for every white woman and that ratio did not decline much over the next thirty years. The costs of the journey from Europe and across the continent and the limited employment prospects at the end made it difficult for single women to come on their own. As a consequence, at the turn of the century, 75 or 80 per cent of the white women in the province were married or widowed and most of these women were homemakers or informal partners in their husbands' farms or businesses. If they lived in rural areas, they managed without much female company because not only was there an excess of single men, but a good many married men were on their own, having immigrated ahead of their families or come for a trial period.

In the 1890s, about one-sixth of the white women in the province had some form of paid work. Most of these employed women were single and, altogether, they comprised only 4 per cent of the paid workforce.[60] Domestic service, teaching, dressmaking or keeping a boarding house were the main possibilities in the 1890s. A handful of women had positions as sales clerks or stenographers and, in the census of 1891, twelve were telephone operators. Yet women willing to take work in the largest field then open to them— domestic service— were scarce and two-thirds of the domestic positions were taken by Chinese men.[61] By this time, women teachers outnumbered men in rural areas as well as in the cities. From the beginning, women had been recruited to teach in the farthest corners of the province where the pay did not support a married man. Seventy-five women owned and operated farms or ranches. Others were self-employed in traditional activities—dressmaking, millinery, and teaching music, art and dancing—which they could do in their own homes.[62] Many women were also involved in their husbands' businesses. Jessie Ann Smith was widowed in 1905 after farming with her husband at Spences Bridge for thirty years. A man came to the door expressing sympathy and saying she must be short of cash and that he could help her out by paying a $30 debt for hay if she just signed a statement "paid in full." She was not deceived because she had kept the farm accounts and knew that he actually owed $250.[63]

After 1900, as the employment sector grew and became more complex, the proportion of women in the workforce increased, reaching 8 per cent in 1911. Domestic service remained the largest single area open to women, though much of this work was part time or short term—helping a mother during a pregnancy or though the infancy of a child or during spring cleaning. The turnover rate for domestics was high: the Vancouver family that advertised for help thirteen times in eleven years between 1896 and 1907 was probably not unusual.[64] In British Columbia, unlike Quebec and Ontario, domestic work attracted mostly immigrant women—English and Scottish. Domestic work was acceptable to these women on first arrival, and frequently it was something they were committed to doing after taking an advance for passage fare from a prospective employer or from an agency.[65] In the first decade of the twentieth century, these women displaced Chinese men as the mainstay of the domestic labour market. In these years as well, women found new opportunities in office work as clerks, typists and stenographers and in retail outlets as sales clerks. With the growth of population, the teaching profession expanded with most of the new positions going to women, two-thirds of whom were Canadian-born. By 1914, domestic work, office work, elementary school teaching and nursing had all emerged as employment enclaves for women. At the same time, there was not much employment for women in manufacturing, in contrast to eastern Canada where industries that employed women—clothing and textiles, canning and food processing, and tobacco—were more developed. In Vancouver, in 1911, women constituted an eighth of the paid workforce. In Toronto they were a quarter and those fractions illustrate a persistent difference in the labour market for women between the west coast and eastern Canada.[66]

The record of immigration into British Columbia in the post-Confederation era is spotty and incomplete. The federal government did not have an immigration office on the west coast until 1884 (when it took over the provincial office opened in 1883), and it had no immigration officials on the Canada-United States border before 1908. Comprehensive figures on British and foreign immigration into British Columbia begin only in 1908.[67] For interprovincial migration, there are no figures at all. Decennial census returns, however, offer some help in determining—roughly—when immigrants came and from where. Between 1870 and 1911, the white population multiplied nearly forty times from approximately 8,500 to 335,000. It increased by tripling between 1870 and 1881; and again between 1881 and 1891; and then doubling between 1891 to 1901; and more than doubling from 1901 to 1911 (when the absolute increase was 235,000). If there had been a census in 1914, it would have shown another substantial gain, because the three greatest years of immigration that British Columbia ever experienced were from 1911 to 1913.

Throughout the period from 1871 to 1914, immigration far exceeded natural increase as the agent of growth. Because the province attracted at least twice as many male immigrants as females right down to 1914, the annual birthrate for whites in British Columbia continued at about half the rate for Canada for the whole period. As late as 1900, 30 per cent of the births in the province were among Native people, a percentage that illustrates a shortage of white women, not the high fertility of the Native people.[68] With the exception of the decade 1891 to 1901 (when the figure was 75 per cent), immigration accounted for 80 or 90 per cent of the new population in the province at the end of each census decade.

In 1881, a majority of the white settlers in British Columbia were British-born or the offspring of British-born parents. With the completion of the transcontinental railway and then a long slump in trans-Atlantic migration, the province took on a more Canadian flavour. This process of Canadianization continued until the turn of the century. In 1901, Canadians from other provinces made up 40 per cent of the white immigrant population, while British-born immigrants were 31 per cent, Americans 17 per cent, other Europeans 9 per cent, and white immigrants from British possessions (Newfoundland, Australia, New Zealand, India, etc.) about 2 per cent.[69] At this point, the trend reversed itself. In the early years of the twentieth century, when British Columbia took its share of a massive movement of people from Britain and Europe to North America, the rank and file of the white population was again Anglicized. In these years, the British made up more than 60 per cent of the white immigrants who came to British Columbia from outside Canada;

and they entered the province at nearly double the rate of Canadians. The percentage of British-born in the British Columbia population rose sharply between 1901 and 1911 (from 17 to 28 per cent) and it continued to increase right up to 1914.[70]

In the small settler population of 1870, there was a noticeable Irish element, but the immigration that followed was overwhelmingly English and Scottish. The Irish were a declining component of British immigration to Canada all through the late nineteenth and early twentieth century, and that trend was observable in British Columbia. In the first decade of the twentieth century, thirty-five English people settled in the province for every fifteen Scots, three Irish and one Welsh person. On the eve of the First World War, British Columbia was the most British province in the country, and the most English. Only in British Columbia were the Anglicans the largest single religious denomination. Only in British Columbia did as much as half the white population claim affiliation either with the Anglican or the Presbyterian church (the church of the English and the church of the Scots).[71]

Seventy per cent of the British-born residents of British Columbia in 1911 were living in the southern coastal region, in the cities of Victoria, and Vancouver, and in the Nanaimo and New Westminster districts.[72] This was a slightly greater concentration than in the white population as a whole. By comparison, 57 per cent of the Americans and 66 per cent of the Canadians from other provinces were living this region. A great many of the British had immigrated as single persons, and men outnumbered women three to one. In the southern coastal region, British immigrants made up one-third of the white population and more than half of the white male workforce. They predominated in the building trades, the manufacturing trades, in office work, in sales, in the arts, in architecture and engineering, in the shipping industry, on the street railway and working for the telephone and telegraph companies.[73] The sound of British accents was unavoidable, wherever one went.

Ontario was the main source of immigrants from eastern Canada. Up to 1900 the Maritimes were the second main source. After 1900, people from the Prairies began arriving in appreciable numbers. In 1911, among Canadians living in British Columbia, for every six from Ontario, there were two from the Maritimes, one and three-quarters from the Prairie provinces and the territories, and one from Quebec. More than half of the immigrants from Quebec were French Canadians.[74] From the Prairie provinces came farming families; some took up land in the Okanagan or in the Kootenays, but a majority were retired farmers who moved to the cities on the coast. Migration from the Prairie provinces included equal numbers of men and women. From other parts of Canada, a large number of the migrants were single men, though the information in the 1911 census suggests that the proportion of women and children was somewhat higher than from the British Isles.

The American portion of the white immigrant population in British

Columbia fluctuated between 14 and 18 per cent. It was more constant in the cities, but rose and fell dramatically in the Interior. In the 1890s, Americans were entering the province in the same numbers as the British but, unlike the British, their main destinations were the farm lands and mining camps of Cariboo-Kootenay region. In 1901, more than half of them were concentrated there; but the miners were a transient population, and a majority did not stay. By 1911, the main concentration of Americans had shifted to the city of Vancouver. In the cities, the ratio between men and women was much closer to parity among the Americans than among the immigrants from Ontario or the Maritimes or the British Isles. They were a settled group who blended easily into the general community. Two-thirds of the Americans who established themselves permanently in British Columbia were members of the mainstream Protestant churches of Canada—Anglican, Presbyterian and Methodist.[75] They were much like the people who came from eastern Canada and moved in the same social circles.

The more rapidly British Columbia grew, the more it became a land of immigrants. When the pace of immigration slowed during the 1890s, there was some increase in the percentage of native whites. But this trend reversed after 1901; and in 1911, fewer than one in five whites was a native British Columbian. Some families could claim several generations in the province; but they were a select group because the base population of 1870 had been so small. In 1911, 80 or 85 per cent of native-born white British Columbians were under twenty years of age.[76] The adult world was an immigrant world. It is not surprising that, of the seven members of the provincial executive at the time, only the premier, Sir Richard McBride, had been born in British Columbia. At the same time, five of the other six members of his executive were from other parts of Canada. In politics, migrants from other parts of Canada were dominant, not the British-born.

By 1911, the top layer of British Columbia society had become more Canadian than the lower echelons. The evidence comes from a study of 245 entries in J. B. Kerr's *Biographical Dictionary of Well-Known British Columbians*, published in 1890, and 1,218 British Columbian entries in the *Who's Who in Western Canada*, published in 1911. Each of these dictionaries gives biographical information on leading merchants, managers, entrepreneurs and professionals of the day. As characteristic productions of their age, these dictionaries do not provide many examples of women—none in the 1890 *Dictionary* and only eighteen in the 1911 *Who's Who*. But they include enough men (with information on their wives) to suggest the nature of the upper strata of British Columbia society. The 1911 *Who's Who*, for example, included half of the doctors, a fifth of the lawyers, and a twelfth of the architects in the province. Three-quarters of the biographical subjects of the 1890 *Dictionary* were people who had arrived in British Columbia before 1870. This group was predominantly British-born: 91 were from the British Isles; 42 from Ontario, the Maritimes and Quebec; 11 from the United States and 17 from other places of origin. The 1911 *Who's Who* identifies 142 people who arrived in the years 1872-1885, another 584 in the years 1886-1903, and 299 after 1903. In all three periods, the Canadian-born outnumbered the British-born. In this sample, for the whole span 1872-1911, the Canadians totalled 474 (46 per cent), the British 376 (36.6 per cent), the Americans 65 (6.3 per cent) and others 68 (6.6 per cent).

Among the Canadian-born in the 1911 *Who's Who*, 90 (77 per cent) of the Maritimers, 33 (63 per cent) of the immigrants from Quebec, and 256 (74 per cent) of the immigrants from Ontario came straight to British Columbia from their home provinces. Those who crossed the continent in stages—leaving the Maritimes for Ontario, or Ontario for Manitoba before moving to British Columbia—were in a minority. Similarly, with the British-born, 279 (65 per cent) immigrated directly from the British Isles to British Columbia; only 110 (26 per cent) first took up residence elsewhere in Canada and only 21 (5 per cent) immigrated initially to the United States. Once settled in British Columbia, these people tended to stay put. A number of them did relocate from Victoria to Vancouver during the 1880s and 1890s; otherwise, they were not people who moved about. Most of them arrived in British Columbia with an economic or educational advantage. The 1911 *Who's Who* gives the pre-immigration occupations of 66 per cent of its biographical subjects. About a quarter had been white-collar workers (retail workers, salesmen, clerks) or artisans, or (in the case of 2.5 per cent) unskilled workers in Britain or eastern Canada or the United States. Nearly three-quarters, however, came to British Columbia as experienced professionals, merchants or managers. They were part of an imported, rather than a made-in-British Columbia, elite.

In the 1890 *Dictionary* and in the 1911 *Who's Who*, Americans were under-represented among professionals and over-represented among merchants and businesspeople. The Canadian-born as well were slightly under-represented among professionals in the 1890 *Dictionary*; but by 1911 the situation had changed. Of the professionals included in the 1911 *Who's Who*, 189 (60 per cent) were Canadian-born, 110 (35 per cent) were British-born, and 15 (5 per cent) were American-born. In this sample, the Canadian-born dominated both medicine and law—the classical professions. The sample included 83 medical individuals, of whom 63 (76 per cent) were Canadian-born and only 15 (19 per cent) were born in Britain. In the legal profession, out of a total of 95, the Canadian-born numbered 78 (82 per cent), and the British-born only 16 (17 per cent). On the other hand, the British-born held a slight edge in engineering with 27 (54 per cent) of the 50 included, and a wide margin in architecture and accountancy with 16 (70 per cent) of 23 and 13 (72 per cent) of 27, respectively. The sample included more Canadian-born among journalists and writers: 18 (67 per cent) of 27. There were slightly more British in the civil service: 36 (58 per cent) of 62; but a majority of the politicians at the federal, provincial and municipal levels were Canadian: altogether 100 (58 per cent) of 171. These results are not surprising. Canadians generally had easier access to training in medicine and law than engineering or architecture. In the civil service, the British-born had a numerical advantage in the beginning and that situation tended to perpetuate itself. In politics, the Canadian-born played a greater role because more of them had immigrated in the 1880s and 1890s and therefore, among the well-established citizens of the province, they were the larger group.

In a social sense, by the early twentieth century, the differences between British-born, Canadian-born and American-born were readily bridged. Marriage patterns are a guide and the 1911 *Who's Who* gives place of birth of spouse in 494 (40.55 per cent) of its 1,218 entries. Among the Canadian-born men, 86 per cent were married to Canadian-born women; but this really doesn't suggest any kind of exclusiveness among people of Canadian origin within the white population; instead, it reflects the probability that a good many of them married before moving to British Columbia. In the small communities of Ontario and the Maritimes, from which so many of them came, there were few immigrants and most marriages were between people of Canadian birth. The more telling indication is with the British-born men: 58 per cent of them were married to Canadian women and another 8.5 per cent to Americans. As a group they were well-connected with the Canadian- or North American-born community.

At the same time, the British held onto their identity with as much tenacity as any immigrants. This was true of merchants, capitalists, professionals, gentlemen farmers and artisans, all of whom tried wherever possible to recreate the atmosphere of home. In Victoria, Vancouver and in the Okanagan, members of the British elite strove to preserve a distinctly British social life for more than a generation.[77] They read British magazines and papers, belonged to sports clubs where they played cricket and tennis, sent for English governesses to teach their daughters, and, for their sons, created private schools based on the English public school system. These schools had been necessary before 1872, when there was no state-supported school system, but they were maintained after that by the advantaged few who wanted a distinctive and superior education for their children. By the 1890s, prominent families were sending their sons back to England for the kind of education that they could not get in Canada. With the increased immigration after 1900, local private schools enjoyed a revival, and by 1914 there were thirty or forty private schools in the province based on the English model.

The towns and cities of British Columbia promised people of British, Canadian or American origin a way of life that was a least as orderly, safe and comfortable as anything they might have enjoyed in Britain, eastern Canada or the United States. It is true that a very different situation prevailed outside urban areas. Rural women had to go to town well in advance of an expected birth if they did not want to wait uncertainly for the arrival of a nurse or midwife. Mine workers, lumbermen or railway workers risked typhoid fever and other infectious diseases in the primitive camps of the day, which provided carelessly for hygiene and drinking water. In the woods, when workers were mauled by machines or crushed by falling trees and logs, or in the mines and on the railways when they were injured by explosives or runaway carts or falling rock, or, in any of these industries, when they fell sick, the nearest doctor was generally too far away to help.[78] Doctors usually attended camps and mines on a contract basis, and, in the 1890s, a conscientious doctor would visit each location in the contract twice a month.[79] Yet the urban areas were not short of medical practitioners. In 1881, in British Columbia, there was one doctor for every 1,595 people compared to one for every 1,233 in the whole country. For British Columbia's urban white people, the situation was much better than these figures might suggest. At that time, white people comprised 40 per cent of the provincial population but got most of the medical attention. Thirty years later the ratio in British Columbia was one doctor for 945 people and this compared well with one for 1,065 in Manitoba, one for 828 in Ontario and one for 970 in all of Canada.[80]

At its inception, Vancouver developed a better public health infrastructure than the major cities of eastern Canada. It came into existence at a time when city governments in Europe and North America increasingly accepted responsibility for effective sewerage, pure water supply, hospitals, and public health and safety standards. As a new city, Vancouver had no legacy from the past to overcome, and moved more readily than older cities like Toronto or Ottawa to meet the advancing standards of the age.[81] In other respects, too, Vancouver was in the forefront. The electric streetcar made its appearance in Europe and North America during the 1890s. Vancouver had an electric streetcar system from 1890, only four years after the city was first incorporated. The world had known about telephones for less than a decade when the first CPR train ran into Vancouver; by then, the Victoria and Esquimalt telephone service was six years old, and Vancouver immediately got a telephone connection with New Westminster.

In the late nineteenth and early twentieth centuries the provincial and municipal governments of British Columbia, like those of the rest of Canada, employed few police. In 1881, there were only twenty-four police officers in the whole province, of whom all but eight were in Victoria and New Westminster.[82] In 1911, there were 365, including a provincial police force of about 140. The police and magistrates were concentrated in the cities of the Lower Mainland and it was here that most convictions for drunkenness, vagrancy or breach of the peace took place. These convictions rarely affected members of the settled Anglo-Canadian population. Most frequently they involved foreign immigrant labourers or Native people. In the off-season, Vancouver, New Westminster and Victoria were filled with jobless men, or seasonal workers who had come down from the Interior or northern coast. These were the people most exposed to the sanctions of the law. The existence of a floating population contributed to the murder rate in British Columbia, which, before the First World War, was four or five times as high as in the rest of the country, though less than half the rate that it is today. Even so, the society of the time was not a violent one. On average, from 1910 to 1914, the courts dealt with about five murder cases and one hundred assault cases a year in a population rising to and exceeding 400,000.[83]

In 1881, close to 60 per cent of the white children in British Columbia aged five to sixteen were enrolled in free public schools and attending, on average, one day in two.[84] These were good figures for the time. Immigrants from small towns in eastern Canada had quickly recreated in Victoria and New Westminster much the same educational environment that they had left behind. From 1872, the province had a centrally controlled school system, modelled on the Ontario example and staffed, in the beginning, mostly by teachers from Ontario and the Maritimes. This system paid teachers more than they could get in Oregon or California, and about double what they could earn in Ontario. It also subjected them to examination and certification.[85] Although many schools in the 1870s and 1880s were taught by untrained and inexperienced people, the same was true in much older and more established parts of the country. In these years, British Columbia moved progressively to upgrade its teachers, at the same time recruiting more women into the profession than men; by 1901, 80 per cent of the teachers in the province had taken professional teacher training and most of these teachers were women

In establishing the principle of free public education in 1872, British Columbia set a progressive standard. Even in a developed province like Ontario, it was not until 1871 that all elementary schools were free. By 1910-1911, daily school attendance in British Columbia had reached an average of 71 per cent of total enrollment over the course of a ten-month school year, with girls attending slightly more frequently than boys. By comparison, the national figure was only 64 per cent for both sexes.[86] The predominantly urban character of British Columbia's white settler population was a factor. In 1911, 57 per cent of the white students attending school in British Columbia were going to graded city schools. Another 21 per cent attended rural schools in farming districts near or adjacent to Vancouver and Victoria or in the Okanagan. The remainder were enrolled in 155 one-room schools located across the province in isolated mining, lumbering and farming communities. The percentage of city students was high for Canada at that time, and that produced a greater focus on the needs of city schools than in other provinces, where rural constituencies had louder voices.

British Columbia's murder rate, which might have suggested social instability, and its school attendance rate, which seemed to indicate the opposite, must be understood in terms of the sharp segmentation of society along economic, racial and ethnic lines. It was one kind of province for the white,

English-speaking population, living in prospering towns and cities or in rural areas, or employed as managers, foremen or skilled workers in fisheries, lumber camps, mines and railways. It could be quite a different province for its other inhabitants.

IMMIGRANTS FROM ASIA AND CONTINENTAL EUROPE

When Rudyard Kipling visited British Columbia in 1907, the province seemed to him to have everything it could want except a sufficient supply of labour. He asked a local about the problems farmers had finding white workers for their fruit farms and dairies, and he got this response:

"Well, you can't expect a man with all the chances that our country offers him to milk cows in a pasture. A Chinaman can do that."[87]

On farms and railways, and in mines, fisheries and forests, British Columbia provided work that most Canadians did not want because it was insecure, seasonal or temporary, hard and frequently dangerous, and very likely required going to isolated places that offered little comfort or intimate companionship. Such work generally demanded a mobile labour force, one that would appear when needed and go away when not needed and that would accept modest wages as compensation. In the early years, Native people were the mainstay of the labour force, but as economic activity expanded, immigrants from Asia and continental Europe moved in. By the first decade of the twentieth century, the immigrant workforce included, in rough order of numerical importance, Chinese, Japanese, Italians, Swedes, Ukrainians, Norwegians, Finns and Sikhs. Among these people, there was a great deal of transience; they shared a view of British Columbia as a place to work but not necessarily a place to settle.

Within this workforce, labour was recruited along ethnic lines. A sawmill operator or a railway contractor might employ men of several nationalities, but each group was hired through its own agencies. The Chinese firm of Lian Chang in San Francisco recruited thousands of Chinese labourers from California and Oregon and from China for the CPR in the 1880s. Twenty years later, when the CPR was recruiting Italian labour into British Columbia, their agent was Antonio Cordasco in Montreal who in turn obtained his men from an Italian employment agency in Boston; and when the CPR imported Japanese labour in 1907, their exclusive agent was the Nippon Supply Company of Vancouver.[88] When Fraser Mills in New Westminster decided to employ French Canadians in 1908, they sent an Oblate missionary and a company employee on a recruiting tour of the Quebec, Montreal and Hull/Ottawa regions.[89] In this way employers sought out specific groups and brought them into the province in large numbers. Much of the time, however, the process was more spontaneous. Immigrants came into the province looking for work and were recruited after they arrived. Even so, employers generally tapped this pool through ethnic employment bureaus or agents. What appeared to be a spontaneous movement was actually the product of highly organized commercial activity. Railway agents, shipping agents, hostelers and those who gave credit to emigrants on both sides of the Atlantic and Pacific all played roles in bringing labour into British Columbia. Initially, this labour came from California and Hong Kong. That began to change in 1886, with the arrival of the first CPR trains, though Asia also became more accessible with the introduction of a trans-Pacific steamer service in 1887.

Most of the labourers imported into the province before 1885 were Chinese. They made up the bulk of the workers on the Cariboo Road in the 1860s and on the Pacific-coast section of the CPR in the 1880s. Subsequently, British Columbia attracted a more diverse force of immigrant workers, particularly in the years from 1903–1914. Trans-Pacific steamers brought in Japanese and East Indian workers as well, and railways from the east carried Italians, Ukrainians and other Europeans, either directly along the Canadian line, or indirectly via the United States. (The American route was cheaper because the American railways sold third-class immigrant fares to the west coast and the Canadian line did not.)[90] Many of the Scandinavians who found their way into British Columbia in these years had worked previously in Washington or Oregon and, some of them, before that in Minnesota or elsewhere in the American midwest. For them, British Columbia was simply an extension of the American frontier. By 1911, continental European workers in British Columbia outnumbered Asians by a small margin, though the Chinese remained the largest single immigrant group (aside from the British and Americans).[91]

In time, transient workers did become settlers, but some groups were slower to root themselves than others. The proportion of men to women gives an indication. The census of 1911 shows a common pattern among central Europeans, Italians and Japanese—about two females for every eight males. The proportion among Scandinavians was close to that—about two and a half females for every seven and a half males. These figures describe populations of unattached male workers augmented by the families of a few merchants, agents and professionals selling goods and services to their countrymen. Among the Chinese and East Indians, the situation was more extreme. In 1911, there were only three women in an East Indian population of 2,292 and only 769 women in a Chinese population of 19,568.[92]

The differences were not cultural but economic. Whether they came from Europe or Asia, the work gangs and bunkhouse men of British Columbia found themselves labouring under conditions that were acceptable only because the wages they earned were higher than they could obtain anywhere else. For a Punjabi or a Chinese worker, wages for hard work in British Columbia were ten or fifteen times as much as they were at home. Men did work in Canada that they would not have considered doing previously, simply because the wages were good. They viewed their experience in Canada as a short-term hardship that would pay off debts or accumulate capital for the benefit of their families, whether in Punjab or Canton or on a homestead in Saskatchewan.

As a way of accumulating capital, many purchased property in British Columbia or started businesses and, in time, became settled and began to think of bringing their families to join them. In this way, in British Columbia as elsewhere, transient communities put down roots. Among the Chinese and East Indians, this did not happen readily because these people faced exceptional immigration barriers. If a Chinese worker set aside his deep-seated longing to go home and thought of bringing out a wife, he had to consider the cost of her passage and of maintaining her in Canada plus the cost of the head tax, which was $500 after 1903. For a man who made $1 a day or less, that was too much. East Indians simply could not bring in their wives and children without challenging the regulations in force against them from 1908 on, and in all probability losing the challenge after a lengthy appeal process. The Japanese and the various European groups were more fortunate in their experience with Canadian immigration regulations and could, more realistically, think of making homes and raising families in Canada. Even so, a majority of them did not do it, or did not do it for a long time. In 1921, there were still fewer than three females for every seven males among first-generation Swedes, Norwegians, Italians, Central Europeans and Japanese.[93] The percentages in each population were so comparable — 29 per cent female among first-generation Norwegians, Japanese and central Europeans and 27 per cent among Italians and Swedes — that they probably reflect more about the nature of British Columbia's social and economic development than the behaviour of particular ethnic groups.

In typical cases, foreign workers felt that they had been Canadianized or North Americanized by living in British Columbia, and, if they went home to their family villages or neighbourhoods, they consciously carried the aura of their foreign experience. However, that experience was generally confined to the community of their own countrymen. As long as they lived as single men, they missed the contact with Canadian society that children might have given them. The Anglo-Canadians that they encountered at work generally had the better jobs — machine operators, accountants, clerks, cooks — or were in positions of authority as supervisors or managers. Language as well as the social order of the camp or mill kept them at a distance.

In many ways, these immigrants knew the province better than most British Columbians because their jobs took them into its most distant parts. If they were seasonal workers, they were constant travellers. The Chinatowns of Vancouver and Victoria wintered a large labouring population that fanned out across the province in the spring. Swedish lumber workers and Norwegians who worked in the fishing industry came back to Vancouver in the off-season, while Italians might go as far east as Toronto or Montreal when cold weather put an end to outdoor work in the east Kootenays. Moreover, these workers were world travellers, and some went home to their villages and families regularly. In the early years of the Japanese fishing community at Steveston, some workers returned to Japan every year, as soon as the fishing season was over.[94] Although that pattern changed when they began to find employment in lumber mills in the months when they were not needed in the fisheries, there were many Chinese, Japanese, East Indians, Italians and Central Europeans who made repeated ocean crossings.

The migrant traffic went two ways. The scale of it is revealed by the fourth-class Oriental steerage figures for CPR steamers on routes between British Columbia and Asia. In the years 1911–1919, when total Asian immigration to Canada was only 37,493, CPR steamers carried 83,578 Asian steerage passengers inbound and 49,927 outbound.[95] Even making allowances for migrants who travelled by other steamship lines and for CPR traffic generated by travel between Asia and the United States, this is evidence of a remarkable amount of coming and going. Much of the going was permanent. Between 1891 and 1921, 61,777 Chinese entered Canada as immigrants for the first time; yet, at the end of that period, the Chinese population in Canada was only 39,587.[96] But men also travelled home to visit, sometimes staying for a few months and sometimes for several years.

Most immigrant workers subjected themselves to a much lower standard of living and to fewer creature comforts in British Columbia than they enjoyed at home. Much of what they gained in high wages, they lost in high prices; and they could not save without cutting their requirements to a minimum. The incentive to do so was great because a modest sum in Canadian dollars represented a small fortune in rupees, yen or lira. These considerations kept men in Canada while their families stayed at home. The equation would have changed if they had been able to get jobs that paid more, but ethnic workers had little chance of job promotion on most work sites. English-speaking workers generally had the inside track whenever anything other than a general labourer's position was available.

Asians, especially, were confined to an extremely limited world of opportunity. The range of industrial jobs open to them actually shrank over time as employers and politicians responded to white labour agitation and to public pressure. Provincial legislation excluded them from employment on public works or on Crown lands; most unions would not accept them as members; and the Western Federation of Miners was able to exclude them from the Kootenay mining districts altogether, though Chinese and Japanese did work in mines on Vancouver Island and the mainland coast.[97] Asian labourers seldom worked east of the Rockies. At Craigellachie, in 1885, the Pacific section of the CPR, built by Chinese labour, met the line from the east, built by European labour. This point marked the limits of the Asian labour zone. European workers came into British Columbia along the CPR, but Asian workers did not go east into country where European labour was already paramount. Anti-Asian feeling was too strong for that.

For most Asian immigrants, Canada yielded nothing more than a succession of menial or low-paying jobs within British Columbia. The only escape was to set up shop as a retailer or tradesman or boardinghouse keeper providing goods, services and accommodation for compatriots. In 1884, 2 per cent of the Chinese in British Columbia were employers and professionals and another 9 per cent were tradesmen, artisans and self-employed workers.[98] Up to this point, however, Chinese businesses served Chinese customers. Only in the 1890s did Chinese begin to operate businesses catering to white clientele,[99] mostly laundries or restaurants. With these enterprises, they breached the Rockies and spread across the country. By 1911, 30 per cent of the Chinese in Canada resided outside British Columbia. But the men who owned and operated small businesses worked hard and long for comparatively small returns, and, for them, family life was still out of the question.

The Japanese did not begin to move into commercial activity until the 1920s.[100] The same appears to be true of the East Indians, the Ukrainians, Gallicians, Finns and, to a lesser extent, the Italians and Swedes. None of these groups made much occupational progress in their first generation in British Columbia. In nearly every group, however, there was a socially and economically advantaged element from the beginning. The early Chinese population included a few well-to-do merchants from Hong Kong who had first settled in San Francisco in advance of the Chinese influx into California, and subsequently shifted their operations to Victoria. Most of the Chinese who came into the province at the time of the gold rush were in the employ of large Chinese companies.[101]

In 1894, the Chinese consul in San Francisco conducted a survey of the Chinese in British Columbia, and counted 188 merchant/employers and professionals in a population of 10,471.[102] These men could afford to bring out wives and raise children in Canada, and in their households a small Canadian-born generation grew up that numbered about three hundred in 1901 and over eight hundred in 1911. Among the Canadian-born, as a rule, the boys went to elementary school but did not continue on to high school, and most of the girls stayed at home; the children of these families were not readily integrated into general Canadian society. In the early years, the merchant elite played a dominant role in the life of the Chinese community. The Chinese merchants of Victoria took the initiative in establishing the Chinese Consolidated Benevolent Association in 1884 and this organization was the principal voice for the Chinese in British Columbia for a few years. With the formation of numerous clan and district associations and Chinese chambers of commerce, and with the organization of separate benevolent associations in Vancouver and New Westminster as well as Victoria, leadership became dispersed.[103]

Every immigrant group included a few merchants or entrepreneurs and professionals who played prominent community roles. However, in the pre-1914 era, except for the Chinese community, most ethnic organizations represented the rank and file. In the absence of any government unemployment scheme or workers' compensation plan, benevolent societies were an early priority. The Aallotar Injury and Sick Benefit Society organized by Finns in North Wellington in 1883, the Giordano Bruno, organized by Italians in Rossland in 1899, the "bratstvo" of the Ruthenian National Union, organized by Ukrainians in 1904 and the Foreningen Svea by Swedes in Vancouver are examples. Among the Ukrainians and Finns, organization began with reading clubs, libraries, temperance societies, community halls and meetings of the local branches of the Ukrainian Socialist Democratic party or the Finnish Socialist Organization. These were all institutions organized by working men.[104]

For Sikhs, organization began with the renting of space for worship and then the building of temples in Vancouver and Victoria. The management of these temples rested entirely in the hands of Sikh mill workers and labourers, and the temples functioned as forums for political and community action with the temple executives providing the leadership. Generally, however, religious institutions were hard to maintain among transient workers, unless they were supported by missionary organizations or had an evangelical impetus. Ukrainians in British Columbia rarely saw a priest and they did not have a church until a few farming families put one up at Mount Cartier near Revelstoke in 1915. When the Gallician Metropolitan Andrey Sheptysky visited Vancouver in 1911 and wished to hold a meeting and a mass, the only Ukrainians he could find who would organize an audience were socialists. They brought out a small and hostile crowd who threw eggs at him when he was leaving.[105]

Many immigrant workers received their first political education in the hothouse atmosphere of an immigrant working community where young men of the same nationality were thrown together in a foreign and none too friendly country, far from the restraining influences of church, family or state. Young men from the province of Galicia or Bukovyna, in the Austro-Hungarian Empire, became radical Ukrainian patriots in towns like Homer, British Columbia, where they met together for readings of Ukrainian books and periodicals at the weekly meetings of the Ukrainian society. Immigrants from Punjab became staunch Sikhs and vehement opponents of British rule in India while working in sawmills in Vancouver or New Westminster and attending the local Sikh gurdwara. These workers were caught up in nationalist movements that emanated from home or from expatriate communities in the United States or elsewhere.

Socialist ideology gave them a basis for common action with immigrants of other nationalities. The Western Federation of Miners, the Industrial Workers of the World, and the United Mine Workers of America (UMWA) all had success in organizing Italian, Ukrainian and other immigrant workers in the Kootenay and Rocky Mountain mining districts. A sense of common class interest, however, stopped at the boundary between European and Asian workers. The UMWA recruited European workers but boycotted Chinese. The Fraser River Fishermen's Union represented immigrant and native-born whites and Native people, but not the Japanese who had their own fishermen's association.[106] Even among the Asians there was no sense of common interest. The Chinese, Japanese and East Indians made no attempt to work together in any form of common front or alliance. The political issues that absorbed their attention were those of their home countries (although the events leading up to the Chinese revolution of 1911 did divide the Canadian Chinese community along class lines). The radicalism of European immigrants was generally more concerned with reform or national independence at home than change in Canada. This was the outlook of transient immigrant workers or of men who still held onto the idea that they would eventually go back home. It was strong among Finns, Ukrainians and Italians and it inhibited co-operation among immigrant groups and involvement in Canadian political issues.

Foreign European immigrants made up approximately 5 per cent of the male workforce in British Columbia in 1891, 7 per cent in 1901, and 12 per cent in 1911. This trend continued until 1914. In the first years of the First World War, thousands of Europeans left the province; and, in the years that followed, very few entered. The exodus was most dramatic among Italians and Ukrainians, but it included Poles, Finns, Norwegians, Austrians, Romanians and others. Only a quarter of the Italian men enumerated in the census of 1911 remained in the province ten years later. Between 1911 and 1921, the number of European-born males in British Columbia fell by a third from 32,519 to 21,499 despite a huge immigration up to 1914.[107] The primary cause of this exodus was the recession of 1914–1915, which produced massive layoffs in the railway, mining and lumber industries, but wartime xenophobia gave added impetus.

Anglo-Canadians demanded the dismissal of enemy aliens (citizens of enemy countries) and, in the face of threats of strikes and violence, many employers complied, even when it might have been in their economic interest to retain cheaper immigrant labour. Ukrainians, Poles and other immigrants from Austro-Hungary, who generally felt little or no loyalty towards their own government, were the main targets of this agitation. In the first few months of the war, these people risked arrest and detention if they attempted to leave the country. It was assumed that they were trying to get home for military service. In reality, most of them were looking for work; if they couldn't find any in Canada, they hoped there might be some in the United States. By late October 1914, unemployment and destitution among them had become so acute that the government began to allow them to cross the border if they appeared to present no security risk.[108] Italians also attracted hostility from Anglo-Canadians until Italy entered the war on the British side. After that, the Canadian government co-operated fully with Italian consulates across the country in recruiting

Italian reservists for service in Europe.[109] Other European immigrants, whether subjects of allied or neutral states, were affected by the vigour with which anti-alien sentiments surfaced in wartime.

The conditions that drove out European workers affected Asians as well, but with somewhat different results. Most accounts associate the departure of hundreds of Sikhs from Vancouver and Victoria in the fall of 1914 with a wartime insurgency movement against the British, though, like the Ukrainians and other Europeans, these men left mainly because they had no work.[110] Similarly, by the estimate of one missionary, 70 or 80 per cent of the Chinese in Vancouver in 1916 were unemployed. Many of them went home, some for the balance of the war. When the economic situation in British Columbia improved significantly in the last two years of the war, Chinese and Japanese workers reappeared in force. The Sikhs had greater difficulty getting back because the immigration authorities were screening any connected with anti-British activities. The Chinese and Japanese, on the other hand, were able to maintain and increase their place in the workforce through the period of the First World War so that by the time of the census of 1921, Asians outnumbered continental Europeans by a wide margin. The fluctuating numbers of both groups, however, demonstrate the transient nature of the foreign-born population.

A SEGREGATED POPULATION

The 1911 *Year Book of British Columbia*, published by the Provincial Bureau of Information, contains a short statement on social conditions promising visitors to the province an atmosphere as thoroughly British as anywhere in the empire and as Canadian as anywhere in the Dominion. The idea now seems contradictory, but at the time it simply claimed a national Canadian identity within a larger British one. This statement did reflect the way that British Columbia appeared to the English-speaking majority. The largest single group in the population was immigrants from the British Isles—English, Scottish and Irish. At the same time, native-born Canadians dominated the professions of medicine and law as well as teaching, journalism and political positions at all levels, so the Canadian perspective was prominent. What would have been out of character for any member of the majority community would have been talk about the multi-cultural character of the province. The residents of the reserve, the camp and the urban ghetto were consigned to a place beyond the gates of the majority community.

In an economic as well as a social and cultural sense, the inhabitants of British Columbia lived and worked within the logic of very different situations. The majority, as members of a global Anglo-Saxon or English-speaking community, were drawn to British Columbia by the high wages, salaries or investment opportunities available to their men, and by the comparatively high standard of living that could be found in a safe, secure and familiar political and cultural environment. For foreign workers, Asian as well as European, British Columbia presented an adventure involving considerable privation but made attractive by the possibility of converting Canadian earnings into the undervalued currencies of their countries of origin. Native people, with a subsistence economy as a support, participated in the general economy as seasonal or casual labour when wages were high enough, while preserving their communities and many of their traditional pursuits.

The growth of the provincial economy provided economic benefits for each element of the population, but on an unequal basis that did nothing to reduce social and cultural gaps. Under the colonial constitution—in theory at least—all residents of British Columbia enjoyed equality before the law and rights of citizenship or, if they were immigrants, the opportunity to become citizens. After Confederation, Canada and British Columbia introduced a number of legal distinctions marking off the "chosen" Canadian or British Columbian from the outsider. In the 1870s, the disenfranchisement of the Chinese and of Native people by the provincial legislature was a significant step in this direction—as was the disenfranchisement of the Japanese in 1898 and the East Indians in 1907. The 1885 act of the federal Parliament introducing the head tax for Chinese immigrants placed them in an administrative and legislative category apart from all other immigrants. In the first decade of the twentieth century, when the federal government moved to limit Japanese and East Indian immigration, it did so without putting them under separate legislation. Section 38 of the Immigration Act of 1910 gave the government the power to exclude immigrants of "any race deemed unsuited to the climate or requirement of Canada." In this measure, Parliament openly sanctioned an immigration policy based on race. British Columbia and Canada never went as far in this direction as states such as California and Washington with their anti-miscegenation and alien land laws, but anti-Asian bills, particularly in the field of employment, were constantly placed before the provincial legislature; and when they failed, the compelling argument was always one of economic consequences, not principle.[111]

With Confederation, the Native population fell under the jurisdiction of the federal government. The immediate consequence of the change was slight. The long-term objectives of federal government policy—the assimilation and integration of the Native people—were never achieved. If they had been, Native reserves would have disappeared. With this future in mind, the advocates of assimilation and integration agreed that the people of the reserves did not deserve full citizenship. Yet Native people had proven adaptable and resourceful; and their communities survived despite the general expectation, even among their best friends, that they would fade away. By the early years of the twentieth century, however, they were coming up against the economic limits of their reserves and the worst and most unhappy aspects of reserve life were becoming evident. There was no ready way up from the bottom rung of the ladder.

NOTES

The author wishes to acknowledge the valuable contributions of Robin Anderson, Ira Chaikin, and Siân Johnston, who collected and analyzed material for this chapter as research assistants while they were students at Simon Fraser University.

1. Only 1 per cent of the people of Canada lived in British Columbia in 1871, but 5.5 per cent in 1911.

2. Bishop of Columbia to Secretary of State for the Colonies, 21 July 1871, *British Columbia, Papers Connected with the Indian Land Question, 1850-1875* (Victoria: Government Printing Office, 1975): 97-98.

3. Department of Indian Affairs (DIA), *Canada, House of Commons, Sessional Papers*, no. 23, 1873: 7.

4. In seven years from 1834 to 1840, the average annual value of furs traded on the northwest coast (including Oregon) was £13,527 or $54,108. In 1862, total exports from Vancouver Island and the B.C. mainland (other than gold) were valued at $60,000 and in 1866 at $213,000. Yet exports of furs and hides alone were worth $177,000 in 1870, $250,584 in 1871 and $413,912 in 1881, with furs representing most of the value (over 98 per cent in 1871, for example). In the 1880s, the value of exports of furs and hides declined to a low of $70,184 but by 1887 had rebounded to $586,745. E. E. Rich ed., *The Letters of John McLoughlin From Fort Vancouver to the Governor and Company, Second Series, 1839-44* (Toronto: The Champlain Society, 1943), appendix A: 338; Paul Phillips, "Confederation and the Economy of British Columbia," W. George Shelton, ed., *British Columbia and Confederation* (Victoria: University of Victoria, 1967): 56, 58; Alexander Caulfield Anderson, *The Dominion at the West: A Brief Description of the Province of British Columbia* (Victoria: Government Printer, 1872): appendix E.; *Canada, Sessional Papers*, no. 6, 1882: 159, no. 3 1885: 122, and no. 15, 1888: 140; and *Guide to the Province of British Columbia for 1877-78* (Victoria: T. N. Hibben and Co., 1877): 151.

5. DIA, *Canada, Sessional Papers*, no. 23, 1873: 4.

6. Duane Thomson, "The Response of Okanagan Indians to European Settlement," *B.C. Studies* 101 (Spring 1994): 106; and "A Problem of Perception: Views of Indians in British Columbia." (Unpublished paper, Okanagan College, November 1986): 7-8.

7. DIA, *Canada, Sessional Papers*, no. 23, 1873: 8.

8. George Edgar Shankel, "The Development of Indian Policy in British Columbia." (Ph.D. thesis, University of Washington, 1945): appendix 1, 332.

9 For a discussion of Indian labour up to 1890 see John Lutz, "After the Fur Trade: The Aboriginal Labouring Population of British Columbia, 1871-1990," *Journal of the Canadian Historical Association* NS 3 (1992): 69-94.

10. James K. Burrows, "A Much Needed Class of Labour: The Economy and Income of the Southern Interior Plateau Indians, 1897-1910," *B.C. Studies* 71 (Autumn 1986): 33; R. E. Gosnell, *The Year Book of British Columbia and Manual of Provincial Information* (Victoria: Bureau of Provincial Information, 1903): 50-80.

11. Rolf Knight, *Indians at Work; An Informal History of Native Indian Labour in British Columbia, 1858-1930* (Vancouver: New Star Books, 1978): 100; Alicja Muszynski, "Race and Gender: Structural Determinants in the Formation of British Columbia's Salmon Cannery Labour Forces," *Canadian Journal of Sociology* 13 (1-2), 1988: 110-17; Evelyn Pinkerton, "Indians in the Fishing Industry," Patricia Marchak, Neil

Guppy and John McMullan, eds., *Uncommon Property: The Fishing and Fish Processing Industries of British Columbia* (Toronto: Methuen, c. 1987): 249-259; Percy Gladstone, "Native Indian and the Fishing Industry of British Columbia," Mark Nagler, ed., *Perspectives on the North American Indians* (Toronto: McClelland and Stewart, 1972): 156-174.

12. Muszynski, "Race and Gender," 103.

13. Gladstone, "Native Indians and the Fishing Industry," 169.

14. DIA, *Canada, Sessional Papers*, no. 27, 1902: 223-243, 263-264, 268, 286-287.

15. *Ibid.*, 1910: 204-266.

16. Thomson, "The Response of Okanagan Indians," 108.

17. DIA, *Canada, Sessional Papers*, no. 5, 1887: 81; no. 10, 1890: 118; no. 15, 1891: 106.; no. 14, 1897: 87-88.

18. My calculation from the returns of Indian agents published in *Sessional Papers*, no. 14, 1897-1900 and no. 27, 1901-1915 which report births and deaths. These returns do not give the number of deaths by age, but they do give populations by age. All of the children born in 1897 through 1901, who were still living in 1901, totalled 3,506. All of the children born in 1902 through 1906, who still living in 1906, totalled 3,459. The sum of these numbers is 6,965 and, if there had been no deaths, this is the number we would expect to find in the population of five- to fourteen-year-olds in 1911. Instead, in this population group, we find only 4,057.

19. See, for example, DIA, *Canada, Sessional Papers*, no. 8, 1875: 66; no. 9, 1876: 55.

20. *Ibid.*, no. 16, 1889: 101; no. 12, 1890: 101; no. 13, 1897: 93; no. 27, 1907-1908: 245.

21. DIA, *Canada, Sessional Papers*, no. 9, 1876: 50,56; no. 5, 1883: 160; no. 18, 1891: 189; no. 14, 1897: 70, 73.

22. The role of venereal disease is emphasized in Helen Codere, *Fighting with Property: A Study of Kwakiutl Potlatching* (Seattle: University of Washington Press, 1950): 54-56.

23. See comments by Indian agents in DIA, *Sessional Papers*, No 16, 1889: 104 and no. 27, 1901: 276. Very few Indian women were arrested as streetwalkers in Victoria after 1880: Marjorie Mitchell and Anna Franklin, "When You Don't Know the Language, Listen to the Silence," Patricia E. Roy, ed., *A History of British Columbia: Selected Readings* (Toronto: Copp Clark Pitman Ltd., 1989): 59.

24. See comments of Indian agents as reported by the Department of Indian Affairs: for example, *Sessional Papers*, no. 4, 1886: 78-79, 81, 84, 122; and no. 27, 1901: 239-298.

25. Robin Fisher, *Contact and Conflict* (Vancouver: University of British Columbia Press, 1978): 175-201; Wilson Duff, *The Indian History of British Columbia* (Victoria: Provincial Museum of British Columbia, 1964): 65-67; H. B. Hawthorne, C. S. Belshaw, and S. M. Jamieson, *The Indians of British Columbia: A Study in Contemporary Social Adjustment* (Toronto: University of Toronto Press, 1958): 49-53; DIA, *Canada, Sessional Papers*, no. 9, 1876: 53-54 and no. 10, 1878: 51.

26. Daniel Raunet, *Without Surrender, Without Consent* (Vancouver: Douglas & McIntyre, 1984): 92-93; Clarence Bolt, "The Conversion of the Port Simpson Tsimshian; Indian Control or Missionary Manipulation?" *B.C. Studies* 57 (Spring, 1983): 449-451.

27. See Indian agents' reports in *Canada, Sessional Papers*, no. 14, 1900: 209-284; and no. 27, 1901, no. 27: 229-295. There were fifty-five missionaries in the province in 1911, including those working with the Chinese and other immigrant groups: Census of Canada, 1911, vol. 6, table v.

28. Codere, *Fighting with Property*, 81-97.

29. Douglas L. Cole and Ira M. Chaikin, *An Iron Hand Upon the People: the Law*

Against the Potlatch on the Northwest Coast (Vancouver: Douglas & McIntyre, 1990): 35-36, 43-44; Tina Loo, "Dan Crammer's Potlatch: Law as Coercion, Symbol and Rhetoric in British Columbia, 1884-1951," *The Canadian Historical Review* 73 (2) (June 1992): 125-156.

30. Cole and Chaikin, *An Iron Hand*, 54-61.

31. James Redford, "Attendance at Indian Residential Schools in British Columbia, 1890-1920," *B.C. Studies* 44 (Winter 1979-1980): 42.

32. DIA, *Canada, Sessional Papers*, no. 27, 1904: 54-55.

33. *Ibid.*, no. 27, 1901: 277.

34. Redford, "Attendance at Indian Residential School," 41-55.

35. Census of Canada, 1921, vol. 2: tables 78 and 99.

36. *Papers Connected with the Indian Land Question*, 153.

37. See Paul Tennant, "Native Indian Political Organization in British Columbia, 1900-1969: A response to Internal Colonialism," *B.C. Studies* 55 (Autumn 1982): 16-27; and F. E. LaViolette, *The Struggle for Survival: Indian Cultures and the Protestant Ethic in B.C.* (Toronto: University of Toronto Press, 1973): 119-132: E. Palmer Patterson, "A Decade of Change: Origins of the Nishga and Tshimshian Land Protests in the 1880s," *Journal of Canadian Studies* 18, no. 3 (Autumn 1983): 40-54.

38. Thomson, "The Response of Okanagan Indians," 96-117; Burrows, "A Much Needed Class of Labour," 27-46.

39. See Robert A. J. McDonald's conclusions in "Working Class Vancouver, 1886-1814: Urbanism and Class in British Columbia," Robert A. J. Macdonald and Jean Barman, eds., *Vancouver Past: Essays in Social History* (Vancouver: University of British Columbia Press, 1986): 33-69. See also the personal histories provided in Robin John Anderson, "Vancouver's Male Employment Agencies, 1896-1915," *B.C. Studies* 98 (Summer 1993): 43-84; and the discussion of the labour outlook reflected in the Vancouver Trades and Labour Council in Mark Leir, "Ethnicity, Urbanism, and Labour Aristocracy: Rethinking Vancouver Trade Unionism, 1889-1909," *Canadian Historical Review* 74, no. 4 (December 1993): 510-534.

40. M. Allerdale Grainger, *Woodsmen of the West* (Toronto: McClelland and Stewart, 1964): 29.

41. J. M. S. Careless, "The Business Community in the Early Development of Victoria, British Columbia," in J. Friesen and Keith Ralston, eds., *Historical Essays on British Columbia* (Toronto: McClelland and Stewart, 1976): 177-200; Robert A. J. McDonald, "Victoria, Vancouver and the Economic Development of British Columbia, 1886-1914," in W. Peter Ward and R. A. J. McDonald, eds., *British Columbia: Historical Readings* (Vancouver: Douglas & McIntyre, 1981): 373-377; and Keith Ralston, "Patterns of Trade and Investment on the Pacific Coast, 1867-1992: The Case of the British Columbia Salmon Canning Industry," Ward and McDonald, eds., *British Columbia*: 296-305.

42. McDonald, "Vancouver, Victoria and the Economic Development of British Columbia," 377-384.

43. Dorothy Blakey Smith, ed., *The Reminiscences of John Sebastian Helmcken* (Vancouver: The University of British Columbia Press, 1975): 76-80.

44. Matthew McFie, *Vancouver Island and British Columbia: Their History, Resources and Prospects* (London: Longman Green, 1865, Coles Canadiana facsimile edition, 1972): 502-505.

45. The fare from New York to Atchison was $41; from Atchison to Placerville, $200; from Placerville to San Francisco, $10: and from San Francisco to Victoria, $45 in a

cabin and $20 in steerage. A headmaster in Toronto in the 1860s earned about $700 a year and rural teachers, male or female, earned $300 or less.

46. Anderson, *The Dominion at the West*, 78-88.

47. For example see Northern Pacific Railway advertisement in Victoria's *The Daily Times* in June 1885 and Canadian Pacific Railway advertisements in *The Daily Times* and Winnipeg's *Manitoba Daily Free Press* in July and August 1886. For immigrants arriving from the U.S. in 1890: Department of Agriculture, *Canada, Sessional Papers*, 1891, no. 6, table A: 140-141.

48. McFie, *Vancouver Island and British Columbia*, 499-500; Norman Macdonald, *Canada, Immigration and Colonization: 1841-1903* (Toronto: Macmillan, 1966): appendix vi, 367-368.

49. Department of the Interior, *Canada, Sessional Papers*, no. 5, 1989: 27, 209.

50. Gosnell, *Year Book*, 1903: 78-79, 332-333.

51. Census of Canada, 1901: vol. 3: xi-xvi.

52. Edgar Wickberg, ed., *From China to Canada: A History of the Chinese Communities in Canada* (Toronto: McClelland and Stewart, 1982): 19.

53. *Guide to British Columbia for 1877-78*: 151; Gosnell, *Year Book*, 1903.

54. Census of Canada, 1665-1871, vol. 4: 376, table 2; 1881, vol. 2: table 14; 1911, vol. 6: table 5.

55. McDonald, "Victoria, Vancouver, and the Economic Development of British Columbia," 379.

56. Census of Canada, 1891, vol. 4: tables 6 and 7.

57. Gosnell, *Year Book*, 1903: 335.

58. Census of Canada, 1891, vol. 4: table 6.

59. R. E. Gosnell, *The Year Book of British Columbia and Manual of Provincial Information* (Victoria: Legislative Assembly, 1911): 239.

60. Star Rosenthal, "Union Maids; Organized Women Workers in Vancouver 1900-1915," *B.C. Studies* 41 (Spring 1979): 39-41.

61. Census of Canada, 1891, vol. 2: table 12.

62. Peter Baskerville, "She has Already Hinted at Board: Enterprising Urban Women in British Columbia, 1863-1896," *Histoire Sociale/Social History* 26, no. 52 (November 1993).

63. Jessie Ann Smith, as told to J. Meryl Campbell and Audrey Wars, *Widow Smith of Spences Bridge* (Merritt, B.C.: Sonotek Publishing, 1989): 85-86.

64. Robin John Anderson, "Domestic Service: The YWCA and Women's Employment Agencies in Vancouver, 1898-1915," *Histoire Sociale/Social History* 20, no. 50 (November, 1992): 307-333.

65. Marilyn Barber, *Immigrant Domestic Servants in Canada* (Ottawa: Canadian Historical Association, 1991): 8-14.

66. Robert A. J. McDonald. "Working Class Vancouver: Urbanism and Class in British Columbia," R. A. J. McDonald and Jean Barman, eds., *Vancouver Past: Essays in Social History* (Vancouver: University of British Columbia Press, 1986): 41-43.

67. On the first immigration agent for British Columbia, F. Henry Johnson, *John Jessop: Gold Seeker and Educator* (Vancouver: Mitchell Press, 1971): 163-165.

68. The registrar-general for British Columbia reported 1,774 births in 1900. This did not include Native people. For the same year, the Department of Indian Affairs reported 779 births among Indians in the province.

69. Census of Canada, 1901, vol. 1: table 13.

70. *Ibid.*, 1911, vol. 2: table 17.

71. *Ibid.*, 1911, vol 2: table, 2.

72. *Ibid.*, 1911, vol. 2: table 17.

73. *Ibid.*, 1911, vol. 6: table 5.

74. *Ibid.*

75. R. H. Coats and M. C. Maclean, *The American-Born in Canada* (Toronto: Ryerson Press, 1943): 150, table lxix.

76. The British Columbia-born population of British or European origin was about 11,000 in 1891 and 64,000 in 1911. See *Census of Canada*, 1891, vol. 1: table 5 and 1911, vol. 2: tables 13 and 17.

77. Jean Barman, "Ethnicity in the Pursuit of Status: British Middle and Upper Class Emigration to British Columbia in the Late Nineteenth and Early Twentieth Centuries," *Canadian Ethnic Studies* 18, no. 1 (1986): 36.

78. Minister of Health, B.C., *Sessional Papers*, 1910, D 8; Department of Labour, Canada, *Sessional Papers*, 1911, no. 36: 190.

79. T. E. Rose, *From Shaman to Modern Medicine: A Century of Healing Arts in British Columbia* (Vancouver: Mitchell Press, 1972): 13.

80. *Ibid.*, 54.

81. Margaret W. Andrews, "Sanitary Conveniences and the Retreat of the Frontier: Vancouver, 1886-1926," *B.C. Studies* 87 (Autumn 1990): 3-22.

82. *Census of Canada*, 1881, vol 2: table 14 and 1911, vol. 6: table 5.

83. *Canada, Sessional Papers*, 1910, no. 17.

84. Gosnell, *Year Book*, 1903: 263.

85. Johnson, *John Jessop*, 144.

86. C. E. Phillips, *The Development of Education in Canada* (Toronto: W. J. Gage, 1957): 186: Public Schools Report, British Columbia, *Sessional Papers*, 1912: lviii.

87. Rudyard Kipling, *Letters of Travel* (London: Macmillan, 1920): 165.

88. Gabriele P. Scardellato, "Beyond the Frozen Wastes: Italian Sojourners and Settlers in British Columbia," Roberto Perin and Franco Sturino ed. *Arrangiasrsi: The Italian Immigration Experience in Canada* (Montreal: Guernica, 1989): 145-146; Howard Hiroshi Sugimoto, *Japanese Immigration: The Vancouver Riots and Canadian Diplomacy* (New York: Arno Press, 1978): 110.

89. John Ray Stewart, "French Canadian Settlement in British Columbia." (M.A. thesis, University of British Columbia, 1956): 43-45.

90. Scardellato, "Beyond the Frozen Wastes," 160.

91. *Census of Canada*, 1911, vol. 2: table 12.

92. *Ibid.*

93. *Ibid.*, 1921, vol. 2: table 50.

94. Ken Adachi, *The Enemy that Never Was: A History of the Japanese Canadians* (Toronto: McClelland and Stewart, 1976): 48.

95. Department of Trade and Commerce, *Canada, Sessional Papers*, 1912-1920 (1912, no. 10e, Canada China and Japan and Japan Service, 162, etc.).

96. Jin Tan and Patricia Roy, *The Chinese in Canada* (Ottawa: Canadian Historical Association, 1985): 9 tables 1 and 2.

97. Gillian Creese, "Organizing against Racism in the Workplace: Chinese Workers in

Vancouver before the Second World War," *Canadian Ethnic Studies* 19, no. 3 (1987): 38; Cole Harris, "Industry and the Good Life around Idaho Peak," *Canadian Historical Review* 66, no. 3 (1985): 303; John Norris, "The Vancouver Island Coal Miners, 1912-1914: A Study of an Organizational Strike," *B.C. Studies* 45 (Spring 1980): 63, table 2; Paul Phillips, "The Underground Economy: The Mining Frontier to 1920," Rennie Warburton and David Coburn, eds., *Workers, Capital and the State in British Columbia* (Vancouver: University of British Columbia Press, 1989): 44.

98. Edgar Wickberg, ed., *From China to Canada: A History of the Chinese Communities in Canada* (Toronto: McClelland and Stewart, 1982): 309, table 13.

99. *Ibid.*, 80.

100. C. H. Young and Helen R. Y. Reid, *The Japanese Canadians* (Toronto: University of Toronto Press, 1939): 35.

101. David Chuenyan Lai, *Chinatowns*, 16.

102. Wickberg, ed., *From China to Canada*, 309, table 13.

103. Chuen-Yan Lai, "The Chinese Consolidated Benevolent Association in Victoria: Its Origin and Functions," *B.C. Studies* 15 (Autumn 1972): 53-62; W. E. Willmott, "Some Aspects of Chinese Communities in British Columbia Towns," *B.C. Studies* 4 (Spring 1970): 30-34; Wickberg, ed., *From China to Canada*, 77-79.

104. J. Donald Wilson, "Finns in British Columbia before the First World War," *Polyphany* 3 (1981): 55-64; Scardellato, "Beyond Frozen Wastes," 145; Michael Huculak, "Ukrainians in British Columbia and Their Contribution to the Cultural Life of the Province." (Unpublished manuscript, 1984): 122-142; Irene Howard, *Vancouver's Svenskar: A History of the Swedish Community in Vancouver* (Vancouver: Vancouver Historical Society, 1970): 44-49.

105. Huculak, "Ukrainians in British Columbia," 319-322.

106. Adachi, *The Enemy that Never Was*, 57-60; Percy Gladstone, "Native Indians and the Fishing Industry of British Columbia," and Stuart Jamieson, "Native Indians and the Trade Union Movement in British Columbia," Mark Nagler, ed., *Perspectives on the North American Indians* (Toronto: McClelland and Stewart, 1972): 146-150, 166-169.

107. Census of Canada 1911, vol. 2: table 17, and 1921, vol. 2: table 52.

108. Peter Melnycky, "The Internment of Ukrainians in Canada," Francis Swyripa and Johns Herd Thompson, eds., *Loyalists in Conflict: Ukrainians in Canada during the Great War* (Edmonton: Canadian Institute of Ukrainian Studies, University of Alberta, 1983): 1-24.

109. Robert F. Harney, "Italians in Toronto," *Italian Americana* 1, no. 2 (1975): 162.

110. Hugh Johnston, "Patterns of Sikh Migration to Canada, 1900-1960," J. T. O'Connell *et al.*, eds., *Sikh History and Religion in the Twentieth Century* (Toronto: South Asian Studies, University of Toronto, 1988): 304.

111. Patricia E. Roy, *White Man's Province: British Columbia Politicians and Chinese and Japanese Immigrants, 1858-1914* (Vancouver, University of British Columbia Press, 1989): 70-77, 134-141.

Chapter 7
THE RESOURCE ECONOMY, 1871–1921
Allen Seager

Between 1871 and 1921, the industrial world took a giant step towards a global economy, with dramatic consequences for once distant and isolated regions. Before that time, the trade that spanned oceans and continents and that brought Europeans to British Columbia was restricted to luxury items and precious metals—furs and gold. It was only in the closing decades of the nineteenth century that international investment in railways and steamships created the carrying capacity that made it economical to ship bulk commodities from the Pacific to Atlantic markets. Freight rates began falling on the Atlantic after 1870, and, within a couple of decades, as the merchant fleet of steamships on the Pacific grew, they fell there as well. The completion of a transcontinental railway and the commencement of regular trans-Pacific steamship services brought British Columbia into the new era after 1885. Up to that point, local producers of coal and timber had access only to Pacific markets, particularly those on the North American coast from California to Alaska. The new economic order, with its increased continental and global trade, encouraged a general expansion of economic activities on the mainland. The development of Vancouver as a larger city and more important economic centre than Victoria followed.[1] In the 1890s, metaliferous mining and smelting, centred in the hitherto remote Kootenays, became viable industries.[2] And a burgeoning forest industry emerged as the most dynamic sector of British Columbia's resource economy after 1900.[3]

While British Columbia's untapped natural resources afforded rich opportunities for the export sector, other elements of the economic equation must be considered. The domestic market of 1921, for example, was qualitatively and quantitatively very different from its analogue in 1871—a much more significant factor in the economy. A steadily rising tide of immigration from overseas, from other parts of Canada, and from the United States produced a spectacular expansion of the non-Native population, particularly in urban areas on the lower coast. By 1921, 42 per cent of the population of British Columbia lived in greater Vancouver, which comprised a dozen municipalities, and another 11 per cent lived in greater Victoria. While these metropolitan areas functioned as interdependent nodes of regional, resource-based development, they were also becoming centres that generated economic activity on their own—activity that had little to do with the economic nature of the rest of the province. Any understanding of the importance of exports must be modified in another way as well. In contrast to the wheat-producing Prairie provinces, British Columbia had a less certain connection with foreign markets. Its primary producers and others struggled instead to find their own niches within the national market and political economy.

THE TRANSPORTATION REVOLUTION: STEAM RAILWAYS AND THE CPR

In 1871, British Columbians understood that the economic success of their province depended on railway construction. Railways meant strengthened ties with Canada. In adopting the Canadian "philosophy of railways," British Columbia gradually turned its back on its sea-borne origins to embrace a continentalist strategy of development. The reorientation had a profound impact on the province's economic history and geography: see Map 4.[4]

If success is measured in railway mileage, British Columbia did well. By 1928, the zenith of the railway age, the province boasted 5,280 miles of track, a network of main and branch lines that included the so-called "extra-transcontinental" railways: the Canadian Northern and the Grand Trunk Pacific, amalgamated by the federal government under the flag of the Canadian National Railways (CNR) in 1919. Their provincial counterpart was the Pacific Great Eastern (PGE), later rechristened the British Columbia Railway, similarly brought under public ownership for reasons of financial necessity during the First World War. As originally conceived by its private promoters in 1909, the PGE aimed to connect Vancouver with Prince (formerly Fort) George in the north-central Interior as an integral part of the grander railway-colonization schemes of the immediate pre-war period. The regional trunk line, although not completed, still linked a string of historic settlements like Lillooet, Williams Lake and Quesnel, which were not served by the national railway grid and would otherwise have withered on the vine. Through such national and provincial railway projects, governments were drawn into direct and sustained involvement in Canadian and British Columbian economic life.

The ribbons of steel that punched through British Columbia's otherwise impassable natural barriers freed up inland resources for exploitation, and to a lesser extent, advanced the agricultural frontier. By 1914, when the first Vancouver grain elevators were established, the railways had also begun to play, in a serious fashion, their modern role as pipelines for continental and international commerce via west coast ports. Today, all but a few of the Canadian railways' western passenger services have been eliminated, but during the age of steam, they were equally critical factors in regional economic development.

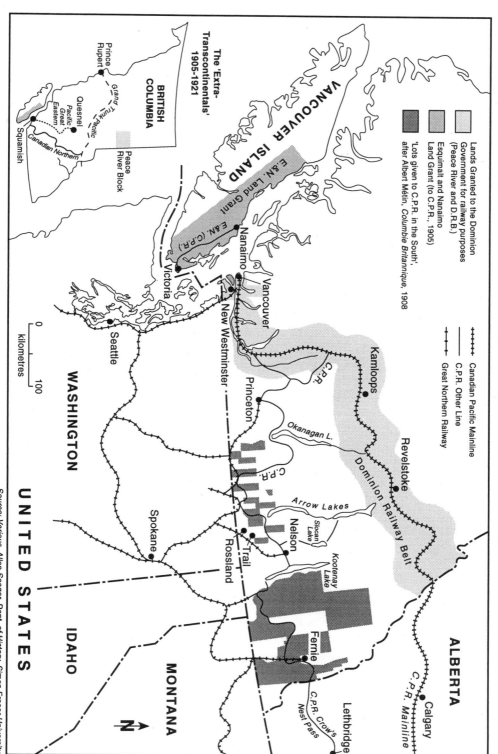

Map 4: British Columbia Major Railways and Rail Land Grants, 1880–1905

Lands Granted to the Dominion Government for railway purposes (Peace River and D.R.B.)

Esquimalt and Nanaimo Land Grant (to C.P.R., 1905)

"Lots given to C.P.R. in the South", after Albert Métin, Columbie Britannique, 1908

+++++ Canadian Pacific Mainline
——— C.P.R. Other Line
+++++ Great Northern Railway

The 'Extra-Transcontinentals' 1905–1921

BRITISH COLUMBIA

Prince Rupert

Quesnel

Squamish

Peace River Block

Grand Trunk Pacific

Pacific Great Eastern

Canadian Northern

VANCOUVER ISLAND

E.&N. Land Grant (C.P.R.)

Nanaimo

Victoria

Vancouver

New Westminster

Seattle

WASHINGTON

Princeton

C.P.R.

Kamloops

Okanagan L.

Revelstoke

Dominion Railway Belt

C.P.R.

Arrow Lakes

Slocan Lake

Nelson

Spokane

Trail

Rossland

Kootenay Lake

UNITED STATES

IDAHO

MONTANA

Fernie

C.P.R. Crow's Nest Pass

Lethbridge

ALBERTA

Calgary

C.P.R. Mainline

0 kilometres 100

N

Source: Various, Allen Seager, Dept. of History, Simon Fraser University

Railway building stimulated unprecedented demands for labour and supplies, and railways were significant employers. Over 8,500 men, a large number of them highly skilled members of the powerful railroad brotherhoods, worked on CNR's and Canadian Pacific Railway's (CPR's) British Columbia lines in 1926. After a fashion, steam railways were the cement that bound the regions to the province and the province to the country. A combination of public enthusiasm and private greed, however, also resulted in a system that was poorly planned, overbuilt, and as a result a drain on the productive forces of the economy. As the authors of a 1942 history of British Columbia put it, British Columbia's railway map "can be explained historically, but cannot be justified as evidence of money spent so as to produce the best results in transportation."[5] The pattern was set with the first railway, the CPR.[6]

It is vital to remember that the legendary CPR was more than a pioneering venture bringing rapid communications to western Canada. It was also a large and, in time, ruthlessly efficient engine of capital accumulation. Even when allowance is made for inflation, the entire capitalization of the Hudson's Bay/North West Company monopoly in 1821—£100,000 sterling or roughly $500,000—pales by comparison with the CPR, capitalized at $228 million in 1905.[7] As a strictly transportation enterprise, a railway built through vast, under-populated regions was a dubious investment. The promise of financial success lay with diversification into more lucrative endeavours—notably land speculation. Because the government subsidized the railway with land grants, the railway had an incentive to overbuild. In Canada, as in the United States, railway investment and western expansion proceeded in tandem, helped along by the state, which typically did the railways' legislative bidding. The outcomes of this dynamic process were usually very different from those hoped for by regional railway enthusiasts. Railways, seen as a liberating technology by their nineteenth century advocates, became synonymous with economic oppression: a "crushing burden" or a "strangling octopus," in the words of their critics.

The land grants that supported the CPR were massive: twenty-five million acres of Dominion lands located primarily in what is now Alberta and Saskatchewan and over thirteen million acres of provincial lands in British Columbia. Under the original terms of union, the province ceded a twenty-mile-wide belt on either side of the proposed line to the federal government for railway purposes. This "railway belt" was later surveyed as comprising 10,976,000 partly timbered and partly arable acres. Subsequently, the province ceded 3,468,000 acres of potentially arable lands in the Peace River district in lieu of lands in the Lower Mainland railway belt. Finally, the province ceded a strip of territory known as the Vancouver Island railway belt, comprising some 2,100,054 acres or about one-third of the Island. The Island belt was by far the most valuable of the three tracts; it was also the most swiftly alienated, ceded to private interests by special federal legislation in 1884. A lone dissenting member Member of Parliament, J. A. R. Homer from New Westminster, objected that the people of British Columbia were being "relieved of property consisting of lands, timber, coal, and other minerals to the value of $20,000,000 . . . to receive a railway, seventy [eight] miles in length." He was referring to the railway mileage proposed for the Island.[8]

The grab for railway lands brought in a host of players besides the CPR. Between 1882 and 1914, the legislature authorized construction of no less than 212 different railways by land-grant charters, which appear to have totalled 6,133,346 acres. Only a fraction of these, however, were actually built, and a large number of the provincial land-grant charters were inevitably cannibalized by the CPR. The company's private property holdings in British Columbia in 1914 are said to have comprised seven million acres. The French geographer Albert Metin produced a map of British Columbia in 1908 that looked like a checkerboard of CPR property (see Map 4), while Englishman Henry Boam wrote in 1912 that "it can be truthfully said that the influence which the Canadian Pacific Railway has wielded over the destinies of the Province has been almost without parallel in modern history."[9]

The title of Pierre Berton's history of the railway, *The National Dream*, makes the CPR sound like a popular project, an achievement of the Canadian people. *Lords of the Line*, the title of a biography of the larger-than-life characters who led the company, suggests something else. The grandees of the CPR belonged to the larger collective of businessmen portrayed in American historiography as "robber barons," the dominant figures of a free-wheeling economic age.[10] The men who spearheaded a new imperial assault on the province during the 1880s were part of this group: William Cornelius Van Horne of the CPR, James Jerome Hill of the U.S.-based Great Northern, or British Columbia's home-grown robber baron, Robert Dunsmuir, successful promoter of the original Esquimalt and Nanaimo (E & N) Railway on Vancouver Island.[11]

The chequered history of the financing and construction of the CPR transcontinental reveals the nature of the enterprise. The men who promoted it moved in a realm that transcended national borders. The abortive first Canadian Pacific Railway Company, chartered by the federal government in 1872, comprised a strange alliance between Montreal shipping magnate Hugh Allan and a secret backer, Philadelphia financier Jay Cooke, who was also a promoter of a projected American line. This CPR project collapsed in the Wall Street Panic of 18 September 1873. Three months later, charges of corruption based on revelations about the relationship of Cooke and Allan to the Tory government in Ottawa forced Prime Minister Macdonald to resign. These events caused considerable consternation in British Columbia. In the gloomy global economic climate of the 1870s, it proved impossible to float another company, and the Liberals, who held power in Ottawa from 1874 to 1878, became the targets of the dissatisfaction felt in British Columbia.[12]

In truth, British Columbia had little reason for complaint. During the 1870s, the national government spent over four million dollars on the transcontinental railway project. The lion's share of this expenditure went for surveys of the projected line, and the provincial economy was buoyed by this money. As it became increasingly clear that Victoria would never be the terminus for any transcontinental railway—Ottawa's promises to the contrary—powerful local interests on the Island took the lead in a so-called provincial protest. What they could not brush aside was the matter of cost. In the opinion of Sandford Fleming, an engineering scientist, seven bridges "of a most formidable kind" were required to connect the mainland to the Island near the mouth of Bute Inlet where the water crossing was narrowest. Building them would have sunk the whole project right then and there. Port Moody, at the head of Burrard Inlet, was briefly designated as the western terminus; and then, as part of a provincial-municipal deal, the transcontinental leapfrogged Port Moody to run its line into what became City of Vancouver where the CPR received approximately 50 per cent of the real estate within the present-day municipal boundaries.[13]

Two routes through the Rocky Mountains would have been more viable from an engineering and economic standpoint than the Rogers' Pass/Kicking Horse Pass route that the main line of the CPR ultimately followed. They were rejected on various grounds by either the company or the federal government. For the company, the Yellowhead Pass was too far north and would have left vast territories open to incursions by rival American railroads. For the government, the Crowsnest Pass was too far south to be defended in a war with the United States, a totally anachronistic argument that was based on a misconception of the evolving relationship between Canada and the United States. Railways were instruments of continental integration as well as national competition. The new rivalries were economic, not military, and these rivalries, as Ottawa's often contradictory railway policies demonstrate, could make very strange bedfellows indeed.

After the collapse of the first CPR company in 1873, the federal government continued slowly with the railway as a public work. Late in 1879, when the government let the first contracts for the construction of the Fraser Canyon section, American interests gained a significant toehold in the western half of the railway. A plethora of local entrepreneurs lost out to a foreign contractor named Andrew Onderdonk who had backers in San Francisco. The investors behind Onderdonk probably aimed at ownership, expecting the Canadian government to divide the transcontinental into two regional entities as Washington had done with the first American transcontinental in the 1860s. The Canadian government, however, continued to view the railway as a single project and to look for a group of entrepreneurs who would take it on.

Once the Fraser Canyon section was well in hand, Macdonald was able to float another transcontinental railway company in 1880–1881. Only two Canadians sat on the new CPR's board of directors, and American citizens dominated its operating management, though American involvement was significantly diluted by the participation of "blue-chip" British and European investors. Thirty per cent of CPR stock was held by Morton Rose and Company of London, Kohn Reinach of Frankfurt, and the *Societé Generale* of Paris. Fifty per cent of the stock was subscribed in the United States.[14]

In 1882, disagreement on the viability of an "all-British" main line for the CPR led to the exodus of a key director, J. J. Hill, an expatriate Canadian based in St. Paul, Minnesota. Hill controlled the St. Paul and Manitoba Railway, which begat the famous Great Northern line, arcing its way across the top of the northern tier of states to reach Seattle by 1886. Ironically, almost no one had greater faith in the economic potential of western Canada than Hill, who waged economic warfare against his former partners for control of a large share of their Canadian traffic and territory. Adding spice to the corporate quarrel was a personal enmity between Hill and the CPR's Van Horne—himself an expatriate American. Hill vowed to vanquish Van Horne "if I have to go to hell and shovel coal."

This falling out among the robber barons accelerated the pace of construction. The CPR management no longer felt that they could take a decade to complete. In 1882 and 1883 Van Horne drove his CPR crews—a motley force of Americans, Canadians and continental Europeans—across the Canadian Prairies. In 1884 and 1885 he pitted a force of up to 12,000 navvies against the Rockies and the Selkirks, while Onderdonk's men conquered the Fraser and raced quickly eastward along the Thompson.

Onderdonk had persuaded Ottawa to allow him to use low-wage Chinese "coolies," as the Americans had done on the Central Pacific. In making this concession, the Macdonald government overrode strenuous protests from legislators and opinion makers in British Columbia. Between 1881 and 1884, 17,007 Chinese workers entered the province, though scarcely half of these people remained behind when the railway was completed in 1885. Many returned to China; others slipped into the United States; and about 1,500 died through accident or disease. The standing force of Chinese railway construction workers in 1883 numbered about 6,500 souls. Despite their posturing, most politicians in British Columbia reluctantly accepted the need to use Chinese labour to get the railway built, but as the railway neared completion they stepped up the anti-Chinese campaign. On 1 January 1886, the Dominion government responded with a discriminatory $50 "head tax" on Chinese workers entering the country.[15]

Van Horne's impetuous gamble on the route west of Calgary through Rogers' Pass and Kicking Horse Pass—a route for which no detailed survey existed—proved monumentally costly. The dangerous grades in this area (addressed by laborious and costly tunnelling after 1900) were cited forever after as a justification for equally steep mountain freight rates. Van Horne's blackjack tactics in forcing the subcontractors to work during the worst of the winter months in 1884–1885 also provoked a rebellion by unorganized white navvies, encouraged by the ascendant Knights of Labor on the coast. Accounts of the first (but by no means the last) railway construction strike in British Columbia vary considerably; all agree that the North-West Mounted Police succeeded in quelling it with a minimum of "disorder."[16]

The driving of the CPR's last spike by company officials at Craigellachie on 5 November 1885 brought British Columbia into the railway age by an all-Canadian route. The monopoly that this route enjoyed, however, proved short-lived. Within a year and a half the Great Northern had reached the 49th parallel at Blaine, Washington, the first of more than a half-dozen American branch lines crossing the British Columbia border between 1891 and 1904 (see Map 4). These branch lines, primarily serving the mineral districts of the Interior, were investments in a new and highly competitive game of industrial expansionism.

MINING AND ENERGY

The miners of pre-Confederation British Columbia barely scratched the surface of one of the most richly mineralized areas of the world. After Confederation, private prospectors, aided by the Geological Survey of Canada, searched relentlessly for an ever larger variety of mineral resources, from platinum to petroleum. Stirred by the first wave of railway building, no fewer than 1,316 British Columbia mining companies were launched between 1886 and 1900. At least 425 (or 33 per cent) were American-owned, hardly a surprising fact considering the regional geography of the British Columbia railways, and the comparative inexperience of Canadians in mining before 1900. English and Scottish investors were present as well, forming at least 161 companies in this period and sharing, with the Americans, ownership of the major producing mines around the turn of the century. Despite legitimate fears of American domination, and high hopes for British involvement, Canadian interests eventually captured the commanding heights of the industry. The Montreal-based Consolidated Mining and Smelting Company, formed in 1906, accounted for one-half of the dividends paid out by all British Columbia mining companies between 1897 and 1941. At the same time, the unregulated environment seems to have discouraged British investors, by no means a healthy situation from either the national or the regional point of view. According to available estimates, British direct investment in the province actually dropped from a turn-of-the-century peak of $80 million, 80 per cent of which was invested in mines, · to $52 million in 1914, 75 per cent outside the mining sector.[17]

The mining boom had a speculative underside. In the words of iconoclastic Kootenay journalist R. T. Lowery, British Columbia was cursed with a "class of crooks who prefer to mine the public instead of the ground," and these were particularly active in the London market. A local historian, writing about the Kootenay mining town of Rossland, adds: "For every legitimate large scale company . . . perhaps ten were floated for the [sole] purpose of enriching those engaged in stock promotion . . . . For years after, the name of 'Rossland' was to be a byword for piles of worthless stock."[18] Far from unusual was the Orphan Boy Gold Mining Company, which had a brief life, in the opinion of a presiding bankruptcy judge, as a "social welfare scheme" for its officers and directors. The *Mining Critic*, a London financial paper devoted exclusively to the arduous task of separating fact from fiction in Canada's mining west, satirized it as "the fatherless one":

> One more unfortunate claim
> Gone to Smash
> Dogged by unkindly Fate
> Lost is the Cash
> Liquidate tenderly
> Wind up with Care
> Left to expend there be
> Nothing per share[19]

The British Columbia *Mining Record*, a semi-official publication of the industry, vigorously denounced "knockers" like Lowery and "mosquitoes" like *Critic* editor Maurice Gradwohl, but felt constrained, in its special Christmas issue in 1899, to solicit a lengthy discourse on "The Introduction of Capital into New Countries" by a professional economist. "There are certain people," Professor D. B. Ogle pontificated, "whose minds are so painfully misguided as to argue that a swindle on outside capital is a good thing because it brings money into the country. But the capital it introduces is destroyed absolutely, except that portion of it diverted into the swindler's pocket, where it seldom remains for any good purpose."

Governments could not be relied on to police the capital market place because government officials, high and low, were deeply compromised in mining speculation. Dominion Minister of the Interior, Clifford Sifton, reflected the lax standards of the age when he gambled in western mining stocks. As a consequence, the commitment to effective action was weak. The British Columbia legislature appeared to respond to complaints of British investors with the mildly regulatory Companies Act of 1897. It compelled the registration of companies, creating a small amount of work for the legal profession, and solemnly prohibited the publication of false prospectuses. Still, promoters did not have to worry that the Companies Act might enforce any serious liabilities on them.[20] In March 1897, sixty mining brokers met in Rossland to form a stock exchange where mining stocks would trade in an open market "so that the public cannot be fleeced by unscrupulous brokers."[21] Unfortunately they failed to agree on the most basic principles, such as to quote or not to quote the daily price of stocks, so the project died stillborn.

In 1897, the putative capitalization of British Columbia mining companies was approaching $1 billion, "an absurd figure," stated one contemporary commentator, "when it is considered that, with a few exceptions, our mines are as yet in their infancy."[22] The Interior mining bubble inevitably burst. A decade later, British Columbia's mining fields still had a reputation as a doubtful place to invest.[23] The mining industry's speculative excesses contributed to the general underdevelopment of the regional capital market. The Vancouver Stock Exchange, formed in 1907, long remained a bastion of "penny stock" promotions, and did not compete with eastern institutions in more substantial promotions. The mining boom left the banking situation in British Columbia very much as it had been before—under outside control. Of sixty-six British Columbia banks listed in R. G. Dun's *Mercantile Reference* for 1907, only the three branches of the Northern Bank of Winnipeg had a western Canadian headquarters.

The productive side of the mining industry seemed to prosper by exploiting a diversity of natural resources, each with rather unique characteristics. (Figures 1 and 2) Lode gold and silver, two "staples" that led the province's

Figure 1: Estimated Value of Mineral Production, 1880–1914

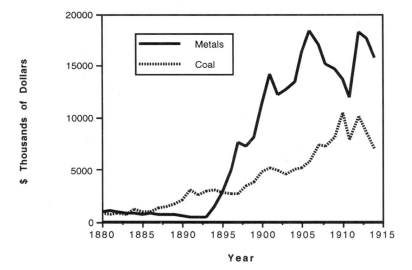

Note on metals: Data on placer gold (virtually all output in the 1880s) include an officially-calculated addition of one-fifth for gold "carried away" and not reported. The values of silver and lead are first reported in 1887, of "lode" gold in 1893 and copper in 1895. All these data are stastistical estimates based on various indices of prices and are especially problematic prior to 1895. Typically "Some silver ore is known to have been sold prior to 1887, but no record has been obtained regarding these small sales." R.E. Gosnell, *The Year Book of British Columbia and Canadian Yukon* (Victoria, 1897), p. 391. For 1894 we have added the "Value of gold, silver, copper and lead ore shipped from Nelson during the year, $784,956," omitted for some reason in the table of production in the "Report of the Minister of Mines," *Sessional Paper* 58 Victoria, p. 723.

Figure 2: Relative Value of Minerals in 1915

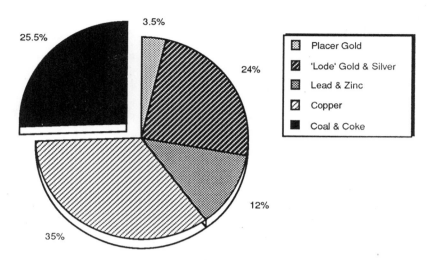

export drive between 1886 and 1901, were more than market commodities: they were, literally speaking, hard currency. The discovery of relatively high-grade ores of gold and silver in the Slocan and Boundary districts were peculiarly electrifying during the general commercial depression of the mid-1890s. The lodes were magnets for labourers, merchants and professionals as well as capitalists. Unfortunately, as an 1899 resolution by the Silverton, British Columbia, miners' union prophesied, the longer-term effect was to "leave only cabins here for houses, while palaces would be built in Spokane, Butte, Salt Lake, and London." Because of the mines, new towns sprang up throughout the area, but only in a minority of cases would local economies become sufficiently resilient to survive once the mines died.[24]

Gold production increased only marginally between 1900 and 1910, while silver production—owing in part to its declining significance as currency—dropped substantially during the same period. The real and/or money value of the index of metal production would have fallen dramatically had it not been for the development of industrial minerals, notably copper, lead and zinc, which became the mainstays of the industry after 1900. The new product mix had definite ramifications for the capital structure. In gold and silver mining, a degree of small-scale enterprise persisted; in the mining of relatively low value industrial minerals only large-scale integrated operations were viable—like Consolidated Mining, Granby Mining and Smelting, or Britannia Mining and Smelting (which commenced operations at Howe Sound in 1905). The smelting or refining end of the business was already littered with cautionary examples of failed enterprises, beginning with a bungled Vancouver smelter, heavily bonused by local taxpayers, that operated for "a day or two" in 1889.[25] British Columbia's first successful smelter opened near the Rossland mines at Trail Creek in 1895-1896. The property of an entrepreneur from Butte, Montana, Frederick Augustus Heinze, it was purchased in 1898 by the CPR Company not, initially, "to make money out of it," but rather, to secure the company's share of regional rail-freight traffic in coal and ores. This was to be the cornerstone of Consolidated Mining, or Cominco, a wholly owned subsidiary of the CPR, which became vertically integrated after the timely acquisition of the valuable War Eagle, Le Roi, Centre Star and St. Eugene mines following 1905.[26]

The CPR acquired hegemony in the mining business as a natural extension of its railway business and with the advantage of support from the federal government. In the opinion of influential nationalists like J. W. Dafoe, Sifton's right-hand man, the Kootenays were destined to become "the greatest mining camp in the world." By 1895, the CPR already had an impressive network of short lines and inland water connections running south of its poorly situated main line track. For example, the coal for Heinze's original smelter was shipped by sternwheeler or barge down the Arrow Lakes. After 1896 the Dominion government underwrote the more ambitious scheme of building a second CPR trunk line through the province, via the Crowsnest Pass. Coastal interests had also promoted the Crowsnest route, though they were to be severely disappointed by the results of the Crowsnest Pass Agreement negotiated by Sifton and Van Horne in 1897. Only the eastern section of the line, from Lethbridge to Nelson, was to be completed forthwith. In return for fresh subsidies, the CPR acceded to a downward revision of western freight rates, primarily to the benefit of central Canadian manufacturers and Prairie grain growers. Work on the remaining section of the Crowsnest Pass or Kettle Valley line, from Nelson to Hope, continued, but the Kootenay boom was already history by the time the line was finished in 1916. Ahead lay decades of political conflict over freight rates that tended to isolate British Columbia interests. Nevertheless, Cominco would become a North American model of the techniques of modern mining, including hard-driving "scientific management" and government-backed research and development, all dedicated to "minimize, so far as possible, the speculative element."[27]

No survey of British Columbia mining would be complete without some discussion of a more prosaic commodity: coal. Coal mining accounted for at least one-quarter of the value of mineral production and closer to half of all mining employment in the province in its pre-1914 heyday, and, if only because of British Columbia's seemingly inexhaustible coal reserves, continued to figure prominently in economic discussions during the 1920s and afterwards. Coal mining, however, was an increasingly insignificant factor in capital formation. The CPR, for example, avoided direct investment in coal mining despite the company's extensive holdings of coal lands in the southeastern part of the province.

Coal mining is remembered best for its "company towns," and its heavy toll in life and limb: 1,147 of 1,600 recorded fatalities in the mining industry between 1878 and 1926. The dynamics of company-town life and the safety issue together contributed to a level of industrial conflict unmatched in other industries. Major strikes of the United Mine Workers of America involving two western Canadian districts rocked the coal towns for periods of up to twenty-five months in duration between 1911 and 1914. Coal owners have not been terribly sympathetic figures in provincial history, but the fact remains that large and important communities were utterly dependent upon their economic fortunes.

Vancouver Island's coal industry enjoyed its most prosperous years in the 1880s. Between 1875 and 1890, production increased ten-fold, largely due to exports to the United States, which accounted for about 75 per cent of the provincial output in this period. The Dunsmuir family, with their mine at Wellington north of Nanaimo on Vancouver Island, were the best-known coal owners in the province. Even so, they were outproduced much of the time by the colliery at Nanaimo, which had begun as a Hudson's Bay Company operation and which continued under English ownership. The Nanaimo company had fewer capital assets than the Dunsmuirs and acted in a more conciliatory way towards labour by tolerating locally based unionism. This company also tried to encourage a "better class" of worker by setting aside five-acre lots for the benefit of established, mainly British stock, mining families. At the Nanaimo mine, Chinese pit-men were excluded by a collective agreement in 1891.[28] The Dunsmuirs relied on a more transient workforce: unattached single men, "foreigners" from continental Europe, and, most controversially, Chinese pit-men. The elder Dunsmuir, Robert, was a formidable foe of organized labour. His death in 1889, however, did little to smooth the local class relations. His son James battled the Wellington miners to a standstill in a prolonged strike that became an international *cause celebre* in 1891.[29] With remarkable prescience, however, both the Dunsmuirs and their English competitors at Nanaimo sold their Vancouver Island properties before the First World War: profits were falling and the actual tonnage of coal mined in the province peaked in 1910 at a level not seen again until the energy-short 1970s. Stagnant markets were complicated by the effects of over-expansion. Between 1898 and 1908 the capacity of the provincial coal industry doubled with the addition of the Crowsnest field. But great expectations for Crowsnest coal fell with the ebbing of the Kootenay boom. Output and employment dropped by 50 per cent between 1913 and 1920.

The emerging crisis in the coal industry had its roots in global competition and in the development of alternative sources of energy. During the 1890s, maritime freight rates fell in such a way that Welsh coal became available in San Francisco at prices almost identical to those for coal from British Columbia. Patriotic expectations that Vancouver Island would have a strategic role as a giant coaling station for the Royal Navy proved groundless, even before the admiralty decided to switch to Persian oil in 1911.[30] The hope that newly developed Interior coalfields might become a source of supply for the mid-western Canadian market proved equally illusory because of distance as well as the obviously discriminatory railway freight rates.[31] Meanwhile, the development of the California oilfields stole all but a fraction of the market for British Columbia coal exports before eating into temporarily buoyant domestic markets as well. The Sante Fe Railroad was the first in the world to convert from coal to oil-fired steam locomotives, beginning in 1892. Two decades later the CPR commenced conversion west of the Great Divide and other railroads—including the provincially owned PGE—eventually followed suit.[32] With the evolution of the internal combustion engine, and the aggressive tactics of U.S.-based oil monopolies, oil soon had a large place in the British Columbia energy picture. (American companies established their beach-head in the Burnaby-Burrard import terminals and refineries long before these facilities were reconverted to handle Alberta oil).

Electrification was already well-advanced throughout the province by the 1920s. The first practical application of electrical power in British Columbia came on the docks of Moody's mill in 1882—introducing the curse of night work for the longshore industry.[33] The first all-electric sawmill—Hanbury's on False Creek—opened in 1911 and promised not only productivity gains, but considerable savings in life and limb, with the elimination of miles of hazardous pulleys and belts. Contemporaries needed little persuasion from "power visionaries" to be attracted to their utopia of warm, well-lit homes, barns and classrooms, or clean, safe and efficient industries.

Electricity could be generated in any number of ways, but by far the most economically efficient and, within limits, environmentally sustainable method was the use of water or hydro-power, known as "white coal." By 1914, even coal operators were generating power for their plants using hydro! The question remained, who would control this vital resource? The first hydro-electric installation in British Columbia, on the Kootenay River's Bonnington Falls in 1897, set a pattern of ownership by private industrial and utility interests. This facility became the nucleus of the regional power monopoly of West Kootenay Power and Light (1916), another important subsidiary of the CPR-Cominco group.[34]

In 1910, the province of Ontario—responding to the needs of local industrial consumers of power—had begun to bring the generating and distribution systems for electric power under public ownership. British Columbia, where there was less demand from local industry, the initiative lay with the producers of electric power, not the consumers. Here, the "trusts" sought to capitalize on the hydro-electric boom with the enthusiastic acquiescence of the provincial government, which constitutionally controlled most water rights, and the active assistance of the federal government, which supplied technical studies and, more controversially, export licences to hydro entrepreneurs.[35] The resulting electrical grid was at first a rudimentary patchwork that left large areas of the province in the dark. Communities such as Alberni, Courtenay, Duncan, Fernie, Grand Forks, Kaslo, Kelowna, Ladysmith, Merritt, Penticton, Prince George, Prince Rupert, Revelstoke, Salmon Arm, Summerland and Vernon did not have power provided by mining, forest or utility companies. Instead, they developed small municipally owned utilities, which purchased from the majors or operated small steam or hydro stations. At the end of the First World War, only four of these experiments with "gas and water socialism" had more than 1,000 subscribers: Kamloops, Nelson, Nanaimo and New Westminster (the largest and longest-lived among them, which had 3,330 meters running in 1919).

These municipal utilities were dwarfed by the electrical distribution system owned by the British Columbia Electric Company, the largest and most lucrative of the utilities in the province. Formed in 1897 out of a consortium of bankrupted tram, power, gas and light companies operating in Vancouver and Victoria, B.C. Electric, as it was generally called, boasted 53,498 residential and 2,229 industrial customers in 1919. While at one time B.C. Electric had a poor public image, it made an important contribution to provincial economic life. Its key plant, the Buntzen Lake facility in Coquitlam, was exceptionally well located. Completed in 1903-1904, it included an engineering marvel—a two-and-a-half-mile long waterspill, tidily bored beneath the ground, reputed to have been the longest hydro-electric tunnel in the world.[36] Until the 1920s, B. C. Electric attracted substantial amounts of British investment capital. All other things being equal, it tended to favour local production, like street-car manufacturing in its New Westminster shops. Its power rates were no higher than Ontario Hydro's were, and because it was a private enterprise, it never saddled the province with debts for grandiose hydro-development schemes.

By degrees, B.C. Electric established a remarkably comprehensive regional transportation system in the cities and rural areas of the Lower Mainland and Victoria regions. With their transcontinental priorities and prohibitively high short-haul freight rates, the steam railways had effectively vacated the market for local agricultural producers. The electric railways filled that gap. By 1923, B.C. Electric streetcars and inter-urbans operated over 311 miles of track on the Lower Mainland and 65 miles on Vancouver Island. The system began to shrink in 1924, when the first of many line abandonments caused by unregulated competition from automobiles and trucks occurred.

From the beginning, B.C. Electric's location near resources and markets laid it open to serious competition from other hydro-electric producers. A would-be competitor called the British Mining Corporation tried but failed to develop a Lower Mainland site at Stave Lake.[37] In 1909, its assets and water rights fell into the hands of an opportunistic group led by Max Aitken, an early Canadian specialist in the "paper entrepreneurship" of corporate mergers and acquisitions, and Thomas Shaughnessy, then-president of the CPR. Their corporate creature, the Western Canada Power Company, finally came on stream with about 50 per cent of the total horsepower of B.C. Electric in 1912. By 1915, B.C. Electric's output of kilowatts had dropped by 30 per cent, and still there was no market for the surplus capacity at Stave Lake. Over local protests, Ottawa authorized the export of about 40 per cent of the Stave Lake power to the state of Washington. (The export of Slave Lake power was later curtailed by a gradual rise in domestic requirements.) Fortunately for the B.C. Electric stockholders, the new company failed to meet its financial obligations, and its assets were purchased by the established competitor in 1920.[38]

Until its nationalization by the provincial government in 1961, B.C. Electric ruled the roost on the Lower Mainland, adapting to changing circumstances as the necessity or opportunity arose. For example, when planners in Ottawa came to the conclusion in the 1920s that the coal industry needed assistance in the form of an advanced technology called the "by-products of coke" only B.C. Electric had the resources to build a federally subsidized coke plant. Unfortunately, it was located in downtown Vancouver where B.C. Electric centralized its operations. The new works did give the Vancouver Island coal miners a small boost, but it also showered more than one city motorist with a coating of coal tar—a by-product of coke that came with a lifetime guarantee.[39]

RENEWABLE RESOURCES: FORESTS AND FISHERIES

Forestry in British Columbia is the only component of the resource economy that fits the dictionary definition of a staple industry—an industry holding chief place in the employment of people and production of commodities. Although it was slow to achieve this status, by 1914, Chief Forester H. R. MacMillan could argue without fear of contradiction that logging and related manufacturing "employs more labour, distributes more money, consumes more supplies [and] produces more wealth and public revenue than any other." The key to its success was of course a natural abundance of timber. No resource extended over more of the province. Approximately 45 per cent of the land surface was high-value virgin forest; only about 8 per cent of that had been logged off by the end of the First World War.[40] The forest sector would be the engine that lifted British Columbia's overall economy out of the post-war doldrums. British Columbia forestry, however, was also a very political economy, deeply enmeshed in the toils of business/government relations.

Official statistics of the timber cut date from 1888 when Victoria passed the first legislation defining the twin aims of provincial forest policy: first, to develop the resource—without encouraging the export of raw logs—and second, to capture (much-needed) public revenues. Accurate measurement was needed to ensure a true tally of the "people's" share of production and to referee disputes among buyers and sellers of timber. None of these objectives was easily met. In 1902, for example, the government created a committee chaired by a prominent Vancouver timber capitalist, R. H. Alexander, to improve rules of estimation and restrict cheating by developing a new "British Columbia log scale." In 1905 the government tried to rationalize conditions in the field by passing a special Timber Measurement Act. Not until 1912, however, were forest companies actually compelled to use the services of provincially licensed timber scalers. Meanwhile, the federal government presided over a somewhat looser regulatory regime in the railway belt, which accounted for as much as half of recorded production before the turn of the century.

Until 1930, when a constitutional amendment returned Dominion lands in the railway belt to the province, the federal and provincial governments competed with each other for resource rents. This situation tended to benefit private bidders for cutting rights. Big eastern-based companies with political influence in Ottawa—like the Canadian Northern Railway subsidiary, Canada Western Lumber (Fraser Mills) drew most of their supplies from the Dominion lands. Because the forest reserves under provincial control were far more extensive than those on Dominion lands, the potential for growth in the timber cut lay almost entirely on provincial lands. As shown in Figure 3, the Dominion lands became relatively insignificant after the turn of the century. American interests gambled heavily in provincial timber leases after 1905, accounting for perhaps 50 per cent of capital assets in the industry by 1914. Not included in Figure 3 is the tally of production from the other joker in the regulatory deck: forests owned in fee-simple by private interests. Major corporate holdings

Figure 3: Lumber/Timber Scale on Public Lands, 1888–1914

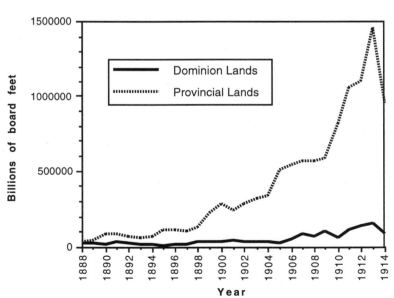

included the successors to Dunsmuir's E & N Railway, whose Island "belt" happened to include the finest stands of Douglas fir. In 1905, the CPR purchased 1.4 million unsold acres of the original Dunsmuir grant for a little less than a dollar an acre—with the rail line and rolling stock thrown in for a bonus. A legal battle over the exact status of this property ensued, but the CPR eventually won its claim to free forest tenure, and the province had to settle for an obscure pledge for the perpetual maintenance of local railway services.

The legislature did not adopt the principle of state ownership of the forests until 1896. Only then did it stop the practice of alienating Crown timber—"let us hope forever," Minister of Lands W. R. Ross ruefully declared in 1912. Ross himself was one of a new generation of progressives, advocates of a "scientific" approach to resource management and inclined to a generally more interventionist role for government. The comprehensive Forest Act of 1912, with a moderately reformist agenda, set the tone of provincial forest policy and administration for another generation.[41] Certainly in the period up to the First World War, provincial forest policy cannot be judged as terribly successful, and provincial revenues from forestry were only impressive in comparison to the pitifully small rents gleaned from the mining industry. (Figure 4).

Forest reformers had to accept structural impediments to the generation of the desired economic surplus. These included frustrating technical failures and a good deal of "fraud, misrepresentation, and surreptitious stealing" by promoters that delayed diversification into pulp and paper until 1912.[42] The manufacture of newsprint from wood chips and small-dimension timber, which accounted for about one-fifth of the value of forestry production by 1918 (see Figure 5), promised more efficient use of resources, the substitution of home production for imports, and an expansion of export markets. The marketing of

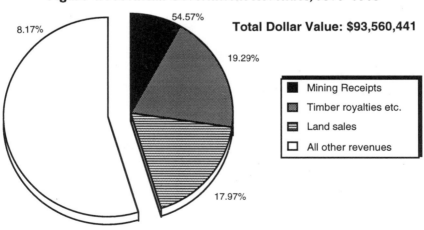

Figure 4: Provincial Government Revenues, 1871–1913

8.17%

54.57%

19.29%

17.97%

Total Dollar Value: $93,560,441

- ■ Mining Receipts
- ▨ Timber royalties etc.
- ▤ Land sales
- ☐ All other revenues

Figure 5: Value of Forest Production (Provincial Lands) in 1918

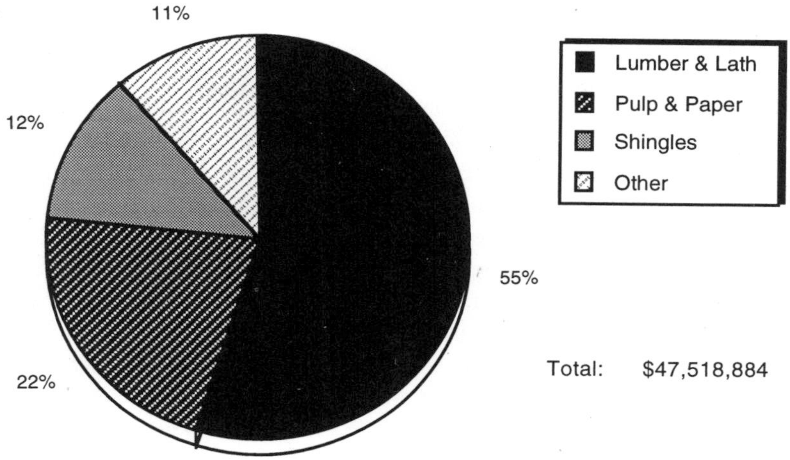

Note: "Other" includes piles, poles, pit props and ties; estimated miscellaneous cut by railways and settlers, and log exports.

British Columbia lumber products was another weak spot. Some lumber products went to Australia, Chile, Hawaii, and a few customers on the Asian mainland. Shanghai, the most westernized of Chinese cities, valued Canadian lumber highly for boat and house construction. However, only two coastal mills were fully employed by the export trade in 1905. In 1913, cargo shipments accounted for only 25 million of 1.6 billion board feet scaled. The Panama Canal project potentially allowed access to markets in Britain and Europe but the canal era opened with a radical disruption of international shipping as a result of the European war. Significantly, the initial push behind state-financed ship building on Canada's west coast came not from military planners, but from hungry timber capitalists who lost 600 million board feet worth of business during the depression of 1913–1915.[43]

During the boom years, as much as one-third of provincial production was absorbed by local building markets, but much more important was the burgeoning Prairie market that forestry leaders in British Columbia wanted to protect. They had to contend with Prairie farmers and town developers who favoured the existing Canadian policy of a one-way free trade in lumber. Western Canadian lumber producers were effectively barred from the United States market but American lumber entered western Canada free of duty. If

Prime Minister Laurier admitted in 1904 the injustice that "the lumberman is taxed on everything he has to use and has no corresponding advantage as against outside competition," he nonetheless bowed to Prairie consumers on this vital question. The abortive Reciprocity Treaty in 1911 might or might not have balanced the ledger.

The "lumberman" may have been targeted for unfair treatment under the tariff but it was the British Columbia taxpayer and the lumber worker who paid the bill. British Columbia lumber workers toiled for small wages in an "open shop" industry where combinations of employers kept unions at bay by highly effective means, like a centralized blacklist of alleged labour agitators. The rise of the Vancouver-based Lumber Workers' Industrial Union, which claimed 13,000 members at the end of the First World War, represented a serious challenge to the open-shop system, but had been successfully beaten back by 1921. The physical carnage within the forest industry was long obscured by the absence of any protective labour legislation that might have generated relevant statistics. After a rudimentary system of state compensation for injury or loss of life at the workplace came into effect in 1918, it became apparent that logging, rather than mining, "was the most costly of our industries from an accident point of view."[44]

In the woods, the logging railway and high-rigging techniques speeded up production; despite bottlenecks caused by universal reliance on the broad axe and the handsaw (the "misery whip"), west coast camps impressed observers as "giant factories, with the sky for a roof." The bulk of production (65 to 80 per cent by value) remained centred upon the exploitation of the large-dimension timber on the coast, notwithstanding expanded investment elsewhere. Vancouver Island mill towns like Chemainus and Port Alberni were shipping up to 90 per cent of their output to the Prairies during the boom. Although farther from the Prairies, they were doing better than the new Interior lumbering centres like Cranbrook on the Crowsnest railway line, or Prince George on the Grand Trunk Pacific. Their main advantage was the size of the timber grown on the coast. They also had more economic clout in negotiating freight rates than ventures such as the United Grain Growers' co-operative mill at Hutton, in the central Interior, which failed because it could not obtain economical transportation from the railway.[45]

It is noteworthy that government did not attempt a comprehensive inventory of forest reserves until after the outbreak of the First World War. This task (in which both levels of government and the CPR participated) fell to the national Commission of Conservation, a body established by the Laurier government in 1909 and chaired until 1918 by ex-minister of the interior, Clifford Sifton, a late-blooming advocate of progressive-style reform. Having a strictly advisory and educative role, the Commission of Conservation sponsored studies on every conceivable topic from saving sea birds to coal-mining safety. In 409 richly illustrated pages, *Forests of British Columbia* appeared in 1918. Beneath a mountain of technical information compiled by authors H. N. Whitford and Roland D. Craig lay an optimistic thesis: current forestry practices were sustainable if relatively modest measures of conservation—like fire-fighting and prevention—were continued and enhanced. Conservationism, the reader was reminded, did not imply a critique of economic growth. "Untilled fields, buried minerals, and standing forests are of no value," Craig and Whitford emphasized, "except for the wealth that, through industry, can be produced therefrom." Even when expressed in these tepid terms, conservationism was not a government priority; budgetary cutbacks and political in-fighting led to the permanent demise of the Commission of Conservation in 1921.[46]

In the fishing industry, as well, the exhaustion of resources was not recognized as a problem, though from 1901 on experts collected evidence that it was happening on a fairly wide scale. Most of the fishery was in-shore and salmon-based: the salmon fishery accounted for at least two-thirds of the value of all fisheries production between the 1870s and the 1920s. Pacific halibut, harvested by British Columbia's relatively small deep-sea fleet, accounted for 14.5 per cent of fisheries production in this period. The herring, cod, oolachan, sturgeon, oyster, clam and crab fisheries were all much smaller. The salmon-packing companies were the largest enterprises in the industry. Best known among them was the B.C. Packers Ltd., an alleged "association" organized in 1902. In a speech given in 1920, its founder and spokesman, Henry Doyle, spoke about the industry with bravado: it was a "A Grown Man's Game" and rivals were "toy fisheries" by comparison. "Ups and down we have had," he said, "and doubtless will have again, but the industry in 56 years has expanded from one to 303 canneries, and from 2,000 to 10,000,000 cases of annual pack; with such a firm foundation established we have nothing to fear for years to come. Today the Pacific Coast salmon canning industry is far and away the greatest fishery enterprise the world possesses."[47]

In the 1880s and 1890s, ever larger numbers of entrepreneurs—local, American, English and Scottish—had cashed in on the Fraser River bonanza. The natural bounty seemed limitless. Export markets were successfully cultivated, especially in Great Britain, where the *oncorhynchus nerka* (sockeye salmon) added needed protein to the working-class diet. In 1888, there were 366 canneries in operation. The harvest proceeded all through the 1890s without any attempt to determine the actual conditions of the salmon run. The only cloud on the horizon that the canneries recognized was the organization of the Fraser River Fishermen's Protective and Benevolent Association in 1892. This association sought to represent the views of European fishermen to government authorities and to engage in collective bargaining with the canneries.

The Fraser River strike of 1900 united upwards of five thousand fishermen for up to one month. Members of the Japanese Fishermen's Benevolent Society joined in support of a demand for twenty-five cents per sockeye; American fishermen, the strikers claimed, were receiving twenty-eight cents for the same commodity. The Japanese settled for eighteen cents, earning the enmity of many whites and Natives, and the rest of the union capitulated at nineteen. This dramatic dispute climaxed with the intervention of troops at Steveston on July 24th. The same pattern of confusingly defensive action was repeated in strikes in the salmon fishery in 1901, 1903, 1907 and 1913. By contrast, the halibut fishery suffered only one disruption in this period, a lengthy coast-wide strike by British Columbia-, Alaska- and Washington State-based boats in 1912.[48]

Pushed over the edge by chaotic competition and the Fishermen's Union, a majority of the canning companies were heading into liquidation by 1902. The formation of B.C. Packers thus came in response to a structural crisis in the salmon fishery, and the declared profits of the company, between $300,000 and $475,000 *per annum* between 1908 and 1916, were not particularly impressive. Capitalists found ways of beating down production costs by fighting the fishermen and introducing exotic labour-saving technology, like the Smith butchering machine for processing fish—the "Iron Chink"—introduced into the canneries around 1906. Dealing with the resource, however, was a different matter. A fisheries expert, John Pease Babcock, pointed out in the *Report of the Commission of Conservation* for 1917: "The salmon industry does not depend on the amount of money invested in canneries, gear, and boats. It depends on the number of salmon which escape capture and spawn." Babcock, who had been chief deputy of the California Fish and Game Commission, served as deputy of the British Columbia fisheries department from its inception in 1901 until 1910, launching the first systematic studies of the spawning beds on the Fraser and the other principal salmon rivers. Early on, he warned that the canneries were seriously depleting the "capital stock" of fish; but the government and the industry were slow to respond.[49]

On the Fraser, the fishing community grappled with the well-known though little understood phenomenon of the "big year." Every four years, the sockeye appeared in huge numbers, their biological cycle oblivious to new human requirements for annual returns on invested capital (see Figure 6). Although these data are not species-specific, they do indicate the effect of the "big year" phenomenon, and also indicate that longer-term yields from the Fraser were declining after 1900. The canning industry increased its productivity, but only by exploiting new territories in the northern waters—the Skeena, the Nass, and Rivers Inlet—which required more investment in an already over-capitalized sector. Almost unbridled competition by the Americans, who intercepted the Fraser River salmon on their way into British Columbia waters, threatened the survival of that resource, as did increasing industrial use of formerly pristine streams. In 1913 railway builders dropped a quarter of a million tons of rock into the canyon at Hell's Gate during the spawning season of a "big year." This created an environmental emergency that had to be swiftly met if the crop for 1917, 1921, 1925, and so forth was not to be completely wiped out. Armed with

Figure 6: B.C. Canned Salmon-Pack, 1876–1928

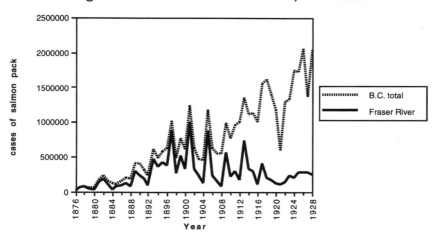

dynamite, nets, and improvised devices, federal Department of Fisheries personnel and volunteers did rescue a large number of sockeye but it was not until the erection of special fish ladders in the 1940s that the unnatural obstacle to their reproduction was overcome.[50]

Even in 1914, the original concentration of canning activity at the mouth of the Fraser was breaking up and the old fleet of dories was shrinking. Canneries encouraged a new type of entrepreneurial fisherman equipped with a more mobile, motor-powered craft that was better able to pursue more and different species at longer range. As one Japanese fisherman testified in 1917: "I stay at Steveston ten years ago and everybody made some money, but, now, all the time they use motor boats and can't make any money . . . . Cost money to fix up, get new nets, all the time in debt to canneries."[51] In an example of the historic overlap between the regulations of the Departments of Fisheries and Indian Affairs after 1876, the Dominion authorities temporarily banned the use of motor boats in the northern waters in 1911, and, in 1917, imposed an additional five-year moratorium to allow Native communities to adjust to the demands of the internal combustion engine. Natives desirous of accessing the commercial market eventually had no choice but to adapt to the new technologies. After 1922, they would put to sea in seiners, large power boats that could capture whole schools of fish with modern offshore nets. The new financial obligations they faced as a result would be the driving force behind the creation of the Native Brotherhood of British Columbia during the Great Depression. The increased efficiency of fishing methods added new dimensions to the complex of regional, class, racial and gear-related tensions within an industry facing the reality of finite resources and static or declining prices.

Sealing and whaling accounted for less than 5 per cent of the measured output of British Columbia's fisheries (by value of commodities) in the period
from 1876 to 1928. Access to sealing waters and management of the seal herds,
however, were significant international issues in the closing decades of the
nineteenth century and in the early twentieth. In the 1880s, Victoria became
the main base of the pelagic sealing industry, a far-flung enterprise ranging
deep into the Bering Sea, where Canadian and American interests clashed.
The peak year of British Columbia's seal harvest was 1894. Fifty-nine vessels
shipping from Victoria gathered 94,474 skins, valued at $10 apiece. (By con-
trast, the numbers of coastal sea otters had so diminished that only 115 were
taken in 1889, fetching a handsome price of $100 per skin). The peripatetic
San Francisco writer, Jack London, offers a semi-fictional account of the sealing enterprise:

> So I shipped on a seal schooner with the lazy Siwashes . . . we were away many
> weary months and spoke of many of the fleet, and heard of the wild doings . . . .
> We went north, even to the Pribolofs, and killed the seals on the beach, and
> brought their warm bodies aboard till our scuppers ran grease and blood and no
> man could stand upon the deck. Then we were chased by a ship of slow steam,
> which fired upon us with great guns. But we put on sail till the sea was over our
> decks and washed them clean, and lost ourselves in a fog.[52]

In 1886, American revenue cutters began arresting Canadian sealing vessels in
international waters, claiming the right to protect the Pribolof Island herd,
whose natural range included a large portion of the North Pacific. In 1894, an
international convention attempted to establish order in the industry and
resolve the dispute. Partly under its restraints, the Canadian-based harvests
declined to about 35,000 *per annum* by the turn of the century and the
American to approximately 22,000. The agreement lapsed after four years.
During abortive negotiations in 1898 the government of Canada "agreed that
pelagic sealing was leading to the extinction of the seal herd." The law of
diminishing returns led to the withdrawal of most of the capital invested in the
industry so that by 1908 fewer than ten boats still plied the Victoria trade. As
the value of the harvest fell, critics of pelagic sealing finally won their point. In
1910, Britain, Canada and the United States signed a pact that effectively
ended the seal hunt—an early and, up to the present, unfortunately rare example of international action to protect marine populations.[53]

AGRICULTURE

Agriculture did not emerge as a vibrant industry in British Columbia until after
1900, but it ranked second only to forestry in measured output by the early 1920s.
Fruit farming proved to be the area with the greatest commercial potential. If

"reforestation" still remained a foreign word in the province, Johnny Appleseed was tramping in the footsteps of Paul Bunyan. Literally millions of apple, peach and other fruit trees were planted in the province before the First World War. During and after the war, the major plantations, concentrated in the Okanagan Valley, finally began to pay off (see Figures 7–9).

Fruit farming, which produced relatively high-value crops from relatively small acreages, represented a more-or-less successful adaptation to British Columbia's unique natural and man-made environments. The high cost of

Figure 7: Number of Fruit Trees in B.C., 1911 and 1921

Figure 8: Spatial Location of Tree-Fruit Production in 1920 (Major Fruits)

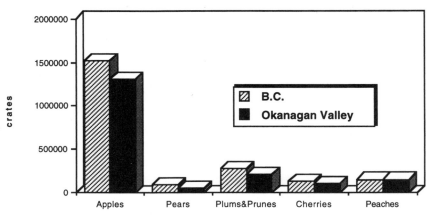

Figure 9: Fruit Production (Value and Volume), 1914–1928

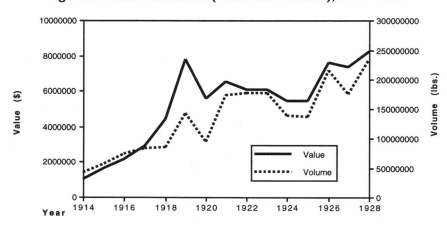

farm land, which was limited in supply and therefore attracted money during the boom years, made low-yield usages untenable. By 1900, if not before, the typical agricultural settler in British Columbia was paying market prices for an initial "homestead." From then on, free government grants were available only under exceptional circumstances, such as soldiers' settlement after the First World War. Land speculators, in turn, maximized their profits by subdividing properties into the smallest possible units, which could be made economically viable only through intensive forms of cultivation like fruit farming.[54]

A letter written in the 1880s reveals something of the less tangible reasoning behind the planting of orchards and vineyards. Henry Alan Bulwer had located near Mission City in the Fraser Valley, which he described as "admirably suited [for] apples, plums, pears [and] cherries . . . Grapes have not been given a fair trial . . . I consider it for an Englishman one of the healthiest and most delightful climates," he noted, buttressing the argument with numerous meteorological data and the observation that most of the local rheumatics were "old miners and prospectors who have spent years of their lives in hardship—wet and cold—washing gold." Bulwer, among other "gentlemen immigrants," hoped to avoid the arduous toil associated with Canadian farms: "Chinamen are cheap . . . their board consists mainly of rice, which costs little. They are capital fruit pickers and pick twice as fast as a white man, and with no injury to the fruit." For the prospective orchardist local conditions seemed idyllic. The resources of science and the state were also called upon from an early date, the Dominion Experimental Farm being established at nearby Agassiz in 1889.[55]

Much of the labour of the early coastal planters, however, proved to be in vain. During the 1890s, the centre of gravity in the tree-fruit industry decamped for sunnier climes in the Interior. Faced by stiff inter-regional as well as international competition, commercial fruit growers in the Lower Mainland abandoned their orchards, switched to other crops, or relocated. "Boosters" of the Okanagan Valley, meanwhile, reaped high short-term profits as the area was aggressively promoted by as many as a dozen fruit-land development companies. Unfortunately, Okanagan fruit lands required a large investment in irrigation, with considerable risk. As one contemporary warned intending British settlers: "As in mining, there are irrigation schemes placed upon the market from time to time that, through either dishonest management or poor judgment are bound to be failures." A "tradition of bitterness on the part of people who had come to the valley under false pretences" added to problems of rust, insects, unsuitable species and, predictably, inadequate transportation. In the Okanagan, however, fruit growers came to wield political clout in pursuit of their economic objectives. Although in 1921 the tree-fruit industry was still developing,[56] the introduction of refrigerated rail cars and the development of local canning facilities promoted the valley's comparative advantages in tree-fruit production.[57]

Producers in other agriculture sectors were also just finding their way. Cereal production, practically wiped out on the Lower Mainland and Vancouver Island by competition from California and later Manitoba in the early national period, had only begun to flourish again in the Peace River district, a geographical-administrative extension of the Prairie region where venturesome settlers like Monica Storrs and her family could still obtain a Dominion land grant in the 1920s.[58] Between 1907 and 1921 the number of non-terminus grain elevators in the province expanded modestly from three to twelve, having a capacity of over half a million bushels. Surprisingly, average wheat yields in British Columbia exceeded all other provinces except Ontario at the census of 1911.

The ranching industry had experienced a spectacular rise during the 1870s, when investors expanded or established a number of impressive spreads in the central interior. Thaddeus Harper, an expatriate Virginian, amassed thirty thousand acres valued at $300,000 in 1880. Like the fruit farmers, provincial stockmen were consistent supporters of the protective tariffs for agricultural products, though, in the beginning, they were prepared to make heroic efforts to reach American markets. In 1876–1877, Harper and nine of his men managed to drive a herd of nearly two thousand cattle from British Columbia to San Francisco. Even routine drives from the Princeton district to New Westminster were an adventure, as the remarkable memoir of English-born ranching "gentlewoman" Susan Allison makes clear.[59] Testifying to their faith in future prospects, British Columbia cattle ranchers were importing eastern Canadian breeding stock (more highly prized than the "miserable wretches" available in the adjacent U.S. states) by sea as early as 1877. Ironically, when the transcontinental railway arrived, it checked the growth of the ranching kingdom. By the 1890s, not only were coastal merchants filling orders with cheaper Alberta beef, but thanks to the peculiarities of the regional railroad grid, Americans as well as Albertans closed B.C. ranchers out of the Kootenay market. The significant enterprises that persisted tended towards even larger units of production, who picked up the holdings of their weaker competitors. In 1910, for example, the Douglas Lake Cattle Company was ranching 100,000 acres valued at $800,000.[60]

That such great estates were not the norm is shown by the average size of provincial farm units at the census of 1911: 136 acres compared to a national figure of 154 acres. Eighty-five per cent of the province's agricultural workforce was self-employed, a statistic due in part to the entrepreneurship of Asian immigrants who were not, generally speaking, content to be a class of cheap labour for white landowners. Most numerous were thousands of smallholders engaged in dairy farming, mixed farming and market-gardening near the major cities in the southern coastal area. Responding to local market opportunities, the limited agricultural land base of the Fraser Valley and Delta had been expanded by dyking and draining. Flooding continued to be a problem in the early years of the twentieth century, requiring further investment in reinforced dykes. Development costs and proximity to markets together contributed to the high capital value of the land.

As a measure of their greater maturity—not, by any means, their uniform prosperity—British Columbia's agriculturalists became increasingly conscious of a distinct class interest and organized to express it. A series of statutes passed by provincial legislators between 1873 and 1897 had enabled the formation of agricultural co-operatives for reclamation, marketing, credit, educational and other purposes. There were about eighty Farmers Institutes and a number of women's auxiliary associations in 1914. At least sixty-seven rural co-operatives were functioning in the province between 1917 and 1925. These ranged in size and scope from the Nechako Valley Co-op Creamery to the British Columbia Fruit Growers Association (BCFGA). In 1919, the socialist leadership of the British Columbia Federation of Labour formed a short-lived "general headquarters" for farming interests in province. The United Farmers of British Columbia (UFBC), founded in 1916, claimed 103 locals at its peak around 1922. Speakers at the UFBC's 1920 convention included Henry Wise Wood, Alberta populist apostle of "Group Government," and James McVety of the Vancouver Trades and Labour Council, a "One Big Union" advocate from the ranks of skilled urban workers. The emerging tradition among British Columbia farmers, however, was collective action through established channels. In 1920, UFBC president R. A. Copeland expressed the sentiments of a majority of the sixty-five rural delegates in emphasizing that the "United Farmers' movement . . . does not mean revolution but reformation."[61] The members of the BCFGA became some of Canada's most vigorous advocates of controlled marketing. Although efforts to form compulsory pooling arrangements for commodities sold in the domestic market were frustrated by constitutional challenges until the

1940s, it is no accident that British Columbia introduced pioneering marketing-board legislation as early as 1927.[62] No less than the industrialists and industrial workers, British Columbia farmers embraced the modern motto of the market-place: organize or perish!

MEASURING THE RESOURCE ECONOMY

Any attempt to compare the output of each sector of the resource economy—mining, energy, forestry, fishing, agriculture—must confront the central *problematique* of economic history: the fragmentary nature of the *measured* economic activity in the past. Patterns of international trade are easier to document than the internal dynamics of the economy, even in basic industries. As an example, for nineteenth century British Columbia there are extant data on the export of timbers and sawn lumber, but no data on the total output of the forest industry, without which it is impossible to say anything at all about its real or imagined "export base."[63] Likewise, although nineteenth century coal statistics offer probably the most comprehensive extant data on a resource industry, they say little about larger patterns in the production and consumption of domestic fuel—mainly firewood and sawdust.[64] The provincial fishery, a seemingly unproblematic example of the resource economy's export base, provides another case in point. According to late nineteenth century estimates, the hypothetical dollar value of "Salmon, consumed by Indians" exceeded that of the tinned commodity as late as 1889.[65] Contemporaries were well aware of the problems of economic measurement. A vast amount of real economic activity remains to this day systematically undocumented, including the informal production and exchange of goods and services among individuals, families and communities that Fernand Braudel calls "the structure of everyday life."[66]

Trade statistics were the first economic data to be compiled by the federal government. Figure 10 summarizes extant data on British Columbia's export trade before the First World War. These data denote the total volume of trade moving *through* the province and therefore include exports of goods originating elsewhere. Prior to the opening of the Panama Canal in 1914, however, inter-regional trade at Canada's west ports was of marginal significance. The figures are at least a reasonable basis upon which to test the assumption of an "export-led" economy.

The first thing to be noted is that Confederation appears to have had no immediate impact on British Columbia's trade relations: the aggregate value of exports neither increased nor declined over a fifteen-year period after 1871. One explanation might be that the provincial economy stagnated in this period, but there is no evidence from population or workforce statistics to support this conclusion. The only thing that is clear is the radical stimulation that railways gave to exports after 1886. In 1881 the province exported $125 worth of goods per capita of gainfully employed workers; twenty years later this had soared to $266

Figure 10: Dollar Value of B.C.'s Export Trade, 1871–1914

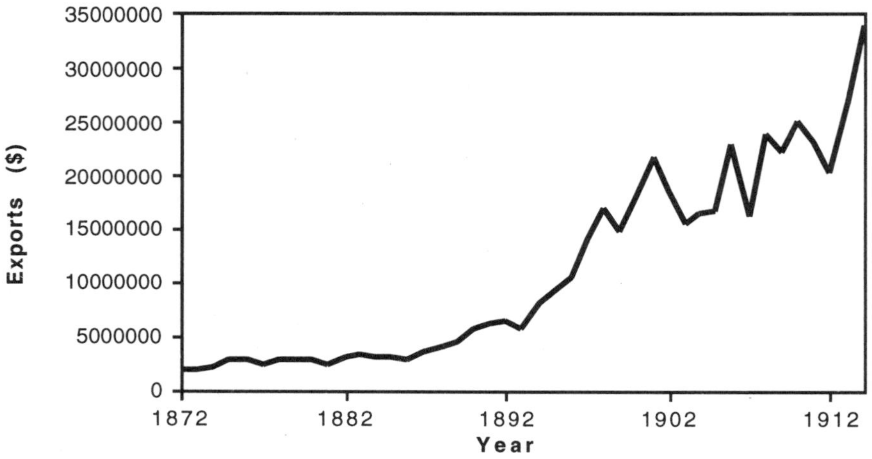

Note: These figures do not account for the depreciation of currency or inflation of approximately 35%, 1900–1913

per capita—astonishingly high by contemporary world standards.

During the period 1900-1914, however, British Columbia's export picture becomes considerably more obscure. How important were exports in stimulating the general Canadian economy during these "boom" years? Economic historians do not agree.[67] In British Columbia, however, exports definitely did not lead the van: at the peak of the boom, in 1913, the value of British Columbia's exports was up only 25 per cent over 1901. In 1911, exports per capita of gainfully employed workers stood at $112, well below the level of 1881. These current-dollar figures disguise the full extent of the decline because they do not account for inflation. Taking average commodity prices between 1890 and 1899 as a basis for a crudely calculated index of the "cost of living," a federal inquiry later showed that Canadian prices in 1913 were, on average, 35 per cent higher than they had been in 1900.[68] This means that the real value of British Columbia's exports actually decreased between 1900 and 1913. Unless the "boom" is dismissed as an economists' fantasy, it is therefore necessary to look beyond exports to comprehend the economic structure.

Figure 11 illustrates the ways in which statistics can be manipulated to present quite different images of underlying structures. It presents two government estimates of British Columbia's combined output for two of the immediate post-war years—the earliest attempts to measure something approximating the gross provincial product available to historians. One model, for 1922, is taken from an interpretation of provincial data done by a provincial commission into

234

Figure 11: Early Estimates of the Gross Provincial Product, Primary and Secondary Industries

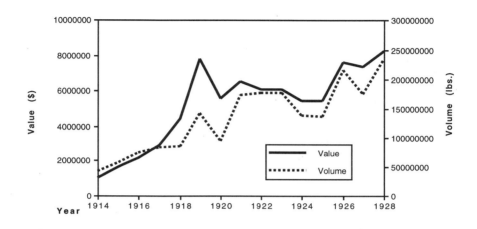

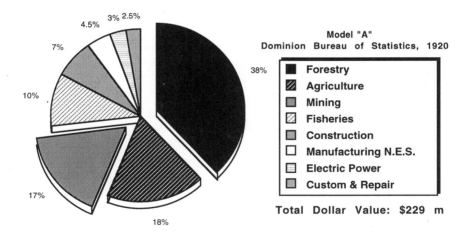

economic governance during the Great Depression. The other model, for 1920, interprets data from the Dominion Bureau of Statistics (DBS)—incidentally, the more advanced and elaborated scheme. The DBS system whittles "manufacturing" down from its status in the provincial model as the largest among five pieces of the economic cake to sixth-ranking among eight. Each model seems to agree on a hierarchy of primary industries—forestry, agriculture, mining and fishing, in descending order. If the reported volume of exports moving through British Columbia ports were factored into these models, the export base of the *goods*-producing side of the provincial economy might be interpreted as representing either 25 per cent of the value of production (1922), or 40 per cent (in 1920). In truth, the export base of the British Columbia economy appears to have been an extremely *variable* phenomenon, necessarily dependent on fluctuations in market demand and on productive capacity.

The only sources of statistical data that give a comprehensive picture of economic activity are returns from the decennial census of occupations after 1881. These are flawed by the cultural bias and conceptual limitations of the census authorities who generally classed women and Native people as not gainfully employed. Moreover, the criteria for defining occupational categories sometimes changed from census to census. Census measurements of the provincial labour force nevertheless provide a more useful guide to the timing of economic growth than any other source; and the problem of changing criteria has been addressed by using corrected historical data created by the census office in the 1930s (see Figures 12 and 13). Estimates of the British Columbia labour force at Confederation do not exceed 7,500 souls. According to the Dominion census, British Columbia's gainfully employed workers—including the self-employed, and the temporarily unemployed[69]—numbered 18,000 in 1881, rising to 50,000 in 1891, 80,000 in 1901, over 200,000 in 1911, and just under 220,000 in 1921. What is immediately apparent is a general trend that was *not* closely correlated with the network or cycles of trade.

Figure 12 illustrates the occupational breakdown of the provincial workforce in two census years for which comparable data are in fact available (1891 and 1921). Perhaps most striking is the broad distribution of occupations across the primary, secondary and tertiary sectors of the economy; the same figure offers an added dimension of comparison by illustrating the occupational breakdown in the country as a whole.

What distinguished British Columbia from other provinces was the nature of its primary sector rather than the size. In the country as a whole, this sector was almost entirely agricultural in 1891, and only marginally less so in 1921. British Columbia's primary sector was more diverse. Census figures can of course be misleading, since the individual could cite only *one* gainful occupation and persons classed as farmers, for example, were often heavily dependent on other primary industries like lumbering or fishing. In Quebec or the Maritimes, such mixed rural economies were especially commonplace. British Columbia evidently had a more pronounced trend towards occupational specialization, with distinct groups from the logging, fishing and farming sectors readily identified in the census.

The shortage of arable land in British Columbia and the industrialization of the province before there was much commercial agriculture help explain this phenomenon. In 1891, the census reported 17 per cent of British Columbia's workforce engaged in agriculture—one-third the Canadian figure; in 1921, the

Figure 12: Occupations of the People, 1921

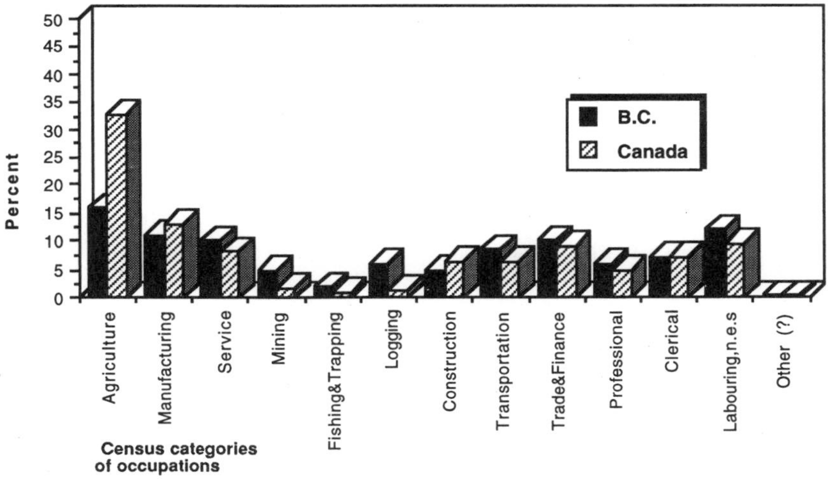

The "Agricultural" category included sons of farmers over 14 years but excluded wives and daughters; "Fishing and Trapping" excluded "nomadic Indians" in 1891 and "Indians living on reserves" in 1921; "Service" included most realms of public, domestic and personal services; "Clerical" included clerical workers in government service in 1921; "Labouring, n.e.s." is the category of "Labourers, nothing else specified" or *Ouvriers sans metier.*

census showed 16 per cent of the workforce engaged in agriculture—about half the Canadian figure. The narrowing gap indicates the unique path of agricultural development in the province. British Columbia had a steadily growing class of (highly commercial) agriculturalists before the 1930s and never had a "surplus" population of agricultural labourers—a distinctly modern feature of its economy. Not until the Second World War did highly industrialized Ontario, for example, reach British Columbia's 1921 level of statistical equilibrium between land and labour.

Other primary occupations formed a large but (unlike farming) declining minority of the labour force. "Timbermen" or loggers, miners and quarry workers, and trappers and fishermen, collectively made up about one-quarter of the census workforce in 1891, and fewer than 15 per cent thirty years later. Any characterization of British Columbia's working class as a "resource proletariat" involves a considerable distortion.[70] Moreover, each primary sector exhibited distinctive—and for the economic historian, suggestive—patterns of change or continuity over time. In all of the censuses between 1891 and 1921, the absolute level of employment claimed for fishing and trapping remained virtually static, at about 4,500 souls. In the same period, agricultural employment grew from 8,000 to 30,000. Measured employment in logging grew by leaps and bounds from roughly 1,200 in 1891 to more than 12,000 in 1921. Mining and quarrying presents a more complicated picture. British Columbia miners numbered fewer than 5,000 in 1891. A preliminary examination of the nominal or manuscript rolls of the census available for that year suggests that a very substantial proportion were not industrial workers in the modern sense. Despite the alleged demise of placer mining after 1866, some 2,000 miners were still working claims along a 150-mile front from Lytton to Richfield in the Cariboo region in 1891. Hundreds of others were scattered throughout the province.[71] Only a decade later, the census netted over 14,000 miners in what became known as "The Mineral Province of Canada." The vast majority of these miners would have been wage or contract employees of collieries and hard-rock metalliferous mining companies. By 1911, however, mining employment had levelled off at 15,000 and by 1921—admittedly a year of recession in the minerals industry—it had apparently dropped to scarcely more than 10,000. Longerterm trends indicate that even a prosperous mining industry required fewer hands to do more productive work. In 1930, the average British Columbia coal miner produced 20 per cent more coal in a year than a counterpart could have done in 1900, while the average hard-rock miner dug five tons of ore in 1930 for every ton produced in 1900.[72] The same trend was evident in the commercial fishery and, to a lesser extent, in forestry.

MANUFACTURING, CONSTRUCTION AND THE SERVICE SECTOR

Employment in all industries was higher than the census sources quoted here imply. These sources put a sizeable proportion of workers under the heading of "labourers, nothing else specified." This class of worker made up 12 per cent of the gainfully employed in 1891 and again in 1921, while the national figure was rising slowly from 7 to 9.5 per cent. People without recognized skills or regular employments—often low-status immigrants or members of subordinated ethnic groups—were drawn into the province as a by-product of industrialization. In the British Columbia context, demand for unskilled labour was periodically high in building and construction—including railway construction—and consistently high in the sawmilling industry. A nominal list of "labourers" recruited into the army in 1914–1918, however, confirms the impression that members of this class were found everywhere. William Farmer drew his last civilian pay from the Stump Lake Land and Cattle Company of Kamloops; Herbert Grant, from the library of the new University of British Columbia. E. Gull, a steam-shovel hand, was one among dozens of former employees of the railway contractors-cum-loggers, Foley, Welch & Stewart. Usaka Shibuta had been toiling for Canada Western Lumber's Fraser Mills while his Japanese-Canadian countryman, Kato Katamasa, had been engaged in a canning factory.[73]

In 1891, as in other census years, British Columbia had a relatively larger force of construction workers than most other provinces, though this was not so in 1921; building and real estate markets had been flat ever since the collapse of the pre-war boom, and did not recover until the mid-1920s.[74] *Occupational Trends in Canada*, published by the Dominion Bureau of Statistics in the 1930s, provides an historical overview that uses consistent occupational categories, though it leaves out a large body of labourers. This source shows 14.5 per cent of the provincial workforce in manufacturing in 1891, the same percentage as the whole country. For 1921, this source shows the national figure at 13 per cent, and British Columbia's at 11 per cent. For Ontario, by contrast, it shows the manufacturing sector at 16.5 per cent of the workforce in 1891 and 17 per cent in 1921.

Given the many historical and geographical advantages that Ontario had, British Columbia's figures actually seem high. All these figures lead us to the contemporary debate about the federal government's policy of tariff protection for domestic producers that allegedly skewed development in the direction of central Canada. Those who believe that tariff protection hurt British Columbia have overlooked the significant place that manufacturing had in the province's economy.[75] The existence of a sizeable manufacturing sector helps explain the behaviour of British Columbia's electorate, which rejected by wide margins the "western" alternative of reciprocity with the United States in each of the three national elections fought in whole or in part over the issue (1891, 1911 and 1921).[76] The whole National Policy package of tariff and transportation policies may not have been ideal for British Columbia; some policies, incidentally or by design, ran roughshod over provincial economic interests. Nonetheless, it is no accident that a wide range of British Columbia producers favoured "protection for home industries" in one form or another. Even export-oriented groups came to be dependent on protectionist measures like the coal tariff, federal bounties on certain end products from the metalliferous mining and smelting industry (notably lead and zinc), or the provincial "manufacturing condition" that tied private rights to cut timber on public lands with the obligation to mill the lumber locally.

Unlike the Prairie provinces, British Columbia had entered Confederation with a peculiar combination of small-scale or artisanal industry and the beginning of large-scale enterprise in resource-related activities. At the census of 1881, British Columbia possessed spectacular per capita ratios of output and investment in manufacturing, though the data are to some extent illusory.[77] Subsequent years witnessed real and sustained growth in manufacturing output. In 1880, British Columbia contributed 1.27 per cent of the net value of Canadian manufactures (or "value-added"—the value of the finished good minus the cost of raw materials); in 1890, 4.61 per cent, more than commensurate with the growth of its share of the national population.[78] Alexander Begg's *History of British Columbia*, published in 1894, remarked:

> From the census of 1891 it appears that although British Columbia is not gener-ally considered a manufacturing province its returns show it to be the largest manufacturing province in the Dominion, relative to population. From the same source it is learned that the value of machinery and tools in use in industrial establishments is $3,248,570 and that the number of employees has increased 300 per cent during the ten years preceding the census.[79]

Begg was a typical National Policy advocate, persuaded by the apparently objective evidence of tariff-supported growth that the census provided. Free traders, for their part, argued that the census "padded" the figures for domestic manufacturing by undiscriminating methods of measurement. In response to these objections from the free-trade wing of the Liberal party, the Laurier gov-ernment created the *Postal Census of Manufactures*, a peculiar economic sounding taken at five-year intervals in 1900, 1905, 1910 and 1915. Arbitrarily, the postal census excluded establishments with fewer than five employees, which made hundreds of artisanal shops disappear from statistical view. The postal census does show that the number of manufacturing establishments employing five or more workers doubled (from 392 to 651) from 1900 to 1910, with the average number of employees in these manufacturing establishments rising to a peak of 51.2 in 1910 (more than twice the national average). The postal census's estimate of the province's manufacturing output—5.67 per cent of national output in 1900, 5.35 per cent in 1905, 6.25 per cent in 1910, and 5.17 per cent in 1915—was commensurate with the province's population, which did not exceed 6 per cent of the national population before 1921. Reported capital investment in manufacturing enterprises rose from $22 mil-lions in 1900 to $158 millions in 1915.[80]

Throughout this period, manufacturing employment—using the criteria of *Occupational Trends in Canada* and omitting thousands of labourers—seems to have risen more steadily than employment in areas such as construction or mining: from 7,000 in 1891 to 21,000 in 1911 and 24,500 in 1921. These fig-ures miss a surge in manufacturing during the First World War, a phenomenon explained by British Columbia's relatively generous (or "fair") share of federal spending for munitions and, especially, shipbuilding. (West-coast contractors launched 118 wood-and-steel-hulled vessels for the Imperial Munitions Board between 1916 and 1919.) In 1917 the Dominion Bureau of Statistics estimated that British Columbia manufacturing establishments of all sizes employed as many as 37,000 workers. Manufacturers in British Columbia contributed an extraordinary 8.7 per cent of net national manufacturing output in 1919, the year the shipyards were wound down. By 1918, capital investment in provincial manufacturing totalled $240 million, declining to $220 million in 1920.

Statistics can only suggest the economic disruption that the end of the war brought. Unemployment among British Columbia trade unionists rose from less than 1 per cent in June 1918 to nearly 25 per cent in June 1921; the total number of trade unionists in "manufacturing and mechanical industries" plummeted from 6,352 in February 1919 to 2,865 in December 1920.[81]

Examination of the employment returns from the 1911 census shows the resource-related nature of manufacturing in the pre-war period. Forty per cent of the people employed in manufacturing were in industries directly tied to resource extraction: for example, there were 4,000 saw and shingle workers, 1,200 smelter workers and 3,000 fish-processing workers. In other manufacturing, employment was distributed over a wide range of occupations. Artisanal enterprises still flourished. British Columbia had a handful of agricultural implement makers, for example, but no factory like Toronto's Massey-Harris.

As was the case in Ontario or Quebec, a large fraction of the manufacturing sector was dedicated to the processing of agricultural products. Food and allied products, not including fish, employed 1,600 people in 1911. This number might have been higher if censuses had been taken in the autumn instead of the spring. Leather goods employed another 600; Leckies Manufacturing, a "palatial" six-storey shoe factory, had recently opened in Vancouver. There appeared to be fewer than 100 clothing and textile workers in British Columbia in 1911; the next year, however, MacKay, Smith, Blair and Company, established importers of British woollens, had developed in Vancouver "a manufacturing business of considerable importance, making the Pride of the West brand of shirts, tweed trousers, overalls, tents, and also hand-knitted sweaters." Seemingly marginal enterprises set their collective face forwards in the optimistic atmosphere of the times.[82]

Metal works of all kinds employed 1,000 blacksmiths, and another 3,000 moulders, pattern makers, machinists, boiler makers, engine builders, or tool-and-die specialists in 1911. That the province possessed such skilled workers was an industrial asset of no small importance. The evidence from wartime experience shows that even a relatively small cadre could be swiftly and effectively mobilized for large-scale endeavours; together with a surplus from the building trades, they formed the core of a workforce of 6,000 to 8,000 in new coastal shipyards in 1917–1919. In peacetime, metal-trades workers tended, mended and manufactured a panoply of industrial equipment including stationary steam engines used in sawmills, or portable "donkeys" used in logging.

The river and inland water transport industry reveals typical patterns in the regional division of labour. Early equipment on such vessels as the famous CPR construction workhorse SS *Skuzzy* included British Columbia-built engines. Later operators found it more convenient to purchase engines from established central Canadian and American firms. The sternwheelers and steam tugs that plied the inland waterways, however, were more often than not built from scratch in British Columbia shipyards. Of sixty-seven vessels identified in the records of this industry between 1885 and 1940, forty-four had British Columbia-built hulls and superstructures.[83]

The Albion Iron Works was among the firms that challenged the provincial trend to specialized piecework. Effectively embracing the National Policy on its own terms, Albion was western Canada's largest engineering-type enterprise at the turn of the century. Founded in 1862, Albion is also a good example of an enterprise that *could* have developed into a sophisticated industry, but did not. At its peak, the Victoria plant employed 230 craftworkers and covered a site of 3.5 acres. Albion workers produced some railway equipment, pipes for water-works, and a well-known line of cast-iron stoves, which found a market as far away as China. By 1882, the chief stockholders in the company, Robert Dunsmuir and R. P. Rithet, were coal owners and merchants. In the 1880s and 1890s, Albion diversified into the manufacture of stationary and marine boilers and attempted to do the same in the field of mining machinery. In the early 1900s, however, the company folded, the victim of financial mismanagement and railway freight rates that gave a competitive edge to eastern engineering firms. In the emerging world of the consolidated, professionally managed corporation and the national marketplace, Albion Iron failed to take off.[84]

Although employment in both the primary and secondary sectors of the British Columbia economy tended to stagnate or decline over time, the relative size of the tertiary or services sector increased. The categories of "trade and finance," "clerical," "transportation," "professional," and "service" occupations are in many ways the most frustratingly inconsistent of census classifications. They include a large number of crucially important activities that either added value to commodities by moving them, selling them, or administering the bureaucracy of industrial production, or contributed to the development of social capital by serving human needs. These categories totalled less than a quarter of the census workforce in 1891, but over one-third of it in 1921. Figure 13, focussing on women and girls, shows subtle changes in the occupational structure. Women and girls were much more likely to be enumerated as gainful workers in 1921 than they had been in 1891. Paid work was becoming accept-able and even obligatory for unmarried women. By the early decades of the twentieth century women were finding work in offices, retail shops, or in "pro-fessional" activities—like school teaching, or hospital or private nursing—as well as in domestic service, though their wages and salaries were lower than those of the men in most occupations.[85] The principal of Vancouver's Fairview High School, one of the new vocationally oriented institutions of the post-war period, took pains to remind his students, "Many of you will find employment in retail stores or wholesale offices. You will then be producers in an economic sense and can render a true service to the public. Efficient workers speed the nation's business . . . . Cheerful, well-trained sales clerks assist the consumer . . . . As a member of either group you will have reason to take pride in your work and demand public respect."[86]

Figure 13: Occupation of Women and Girls, 14 Years or Older, Enumerated by the Census, 1921

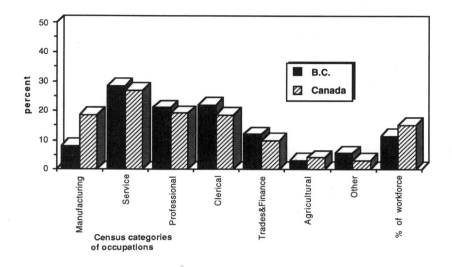

The "Agricultural" category included sons of farmers over 14 years but excluded wives and daughters; "Fishing and Trapping" excluded "nomadic Indians" in 1891 and "Indians living on reserves" in 1921; "Service" included most realms of public, domestic and personal services; "Clerical" included clerical workers in governments service in 1921; "Labouring, n.e.s." is the category of "Labourers, nothing else specified" or *Ouvriers sans metier*.

THE EXPECTATION OF GROWTH

The economic history of post-Confederation British Columbia does not fit a single-dimensional theory of development, or of dependency. While the main theme is the expansion of a capitalist frontier, with "production for profit" displacing "production for use," subordinate themes run in many directions. The resource economy of the late nineteenth and early twentieth centuries had no given set of characteristics. It was a dynamic process of exploitation shaped by the environment, markets, state policies, patterns of investment, the application of technology and the choices that individuals made. Growth was accompanied by dubious and failed experiments, the wastage of natural and human resources, and the massive leakage of economic benefits outside the region. Moreover, growth was uneven and problematic long before the deepest round of cyclical crises in the 1930s. This is not even to mention the unequal distribution of wealth among British Columbia's economic classes. But the province's economic communities were increasingly numerous and diverse; and development depended on the speculative enterprise of ordinary British Columbians of all backgrounds. The expectation of growth was a vital force and it infected the whole society. Militant reformers might still imagine that a new society could discard "production for profit," yet even the discourses of socialism or radical agrarianism voiced within the province were products of the capitalist revolution taking place.

SOURCES FOR FIGURES

Figure 1, p. 214: British Columbia, Reports of the Minister of Mines (various).

Figure 2, p. 215: British Columbia, Reports of the Minister of Mines (various).

Figure 3, p. 221: Canada, Commision of Conservation, H. N. Whitford and Roland D. Craig, *Forests of British Columbia* (Ottawa, 1918): 175-176.

Figure 4., p. 222: Robert E. Cail, *Land, Man and the Law: The Disposal of Crown Lands in British Columbia, 1871-1913* (Vancouver, 1974): 271.

Figure 5, p. 223: Economic Council of British Columbia, *Statistics of Industry in British Columbia, 1871-1934* (Victoria, 1935), Table FY1.

Figure 6, p. 227: Various.

Figure 7, p. 229: *Report of the Royal Commission on the Tree-Fruit Industry of British Columbia* (Victoria, 1958): 226.

Figure 8, p. 229: *Report of the Royal Commission on the Tree-Fruit Industry of British Columbia* (Victoria, 1958): 225.

Figure 9, p. 230: Province of British Columbia, *Manual of Provincial Information* (1929): 80.

Figure 10, p. 234: Province of British Columbia, *Manual of Provincial Information* (1929): 142.

Figure 11, p. 235: Various

Figure 12, p. 237: Dominion Bureau of Statistics, Census Branch, *Occupational Trends in Canada, 1891-1931* (Ottawa, 193?), courtesy of Mr John Lutz.

Figure 13, p. 243: Dominion Bureau of Statistics, Census Branch, *Occupational Trends in Canada, 1891-1931* (Ottawa, 193?), courtesy of Mr John Lutz.

NOTES

The writer acknowledges the collaboration of all other members of the *Pacific Province* team in the construction of this text, particularly general editor Hugh Johnston. Researcher David Roth made a key contribution, especially to the "Mining and Energy" section, as did Stephen Gray to the forestry section.

1. See R. A. J. McDonald, "Victoria, Vancouver, and the Economic Development of British Columbia, 1886-1914," reprinted in W. Peter Ward and R. A. J. McDonald, eds., *British Columbia: Historical Readings* (Vancouver: Douglas & McIntyre, 1981): 369-395; J. M. S. Careless, "The Business Community in the Early Development of Victoria, British Columbia," in J. Friesen and H. K. Ralston, eds., *Historical Essays on British Columbia* (Toronto: McClelland and Stewart; Carleton Library, 1976): 177-200; R. E. Caves and R. H. Holton, "An Outline of the

Economic History of British Columbia, 1881-1951," *ibid.*, 152-153, passim; Daniel T. Gallacher, "Men, Money and Machines: Studies Comparing Factors of Production in British Columbia's Coal Industry to 1891." (Ph.D. dissertation, University of British Columbia, 1979); Duncan Stacey, *Sockeye and Tin Plate: Technological Change in the Fraser River Canning Industry, 1871-1912* (Victoria: B.C. Provincial Museum, 1982).

2. Martin Robin, *The Company Province: The Rush For Spoils, 1871-1933* (Toronto: McClelland and Stewart, 1971): 12; Paul Phillips, "The Underground Economy: The Mining Frontier to 1920," in Rennie Warburton and David Coburn, eds., *Workers, Capital, and the State in British Columbia: Selected Papers* (Vancouver: University of British Columbia Press, 1988): 35-54; G. W. Taylor, *Mining: The History of Mining in British Columbia* (Saanichton: Hancock House, 1978): chapter 7.

3. G. W. Taylor, *Timber: History of the Forest Industry in B.C.* (Vancouver: J. J. Douglas, Ltd., 1975); Donald MacKay, *Empire of Wood: The MacMillan Bloedel Story* (Vancouver: Douglas & McIntyre, 1982).

4. R. E. Gosnell quoted in Allan Smith, "The Writing of British Columbia History," reprinted in Ward and McDonald, *British Columbia: Historical Readings* 8; H. V. Nelles, ed., *Philosophy of Railroads*, by T. C. Keefer (1853: reissued with an introduction, University of Toronto Press, 1972).

5. F. W. Howay, W. N. Sage, and H. F. Angus, *British Columbia and the United States* (Toronto: The Ryerson Press, 1942): 263.

6. For later chapters see Patricia E. Roy, "Progress, Prosperity and Politics: The Railway Policies of Richard McBride," *B.C. Studies* 47 (Autumn 1980): 3-28; Frank Leonard, "A Thousand Blunders: The Grand Trunk Pacific Railway Company and Northern British Columbia, 1902-1919." (Ph.D. thesis, York University, 1988.)

7. Figure from Christopher Armstrong and H. V. Nelles, *Monopoly's Moment: The Organization and Regulation of Canadian Utilities, 1830-1900* (Philadelphia: Temple University Press, 1986): 116.

8. Homer quoted in Robert E. Cail, *Land, Man, and the Law: The Disposal of Crown lands in British Columbia, 1871-1913* (Vancouver: University of British Columbia Press, 1974): 139-140; see also James B. Hedges, *Building the Canadian West: The Land and Colonization Policies of the Canadian Pacific Railway* (New York: Russell and Russell, 1939) and John Eagle, *The Canadian Pacific Railway and the Development of Western Canada 1896-1914* (Montreal: McGill-Queen's Press, 1989). Other instructive works include A. M. Sakolski, *The Great American Land Bubble* (New York: Harper, 1932) and Gustavus Myers, *The History of Canadian Wealth* (Chicago: Chas Kerr, 1914).

9. Cail, "Appendix C"; Albert Metin, *La Columbie Britannique: Étude sur la colonisation au Canada* (Paris: Armand Colin, 1908), Carte d'ensemble, "showing railway cadasters" and "Lots donné au CPR dans le sud"; Boam, *British Columbia*, 426.

10. Pierre Berton, *The National Dream: The Great Railway 1871-1881* (Toronto: McClelland and Stewart, 1970); David Cruise and Alison Griffiths, *Lords of the Line: The Men who built the CPR* (New York: Viking, 1988); Matthew Josephson, *The Robber Barons: The Great American Capitalists 1861-1901* (New York: Harcourt, Brace & Co., 1934): vii.

11. On Dunsmuir and the E & N (1884-1905) see Robert D. Turner, *Vancouver Island Railroads* (San Marino, Calif: Golden West Books, 1974); Lynne Bowen, *Three Dollar Dreams* (Lantzville: Oolichan Books, 1987): 243-247.

12. Quotation from Eric Hobsbawm, *The Age of Empire, 1875-1914* (London: Weidenfeld and Nicholson, 1987): 34-35; A. A. den Otter, "Nationalism and the Pacific Scandal," *Canadian Historical Review* LXIX, no. 3 (September 1988): 315-339.

13. P. B. Waite, *Canada: 1874-1896: Arduous Destiny* (Toronto: McClelland and Stewart, 1971): 25-31, 54-61; Norbert MacDonald, *Distant Neighbours: A Comparative History of Seattle and Vancouver* (Lincoln: University of Nebraska Press, 1988): 28, passim.

14. J. T. Saywell, *Across Mountain and Muskeg: Building the Canadian Transportation System* (Ottawa: Economic Council of Canada, 1975): 41-45, passim; For a list of the original directors, *Canadian Pacific Facts and Figures* (Montreal: General Publicity Department, 1937): 14.

15. Patricia E. Roy, "A Choice Between Evils: The Chinese and the Construction of the Canadian Pacific Railway in British Columbia" in Hugh A. Dempsey, ed., *The cpr West* (Vancouver: Douglas & McIntyre, 1984): 13-34; see also Anthony B. Chan, *Gold Mountain: The Chinese in the New World* (Vancouver: New Star Books, 1983); British Columbia Archives and Records Service, Vertical Files, "Andrew Onderdonk."

16. Jack Scott, *Sweat and Struggle: Working Class Struggles in Canada, 1789-1899* (Vancouver: New Star Books, 1974): 185-194. T. D. Regher, "Letters From the End of Track," in Dempsey, cpr *West*, 48-51; P. Turner Bone, *When the Steel Went Through: Reminiscences of a Railroad Pioneer* (Toronto: MacMillan, 1947): 104-106.

17. John S. Church, "Mining Companies in the West Kootenay-Boundary Regions of British Columbia 1890-1900," Appendix E. (M.A. thesis, University of British Columbia, 1961); D. G. Paterson, "European Finance Capital and British Columbia: An Essay on the Role of the Regional Entrepreneur," *B.C. Studies* 21 (Spring 1974): 33-47.

18. "Class of Crooks," from *The Ledge* (Fernie), 4 January 1905; "Worthless Stock" from Edward L. Affleck, *Kootenay Pathfinders* (Vancouver: The Alexander Nicolls Press, 1976): 25; Charles Hanbury-Williams, "In the Kootenays," *Blackwoods Magazine* (April 1903): 501.

19. "The Orphan Boy Swindle," *Mining Critic*, 6 May 1897; "Orphan Boy Prosecution," *ibid.*, 15 January 1898.

20. National Archives of Canada, Clifford Sifton Papers, vol. 95, 74417-8, private correspondence re: B.C. Companies Act and mining investment, J. M. Chrysler to Sifton, n.d. 1900.

21. British Columbia Archives and Records Service, G. T. German mss, "The Stock Exchange of Rossland, 1897-1905," typescript 21 pp.

22. Quoted in Church, "Mining Companies, 1890-1900," 146.

23. R. E. Gosnell, A. *History of British Columbia* (Victoria: Lewis Publishing, 1906): 61, 278-280.

24. See Cole Harris, "Industry and the Good Life Around Idaho Peak," *Canadian Historical Review* XVVI, no. 3 (September 1985): 315-343; quotation from Public Archives of British Columbia, RG 441, vol. 25, F.5. "Resolutions Passed by the Silverton Miners Union," 10 June 1899.

25. S. S. Fowler, "Early Smelters in British Columbia," *BC Historical Quarterly* 11, no. 3 (1939), reprinted in *The Cominco Magazine* 1, 5 (June 1940): 1-24; Vancouver City Archives, add mss 108, David Oppenheimer, "Address to the Board of Trade," 1888, "Vancouver City; its Progress and Industries," 1889.

26. Thos. Shaughnessy quoted in Church, "Mining Companies, 1890-1900," 156; Robert Chodos, *The cpr: A Century of Corporate Welfare* (Toronto: James Robert Lewis & Samuel, 1973): 59-72; D. J. Hall, *Clifford Sifton: The Young Napoleon, 1861-1900* (Vancouver: University of British Columbia Press, 1982): 150-157; see also sources listed in note below.

27. On the Crow's Nest line and the "greatest mining camp in the World" see J. W. Dafoe, *Clifford Sifton in Relation to his Times* (Toronto: MacMillan, 1931): 145-146; text of agreement published in the Toronto *Globe*, 12 August 1897. On Consolidated Mining and "modern mining," see Logan Hovis, "The Origins of 'Modern Mining' in the Western Cordillera, 1880-1930." (Paper read at the Second Canadian Business History Conference, Victoria, 1988.) Jeremy Mouat, "Mining in the Settler Dominions; A Comparative Study of the Industry in Three Communities, 1880s — First World War." (Ph.D. thesis, University of British Columbia, 1988), "speculative element" from *ibid.*, 148.

28. See John Douglas Belshaw, "Mining Technique and Social Division on Vancouver Island, 1848-1900," *British Journal of Canadian Studies* 1:1 (June 1986): 45-65; Jeremy Mouat, "The Politics of Coal: A Study of the Wellington Miners" Strike of 1890-1," *B.C. Studies* 77 (Spring 1988): 3-29.

29. Adele Perry and Allen Seager, "Mining the Connections: Structure and Experience in a Nineteenth Century Coalfield." (Paper read at the B.C. Studies/Atlantic Canadian Studies Conference, St. John's Newfoundland, 1992.)

30. A prominent Canadian imperialist devoted an entire chapter of one nineteenth-century book to the alleged strategic signifcance of Canadian coal. George Parkin, *The Great Dominion* (London: MacMillan, 1895): chapter IV, "Coal."

31. "To give one instance: the mileage from Fernie, B.C. to Winnipeg is approximately the same as that from Sydney, N.S. to Montreal. But the rates are $5.10 and $3.80 respectively." Martin Nordegg, *The Fuel Problem of Canada* (Toronto: MacMillan, 1930): 45; see also Ken Cruikshank, *Close Ties: Railways, Government and the Board of Railway Commissioners, 1851-1933* (Montreal & Kingston: McGill-Queen's University Press, 1991): chapter 8-9.

32. An early study of fuel consumption on the railways showed that even the former E & N railway ran on oil by 1914. W. J. Dick, *Conservation of Coal in Canada* (Canada Commission of Conservation, 1914) map opposite p. 32. Documents relating to the long-standing controversy over railway fuel policy include Justice M. A. Macdonald, *Report of the Coal and Petroleum Products Commission* (Victoria, 1938) III: 130-140; *Submission of the Canadian Pacific Railway to the Royal Commission on Coal* (Ottawa, 1945): 18-19. Canadian National Railways Research Library, Montreal.

33. On Hanbury's mill see G. W. Taylor, *Timber*, 101; for the Moody docks, G. W. Taylor, *Builders of British Columbia; An Industrial History* (Victoria: Morriss Publishing): 173.

34. Maureen D. Taylor, "Development of the Electricity Industry in British Columbia." (M.A. dissertation, University of British Columbia, 1965): 21, passim.

35. For an overview of hydro development and policy see Arthur V. White, *The Water Powers British Columbia* (Canada, Commission of Conservation, 1919); where not otherwise indicated, the following data has been taken from this source. For public power and the "trusts," H. V. Nelles, "Public Ownership of Electrical Utilities in Ontario and Manitoba," *Canadian Historical Review* LVII, no. 4 (1976): 461-484; Christopher Armstrong and H. V. Nelles, *Monopoly's Moment: The Organization and Regulation of Canadian Utilities, 1830-1900* (Philadelphia: Temple University Press, 1986).

36. The definitive scholarly history of the company remains Patricia E. Roy, "The British Columbia Electric Railway Company: A British Company in British Columbia." (Ph.D. dissertation, University of British Columbia, 1970); see also Brian Kelly and Daniel Francis, *Transit in British Columbia: The First Hundred Years* (Madeira Park: Harbour Publishing, 1990).

37. G. W. Taylor, *Builders of B.C.*, 181.

38. On the Stave Lake project see also Nelles and Armstrong, *Monopoly's Moment*, 99-100; Vancouver City Archives, B.C. Electric Papers, fol., "General History," mss, 17-18.

39. Canada, Commission of Conservation, *Ninth Annual Report* (Ottawa, 1917): 15; Vancouver City Archives, B.C. Electric Papers, f. 4, "Appraisal of Property . . . June 30, 1939"; interviews, former gas and tram workers Clifford Ray and Russell Hicks.

40. MacMillan quoted in Gordon Hak, "On the Fringes: Capital and Labour in the Forest Economics of the Port Alberni and Prince George Districts, British Columbia, 1910-1939." (Ph.D. dissertation, Simon Fraser University, 1986): 1; where not otherwise specified statistics of forestry are taken from H. N. Whitford and Roland D. Craig, *The Forests of British Columbia* (Canada, Commission of Conservation, 1918): 238-241, passim.

41. *British Columbia's Forest Policy, Speech by the Hon. William R. Ross* (pamphlet, n.p., 1912): 1, 21. Recent surveys of forest policy and administration in British Columbia include William McKillop and Walter J. Mead, eds., *Timber Policy Issues in British Columbia* (Vancouver: University of British Columbia Press, 1987); R. Peter Gillis and Thomas R. Roach, "A Touch of Pinchotism: Forestry in British Columbia, 1912-1939," in Roy, *British Columbia Selected Readings*, 72-107; Jeremy Wilson, "Forest Conservation in British Columbia; Reflections on a Barren Political Debate," *B.C. Studies* 76 (1987/8): 3-32. Stephen Gray, "Forest Policy and Administration, 1888-1912." (Unpublished manuscript, courtesy of the author); Stephen Gray, "The Government's Timber Business: Forest Policy and Administration in British Columbia, 1912-1928," *B.C. Studies* 81 (Spring 1989): 24-49.

42. British Columbia Archives and Records Service, GR 441, Box 25, F. 1048, correspondence re: Pulp Frauds, J. S. Emerson, President B.C. Loggers' Association to Premier Richard McBride, 10 January 1905. For a devastating public critique of pulpwood speculators and bankrupt paper promoters see the Ministerial Union of the Lower Mainland, *The Crisis in B.C.: An Appeal for Investigation* (pamphlet, E.C. Appleby, 1915): 17-18. Estimate of the local market found in "Tariff Commission Sits: Important Statements by Millmen and Others," *British Columbia Lumberman and Contractor* 2, no. 10 (October 1905).

43. Hak, "On the Fringes," 46-47; Elizabeth Lees, "Business Not as Usual: Shipbuilding in British Columbia, 1917-1920." (Paper read at the Canadian Historical Association Annual Meeting, Windsor, Ont., 1988): 3-4.

44. "Most costly of our industries" from the British Columbia Workmen's Compensation Board, *Fifteenth Annual Report* (1931), quoted in Hak, "On the Fringes," 9.

45. On industrial development in the woods, Richard Rajala, "Technical and Managerial Control in the West Coast Lumber Industry." (Unpublished paper, University of Victoria, 1986); "The Emergence of the Profession of Logging Engineering on the West Coast." (Paper read at the Second Canadian Business History Conference, Victoria, 1988.) The appearance of a farmer-owned mill at Hutton alarmed some circles but as the *Nelson Daily News* prophetically commented: "A few more mills so operated would be sufficient to demonstrate to the prairie farmers that if they are paying more for their lumber than they should, this is not because (our) lumbermen . . . are making an undue profit." Quoted in Hak, "On the Fringes," 78-79.

46. Whitford and Craig, *Forests of British Columbia*, 1; David J. Hall, *Clifford Sifton: The Lonely Eminence 1901-1929* (Vancouver: University of British Columbia Press, 1985): chapter 11, "The Commission of Conservation, 1909-1921."

47. Diane Newell, *The Development of the Pacific Salmon-Canning Industry: A Grown Man's Game* (Montreal: McGill-Queen's Press, 1989): xi.

48. Harry Keith Ralston, "The 1900 strike of Fraser River Sockeye Salmon Fishermen." (M.A. thesis, University of British Columbia, 1965.) For a first-hand account of class and communal conflicts in the salmon fishery see Rolf Knight and Maya Koizuma, *A Man of Our Times: The Life History of a Japanese Canadian Fisherman* (Vancouver: New Star Books, 1979). The particularities of salmon, halibut and other species are emphasized in Frank W. Millerd, "Windjammers to Eighteen Wheelers: The Impact of Changes in Transportation Technology on the Development of British Columbia's Fishing Industry," *B.C. Studies* 78 (Summer 1988): 28-52. Less well known are the circumstances of shoreworkers in the fishing industry, who were unorganized and collectively voiceless in this period: see Alicja Muszynski, "Race and Gender: Structural determinants in the Formation of British Columbia's salmon cannery labour force," in Gregory S. Kealey, ed., *Class, Gender and Region: Essays in Canadian Historical Sociology* (St. John's: Committee on Canadian Labour History, 1988): 103-120.

49. R. E. Gosnell, *The Year Book of British Columbia, 1911 and Manual of Provincial Information* (Victoria: Government of B.C., 1911): 202-203.

50. The Hell's Gate incident was described as "the greatest disaster that has been recorded in the history of the fishing industry in the world." J. P. Babcock, "Salmon Fishery of the Fraser River District" (Canada, *Commission of Conservation, Ninth Annual Report* [1917]): 147.

51. Quoted in James Conley, "Relations of Production and Collective Action in the Salmon Fishery, 1900-1925," in Warburton and Coburn, *Workers, Capital and the State*, 99.

52. Quoted in Donald G. Paterson, "The North Pacific Seal Hunt, 1886-1910: Rights and Regulations," in Ward and McDonald, *British Columbia: Historical Readings*, 343.

53. *Ibid.*, 343-366; R. C. Brown and Ramsay Cook, *Canada 1896-1921: A Nation Transformed* (Toronto: McClelland and Stewart, 1974): 36-37.

54. See Jean Barman, *The West Beyond the West* (Toronto: University of Toronto Press, 1991): 186; Paul Koroscil, "Boosterism and the Settlement Process in the Okanagan Settlement, 1890-1914," *Canadian Papers in Rural History*, 73-103. Koroscil, "Soldiers, Settlement, and Development in British Columbia, 1915-1930." An early overview of the topic is Margaret Ormsby, "Agricultural Development in British Columbia." [1945], reprinted in Dickson M. Falconer, ed., *British Columbia: Patterns in Economic, Political, and Cultural Development* (Victoria: Camosun College, 1982): 152-165.

55. Vancouver City Archives, Add. mss. 71, Henry Allan Bulwer, letter to his father, n.d. 1887 (Foolscape, handwritten, 7 pp.); See also Patrick Dunae, *Gentlemen Emigrants: From the British Public Schools to the Canadian Frontier* (Vancouver: Douglas & McIntyre, 1981): especially 113-115. For the Dominion Farm at Agassiz, see Boam, *British Columbia*, 286.

56. Ormsby, "Agricultural Development," 160.

57. Quotations from H. W. E. Canavan, "Irrigation," in Boam, *British Columbia*, 301-302, Dean E. D. MacPhee, Commissioner, *Report of the Royal Commission on the Tree Fruit Industry of British Columbia* (Victoria: Government of British Columbia, October 1958): 22. Unpublished literature on the orchard community includes Margaret Ormsby, "A Study of the Okanagan Valley of British Columbia." (M.A. thesis, University of British Columbia, 1932); David Dendy, "One Huge Orchard: Okanagan Land and Development Companies before the Great War." (B.A. Hons thesis, University of Victoria, 1976); and Jane Sproule, "The Polarization of

Okanagan Fruit Farming Communities and the 1955 Packing House Workers' Strike." (M.A. thesis, Simon Fraser University, 1991.)

58. See W. L. Morton, ed., *God's Galloping Girl: The Peace River Diaries of Monica Storrs 1929-1931* (Vancouver: University of British Columbia Press, 1979).

59. David H. Breen, *The Canadian Prairie West and the Ranching Frontier 1874-1924* (Toronto: University of Toronto Press, 1983): 10; M. A. Ormsby, ed., *A Pioneer Gentlewoman in British Columbia: The Recollections of Susan Allison* (Vancouver: University of British Columbia Press, 1976).

60. Gregory E. G. Thomas, "The British Columbia Ranching Frontier, 1858-1896." (M.A. thesis, University of British Columbia, 1976): 131-132, passim; Nina Wooliams, *Cattle Ranch*.

61. Robin, *Rush for Spoils*, 174.

62. R. E. Gosnell, "History of Farming," in Adam Short and Arthur G. Doughty, eds., *Canada and its Provinces* (Toronto: Glasgow, Brook, 1914-1917) xii: 551; Ian MacPherson, "Creating Stability Amid Degrees of Marginality: Divisions in the Struggle for Orderly Marketing in British Columbia, 1900-1940," *Canadian Papers in Rural History* vii (1990): 310, 319; Barman, *The West Beyond the West*, 243.

63. Early data on cargo exports are drawn together in C. James Taylor, *The Heritage of the British Columbia Forest Industry* (Ottawa: National Historic Parks and Sites, 1987). Significant customers in 1869 included Australia, China and Peru, all taking more than 1 million board feet. *Ibid.*, 29.

64. Comprehensive coal statistics were routinely gathered in the annual reports of the British Columbia Minister of Mines, after 1874. "Home consumption," including railway and steamer coal, typically accounted for 17 to 26 per cent of annual output in the period 1880-1895. On the significance of firewood, see survey results published in Canada, Commission of Conservation, *Report of Committees on Lands, Fisheries, Game and Minerals* (Ottawa: The Mortimer Company, 1911): 445.

65. R. E. Gosnell, *British Columbia; A Digest of Reliable Information Regarding its Natural Resources and Industrial Possibilities* (Vancouver: News-Advertiser Printing and Publishing, 1890): 1, 18, gives the Indian salmon food fishery in 1889 a value of $2.7 million; the salmon-packing industry, $2.4 million; coal mining, $2.5 million; lumber exports, $400,000.

66. For R. E. Gosnell's statistics see Patricia E. Roy, *A History of British Columbia: Selected Readings* (Toronto: Copp Clark Pitman, 1989): 70-71; Fernand Braudel, *The Structure of Everyday Life: Civilization and Capitalism, 15th to 18th Centuries*, vol. 1 (New York: Harper and Row, 1981). One of the few Canadian studies to confront the issue of measured/unmeasured activity in a theoretical way is Marjorie Griffin Cohen, *Women's Work: Markets, and Economic Development in Nineteenth-Century Ontario* (Toronto: University of Toronto Press, 1988).

67. See Douglas McCalla, ed., *Perspectives on Canadian Economic History* (Toronto: Copp Clark Pitman Ltd., 1987): 200-242.

68. Canada, Department of Labour, *Report of the Board of Inquiry into the Cost of Living* (Ottawa: The King's Printer, 1915): x, passim. Taking the average prices of 272 commodities, 1890-1899, as 100, the resulting index of prices surpassed 110 in 1904, 120 in 1906, 130 in 1911, and 135 in 1913. This inflation was "moderate" in comparison with 1915-1920, when the cost of living may have increased by 60 per cent or more. See E. A. Bartlett, "Real Wages and the Standard of Living in Vancouver, 1901-1929," *B.C. Studies* 51 (Autumn 1981): 3-62.

69. See Peter Baskerville and Eric Sager, "The First National Unemployment Survey: Unemployment and the Canadian Census of 1891," *Labour/le Travail* 23 (1989): 171-178.

70. Daniel Drache, "The Formation and Fragmentation of the Canadian Working Class, 1880-1920," *Studies in Political Economy* 15 (Fall 1984): 43-90.

71. In an unpublished study (Simon Fraser University, 1988) researcher Marilyn Janzen was able to identify most of the 4,700 individuals classified as miners in the 1891 census: 56 per cent worked in collieries; 5 per cent in hard-rock mining, and the remaining 39 per cent were placer miners, "prospectors," etc.

72. Allen Seager, "Miners' Struggles in Western Canada," in Deilan R. Hopkin and Gregory S. Kealey, eds., *Class, Community and the Labour Movement: Wales and Canada, 1850-1930* (Society for Welsh Labour History and the Canadian Committee on Labour History, 1989): 160-198.

73. British Columbia Archives and Records Service, GR 126, Provincial Secretary's Papers, Box 15, F.41, enlistment records filed under "Labourer" (15 pp. foolscap, typed, single-spaced).

74. Carpenters' Pensioners' Association, *Building British Columbia!: The Story of the Carpenters' Union and the Trade Union Movement since 1881* (Vancouver: College Printers, 1979): 21.

75. John Lutz, "The Rise and Fall of Secondary Manufacturing in British Columbia, 1860-1910." (Paper read at the Second Canadian Business History Conference, Victoria, 1988); "Losing Steam: The Boiler and Engine Industry as an Index of British Columbia's Deindustrialization, 1880-1915," *Historical Papers* (Canadian Historical Association, 1988): 168-208.

76. See, for example, John Conway, *The West: The History of a Region in Confederation* (Toronto: Lorimer, 1983): 51-61.

77. Lutz, "The Rise and Fall of Secondary Manufacturing," Allen Seager, "Workers, Class and Industrial Conflict in New Westminster," in Warburton and Coburn, *Workers, Capital and the State in British Columbia*, 117-140.

78. Where not otherwise indicated the statistics on manufacturing production and investment cited here are taken from Stephen F. Kaliski, "The Growth and Development of the Manufacturing Industry in British Columbia." (B.A. Hons thesis, University of British Columbia, 1952.)

79. Alexander Begg, *History of British Columbia From its Earliest Discovery to the Present Time* (Toronto: McGraw-Hill Ryerson reprint, 1972): 564.

80. Economic Council of British Columbia, *Statistics of Industry in British Columbia 1871-1934* (Victoria 1925): tables MG2, FY2.

81. Unemployment among trade unionists was the only available measure of joblessness: see the *Labour Gazette*, November 1921, 139, (Table 1) and regular monthly reports. A typical distribution of union membership within the "manufacturing and mechanical industries" in British Columbia is as follows: metals, machinery and conveyances (2,561); printing and publishing (650), pulp, paper and fibre (560); food, tobacco and liquors (502); oil refining (165); clothing (195); leather (104); jewelry (92), woodwork and furniture (38). *Ibid.*, December 1919, 78-79.

82. "Mackay, Smith, Blair & Co." in Henry J. Boam, ed., *British Columbia: Its History, People, Commerce, Industries and Resources* (London: Sells Ltd., 1912): 183; "A Great British Columbia Industry," *The British Columbia Mining and Engineering Record* (June 1911): 302-303, for boot and shoe.

83. Robert D. Turner, *Sternwheelers and Steamtugs: An Illustrated History of the Canadian Pacific Railway's British Columbia Lake and River Service* (Victoria: Sono Nis Press, 1984).

84. Lutz, "Losing Steam"; see also British Columbia Archives and Records Service, "Albion Iron Works," *Directors' Minute Books*, 1882-1902; K. R. Genn Collection,

vol. 40, fl "Albion Iron Works" (liquidated 8 September 1910); Harry Gregson, *A History of Victoria, 1842-1970* (Victoria: Observer Publishing Company, 1970): 146.

85. See Elaine Bernard, *The Long Distance Feeling: A History of the Telecommunications Workers Union* (Vancouver: New Star Books, 1982); Marjorie MacMurchy, "Women and the Nation," in J. O. Millar, ed., *The New Era in Canada* (Toronto: J. M. Dent & Sons, 1917): 212.

86. Graham Bruce, Principal, Fairview High School, *et al.*, *Business Fundamentals* (Toronto, Gregg Publishing, 1945): 244.

PART IV

Since the First World War

Chapter 8
PATTERNS OF PROVINCIAL POLITICS SINCE 1916
Robin Fisher and David J. Mitchell

It sometimes seems that British Columbia politics are regarded as a joke, and not even a very funny one. Commentators frequently use catchwords such as "polarization" and "volatile" as substitutes for careful analysis of political developments. Eastern reporters, in particular, sometimes write on west coast politics as a form of light relief from the more important events in Ottawa, Ontario and Quebec. In the current climate of contempt for politicians, even British Columbians themselves find it difficult to take provincial politics very seriously. Historians have not helped much either. The current generation of historical scholarship has concentrated on social and economic themes and there has not been an abundance of thoughtful historical writing on British Columbia politics in the twentieth century.[1] In this context, it might be challenging for students of British Columbia history to see the study of provincial politics as particularly significant.

Yet politics are important. If we believe in democracy, then elections are an expression of the collective opinion and will of British Columbian. The kinds of governments and leaders that we elect reflect something of the provincial character. If politics are an expression of ourselves, then we need to understand politics in order to know ourselves. And it is particularly important for us, as students of history, to see beyond the intriguing details of the particular political moment or personality and seek out the patterns and continuities of this province's politics.

PARTIES AND ELECTIONS

The election of 1916 ended an era in British Columbia politics. The Conservatives had been in power for more than a decade, but their government was running out of steam and tainted with charges of corruption. The old smoothy Richard McBride had been replaced as Conservative leader by William Bowser, who had all the charm of a pit bull. The Liberals, under Harlan Brewster, were better organized, had some strong candidates and looked as though they had some new ideas. At dissolution there were two Liberals, who had recently won by-elections, in the Legislature, but, after the voters had spoken in the general election of 1916, there were thirty-six Liberal members opposed by only nine Conservatives.[2] It looked as though the electorate had voted for a complete change and the Liberals began a quarter-century in which they would be the governing party for all but five years.

There have been other watershed elections in British Columbia since 1916. The 1933 election involved a new party, the Co-operative Commonwealth Federation (later the New Democratic Party), which became a major force in British Columbia politics. This party would, however, have to wait nearly forty years to form a government: in 1933, it was the Liberals who came to power. In 1941, a Coalition government made up of Liberals and Conservatives was elected, and in 1952 Social Credit took over the government for the first time. In each of these four elections there were apparent switches in political direction by the voters. New parties, or in the case of the Liberals in 1933, renewed parties, were elected to power with fresh agendas and mandates for change. In each case the party elected went on to win at least one other election and stay in office for an extended period.

More recently, the swings in political direction have been shorter as new governments have fallen into disfavour more rapidly. The New Democratic Party finally formed a government in 1972, but it lasted for only one term. In 1986 a new, right-wing, revivalist form of Social Credit was elected and then discredited by the next election. The New Democratic Party was elected again in 1991 and, as it approached the end of its first term, appeared unlikely to survive the next election. These electoral swings, whether long or short, contribute to the British Columbia electorate's reputation for volatility.

Figure 1:Premiers of British Columbia 1916–1995

Name	Dates	Party
BREWSTER, Harlan	1916–1918	Liberal
OLIVER, John	1918–1927	Liberal
MACLEAN, John	1927–1928	Liberal
TOLMIE, Simon Fraser	1928–1933	Conservative
PATTULLO, T. Dufferin	1933–1941	Liberal
HART, John	1941–1947	Liberal-Conservative Coalition
JOHNSON, Byron	1947–1952	Liberal-Conservative Coalition
BENNETT, W. A. C.	1952–1972	Social Credit
BARRETT, David	1972–1975	New Democratic
BENNETT, William R.	1975–1986	Social Credit
VANDER ZALM, William	1986–1991	Social Credit
JOHNSTON, Rita	1991–1991	Social Credit
HARCOURT, Michael	1991–1996	New Democratic

THE DECLINE AND FALL OF GOVERNMENTS

Yet change is never absolute. Although the party labels have changed, all four of the major watershed elections of 1916, 1933, 1941 and 1952 were contests between parties that believed in the efficacy of private enterprise and maintaining the status quo and parties that contemplated government intervention and advocated moderate reform. In 1916, for example, the Conservatives ran on their record. In the early years of their mandate they had provided every encouragement to private enterprise to exploit natural resources and develop infrastructure. By the teens of the century, as the economy took a downward turn, they began to think about the consequences of uncontrolled economic growth. To take the case of forestry, private industry began to convince the government that rampant exploitation could not go on forever. The Royal Commission on Timber and Forestry of 1909 and the Forest Act of 1912 were small steps in the direction of controlling the province's most valuable natural resource. None of this went far enough for the Liberals, who, in the campaign of 1916, called for an end to resource give-aways, more government planning, improvement of working conditions and wages, and some minimal provision of social services by government. The Liberals seemed reformist enough to be supported by the socialists in some ridings.[3] In the electoral battles between conservatism and reform that produced long swings, the results have been an even split. Elections were won by reformist Liberal parties in 1916 and 1933 and the conservative Coalition and Social Credit parties in 1941 and 1952.

Of course, governments that stayed in power for more than one term did not necessarily remain the same throughout their tenure. The Liberal administration of 1916 to 1928 is a good example of a government that began with lots of reformist steam, but fizzled out in the 1920s. This pattern would also be repeated throughout the province's political history.

Liberal candidates had campaigned in 1916 on an end to Conservative corruption, clean and open government, and the idea of governing in the interests of all British Columbians rather than just the privileged few. Once in power, it became clear that their commitment to reform went beyond mere election rhetoric. The new government had to deal with a host of problems as the disruptions of war were followed by the demands of reconstruction. The province was faced with major financial problems. The federal government had moved into what had been the provincial preserve of income tax, and the primary extraction industries that normally drove the economy were all in a bad way. In the face of these difficulties, the Liberal government introduced a long list of reformist measures in the early years of its mandate. The province became the first in Canada to establish a Department of Labour, and there was legislation to extend the eight-hour day to a greater number of workers, to improve workers' compensation and working conditions, and to provide a minimum wage for women. Enacting female suffrage in 1917 was the most dramatic move on behalf of women, but the government also established mothers' pensions, maintenance for deserted wives, and made both parents the legal guardians of their children. There was an effort to supervise and regulate public utilities and a good deal of legislation to improve both health and educational services. Provisions were made to open up new areas of the province and to help new settlers, particularly returning soldiers, acquire and develop land. The government also moved to impose some control on the forestry industry, which was now the province's largest, in the interests of acquiring a people's share of the resource revenue. All of these policies were predicated on a belief that government intervention was the best way to deal with the social and economic problems of the province. This bright burst of reform would not, and perhaps could not, last.

Governments never satisfy everyone and may alienate more people the longer they stay in power, particularly in times of economic uncertainty. By the early 1920s, the Liberals were facing pressure from all directions. Even a reformist government could not solve all of the problems of postwar reconstruction and a brief upswing in the provincial economy at the end of the war soon turned to a recession. Many veterans felt that not enough was being done to help them start new lives, workers expressed their dissatisfaction when they went out in support of the Winnipeg General Strike in 1919, and farmers showed that they were unhappy with their lot by forming a new political party, the United Farmers of British Columbia, in 1917. When the Liberals went to the people again in 1920, the overwhelming victory of four years earlier would not be repeated. After the election they were still in a comfortable position with twenty-five seats to the Conservatives' fifteen, but they were no longer new and shining brightly.

The reform impulse grew even dimmer as time went on. The 1920s were an economically uncertain decade even before the stock market crash of 1929 heralded the beginning of the Depression. It seemed to cautious politicians that revenues from the primary resource industries such as forestry were not reliable enough to support an expensive agenda of social reform, and John Oliver, the Liberal leader after the death of Harlan Brewster in 1918, was a very cautious man. He grew increasingly fidgety about the expenditure side of his ministers' annual estimates and demanded that they justify every line. Even the big spending ministers with expansive plans, like Duff Pattullo, the minister of lands, had to admit that "we can move just as fast and no faster than economic conditions will permit."[4]

The Liberals' enthusiasm for reform also diminished in the 1920s because the political challenges came from the right rather than from the left. Support for Labour and Socialist parties declined from 16.15 per cent of the total vote in 1920 to 5.04 per cent in the 1928 election.[5] Meanwhile another political party attracted a brief flurry of attention. The Provincial Party was difficult to define ideologically, but it was certainly to the right of centre. Its leader, in fact if not in name, was a Shaughnessey millionaire named Major-General A. D. McRae. He hijacked the United Farmers of British Columbia and turned its organization to his own purposes, added some disgruntled Conservatives, and held the founding convention of his new party in December 1922. The Provincial Party called in ringing tones for the elimination of corruption and waste in government and an end to the party system, but its interests were those of big business and not the disadvantaged of society.

Business was on the offensive against the Liberals in other ways as well. Through 1923 and 1924 there was, for example, a running battle with the forest industry when the government wanted to raise the timber royalties charged to the forest companies for cutting trees. The Timber Industries Council had developed into a powerful lobby group and it was eventually able to convince the government to retreat from its initial position.

It is hard for a government to focus on reform when it is beset on all sides and in 1924 the Liberal government was given a jolt by the electorate. When the votes were counted a fairly comfortable majority had been transformed into a minority with the support of only slightly more than 30 per cent of the electors. The Liberals had barely squeaked into office because the Conservative and the Provincial parties (which together received nearly 54 per cent of the votes) had split the right-wing vote in half.[6] In the Legislature, the Liberal government only held on with the dubious support of a couple of independent Liberals. It was not a situation likely to produce vigorous government and so it proved: the reform impulse faded away entirely. The premier, John Oliver, died in 1927 and was replaced by John MacLean, a party politician who was long on experience but short on new ideas and charisma. He could not save his government and, in an election the following year, the Liberals were decisively defeated.

It was not entirely a bad thing to lose an election in 1928 for the Conservatives, led by Simon Fraser Tolmie, were now faced with the economic and social consequences of the Great Depression that began in 1929. Tolmie was an amiable man, more at home at a country garden party than in the rough and tumble of British Columbia politics. The Depression posed problems that would defeat stronger leaders and governments than Tolmie and the Conservatives. They stumbled around looking for solutions and then, towards the end of their mandate when people were looking to government for help, they decided that savage cutbacks and reducing government services were the means of reviving a devastated economy. It was not the last time in British Columbia's political history that right-wing doctrine would be served up as a starvation diet to a hungry population. In 1933, the people of British Columbia declined the invitation to dine on such bitter fare.

The 1933 election was a crucial one, not just because it brought a change of government, but also because of the advent of the Co-operative Commonwealth Federation. By election time, the Conservatives were in complete disarray and not a single candidate running under that party label was elected. The real contest was between the Co-operative Commonwealth Federation and the Liberals led by a confident and dynamic Duff Pattullo. Although it ended up with only seven members, the Co-operative Commonwealth Federation, by getting 31 per cent of the popular vote with strong support in the cities and suburbs, announced that it was likely to be a continuing factor in provincial politics. But with thirty-four seats in a legislature of forty-seven, Pattullo and the Liberals were clearly the winners.[7]

The first Pattullo administration offered the most vigorous political response to the Depression of any government in Canada. The new premier firmly believed that the power of the state should be used to redistribute wealth. He did not believe in socialism, but rather in reforming capitalism in order to ensure its continued survival. His government passed legislation to improve wages and working conditions, to assist economic development, to raise the level of welfare and relief, to increase funding to education, and to provide aid to municipalities. Pattullo also tried to convince the federal government to face the problems of the day, for example, by setting up unemployment insurance and improving old age pensions. But the real way out of the Depression for the provincial Liberals was for the government to inject money into the flagging economy by spending on major public works projects such as the Pattullo bridge or the Alaska highway. In fact, nearly all of Pattullo's ideas required his government to spend money and the rub was that it did not have any. And when Pattullo went to Ottawa to raise money from the federal government he usually returned to the west coast empty handed.

Because of the vigorous reformism of their first term in office, the British Columbia Liberals were the only government in Canada to be re-elected during the depths of the economic crisis of the 1930s. Yet it was clear that the second Pattullo administration had run out of reformist steam. Apart from an ongoing effort to impose government regulation on multi-national oil companies in British Columbia, little remained of the reform agenda. Pattullo still wanted to build a highway to Alaska as a way of opening up the northern part of the province, but, as with most things that required federal assistance, he ran into a brick wall in Ottawa. Even after another Liberal, and an old family friend, William Lyon Mackenzie King, became Prime Minister of Canada in 1935, Pattullo could not convince the federal government to assist with any of his expansionist policies. A strong, provincial-rights advocate, Premier Pattullo became increasingly frustrated by the limits of British Columbia's jurisdiction within Canada's federal system. Much of his political energy in his second term of office was expended in the endless struggle to convince Ottawa to take more decisive action to deal with the effects of the Depression. These tussles with the federal government undoubtedly contributed to his unexpected political overthrow in 1941

The Coalition government from 1941 to 1952 was perhaps an example of the reverse trend: an administration that in some respects became more reformist in office. When it was first elected with John Hart, Pattullo's former finance minister, as its leader, the Coalition emphasized the need to downsize government and give the private sector a freer reign in the economy. But when such small "c" conservatism was seen to be out of tune with postwar reconstruction and the development of the welfare state by the Liberal government in Ottawa, the coalition came under the influence of more reformist politicians. The introduction of a hospital insurance scheme in 1949 was a signal of this development, though it also has to be said that the debate within the caucus over first the legislation itself and then its implementation, was indicative of the tensions that ultimately tore the Coalition apart.

Social Credit came to office in 1952 fueled by an initial enthusiasm for and expectation of change. Led by a maverick former Tory, W. A. C. Bennett, Social Credit was, from the start, mildly reformist but also clearly pro-business. The new administration concentrated on keeping Victoria's fiscal house in order and provided moderate support for social programs. In spite of the Social Credit Party's avowedly "free enterprise" bias, the government was decidedly interventionist. For instance, as a result of Premier Bennett's interceding in a labour dispute in 1958, the provincial government ended up purchasing a privately owned ferry service that became the British Columbia Ferry Corporation, the world's largest publicly owned ferry fleet. In 1960, the Social Credit government shocked most observers by expropriating the B.C. Electric Company, thereby creating the British Columbia Hydro and Power Authority. The Socreds also enjoyed boasting about expanding the provincially owned Pacific Great Eastern Railway (later renamed the British Columbia Railway Company) in order to open up the northern Interior of the province.

The Social Credit government made extensive use of Crown corporations as aggressive agents of provincial development. The role of the state, however, was largely limited to providing the infrastructure for the development of British Columbia by private capital. It was no surprise, therefore, when large corporations, particularly those active in the province's resource industries, offered vocal support for Social Credit. Indeed, towards the end of W. A .C. Bennett's twenty years as premier, his government became increasingly identified as a conservative administration committed to the status quo.

PERSONALITY POLITICS

The decline and fall of initially reformist governments is a consistent pattern in British Columbia politics, though other recurring themes have both a descriptive and an explanatory role. For example, personality politics have long dominated the province, with an unusual procession of outgoing, flamboyant characters governing in Victoria. Well before the age of television and electronic news media, that so often exaggerate the role of leadership and turn political leaders into caricatures of themselves, British Columbia was renowned for producing larger-than-life politicians who gave voluble expression to the province's distinctive frontier culture.

Thomas Dufferin Pattullo, who was premier during the tumultuous years from 1933 to 1941, was a case in point. "Duff" Pattullo was assertive and gregarious and he liked nothing better than getting away from Victoria and talking turkey with the people of the Interior and the north. He was born in Ontario in 1873 and headed west as a young man. He worked in Dawson City as a government official and later entered the real estate business. In 1908 he moved to the coastal town of Prince Rupert where he became involved in municipal politics before being elected to the provincial legislature as a Liberal Member of the Legislative Assembly (MLA). For a dozen years Pattullo served as minister of lands, responsible for the province's largest industry: forestry. Between 1928 and 1933, during the bumbling and chaotic administration of Premier Tolmie, Pattullo served as Leader of the Opposition, during which time he revitalized the provincial Liberal party. As premier, after the Grits were returned to office, he led a pugnacious government, shaped largely by the force of his own determined personality. Pattullo was a precise thinker and a clear speaker who reveled in the use of the English language. It was, indeed, his consistency and clarity on some issues that eventually led to his political downfall. The Liberals turned their backs on him when he refused to consider a coalition with the Tories. After he was defeated at a party convention, a Pattullo loyalist made the comment, "His strength is his only weakness."[8] Ousted as Liberal leader and premier, Pattullo was bitter but also prescient when he warned that "the great Liberal party would start downhill and wouldn't come up for a generation."[9] For almost a decade, however, his boisterous voice had been British Columbia's, and he fashioned a strident image for the province that, unlike the provincial Liberal party, has endured.

Pattullo may have been the quintessential British Columbia politician, but not all the province's premiers were Pattullos. In fact, one of the features of personality politics in British Columbia has been the alternating pattern of strong, flamboyant leaders followed by comparatively bland, but efficient administrators. The province seems to require occasional respite from its colourful demagogues.

Thus, when Duff Pattullo was replaced by a Liberal-Conservative coalition, the province was led first by John Hart, a shrewd and cautious Irishman who had served as Pattullo's finance minister, and then by Byron "Boss" Johnson, a genial gentleman of Icelandic origin who succeeded Hart as a compromise candidate among old-time Liberal machine politicians.

The break-up of the coalition led to a watershed electoral contest in 1952, which unexpectedly gave rise to a remarkable political leader: W. A. C. Bennett. Born in rural New Brunswick in 1900, Bennett moved to northern Alberta as a young man and settled in British Columbia's Okanagan Valley during the Depression, where he launched a successful hardware business. He was first elected to the provincial legislature in 1941 and pursued a quixotic political path notable for a long string of failures. Bennett was twice unsuccessful in seeking the leadership of the British Columbia Conservative Party; he lost his bid to go to Ottawa in a 1948 by-election; he failed to attain a coveted Cabinet post. Yet, in 1952, the renegade Tory confounded all observers by becoming the province's first Social Credit premier. He would go on to become British Columbia's longest-serving occupant of the office.[10]

W. A. C. Bennett was influenced by, and to some extent styled himself after, Duff Pattullo. Bennett, however, carried the politics of personality to a new level by pitting his own irrepressible, outgoing disposition directly against those of struggling leaders of other parties. It proved a successful formula, as his party won seven consecutive general elections, sending a legion of impressive opponents to oblivion. Bennett fought issues and argued policy, but most of all he demonstrated a genius for reducing complex questions to a lowest common denominator: the character of the politician espousing the idea. "Wacky" Bennett became as famous for his personality as for his accomplishments as premier. And because his well-developed, somewhat eccentric style dominated public life for so long, personality politics became deeply ingrained in British Columbia. More than ideology, more than political philosophy, it has been powerful personal loyalties, animosities and grudges that have shaped the province's development, its identity and its image abroad.

With the defeat of the Socred administration in 1972, the province's first New Democratic Party government came to office, led by Dave Barrett. A former social worker who had been an MLA for over a decade, Barrett was a generation younger than W. A. C. Bennett. He was, however, no less flamboyant nor outspoken. In fact, having served so long in opposition to Bennett, he appeared to model himself after his old foe, often seeming a political progeny of his ideological nemesis. Public servants in Victoria quietly referred to the new premier as "W. A. C. Barrett."[11]

Although he would serve as New Democratic Party leader for fifteen years, Barrett would occupy the premier's office for only one short but noisy term. In 1975, he surrendered to Bill Bennett, son of W. A. C. This unprecedented family dynasty prolonged the life of Social Credit, with the younger Bennett serving as premier for more than a decade. Early on, Bill Bennett was derided as "Daddy's Boy" and "mini-WAC." In terms of political style, however, it was the gregarious Barrett who actually played the role of "mini-WAC" whereas Bill Bennett's dry almost plodding approach made him more of an "anti-WAC." In this sense, Bill Bennett provided the necessary antidote to the overdose of bombast experienced during the regimes of both his father and Dave Barrett.

By 1986, when the younger Bennett stepped down as premier, the province had endured years of political leadership characterized by the dull language of public administration and the tough message of fiscal restraint. British Columbia seemed to long for a return to personality politics. There was an almost palpable desire for change, for a return to tradition, and possibly some fun and adventure. With Bennett's successor, Bill Vander Zalm, British Columbians got more than they ever bargained for.[12]

Bill Vander Zalm was born in Holland in 1934 and came to Canada following the Second World War, when his family settled in the Fraser Valley. After developing a successful gardening and nursery business, Vander Zalm entered municipal politics in Surrey where he became mayor in 1969. As a controversial, attention-seeking politician, he made headlines by loudly quarrelling with Victoria and by taking strong stands on issues such as nuclear power, marijuana and pornography. Surrey was ridiculed as the only municipality in the land with a foreign policy, and its charismatic mayor clearly had ambitions that went beyond the borders of his suburban community.[13]

Vander Zalm was unsuccessful in an attempt to be elected as a federal Liberal and in 1972 also lost his bid to become leader of the provincial Grits. Undaunted, he joined the new Social Credit coalition under Bill Bennett's leadership and, following the 1975 provincial election, became a controversial, outspoken Cabinet minister. As minister of human resources, Vander Zalm's popularity seemed only to increase when he publicly mused about giving employable welfare recipients shovels if they would not work. Later, as minister of municipal affairs, he committed the single most significant breach of solidarity during Bill Bennett's premiership when he referred to his Cabinet colleagues as "gutless" after they refused to endorse one of his legislative initiatives.

Vander Zalm did not seek re-election in 1983. He returned to his family business, ran for mayor of Vancouver and was soundly beaten by Mike Harcourt. He was generally regarded as a spent political force, until 1986 when Bill Bennett stepped down. Then Vander Zalm became a leading contender to succeed his former boss. In the summer of 1986, at a highly charged and bitterly fought leadership convention at Whistler, Bill Vander Zalm's last-minute, grassroots campaign defeated the assembled establishment forces of the governing Social Credit party. One of the dozen candidates who sought the job, Kim Campbell, warned: "Charisma without substance is a dangerous thing."[14]

Later that year the smiling gardener-premier breezed through a provincial election. Campaigning like a born-again folk hero, he won a solid victory for Social Credit. As premier, however, Vander Zalm became living proof that the qualities and abilities required to attain power are very different from those needed to exercise it competently or responsibly. Although he enjoyed an extended political honeymoon in office, he never consolidated power within his party, which still suffered from unhealed wounds caused by the divisive leadership race. Perhaps more important, Premier Vander Zalm, a devout Catholic with a strong appeal to fundamentalist Christians, railed against sex education, birth control and advertisements for contraceptives, and used his standing in the legislature as a kind of bully pulpit against abortion rights advocates. Many British Columbians grew perplexed, confused and exasperated by their premier's inability to separate church from state.

Vander Zalm soon lost his folk-hero status. He also suffered numerous embarrassments in office, including the resignations of high-profile cabinet ministers and a series of by-election defeats. His ultimate undoing, however, was the revelation that he may have used the influence of his office to benefit personally from the sale of his Fantasy Gardens biblical theme park to a Taiwanese billionaire. In the spring of 1991, Vander Zalm was finally forced to resign in disgrace for violating the province's conflict of interest rules.

Rita Johnston, a Vander Zalm loyalist, was selected to lead the Social Credit government into the next election. The first woman in Canada to serve as a premier, Johnston was not, however, given a mandate by British Columbians. Indeed, Social Credit—one of the most successful political parties in the history of the country—did not long survive Bill Vander Zalm. The province lurched from the vehemence of his extremism towards a moderate alternative offered by former Vancouver mayor Mike Harcourt. In 1991, Harcourt led the New Democratic Party to victory for the second time in British Columbia. As premier, his bland—some would say boring—style of leadership served as a direct and effective counterpoint to the excesses of the Vander Zalm era. Although Harcourt served only one term in office, it appears unlikely that British Columbia will quickly return to the kind of personality politics that have thus far shaped its identity.

Harcourt was a rarity in British Columbia politics. First, he was a lawyer, and few British Columbia premiers have come from the professional classes or even attended university. Second, he came from Vancouver, which has been the province's largest city since the turn of the century. Most British Columbia premiers have hailed either from smaller towns of the Interior or from the outer suburbs of Vancouver. This pattern helps highlight another dominant theme in British Columbia's politics: populism.

The province has been led predominantly by small-town politicians with backgrounds in small business; their orientation has been distinctly anti-establishment. John Oliver, the Liberal premier in the 1920s, came from Delta when it was still a farming area and, though he was a shrewd politician, he cultivated the image of honest John Oliver who was just one of the down-home, country folks.[15] Such leaders often have an uneasy relationship with the representatives of the metropolitan centres within their party or caucus. Duff Pattullo, whose roots were in the north, always felt that his leadership was never entirely accepted by the Vancouver wing of the Liberal machine, and he was not mistaken. Likewise, W. A. C. Bennett was an outsider from the hinterland. Social Credit was forged in his image as an aggressive populist party, drawing its electoral strength from the rural Interior of the province. Bennett carefully adopted the stance of a leader who sought to represent the concerns of ordinary citizens rather than elites or moneyed interests. This attitude has helped induce in British Columbia a tradition of distrust of large powerful organizations such as big business, big labour or big government—particularly the federal government in far-off Ottawa.

As premier, Dave Barrett was also prone to populist flourishes and political rhetoric culminating in his desperate 1975 election campaign appeal: "Don't let them take it away!" With much less flamboyance, Bill Bennett was no less affected by this well-established political motif. This was aptly demonstrated in 1978 when he threatened eastern-based Canadian Pacific during their attempted takeover of MacMillan Bloedel, the province's largest forestry firm, with his public admonishment: "B.C. is not for sale!" Certainly Bill Vander Zalm was at heart a populist leader who took great delight in ignoring the counsel of experts or professional public servants, preferring instead to govern by gut instinct or on the basis of advice from taxi drivers or glad-handers on street corners. Even Mike Harcourt succumbed to the populist tradition. Early in 1995, for instance, when he announced that the New Democratic Party government was cancelling Alcan's massive Kemano project in the province's northwest, he did so by attacking the large corporation and suggesting that any compensation owing for the decision was the responsibility of the federal government.

THE POLITICS OF THE CENTRE, LEFT AND RIGHT

If British Columbia's populist tendencies crossed party lines, so too did the general reformist tendencies inherent in the province's politics. Until the 1930s, the impulses to reform both government and society were most effectively represented by the Liberals. After 1933, when the Co-operative Commonwealth Federation became British Columbia's Official Opposition, the province's party system was significantly restructured. From that time forward, the Co-operative Commonwealth Federation, and later the New Democratic Party, captured a third or more of the votes cast in provincial elections. The socialist alternative appropriated the mantle of reform and emerged as the perennial party of opposition, forcing others to conspire in order to prevent them from assuming office. This has contributed to another major theme in British Columbia politics: polarization.

It has often been asserted that politics in Canada's west-coast province are ideologically charged, with the left further left and the right further right than elsewhere in the country. Thus British Columbia politics appears to be a morality play, and the "good guys" versus "bad guys" syndrome has certainly had an impact on political discourse.[16] Like any morality play, however, this view is an oversimplification of real life. In fact, extremism has existed more around the edges than at the centre of British Columbia society. Evidence suggests that most British Columbians have viewed themselves more moderately, towards the centre of the political spectrum. The province's reputation for political militancy is accounted for by a relatively small number of "true believers." In this respect, it is the party activists who have successfully steered the political agenda in British Columbia, thereby perpetuating the potent myth of polarization.[17]

When the Co-operative Commonwealth Federation declined an offer to join the Coalition government in 1941, the polarity of British Columbia politics became firmly established. From that time on, the province's other parties competed with each other to become the province's preferred non-socialist alternative. Following the Coalition years, Social Credit was consistently successful in presenting itself as the "free enterprise" choice for British Columbia. W. A. C. Bennett laboured to preserve this favoured position, warning voters during election campaigns that, "The socialist hordes are at the gate!" This was but one example of the exaggerated political rhetoric inspired by the drive towards polarization and practised by both right- and left-wing politicians.

W. A. C. Bennett sought to destroy the Liberals and Conservatives in provincial politics, leaving the field open to Social Credit as the sole alternative to the New Democratic Party in British Columbia. Although he was surprisingly successful in his advocacy of a polarized political culture, it is noteworthy that during his two decades as premier W. A. C. Bennett always faced Liberal and Conservative opponents both on the hustings and in the House. In fact, it was not until 1979, during his son Bill's second term as premier, that the provincial legislature was completely polarized, with only two parties electing MLAs. This was the first such occurrence in British Columbia since the introduction of party politics in 1903. The poisonous polarization of the 1980s, when the Socreds and the New Democratic Party squared off against each other, was an aberration in the larger sweep of the province's history. Multi-party politics is actually the norm in British Columbia, reflecting a tradition of pluralistic diversity rather than a strict class-based society.

The province's supposed polarization also gives rise to a reputation for volatility. Although British Columbia has provided a fertile field for outspoken politicians, politics and political parties have actually been remarkably stable over the course of the twentieth century. And while there have been watershed elections, there have also been enduring lines of continuity between these watershed elections. Once governments are elected in British Columbia, they tend to stay in power for extended periods of time. The exceptions were the Conservative government elected in 1928 and the New Democratic Party government elected in 1972. Each of these was a one-term administration. Other governments have survived at least a second election. After they were first elected in 1916, the Liberals won elections in 1920 and 1924 and governed for twelve years before they were defeated by the Conservatives in 1928. The Liberals came to power again in 1933 and were one of the very few governments in Canada to win re-election during the Depression when they were returned in 1937. After an inconclusive election in 1941, the province was governed by a coalition of Liberals and Conservatives that won two more elections to stay in power for more than a decade. The Social Credit regime of W. A. C.

Bennett that won a tenuous electoral victory in 1952 became the longest serving government in the history of the province, winning six subsequent elections and controlling the province for twenty years. In every one of those six elections, Social Credit never won less than twice as many seats as its nearest rival, the Co-operative Commonwealth Federation/New Democratic Party. A revised version of Social Credit, led first by William Bennett and then by William Vander Zalm, won four elections between 1975 and 1986. Admittedly such victories, especially during the 1920s and the 1950s and 1960s, were possible partly because the opposition was divided. Nevertheless, Social Credit's string of electoral victories in every contest but one between 1952 and 1991 is quite remarkable in a province that is often said to be characterized by voter volatility. Since 1916, British Columbians have, much more often than not, voted for the status quo.

What is true for governments is also true for political leaders. Parties have come and gone, and some have lasted longer than others, but the longevity of party leaders has been striking. Richard McBride started this tradition in British Columbia by serving as the first Conservative leader for more than a dozen years. When John Oliver died in office in 1927, he had been leader of the Liberals for almost a decade. Duff Pattullo served as Liberal leader during a turbulent period from 1929 until his sad departure as premier in 1941. Harold Winch led the Co-operative Commonwealth Federation in opposition from 1938 to 1953. Robert Strachan served as leader of the Co-operative Commonwealth Federation, and then the New Democratic Party, from 1956 to 1969. Dave Barrett guided the party for a decade and a half and Mike Harcourt served as New Democratic Party leader for almost a decade. The Social Credit party was dominated by W. A. C. Bennett for a generation, from 1952 to 1972, and he was succeeded by his son, who was leader until he stepped down in 1986. To be sure, there were other, more forgettable, personalities who waltzed only briefly across the brightly lit stage of political leadership in British Columbia, but the extraordinary catalogue of long-serving party leaders suggests a steadiness that belies the province's reputation.

For many citizens, involvement in the formal political process is restricted to casting a ballot on election day. Nevertheless, the province's party system still offers a useful lens through which British Columbia can be better understood. In the structure of this party system there has been a surprising degree of continuity, created in large measure by the emergence of a viable left-wing political option. Since the 1930s, the existence of a serious socialist alternative has provided an important thread of political continuity, offering an oddly stabilizing influence to the dynamics of provincial partisanship. The alliance of the so-called "free enterprisers" to keep the "socialists" out of office has been been a continuing theme in British Columbia politics.[18] Accordingly, the New Democratic Party has only twice formed a government and each time it was largely because the forces on the right were divided.

RELATIONS WITH FEDERAL PARTIES

Another aspect of British Columbia's party system involves relationships between provincial and federal parties. The introduction of party labels in provincial politics early in the century was the direct consequence of the designs of federal politicians who wanted to end the awkwardness of fighting national election campaigns in a province where they had no junior counterparts to bolster their efforts. Thus, when provincial Conservative and Liberal parties were founded it was not the result of attempts by British Columbians to organize indigenous political movements or electoral organizations; rather, the parties can more accurately be seen as labels of convenience imposed by easterners.

From the beginning, there was a strong sense that Tories and Grits in British Columbia were more independent than elsewhere. Even within the federal parties, politicians from Canada's westernmost province were often viewed from Ottawa with a mixture of curiosity and disdain. In 1922, for instance, Liberal Prime Minister Mackenzie King confided to his diary serious concerns about his own party's representatives and appointments on the west coast: " . . . the B.C. lot seem a poor lot. . . . I find it hard to conceal my distrust."[19] When the question of the relationship between federal and provincial wings of parties was raised, that distrust grew even deeper.

It is often assumed that in a federal state like Canada, the natural tendency should be for political parties to be organized on a parallel basis at the different levels of government. In Canadian politics, however, the close workings of the federal and provincial governments has actually induced the separation of parties at the federal and provincial levels.[20] In no other province, save Quebec and perhaps Alberta, has this been more apparent than British Columbia. Indeed, ever since the 1930s, British Columbia's federal and provincial party systems have moved increasingly apart. Not only has this resulted in political parties that were often ideologically and organizationally distinct at the federal and provincial levels, but in British Columbia this has also meant that completely different parties have competed for dominance in the province's "two political worlds." [21]

Duff Pattullo's aggressive brand of reform-oriented Liberalism was certainly at odds with the cautious approach of federal Liberals under Mackenzie King. Pattullo rejected the 1940 Report of the Rowell-Sirois Commission, which recommended increasing the taxing powers and program responsibilities of the federal government at the expense of the provinces. His strong provincial rights stance at the Dominion-Provincial Conference of 1941 was the logical outcome of years of frustration with Ottawa. It set him firmly in opposition to his federal counterparts — and may have contributed to his ouster as provincial party leader.[22] With Pattullo's departure and the formation of a coalition government, British Columbia politics experienced a decisive shift after which Canada's two major national parties would play only supporting roles in the province. Following the coalition years, Liberals and Conservatives became fringe parties in British Columbia, whereas Social Credit and the Co-operative Commonwealth Federation/New Democratic Party emerged as the province's two dominant political alternatives. Under W. A. C. Bennett, the Socreds succeeded in presenting themselves as an independent, made-in-British Columbia party with a mandate to fight Ottawa. Because the New Democratic Party was a perennial third party at the national level, provincial New Democrats were never too concerned about appearing to take orders from a distant head office.

That British Columbia politics has two separate and distinct worlds cannot be explained simply by reference to broad social and economic forces. The fact that as many as two-thirds of British Columbians have voted for different parties provincially and federally is, rather, a consequence of Canadian federalism, which requires both the electorate and the party elites to respond to different sets of issues, events and personalities.[23] Unlike most other provinces, however, British Columbia has not been content simply to adopt the labels and machinery of federal politics but has instead developed a uniquely differentiated system characterized by strongly independent parties.

The party system itself has often been challenged in British Columbia. From the beginning, the province had a strong non-party tradition, and it was not a simple task for federal politicians to transfer their organizational techniques or discipline to British Columbia. Less than a generation after the introduction of party politics at the provincial level, it was clear that British Columbia voters were not strongly committed to the traditional Canadian two-party system of Liberals versus Conservatives. In fact, since 1920 there have been numerous efforts to reform British Columbia politics by advocating the election of a non-partisan government unrestricted by any direct ties to federal parties or political machines.

The Provincial Party was a notable attempt to achieve such a goal. In the 1924 election it received almost a quarter of the total vote and jarred both the Liberals and Conservatives by helping defeat both their leaders.[24] Although the Provincial Party soon disintegrated, the impulse behind it continued as both a popular idea and a political force in British Columbia. This was evident in 1932 when the province's last Conservative administration, led by Simon Fraser Tolmie, agreed to the appointment of a group of high-powered businessmen to advise the government on the deepening financial crisis created by the economic depression. The Kidd Commission, as it was called, recommended a radical reduction of the size and influence of government as well as the elimination of parties, since they were seen as part of the general inefficiency of the state.[25] In 1941, part of the impetus behind the formation of a coalition government was the notion that political parties were inappropriate—at least during wartime. And the origins of both Social Credit and the Co-operative Commonwealth Federation as populist movements were also characterized by strong anti-party sentiments. The modern history of British Columbia has been marked by persistent attempts to reform parties or to change the party system. Most recently, this tradition can be identified as a key element in the platform of the Reform Party, which calls for politicians to be directly accountable to their constituents, rather than party bosses or party whips, and in the Liberal Party proposal to reduce the number of members in the legislature.

CONCLUSION

We can learn a great deal about the character of Canada's Pacific province through the study of politics. This is not to deny the importance of the social and economic history that has preoccupied historians in recent years: as the other chapters in this book show, scholars looking at these aspects of the past have important things to say about British Columbia, its people, and how they lived their lives. But let us not forget that politics are also about people. Politics involve individuals, both the important and the seemingly unimportant, and politics are also the expression of the collective will of British Columbians. Nor should the study of politics be left to political scientists and journalists, for it is only through the perspective of time and history that we can see beyond the allure of the moment to the enduring patterns of change and continuity that make up our past and present.

It may seem from the daily news that the only thing that is constant in British Columbia politics is change. Clearly, contemporary politics are unlike the politics of 1916. The parties are different and have more sophisticated organizations. British Columbians expect more of their politicians, and of their governments. Elections are organized more efficiently. Politicians communicate through a greater range of media. There are more members in the legislature and they represent larger constituencies.

Yet through all these changes, the continuities in British Columbia's politics are striking. The personality of political leaders remains a crucial factor. Reformist governments still run out of energy. West coast politicians still have an uneasy relationship with their Ottawa counterparts. Perhaps most important of all, if we make the effort to look at our politics over the long term, they are not nearly as polarized and volatile as some commentators would have us believe. British Columbia is a special province that often marches to a different tune than the rest of the country, but if we listen carefully, there is a distinctive rhythm to our politics.

NOTES

1. In some historical texts, politics and politicians scarcely exist at all. See, for example, Jean Barman, *The West Beyond The West: A History of British Columbia* (Toronto: University of Toronto Press, 1991).

2. *Electoral History of British Columbia* (Victoria: Elections British Columbia, 1988): 123.

3. Robin Fisher, *Duff Pattullo of British Columbia* (Toronto: University of Toronto Press, 1991): 118.

4. Pattullo to Oliver, 20 November 1922, British Columbia, Premier, Papers, vol. 345, file 6, British Columbia Archives and Record Service (BCARS); Fisher, *Duff Pattullo*, 147-148.

5. *Electoral History of British Columbia*, 139, 149, 159. Voting percentages in British Columbia are complicated by the existence of multi-member constituencies in the Vancouver and Victoria areas. Voters in these electoral districts have as many votes as seats to be filled, though they are not obliged to exercise all their votes and vote for a full slate. Thus the percentages are of votes cast rather than of the number of voters. See *Electoral History of British Columbia*, 5.

6. *Ibid.*, 149.

7. *Ibid.*, 173.

8. Fisher, *Duff Pattullo*, 351.

9. *Ibid.*, 348.

10. See David J. Mitchell, *W. A. C.: Bennett and the Rise of British Columbia* (Vancouver: Douglas & McIntyre, 1983)

11. A useful review of Barrett's term of office as premier is provided in: Dave Barrett and William Miller, *Barrett: A Passionate Political Life* (Vancouver: Douglas & McIntyre, 1995). This is the first published memoir of a B.C. premier.

12. For a detailed description of the 1986 Social Credit leadership convention, see David J. Mitchell, *Succession: The Political Reshaping of British Columbia* (Vancouver: Douglas & McIntyre, 1987): 92-124.

13. The best source on Vander Zalm's personal background is Alan Twigg, *Vander Zalm: From Immigrant to Premier* (Madeira Park, B.C.: Harbour Publishing, 1986).

14. Quoted from Mitchell, *Succession*, 113.

15. Such a view is expressed in James Morton, *Honest John Oliver: The Life Story of the Honourable John Oliver Premier of British Columbia 1918-1927* (London: J. M. Dent, 1933).

16. The point is made by Terry Morley, "Politics as Theatre: Paradox and Complexity in British Columbia," *Journal of Canadian Studies* 25 (Fall 1990): 19.

17. This thesis is persuasively argued in Donald E. Blake, R. K. Carty and Lynda Erickson, *Grassroots Politicians: Party Activists in British Columbia* (Vancouver: University of British Columbia Press, 1991).

18. Morley, "Politics as Theatre", 25.

19. W. L. M. King Diaries, 4 November 1922, National Archives of Canada.

20. See D. V. Smiley, *The Federal Condition in Canada* (Toronto: McGraw-Hill Ryerson Limited, 1987), Chapter eight "Political Parties and the Federal System": 110-124.

21. The phrase comes from Donald E. Blake *et al.*, *Two Political Worlds: Parties and Voting in British Columbia* (Vancouver: University of British Columbia Press, 1985).

22. For a useful discussion of this period see George M. Abbott, "Pattullo, the Press and the Dominion-Provincial Conference of 1941." (Paper presented at the B.C. Studies Conference, Okanagan University College, Kelowna, B.C. October 7-10, 1994.)

23. See Alan C. Cairns and Daniel Wong "Socialism, Federalism and the B.C. Party Systems 1933-1983" in Hugh Thorburn, ed., *Party Politics in Canada*, 6th edition (Scarborough, Ontario: Prentice-Hall Canada, 1991).

24. See Ian Parker "The Provincial Party," *B.C. Studies* 8 (Winter 1970-1971).

25. For summaries of the Kidd Commission's recommendations, see Robert Edmund Groves, "Business Government: Party Politics and the British Columbia Business Community, 1928-1933." (M.A. thesis, University of British Columbia, 1976):143-146.

Chapter 9
SOCIETY IN THE
TWENTIETH CENTURY
Veronica Strong-Boag

British Columbia is a prosperous province, but it contains persistent and fundamental inequities based on class, race and gender. The existence of class consciousness—as demonstrated by union membership or voting patterns—is not easy to show; but, as one sociologist puts it, class is a matter of experience, not only of consciousness, and in British Columbia the consequences of class have been inescapable, if not always recognized.[1] The perception of racial or ethnic difference has been a powerful force in the lives of individual British Columbians—as for example, when discriminating legislation barred Asian residents from the franchise and various employments. Gender in British Columbia—as in the rest of the country—has also been a major determinant of opportunity, whether it be in immigration, family life, waged labour or politics.[2] Whatever the precise weight to be given race, class or gender, or, for that matter, ethnicity or (dis)ability, there is no doubt that such factors have distinguished members of the province's population in crucial ways.

DEMOGRAPHIC TRENDS

The shifting character of the province's population explains some of the social patterns that have emerged over time. Especially noticeable in the early decades of the twentieth century was the male majority in the age group twenty to sixty-four years. In 1911 men outnumbered women 2.3:1. Two decades later, thanks to the impact of changing immigration flows and natural increase, the ratio had dropped to 1.4:1 but both figures remained higher than the Canadian average, which never exceeded 1.2:1 in the same years. After 1971 the numerical discrepancy between the sexes largely disappeared, as it did for Canada as a whole: women's greater longevity, together with the decreased birth rate, contributed to a national sex ratio of 97:100 in 1991. The effect of the long-time male majority is difficult to judge but it may be that minority status means not so much that women benefit from short supply in the marriage market, as traditional assumptions would suggest, as that they suffer from lack of power and the reaffirmation of roles limited to wife and mother or sexual commodity. As the numbers of each sex in the population evened out, women often found enhanced opportunities in association with one another and with men. The shift in the average age of marriage for women and men that saw a substantial reduction in the age difference between spouses—for example, from 7.8 years in 1911 to 2.5 in 1971—may well have also improved women's ability to negotiate a fair deal. The other obvious change in intimate relations between the sexes has been the growing phenomenon of common-law marriage. Always an option, especially for the poor, "living together" had largely lost its opprobrium by the last decades of the century. In 1991, for example, 11 per cent of all British Columbia couples lived common law; only Quebec reported more at 19 per cent.

The age structure of its population has also shaped the province's history. In the early part of the century a median age that was higher than the rest of Canada (Figure 1) owed much to the fact that fertility rates were lower than the national average and that the most common arrivals were not families with young children, or for that matter equal numbers of both sexes, but young male immigrants searching for work in the province's fishing, mining and logging industries.

Figure 1: Median Age of the Population: Canada and B.C., 1911–1991

	Canada	B.C.
1911	23.8	28.0
1921	24.0	29.8
1931	24.8	30.6
1941	27.1	32.1
1951	27.7	32.0
1961	26.3	29.8
1971	26.3	28.0
1981	29.6	30.9
1991	33.5	34.7

The higher median age in the early part of the century also meant a comparatively small population of children in British Columbia. After 1941 it reflected lower fertility and growing numbers of elderly residents, many of whom retired from elsewhere in Canada to places like Kelowna, Penticton, White Rock, Parksville and Victoria. The aging of Canada's population as a whole has been matched in British Columbia. In 1991 the province reported the highest median age in the country. The rising numbers of seniors put new pressures on the social security system as it evolved in the course of these decades. Demographic change underlay the activism of the Old Age Pension Clubs that sprang up soon after the inauguration of the shared federal-provincial plan in 1927 and of the Raging Grannies from the Gulf Islands who championed the cause of peace in the 1980s and the 1990s.

Female fertility fell after the First World War, reflecting the widespread use of contraceptive measures of all kinds, and changing views about appropriate family size. Indeed the birth control movement in Canada was launched in British Columbia in the 1920s. Shortly after the visit of the famous American birth control advocate, Margaret Sanger, to Vancouver in 1923, the Canadian Birth Control League was founded. Later, in the hard times of the 1930s, a birth control clinic appeared in the same city.[3] By the 1960s agitation over access to abortions again made the province a national leader. Such initiatives inspired fierce controversy among supporters and opponents. Not surprisingly, questions about fertility control—who has babies and how many—have regularly troubled British Columbia politics over the course of the twentieth century. Female fertility has dropped again very dramatically in the last decades of the twentieth century as a result of access to abortions and the changing roles of women.

Figure 2: General Fertility Rates and Death Rates, Canada and B.C., 1911–1991[4]

(Births per 1,000 women aged 15–49 and deaths per 1,000 of population)

	Canada		B.C.	
	Fertility	*Mortality*	*Fertility*	*Mortality*
1911	144		149	9.3
1921	120	10.6	84	8.0
1931	94	10.0	62	8.8
1941	87	10.0	73	10.4
1951	109	9.0	99	10.0
1961	112	7.7	104	8.8
1971	67.7	7.3	67.0	8.1
1981	57.9	6.7	56.7	7.2
1991	55.6	6.6	54.0	7.1

Throughout the twentieth century, British Columbia has had a comparatively low rate of natural increase—a consequence of the excess of men over women in the early decades and the decline in female fertility subsequently. In-migration from other provinces and immigration from abroad have been more important agents of growth than natural increase. This has strengthened ethnic and racial diversity over the course of the twentieth century and contributed to the distinctiveness of British Columbia's society The persistence of particular communities among immigrants and their descendants has continued the cultural heterogeneity that long characterized the Native tribes of the Interior and the coast. It has also inhibited the development of province-wide loyalties. And yet, as the marriage of Yip and Nellie Gong, one of Vancouver's early inter-racial couples demonstrates,[5] boundaries could be crossed. Sky Lee illustrates this point in her 1990 novel *Disappearing Moon Cafe*. The decision in the 1981 Canadian census to drop the long-standing requirement that citizens report only paternal ancestry reflected the reality of a population where ethnic/racial intermarriage was a fact of life and where maternal kin were also significant.

Figure 3:

Percentage of Provincial Population by Ethnic Origins, 1911–1971

Year	British Isles	French	Other European	Asian	Native	Other/ Not Stated
1911	67.8	2.4	15.4	7.9	5.1	1.4
1921	73.9	2.1	11.7	7.6	4.3	0.4
1931	70.6	2.2	16.2	7.3	3.5	0.2
1941	69.9	2.7	18.8	5.2	3.0	0.5
1951	65.8	3.6	23.8	2.2	2.4	2.2
1961	59.4	4.1	29.9	2.5	2.4	1.7
1971	57.9	4.4	30.1	3.5	2.4	1.7

Figure 4:

Number and Percentage of Provincial Population by Ethnic Origin

		1981 (%)
Single Origin	2,407,045	88.7
British	1,385,165	57.6
French	92,305	3.5
Other	929,575	8.6
Multiple Origins	306,570	11.3

Figure 5:

Number and Percentage of Provincial Population by Ethnic Origin

		1991 (%)
Single Origin	1,952,850	60.1
British	812,470	25.0
Chinese	181,185	5.9
German	156,635	4.9
Aboriginal	74,420	2.3
French	68,795	2.1
Dutch (Netherlands)	66,525	2.0
Other Single Origins	503,560	15.5
Multiple Origins	1,294,650	39.9

As Figures 3 to 5 suggest, the dominance of the British population has been increasingly challenged by residents whose roots lie elsewhere. John Norris's *Strangers Entertained: A History of Ethnic Groups of British Columbia*, published by the B.C. Centennial '71 Committee, described a world that changed remarkably after the Second World War. Before 1945, many arrivals of European origin came to British Columbia after a period, sometimes amounting to a generation or two, elsewhere in Canada, especially the Prairies; after 1945, a war-torn continent and Soviet repression increased the flow of European immigrants who travelled directly to the Pacific coast. Some of them arrived as members of such organized groups as the "Netherlands Farm Families Movement," which planted Dutch farmers in the Fraser Valley, and the Sopron University School of Forestry whose staff and students, in the aftermath of the Russian invasion of 1956, helped double the province's Hungarian population. They also turned up individually as part of chain migrations from nations like Italy, Portugal and Greece to invigorate towns such as Powell River where Italians joined a nucleus of their compatriots at work in the pulp mill.[6] In large part depending on the capacity of the economy to absorb them as waged workers, European migrants were generally welcomed, although the post-war tagging of many arrivals as "Displaced Persons" or "DPs" expressed the prejudice they sometimes encountered.

Such reservations were minor compared with the overt hostility to Oriental residents expressed by popular writers like Hilda Glynn-Howard in *The Writing on the Wall* (1921, 1974). The so-called "Gentleman's Agreement" of 1908 between Japan and Canada that limited the entry of Japanese nationals, the "continuous journey" federal regulation of the same year that excluded immigrants from the Indian sub-continent, the Chinese Exclusion Act of 1923, and internment and later dispersal of Japanese Canadians during the Second World War helped bring about a steady decline in the percentage of the provincial population claiming Asian ancestry. The census of 1961 marked the lowest point. Although Chinese storekeepers and East Indian fruit and vegetable pickers, among others, were both visible and industrious and some citizens of Asian origin—like David Lam who was appointed lieutenant-governor in 1988 and Moe Sihota who was first elected as a New Democratic Party MLA in 1986—won positions of distinction, British Columbians remained susceptible to long-standing prejudices about the economic and cultural impact of non-Europeans. In the 1980s, books such as *Hong Kong Money* (1989) by John DeMont and Thomas Fennell and *The China Tide* (1989) by Margaret Cannon documented the fear and anger focussed on off-shore, especially Hong Kong, capital with its perceived threat to real estate prices, organized labour and the social security system. Such fears did not, however, stem the numbers of Asian, especially Philippino, nannies who, recruited under the federal government's foreign domestic worker program, came to labour for middle-class families seeking to escape the consequences of the state's failure to fund childcare adequately. Like other domestic and agricultural labourers, these women made important contributions to the province, receiving in return little legislative protection or financial reward.

The percentage of Native people in the provincial population continued to fall until just before the Second World War. Often shoved into marginal reserve lands that were still further whittled away by the McBride Royal Commission of 1913–1916 (which, in one of many cases, cut about 130 acres from the Capilano reserve in North Vancouver), Natives faced infant mortality rates that, in 1954, reached 105.2 per 1,000 live births, far above that of the non-Natives at 22.4. The sad line of "little graves" tended by Emily Carr's friend, Sophie Frank of the Capilano Band, was matched on reserves around the province.[7] Although poverty made them especially vulnerable to tuberculosis and drug abuse, the essential vitality of the tribes, especially those more insulated on the north coast and in the Interior from the full weight of European contact, contributed to a demographic, as well as a political, revival that became obvious in the third quarter of the century. The success of the sobriety movement among the Alkali Band of the Shuswap people in the 1970s and 1980s, and of the university courses organized jointly by the Shuswap's Secwepemc Cultural Education Society and Simon Fraser University beginning in 1988, provided a powerful example of how Native communities could muster resources in defence of cultural survival. The announcement of the Haida Nation's claim to effective sovereignty over the Queen Charlotte Islands and their institution in 1989 of a passport system for those who wished to visit Haida Gwaii reflected the same determination to assert a unique identity.

Over the course of the twentieth century racial prejudice has ebbed and flowed in response to perceived threats from one group or another. Although some individuals and groups, such as Mildred Fahrni and the Women's International League for Peace and Freedom in the 1930s, always advocated tolerance and understanding, the horrors of the Second World War sensitized many more to the dangers of racial hatred. This heightened sensitivity fostered a climate that at long last permitted, among other things, the enfranchisement of the Chinese and East Indians in 1947, the Japanese, Mennonites and Natives in 1949, and the Doukhobors in 1952. In 1949, Frank Calder, a Nishga, became the first Native to serve in a provincial legislature. The adoption in 1971 of a federal policy of multiculturalism, and growing evidence of racial intermarriage were also signs of a more open cultural environment.

Many new arrivals came from other parts of Canada: indeed internal migration has always supplied the bulk of in-migrants. The refugees from the Depression and drought of the Prairies in the 1930s are a case in point. Many in-migrants were foreign-born residents seeking another start but the native-born were also numerous. The proportion of the province's population born elsewhere in Canada has been significant:

Figure 6: Percentage of British Columbia Population Born in Other Parts of Canada

1911	21.6
1921	20.4
1931	20.4
1941	24.1
1951	30.8
1961	27.3
1971	28.9
1981	30.5
1986	28.7

In the period 1976–1991 British Columbia was the only province to experience a net gain through interprovincial migration. In spite of the squabbles between Victoria and Ottawa, kin ties and attachment to other provinces helped maintain British Columbia's connections to the Dominion as a whole.

Religion was another force shaping the lives of many citizens. Early in the century religious faith inspired a "social gospel" that called for the application of Christ's teachings to the social problems of the day. Women's auxiliaries funded many religious enterprises from day camps to foreign missions. Although religious affiliation was a significant enough indicator of status to encourage some Japanese residents to convert to Christianity as a sign of integration before the Second World War, its meaning and expression shifted from decade to decade. Anglicans and United Church adherents, for example, dropped from 22.5 per cent and 31 per cent respectively of the population in 1961 to 13.4 per cent and 20.2 per cent in 1981. Still more impressive was the increase in the "Other and none" category from 9.4 per cent to 29.2 per cent.[8] By 1991 30.1 per cent of the population reported no religious affiliation whatsoever.

Although racial, religious and ethnic communities are scattered throughout British Columbia, many of them are associated with specific locations. By 1989, Vancouver's public schools had a majority of "English as a Second Language" students, a clear indication that, like Montreal and Toronto, Vancouver had become home for many newcomers. In 1981, for example, metropolitan Vancouver housed 84,000 of the province's 97,000 residents of Chinese origin, 8,000 of the 16,200 Portuguese, and 11,500 of its 13,200 Jews. Elsewhere, Doukhobors have been identified with the Slocan and Kettle Valleys, Mennonites with the Fraser Valley, Norwegians with Bella Coola, and French Canadians with Maillardville. Such associations helped give rise to a strong sense of local identity in regions such as the Cariboo, the North Island, the Kootenays, and the Lower Mainland. Larger-than-life characters like newspaper editor "Ma" Murray of Lillooet, minister-politician "Flying" Phil

Gaglardi of Kamloops, and socialist activist Ernie Winch of Burnaby voiced the preoccupations of their communities and their presence helped give their regions imaginative form.

Some forty years after W. A. C. Bennett's efforts to connect all parts of the province with pavement, British Columbians still struggle with isolation, both physical and spiritual. People of many heritages living everywhere from company towns to logging camps, utopian communities to Native reserves, wealthy suburbs to working-class neighbourhoods, have not easily found common cause. Their needs and desires in matters ranging from schooling to land development and transportation have often been far from complementary.

CITY, TOWN AND COUNTRY

For a large part of the population, cultural and geographical differences have been mitigated by the increasingly common experience of city and town life. As Figure 7 suggests, British Columbians have been less and less inclined to choose the country.

Figure 7: Provincial Population, Urban and Rural, 1911–1991[9]

Year	Population	Urban (%)	Rural (%)
1911	392,480	51.9	48.1
1921	524,582	47.2	52.8
1931	694,263	43.1	56.9
1941	817,861	54.2	45.8
1951	1,165,210	52.8	47.2
1961	1,629,082	72.6	27.4
1971	2,184,620	75.7	24.3
1981	2,744,465	78.0	22.0
1991	3,282,061	80.4	19.6

Dorothy Livesay, winner of two Governor General's Literary Awards for poetry (1944, 1947), celebrated the vitality of 1940s Vancouver in the lines:

> The City is male, they said: smelling the sweat
> Squeezed as a log boom's launched
> Into False Creek; as a Stevedore unloads
> The sick-sweet copra; hoists high
> The out-going wheat, matey and muscular.[10]

Her successors as poets and social critics, like Tom Wayman in *East of Main: An Anthology of Poems on East Vancouver* (1989), have also taken the city as their theme. Yet, although the city asserted its dominance in the second half of the century, the ranches, mines, railroads, fishing and logging communities, and isolated farmsteads of the countryside have imprinted themselves, not only economically and socially, but imaginatively as well. Many volumes of popular history, not to mention the folk songs collected by Phil Thomas in *Songs of the Pacific Northwest* (1979), suggest the impact that the province's remote places have had on the minds of British Columbians

Throughout the twentieth century a proliferation of novels, travel accounts, biographies and autobiographies have focussed on life in boats, lighthouses, and isolated maritime holdings and settlements. Radio and airplane pioneer Jim Spilsbury recalled, in *Spilsbury's Coast: Pioneer Years in the Wet West* (1987), a coastal world of dispersed settlement that depended on boats in ways that other communities depended on trains and, later, cars to get to work, to hospital, to school, to church. The appeal of sea-bound solitude and beauty also drew amateur explorers like the widow Muriel Wylie Blanchet whose *The Curve of Time* (1968) vividly depicted the long inter-war summers spent with her five children boating up and down the lonely Inland Passage. Although coastal communities dependent on disappearing resources and steamships grew steadily fewer, visitors in the last decades of the century, like New Yorker Edith Iglauer in *Fishing with John* (1988), still chronicled the sea's fascination. By the 1990s, however, people were more likely to go to the ocean on holiday than to live and work close to the ocean as loggers, fisherfolk, farmers and miners had traditionally done.

Like the sea, inland locations also drew those hoping for a better life. Optimistic portraits drawn by journalists, businesspeople, and politicians spurred land rushes, such as the 20,000 homesteads claimed between 1928 and 1931 in the Peace River region.[11] Settlers' hopes persisted in the face of, or even perhaps for some heroic souls because of, the difficulties of existence outside the metropolitan centres. Cariboo pioneers Gloria and Richmond Hobson recalled the struggle to cattle ranch in the 1930s and 1940s in *Nothing Too Good for a Cowboy* (1955) and *The Rancher Takes A Wife* (1961). Veterans of the First World War, in the face of over-production, strong competition and under-capitalization, tried to find financial independence with marginal tree fruit farms in the Okanagan Valley in the 1920s and the 1930s; such rural dwellers for many years went without amenities such as electricity and indoor plumbing, which at least middle-class residents of the province's cities were learning to take for granted. The abandonment of rural settlements such as Wallachin in the Thompson area, whose British orchardists succumbed to a mixture of bad planning, half-hearted commitment and the First World War, reflected the marginality of farming as way of life in many parts of the province.

A landscape littered with abandoned homesteads never, however, deterred a stubborn minority who were rich, industrious or idealistic enough to chance life on the land. Such was the case with some adventurous anti-Nazi survivors like Bet and Patrick Dalzel Job, whose interior homesteading in the 1940s and

1950s, recounted in *The Settlers* (1957), collapsed only when the province's schools failed to meet the standards they wanted for their son and they returned to Britain. The province also has a long history of romantic refugees from urban materialism. Until their money ran out, music teacher Margaret McIntyre and her friend, clerical worker Gerry, deserted busy Vancouver of the 1950s for a Gulf Island refuge they named the *Place of Quiet Waters* (1965). A decade later, Mark Vonnegut, an American critic of the Vietnam War, brilliantly evoked the 1960s counter-culture in his description of a Sunshine Coast commune in the autobiographical *The Eden Express* (1975).

The efforts of privileged romantics to "live off the land" stood in stark contrast to the day-to-day struggles of farm labourers who could not afford to fail. When tragedy visited these labourers, there was no easy retreat to another style of life. In 1970, for example, Indo-Canadian parents gathering crops in the Fraser Valley returned to their shelter to find an infant dead in a bucket of drinking water, and in the same year other parents left the fields only to discover three young boys drowned in an Aldergrove gravel pit. To compound their pain, their health was threatened by pesticides and heavy work, and they had to work long hours for low pay. But this was just part of the cost of survival. Such labourers played an essential role in an agricultural sector that, directly or indirectly, accounted for 22.8 per cent of the province's economic activity in 1981.[12]

Although farms continued to produce fine crops and good lives for the lucky few, such as the Okanagan family portrayed in Sandy Wilson's movie, *My American Cousin* (1985), few stayed in farming unless they were particularly stubborn, hopeful or well-capitalized. Not even the efforts of the Farmers' and Women's Institutes or the early travelling educational programs developed by the National Film Board and the University of British Columbia's Department of University Extension could stop the human hemorrhage from the hardships of life on the land.[13] Although farmers made up only 1.9 per cent of the province's population in 1991, as compared to 3.2 per cent of Canada's, it is interesting to note that the province reported the highest percentage (35 per cent) of female farm operators of any jurisdiction, with Ontario the next at 29 per cent.

Single men, and sometimes whole families of workers, sought paid labour and better lives in the shanties, canning villages and floating houses associated with fish and timber production. For many years the shoreline was dotted with:

> . . . whole colonies of these little houses . . . mounted on log booms with runways leading up to the land, and on the platforms surrounding the dwellings women were hanging out washing on improvised clothes-lines. Children were playing, oblivious of the deep water all around, and far up the mountains . . . the men were working . . . .[14]

Such floating villages, like the trailer camps that were their land equivalents in the many smaller centres linked to mines, forests, and canneries, disappeared as resources were exhausted and processing centralized. Except for Native communities and occasional tourists, much of the coast is now deserted for months at a time. The 1989 decision to eliminate the United Church's last mission ship serving these waters reflected the disappearance of the small population centres, like Ocean Falls, that had once characterized the region.

Over the course of the twentieth century many British Columbians have sought better times and places in single-industry company towns with predominantly male labour forces. Many such settlements were short-lived, rapidly becoming the ghost towns that have been so common a feature of the province's landscape. Their authoritarian administration with its inevitable clashes between labour and capital also made them the target of mounting criticism. They were unacceptable, in J. S. Woodsworth's words, because they allowed no "economic freedom and political and religious freedom have become a sham." Between 1962 and 1972, company towns disappeared as the provincial government eagerly set about attracting investment. The company town was replaced with a legislated "instant town." Old settlements like Port Alice, long associated with a pulp and paper mill on Vancouver Island, and new ones like Mackenzie, located to exploit the mining and timber resources of the northern Interior, became part of the Social Credit government's efforts to absolve "companies of the responsibility and costs of running their single-enterprise settlements" and to transfer "the social overhead costs of resource extraction from companies to workers."[15] Unfortunately, as the National Film Board film *No Life for a Woman* (1979) movingly demonstrates of Mackenzie, community-planning models developed in different climates and for different economies very largely failed to address the economic, social and cultural needs of the inhabitants of these communities, especially women. Nevertheless, when good jobs elsewhere were scarce, towns like Tumbler Ridge and Mackenzie continued to attract families, many of whom could not afford to buy houses in the over-heated real estate market of the Lower Mainland and southern Vancouver Island in the 1980s and 1990s.

Like more permanent centres of all sizes from Yale to Vancouver, semi-permanent settlements located to exploit a particular resource were commonly segregated by race, class and ethnicity. Only rare individuals, like the Native and non-Native women in Burns Lake in the 1980s who together designed a women's centre for counselling and education, were able to cross such boundaries. Reserves on the periphery of towns like Kamloops, Squamish and Vancouver were perhaps the most obvious expression of such divisions but every community also had sections reserved for the poor of all ethnic and racial backgrounds. Elderly refugees from a lifetime of labour on resource frontiers settled in "coolie cabins" or bunkhouses, rooming houses and firetrap hotels near Vancouver's Hastings Street until forced out by speculative land development.

In the 1960s housing for Victoria's poor in James Bay and the Rose-Blanshard district was similarly sacrificed to corporate interests.[16]

Small-town British Columbia has remained vibrant both economically and socially. The growth during 1986–1991 of centres such as Kelowna (19.7 per cent), Kamloops (8 per cent), Penticton (15.4 per cent), Prince Rupert (16.4 per cent), Qualicum Beach (29.2 per cent), Nanaimo (22.5 per cent), and Grand Forks (10 per cent) confirmed this vitality. The population in and around Vancouver and Victoria has nevertheless always been large relative to that in the rest of the province. In 1911, for instance, Vancouver contained 31 per cent of British Columbians, and the Greater Vancouver Regional District was home to 47 per cent in 1971 and 44 per cent in 1981. Not even the bankruptcy of urban areas like Burnaby, North Vancouver City and North Vancouver District in the 1930s or the unhappy prospect of flop houses in Vancouver's Strathcona district deterred the city-bound. Some female migrants like Phyllis Knight, as she recalled in *A Very Ordinary Life* (1974), sought to establish home bases where they could more easily add to family income while husbands worked on fish boats or in logging camps. But, like the Knights, most residents struggled to find paid employment for men, as well as women, close to where they lived. While the well-to-do could turn to the wide boulevards, large lots and substantial houses of inter-war inner suburbs like Kerrisdale, a majority of urban residents lived in areas like East Side and South Vancouver with their small lots, narrow streets and rows of similar houses.

After the First World War Vancouver, like most British Columbia centres, was a "city of homes and gardens." Cheap land, materials and houses made modest bungalows possible for many people in areas like Grandview, South Vancouver and Mount Pleasant.[17] During the Great Depression, widespread unemployment and the paralysis of residential construction pushed many British Columbians into increasingly crowded and substandard accommodation. Although tenants organized on Vancouver's East Side to prevent evictions and the Vancouver Mothers' Council composed of progressive women championed the cause of the unemployed, government solutions were short term and often brutal. Single males out of work were offered the hopeless discipline of relief camps; the aged poor were given the dark dormitories of the city's refuge for the elderly. For all the efforts of champions like Helena Gutteridge in Vancouver and Agnes MacPhail in Ottawa, the lot of unemployed women was at least as brutal: they were often ignored altogether, or forced into domestic service, and always eligible for less assistance. Domestic comfort and security became a forlorn hope for such victims of a failing economy.

The Second World War energized governments previously reluctant to improve housing prospects for their citizens. The demands of North Vancouver's shipyards for male and female workers brought state-sponsored accommodation that Dorothy Livesay summed up as:

> . . . boxes set in tidy rows, a habitation for
> A thousand children swept from farm to mine.[18]

The demand for housing was not restricted to the Lower Mainland. In Prince Rupert, as numbers of shipyard workers jumped from one hundred to two thousand, Ottawa built bunkhouses for single workers and over five hundred "wartime houses" for their families. For all the relief they offered to a lucky few, such initiatives did little to alleviate the city's long crisis in affordable accommodation or counteract a cost of living reckoned to be 14 per cent higher than Vancouver's.[19] To the east, Prince George's population doubled during the Second World War and people found themselves living in tents, shacks and converted brothels; even then mothers and children were turned away.[20] In Victoria overcrowding in 1942 contributed to cases of communicable diseases jumping almost five-and-a-half times when compared with 1939.[21]

Crowding did not end with the war. In 1946 veterans occupied the old Hotel Vancouver to dramatize a residential crisis worsened by the removal of wartime rent controls.[22] Between 1945 and 1949 University of British Columbia student veterans and their families crowded together in the former army huts. By 1951 more than thirteen thousand families in the City of Vancouver were doubling and tripling up. With an eye on the electorate and the benefits to the labour-intensive construction industry, not to mention private contractors and developers, governments slowly moved to address the post-war housing shortage. With assistance from Central Mortgage and Housing Corporation (CMHC), inner city suburbs, like Renfrew Heights and Fraserview in Vancouver and Victory Heights in New Westminster, sprang up full of single family bungalows. Relatively low-cost loans from CMHC also supported public housing initiatives such as those in Vancouver's Skeena Terrace and Little Mountain areas, which, in tandem with the steady transformation of the West End into an area of boarding houses, apartments and, later, condominia, slowly changed the city's low density and replaced the overwhelming predominance of detached homes. In spite of great expectations nourished in the pre-First World War housing boom, the development of convenient locations like Vancouver's Grandview had been slow and haphazard during the 1920s and 1930s, but they became home to successive waves of immigrants after the Second World War—in this case British, Italians and Asians. Not for such people were the lots in University Hill pre-landscaped by the provincial government in the 1920s or the majestic homes erected earlier in the CPR inner suburb of Shaughnessy.

In the Lower Mainland and Victoria in the 1960s, a great debate raged over the construction of freeways. This debate made the public more aware of the issues involved in urban planning and growth. The cheap housing traditionally offered to the working class in Strathcona and the Rose-Blanshard district stood in the way of developers whose plans did not include sheltering the low-waged in the urban core. Although Dr. Leonard Marsh of the University of British

Columbia, had earlier proposed in *Rebuilding a Neighbourhood* (1950) a way of preserving, while improving, accommodation for the traditionally poorer inhabitants of Strathcona, much affordable housing was lost in the redevelopment of the 1960s, and again in the clearances preceding Expo '86. In Victoria, although the Rose-Blanshard district was razed, its Chinatown like Vancouver's largely escaped the bulldozer.

Although the freeway proposals of the 1960s were halted by a timely — if short-term — alliance of middle-class professionals and workers, Vancouver and other cities became increasingly captive to corporate development. Planning for the redevelopment of Coal Harbour and False Creek in Vancouver, downtown Victoria, and the CNR Park in Prince Rupert was critically influenced by private investors who had no interest in affordable housing, public parks or the maintenance of traditional retail areas. By the 1960s even areas adjacent to Vancouver such as Burnaby, a traditional refuge for those wishing larger lots at cheap prices, were becoming expensive. Between 1963 and 1973 the land costs for a new bungalow in that municipality jumped 250 per cent and property taxes 147 per cent while the cost of financing such a new home increased by 191 per cent. The so-called crisis of house purchases by off-shore buyers in the 1980s in Vancouver was no more than a logical continuation of urban development that had regularly made only minimal provision for any but the well-to-do minority of citizens. What differed in the last quarter of the twentieth century was the disappearance of cheap land that had permitted the "do-it-yourselfer" to build homes near to jobs in major cities. Sheila Baxter's *Under the Viaduct* (1991) chronicled the human tragedy of homelessness in the province. It is hardly surprising that protests by "squatters" and tenant rent boycotts troubled Vancouver politics in the 1980s and 1990s.

Families did not readily give up dreams of home ownership and were prepared to make numerous sacrifices, from doubling up to going without, in order to achieve it. Their determination helped keep home ownership relatively high, especially in smaller communities.

Figure 8: Housing, 1971

	Owner-Occupied	Rental
British Columbia	60.9	39.1
Vancouver	58.8	41.2
Vernon	64.4	35.6
Victoria	61.4	38.6
Williams Lake	63.0	37.0

Families that were willing and able to leave the opportunities of city centres or to assume the burden of commuting from increasingly remote locations turned to outer suburbs and small towns. Here they could hope to own their own homes. With the help of CMHC, areas such as Richmond, Surrey and Coquitlam in the three decades after the Second World War offered relatively affordable housing. By the end of the 1960s Vancouver workers were commuting to tract homes in Port Coquitlam and Port Moody; two decades later they were driving to Mission and Abbotsford. In 1975 the Greater Vancouver Regional District published its "Livable Region Plan" that, based on the existing bus system, new commuter rail links, and continued reliance on the private automobile, envisioned extensive residential and workplace decentralization: by the late 1980s Coquitlam, Port Moody and Port Coquitlam housed more than 113,000 people and forecasters predicted many more before the turn of the new century.

Most residents of these outer suburbs were young families. Parents wanted a safe place to raise children, so, unable to afford suitable accommodation in older areas, they turned to newer developments where homes and lots were less expensive and more spacious. On the other hand, services, amenities and jobs were not likely to be available in the immediate neighbourhood. Suburban living therefore divided communities by gender, as well as by age. Men more often spent greater time on the road and less time with their families, whereas women were left to cope individually and collectively, with the isolation of urban sprawl.[23] One response, echoed in small and large communities in the 1970s and 1980s, was the Port Coquitlam Women's Centre, which opened in 1975 to offer advice and assistance on everything from abortion and childcare to equal pay and pensions. The decision of the federal Conservative government to remove core funding from all women's centres in 1990 jeopardized initiatives designed to overcome the disadvantages women encountered in trying to make decent lives for themselves and their children. After a wave of public protest, this negative decision was withdrawn, though only for a year. Fortunately matters improved in 1991, when the new provincial NDP government established the Ministry of Women's Equality—Canada's first free-standing ministry dedicated to improving women's lives—which began to provide operational funding for the province's twenty-eight women's centres.

With the exception of rare initiatives such as the NDP's creation of the Agricultural Land Reserve in 1973, provincial and federal governments have shouldered little responsibility for creating a humane balance between country and city. On the other hand, they have proved to be enthusiastic promoters of highways, and, to a more limited degree, railways and ferries to diminish the physical distances that separated citizens from each other and capital and labour from resources. Significant transportation linkages have been completed: the Banff-Windermere Highway (1923), the Second Narrows Bridge (1925, 1960), the Lion's Gate Bridge (1938), the Port Mann Bridge (1964), Oak Street Bridge (1957), the Hope-Princeton Highway (1949), the Lougheed Highway (1950), Route 98 between North Vancouver and Squamish (1958), the Deas Island Tunnel (1959), and the highways from Prince George to

Quesnel (1953), Prince George to Chetwynd (1955), Fort St. John to Dawson Creek (1958), Kennedy to Mackenzie (1966), Fort St. John to Fort Nelson (1971), and the Coquihalla between Hope and Kamloops (1986). Provincial ferry service was initiated in 1960 and the province purchased Black Ball Ferries a year later. These projects facilitated continuous expansion in the use of private gas-fuelled transport. In 1960 Alert Bay was recognized by the *Guinness Book of World Records* for the "Most Cars Per Mile of Road." The province's love affair with trucks and cars, as illustrated in Figure 9, undermined support for collective transit of all kinds.

Figure 9: Number of Private Cars in B.C., 1941–1971

1941	77,182
1951	153,325
1961	329,739
1971	544,310

Although buses remained at the core of public transit throughout the province, the inter-urban rail line between Vancouver and New Westminster, for all its efficient, relatively non-polluting movement of large numbers of travellers, succumbed after the Second World War. Energy-efficient trolley cars also disappeared from Victoria in 1948 and from Vancouver in 1949. The short-comings of the provincially owned Pacific Great Eastern Railway, nicknamed "Please Go Easy" and the "Province's Greatest Expense," did little to encourage rail passengers in the north. Yet, in response to congestion and environmental concerns, there were signs in the late 1980s of renewed interest in collective forms of transportation. The introduction of the inter-urban's much-needed successor, the Light Rapid Transit System or "Skytrain" in 1986, and the immediate calls for its extension both east and south, sprang from a slow-dawning realization that the price paid in urban sprawl, traffic congestion and air pollution—in 1973 alone Greater Vancouver's air received more than 400,000 tons of carbon monoxide from gas-fuelled vehicles—was too high.

HOUSEHOLD, FAMILY, AND CHILDHOOD

Just as new technologies transformed transportation, they also changed domestic life. The widespread introduction of household science as a school subject in the first three decades of the century signalled that old ways of keeping house were no longer sufficient. Where previously girls had learned from older family members the responsibilities traditionally allocated to their sex, students were now being "introduced to new foods and recipes whose selection was justified on scientific grounds and whose preparation was taught according to standardized procedures . . . [and] to new consumer goods—the carriers of new technologies—and new patterns of consumption."[24] The repetition, in newspapers and magazines as well as in schools, of information about new appliances and food products changed aspirations faster than practices. Limited family budgets and the household traditions of religious and ethnic communities were major deterrents to innovation. While "making do" was not limited to any one decade, one Vancouver Islander singled out the Great Depression of the 1930s for its effect on family finances:

> When your sheets started to wear out, you tore them up the middle and put a seam down the middle and hemmed the sides . . . . You patched . . . you canned, you jammed . . . . You had to be very ingenious . . . to stretch your dollar."[25]

Although the benefits of mass production and, later, the electronic and computer revolutions promised a lifestyle revolution, British Columbians' relationship to domestic innovations was critically mediated by class and gender. To take just one example: domestic hygiene required a markedly different commitment from middle-class women—whose options in the course of the century included employing a servant, sending out heavier linen to the local Chinese laundry, and operating washers and, later, dryers—and their poorer sisters for whom the scrub board remained a key piece of domestic equipment until well after the Second World War. One Coast Salish mother and wife remembered routines that wore out hard-working women around the province:

> And I used to wash all day sometimes. Of course when you're washing diapers you have to be washing every day, every morning. You can't miss a morning. Then you have a certain day for washing your clothes, another day . . . if you have to wash your sheets and blankets and all that, because we had a hard time getting water . . . . Every weekend I'm scrubbing the house.

Her proud insistence that "Indians aren't dirty,"[26] was echoed by Native and non-Native poor who remained sensitive to slights from the economically privileged.

By 1910, thirty-eight British Columbia communities had organized some kind of electric service and, a decade later, the B.C. Electric Railway Company was actively marketing washing machines, electric fires, vacuum cleaners, sewing machines, fans and toasters. The initial cost of major appliances kept many women in thrall to time-consuming domestic regimes. In 1941, for example 57 per cent of Vancouver tenants and 53.4 per cent of home-owners possessed neither refrigerators nor ice boxes, while 42.3 per cent of the province's households owned neither electrical, oil nor gas stoves. The situation was likely to be much worse up-country where, well past the booming 1950s, families routinely struggled with coal, wood and sawdust for cooking and heating. On the other hand, by 1971 21.3 per cent of the province's dwellings reported a colour television, and by the 1980s the emergence of "new necessities," as they were called, still further highlighted the differences between privilege and poverty.

Figure 10: Percentage of British Columbia Households with "New Necessities," 1987[27]

Cable television	84
Freezer	60
Two or more telephones	54
Two or more TVs	40
VCR	44
Microwave oven	45
Dishwasher	45
Air conditioning	7
Pay television	9
Home computer	10

Not surprisingly, innovations like disposable diapers, in wide use by the 1970s, were reckoned a boon by many mothers. The so-called "green revolution," which identified these products as environmental disasters and proposed the return to cloth, could be relatively easily espoused by consumers with access to washers and dryers or diaper services, but would mean a return to hard household labour for those too poor or too isolated to have such conveniences available. Although problems of pollution were by no means new (in the 1920s and 1930s, for example, beehive burners regularly threatened visibility in Burnaby), protection of the environment appeared on the agenda of many households in the 1980s. The failure to prevent industrial pollution (dioxins remained a significant product of pulp and paper mills) or to provide satisfactory treatment for human waste (many coastal communities, including Vancouver, Victoria and Prince Rupert, continued to flush sewage into the ocean) together with the consumption of a wide range of non-biodegradable products, helped create an environmental time bomb in the province. The best-selling *The Canadian Green Consumer Guide* (1989) summed up public concerns. Efforts as diverse, but related, as the struggle to save Meares Island and the Carmannah Valley from logging and to establish curbside recycling programs reflected these concerns, and women found their domestic concerns increasingly included responsibility for the four Rs: "Refuse, Reduce, Reuse, Recycle." Households varied tremendously not only in their consumption of environmentally dangerous products but also in their ability either to substitute or to go without. Threats, like the massive oil spill that killed many marine animals along the west coast of Vancouver Island or the relevations about dioxins that turned milk consumers in record numbers from paper to glass containers, both in 1989, helped citizens understand the connections between patterns of consumption and threats to the environment.

Like other Canadians, British Columbians looked to continuous economic growth to improve the quality of life. Substantial increases in average family incomes in the decades after the Second World War ended abruptly in the

1980s. Despite considerable economic growth, "average real disposable family income actually fell," only spared a much more dramatic collapse by the increased number of wage-earning wives and mothers.[28] By 1990 14.6 per cent of the province's households were defined as living below Statistics Canada's low income cut-off line. Families with only one income earner or those hurt by ill health, disability or prejudice were especially likely to face few real choices in their purchases. The fact that other provinces often offered worse prospects, not to mention climates, however, continued to fuel migration to the "wet coast," which has been the only region to show a continuous increase in its share of the Canadian population since 1901.

Although the timing and meaning of changes in domestic consumption are often far from certain, understanding intimate relationships among British Columbians and between families and the wider community is still more difficult. In face of much evidence to the contrary, many people, including leading politicians, have preserved a belief in a golden age when patriarchal kin groups of several generations supposedly lived harmoniously together. That the past has had higher death rates, lower life expectancy, authoritarian relationships, and a long history of same-sex relationships and mother-headed families tends to be conveniently forgotten. The phenomenon of "coming out" among the province's lesbian and gay population, which became evident in the 1980s, was especially troubling to those who assumed the immutability of sex roles. Ironically enough, belief in a golden age of the family frequently existed simultaneously with criticism of the family life of non-Anglo-Celtic immigrants. In point of fact, recent Chinese, Fijian and Italian communities, among others, have employed many of the same strategies—such as crowding households with several generations to pool resources—that have traditionally characterized new arrivals, whatever their origin.

Although the ideal of conservative social critics has normally been the nuclear family headed by a male breadwinner, families in British Columbia as elsewhere have regularly come in different configurations and sizes, ranging from single individuals to various combinations of ages and sexes. At the beginning of the 1990s, the province was home to over seventy-four thousand lone-parent families, 95 per cent of them headed by women. Of the province's children and youth, 13.3 per cent lived with only one parent. Although many mother-headed families functioned far better than they had with a male breadwinner present, the increasing economic necessity for two incomes, together with the lower wages earned by women, meant that over 62 per cent of lone-parent families needed social assistance.[29] The fact that British Columbia's expenditures on childcare remained lower than other "have" provinces such as Ontario and Alberta helped ensure that most mother-headed households stay poor even during more sympathetic NDP administrations.

Tensions within the family have frequently occurred as immigrants struggle to sort out their obligations to kin and community in their new land and as British

Columbians in general endeavour to come to terms with limited budgets, traditions of patriarchal violence, and changing views of appropriate behaviour for women and men, and children and adults. In the 1980s young Indo-Canadian women began to challenge arranged marriages and immigrant men, alarmed by the independence of women born or long-settled in British Columbia, sought wives from the homeland—whether Italy or the Philippines—hoping that mail-order brides would be more accepting of male power. Disrespectful children also appeared to threaten the old order. The emergence of Asian youth gangs in Vancouver in the 1980s dismayed their communities at least as much as it shocked other citizens. Such gangs reflected not only the problems of racial integration but also the domestic upheaval that was endemic as different generations and sexes sought solutions to the problems of resettlement.

Controversies evoked by issues like birth control, venereal disease, abortion and Acquired Immunity Deficiency Syndrome (AIDS) reflected popular anxiety about the proper relationship of women and men.[30] Debates about the preferred ways for people to live together have often in British Columbia, as elsewhere, focussed on the role of women and gender roles. The failure to give women the provincial franchise until 1917 has been part of a more general unwillingness to implement meaningful equality, as the continued reluctance to offer female children and adults equal opportunity in the school, the workplace or the bedroom reveals. Girls and women have regularly been targets of male violence: the murder on 6 December 1989 of fourteen young women in Montreal's L'Ecole Polytechnique by an anti-feminist madman finds echoes in such events as the destruction of Vancouver's Women's Bookstore by an arsonist in October 1979 and the November 1994 attack on a Vancouver doctor who performed abortions. Yet, as indicated in the report of the B.C. Task Force on Family Violence, *Is Anyone Listening?* (1992), and the accompanying *Family Violence in Aboriginal Communities: A First Nations Report* by Sharlene Frank, most violence is not usually by strangers. The founding of Women Against Violence Against Women (WAVAW), Rape Relief, transition houses for battered women and their children—by 1978 there were six transition houses—and the inauguration of the "Women Reclaim the Night" marches in 1978 responded to a need for protection for women that courts, the police and women had been identifying since the turn of the century. The lack of agreement even in the feminist community about the connection between violence and pornography is summed up by the Wimmins Fire Brigade's firebombing of three Red Hot Video outlets in the Lower Mainland in 1982 and the struggle of the Little Sister's Bookstore to prevent censorship of gay and lesbian materials by Canada Customs in the 1990s.

In the twentieth century the very definition and experience of family life have been challenged, not only by family members but by a variety of external authorities. Caught between increasingly authoritative childcare professionals in medicine and education on one hand and their own desires and cultural traditions on the other, parents throughout the century have had to work out relationships between themselves and their children. Thousands of advisory "Little Blue Books" and, later, copies of *The Canadian Mother and Child* came from Ottawa to join pamphlets from the provincial government, the Canadian Council on Child Welfare, the Canadian Red Cross, and the Victorian Order of Nurses in the battle against parental ignorance.[31] After the Second World War, Dr. Spock's baby books with their more liberal views on family relations (in the 1980s he issued a non-sexist edition) became household stand-bys, contributing something—though it is impossible to say how much—to increasing consensus about appropriate methods of child-rearing.

The toll of injury and death suffered by Canadians has been considerably reduced by scientific and technological advances, ranging from the introduction of sulfa drugs in the 1930s to the use of ultrasound machines in the 1970s. Conscious of the promise of modern medicine, women demanded improvements in care before, during and after childbirth. For the first half of the century this meant concurring with physicians' desire to control labour and delivery within the confines of the modern hospital and demanding apparent advances like the anaesthetic nitrous oxide, which produced "twilight sleep" during delivery.[32] Beginning in the 1940s, however, doubts about the over-medicalization of childbirth led to campaigns for more natural deliveries. In the 1980s women demanded home births and the legalization of midwifery. Improved medical care, more knowledgeable and demanding mothers, and a healthier population reduced the provincial maternal mortality rate from 1.7 deaths per 10,000 live births in 1971 to 0.7 in 1981 and 0.2 in 1986, and the infant mortality rate from 18.7 deaths per 1,000 live births in 1971 to 10.2 in 1981 and 8.5 in 1986. For all the improvement they represent, these rates obscure the very different experience of the poor and, especially, of Native peoples. In 1971, for example, neonatal (infants four weeks or younger) deaths in the population at large amounted to one in every 58 live births; in contrast, Native neonatal deaths were one in 18. Not surprisingly, Native life expectancy remained below that of more privileged groups throughout the twentieth century.

Although children have always preoccupied parents and experts, most traditional histories leave them out. Youngsters' experience reveals a great deal about society, however. Until very recently, for example, most children spent much of their time assisting families economically, as waged and unwaged labourers both in and beyond the home. Although their contribution was essential to the survival of many households, work of some kind, whether it was in minding younger siblings or helping out in the family store, was also viewed as important training in values by most middle- as well as working-class families. For all that youngsters had in common, however, very different experiences of childhood reflected and contributed to the divisions that have marked British Columbia society. Expectations regularly differed by gender, with girls more responsible for unceasing domestic routines and boys for outside chores and income.[33] Class comparisons could also be stark: compare the "training" undergone by the unfortunate residents of the Girls' Industrial Home opened in Vancouver in 1914[34] with the education offered to the comparatively well-to-do boarders at the select Vernon Preparatory School for boys founded in the same year.[35] The situation of "neglected and dependent" children placed by the Vancouver Children's Aid Society and the Catholic Children's Aid Society, first in orphanages and then, increasingly, with foster parents, remained far from ideal throughout the century. The state's increasing interest in children and long-standing hostility to cultural non-conformity were both evident when 306 Doukhobor girls and boys were seized and placed in provincial institutions from 1932 to 1935 in an effort to force their parents to accept compulsory schooling. At least as troubling has been the on-going predicament of Native youngsters apprehended by the province and frequently placed with white families who, whatever their good intentions, could not root their charges in their original culture.[36] Not surprisingly, by the end of the century Native communities were making strenuous efforts to foster children unable to remain with their parents.

The lot of immigrant youngsters could also be rough. Poorer children who, right up to the Second World War, were being sent to Canada by British philanthropic societies like Dr. Barnardo's Homes, regularly benefitted fostering families by contributing long hours of labour, often receiving little education or affection in return.[37] Even the more fortunate "guest children" sent to British Columbia beginning in 1940 to escape wartime Britain turned up in the province's child guidance clinic as they suffered the traumas of sorting out the meaning of new surroundings and relationships.

If, as historians have argued, "modern" childhood is to be distinguished from that of the past by its prolonged period of dependence, delayed responsibilities, protection and segregation,[38] then it is clear that poorer British Columbia children, whether in the hands of strangers or of their families, experienced few of the benefits of "modernity."

EDUCATION

The school, the institution outside the family most closely associated with modern childhood, has been a source of controversy from the early decades of the twentieth century. A series of public investigations, from the *Survey of the School System* by J. H. Putman and G. M. Weir in 1925, with its advocacy of initiatives such as IQ tests and junior secondary schools, to the 1988 Sullivan Royal Commission on Education, *A Legacy for Learners*, with its proposed non-graded primary program, have attempted to apply the newest insights on child development to the province's educational system. Despite the continuing failures of the system, as illustrated by pupils who had not kept up with their age group, absenteeism, and a drop-out rate that meant that 30 per cent of pupils in 1988 failed to graduate from high school (although many would return later on), public support for education expanded steadily throughout the century.

The 1901 Public School Act made schooling compulsory for children aged seven to fourteen living in a city district. In 1921 legislation provided for free education for youngsters aged six to sixteen and compelled the attendance of those aged seven to fourteen throughout the province. Even then many potential pupils remained absent for much of the year, deterred by some combination of over-crowding, unsuitable instruction, the need to add to family income, parental indifference and isolation. The situation of children in mining, forestry and railway camps was especially difficult as schooling depended on the uncertain ability of local industry to sustain employment for sufficient number of parents to guarantee a school. Bad housing and pay, a shortage of congenial company, and the lack of fundamental resources like textbooks in many rural and isolated schools encouraged high levels of teacher turn-over, as did the reluctance of some parents to pay school taxes. Although some dedicated teachers nourished pupils' aspirations, their own ambitions frequently included a post in Victoria or Vancouver and, for men, a principalship or a superintendentship. Throughout the century, children in outlying districts suffered from a highly transient teacher labour force.

Nevertheless, by the 1920s growing opposition to the employment of children and young people and an emerging consensus that longer periods of schooling were an important asset in life increased the enrollment of the province's fifteen-year-old girls from 69.4 per cent in 1921 to 83.2 per cent in 1931 and the same aged boys from 64.1 per cent to 81.8 per cent. Yet, as one Vancouver East Sider remembered, "If you went to high school, your parents had money and anybody who didn't have money, the kids left school at 13, 14 or 15."[39] In the 1930s the lack of alternative employment helped keep poor children at school longer but in 1932 conservative interests mobilized behind the Kidd Report (the report of five businessmen appointed by Premier Simon Tolmie to investigate provincial finances) demanded that free schooling be restricted to ages six to thirteen and that the University of British Columbia be closed. Working people determined to obtain a fairer deal for their offspring and progressive middle-class organizations like the Parent-Teacher Associations and the Vancouver University Women's Club successfully blocked such proposals, but schools proved no panacea for social inequities in the 1930s or later.

Schools did, however, change, at least in some respects. In response to the progressive philosophy embodied in the *Survey of the School System* (1925), British Columbia "standardized the curriculum and the time allotments for each subject, adopted the notion of the junior high school, eliminated high school entrance examinations, tightened standards for admission to the Normal (teacher training) schools and promoted school consolidation."[40] Such developments did not meet with universal approval. Historian Hilda Neatby, in her best-selling *So Little For the Mind* (1953), blamed so-called progressive reforms for worsening education across the Dominion. Ironically, despite an abundance of administrative changes, the actual learning situation for children within schools appears to have hardly changed between 1920 and 1960. For most pupils, schools continued to evoke a complex mixture of fear, enthusiasm and boredom. Classes that regularly numbered forty and above, inadequate teacher training and limited resources meant that "good" teachers continued to drill incessantly and bad ones to exercise their frustrations on the unfortunate. As attendance laws became more regularly enforced and parents and the public more convinced of the need for at least some high school training, unhappy youngsters found it increasingly difficult to drop out.

Not until the 1960s and later did smaller classes managed by better-educated teachers begin more regularly to reflect the tenets of the child-centred education that Putman and Weir had advocated. In the last decades of the century the appearance in many school districts of federally supported French immersion classes, and the concurrent development—for a very different set of educational "consumers"—of English as a Second Language instruction constituted unprecedented recognition of the province's and the Dominion's diversity. Such developments did not go unchallenged. The expansion of Christian schools after 1945 marked the growth of fundamentalist religion in the province and the resistance of groups like the Dutch Reformed Church to the increased secularization of public education as it slowly moved to address mounting religious and cultural diversity.

Progress within the public sector ground to a halt with the restraint budgets of the early and mid-1980s. Not so constrained were private schools, which were eligible for public funding after 1978. The tax loophole that permitted a number of private institutions to offer tax-deductible tuition for 1989 was yet further reflection of their increasingly favoured status. In contrast, pupils, teachers and parents in the public system struggled to implement recommendations of the Sullivan Report without any significant infusion of new revenue. In May 1990 the Social Credit government's option of public referenda as the sole means to secure additional moneys for school districts was employed by nine desperate school boards but, whether due to opposition to the referendum policy itself or to resistance to increased funding, only the referenda in Vancouver and Richmond passed. Such results helped ensure that at the end of the century, as at the beginning, teachers and schools around the province varied tremendously in their offerings.

Although obvious distinctions separated private and public schools and those in one district from another, differences also surfaced within individual school systems. In Vancouver, Main Street divided the city and its schools. East of that great divide children during the Great Depression were much more likely to go hungry, to doze through classes, and to drop out. Fifty years later, the demarcation remained critical. A number of East Side primary schools whose pupils were discovered to be regularly under-nourished offered free meals while schools west of Main Street benefitted from fund-raising by middle-class parents eager to have offspring enter the computer age. The special difficulties of children whose first language was not English prevented some from realizing their full potential. Stereotyped representations in curriculum materials and stereotypical expectations from many teachers handicapped girls and children of colour in particular. As it had from the beginning, the province's educational system remained geared, to a significant degree, to the learning patterns and needs of white middle-class males.[41] The disadvantages of the public school system for girls were used strategically in the 1990 advertising of York House, a private girls' school in Vancouver, which asked parents, "Did you know that recent research shows that girls-only schools are the best environment for the education of girls?"[42]

Students of non-European origin have long experienced special disadvantages. In Vancouver and Victoria, Chinese parents have had to maintain a strong common front to meet periodic proposals to segregate their children. The most serious crisis came in Victoria in 1922, when the school board decided to place the 240 Chinese students in the city in a separate (and inferior) building. Chinese parents responded by boycotting public schools, organizing their own classes, and agitating against official policy. After a year the school board backed down and Chinese students were reintegrated into the public schools.[43] For Native people, segregated education was the common experience. For the first half of the century many Native children attended residential schools run by the Catholic and Protestant churches. Among others, the Kamloops Indian Residential School run by the Oblate Fathers and the Sisters of St. Ann concentrated on Shuswap children, the Lejac Residential School operated by the Oblates and the Sisters of Child Jesus had a special interest in Carrier girls and boys, and the All Hallows' School managed by an Anglican sisterhood offered classes to Native girls often from the Lillooet and Lytton bands. Although such institutions were not without some advantages (the Lejac school, for instance, is credited with helping to produce a number of outstanding female leaders among the Carrier),[44] they also did terrible damage, isolating children from their families, and applying more or less equal doses of academic training and physical labour in an often brutal effort to force the abandonment of Native traditions.

Despite the compulsion and mistreatment involved in the education of Native children, Native mothers and fathers were eager to obtain benefits of schooling for their youngsters. They had expectations and demands of the schools and were critical when these were not met. Like many vulnerable working-class parents who used orphanages and child welfare agencies to care for children when families were in crisis, Natives were also likely to employ schools to help them over bad times. By mid-century, however, First Nations' peoples had increasingly concluded that, whatever the benefit to an occasional child or family, the costs of segregated residential instruction were too high. In 1951 the Indian Act permitted reserve children to attend public schools. In 1955, for instance, Native students in Alert Bay began attending the public school in the white end of town. By the late 1980s only the Catholic Prince George College still functioned as a boarding school for Native students.

Although some youngsters excelled in the white school system, many encountered racism in playground and classroom. The obvious shortcomings of attempts at integration led, in 1972, to a policy statement from the National Indian Brotherhood that affirmed the importance of local control, the need for more Native teachers, and the value of Native studies in the curriculum. Two years later the University of British Columbia's Native Indian Teacher Education Program began to train Native teachers. In the same year the Nishga created the province's first Native school district.[45] By the 1980s band-run schools had emerged in such communities as Mt. Currie, Alkali Lake, Canim Lake and Bella Coola. Institutions of higher learning also began addressing the needs of the Native community. Chilliwack's Fraser Valley College developed a college preparation course specifically geared to First Nations' students and the University of British Columbia inaugurated a Native Law program. In Vancouver the Native Education Centre, affiliated with Vancouver Community College, introduced a wide range of programs. In the late 1980s Simon Fraser University offered, for the first time in the province's history, a university-level course in a Native language—Shuswap. The emergence of educational initiatives controlled or heavily influenced by the First Nations' people themselves was an outgrowth of a long history, not only of prejudicial treatment, but also of distinctive cultures that had a major stake in shaping an educational system that could guarantee their future.

With the inauguration of classes at the University of British Columbia in 1915, the province became the last in the country to possess an independent institution of higher learning (colleges in Victoria and Vancouver had earlier been affiliated with McGill University). Although nursing was associated with the university from 1919, other specialized programs were late to appear: law in 1945, graduate studies in 1948, pharmacy in 1949 and medicine in 1950. These initiatives served the privileged especially well. Talented young people whose parents belonged to the working class—that is, 67.5 per cent of the province's population in 1928–1929—contributed only 21.5 per cent to the university's student body in that year. The odds of entering university were also overwhelming biased in favour of males. In 1949–1950, for example, 1,684 women were registered and 5,924 men. Female students were routinely discouraged from considering university or routed to a narrow range of programs in arts, education or nursing. Nor was that all. Until 1941, for example, separate English classes taught by junior faculty were the order of the day for co-eds, while male professors set the exams taken by all students and organized the courses they taught personally to young men.[47]

Although women approached numerical parity among full-time undergraduates in the 1970s and 1980s, as late as 1987–1988 British Columbia had the dubious distinction among all provinces of enrolling the lowest proportion of women. Even a lofty position could not guarantee fair play as Dr. Pauline Jewitt, president of Simon Fraser University, discovered when she was denied membership in the all-male University Club in 1975. Despite such tardy progress, prejudice against women in higher education gradually became considerably less overt; UBC's engineering society's notorious Lady Godiva ride was forcibly shut down, women's studies programs were developed through the 1970s and specific policies against sexual harassment were put in place during the 1980s.

Starting in the 1960s, opportunities for disadvantaged groups improved tremendously. A community college system was created in the 1960s; two new universities, Simon Fraser and the University of Victoria, were established in 1963, and a third, the University of Northern British Columbia, in 1991; new options were provided by the British Columbia Institute of Technology (1964) and the Open Learning Institute (1978); and Notre Dame University, originally a Catholic college, and the evangelical Christian Trinity Western College (later Trinity Western University) achieved new stature in the 1970s. The development of university colleges in cities like Kamloops and Nanaimo in the 1980s at long last offered the possibility of degree completion outside of metropolitan Victoria and Vancouver. There were also setbacks, however. In the early and mid-1980s educational cutbacks hit poorer, part-time, and older students disproportionately, threatening to undercut gains. The closure of Notre Dame University in Nelson confirmed long-standing regional inequalities in access to higher education. In the 1990s, which began with a major economic downturn, the future of higher education looked less than bright as institutions struggled to maximize efficiencies and cut budgets. Yet if the province continued to report some of the lowest rates of participation in higher education in Canada among the age group nineteen to twenty-four, the closing decades of the twentieth century did bring unprecedented educational opportunities to new groups of citizens.

HEALTH AND SOCIAL SECURITY

Slow improvements in education over the century were matched by the cautious emergence of health care and social security programs that directly affected all British Columbians. Public education initiatives launched by schools and governments and, after the First World War, the Red Cross encouraged families to improve their nutritional, dental, physical and medical regimes. Domestic science and health classes targeted girls as the managers of future households and school children in general were among the first beneficiaries of the bacteriological revolution that included the discovery of the anti-toxin for diphtheria, one of childhood's greatest threats. By 1910 British Columbia legislation provided for health inspection of teachers, pupils and janitors, though check-ups were the order of the day only in Victoria, Vancouver, New Westminster, South Vancouver and Nelson. Rural children had to await the introduction of provincial public health nurses in the 1920s.

Campaigns in magazines and newspapers and by governments against infant and maternal mortality, tuberculosis and venereal disease also raised general awareness of threats to good health. The First World War's heavy casualties also alerted Canadians to the implications of the high rate of infant death. Childhood's special dangers were chronicled by many a tombstone, such as the matter-of-fact list of tiny victims on one Ladner monument: "Lena Aged 21 Days/Freddy Aged 1 year 1 month/Edith Aged 3 Years 11 Mos/Ella Aged 3 Years 10 Mos."[48] The home remained at the centre of disease prevention and cure. The Victoria Order of Nurses, and Red Cross and public health nurses went into private residences and schools around the province, encouraging children and adults to seek vaccinations, regular check-ups and remedial assistance of every kind, and urging communities to safeguard water, milk and food supplies.

Although women as mothers and nurses remained on good health's front line throughout the twentieth century, doctors and hospitals became increasingly powerful influences on medical care. Like many other residents, doctors generally preferred to settle in urban centres and many, especially in the first half of the century, relied heavily on contract work for logging, fishing and railway companies, as well as for the federal Department of Indian Affairs.[49] Self-diagnosis and medication, including the use of a wide variety of patent medicines such as Dr. Chase's nerve pills and Lydia Pinkam's Pink Pills for Pale People, remained widespread. However, as a result of public health education programs, the experience of both world wars, which alerted many to the value of regular check-ups, and the provision of medical treatment under workers' compensation laws, citizens grew more ready to consult physicians. Confidence in professionals was increased by their monopoly of many scientific, surgical and drug advances. The outlawing of midwifery until 1993 and the marginal position of so-called "irregular" practitioners like chiropractors and massage therapists also helped maintain the demand for orthodox services. The power of new medical technologies, in matters ranging from sex selection to the prolongation of life, further empowered medical practitioners. The tragic case of Sue Rodriguez, a Victoria woman suffering from Lou Gehrig's disease who asked for medical assistance in ending her life, captured some of the ethical dilemmas facing citizens at the end of the century.[50]

Although health services did improve over the century, the 1979 appendicitis death of an eleven-year-old member of Alert Bay's Native community, after inadequate treatment by the district's sole doctor, highlighted regional and racial inequalities. In the 1980s another highly publicized case demonstrated the same disparity. In response to the reluctance of physicians to move to rural and small-town British Columbia, the federal Department of Indian Affairs began flying specialists to remote communities. In 1985, one such visitor, a former president of the B.C. Medical Association, charged the medical insurance scheme for eye examinations for Native children that averaged seventeen seconds.[51]

From the 1870s onward, hospitals in Canada came increasingly to depend on grants from the federal and provincial governments, and in British Columbia all major hospitals were set up with government backing. Public funding ensured the domination of large institutions like Royal Jubilee in Victoria, Royal Inland in Kamloops, and the Vancouver General, Grace, Shaughnessy, and B.C. Children's hospitals in the Lower Mainland. Although private hospitals never entirely disappeared, they emerged, unlike the United States, as small players in the provincial health care system. By the 1990s small communities—understanding full well the benefits of the high-cost, highly specialized facilities like those available in the intensive care nursery of B.C. Children's Hospital—clamoured for the air ambulance connections that could mean the difference between life and death. Those small hospitals that remained increasingly dealt only with straightforward cases, referring the more serious to regional medical centres. Ironically enough, the tendency to limit the type of medical assistance provided locally also contributed to the disinclination of doctors to settle outside metropolitan areas.

The emergence of health insurance schemes lay at the heart of the expansion of medical services in the twentieth century. However convinced of the merits of medical treatment, the majority of citizens could not readily assume its costs. In 1921, in the wake of labour unrest and a deadly flu epidemic, a provincial Royal Commission unsuccessfully recommended a health insurance program for wage earners who earned less than $3,000. Eight years later a second provincial commission again scrutinized health insurance. Doctors of the day, whose unpaid work was estimated in 1929 to include 29 per cent of patients, and in 1933, the worst year of the Depression, 52 per cent, seemed initially sympathetic. When polled, however, they overwhelmingly rejected the 1936 provincial Health Insurance Act. In face of such opposition, and despite a 1937 referendum that favoured health insurance by about three to two, Premier Pattullo postponed implementation. Three years later British Columbia doctors inaugurated the voluntary Medical Services Association (MSA) plan with prepayment by contributions collected by employers. By 1950 about 14 per cent of the province's population was enrolled in MSA.

In 1948 the province introduced the B.C. Hospital Insurance Service. After birthing pangs that helped defeat the Liberal-Conservative coalition in 1952, universality was introduced with the abolition of hospital insurance premiums two years later.[52] The prosperous 1950s prompted Ottawa to introduce the Hospital Insurance and Diagnostic Act of 1957, providing for federal-provincial cost-sharing of hospital plans; British Columbia joined in 1958. In wake of a federal Royal Commission chaired by Justice Emmett Hall, nation-wide medicare was next. With the introduction of medical insurance in 1968 doctors enjoyed the security of good incomes and patients discovered protection from disastrous health costs. Medical and hospital insurance removed a spectre that had haunted all but the richest and contributed, along with rising wage rates and improved social services, to the better health of the general population.

Unlike many other provinces, however, British Columbia's hospital plan from the beginning included daily patient fees. Increases in these fees and those for long-term-care residents, which jumped 56 per cent between 1981–1984, have continued to hit poorest families disproportionately. The Social Credit government's support of the expansion of for-profit medical services in the 1980s led to the entry of multi-national corporations, such as Extendicare and American Medical International, into the province's health care delivery system, soon compromising wage rates for workers and conditions for patients.[53] Nevertheless, despite the advance of privatization, publicly funded hospital care remains one distinction from the United States that British Columbians prize.

At least as critical to improvements in the standard of living in the twentieth century has been the introduction of social security programs, ranging from workers' compensation (1916), mothers' pensions (1920), old age pensions (1927), war veterans' allowances (1930), pensions for the blind (1937), unemployment insurance (1940), family allowances (1944), disabled persons' allowances (1954), to the Canada Pension Plan (1965). During the First World War and the decades that followed, governments recognized that social assistance programs provided a useful means, not only of gaining election, but also of ensuring social peace and of addressing, to a limited degree, the problems of widespread poverty. Mothers' pensions (or allowances as they later became) and old age pensions identified two groups—single mothers and the elderly— who were especially vulnerable to the vicissitudes of the market economy.

Mothers' pensions, pushed by a powerful feminist lobby,[54] were introduced four years after similar legislation had been passed in Manitoba, also by a Liberal government. A rising tide of applicants for its small, means-tested program quickly uncovered unanticipated levels of distress. Although there was plentiful evidence of women employing a variety of strategies to stay afloat (everything from operating boarding houses, going without food themselves, and wresting what they could from gardens and the ocean),[55] 636 women were enrolled with their young children by November 1920, 847 by 1925, and 1,370 by 1930. There were significant restrictions in coverage, as the following case illustrates:

> A woman with three children, one of whom was crippled, was granted a pension after the death of her husband. Three years later she remarried and her pension ceased forthwith. Although she had married her second husband in good faith, it

turned out to be a bigamous union. Her second husband was jailed and on his release disappeared from the scene. With no means of support, the woman reapplied for a mothers' pension but was told that in view of her bigamous marriage she was not a "fit and proper person" to receive a pension.[56]

British Columbia's early pensions, among the most generous in the Dominion, often kept families together. Yet, for all the evidence of suffering they uncovered and the good they did, rising costs often made pensions the target of provincial cost cutting. In the hungry 1930s mothers with one child were generally refused aid and rates overall were lowered. First Nations women continued to be ineligible.

After the Second World War and an upturn in the British Columbia economy, criteria for support were relaxed and benefits increased. Yet not even the inauguration of the Canada Assistance Plan in 1966 changed the fact that the overwhelming majority of single mothers, while better off than in many other jurisdictions, remained trapped in poverty. The New Democratic Party government's experiment with Community Resource Boards (1972–1975) promised much in terms of more humane and fair treatment, but it was too short-lived to do more than raise hopes. The Social Credit government that was returned to power in 1975 responded to the substantial numbers of sole-support mothers on assistance, the greater acceptability of wage-earning mothers, and the availability of so-called female jobs in the service and trade sectors by trying, through the "imposition of work requirements, attempts to alter the benefit system to increase the rewards of low-paid work, and the provision of a variety of employment-related services," to move single mothers off welfare.[57] Under provincial "restraint" in the early 1980s, this group was specifically targeted for reduced benefits and so-called "employables" were subject to more stringent work requirements.[58] Not surprisingly, single mothers provided the first clients for food banks when they appeared in 1982. By 1984 British Columbia led all provinces and territories with forty-seven of Canada's seventy-five food banks; second place Alberta was far behind with twelve.[59] Although the worsening situation was challenged by clients, feminists and the election of an NDP administration in 1991, single mothers remained among poverty's saddest victims.

As evictions of long-time tenants by developers in Vancouver in the late 1980s revealed, the situation of the elderly was also often precarious. Before the introduction of old age pensions by the federal government in 1927 and their immediate implementation by British Columbia, the provincial pioneer, conditions were far worse. Vancouver's home for the aged, Taylor Manor, was as humiliating and uncomfortable as the shacks and fleabag hotels that became refuges for many male veterans of the resource economy. Means-tested pensions at a maximum of $20 per month could provide little comfort in themselves but they offered, especially during the deflationary 1930s, some prospect of independence.

The appearance of the earliest active pensioners' associations in Canada helped keep the heat on politicians. The Old Age Pensioners' Organization of British Columbia, formed in 1932, challenged the increasingly restrictive interpretation of the means test, especially the demand that children prove they could not support their parents.[60] By 1947 the rising cost of living prompted an increase in the maximum benefits, the elimination of some restrictions, such as the exclusion of aliens and provincial residence requirements, and an increase in the maximum allowable income. Four years later, the means test was eliminated for those seventy and older, but retained for a new group of recipients aged sixty-five to sixty-nine. At long last, too, the exclusion of Native people from the benefits of old age pensions was dropped. In 1965 Ottawa introduced the contributory Canada Pension Plan and, in response to the "grey" lobby, added a guaranteed income supplement one year later. Pressed hard by its pensioners, British Columbia led, from their introduction in 1942, in providing supplementary benefits to the needy. In 1972, after an election skilfully managed by the British Columbia members of Pensioners for Action Now, the province promised residents over sixty-five a minimum income of $200 a month.

Although the elderly benefitted most from the attention focused on poverty in the 1960s—reflected in the *Report* of the Royal Commission on the Status of Women (1970) and in *Poverty in Canada* (1971), a report by the Special Senate Committee on Poverty—government policy of holding down old age benefits to a maximum of 25 per cent of the average industrial wage meant that distress for many was never far away.[61] The introduction of a contributory program did not change matters: a work life of low or little earnings meant penury continued into old age, particularly for women. Yet, for all their failure to transform the hierarchy of gender or class, pensions did upgrade the lot of many of the province's most vulnerable citizens. Improved savings, pensions and other government benefits caused the percentage of low-income seniors to drop from 20.5 per cent in 1980 to 8.2 per cent in 1990.[62]

SPORTS AND RECREATION

Improvements in the general standard of living in the twentieth century were also illustrated by the development of sports and leisure activities, many created by the province's numerous voluntary organizations. In the early 1960s, for example, Penticton was typical in having a large number of clubs. These ranged from service groups such as the Kinsmen and Jaycettes, fraternal organizations such as the Elks, the Knights of Columbus, and the Imperial Order of the Daughters of the Empire, community service organizations such as the John Howard Society and the Women's Institute, sports bodies such as the Figure Skating Club, the Senior Soccer Club, and the Ladies' Lawn Bowling Club, youth groups such as the Scouts and Guides, cultural organizations such as the Alliance française de l'Okanagan du sud, the Okanagan Historical Society, the civic orchestra and the Accordion Band, and many others. Penticton's roll call could be matched in most communities, with each contributing associations that reflected its own particular ethnic, racial and socio-economic history.

Voluntary groups were the mainstay of cultural and sports programs and facilities. They not only acknowledged differences among citizens—as with Vancouver's Scottish and Italian Cultural Centres with their celebration of specific ethnic identities and, less innocuously, the Vancouver Club with its long-time resistance to women, Jews and Asians—but were also instrumental in bringing together British Columbians of diverse origins and sentiments through such undertakings as the highland games that were staged all through the century, the construction of community centres, and support for children's clubs. Such activities contributed something to the population's always fragile sense of common interest.

Of course, not all pleasures were highly organized. Easy access to the natural environment continued to offer most children and adults opportunities for recreation. The human landscape marked by docks, railway lines and derelict buildings also opened worlds to the adventuresome. In his recollections of Vancouver's East Side in the 1940s, Rolf Knight recalled:

> Ball park playgrounds couldn't compete with vacant lots as places to play. The lots offered a tangle of salmonberry and thimbleberry brush, with grassy glades and thickets of willow . . . . Deep hollows . . . filled with spring rain, soon followed by a succession of tadpoles, frogs, and children bearing glass jars and improvised scoops. A few of the largest ponds spawned a fleet of flimsy rafts. But by age ten we were smugly superior to such fresh-water sailoring. We had an ocean at our doorstep, and a rowboat to sail on it.[63]

Although much play remained informal, British Columbians also developed new habits. The youth culture of the 1920s, fuelled by modern advertisers and improving public health, spurred major developments in individual and team sports, ranging from track and field to golf, softball and lacrosse. Young women, liberated by less restrictive dress and moral codes, and supported by the expansion of school and company sports programs, not to mention the enthusiasm generated by surging enrollment in the Canadian Girls in Training and the Girl Guides, increasingly took their turn in swimming pools and on basketball courts and softball diamonds. Home town sports' heroines provided new models of female behaviour. Such was the case with thirteen-year-old Audrey Griffin of Victoria who, beginning in 1915, drew thousands to watch her win provincial women's swimming championships and go on to become the Canadian champion in the 50- and 100-yard freestyle events.

After 1945, improvements in the general standard of living permitted an unprecedented devotion to sports and recreation. Particularly important for families was the emergence of camping as a widespread phenomenon in the 1950s. The expansion of provincial parks gave the urban majority greater understanding and sympathy for the wilderness. Not coincidentally, the children who camped then were often those citizens who, thirty and forty years later, were committed to saving the Stein and the Carmannah Valleys from destruction and insisting that governments expand the number of protected parks and wilderness areas. These same baby boomers' discovery of exercise and clean living, through Participaction Canada first in the 1970s and a host of fitness centres in the 1980s, made them all the more intolerant of the environmental costs of economic development. The fact that their employment no longer depended to the same degree as had their parents on resource development also made it a good deal easier for this generation, especially those living in Vancouver and Victoria, to be environmentally friendly.

The construction of indoor and outdoor facilities, the inauguration of public sports programs, the emergence of national and international sporting events, and the proliferation of voluntary sporting associations involved almost all British Columbians at some time in their lives. Many ties spanned the entire Pacific Northwest, with teams from cities like Seattle, Portland and Port Angeles as regular visitors. From 1921 to 1940, for instance, the University of British Columbia rugby team suited up against Stanford and the University of California for the World Trophy. After 1965 north-south sporting links were continued by teams from Simon Fraser University that battled rivals in Washington, Oregon and other northwest states. Professional baseball and hockey also linked Pacific coast and Interior communities. Teams from cities in British Columbia and northwestern states played in the Pacific Coast Hockey League in the 1920s. In 1939 the Western International Baseball League included Vancouver and five American centres.

Yet, in spite of the proximity of the United States, British influences encouraged devotion to rugby and soccer throughout the century. Many post-war European immigrant groups, like the Italians, also had a long soccer tradition and it was the combined impetus of these enthusiasts that launched the Vancouver Whitecaps in 1974 and, after they folded, the Vancouver 86ers. Even cricket drew dedicated followers, especially after it was introduced in Vancouver high schools in the 1930s.[64] Those in search of a "Canadian" sport kept lacrosse as the staple of life in many communities. Throughout much of the century athletics remained an uncertain amalgam of influences from Europe, the United States, and the rest of Canada.

For many years, despite the national stature of an occasional British Columbian, such as Percy Williams of Victoria who won the 100- and 200-metre sprints in the 1928 Olympics, cross-Canada links were undeveloped. The inauguration of provincial and federal involvement in athletics, beginning with the Provincial Recreation Program in 1934 and the Dominion-Provincial Youth Training Scheme in 1937, strengthened Canadian loyalties. The shared excitement of the British Empire and Commonwealth Games in Vancouver in 1954, where the "Miracle Mile" was run by Roger Bannister and John Landy in Empire Stadium, and the Commonwealth Games in Victoria in 1994, as well as the pace-setting races of sprinter Harry Jerome in the 1960s and the world hockey championships won by the Trail Smoke Eaters (1939, 1961) and the Penticton 'Vs' (1955), helped make British Columbians more conscious of themselves as a group and as Canadians. Support for participation in international events through the creation of Recreation Canada and Sport Canada in 1973 reflected the state's interest not only in keeping young people out of mischief but also in improving national health. Concern about a decline in fitness levels led to the introduction of the Canada Games and the B.C. Youth Games. Nancy Greene of Rossland, who won Olympic gold in the giant slalom in 1968, was an early beneficiary of a program of state aid to sports designed to enhance national and provincial prestige through athletic competition and to improve public fitness.

Yet, for all the wide appeal of major national and international events, many sports have drawn on distinctive local constituencies. Choices often depended on the pocketbook. In the 1930s, for instance, the unemployed drifted to inexpensive games like baseball, softball and soccer whereas the more well-to-do played tennis and golf, rode and sailed. Traditionally, gender was also a determining factor in the choice of leisure activities, but after the First World War, "women of the new day" widened their participation in individual and collective sports. In 1924, for instance, Isobel Coursier of Revelstoke won the ladies' world title in ski jumping. Ethnic and racial communities also sponsored their own favourite pastimes. Finns and Scandinavians introduced many British Columbians to skiing, producing heroes like Nels Nelson from Revelstoke, who took the world ski-jumping record in 1924. With the founding of the Vancouver Judo Club in the 1920s Japanese residents introduced a new sport to the Dominion. Some sixty years later, Terry Fox of Coquitlam and Rick Hansen of Williams Lake broke new barriers in demonstrating the ability of handicapped athletes. The hosting of the Special Olympics and the World Gay Games in Vancouver in 1990, with all the controversy the latter in particular engendered, provided yet further illustration of how sports mirrored other social divisions in the province.

Professional or commercial sport, developing rapidly after the 1920s, promised to unite enthusiastic fans whatever their individual background. Although the B.C. Lions played their first Canadian Football League game in 1954 and the Vancouver Canucks did not make their appearance in the National Hockey League until 1969, the Canadian Broadcasting Corporation began broadcasting Hockey Night in Canada in 1952 and the Grey Cup games two years later. Both, like the Rose Bowl also first aired in 1950s, captured mostly male audiences around the province. By the 1970s, sporting events had become big business. Promoters like Murray Pezim helped make teams like the

B.C. Lions increasingly indistinguishable from their American counterparts, and the increasing commercialization more fully integrated British Columbia audiences into a North American spectator economy.[65]

Spectator events that have mass appeal in one generation can lose it rapidly in the next. The rise and decline of the Pacific National Exhibition (PNE) is an example. Prior to the opening of the then-named Vancouver Exhibition in 1910, the province's farm population had long supported agricultural displays. Closely tied to the development of its city, specifically the East Side, the Vancouver extravaganza soon saw agricultural exhibitors shifting from familiar competitions among themselves to consumer education for urban dwellers. In the 1920s and 1930s the emphasis on amusements and sports grew steadily, as did attendance, reaching 390,000 by 1941. The prominence of Happyland and then, from 1958, Playland, like the Sunday openings after 1968, reflected a world that was overwhelmingly urban and secular. "B.C.'s Fair" always had strong critics. From the beginning the Women's Christian Temperance Union challenged gambling and over the years its moral objections to a variety of PNE events were echoed by a host of religious groups. More significantly, in the 1970s as the fair reached out to a mass audience, it increasingly ignored its old constituency of local sporting enthusiasts. East Side voters, traditionally so useful for majorities in city referenda authorizing municipal support for the PNE, were further alienated by the expressway debates of the 1960s and a shortage of local park land, which became all the more visible as the PNE with a board of directors loyal to the city's business community ate up more space.[66] The glamour of a world's fair, Expo '86, made the PNE seem rather dowdy. Expo's robot mascot, Ernie, symbolized just how much the province had changed since the days of the early agricultural fairs. Just as farmers and their interest in exhibitions had succumbed to the demands of industry and commerce, so too it seemed, by the end of the century, would the PNE give ground before a new generation's realization that, in a computer age, they valued the parkland occupied by the Exhibition more.

Any examination of British Columbia society in the twentieth century inevitably raises the question of community: is there a shared identity or only a shared territory? The gulf that separated the rich and the poor at the turn of the century has not disappeared. For all the expansion of social programs and undeniable improvement in the conditions of life, no significant redistribution of wealth has occurred.[67] "Supernatural British Columbia" is most accessible for a male economic elite of European origin largely based in the Lower Mainland—and for out-of-province tourists. Other groups, like the Solidarity coalition in the early 1980s, struggle to claim their share. Class, ethnicity, race, region and gender, among other factors, continue to divide citizens and to shape fundamentally their experience of the world. Long-standing differences of experience and outlook rooted in the very fabric of British Columbia society exist even when women and men articulate little or no organized expression of them. Whereas traditional written histories tend to focus on the privileged, social history reveals a complex interplay of influences. It comes as no surprise that provincial politics—like the population itself—is fragmented, often polarized, torn among divergent views not only of the future but of the past.

NOTES

My thanks to Jean Barman, Ellen Gee, Arlene Tigar McLaren, and Don Wilson and the members of the B.C. Book group for their comments on earlier drafts of this chapter and to Mary Ellen Kelm and Douglas Cruikshank for their research assistance.

1. Peter Ward, "Class and Race in the Social Structure of British Columbia, 1870-1939," *B.C. Studies* 45 (Spring 1980): 17-35 and René Warburton, "Class and Race in B.C.: A Comment," *B.C. Studies* 49 (Spring 1981): 79-85.

2. Gillian Creese and Veronica Strong-Boag, eds., *British Columbia Reconsidered: Essays on Women* (Vancouver: Press Gang Publishers, 1992).

3. See Angus McLaren and Arlene Tigar McLaren, *The Bedroom and the State: The Changing Practices and Politics of Contraception and Abortion in Canada, 1880-1980* (Toronto: McClelland and Stewart, 1986): inter alia.

4. General Fertility Rate refers to the annual number of births per 1,000 women aged 15-49 years of age and Death Rates refer to the annual number of deaths per 1,000 of population. It should be noted that the data prior to the 1920s when the federal government significantly improved collection procedures can only be regarded as an approximate measure.

5. Paul Yee, *Saltwater City. An Illustrated History of the Chinese in Vancouver* (Vancouver: Douglas & McIntyre, 1988): 55.

6. See G. P. Scardellato, "Italian Immigrant Workers in Powell River, B.C.: A Case Study in Settlement before World War Two," *Labour/Le Travail* 16 (1985): 145-163.

7. See Emily Carr, "Sophie," Carole Gerson, ed., *Vancouver Short Stories* (Vancouver: University of British Columbia Press, 1985) or Carr's *Klee Wyck* (1941).

8. See Table 10, Jean Barman, *The West Beyond the West: A History of British Columbia* (Toronto: University of Toronto Press, 1991).

9. The definition of urban and rural population has shifted several times. Up to and including 1951 urban meant population living in incorporated villages, towns and cities regardless of size while the rest was described as rural. In 1961 and 1971 urban meant residents living in (a) incorporated cities, towns and villages with a population of 1,000 or over, (b) unincorporated cities, towns and villages with a population density of at least 1,000 per square mile, (c) the built-up fringes of (a) and (b) having a minimum population of 1,000 and a density of at least 100 per square mile; all others were designated rural. In 1981 and 1986 urban residents were defined as living in an area having a population concentration of 1,000 or more and a population density of 400 or more per square kilometre; all others were designated rural.

10. Dorothy Livesay, "Vancouver," in *The Documentaries* as cited in C. R. Boylan, "The Social and Lyric Voices of Dorothy Livesay." (M.A. thesis, University of British Columbia, 1969): 71.

11. Morris Zaslow, "The Struggle for the Peace River Outlet: A Chapter in the Politics of Canadian Development," Thomas Thorner, ed., *Sa Ts'e.: Historical Perspectives on Northern British Columbia* (Prince Rupert: the College of New Caledonia Press, 1989): 368. For a contemporary account see Monica Storrs' diaries, W. L. Morton, ed., *God's Galloping Girl* (Vancouver: University of British Columbia Press, 1979).

12. Sadhu Binning, "The Canadian Farmworkers Union: A Case Study in Social Movements." (M.A. thesis, Simon Fraser University, 1986): 38.

13. On the efforts of public education to encourage rural living see D. C. Jones, "Education and the Myth of the Land," J. D. Wilson and D. C. Jones, eds., *Schooling and Society in Twentieth Century British Columbia* (Calgary: Detselig Enterprises, 1980).

14. M. McIntyre, *Place of Quiet Waters* (Toronto: Longmans, 1965): 10.

15. John Bradbury, "Instant Towns in British Columbia: 1964 to 1972." (Ph.D. thesis, Simon Fraser University, 1977): 162-163.

16. Peter Baskerville, *Beyond the Island. An Illustrated History of Victoria* (Burlington, Ontario: Windsor Publications, 1986): 108-109.

17. Gillian Wade, "Modest Comforts," *Working Lives: Vancouver 1886-1986* (Vancouver: New Star, 1986). See also her *Houses for All* (Vancouver: University of British Columbia Press, 1994).

18. Dorothy Livesay, "West Coast," in Boylan, "The Social and Lyric Voices of Dorothy Livesay," 55.

19. On Prince Rupert during the war see Phyllis Bowman, *Muskeg, Rocks and Rain* (Prince Rupert, B.C.: s.n., 1973) and for a useful overall assessment of the town's history see K. E. Luckhardt, "Prince Rupert: a 'Tale of Two Cities'," Thorner, ed., *Sa Ts'e.*

20. Tom Malkowsky, "Prince George At War," in Thorner, ed., *Sa Ts'e.*

21. Peter Baskerville, *Beyond the Island: An Illustrated History of Victoria* (Burlington, Ontario: Windsor Publications, 1988): 101.

22. Jill Wade, "A Palace for the Public: Housing Reform and the 1946 Occupation of the Old Hotel Vancouver," *B.C. Studies* (Spring-Summer 1986): 288-310.

23. See Isabel Dyck, "Integrating Home and Wage Workplace: Women's Daily Lives in a Canadian Suburb," *The Canadian Geographer/Le Géographe canadien* 33, no. 4 (1989): 329-341.

24. Barbara Riley, "Six Saucepans to One: Domestic Science vs. the Home in British Columbia 1900-1930," Barbara Latham and Roberta J. Pazdro, eds., *Not Just Pin Money: Selected Essays on the History of Women and Work in British Columbia* (Victoria: Camosun College, 1984): 161.

25. As quoted in Veronica Strong-Boag, *The New Day Recalled: Lives of Girls and Women in English Canada, 1919-1939* (Toronto: Copp Clark Pittman, 1988): 127.

26. Leona M. Sparrow, "Work Histories of A Coast Salish Couple." (M.A. thesis, University of British Columbia, 1976): 20.

27. Mary Sue Devereaux, "New Necessities: Popular Household Appliances," *Canadian Social Trends* (Autumn 1988): 31-33.

28. See *The Challenge of Change: Maintaining British Columbia's Social Safety Nets* (Victoria: British Columbia Ministry of Social Services, 1993): 3.

29. *Ibid.*, 5.

30. See McLaren and Tigar McLaren, *The Bedroom and the State.*

31. See Norah Lewis, "Reducing Maternal Mortality in British Columbia: An Educational Process," Latham and Paxdro, eds., *Not Just Pin Money.*

32. V. Strong-Boag and K. McPherson, "The Confinement of Women: Childbirth and Hospitalization in Vancouver, 1919-1939," in R. A. J. McDonald and J. Barman, eds., *Vancouver Past: Essays in Social History* (Vancouver: University of British Columbia Press, 1986).

33. See Neil Sutherland, "We always had things to do: The Paid and Unpaid Work of Anglophone Children between the 1920s and the 1960s," *Labour/Le Travail* 25 (Spring 1990): 105-141 which focuses on B.C.

34. Indiana Matters, "Sinners or Sinned Against?: Historical Aspects of Female Juvenile Delinquency in British Columbia," Latham and Paxdro, eds., *Not Just Pin Money*.

35. See Jean Barman, *Growing Up British in British Columbia* (Vancouver: University of British Columbia Press, 1984).

36. See Patrick Johnson, *Native Children and the Child Welfare System* (Toronto: Canadian Council on Social Development, 1983).

37. See Joy Parr, *Labouring Children* (London and Montreal: Croom Helm, 1980).

38. See Patricia Rooke, *Discarding the Asylum: From Child Rescue to the Welfare State in English-Canada, 1800-1950* (New York: University Press of America, 1983).

39. Cited in Jean Barman, "Knowledge is Essential for Universal Progress but Fatal to Class Privilege: Working People and The Schools in Vancouver During the 1920s," *Labour/Le Travail* 22 (Fall 1988): 9-66.

40. Neil Sutherland, "The Triumph of Formalism: Elementary Schooling in Vancouver from the 1920s to the 1960s," McDonald and Barman, eds., *Vancouver Past*, 202.

41. See Jane Gaskell, Arlene McLaren and Myra Novogrodsky, *Claiming an Education: Feminism and Canadian Schools* (Toronto: Our Schools/Our Selves Education Foundation, 1989).

42. Ad by York House School, *The Vancouver Courier* (7 January 1990): 12.

43. Harry Con *et al.*, *From China to Canada: A History of the Chinese Communities in Canada* (Toronto: McClelland and Stewart, 1982): 128-130.

44. Joanne Fiske, "Life At Lejac," Thorner, ed., *Sa Ts'e*.

45. See Alvin McKay, Bert McKay, "Education as a Total Way of Life: The Nisga'a Experience," Jean Barman, Yvonne Herbert and Don McCaskill, eds., *Indian Education in Canada: vol. 2, The Challenge* (Vancouver: University of British Columbia Press, 1987). See also in the same volume, Lorna Williams, June Wyatt, "Training Indian Teachers in a Community Setting: The Mount Currie Lil'wat Programme."

46. Barman, "Knowledge is Essential," 66.

47. Lee Stewart, *It's Up to You: Women At UBC in the Early Years* (Vancouver: University of British Columbia Press, 1990).

48. Cited by Neil Sutherland, *Children in English-Canadian Society* (Toronto: University of Toronto Press, 1976): 57.

49. John Norris, "The Country Doctor in British Columbia: 1887-1975," *B.C. Studies* 49 (Spring 1981): 15-39.

50. See Lisa Hobbs Birnie, *Uncommon Will. The Death and Life of Sue Rodriguez* (Toronto: Macmillan, 1994).

51. For discussion of this case and the problems of Natives requiring medical treatment see Dara Culhane Speck, *An Error in Judgement. The Politics of Medical Care in an Indian/White Community* (Vancouver: Talon Books, 1987).

52. See Malcolm G. Taylor, *Health Insurance and Canadian Public Policy* (Montreal: McGill-Queens University Press, 1979): 178.

53. See William K. Carroll, Charles Doyle, Noel Schacter, "Medicare at Risk," Warren

Magnussen *et al.*, eds., *The New Reality. The Politics of Restraint in British Columbia* (Vancouver: 1984).

54. Diane Crossley, "The B.C. Liberal Party and Women's Reforms, 1916-1928," Barbara Latham and Cathy Kess, eds., *In Her Own Right: Selected Essays on Women's History in B.C.* (Victoria: Camosun College, 1980).

55. See Megan Davies, "Services Rendered, Rearing Children for the State: Mothers' Pensions in British Columbia 1919-1931," *Not Just Pin Money* and Strong-Boag, "Wages for Housework: Mothers' Allowances and the Beginnings of Social Security in Canada," *Journal of Canadian Studies* (May 1979): 24-34.

56. Cited in Dennis Guest, *The Emergence of Social Security in Canada* (Vancouver: 1985): 60.

57. Patricia Evans, Eilene L. McIntyre, "Welfare Work Incentives, and the Single Mother," Jacqueline S. Ismael, ed., *The Canadian Welfare State: Evolution and Transition* ed. (Edmonton: The University of Alberta Press, 1987): 101.

58. Chris R. McNiven, "Social Policy and Some Aspects of the Neoconservative Ideology in British Columbia," in Ismael, ed., *The Canadian Welfare State.*

59. Graham Riches, "Feeding Canada's Poor: The Rise of the Food Banks and the Collapse of the Public Safety Net," in Ismael, ed., *The Canadian Welfare State.*

60. Ontario in contrast did not produce its first province-wide organization until 1956.

61. See Kenneth Bryden, *Old Age Pensions and Policy-Making in Canada* (Montreal: McGill-Queens University Press, 1974) and Guest, *Emergence of Social Security.*

62. *The Challenge of Change. Maintaining British Columbia's Social Safety Nets* (Victoria: B.C. Ministry of Social Services, 1993): 6.

63. Rolf Knight, *Along the No. 20 Line: Reminiscences of the Vancouver Waterfront* (Vancouver: New Star Books, 1980): 61.

64. See Ronald Lappage, "The Canadian Scene and Sport, 1921-1939," M. L. Howell and R. A. Howell, eds., *History of Sport in Canada* (Champaign, Illinois: Stipes Publishing, 1981).

65. See Dr. Gerald Redmond, "Developments in Sport Since 1939," Howell and Howell, eds., *History of Sport in Canada.*

66. See D. Breen and K. Coates, *Vancouver's Fair. An Administrative and Political History of the Pacific National Exhibition* (Vancouver: University of British Columbia Press, 1982).

67. See Eleanor Bartlett, "Real Wages and the Standard of Living in Vancouver 1901-1929," *B.C. Studies* 51 (1981): 3-62 and W. I. Gillespie, *The Redistribution of Income in Canada* (Ottawa: Gage Publishing, 1980).

Chapter 10
THE ECONOMY
SINCE THE GREAT WAR
John Douglas Belshaw and David J. Mitchell

ajor shifts in British Columbia's economy have occurred in almost every
generation since the First World War. The transitions and turmoils of the
interwar years, the restructuring that took place in the 1940s, the boom years
following the Second World War, and the uncertainties of the post-OPEC era
have produced a succession of distinctive environments for those working and
investing in the province. Individuals who have lived through the past eighty
years have witnessed remarkable changes in market orientation, in the composition of the workforce, and in the industrial character of British Columbia.
Underlying all these changes, however, has been the persistence of the
resource extraction base, with its low level of secondary processing. In an age
when British Columbia has been described both at home and abroad as "the
Brazil of the North," and when talk continues of diverting Interior rivers to
slake the thirst of Californian farmlands, British Columbians remain characterized as hewers of wood and drawers of water.

THE INTERWAR YEARS

This survey begins in a period of economic dislocation. At the end of the First
World War, British Columbia seemed derailed and unlikely to ever reach her
economic destination. Organized labour, for example, bounced back from its
pre-war reverses and mounted a campaign of strikes in the immediate postwar
period. In 1918 alone there were more than a dozen strikes in Vancouver, a
major factor in the constitution of renewed managerial assaults on labour.
Conflict carried on into the next decade, when the recession of 1920–1923 finished off what the employers' associations had begun.

The interwar years therefore began with a sense of uncertainty, a sense that
grew out of lower-than-expected property values, fewer-than-anticipated new
farms, and leaner-than-hoped profits from the export sector. Government policy at the time included John Oliver's much-touted settlement scheme, which
aimed at funnelling Old World emigrants into the agricultural belt of the south
and the newly opened granary of the Peace River district. The strategy was only

a partial success, though the draining of Sumas Lake, the dyking of the upper reaches of the Fraser Valley, and improved access to the Peace District were to be assets over the longer haul.

The project that influenced provincial economic development most decisively in these years was an American one, far to the south. The Panama Canal, though completed before the First World War, became the main conduit for British Columbian exports in the late 'teens and early 1920s. Its implications for the British Columbia economy are still startling to recount.

When the canal across Central America opened in 1914 it had the effect of chopping freight costs for heavy commodities by about two-thirds. For example, British Columbian timber shipped to New York by rail carried a $27.30 freight bill per thousand feet; via the canal shipping charges fell to only $10.11. This placed British Columbia wood in a competitive position *vis-á-vis* American pine and fir products in the same market.[2] Although Prairie demand for west coast wood products caught up to pre-war levels in 1928, its share of British Columbia's exports had been eclipsed by growing demand in Atlantic and central Canada and the eastern United States during the intervening years, an indication of the impact the canal had upon the regional economy.[3] By 1924 British Columbia was exporting over one million long tons through the canal (see Figure 1), hardly more than one-fifth of which wound up in eastern Canada. The other side of this particular coin was that exports from Atlantic ports to British Columbia also grew dramatically. In 1921, 39,561 long tons of freight left eastern Canadian ports bound for British Columbia; three years later that figure had grown to 110,677 long tons.[4]

Running against vastly boosted shipments to Atlantic ports was a steady decline in British Columbia's business around the Pacific Rim. The foremost example of this atrophy was the downward spiral in the coal industry. San

Figure 1: Shipping from B.C.'s Pacific Ports via Panama Canal, 1921–32 (in long tons)

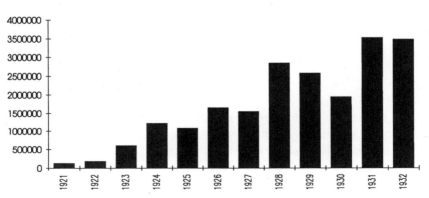

Francisco had been the greatest importer of Vancouver Island coal prior to the 1906 earthquake, but from 1896, for reasons unrelated to seismic thrills, the Californian fuel economy became oriented towards petroleum and oil products. Vancouver Island coal exports slumped from 1 million tons at the turn of the century to 350,000 tons in 1922 and to only 50,000 tons in 1930.[5] Changes in shipping technology were also critical in this regard, as 80 per cent of world shipping was by 1924 using oil rather than coal for fuel; similar patterns affected rail transport in the 1940s. The transition to mineral oils had an equally lethal effect on the provincial whaling industry, albeit over a much shorter period of time. In 1911 (a peak year) 812 whales had been landed on Vancouver Island's west coast; by 1921 the industry had closed down on the Island's Pacific shore and in the Gulf of Georgia. Although whaling persisted in the Queen Charlotte Islands and would reappear briefly around Vancouver Island after the Second World War, it was effectively destroyed when mineral oils replaced animal oils.[6]

Other parts of the Pacific Rim offered few new opportunities in the 1920s. International politics gradually closed off Japan and the Soviet port of Vladivostok from British Columbia's trade, and the development of new, largely parallel economies in Washington, Idaho, Oregon and even Alaska cut into the province's trade with California. By the 1920s, then, external factors including external infrastructural improvements and changes in international markets drew British Columbia further from its nineteenth century orientation. Britain's "little window on the Pacific" quietly closed as British Columbians turned towards North America and Europe.

Trade with eastern Canada and the Prairie provinces accelerated in this decade, largely due to heavy capital investments in freight handling, most notably in and around Vancouver harbour. The recommendations of a 1906 Royal Commission resulted in the construction of the port's first grain elevator during the First World War. By 1925, five more elevators had been added to speed service, giving Vancouver a total storage capacity of 6.9 million bushels.[7] Another elevator was added in the same year at Prince Rupert to handle the Grand Trunk Pacific's (GTP's) grain shipments from the north/central Prairies. The impact on Vancouver's economy was especially profound. From a lowly 4 per cent share of Canadian grain in 1921–1922, the terminal city's exports grew to 41.9 per cent by 1932–1933.[8] These expensive handling facilities were, however, underused for the next four decades, having to await the revival of trade links with Asia.

Transportation corridors *within* the province also improved during the interwar years. In the south, the Kettle Valley Railway (KVR) was completed in 1916, enabling mineral wealth to be shipped from the Kootenays and Tulameen, and apples from the Okanagan. The line had its problems, some of them very serious too: its route through the treacherous Coquihalla exposed the KVR to avalanches and shut-downs during the winter that repeatedly crippled the railroad and hobbled the local economy.[9] The Canadian Northern Railway (subsequently the Canadian National Railway [CNR]) entered British Columbia near Jasper, descended along the banks of the North Thompson River, and thereafter ran roughly parallel to the Canadian Pacific Railway (CPR) all the way to the coast. Cutting through the Rockies at the same point as the CNR, the GTP arrived at the purpose-built port city of Prince Rupert, holding out high hopes of a second Vancouver-style boom in shipping and real estate. The GTP had broader regional implications as well, but these awaited the arrival of the hapless Pacific Great Eastern (PGE) from the south.[10] The PGE's construction got infamously stalled in the 1920s: it stretched only between Squamish and Quesnel (1931 population: 450) and thus linked up with neither the GTP in the north nor Burrard Inlet in the south. To 1929, the PGE had cost the provincial treasury more than $63 million; subsequent governments were inclined to cut their losses and therefore neglected the province's missing link until the 1950s. The GTP's performance was no more inspiring, due to a decline in British shipping across the Pacific and Prince Rupert's distance from other coastal ports: the line's potential was never fully realized. "Behind its miles of track lay millions of English pounds squandered in Canadian railways like lives in the trenches."[11]

More generally successful was the growth of private transport, as well as the roads and highways. In the twelve years before the Depression, automobile ownership leapt from 15,000 units to approximately 100,000 units.[12] However, except for the Pattullo Bridge (which connected New Westminster with the south shore of the Fraser River in 1937), there were few remarkable improvements in highways. Roads grew in numbers but remained largely unpaved; some were barely better than wagon trails. Blacktopping a road from Vancouver through to the Rockies would have to wait until after the Second World War, as would 1930s-era hopes for an improvement in tourist visits.[13]

Even so, the arrival of the automobile industry had other ramifications because it required new supporting industries. In typical British Columbia fashion these industries were long on resource extraction and short on processing, but at least they opened up areas hitherto largely untouched. Lead output, for example, expanded in the 1920s from 20,000 tons to 160,000 tons and zinc output grew at roughly the same rate. By mid-century these two sectors of the mining industry towered over the tiny contribution by then being made by the founding minerals of the industry in British Columbia: coal and gold.[14] Demand for copper was similarly brisk in the interwar years. A massive new mine was opened at Anyox in 1916, along with a port on Observatory Inlet. Geared to servicing the needs of the Laurel Hill Refining Company of Long Island, New York, the little town of Anyox grew, blossomed, wilted and died, all within the space of twenty years.[15] The experience of Anyox was not, in most respects, exceptional. "A good number of the settlements of the last half-century," wrote Edwin Black in 1968, "have had something of the nature of 'instant towns', and a few in recent years have even sprung from bush to beer parlour within the space of several months."[16] Especially in the precarious mining sector, the return to "bush" could be equally expeditious, as the recent experience of Cassiar demonstrates.

Uneven capital improvements and mining ventures aside, the provincial economy took on important new features in the interwar years. Expectations were raised with respect to living standards, and by all indications Vancouverites (if not other British Columbians as well) were enjoying a better life in the 1920s than they had less than a generation earlier.[17] Individual wages remained relatively buoyant because of a continuing shortage of labour in most sectors.[18] Household incomes were improving thanks in part to the growing participation of women in wage labour prior to the crash.

Opportunities for employment were, however, finite. The dependence on a narrow export sector only intensified between the wars, and that sector was typified by unprocessed, unrefined goods. Over half of the value added in manufacturing in 1927 occurred in "fish-packing, sawmilling, pulp and paper, and non-ferrous metal smelting."[19] The consequences of this concentration were evident around the port of Vancouver, where sawmills, grain elevators, shipyards and canneries were the norm. If the economy of Vancouver was "very much underindustrialized," so too was the rest of British Columbia.[20]

This is not to say that sectors other than mining, logging and freight handling were inconsequential. In 1921, nearly three times the number of men and women employed in the logging sector were engaged in service industries. More than one-in-seven British Columbian workers earned wages either in the professional or "private" service sectors, about one-in-nine were engaged in the trade and finance sector, and an almost identical number in manufacturing. By 1931 (two years into the Depression) the number of workers in each of these areas had increased while the numbers of wage earners employed in logging and mining had failed to grow with the population. Ten years further along, in 1941, the real numbers had enlarged still more in manufacturing and service: jobs in these sectors had nearly doubled since 1921. The temporary and shallow depression of the early 1920s, the boom that followed, the sharp and prolonged downturn of the 1930s and the disruption entailed in the Second World War all contributed to an economy that was far from settled or predictable. At any given point, there are considerable shifts in employment, but the most arresting and consequential involve the employment of women.

Female involvement in paid work grew rapidly, at least in absolute numbers. From 9,722 in 1921, the number of women in wage labour grew to more than 20,000 in 1929, suffered a brief and slight reverse in the early 1930s, then resumed its upward march to 27,489 in 1939, 59,176 in 1949 and 70,776 in 1955.[21] It was in the first half of the interwar period that Vancouver's West End began to develop features of a bedroom community for young women in secretarial work. From 1921 to 1941 female involvement in the service sector nearly trebled and the proportion of the service sector (outside of professional

Figure 2:
Employment of Women in British Columbia, by Sector, 1921–1986

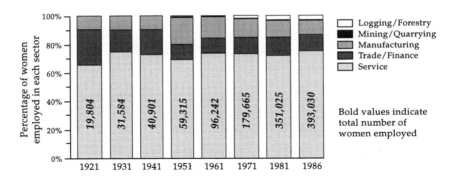

categories) that was female passed the 50 per cent mark sometime during the Depression. Domestic service, however, declined in the 1930s and some of this slack had to be taken up by opportunities for female labour in manufacturing and services. The majority of women working for wages in 1941, as in 1921, however, were still in the service sector (as can be seen in Figure 2), but only just—47 per cent found jobs elsewhere.

Spending power, of course, was to diminish generally throughout British Columbia in the 1930s, but the 1920s held out the hope of unending prosperity right to the end. The few months between the election of S. F. Tolmie's Conservative Party in July 1928 and the Wall Street Crash of October 1929 were to witness some of the most remarkable economic bursts in the history of the provincial economy. Mining stocks in particular traded fast and furiously on the Vancouver Stock Exchange, an institution that had already "acquired a lasting and dubious fame."[22] Wage incomes and housing construction peaked, as did exports in grain through both the port of Vancouver and the port of Prince Rupert. What was to follow was nothing less than devastating. In the 1920s British Columbians enjoyed the highest per capita incomes in the country, generally as much as 15 per cent higher than those of their nearest rivals in Ontario; from 1929 to 1933 British Columbia's per capita incomes fell by nearly half and their recovery to 1936 was slower than that in all provinces apart from Saskatchewan and Alberta.[23]

The immediate source of this grief was the province's heavy reliance on vulnerable commodities exports.[24] World demand for tinned salmon packed in Steveston, grain shipped west from Saskatchewan, orchard fruits from the Okanagan, and minerals won from the deep and dangerous mines of the Kootenays and the Crowsnest Pass simply fell away. Secondly, the imposition of tariffs by the United States in 1930 (increased in 1932) had dramatic effects. In 1929, 350 million board feet of British Columbia timbers had gone to the eastern United States; by 1933 it had fallen to only 29 million.[25] These exports were in decline earlier in the 1920s, but a growing amount of output was being shipped to the United Kingdom and the Empire. For example, British Columbia's share of Australian lumber purchases leapt from 16 to 92 per cent from 1929–1935, and the provincial share of the British market for lumber grew from 20 to 83 per cent. But these were relatively small markets, poor substitutes for the American trade. When Britain imported more of British Columbia's lumber than the United States in 1936, it was a bitter benchmark for the provincial economy.

The fate of exports told only part of the story. In 1929 alone, much of the year's output of 2,400 million board feet of lumber was taken up by the very busy construction industry in booming Vancouver.[26] The population of the province's largest city swelled by 50 per cent in the years between 1921 and 1931, so housing was a prime engine of growth. Domestic purchases were, however, closely tied to the health of exports. When demand for housing on the Prairies dissipated, for example, so too did the Interior logging industry.

The unemployment that resulted from the collapse of international commodity sales was further compounded by the arrival on the west coast of transient labourers, many of them displaced from jobs on the Prairies in the early days of the downturn. As Vancouver became known as "Mecca to the Unemployed," household incomes and the breadth of hardship attributable to the Depression increased. In the year ending 1 June 1931, 45.76 per cent of all male wage earners in all Vancouver industries had lost time through either temporary or permanent layoffs. In forestry and logging more than 87 per cent of the male wage earners had lost time.[27] Housing starts in Vancouver plummeted from 2,400 in 1928 (including houses and suites) to 200 in 1933 and 1934.[28] Nevertheless, per capita incomes—regardless of how badly pared back—were estimated to be higher on the west coast than in any other part of the Dominion, notwithstanding glaring inequities in the distribution of that income.[29]

Government involvement in the social economy marked a new development, one necessitated by the 1930s crisis. From 1912 municipal governments, especially those in Vancouver, began developing welfare programs of a kind. At the provincial level, John Oliver's Liberal government introduced the Old Age Pensioners Act in 1924, following on the Mothers' Pensions Act of 1920 and preceding the federal government's Old Age Pension Act of 1927. Many such initiatives were hurriedly pruned or abandoned as the tax base shrank in the 1930s.[30] The pressure on civic and provincial politicians to intervene with grants for direct relief or work relief quickly intensified. Mayor Gerry McGeer of Vancouver trumpeted that "humanity is going to come first and usury is going to take second place as far as I'm concerned," but repayments on loans and bonds dwarfed what was spent on relief.[31] One alderman telegraphed the Dominion minister of labour and the provincial minister of public works in September 1931 to indicate the anxieties and desperation felt by many at the local level:

> Rain bringing unemployment conditions to a crisis. More than 15,000 registered [for relief in Vancouver]. Twenty-five hundred relief families now requiring clothing and rent. Two thousand homeless single men increasing by seventy floaters daily. One thousand men in [hobo] jungles one man found dead this morning with possible typhoid. Medical officer states epidemic possible.[32]

The situation was hardly better in the countryside, where the prospect of eking out a life through subsistence farming appealed to few, despite the possibilities of some small bonus through trapping, prospecting or guiding wealthy southern tourists. Even in the remote northeast and northwest of the province "quite a few" were dependent on government relief work.[33] Provincial and Dominion governments might have sought to reduce their welfare spending as costs inflated and revenues shrank, but their alternatives were limited and the prospect of widespread disorder (if not outright insurrection) was a terrifying reality. Relief camps administered by the Department of National Defence were one stop-gap measure to deal with unemployment, as was direct payment of relief by municipalities. In order to maximize the effectiveness of their own programs and either to genuinely discourage fraud or to give the impression of wanting to do so, the City of Vancouver and some other communities employed relief inspectors whose task it was to uncover "welfare fraud" cases. This measure itself, of course, had the effect of increasing civic bureaucracies and expenditures. With the advent of professional social work in the 1930s and 1940s, the role of the state as a player in the social economy became more fully developed.

RECOVERY AND EXPANSION IN THE 1940S AND 1950S

The recovery, when it finally came, was as rapid in British Columbia as anywhere else in Canada. As an agent of change, the Second World War had a significant impact on the economy of British Columbia. It spurred demand for the province's natural resources and set the stage for an extended period of rapid economic expansion and development in the 1950s and 1960s. British Columbia's Pacific coast location during the war against Japan ensured a prompt end to the Depression. Military spending on the coast was an important factor, perhaps best symbolized by beach assault practices at Kitsilano.[34] In manufacturing, shipbuilding along False Creek and Burrard Inlet fired a rapid recovery. The number of employees in the shipyards of Vancouver surged ahead, with the Burrard Dry Dock Company leading the way. Its number of workers grew from 200 to a peak of 17,000 in 1943.[35] Nevertheless, there was nothing like the postwar hangover of the late 'teens and early 1920s in the aftermath of the Second World War. "By freeing shipping lanes and markets and reviving worldwide demand for raw materials, the end of the war caused B.C. exports to increase to almost 4 times the 1940 value by 1949."[36] Reawakened world need for primary products was "voracious," welcome news for the province's minerals, wood and pulp sectors.[37]

It was also music to the ears of a society still smarting from the material hardships of the Depression. In 1944, the Canadian Chamber of Commerce polled residents of Vancouver to learn what they hoped for and expected in the postwar world. The daydreams of urban British Columbians were lush with modern conveniences and other trademarks of an improved standard of living: refrigerators, automobiles and a house in the suburbs.[38] For many Vancouverites — as well as for British Columbians beyond the Lower Mainland — these fantasies would be realized. However, they could not have anticipated all of the consequences of their desire for the good life. British Columbia was poised to join with the rest of the postwar western world in an unprecedented boom. And Canada's Pacific province, with the combination of resource wealth and almost chronic underdevelopment, had comparatively greater potential for growth.

The global conflict just ended had stimulated increased production in virtually all industries and in all parts of the province. During the 1940s, the real domestic product of British Columbia almost doubled.[39] This spectacular economic surge went hand in hand with a rapid increase in population. Even prior to the postwar "baby boom," British Columbia experienced a continuing growth based upon steady in-migration from other Canadian provinces as well as from abroad. To place this in a national context, British Columbia had ranked sixth among all provinces in total population until 1931, when it grew to fifth largest. At the outset of the Second World War, British Columbia had moved into fourth position. By the end of the war, when the provincial population surpassed one million, British Columbia trailed behind only Ontario and Quebec.[40]

During the early 1940s, the National Selective Service (NSS) registered women from coast to coast, with an eye to meeting wartime workforce exigencies. The NSS observed that, not only were women entering the job market in larger and larger numbers, women were moving from less well-paid positions to those offering higher rates of remuneration.[41] This phenomenon was observed most clearly in the Cominco works at Trail:

On a trip through the hydrogen and ammonia plants in November 1942, a reporter found two young women using testing equipment while other women were scrubbing dirty cathode plates, and two hydrogen workers were shovelling sand for cell covers. Hearing the sound of a hammer tapping metal, he discovered another young woman shaping plate clips. In the assay office, 'beaker girls' were learning how to assay metals, while in lead and zinc tank rooms women took over light jobs such as testing acid thickener samples.[42]

This wartime program was probably the single most aggressive and effective attempt on the part of government to intervene directly in the labour supply since 1918. There was, to be sure, opposition from those who continued to regard women as intruders in the house of industrial labour. Although demands mounted towards the end of Second World War to withdraw women from "men's work," female participation did not disappear. Nor, unhappily, did the yawning gulf between men's wages and women's wages. Before mid-century British Columbian women received weekly wages that were, on average, less than half those paid to men. As consumers, women could play only a limited role with their own money between the wars.[43]

In the decade following the Second World War, the province's industrial labour force expanded by more than a quarter. During the same time period, organized labour grew at a phenomenal rate, increasing its membership by more than three-quarters to almost 200,000. British Columbia became the most unionized province in Canada, with 46 per cent of eligible workers organized in trade unions. By comparison, throughout Canada and the United States only one-third of the labour force was unionized during this period.[44]

The remarkable rise of organized labour in these years can be seen as a direct response to the rapid but haphazard pattern of economic growth in the province. The organizational structure of the resource industries, and the nature of the export markets on which those industries depended, created seasonal and cyclical instability in employment. Industrial relations were increasingly characterized by confrontations between the unions and powerful employer associations over the terms of employment in an expanding but potentially unstable economy. British Columbia would soon become renowned for its long and bitter industrial conflicts and hold the record as Canada's leader in working days lost due to strikes and lockouts.[45]

Industrial conflict, however, could not forestall the rise of British Columbia. The war had stimulated the provincial economy to new heights; the forest, fishing, mining and service industries were operating at or near full capacity. After 1945, the release of wartime savings, the need for investment in new plant and equipment, housing shortages in all regions of the province, capital investments from central Canada (as well as Europe and, increasingly, the United States), and government spending at unprecedented levels helped drive the economy in new directions at high speeds.[46]

THE RESOURCE INDUSTRIES SINCE 1950

New technologies, improved transportation networks and the stirring of large-scale corporate concentration all contributed to a thriving rugged capitalism in British Columbia. Nowhere was this more evident than in the province's forest industry. The postwar housing boom in North America, combined with a strong worldwide demand for pulp and paper products, forced a significant restructuring of British Columbia's most important industry. Less frequently now were logging camps and milling operations independent entities. Rather, previously small-scale forestry enterprises were integrated within larger and larger corporations that added new production facilities to serve growing markets. Soon, new sawmills and pulp mills were being designed and deployed to exploit the forests of the Interior, the region of greatest growth for the industry from the 1950s on.[47]

These developments were expedited by significant changes in the policies governing the publicly owned forest resource. A 1945 inquiry into the state of the industry, the Sloan Commission, favoured larger timber holdings and longer-term harvesting rights. Eleven years later, in a second Royal Commission report on the subject, Gordon M. Sloan reiterated his arguments in favour of "sustained yield" forestry, and security of tenure for forest companies.[48] The recommendations of these reports provided an important part of the institutional and legal context within which the forest industry would act as the key element in the postwar provincial economy.

During the hearings before the second Sloan Commission, one of the province's most celebrated "timber barons," H. R. MacMillan, spoke up against the proposed policy of providing perpetual timber supplies to selected companies. "A few companies would acquire control of the resource and form a monopoly," he warned.

It will be managed by professional bureaucrats, fixers with a penthouse viewpoint who, never having had rain in their lunch bucket, would abuse the forest. . . . Public interest would become victimized because the vigourous innovative citizen business needed to provide the efficiency of competition would be denied logs and thereby prevented from penetration of the market.[49]

MacMillan foretold a dominant future trend in British Columbia's resource industries, one in which his own firm would play a leading role.[50] The merger of the H. R. MacMillan Export Company in 1951 with Bloedel, Stewart and Welch Ltd. was the largest corporate amalgamation in the province's history and from its very inception MacMillan Bloedel has been the dominant forest company in the province.[51]

In the 1950s, the total volume of timber logged in the province began to increase dramatically, feeding larger, more automated sawmills and new sulfite pulp mills, which were significantly more efficient than the older sulfate kraft mills. As the coastal industry was modernized, forestry operations moved aggressively inland, exploiting a different kind of forest resource. The regional nature of the British Columbia forest economy, with the smaller trees and different mix of species in Interior valleys, was only beginning to be understood. As the forest industry grew, so too did the degree of domination by larger, integrated companies. By 1954, the ten largest companies already controlled more than 37 per cent of the total provincial harvest. Within twenty years, ten forestry giants would control 54.5 per cent of the yield of British Columbia's enormous timber wealth.[52]

British Columbia's other resource industries experienced similar concentration of ownership during this heady period of postwar expansion. For example, the main action in the fisheries was drawn away from the isolated fishing communities scattered along the coast that depended on local species. Most of the fishing fleet and processing facilities became increasingly centralized near the mouths of the Fraser and Skeena Rivers. While no longer a leading player in the British Columbia economy, the fishing industry continued to represent up to 5 per cent of the gross provincial product during the post-Second World War era.[53] New pressures on this export-oriented business, however, would alter both its character and its dimensions.

Ships from other nations, particularly the United States, began to compete for fish off the coast of British Columbia in these years. Salmon, herring and halibut stocks were acutely affected, especially when technological improvements in fishing vessels, gear and navigational aids made competition fiercer still. Modern fishing fleets developed the capability to deplete a salmon run critically in just a few days of fishing.[54] In addition, conflicts over government jurisdiction, aboriginal fishing rights and environmental concerns contributed to a long-standing climate of uncertainty for the provincial fishery.

After decades of open access to the commercial salmon fishery, these challenges were partially addressed by shortening the fishing season, improving salmon spawning grounds and regulating licensed fishing vessels. Nevertheless, the federal government's licence limitation program in 1968 produced mixed results and may have placed even greater strains on the resource.[55]

The trend towards a decreasing number of fish canneries, already evident before the war, accelerated in the years that followed. Fish-processing facilities became larger, more efficient, and consolidated predominantly in the Vancouver and Prince Rupert areas. Almost inevitably, this traditional resource industry evolved into a highly capitalized business, dominated by a few major companies. By 1972, for example, the four top companies accounted for 65 per cent of the salmon production in the province, with more than half the entire catch taken by B.C. Packers alone.[56]

Even in agriculture, always one of the least consequential export sectors of the British Columbia economy, manufacturing firms shrank in numbers while growing in scale. This was most apparent towards the end of the century. In 1970, there were fifteen vegetable and fruit processing firms operating in the province; by 1993 there were only three, all with centralized operations in the Fraser Valley, all owned by corporations with head offices outside of British Columbia.[57]

Despite the scarcity of good farmland in British Columbia, a diversified and specialized agricultural economy showed steady growth in the postwar period. Even prior to 1940, the pattern of agricultural production was well established and concentrated in the Fraser Valley, southern Vancouver Island, as well as the Okanagan and other Interior valleys. Improved transportation systems allowed the various farming districts to become better integrated into the provincial economy. For example, the completion of the Hope-Princeton highway gave fruit and vegetable producers in the Okanagan better access to the growing metropolitan market on the coast. Likewise, the extension of the PGE to the Peace River region permitted feed grains to be transported directly to cattle-feeder lots in the Fraser Valley.[58]

Although the total value of farm cash receipts grew at a steady rate, ultimately making agriculture a billion-dollar industry in British Columbia, one key characteristic differentiated it from other resource industries: most of the products were consumed within the province. However, the industry would never meet the province's expanding food requirements and, therefore, it was forced to compete against imported—mainly American—produce. Unique forms of co-operative marketing were one result. The tree fruit business, which for many decades produced the industry's only major export crop, continued to lead the way. As early as the 1920s, co-operative marketing schemes had been established by Okanagan fruit producers to combat the challenges of competition and distant markets.[59] The next step was the formation of the first agricultural commodity boards in the late 1930s as a defensive response to improved technologies such as refrigerated rail cars, which allowed fruit and vegetable production from other regions, like California, to be shipped to the British Columbia market. Thus the early co-operatives and grower associations evolved into regulatory bodies whose goals were to stabilize production and sales.[60] Postwar marketing boards had a great impact on provincial agriculture, one that gave rise to a prolonged debate over whether the boards served the public interest.[61]

Supply management through marketing boards and anti-dumping legislation undoubtedly helped stabilize and diversify British Columbia's agriculture industry. The provincial government's preservation of all agricultural lands for farm use through the Agricultural Land Reserve in 1973 had a similar effect. There can be no denying that agriculture, as a productive, reliable resource industry, has played an important part in the life of the province. However, "agribusiness" has not been immune to the threats and challenges faced by other sectors of the economy. High capital and operating costs and the global drive to reduce and eliminate trade barriers ensured that British Columbia farmers would confront increased competition from imported produce.

The British Columbia economy has other enduring weaknesses, the most important of which has consistently been the small volume of processing or secondary manufacturing. The province's dependence on resource extractive industries continued as the dominant characteristic of the economy during the course of the whole twentieth century. Both of these trends are evident, for example, in the postwar history of the province's largest non-renewable resource industry: mining. Attempts to keep the minerals sector in an expansive mode after 1945 were largely unsuccessful. What temporary flourishes there were—like the 1939 mini-gold rush in the Cariboo—disguised an embarrassing economic truth: British Columbia's was the slowest growing mining sector in Canada from 1945 to 1960.[62] Iron production and export, despite legislation designed to stimulate both ore output and the manufacture of steel, was virtually non-existent from 1919. The growing demand for materials with which to rebuild war-ravaged Japan coaxed 150,000 tons out of the ground and into the Pacific Rim in 1951; growth of iron-ore mining thereafter was rapid and unrelenting, much of the industry concentrating its efforts around old ore bodies on Texada Island and in new finds on the west coast of Vancouver Island.[63]

A similar tale was told in the copper industry. Anyox was never revived, but production was renewed at Britannia Beach, near Squamish. New mines also appeared in the triangle bounded by Merritt, Ashcroft and Kamloops, including the prodigious open pit operations at Logan Lake. In the 1950s and 1960s it would become apparent that the spine of the inland copper ore body stretched south between the Coquihalla and Nicola Valleys to Princeton as well.

In the mineral export trade British Columbia enjoyed unanticipated special advantages. First, the ore bodies were so impure that concentrators had to be introduced at most mines. The technology necessary to accomplish this on a large scale had been one of the more important economic legacies of the First World War. Combined with the first wave of hydro-electric developments in the province, the erection of concentrators across the province allowed the mining sector to advance quickly in the second half of the 1920s. As a consequence, British Columbia could boast tidewater delivery of some of the highest grade mineral wealth anywhere. Second, the province's main competitor in the copper market, Chile, could not avoid a fifty cent a pound freight differential. Finally, Japanese shipping in the north Pacific was loathe to return home with little in ballast so Canadian exporters exploited surplus Japanese shipping capacity without having to construct a special merchant fleet.[64] Nonetheless, ownership and capital accumulation in the mining field favoured offshore interests. Mining licences were made generously available to foreign investors who, typically, developed the final processing aspects of the metal industries elsewhere. British Columbia continued to boom as a mining centre from the 1960s through to the 1980s, but precious little secondary development took place within the province's boundaries.[65]

It was long assumed that an area rich with mineral resources would go through three well-defined stages of development. First, an increasing number of mines would export ores and concentrates. Second, a smelting industry would develop, producing metals to be manufactured into finished product elsewhere. In the third stage, secondary industries would be established for local manufacture of finished products.[66] Despite profound technological changes in the mining industry in the 1950s, and a greatly expanded range of minerals produced in subsequent decades, this seemingly natural course of development was not followed in British Columbia. Instead, the province appeared stuck largely in the first stage, with only two major smelters being developed: Alcan's Kitimat complex producing aluminum, and the Trail smelter producing lead, zinc and sulphur. Although secondary manufacturing, such as steel fabrication, was actively pursued as public policy, distance from markets, the absence of considerable local demand, and the lack of necessary capital to launch such ventures were obstacles not surmounted.[67]

The failure of the mining industry to move from primary extraction to the processing stage and the rapid growth in exporting unprocessed materials abroad was illustrated by the remarkable expansion of the province's coal sector. British Columbia's southeast coalfields were developed in the late 1960s, primarily to mine rich metallurgical seams for export to the Japanese steel industry. Strong demand and impressive increases in productive capacities soon vaulted coal back into first position among the solid minerals mined in the province. In the 1980s, a significant new expansion occurred with the opening of the northeast coalfield at Tumbler Ridge, a "megaproject" that undoubtedly contributed to a world oversupply of the commodity. Coal prices and production soon faltered in both the northeast and southeast, bringing about a painful rationalization of the industry.[68] Any hope of adding secondary processing to this grandiose scheme was thus stymied.

The boom-and-bust cycles so idiosyncratic to British Columbia's resource economy were somewhat less pronounced in the rise of energy and petroleum resources industries following the Second World War. Discoveries of oil and gas in the Peace River region ushered in an era of unprecedented economic activity. In the 1950s, the first oil pipeline crossing the mountains to the coast was being assembled and in 1957 Westcoast Transmission completed the first natural gas pipeline through the Rocky Mountains to the Lower Mainland. Additional pipelines were later built to serve markets throughout British Columbia and, in the case of natural gas, for export as well. The exploration for and development of these energy resources added an important new dimension to the industrial base of the burgeoning provincial economy. In the early 1970s, for instance, the shock of the first OPEC oil crisis was muffled in the province. British Columbians remained relatively unconcerned and, in fact, optimistic about the province's future energy potential. Rather than worry about scarcity, the challenge was one of developing more of the province's energy resources quickly enough to meet growing demands.[69] This pro-development cast of mind was based in large part upon the elaboration of a dynamic, capitalist economy that was, in turn, fuelled by cheap energy.

DEVELOPMENT AND DIVERSIFICATION

The provincial government's desire to develop British Columbia's massive potential for hydro-electric power generation was one of the most crucial factors in the industrial expansion of the 1960s and beyond. With more than 8 per cent of the world's fresh water supply within its boundaries, large-scale hydro development had long been a part of British Columbia's dream of future prosperity. Unlike fossil fuels, water power is renewable and, therefore, probably the province's most important natural resource. The harnessing of mighty rivers and production of immense amounts of electrical power was a distinguishing feature of the provincial economy, one that helped focus international attention as never before on Canada's westernmost frontier.

Until 1961, the private sector—in the form of the B.C. Electric Company—held sway in the hydro-electric business. In that year, however, the ostensibly free enterprise Social Credit government led by W. A. C. Bennett expropriated B.C. Electric and merged it with the provincial Power Commission, forming the B.C. Hydro and Power Authority.[70] This new Crown corporation became an aggressive factor in economic development, overseeing the implementation of the Columbia River Treaty concurrently with the exploitation of the power potential of the Peace River.[71] This was Bennett's famous "Two Rivers Policy." A controversial economic and political strategy, the overall result was the tripling of the province's hydro-electric generating capacity over the quarter-century that followed and the provision of inexpensive power as an incentive for energy-intensive industries. Hydro-electricity became a potent symbol for regional economic growth and greatly facilitated the resource-led expansion of the provincial economy.

The practice of using large-scale public works as tools for province building set the pace for an increased participation by government in the economy. British Columbians' views about an appropriate role for the state had been fundamentally altered by the signal experiences of the Depression and the Second World War. Across Canada provincial government expenditures thereafter grew rapidly, regardless of the ideologies propounded by the political parties in office.[72] In British Columbia, however, public policy in the 1950s and 1960s was more explicitly directed towards growth and facilitating the development of resource industries than to equality or social concerns. It has been suggested that this may be typical of policy making on any frontier.[73]

Cheap electricity was one prong of Social Credit's developmental agenda; the construction of new transportation corridors into and throughout the Interior was another. The PGE railway was not only extended north to the Peace River country, but southward at last from Squamish to the north shore of Burrard Inlet. Renamed the British Columbia Railway (BCR) in 1972, this Crown corporation served as an economic spine connecting the central and northern Interior to the Port of Vancouver and tying into established east-west rail networks such as the Canadian Pacific and the Canadian National. In the 1980s, the BCR was extended from the northeast coalfields to the Port of Prince Rupert, serving numerous industrial customers across the province's north.

Victoria played a key role in shaping this revolutionary transportation era. In 1958, for example, the government went into the ferry business by taking over a private firm. The ships of this new Crown corporation, the B.C. Ferry Corporation, threaded the Strait of Georgia and the Gulf Islands, stitching together a regional economy. In the process the corporation assembled one of the largest and most modern ferry fleets in the world. In addition, various branches of the provincial administration operated ferry services on the lakes and rivers of the Interior, especially in the Kootenays and the southeast; these were expanded and improved, too, during the 1950s and 1960s.

What happened on the waterways and railways was, however, easily overshadowed by postwar road-building projects. In the 1950s, thousands of miles of new highways were constructed, often through extremely rugged terrain. Practically all existing roads and highways were paved and repaved. New bridges built across the province's many rivers ensured that virtually every British Columbia community would be served by a modern highway. W. A. C. Bennett and his government were hailed as "the New Romans" and the premier may well have been correct when he boasted in 1960 that it was "the greatest highway building program, not just in British Columbia's history, but per capita in the entire western world."[74]

There can be no doubt that the province's resource industries profited from the new highways and transportation routes. Major industrial plants began to appear in what had previously been remote, inaccessible areas. In some cases instant communities—often "company towns"—emerged along rail lines or new roadways. The rationale for updated transportation systems was the building of a modern, efficient resource-based economy, but the immediate beneficiaries included an entire generation of engineers, contractors and construction workers[75] who enjoyed almost full employment and rising incomes. In fact, it may be more accurate to describe these years not so much as the time of a "natural resource boom" as of a "construction boom."[76]

Nevertheless, by developing the energy resources and transportation infrastructure in so bold a fashion, the rate of investment in the province's resource economy was certainly accelerated. Also, British Columbia became much more integrated as an economic region. The historic concentration of population and activity in the province's southwest corner was successfully challenged to the extent that Interior and coastal regions experienced steady growth while, at the same time, becoming more closely interconnected to the larger provincial, national and international economies. New dimensions were added to the traditional metropolitan-hinterland relationships between Victoria, Vancouver and the rest of the province as regional centres like Kelowna, Kamloops, Prince George, Prince Rupert and Nanaimo fostered their own expanding spheres of economic influence.

In addition, British Columbia's economic base slowly began to diversify. While forestry, mining and other resource industries would continue to drive the economy, a gradual increase was evident in complementary service-related activities. The growth of government bureaucracy in the form of an array of public sector agencies and Crown corporations also contributed to the changing character of the provincial workforce. In fact, with a growing public service and the advent of Big Government, especially in the 1970s, the province of British Columbia became the largest single employer west of the Rockies.

Perhaps the best example of diversification has been the emergence of tourism as a leading economic sector. Tourism's worldwide expansion in the postwar era was based on rising incomes, increased leisure time and improved modes of travel. These were among the main factors that brought visitors from other parts of Canada and from abroad in ever-increasing numbers, primarily to enjoy the spectacular natural beauty of British Columbia. By the 1980s, the hospitality industry had grown to the point where it had become a significant element of the gross provincial product, attracting millions of tourists and billions of dollars of revenue to the province.[77] The enormous resources expended on Expo '86 in Vancouver were simultaneously a recognition of and an investment in tourism.

As the landscape and natural environment became important generators of wealth, however, tourism and outdoor recreation came into increasing conflict with the primary industries that underpinned the provincial economy. Tensions mounted between conservationists and those who sought continued access to British Columbia's natural resources. As a result, a serious public debate was engendered about the sustainability of the province's one-hundred-year-old economic foundation.[78] In the 1990s, these two visions for British Columbia—a future rich with jobs in resource extraction and a handsome balance of payments in trade, versus one typified by a pristine wilderness environment of unparalleled splendour that would yield a bounty from international tourism— moved further and further apart. It would be incorrect, however, to assume that these concerns are rooted exclusively in the late twentieth century. Progressive reformers in the pre-1914 era called for prudence and an end to an "epoch of reckless devastation . . . that we may hand down [to subsequent generations] their vast heritage of forest wealth, unexhausted and unimpaired."[79] Their victories were briefly savoured: by 1923, Victoria's policy emphasized short-term profits for companies and revenues for the government over future considerations. The accusation levelled at the government of the day, that, by their policies, they were "turning Vancouver Island into a 'howling wilderness,' " should have a familiar ring in the 1990s.[80] Confrontations over the destinies of the Stein Valley, Clayoquot Sound and the Tatshenshini watershed are typical of the variety of conflicts that have occurred well beyond the historically more familiar barricades of race and class.

Even though a rich endowment of natural resources meant that the character of British Columbia's economy remained essentially unaltered throughout the course of the twentieth century, a most significant structural change took place during the postwar years as the result of the steady growth of the service sector. Although secondary manufacturing failed to emerge as part of what some believed to be a "natural course of development," service-producing industries increased their output each and every year. These businesses, sometimes tied only indirectly to the resource-based goods-producing sector, included transportation, communications, storage, wholesale and retail trade, finance, insurance, real estate, personal business services, and public administration.

An analysis of the industrial distribution of the province's gross domestic product (GDP) reveals that by 1961 British Columbia was already a service economy, with more than 60 per cent of total economic output derived from service industries.[81] Over the next thirty years, the percentage of GDP attributable to services would rise to approximately 70 per cent. What is more, in excess of 60 per cent of the provincial labour force was employed in services in 1960: by the early 1990s, that share had surged to almost 80 per cent.[82] Indeed, not only was the percentage share of services-related employment in Canada amongst the highest of western industrialized countries during the period from 1960 to 1990, but British Columbia's service sector employment was also consistently higher than the Canadian average.[83] During roughly the same period, the resource-based share of British Columbia's GDP declined from approximately 30 per cent to about 20 per cent.[84] These shifts in employment and economic output were generally consistent with the kinds of changes evident throughout the postwar western world. As a result, some observers suggested that British Columbians no longer needed to be concerned about developing new secondary manufacturing industries, because they had already progressed to a new stage of development: a post-industrial economy.

Such a view was misguided and demonstrated a fundamental misunderstanding of the nature of the service sector. In fact, the myth of a post-industrial economy fails to appreciate how resource and manufacturing industries are the drivers of an export-oriented economy such as British Columbia's.[85] It is important to recognize that service industries provide primarily for the domestic economy and are largely auxiliary to the resource sector, which generates growth through exports. In this sense, the service sector is at least indirectly tied to the dynamism of primary resource industries. Although services have grown remarkably in British Columbia since the Second World War, and have contributed to both the diversity and stability of local economies, it is not yet possible to say with certainty whether they have simply supported other industries or generated activity elsewhere in the economy as well.[86] However, it is clear that without the profits and incomes generated by the resource extraction and primary manufacturing sectors, the province's service industries would have been much smaller.

THE CHANGING WORKFORCE

The exceptional growth of the service sector can be partially explained by the province's relatively high rate of population increase. In 1950, Canada's westernmost province had about 8 per cent of the country's total population. By 1990, British Columbia had more than three million residents, representing more than 12 per cent of Canadians. This population boom resulted in employment expansion in fields such as health care, education, the food industry and a wide variety of business services. In the meantime, postwar increases in productivity through technological change and specialization led to net employment decreases in the province's resource industries.[87]

However, this shift from goods-producing to service-based jobs masks a significant point: although total employment was declining in resource industries and manufacturing, these jobs were generally better paying and, indirectly, supported service employment. When forestry workers spent their paycheques, for example, stores hired retail clerks. Just as importantly, the forest industry created jobs when it hired trucks to deliver logs to mills or accountants to audit its books. This kind of functional externalization, or contracting out of services, was typical of the specialization practised by British Columbia's resource industries in the postwar period, contributing to a healthy multiplier effect for employment sustained in the goods-producing sector of the economy.[88]

The forest industry accounted for only 7.6 per cent of the province's jobs in 1984, but generated 15.4 per cent of all employment in British Columbia. In effect, the industry contributed more to employment in other sectors of the economy than those other sectors contributed to the forest industry. The same can be said of mining, which provided 2.1 per cent of British Columbia's jobs directly, but generated 4.5 per cent of the province's total employment. While the multiplier effect for employment in fishing and agriculture was not as strongly felt, the resource industries as a whole accounted for almost one-quarter of all the province's jobs in 1984, though on a direct basis they employed only 15 per cent of British Columbians. Approached from a different angle, although the business service sector employed 54 per cent of British Columbia's workers, many of those jobs were in fact generated by primary resource industries. Without those economic engines, business services would have accounted for only 30 per cent of the province's jobs in 1984.[89]

Nevertheless, the general trend in private sector employment was away from large corporate employers, especially those involved in resource extraction or manufacturing, and towards smaller, service-oriented businesses. Meanwhile, employment in the public sector (notwithstanding major and painful excisions under Bill Bennett's government in the mid-1980s) continued to grow, with about one in five British Columbia workers employed in the broader public service by the early 1990s. The core civil service represented approximately 40,000 government jobs. However, when teachers, nurses, police and employees of

Crown corporations were added, the number of public sector workers totalled more than 300,000.[90]

In 1973, provincial government employees obtained bargaining rights through representation by the British Columbia Government Employees Union (BCGEU). From that time forward, most public sector employees were unionized and public sector unions grew to dominate the organized labour movement in British Columbia. As the industrial structure of the province was transformed, private sector union membership plummeted. For instance, the largest forest industry union, the International Woodworkers of America, was reduced in membership from a high of over 50,000 in the late 1970s to 27,000 by 1993. Most of the new employment created in the private sector over the past two decades has been in small businesses, which tend to provide non-union jobs. In total, the percentage of British Columbia's workforce that was unionized dropped from a peak of more than 55 per cent in 1958 to 38 per cent in 1990—still higher than the Canadian average of less than 35 per cent.[91]

In small businesses, big government, and in some cases even the traditional resource industries, one of the most significant changes in the province's employment structure after the Second World War was the dramatic increase in the rate of female participation in the labour market. Partially a consequence of the rise of service industries, which provided proportionately greater numbers of jobs to women, female participation in the workforce became the norm rather than the exception. At the end of the Second World War, women comprised only 18 per cent of British Columbia's labour force; by 1970, that percentage had grown to 34. In 1984, the proportion of jobs in British Columbia held by women had reached 40 per cent; by the early 1990s the percentage was 45.[92]

The social revolution of this era, which included significant changes in marriage patterns, contributed to the transformation of the province's workforce. Particularly through the last two decades of the century, British Columbia women have been marrying later, having fewer children and more frequently working outside the home while raising children. At the same time as increasing numbers of single women and single mothers were entering the labour market, an influx of married women into the workplace occurred. In 1967, two-income families made up 32 per cent of all husband-wife families in British Columbia; in 1981, the number of dual-earner families had increased to 55 per cent; by 1990, the percentage had increased again to 62.[93]

Between 1975 and 1990, women obtained more than 60 per cent of the new jobs created. However, women still remained concentrated primarily in a small number of occupations that were usually at the lower end of the pay scale. In 1990, the two lowest paid occupation categories—clerical and service—accounted for 52 per cent of working women and only 17 per cent of men. As a result, a significant earning differential between women and men has been a constant feature of the British Columbia labour market. Although the gap has gradually narrowed, as late as 1991 it was estimated that men still earned, on average, 30 per cent more than women.[94] This income disparity was in part a reflection of the overall structure of the provincial economy: the lower-paying service sector was more likely to employ women, whereas the resource industries, such as well-paying wood-manufacturing jobs, have historically provided employment for men.[95] And, as the service sector was regarded (rightly or wrongly) as less significant than the resource sector, it continued to pay lower wages and attract workers with fewer skills (in practice, women).

CONTINUING THEMES

The British Columbia economy, though subject to the inevitable stops, starts and externally induced market "corrections" characteristic of export-oriented capitalism, was remarkably resilient in the postwar period. When the Canadian economy entered a period of economic instability in the late 1950s, British Columbia suffered a brief recessionary interlude. In the early 1970s, coinciding with the province's first New Democratic Party (NDP) government, a more serious recession occurred, caused primarily by the OPEC oil crisis and consequent sharp fluctuations in world prices for resource commodities. However, the most severe setback since the depression of the 1930s was experienced in the early 1980s, forcing widespread concern about British Columbia's economic vulnerability and dependence on a limited range of natural resources. As the worldwide recession of the 1980s played havoc with British Columbia's small, open economy, the province was forced to grapple with a set of conditions never before experienced simultaneously: declining prices for export products, high inflation, falling government revenues and soaring unemployment rates. The term coined by economists, "stagflation," was inadequate to describe the depth of the crisis that hit British Columbia's economy harder than that of any other Canadian province. From 1981 to 1984, employment in British Columbia fell by 79,000 with losses of 3,100 in forestry, 10,400 in mining, 23,600 in construction and 37,700 in manufacturing. Nearly half of the manufacturing employment decline was in the forest industry, with total primary sector jobs dropping by more than 8 per cent. The resource dependence of the provincial economy was devastatingly evident in these slash-and-burn job losses, which cut deeply into the service sector as well.[96]

The responses to this desperate situation did not ease the pain of the recession over the short term, but did point the struggling British Columbia economy in new directions. The Social Credit government, with a new mandate safely secured at the polls in 1983, initiated a policy of radical "restraint" in public spending. Sharp reductions and cutbacks in a wide range of government services, intended to counter the effects of the economic downturn, provoked Operation Solidarity, a massive but unsuccessful popular opposition movement.[97] In the private sector, the province's resource industries also "downsized," embarking on a determined effort to become more competitive by reducing costs, increasing mechanization and automation, and operating with fewer employees. Against this backdrop of hardship and dislocation, the carriage trade in British Columbia—its flagships being the exclusive boutiques of Vancouver's Robson Street and West Vancouver's chic Park Royal—flourished in the "me" decade, an epiphenomenon against which the province could not be immunized, even by high rates of unemployment.

The recession of the 1980s was viewed by some not simply as an ordinary stage in the business cycle, but as a significant restructuring of British Columbia's economy. Certainly, many of the jobs eliminated would never return. In fact, permanent job loss affected the labour force in British Columbia more seriously than in any other part of Canada during this period. Between 1981 and 1985, almost 20 per cent of British Columbians lost jobs that would not be replaced.[98]

This extraordinary reconfiguration can perhaps best be understood by reference to the export orientation of the provincial economy. British Columbia has long been familiar with boom-and-bust cycles; the comparative advantage of bountiful natural resources has been both a blessing and a curse. The overall performance of the provincial economy remained closely tied to international resource markets, over which British Columbia had no control. Early in the century a trading pattern was established that carried through well into the postwar period: British Columbia exported industrial raw materials to the world in order to pay for imports of manufactured goods from the rest of Canada.[99] In the aftermath of the 1980s recession, however, it became clear that this pattern had been altered in a significant way. Although the extreme dependence on resources and exports continued, imports from the rest of Canada dropped and were replaced by purchases from other countries.

Economic "delinking" from Canada was also evident in British Columbia's unique export trade patterns. Whereas other provinces sent more than 80 per cent of their exports to the United States, British Columbia now took full advantage of its waterfront location, shipping more of its products across the Pacific than to the United States. This is not to say that the province was turning its back on North America during a period of nascent continental free trade. On the contrary, by 1991 the Pacific Northwest states purchased more of British Columbia's exports than all of Europe.[100] These increased economic linkages with Washington, Oregon and Idaho generated discussion on both sides of the Canada-U.S. border about the formation of a powerful new economic region, referred to by some as "Cascadia."[101]

Although British Columbia was successfully diversifying its export markets, it was not similarly broadening the range of its exported products. Since 1980, some limited progress has been made in the marketing of remanufactured wood products, telecommunications and electronics equipment, and clothing and apparel; however, 80 per cent of exports are still resource-based products. As late as 1989, two-thirds of all foreign sales of British Columbia goods came from five commodities: pulp, coal, copper, newsprint and softwood lumber.[102] The cityscape of Vancouver has silently reflected this industrial immaturity. In the 1940s, office buildings downtown were more likely to house "doctors, dentists, insurance agents, brokers, bailiffs, and accountants than . . . captains of finance and industry."[103] Most of the firms along False Creek—long the rust bowl of the provincial economy—typically employed fewer than fifty workers in the postwar period.[104] The inability to translate the dynamism of the Second World War boom into a long-term recipe for industrial growth was to be capped in the 1970s, when Granville Island was transformed from a jumble of boatyards and steelyards into a genteel shopping oasis. The nearby flanks of False Creek and the hillsides to the south were simultaneously made over into a warren of expensive condominiums, displacing or "gentrifying" the clapboard-sided rooming houses that had only recently played host to hundreds of white and Asian labourers. The further, post-industrial development of the Creek's north shore continues to provoke controversy, but its trajectory is decidedly away from any manufacturing future. What little remains of that past has taken the form of silent museum pieces, like the CPR roundhouse, tellingly overshadowed by gleaming residential towers and buzzed annually by an Indy-style auto race spectacular.

As the province approaches the end of the century, little comfort can be taken in the knowledge that it continues to have a high dependence on primary resource exports: exports have represented about a third of the value of the province's gross domestic product over the past thirty years.[105] The path of least resistance has led to a continuous process of exploitation of natural resources, which in turn has done much to inform the mindset of policy makers, investors and workers alike. Both at home and abroad, resources have become a metaphor for British Columbia.

The critics' refrains have been largely unchanging. In a book on British Columbia and the United States published in 1942, the head of the Economics, Political Science and Sociology Department at the University of British Columbia, H. F. (Harry) Angus, expressed the hope that the establishment of rudimentary resource management commissions and regulations pointed the way from "wasteful exploitation to conservation." His optimism, unfortunately, was premature.[106] Something had to be done, he argued, because mid-century approaches to logging would lead to a resource catastrophe. This message has been echoed in more recent years by those concerned about the province's ancient forests. Angus, who witnessed a Second World War boom in commodity demand, voiced a now-familiar frustration: "in the case of stands of large trees the date of depletion [is] not far removed and nothing can be done to prevent the process."[107]

By the century's final decade, a pervading sense of the depletion of the province's natural resource base coloured British Columbians' sense of economic well-being. Widespread discussion of the end of resource-led growth and the closing of the resource frontier created a heightened urgency for the drive towards economic diversification and new knowledge-based industries. Diverse voices contributed to the insecurity of those living and working in a prosperous but unstable economy. For example, Gordon Shrum, who helped build and manage the megaprojects of the expansive W. A. C. Bennett era, would write in his 1986 memoirs that "the easy good times are over."[108] Shrum argued that British Columbians needed to be more innovative, productive and efficient in order to maintain their high standard of living. Later, the B.C. Round Table on the Environment and the Economy, in a 1993 report, told the citizens of the province that their lifestyles were unsustainable:

> People of B.C. have become accustomed to steady improvements in their standard of living, and we have now inherited strong expectations of ever-expanding economic fortunes—expectations which can no longer be met.[109]

Other themes have also remained constant in the context of the provincial political economy. For instance, the exploitation of the resources of the Interior to benefit the metropolitan area of Vancouver-Victoria was described by George Woodcock as "a kind of giant squid sending out its tentacles and sucking in the wealth of the province." Professor Ronald Shearer was more charitable when he called the relationship a "symbiotic" one, whilst Dr. Martin Robin drew on imagery worthy of a bodice-ripper: "A lady-in-waiting with great expectations, British Columbia blushed and palpitated with each new thrust into its interior."[110]

In the early 1990s, the relationship between the "two economies of British Columbia"—one based in the coastal metropolis and the other in the Interior valleys and plateaus—is less certain. There have been signs that the two regions are in fact developing into distinctly separate economic zones.[111] With more than half of the province's total population, Vancouver and the Lower Mainland as a whole have become increasingly oriented to a service economy, being described as "an urban node in the network of increasingly interdependent cities of the Pacific Rim."[112] Meanwhile, the Interior region of British Columbia continues to be distinguished by its dependence on the resource-based industries. Of course, this simplistic dichotomy ignores the multi-regional nature of the provincial economy, where metropolitan Victoria relies on public sector activities and sub-regional service centres are growing throughout the province.

Historically, these have been inequitable relationships that were probably avoidable in the context of a sprawling resource-based economy. Vancouver has driven much of the economic change in the province since 1886, but it remained reliant on a hinterland it never completely dominated. This serves to emphasize that, in economic terms, there is no single British Columbia. Rather, there are numerous dimensions to a changing provincial economy that continues to repeat patterns established prior to the advent of the twentieth century. The tiny spots of light throughout the Interior and along the coast will likely continue to manufacture the materials and energy necessary to fuel the Big Smoke for many years to come.

NOTES

1. Andrew Yarmie, "The Right to Manage: Vancouver Employers' Associations, 1900-1923," *B.C. Studies* 90 (Summer 1991): 61, 69.
2. W. A. Mackintosh, *The Economic Background of Dominion-Provincial Relations* (Toronto: McClelland and Stewart, 1964): 91.
3. *Ibid.*, 92.
4. Canada, *The Canada Year Book, 1926* (Ottawa: Bureau of Statistics, 1927): 639-640.
5. Denis E. Kerfoot, *Port of British Columbia: Development and Trading Patterns* (Vancouver: Tantalus Research, 1966): 66-69.
6. Charles Lillard, *Seven Shillings a Year: The History of Vancouver Island* (Ganges, B.C.: Horsdal & Schubart, c. 1986): 230-231.
7. Kerfoot, *Port of British Columbia*, 7, 25-26.
8. *Ibid.*, 27, 31.
9. Barrie Sanford, *McCulloch's Wonder: The Story of the Kettle Valley Railway* (West Vancouver, 1977): 213-214.
10. J. Lewis Robinson and Walter G. Hardwick, *British Columbia: One Hundred Years of Geographical Change* (Vancouver: Talon Books, 1973): 39.
11. Cole Harris, "Moving Amid the Mountains, 1870-1933," *B.C. Studies* 58 (Summer 1983): 21-22.
12. *Ibid.*, p. 27.
13. Robin Fisher, *Duff Pattullo of British Columbia* (Toronto: University of Toronto Press, 1991): 277-279.
14. R. E. Caves and R. H. Holton "An Outline of the Economic History of British Columbia, 1881-1951," J. Friesen and K. Ralston, eds., *Historical Essays on British Columbia* (Toronto: McClelland and Stewart, 1976): 158.
15. Kerfoot, *Port of British Columbia*, 76-77; Pete Loudon, *The Town That Got Lost: A Story of Anyox, B.C.* (Sidney: Gray's Publication, 1973).
16. Edwin R. Black, "The Politics of Exploitation," Ronald A. Shearer, ed., *Exploiting Our Economic Potential: Public Policy and the British Columbia Economy* (Toronto: Holt, Rinehart and Winston, 1968): 25.
17. Eleanor Bartlett, "Real Wages and the Standard of Living in Vancouver, 1901-1929," *B.C. Studies* 51 (Autumn 1981): 60.
18. Ronald A. Shearer, "The Economy of British Columbia," Ronald A. Shearer, John H. Young and Gordon R. Munro, eds., *Trade Liberalization and a Regional Economy: Studies of the Impact of Free Trade on British Columbia* (Toronto: University of Toronto Press 1971): 34.
19. *Ibid.*, 16. For the decline in indigenous manufacturing prior to the war, see John Lutz, "Losing Steam: The Boiler and Engine Industry as an Index of British Columbia's Deindustrialization, 1880-1915," *Historical Papers/Communications Historiques* (1988): 168-208.
20. Alan J. Morley, *Vancouver: From Milltown to Metropolis* (Vancouver: Mitchell Press, 1961): 174-175.
21. Minimum Wage Board/Industrial Relations Board, *Reports*, 1921-1955, quoted in J.

Bannerman, K. Chopik, and A. Zurbrigg, "Cheap at Half the Price: The History of the Fight for Equal Pay in B.C.," Barbara K. Latham and Roberta J. Pazdro, eds., *Not Just Pin Money: Selected Essays on the History of Women's Work in British Columbia* (Victoria: Camosun College, 1984): 303.

22. George Woodcock, *British Columbia: A History of the Province* (Vancouver: Douglas & McIntyre, 1990): 211.

23. MacKintosh, *The Economic Background of Dominion-Provincial Relations*, 134-137.

24. L. Blain, D. G. Paterson, J. D. Rae, "The regional impact of economic fluctuations during the inter-war period: the case of British Columbia," *Canadian Journal of Economics* VII, no. 3 (August 1974): 381-401. See also W. A. Carrothers, "The Barter Terms of Trade Between British Columbia and Eastern Canada," *Canadian Journal of Economics and Political Science* I (1935): 568-577.

25. Kerfoot, *Port of British Columbia*, 47.

26. *Ibid.*, 93.

27. John Belshaw, "The Administration of Relief to the Unemployed in Vancouver, 1929-1939." (M.A. thesis, Simon Fraser University, 1982): 27-29.

28. British Columbia Archives and Records Service, G. G. McGeer Papers, Add Mss 9, v.xvi, file 1, "Vancouver—Relief—Work-Housing."

29. MacKintosh, *The Economic Background of Dominion-Provincial Relations*, 134-137.

30. See Patricia Roy, "Vancouver," in Alan Artibise, ed., *Town and City: Aspects of Western Canadian Urban Development* (Regina: Canadian Plains Research Centre, 1981): 493-513; Megan Davies, "Services Rendered, Rearing Children for the State: Mothers' Pensions in British Columbia, 1919-1931," *Not Just Pin Money*: 250-263.

31. Quoted in Norbert MacDonald, *Distant Neighbors: A Comparative History of Seattle and Vancouver* (Lincoln, Nebraska: University of Nebraska Press, 1987): 131-132.

32. Alderman W. Atherton to Hon. Gideon S. Robertson, Dominion Minister of Labour, and Hon. R. W. Bruhn, Minister of Public Works, British Columbia, reprinted in *The Province*, 4 September 1931: 2, 3.

33. Arthur and Cyril Shelford, *We Pioneered* (Victoria: Orca Book Publication, 1988): 184.

34. Bruce Macdonald, *Vancouver: A Visual History* (Vancouver: Talon Books, 1992): 46-47.

35. N. MacDonald, *Distant Neighbours*, 141-143.

36. B. Macdonald, *Vancouver: A Visual History*, 49.

37. Tom Kemp, *Historical Patterns of Industrialization*, 2nd edition (London: Longman, 1993): 155.

38. Robert Bothwell, Ian Drummond, John English, *Canada Since 1945: Power, Politics and Provincialism* (Toronto: University of Toronto Press, 1981): 457.

39. Robert C. Allen, "The B.C. Economy: Past, Present, Future," Robert C. Allen and Gideon Rosenbluth, eds., *Restraining the Economy: Social Credit Economic Policies for B.C. in the Eighties* (Vancouver: New Star Books, 1986): 14, table 1.

40. British Columbia, *A Review of Resources, Production and Government Finances* (19th edition), August 1959 (Victoria: Department of Finance, 1959): 58.

41. *Ibid.*, 305.

42. Elsie G. Turnbull, "Women at Cominco During the Second World War" in *Ibid.*, 430.

43. *Ibid.*, 307-309.

44. Paul Phillips, *No Power Greater: A Century of Labour in British Columbia* (Vancouver: Federation of Labour, 1967): 138-153.

45. Stuart Jamieson, "Regional Factors in Industrial Conflict: The Case of British Columbia," *Canadian Journal of Economics and Political Science* XXVIII, 3 (1962): 405-416.

46. Economist Ronald Shearer shows that capital formation in British Columbia during this period could not have been financed out of provincial savings alone. Shearer, "The Economy of British Columbia," 33.

47. Mary L. Barker, *Natural Resources of British Columbia and the Yukon* (Vancouver: Douglas, David & Charles, 1977): 84-88.

48. British Columbia, *Report of the Royal Commission on the Forest Resources of British Columbia*, Gordon M. Sloan, Commissioner (Victoria 1945); *idem, The Forest Resources of British Columbia: Report of the Royal Commission on the Forest Resources of British Columbia*, 2 vols., Gordon M. Sloan (Victoria 1956).

49. Quoted in Patricia Marchak, *Green Gold: The Forest Industry in British Columbia* (Vancouver: University of British Columbia Press, 1983): 37.

50. For an overview of the long-term failure to plan in the forestry sector, see Jeremy Wilson, "Forest Conservation in British Columbia, 1935-85: Reflections on a Barren Political Debate," *B.C. Studies* 76 (Winter 1987/88): 3-32.

51. Donald MacKay, *Empire of Wood: The MacMillan Bloedel Story* (Vancouver: Douglas & McIntyre, 1982): 163.

52. Marchak, *Green Gold*, 51.

53. William M. Ross, "Fisheries," Charles N. Forward, ed., *British Columbia: Its Resources and People* (Victoria: Dept. of Geography, University of Victoria, 1987): 179.

54. Barker, *Natural Resources*, 118.

55. Brian Hayward, "The B.C. Salmon Fishery: A Consideration of the Effects of Licensing," *B.C. Studies* 50 (Summer 1981): 41-45.

56. Geoff Meggs, *Salmon: The Decline of the British Columbia Fishery* (Vancouver: Douglas & McIntyre, 1991): 210.

57. David Hogben, "Royal decree means hill of beans to vegetable growers," *Vancouver Sun*, 8 January 1993: D1. See also John Stewart, "The Kamloops Canneries: The Rise and Fall of a Local Industry," *B.C. Studies* 93 (Spring 1992): 30-47.

58. Robinson and Hardwick, *British Columbia*, 44.

59. British Columbia, *Report of the Commission on the Tree Fruit Industry of B.C.* (Victoria 1958). See chapter 2, "The Growth of the Tree Fruit Industry in British Columbia."

60. Margaret A. Ormsby, "Agriculture Development in British Columbia," *Agricultural History* 19 (1945).

61. See for example, Herbert G. Grubel and Richard W. Schwindt, *The Real Cost of the B.C. Milk Board—A Case Study in Canadian Agricultural Policy* (Vancouver: Fraser Institute, 1977).

62. Raymond W. Payne, "Corporate Power, Interest Groups and the Development of Mining Policy in British Columbia, 1972-77," *B.C. Studies* 54 (Summer 1982): 5-6.

63. Kerfoot, *Port of British Columbia*, 72-73.

64. *Ibid.*, 77-78.

65. Patricia Marchak, "The New Economic Reality: Substance and Rhetoric," Warren Magnusson *et al.*, eds., *The New Reality: The Politics of Restraint in British Columbia* (Vancouver, 1984): 26-27.

66. Roderick Haig-Brown, *The Living Land: An Account of the Natural Resources of British Columbia* (Toronto: Macmillan, 1961): 173-174.

67. See for example, British Columbia, *Reports of the Postwar Rehabilitation Council, Interim Report, 1943* (Victoria 1943) and *Supplementary Report* (Victoria 1944).

68. Don Mitchell, "Northeast Coal: Megaboom or Megabust?" *B.C. Business* (April 1986): 10-19.

69. Derrick Sewell, "Energy," *British Columbia: Its Resources and People*, 227.

70. See David J. Mitchell, chapter 8 in *W. A. C.: Bennett and the Rise of British Columbia* (Vancouver: Douglas & McIntyre, 1983): 296-327.

71. The best single-volume study of the public policy debates surrounding the negotiation of the Columbia River Treaty and the "Two River Policy" is Neil A. Swainson, *Conflict Over the Columbia: The Canadian Background to an Historic Treaty* (Montreal: McGill-Queen's University Press, 1979). The much neglected developmental programs of the 1940s governments are examined in John R. Wedley, "Laying the Golden Egg: The Coalition Government's Role in Post-war Northern Development," *B.C. Studies* 88 (Winter 1990-91): 58-92.

72. Sohal Abizadeh and John A. Gray, "Politics and Provincial Government Spending in Canada," *Canadian Public Administration* 35 (4): 519-533.

73. A. D. Scott, "Introduction: Notes on a Western Viewpoint," *B.C. Studies* 13 (Spring 1972): 7.

74. Quoted in Mitchell, *W. A. C.*, 260.

75. Not to mention land speculators. Controversy continues to rage over the extent to which the Social Credit administration's pavement policy was used to reward the party faithful in the hinterland. Two recent biographies of prominent individuals involved in alleged land and construction scams fail to clear away enduring suspicions. See Mel Rothenburger, *Friend o' Mine: The Story of Flyin' Phil Gaglardi* (Victoria: Orca Books, 1991); Jan-Udo Wenzel, *Ginter* (Prince George: Caitlin Press, 1993).

76. Shearer, "The Economy of British Columbia," 25.

77. British Columbia, Ministry of Finance and Corporate Relations, "British Columbia's Tourism GDP," *1992 B.C. Economic and Statistical Review*, 90-91.

78. Peter E. Murphy, "Tourism," *British Columbia: Its Resources and People*, 424.

79. Quoted in Stephen Gray, "The Government's Timber Business: Forest Policy and Administration in British Columbia, 1912-1928," *B.C. Studies* 81 (Spring 1989): 49.

80. *Ibid.*, 48.

81. Ronald A. Shearer, "The Development of the British Columbian Economy: The Record and the Issues," *Exploiting Our Economic Potential*, 8-9.

82. Bruce Little, "Service Sector Drives B.C. Job Market," *Globe and Mail*, 12 August 1991.

83. Ernest B. Kayeampong and Jennifer Winters, "International Employment Trends by Industry—A Note," *Perspectives* (Statistics Canada: Summer 1993): 33-37.

84. B.C. Round Table on the Environment and the Economy, *The Structure of the British Columbia Economy: A Land Use Perspective* (Victoria 1991): 4-10.

85. For an effective debunking of the notion of the post-industrial economy, from an American perspective, see Stephen S. Cohen and John Zysman, *Manufacturing Matters: The Myth of the Post-Industrial Economy* (New York: Basic Books, 1987).

86. B.C. Round Table, *The Structure of the British Columbia Economy*, 10.

87. For a more detailed analysis of the shift of employment to service industries in British Columbia see: H. Craig Davis and Thomas Hutton (B.C. Round Table on the Environment and the Economy), *The Role of Services in Metropolitan Growth* (September 1992): 5-12.

88. See Herbert G. Grubel and Michael A. Walker, *Service Industry Growth: Cause and Effects* (Vancouver: Fraser Institute, 1988).

89. British Columbia, "Conclusion" in *The Structure of the British Columbia Economy*, 39-450, and 28, table 5.

90. British Columbia, *The Report of the Commission of Inquiry into the Public Service and Public Sector, Interim Report* (December 1992): 2, and idem., vol. 1, *Final Report* (June 1993): 9.

91. British Columbia, Ministry of Labour and Consumer Services, *B.C. Labour*

Directory, 1993 (Victoria 1993): 9, table 1, and 57; Statistics Canada, *Labour Unions/Syndicats, 1990* (Ottawa 1990): 9.

92. British Columbia, Ministry of Finance and Corporate Relations, "Women in British Columbia: Their Changing Role," *1990 B.C. Economic and Statistical Review* (Victoria 1990): 42-43; British Columbia, Ministry of Women's Equality, *Women Count: A Statistical Profile of Women in British Columbia* (Victoria 1993): 6.

93. *Ibid., Women Count,* 6.

94. *Ibid.,* British Columbia Task Force on Employment and Training, *Learning and Work: The Way Ahead for British Columbians* (Victoria 1991): 6.

95. Daphne Bramham, "Men beat women in race for jobs," *Vancouver Sun* (4 December 1993): D1.

96. George Pederson, "The British Columbia Economy: Performance and Prospects," *Canadian Business Economics* I, no. 4 (Summer 1993): 36.

97. The political and economic background to the government's restraint program is described in David J. Mitchell, *Succession: The Political Reshaping of British Columbia* (Vancouver 1987): 48-64.

98. British Columbia Task Force on Employment, *Learning and Work,* 10.

99. Shearer, "The Economy of British Columbia," 29.

100. British Columbia, Ministry of Finance and Corporate Relations, "Recent Economic Performance of British Columbia and the Pacific Northwest States," *1992 B.C. Economic and Statistical Review* (Victoria 1992): 6-7.

101. See for example, Clay Hathorn and Ben Parfitt, "Cascadia: A Regional Perspective," *B.C. Business* (September 1993): 31-42.

102. British Columbia, Ministry of Finance and Corporate Relations, "British Columbia's Diversifying Economy," *1991 B.C. Economic and Statistical Review* (Victoria 1991): 56-57.

103. Robert N. North and Walter G. Hardwick, "Vancouver since the Second World War: An Economic Geography," Graeme Wynn and Timothy Oke, eds., *Vancouver and Its Region* (Vancouver, 1992): 200-201.

104. *Ibid.*

105. B.C. Round Table, *The Structure of the British Columbia Economy,* 17, fig. 8; B.C. Round Table on the Environment and the Economy, *Strategic Directions for Community Sustainability* (Victoria 1993): 70.

106. F. W. Howay, W. N. Sage and H. F. Angus, *British Columbia and the United States* (Toronto: The Ryerson Press, 1942): 379.

107. *Ibid.,* 392-393.

108. Gordon Shrum, with Peter Stursberg, *Gordon Shrum: An Autobiography* (Vancouver: University of British Columbia Press, 1986): 144-154.

109. B.C. Round Table on the Environment and the Economy, *An Economic Framework for Sustainability* (Victoria 1993).

110. Woodcock, *British Columbia,* 211; Shearer, "The Development of the British Columbia Economy," 8; Martin Robin, *The Rush for Spoils* (Toronto: McClelland and Stewart, 1972): 40.

111. H. Craig Davis and Thomas A. Hutton, "The Two Economies of British Columbia," *B.C. Studies* 82 (Summer 1989): 3-15.

112. H. Craig Davis, "Is the Metropolitan Vancouver Economy Uncoupling from the Rest of the Province?," *B.C. Studies* 98 (Summer 1993): 3-19.

PART V

Cultural History

Chapter 11

LEISURE, TASTE AND TRADITION IN BRITISH COLUMBIA

Douglas Cole

Although a great variety of cultural traditions now flourishes in British Columbia, most have yet to assert distinctively British Columbian voices: they concern themselves principally with old country cultures. The voices, images and pursuits that speak of British Columbia or claim to be British Columbian are mainly European or Native. Even within the European tradition, it is the larger English-speaking world that dominates British Columbian post-contact culture. With the very significant exception of the Native people, almost all the province's intellectual and creative achievements have been within the English-language community and with an acute consciousness of that community's tradition. Influences have thus been overwhelmingly English, primarily from Britain itself, but increasingly from the United States and anglophone Canada. Popular culture has been even more moulded and constrained by the English-speaking world. The province's sports are British, American, or central Canadian; its popular tastes in reading, music, cinema, radio and television are conditioned by that world's tastes. Distance has been a pervasive counter to the influence of the outside world. Remoteness has always pulled the province toward marginality, provincialism and insignificance. The tensions of margin and centre, of provincial and cosmopolitan civilization, are a major theme in the cultural development of British Columbia.

Exploring, discovering, taking possession or "making a home" have also been discerned as major themes of European civilization in British Columbia.[1] Such is a usual pattern in settlement colonies, though British Columbia has its own history and variations on the theme. A central feature has been the accommodation of settlers to a region temperate enough to be akin to European memory, yet a little strange and alien, characterized (until recently) not by settlement but by wilderness beyond the coastal and riverine fringes. As in other colonial contexts, the Europeans who explored and described the province characteristically came from abroad, with resident British Columbians contributing only late to the process.

THE FIRST HUNDRED YEARS OF
THE EUROPEAN TRADITION

The earliest European visitors scarcely appreciated British Columbia's nature. Its coast lacked variety, possessing neither the essential elements of the picturesque nor the gentle undulations of the beautiful. To the eighteenth-century European eye, nature wore a dreary, gloomy and comfortless appearance. George Vancouver left his impression in the name "Desolation Sound," a reach of water that presented "as gloomy and dismal an aspect as nature could well be supposed to exhibit."[2] Even Vancouver, however, could sometimes find in the landscape an element of the sublime, an expression of nature's awesome immensity and power. Alexander Mackenzie, ascending the first mountain after leaving Bentinck Arm, could not help but contemplate the "astonishing and awful combination of objects" below him.[3]

This desolate and inhospitable shore was mapped by the explorers, notably by Vancouver whose charts remained basic navigational aids for a century and more. The Spaniards, who assisted, left little record because they seldom published their results whereas the achievements of Cook and Vancouver and the latter's coastal delineation were there for the world to know. Mackenzie, Thompson and Fraser did something the same for the maze of waterways of the interior of the province, though their maps gave a mere skeleton rather than the full-fleshed results of Vancouver's hydrography. They drew only sketch maps, fundamental but basic.

Like most new lands, British Columbia's chief importance in terms of culture and intellect for its first century after European discovery was as a scientific field. Part of the northern and temperate zone, it did not possess the exotic strangeness of the South Pacific or South America. It did not, therefore, attract the great names of eighteenth- and nineteenth-century natural science. No Banks, Humboldt, Hooker, Brown or Darwin visited British Columbia. Its natural history came to be known only slowly. Cook's voyage yielded "virtually nothing" for botany and little more for zoology.[4] The great Malaspina expedition did little better. Tadeo Haenke collected only a few plants at Nootka, because he did not find many that he believed were distinct from those in Europe.[5] José Mariano Moziño, with Quadra at Nootka Sound in 1792, did better, though his significant contribution, *Noticias de Nutka* was as much ethnological as biological.[6] From Vancouver's voyage and an earlier visit, Archibald Menzies, an Edinburgh naturalist sponsored by the great Sir Joseph Banks, contributed many specimens new to science, notably the dogwood, maples, hemlock, red cedar, the Pacific rhododendron, and the arbutus, which bears his latinized name.[7] "It was because of the wonders which he reported on his return that British botanists and horticulturists in later years were to send a succession of collectors to our Pacific coast."[8] Among them was David Douglas, famed as "Douglas of the Fir," though the species is *pseudotsugo taxifolia menziesii* after Menzies who first collected it. The youthful Scot, a student of W. J. Hooker, was sent by the Horticultural Society of London to Fort Vancouver in 1824; and, after collecting in Oregon, he took back to Britain a record number of species for a single individual. Returning in 1830 he collected in the Okanagan, on the Fraser River, and at Stuart Lake, but his entire collection was lost in an overturned canoe.[9]

The Hudson's Bay Company was less interested in science than in zoological exploitation. Nevertheless, it kept a museum in London whose specimens Sir John Richardson found valuable, and it presented others to the Zoological Society and the British Museum. It acted as patron to John Scouler and to David Douglas, providing them with transportation and supplies. One of its employees, surgeon William Fraser Tolmie, was an enthusiastic field collector: "one of my most zealous Botanical students," commented Hooker.[10] By 1841, Hooker's Glasgow herbarium contained numerous plants sent by Scouler and Tolmie. The assistance of the Hudson's Bay Company and contributions of Douglas, Scouler and Tolmie are plain in the great compendiums of Richardson and Hooker, respectively *Fauna Boreali Americana and Flora Boreali Americana.*[11]

The most appealing areas of the coast were chosen for the earliest permanent settlements. The first Hudson's Bay Company posts had been located in areas strategic to trade and supplies, but when James Douglas chose Victoria as the future headquarters of the Company, he also had an eye for the beautiful. "The place itself," he wrote, "appears a perfect 'Eden,' in the midst of the dreary wilderness of the Northwest Coast."[12] Victoria, with its undulating surface of hill and dale, meadows of knee-high grass and fern, and picturesque groups of fir and oaks, was full of associations with "Home." The Cowichan Valley and the Courtenay district were similarly blessed with "smiling tracts" that separated them from the rest of the Island's wilderness. The first settlers were British and, few though they were until the gold rushes, they easily put a British stamp upon the countryside as well as giving a Home character to society. The similarities of climate and nature allowed both Island and mainland to reproduce Home more easily than almost any other area of Canada. The first non-Company settler planted broom, which quickly became a weed along the Island's roads. Imported stock—Durham and Devon cattle, Southdown and Merino sheep—though most often brought from San Francisco, were largely of British derivation.

The discovery of gold changed quiet colonial society. The mainland suddenly became important as something more than a fur farm for the Company. Geographical knowledge became vastly more important, both for transportation to the fields and for the potential of finding more gold. The major rivers and Native trails were already known from the fur trade, but the rush put a premium on easier and quicker routes. The more systematic exploration and surveying was done by Royal Navy and Royal Engineers personnel, notably R. C.

Mayne on the Thompson, Fraser, Harrison and Lillooet Rivers. As a result of additional surveys, the Admiralty's Hydrographic Office published its first *Vancouver Island Pilot* in 1861.

Two British-sponsored initiatives brought new knowledge. The Palliser overland expedition concerned itself largely with the prairie region, but geologist James Hector and botanist Eugène Bourgeau penetrated across the Rockies to the Columbia and Kootenay Valleys. Geologist Thomas Blakiston, quitting the expedition, did further work, including zoological observation, in British Columbia before leaving for Asia. The International Boundary Survey of 1858–1862 brought geologist Herman Bauerman and naturalist J. K. Lord to the province. The latter made significant collections for the British Museum (Natural History), and his 1866 *The Naturalist in British Columbia* may be treated as the first contribution to a major and enduring British Columbia genre.

From Victoria came the first colonial expeditions, including a government exploration of the Columbia River district led by Walter Moberly and Ashdowne Green, and a business- and government-sponsored Vancouver Island Exploring Expedition to ascertain the resources of central Vancouver Island. Its leader, Robert Brown, who had come to the colony to collect seeds of horticultural interest, made a few contributions on conifers, oolichan and Island birds to learned journals.[13]

The gold rush's visitors produced an avalanche of descriptive literature, much of it ephemeral advice to intended immigrants. The colonies were seen either as "a wild, romantic, mountainous country" or "a miserable country" unfit for cattle or cereals.[14] The colonies still lacked many of the attractions associated with Home, most strikingly songbirds. "There is not a single note to bring to memory the sweet moment of youth."[15] English songbirds—the skylark, blue tit, and robin redbreast—were imported to fill the lacunae. None succeeded in acclimatizing. Game birds—quail, pheasant and partridge—were more successful.

The colonies' gold-rush growth established the basis for a transplanted British culture with American and even Canadian tinges. An influx of Americans was offset by assertions of British supremacy: by the Royal Engineers at New Westminster, by the Royal Navy base at Esquimalt, by the importation of British officials, and by the invocation of a British-style government. By 1865 the major British religious denominations had established themselves in Victoria; there were newspapers, two girls' schools, a literary and a mechanics' institute, and even a race track at Beacon Hill. On the other hand, architecture reflected American as much as British influences; initially, California versions of the Victorian Italianate villa prevailed in domestic building, and soon this style vied with variations of San Francisco Queen Anne. The buildings were almost universally of wood, often imported California redwood, which gave a North American, rather than British, stamp to the domestic urban landscape.

The majority of permanent settlers were British and regarded themselves as such. A British element constituted itself as an aristocracy of talent and taste. They were literate, read *The Times*, and even published in England (though occasionally in California). They, along with Royal Navy officers, set the standard of polite society in the colony. Among the early Hudson's Bay Company settlers, Alexander Anderson was able and literate, Charles Ross a tolerable classicist, and Tolmie a knowledgeable botanist.[16] Culture had its tasteful place. Most were "trained from childhood to a reasonable level of competence in the use of voice and instrument" and isolation forced them to use this training for their own pleasure and amusement.[17] Settlers hung art on their walls (though few of them painted); they performed in dramas, and read and discussed books. The gold rush brought new talent, including W. G. R. Hind with the Overlanders, who painted a rich and intriguingly idiosyncratic record of the experience of mining in the colony. Victoria's new residents founded choral societies (in which the booming bass of Justice Begbie was often notable) and a short-lived philharmonic orchestra. If colonial culture was entirely derivative, it would be absurd to expect otherwise.

THE LATE NINETEENTH AND EARLY TWENTIETH CENTURIES

What British Columbians had in common with the rest of Canada after Confederation in 1871 was more a shared loyalty to a common motherland than any common loyalty to a British North American home. The new connection had limited effect until the completion of the transcontinental railway in 1886. As discussed in previous chapters, the arrival of the Canadian Pacific Railway (*CPR*) promoted Canadian influences, especially on the mainland, where Canadian capital, settlers and institutions began to mould the new terminus of Vancouver. The Bank of Montreal reached the Pacific almost in the railway's caboose, establishing a Vancouver branch in 1887 and one in Victoria two years later. The old London-based Bank of British Columbia soon became one of nine banks in the province, eventually to be absorbed by the Canadian Bank of Commerce. British Columbia politicians adopted national party labels in the 1896 federal election, though it took another seven years before the same labels were used in provincial elections. Churches gradually connected to their Canadian counterparts. Methodists from Ontario had entered British Columbia before Confederation. Local Presbyterians moved from a direct tie to the Church of Scotland to links with their Canadian co-religionists, and Anglicans from Lambeth to a Canadian primate in 1893. Canadian lay organizations, such as the National Council of Women, the Royal Canadian Humane Society, the Dominion Education Association, and the Canadian Club founded British Columbia branches. By 1891 the number of British Columbians born in other Canadian provinces equalled the number born in Britain; at the end of the century, the proportion of whites born in Britain dropped to one-quarter, those born in Canada doubled to almost a third. It appeared that British Columbia was becoming a Canadian province.[18]

In the field of science, the description of British Columbia remained the task of outsiders, visitors and neighbours. The most complete naturalist survey of the Pacific northwest region was *The Natural History of Washington Territory*, done for the U.S. Pacific railway surveys.[19] Americans continued to make significant contributions, and visitors from eastern Canada played an increasingly important role, though input from the British declined. Survey parties for the Canadian transcontinental railway were in the field from 1871, long before the railway was constructed. With them came the expertise of the Geological Survey of Canada, with Director A. R. C. Selwyn and geologist John Richardson reconnoitering the Fraser River that year. The major figure in the Survey's distinguished history in the province was George M. Dawson, who refused to let his tiny, hunch-backed physique hinder his field assignments. From 1875 until his death in 1901, Dawson explored the province almost annually, contributing to knowledge of topography and resource potential as he established the outlines of its complex stratigraphy and glacial history. Largely because of Dawson, within a decade of British Columbia's union with Canada "the general outlines of its geology were fairly well understood."[20] R. G. McConnell succeeded Dawson as the master of Cordilleran geology, a role he performed with the assistance of R. W. Brock, Charles Camsell, and others.

Basic description and classification were done elsewhere, in the laboratories and studies of central Canada and the United States. The province's marine mollusks, for example, were described by P. P. Carpenter of McGill and the Smithsonian and by W. H. Dall of the U.S. Coast and Geodetic Survey and the Smithsonian, fossil insects by S. H. Scudder of the Geological Survey of Canada, coniferous trees by George Engelmann of St. Louis, and Californian H. T. A. Hus did pioneering description of marine algae. C. D. Walcott of the Smithsonian first worked on the paleontology of the remarkable Cambrian fossils he found in 1909 among the Burgess shale of the Rockies, though the full import of those arthropods awaited "repatriation" by the Geological Survey and rediscovery by a set of Cambridge scientists some sixty years later.[21]

The unquestioned master of field naturalists in the province (and in Canada) was the self-taught John Macoun, who first visited British Columbia on Stanford Fleming's 1872 survey expedition for the CPR. Hired permanently by the Geological Survey a decade later, Macoun collected, with the assistance of his son James and William Spreadborough, an enormous number of specimens, primarily botanical but also of mammals and birds. Much of his field work "was little more than a mad scramble," with cataloguing, inventory, and description always far behind the often chaotic collecting. By 1900, however, he had completed his *Catalogue of Canadian Plants*, and by 1904 his *Catalogue of Canadian Birds*. Macoun's work depended upon American specialists' assistance for the identification of specimens and even for the direction and scope of field work.[22] He retired in 1912 to Vancouver Island, where his collecting continued to be "nothing short of astonishing," including twenty flowering plants new to Island flora and eight species of fungi new to science.[23]

The Natural History Society of Victoria and the Provincial Museum, both established in 1886, did not contribute a great deal, though the latter's 1891 check list of provincial birds was the first in the field, followed by lists from Allan Brooks, A. R. Davidson, Mack Laing, and Theed Pearse.[24] Representatives of the Philadelphia Academy of Natural Sciences, New York's Museum of Natural History, and the U.S. Biological Survey worked in the province (notably Samuel N. Rhodes, Clark P. Streator and E. A. Preble in ornithology, and Wilfred Osgood who prepared the landmark 1901 natural history survey of the Queen Charlotte Islands). The first major distribution list of provincial birds was published in California, a collaboration between Harry S. Swarth of the University of California and senior author Allan Brooks, a British Columbian widely recognized as an ornithological illustrator.[25] Neighbouring science was still important: Charles V. Piper's 1906 list of Washington State flora, for example, was of value in identifying many provincial plants. In 1915 J. K. Henry could justly complain that, though "there has been much collecting done in British Columbia, collectors have in general taken their material away with them." There was no herbarium in the province and plant descriptions were scattered through many books, reports and periodicals.[26] Henry's own description of southern British Columbia plants was an attempt to overcome that deficiency. It was followed by James R. Anderson's descriptive 1925 flora list and J. A. Munro's *Introduction to Bird Study in British Columbia*, all published under the sponsorship of the provincial department of education.[27]

The situation was by then beginning to change. John Davidson, a Scot, was appointed provincial botanist in 1911, then went on to found that department at the University of British Columbia. There he instituted an herbarium, which would eventually answer some of Henry's complaint. The new university took Brock from the federal Geological Survey as dean of applied science and with him came M. Y. Williams in paleontology. With strength in the applied and agricultural sciences, supported by biology, chemistry, and physics, the university offered a nucleus of resident professional scientists at the same time as a community of such specialists was building through other governmental initiatives. Ornithologist Munro was with the federal migratory bird office and other scientists staffed federal and provincial agricultural research farms, forest and fisheries research stations, and similar bodies. Professional science was beginning to establish itself in British Columbia.

Anthropology remained more a natural than a social science. Although thought was given to an appointment in anthropology at the new university, the opporunity was passed over and the task of describing the rich and diverse Native groups remained a field for outsiders. Dawson of the Geological Survey of Canada had made major contributions on the Haida, the Kwakiutl and the Interior Salish cultures. He also served as a member of the North-West Tribes Committee, funded by the British Association for the Advancement of Science and the Canadian government, which in 1888 began a study of the province's Natives and the threat to their way of life represented by the CPR's transformation of the west. The committee dispatched to British Columbia the German-American Franz Boas, who, in a series of reports from 1887 to 1897, established the basic ethnological and linguistic outlines of the province. From 1896 to 1905, Boas continued the work through New York's American Museum of Natural History. By then detailed work was also being done by a few residents, notably the British-born Charles Hill-Tout. Boas used the Scottish-born James Teit and the native-born George Hunt as local collaborators. Both made major contributions, Teit on the Interior Salish, especially the Thompson, and Hunt on the Kwakiutl. After 1912 the Anthropological Division of the Geological Survey, part of the new Victoria Memorial Museum in Ottawa, assumed a major role under the leadership of Edward Sapir, who, in addition to his own important work among the Nootka, sent Harlan Smith (archaeology), Marius Barbeau (Tsimshian), and T. F. McIlwraith (Bella Coola) to the region. The Provincial Museum made few contributions until the 1950s, and the University of British Columbia only in the next decade.

The trend to Canadianization in the 1886–1900 period did not affect Victoria and the Island as much as the mainland. In the early twentieth century, the province's natural beauty, its climate, and its possibilities for gentlemanly farming and sport attracted an increasing number of migrants from Britain. Throughout these years, Victoria's leading families remained British, and they persisted in part by welcoming suitable newcomers into their ranks. *Punch, The Graphic, The Times* and *The Standard* could be found in the drawing rooms and clubs, and some families—the Creases, the Tyrwhitt-Drakes, the Helmckens and the Pembertons—sent their sons to Britain's public schools.[28] The province's cultural leaders, those with education, money and taste, were predominantly from this level of provincial society, and they stamped an indelible imprint upon the developing area.

British Columbia's natural world was always a little strange to British newcomers. Parts of the Interior could be viewed as extensive parklands and the areas around Victoria and other Vancouver Island locales could present themselves as "demi-Englands," but wilderness clothed most of the province. A lack of history and association could still wound the susceptibilities of the sensitive. Visitor Rupert Brooke found the "unmemoried heights" of the Rockies "inhuman," even irrelevant to humanity. British Columbia, like the rest of the continent, was seen as a desolate, empty land, without haunted woods, friendly ghosts or the decaying stuff of past generations. In its empty forests "a European can find nothing to satisfy the hunger of his heart."[29] This perception gradually lost its grip as both migrants and the native-born found that "lonely places with no human habitation" possessed their own romantic and aesthetic appeal.[30]

Nineteenth-century leisure hours were marked by British customs: picnics at the park or beach, church conversazione that mixed music and recitation with informal conversation, and summer campouts for the middle and upper classes. Transportation determined holiday and weekend excursions. In Victoria, the destinations were Beacon Hill, the Gorge, Cadboro Bay, or, via the Esquimalt and Nanaimo Railway, Shawnigan Lake's Strathcona Lodge, with its 45-room resort hotel that boasted tennis courts and croquet grounds. Nanaimo had Newcastle Island and up-island beaches. Vancouver was no less blessed with its Stanley Park, but much of the excursion and summer holidaying focussed on day steamers to Deep Cove and Bowen Island. Cottages, more North American and especially Canadian than British, became increasingly popular. Vancouver's Colonial Portable Home Company made a specialty of prefabricated summer cottage/bungalow "boxes" with oversized verandahs. Jack Cates's Terminal Steam Navigation Company developed transportation to the cottage area of the north arm of Burrard Inlet where 100- by 500-foot lots were available starting at $200. Cates's major innovation was the development of Bowen Island as a summer resort. An hour from the city, it catered especially to company, union and church groups. The Union Steamship Company also ran excursion boats to Gibsons, Buccaneer Bay and Pender Harbour, all resort and camp communities before the First World War.

Other leisure hours might be filled with sport. Field sports appealed to many upper-class migrants; British Columbia remained a home for hunters and anglers. Mountaineering, another British enthusiasm, was quickly adapted to British Columbia and the Rockies. Team sports were initially British — cricket, rugby and soccer — and often confined largely to the leisured classes. These sports were later adopted by private boys' schools. Soccer was favoured over rugby in the towns of the Interior, rugby over soccer on the coast. Rugby's popularity was assisted by occasional international competition: New Zealand's All Blacks team devastated the select provincial team in 1906 by scores of 41–6 and 65–6. Canadian field lacrosse came to British Columbia in the 1880s, and its roughness, even brutality, soon made it the province's most popular spectator sport with thousands attending the inter-city Vancouver, Victoria and New Westminster matches. The New Westminster entry, formed in 1889 and nicknamed the Salmonbellies within a year, soon established themselves as a team of national rank.

Ice hockey was restricted to the lakes of the Interior until 1911 when Lester and Frank Patrick built Canada's first artificial rink in Victoria (a year before Toronto had a rink), opened another a month later in Vancouver, and imported eastern players, including the great Fred "Cyclone" Taylor, to begin professional hockey in British Columbia. By 1915 the Vancouver Millionaires were prepared to take on the Ottawa Senators at the city's Denman Arena and beat them in three straight games for the Stanley Cup.

The most popular participant sport by 1914, however, was neither British nor Canadian, but North American baseball. That game, wrote P. H. Morris in 1912, was enthusiastically played by scores of teams throughout the province, with every town and hamlet possessing its team. Baseball benefitted from its simple field requirements and its lack of invidious associations. Cricket was seen as an elite game, but, as importantly, it was "sadly handicapped by the lack of suitable playing areas." Even with "the aid of cocoa-nut matting" most fields could not provide the smooth, level ground essential for the game.[31] Cricket survived in the larger cities, and some smaller ones like Revelstoke and Kelowna, and certainly in the boys' schools, but remained minor compared to baseball. In cities (Vancouver had almost ninety baseball clubs by 1911), in the small towns of the province (Mt. Olie, Chu Chua and Barrière played a tournament at the 1905 Barrière Fair), and among Indian residential schools (a Saanich team devastated the Kuper Island nine in 1903), baseball was king. By 1905, Vancouver and Victoria had professional franchises in a Northwest League with Portland, Seattle and Tacoma.

Among non-team sports, lawn tennis was played in private gardens and at club grounds in Vancouver, Victoria and Cowichan; "its chief adherents are natives of the Mother Land."[32] Vancouver's parks board provided twenty-four courts by 1915, but most were allocated to private clubs.[33] Rowing and dinghy sailing were popular turn-of-the-century middle-class sports, yachting an upper-class one. Winter sports, such as snowshoeing, tobogganing and skating, were popular: skiing came later, largely introduced by continental Europeans.

In other ways people struggled to keep up the activities and experiences of home, whether British or European. Bands, orchestras and choirs were founded wherever there were enough players or singers to form ensembles. Most struggled for a few years, then disbanded only to be succeeded by another. Victoria's Amateur Orchestra, for example, lasted for almost twenty years from its 1878 foundation, to be succeeded by the Euphonic Orchestral Society that survived only two concerts and then the Victoria Philharmonic that seems to have lasted only one. The story was much the same in Vancouver and elsewhere. Wind bands and choral groups, the latter sustained by a multitude of church choirs, often had longer careers. Despite discontinuity, there was always, in one form or another, a relative richness of opportunity for musical enjoyment. The Dyke brothers, George and Fred, sold sheet music and instruments, performed, and hosted musical events. The CPR's 1891 Opera House was inaugurated with an immense production of *Lohengrin* performed by an American touring company, and Albani, Paderewski, Rachmaninov, and the New York Symphony under Walter Damrosch gave visiting performances. Popular and professional entertainment was almost entirely North American, with the province part of the Pacific touring circuit.[34]

Societies of artists similarly came together, but institutions were small and fragile, patronage thin and insecure. Whether in art, music, literature or architecture, taste remained derivative, conservative and outmoded in an immigrant community removed from developments in distant metropolitan centres and as yet without centres of its own. Music and literature, more than other arts, served to bind the immigrant population to metropolitan traditions not found in the new and isolated settlements of the province. In neither art were there, as Helmut Kallmann has put it for music, "creative giants who determine the course of world music history but humble musicians who instill a taste for their art among pioneers."[35]

Literature remained largely a matter of consumption not production. The province did have its novelists and poets, including Clive Phillipps-Wolley, a British-reared sportsman who told tales of the Cariboo and remittance men. Much of the fiction portrayed life in the mining camps, but a good deal was "concerned with communicating the excitement of life in a new British Columbia Eden, an open, awesomely beautiful land which promised the good life to the venturesome, the courageous, and the flexible."[36] Little of the work of Phillipps-Wolley, Frederick Niven or Bertram Sinclair is appreciated today, though M. A. Grainger's 1908 *Woodsman of the West* remains a minor classic account of coastal logging life thinly constructed as a novel.

In painting, the most impressive pre-war artist was Thomas Fripp, an English-born watercolorist who continued that great tradition among the mountain clouds and misty atmosphere of the Fraser Valley and the southern coast. Traditional, certainly old-fashioned, but an outstanding artist, Fripp symbolized the longevity of the best Home traditions overseas.[37]

Housing, the most basic and ubiquitous element of human culture, reflected British Columbia's nature, its external influences, and the technological innovations of the time. Land was relatively cheap, building material—almost entirely local softwoods—was abundant and inexpensive. The electric streetcar allowed a sprawl of housing even in the cities, replacing the compact housing characteristic of earlier, mid-Victorian urban centres. British settlers preferred detached homes, not apartment flats. The province thus developed as a land of home dwellers. Promoters recognized the bias: "the dweller in flats," wrote one, "is an uncertain and unsettled quantity"; "homes alone indicate the extent and quality of citizenship" and were "the heart, the life and the index of a city."[38]

The prosperous built their homes in solid English-derived style. Victoria's Rockland Avenue and Vancouver's Shaughnessy Heights are showpieces of the Tudor revival, of shingle, chalet and colonial bungalow styles, though similar examples can be found wherever there were merchants or bankers in the province during the years between 1900 and 1915. In Victoria, F. M. Rattenbury, T. C. Sorby, Thomas Hooper, and especially Samuel Maclure mixed various arts-and-crafts and revival motifs. R. Mackay Fripp brought English and California arts-and-crafts styles to turn-of-the-century Vancouver and was soon joined by W. T. Dalton, G. L. T. Sharp, and then by Maclure, whose Vancouver office was staffed by the English-trained C. C. Fox and later

Ross Lort. The influence of the arts-and-crafts revival was not confined to Maclure's major Tudor mansions for the Rockland set; it passed down to more modest half-timbered bungalows and schools scattered throughout the province. Continually influenced by British styles, including those of Baillie Scott and Edwin Lutyens, the province's domestic architecture was characterized by Edwardian rather than Victorian taste. Although English in derivation, Maclure's homes (and, to a certain extent, those by other architects) were "absolutely suited" to their environment.[39]

Although the "better" residential areas stressed a taste for Englishness (and for views), the all-important factor for the lower-income homeowner was cost. Few architect-designed homes were found in the province's smaller towns, on its farms, or in Victoria's James Bay or Vancouver's East Side and south slope. Homes there were largely pattern-book designs, taken from plans developed in the United States, most often in California, Seattle or Chicago. The ready-made designs were from areas similarly dominated by wood rather than brick construction, and wood construction was universal in British Columbia. Prefabricated houses, an innovation by British Columbia Mills, could cost one-third less than site-built homes; they housed many of the immigrants of the first decade of the twentieth century. The two-storey Queen Anne- and Stick-style houses and the box-like two-and-a-half-storey clapboards of the turn of the century mixed with craftsman and shingle styles after 1910, then gave way to the California bungalow, a one-, sometimes one-and-a-half-storey home taken from west coast pattern books but modified in British Columbia to provide a basement furnace.

Rockland's lovely arts-and-crafts homes were surrounded with English-style gardens, with alpine and rose gardens a favourite. The same was true of Vancouver's Shaughnessy, while Marine Drive could contain a woodland garden adapted to the province's own trees, shrubs and flowers. The same mix of adoption and adaptation appeared in the Cowichan Valley, on the Gulf Islands, and in the fruit-farming areas of the Interior. For the horticulturists, everything grown in the Home Isles flourished on the British Columbia coast and, for imaginative gardeners, there was the challenge of using the native camus, erychthium and trillium to embellish a woodland garden. (Salal and Oregon grape had already succeeded in British gardens.) The native garden cultivated by R. H. Beaven next to his 1902 Maclure bungalow survives as an Oak Bay public park.

THROUGH TWO WORLD WARS

Although in 1901 it had appeared that British Columbia was becoming a province populated by the Canadian-born, this new identity was short-lived. The wave of immigration that flooded the province in the years before the First World War reaffirmed British Columbia's Britishness. The majority of adult

British Columbians were, for decades, born in Britain, not Canada.[40] The First World War altered this temporarily as thousands of the British-born enlisted for European service. Joined by the Canadian-born, the province contributed a disproportionate number of men for the mud of Flanders. The war seemed a tragic interlude, the armistice a return to normality. To some degree it was, but, though British influences continued to dominate, their strength was challenged from Canadian and American sources. At the same time the province was struggling to establish stronger cultural institutions of its own.

Henry Esson Young, a Queen's- and McGill-educated medical doctor, presided, as provincial secretary and minister of education in the McBride government, over a brief renaissance permitted by surplus revenues in the 1909–1913 boom. The provincial library, archives and museum received large funding increases, allowing all to expand their collections; and Young was responsible for the opening of the University of British Columbia in 1915. The education minister's determination to found a university in British Columbia came late in the day: all the other provinces, even the most recent (Alberta and Saskatchewan), already had public universities. Young's choice of F. F. Wesbrook was fortunate; the new president, determined to establish "a provincial university devoid of provincialism,"[41] recruited a group of solid academics to its three faculties. Wesbrook's death in 1918 opened the way for the long tenure of L. S. Klinck, from 1919 to 1944, who presided over the student-driven move from the Fairfield shacks to Point Grey. The presence of a learned community on campus, more dedicated to the diffusion than to the creation of knowledge, was important to the province. Professors such as Harry T. Logan in classics, Henry Angus in economics, Walter Sage and Mack Eastman in history, Garnet Sedgewick, Ira Dilworth and Frederick Wood in English, and Dorothy Dallas in French brightened the lamp of culture and learning in the community.

Budget restraint meant that no medical school existed (though nursing and health began in 1919); practicality determined that neither music nor fine arts were part of the curriculum. Practicality also meant an emphasis upon agriculture, engineering and forestry, though the sciences, especially under Dean Daniel Buchanan, achieved modest success in research. The biological sciences gained the greatest prominence, especially microbiology after the arrival of bacteriologist C. E. Dolman in 1936, followed by chemistry and physics. Gordon Shrum, co-discoverer of the auroral green line and the liquification of helium at the University of Toronto, arrived in 1925 and became head of the physics department in 1938. His support of astronomy as a field of study and the interest of Dean Buchanan, whose doctorate was in celestial mechanics, made this one area in which research could be conducted without any sense that living in British Columbia meant intellectual isolation. The university made the best use of the summer assistant program at the Dominion Astrophysical Observatory at Saanich Hill, near Victoria.

From its opening in 1918 until the 1950s, this observatory was the centre of Canada's international importance in astronomy. It began with a ready-made reputation under J. S. Plaskett and Reynold K. Young, a fame that continued with the recruiting of bright young astronomers, including UBC-trained Robert M. Petrie and Andrew McKellar. Although dedicated to the routine yet essential work of collecting and measuring thousands of plates for binary star orbit calculations or for absolute magnitude reckonings, Plaskett and his associates and successors tied these tasks to exciting questions of galactic research: the nature of the interstellar medium, the rotational dynamics of the galaxy, and the nature of massive and peculiar stars. The result was a tremendous output of research that moulded the character of Canadian astronomy. Among British Columbia students that it fostered were, besides Petrie and McKellar, Anne Underhill, Arthur Covington, and George Volkoff, the latter co-author with J. Robert Oppenheimer of the classic paper on neutron stars.[42]

One lacuna in education was filled when the Vancouver School of Applied and Decorative Arts was established in 1925, attracting to it an excellent staff, including the already well-known Group of Seven painter, F. H. Varley. The school suffered severely in the Depression, but retained its eminence under B. C. Binning and later Jack Shadbolt. The work of the school was handsomely complemented by the 1931 establishment of the Vancouver Art Gallery on Georgia Street.

The city had long had an active group of artists and art supporters, but, until the art school and gallery, had lacked focal institutions. Like the rest of the province, Vancouver had suffered from isolation, with no permanent exhibition facilities and few travelling shows. The National Gallery had a loan program, but British Columbians complained of their high cost and the mediocre quality of offerings. Isolation led to conservatism: a loan exhibition of Tom Thomson and Group of Seven works in 1928 brought a flurry of outraged anti-modernism, but the indignant were met with tempered replies by architect Willie Dalton, who, along with mining engineer H. Mortimer-Lamb and photographer John Vanderpant, led in the promotion of modernist styles. By then Varley was painting mountains and sea in his inspired way, passing that inspiration on to his younger colleague, J. M. G. (Jock) Macdonald, and students, while W. P. Weston, instructor at the Normal School (the teacher training school), was setting his mountains in the distinctive style of the Group of Seven.

In Victoria, Emily Carr, approaching her sixtieth year, began to stir from her own isolation. In 1911 she had brought back from a year's study in France the first modernist paintings ever seen in the province. The reception was polite, occasionally jeering. That, but even more the failure of her plan to live as a *rentier* in her Victoria apartment house, led her to neglect her art. In the mid-twenties she met some Seattle artists and showed a few works at the gallery there, but was oblivious of even the existence of the Group of Seven. Mortimer-Lamb had tried to call her to the National Gallery's attention in

1921, but it stirred from its own central Canadian provinciality only in 1927 when Marius Barbeau interested it in an exhibition of west coast painting, Native and modern. Carr travelled east for the opening, meeting Varley in Vancouver, then other members of the Group in Toronto. Lawren Harris's work stirred her so deeply that she was moved beyond expression. She returned to Victoria determined "to wrestle something out for myself, to look for things I did not know before, and to feel and strive and earnestly try to be true and sincere to the country and to myself."[43] The meeting had been an epiphany and, aided by reading, by Seattle artist Mark Tobey, and by Harris's continued encouragement and advice, Carr launched into the remarkable creativity that allowed her to interpret the spirit and essence of Native art, as represented by house structures and totem poles, and then to capture the powerful feelings conveyed by the forests, clearings, shores and skies of coastal British Columbia. This native-born genius became the dominant painter of the province, unequalled (except by Harris) among her generation of Canadian painters, and a heroic influence on later generations of writers and artists. No longer isolated, Carr remained distant. She needed the stimulation of external contacts, but she required as much her solitude with forest and sea.

The landscape—British Columbia's mountains, forests, seas and skies—were the dominant interwar subject matter, as artists sought the essential structures and vital forces of the nature around them. Carr's pictures searched for the spirituality of nature, attempting to find "the underlying spirit" and "the mood, the vastness, the wilderness" of British Columbia.[44] Weston dramatized trees defiant against the elements, mountains standing boldly against the horizon, and driftwood thrown up by the sea. The vision was heroic, differentiating "the old civilized landscape of Europe" from "nature as it could be—in the raw—before man interfered with it."[45] The province's natural landscape was inspiring, its cultural climate considerably less so. "I'm pretty active here," Varley wrote in 1928, "but at times feel keenly the lack of an understanding atmosphere—One is very isolated. Not merely isolated but occasionally at enmity with people possessing appalling ignorance."[46] It hardly improved in the 1930s; Varley left in 1936 and Vanderpant died in 1938. Of the younger generation, only Jack Shadbolt and B. C. Binning "had made contact with the larger outside world by going abroad."[47] Aside from Carr, Victoria was "really *hopeless*."[48]

Shadbolt, from Victoria where he had admired Carr's painting, and then in Vancouver as a part-time student of Varley, courted the wider world. He read omnivorously, travelled to the 1933 Chicago World's Fair to see the art there ("sixty Cézannes together pole-axed me")[49] and to New York where he saw O'Keefes, Marins, Hoppers and Burchfields, and then in 1937–1938 studied in London and Paris. He returned "surprised to realize how insular younger artists were."[50] At the art school, where he joined the staff, there seemed few ideas. Shadbolt, along with Binning and Jock Macdonald, struggled against

such isolation, with Macdonald's experiments in abstraction, under the influence of visiting surrealist Grace Pailthorpe, and those of Lawren Harris, who
settled in Vancouver in 1940, at the leading edge.

As a creative endeavour, painting led literature. Before 1939 only Annie
Dalton, Audrey Alexandra Brown, and, for other reasons, Pauline Johnson left
verse at all remembered. In prose there were few beacons. The most creative
writing was by Roderick Haig-Brown whose essays and books about nature
began to appear in 1931 and continued to do so for the next thirty years, making him preeminent in a genre always important in the province. The end of
the decade saw the publication of two exceptional novels. Howard O'Hagan's
Tay John (1939), a powerful parable of Native primitivism and white civilization, is perhaps the best fiction done in the province before Ethel Wilson and
Malcolm Lowry. Although melodramatic and unsophisticated to some, no one
else captures the "raw power of myth" in the way O'Hagan does as he "single-
handedly moves an indigenous myth through all the genres considered essential for a 'proper literary history.'"[51] Many value the social consciousness of
Irene Baird's *Waste Heritage* (1939), a powerful portrait of the Depression's
unemployed.[52]

Haig-Brown and O'Hagan gave literary expression to the "wilderness ethos"
of Carr and other interwar landscape painters. There is also a strong resonance
of this theme in Earle Birney's "David" (1942), as much a Canadian icon as
any single poem could be. *David and Other Poems* established Birney as the
most sensitive poet of British Columbia nature. Birney was then living in
Toronto and would soon leave for the war, but a certain critical mass of poetic
expression existed already in Vancouver and Victoria, enough to produce from
Allen Crawley's West Vancouver home the best Canadian poetry magazine of
the 1940s.

The impetus for *Contemporary Verse: A Canadian Quarterly* came not just
from Crawley but from four other British Columbia poets, Dorothy Livesay,
Doris Ferne, Anne Marriott, and Floris McLaren—all of Vancouver or
Victoria—who pushed Crawley into the editorship. "Handicapped by blindness
and cornered in the far west" (as Louis Dudek unkindly put it), Crawley, a
sightless ex-lawyer from Winnipeg, was conscious of his problems; he admitted
that "the isolation of this western coast is hard to overcome," but the larger
problem was that there was little enough good Canadian poetry, east or west, to
be found.[53] Determined that *Contemporary Verse* avoid being "the chapbook of
a limited or local group of writers," Crawley soon found his stride and published virtually every modern Canadian poet between 1941 and 1951, more or
less introducing James Reaney, Anne Wilkinson, Margaret Avison, Phyllis
Webb, Jay Macpherson, and Marya Fiamengo to Canadian readers.[54] Two of
Crawley's associates were among the strongest voices in the province, with
Marriott's *Calling Adventures* winning the Governor General's award in 1941
(the year Carr won for *Klee Wyck* in non-fiction) and Livesay in 1944 for *Day*

and Night and three years later for *Power for People.*

A decade earlier the Vancouver Symphony Orchestra had been revived under the Dutch-born conductor Allard de Ridder and the Vancouver Bach Choir had been founded. The symphony owed its existence to Mary Isabella Rogers, widow of Vancouver sugar magnate, B. T. Rogers. She had helped with the 1919 orchestra that began with a program of Tchaikovsky, Sibelius and Haydn, as well as compositions by conductor Henry Green. There were disagreements between Green and Mrs. Rogers over a Debussy prelude, and the orchestra collapsed after its second season.[55] For the next decade the city existed with scratch orchestras and with visiting artists such as Ravel, Casals and Kreisler. The revived 1930 Vancouver symphony began its career with a Webern, Chabrier and Wagner program, with local soloist Ursula Malkin performing a Beethoven piano concerto. That same season's audiences heard Vancouver's Jan Cherniavsky, and, together, Mrs. Walter Coulthard and her daughter Jean. Only in 1939 did the symphony begin its long collaboration with the Bach Choir. In 1934 Ira Dilworth had assumed choir direction and, as a symphony board member, helped promote the joint venture that would continue with great success. By then Dilworth had moved from UBC to the CBC's Vancouver radio station where he almost immediately formed the CBC Vancouver Chamber Orchestra, with John Avison, a Vancouver-born pianist, as its long-standing (until 1980) conductor. It played an important part in keeping professionals in Vancouver. Victoria and other cities were not so fortunate. The capital had a long history of musical performances and was noted for its appreciative audiences, but lacked permanent institutions in either music or art for another decade or more.

Amateur and touring companies were the mainstay of British Columbia theatre for most of its history. "No one has ever doubted," a writer commented in 1914, "that British Columbia is a good province for the theatre business." The stage at that time was dominated by touring circuits sponsored by the Pantages and Orpheum chains. Already, it was noted, the "business of the traveling stock company has been very much cut into by the moving picture business."[56] The 1920s saw a revival of touring companies and, more important, a boom in Little Theatre groups, a trend reinforced in the next decade by the Dominion Drama Festival's regional competitions. Victoria was especially active under the spur of Llewelyn Bullock-Webster, a British emigre who had begun his British Columbia Dramatic School there in 1921 after having founded the Prince Rupert Little Theatre a decade earlier. In Vancouver, the UBC Campus Players began in 1915 a long tradition of amateur drama with which the names Frederick Wood and Dorothy Somerset are associated. Both helped the Vancouver Little Theatre start in 1920. In the following decade there were nine theatres in Vancouver with resident stock or touring companies.[57] This strength in legitimate stage was devastated in the thirties as much by the popularity of radio and talking movies as by the Depression.

The interwar period saw an increase in women's participation in a number of sports, particularly softball, golf and tennis. Professionalism increased in the major men's sports, especially hockey. The Western Hockey League's Victoria Cougars—owned by Frank and Lester Patrick—won the 1925 Stanley Cup, but by then the eastern National Hockey League had become continental. In 1926 six of its ten teams were American. The Patricks could not compete against such money and sold their Cougar and Vancouver Millionaire stars to NHL teams. Decades would pass before a British Columbia team could again compete for Lord Stanley's trophy.

Lacrosse was transformed in a different way as it changed from field to box in the 1930s. The New Westminster Salmonbellies dominated the new version as they had the old, though in the 1930s the North Shore Indians, coached by Andy Paull and led by the Baker brothers, were equally exciting. Percy Williams became British Columbia's most famous athlete of the period as a gold medal winner in the 100- and 200-metre races at the 1928 Olympics. The most famous team, perhaps, was the Trail Smoke Eaters who capped a sensational 1938 season on the ice by winning the world championship in eight games, outscoring their opponents 42 goals to 1.

The 1920s were the heyday of outdoor excursions. The motor car was becoming important, but, with roads poor or non-existent and private autos beyond the means of many, trams, inter-urbans, railways and boats retained their overwhelming importance. The Union Steamship Company dominated Vancouver's holidaying. Taking over the Bowen Island route in 1920, it expanded the cottages at that Howe Sound resort to over one hundred, renovated the hotel as Mount Strachan Lodge, installed a huge dance pavilion, and improved the salt-water pool. The Longshoremen, Woodward's, Kelly Douglas and British Columbia Telephone all had group excursions to this holiday rival of Stanley Park. The company virtually invented the "Sunshine Coast" with its routes to Gibsons, Granthams, and Sechelt. The popularity of day-steamer outings peaked between 1925 and 1929 with as many as six vessels leaving Union pier on summer weekends. Day-return tickets to Bowen were less than a dollar, to Sechelt two. Even in 1933, the company introduced popular day-return tickets to Powell River and Savary Island.

THE POSTWAR DECADES

By 1950 the province seemed to be verging on a new era of robust creativity. George Woodcock, an English intellectual transplanted to British Columbia, sensed it in the Vancouver of that year. The city was, he found, "metropolitan in its disadvantages, yet provincial in amenities." With no permanent professional theatre, no hall acoustically fit for a good symphony orchestra, Vancouver nevertheless was a place "stirring with all kinds of small intellectual impulses and artistic currents," with hints of "all the genuine creative urges which are trying to break through the materialism and semi-colonial smugness of general Canadian life."[58] Woodcock's was a fair characterization. The city still lacked some of the basic cultural necessities and hovered between metropolitanism and provincialism.

For a very long time, the most important cultural vehicle was doubtless the Canadian Broadcasting Company (CBC). Although it was an important instrument linking the province with the outside world, its strength lay as much in local production as in network broadcasting. Music and drama were the cornerstone of regional CBC programming from the 1940s to the mid-1960s. The drama department, under the inspired direction of Dilworth, Andrew Allan, Ross McLean, Robert Harlow and Gerald Newman, was the most active and creative regional studio in the country, producing plays by Ibsen, Shaw and Chekhov, newer works by Elliot, Pinter and Robert Low, as well as commissioning works by Betty Lambert, George Woodcock and, notably, Birney's *The Damnation of Vancouver*. With similar intensity and creativity, the music department broadcast both classical and contemporary work, recreating the first performance of Handels' *Water Music*, highlighting chamber music, and leading the Baroque revival in Canada. The CBC provided work for actors and musicians that fostered the sustenance of professional theatre and music. The quality of its productions, rivalled in the English-speaking world only by the BBC, caught the attention of the national network. Regional radio thrived even after the advent of television: corporation management overlooked radio in its concern with the new medium, allowing the creativity of the drama and music producers to thrive unfettered. Only in the late 1960s did the situation change as the regional management shifted towards engaging outside "stars" and, with a perverse anti-intellectual elitism, sought to take radio "back to the people."[59]

In the postwar decades, musical activity reached new levels of diversity and sophistication. Vancouver's musical life was crowded by new outlets such as the Vancouver Chamber Choir, early, chamber and new music groups, and by the Vancouver Opera Association. In 1941 Victoria established its permanent symphony orchestra, which gradually grew in size, number of performances and quality, especially under Laszlo Gati from 1967 to 1979.

The Vancouver Symphony Orchestra (VSO), however, has tended to remain the centrepiece of music in the province. It thrived on the expatriate conductors Arthur Benjamin, Sir Thomas Beecham, Sir John Barbirolli and Otto Klemperer from 1941 through 1947. Irwin Hoffman, director from 1952 to 1964, supervised the 1959 move to the Queen Elizabeth Theatre, but by then was seen as unexciting and no longer suited to "the high-spirited city of the sixties."[60] Under his successor, Meredith Davies, the orchestra led the city "into a new and exciting period of musical growth." Difficulties with the symphony's management (not helped by their concern at his being gay) led to the controversial departure of Davies in 1971. By that time the VSO was a very good orchestra and its success was further enhanced by Kazuyoshi Akiyama who

presided from 1972 to 1985. In 1978 the symphony had over 40,000 subscribers, more than any other performing arts organization in North America.
The eighties, however, saw it accumulating deficits, having difficulties with its
musicians' union, reeling from the effects of a civic strike that closed its recently renovated Orpheum Theatre site, and losing its audience. In 1988 it collapsed under a $2,311,000 deficit, then revived later that year after an almost
complete reorganization and a bail-out by private and public benefactors.

The Vancouver Opera Association had already endured similar difficulties.
Irving Guttman, the "unlikely pioneer" of opera in western Canada, had begun
its productions with *Carmen* in 1960 and remained artistic director for fourteen
years.[61] The board and the public insisted on popular operas that kept houses
reasonably full and deficits modest. Guttman left in 1974, to be succeeded by
Australian Richard Bonynge, husband of soprano Joan Sutherland, who had
ambitions for an innovative repertoire and much more. Things quickly fell
apart as the board broke into factions, the deficit rose to half a million dollars,
and Bonynge lost interest. The organization never went under and, especially
with Guttman back for five operas in 1982–1984, recovered something of its
1960s lustre.

Musical growth was accompanied and promoted by the growth of musical
education. UBC opened its faculty of music in 1946, and the University of
Victoria followed suit in 1967; the Victoria Conservatory of Music was established in 1964, the Vancouver Academy of Music in 1969. The creation of
salaried staffs allowed composition to be nourished. Early appointments to the
department of music at UBC included Jean Coulthard in 1947 and Barbara
Pentland in 1949. Coulthard, born in Vancouver, learned her music at her
mother's knee before studying abroad. Long before her UBC appointment she
had earned recognition, but her best work, characterized by an eclectic
approach that was both contemporary and comprehensible, came after it.[62]
Pentland, born in Winnipeg, was influenced first by César Franck, then in
New York by Hindemith, Stravinsky and Copland, by John Weinzweig while
teaching in Toronto, then, through exposure during visits to the United States,
by serial technique, and, finally, by Webern after a summer in Germany. "Alert
to all significant trends and techniques,"[63] she required external stimulation and
sensed the isolation of the province. "I would like to feel I'm part of the culture," she said in 1968; "occasionally I get an inkling that I may be, but it's not
a permanent feeling."[64]

The establishment of Simon Fraser University brought Murray Schafer to
the province for what was both his and the university's most exciting decade.
Raised in Ontario, Schafer studied in Toronto where he was strongly influenced by John Weinzweig in music and Marshall McLuhan in other, equally
important, ways. Expelled from the conservatory there, he spent six enormously
rewarding years in Europe before returning to Canada. His decade in
Vancouver was astonishingly productive in compositions, often multi-media

studies on themes of urban alienation and psychoneurosis. *Requiems for the Party Girl* (1966), for example, documents the mental collapse and suicide of a young woman in the alienated, dehumanized labyrinth of the city. Moving into "acoustic ecology," Schafer concerned himself with the "sonic sewers" created by technology. He established the World Soundscape Project dedicated to the study of human relationships to the acoustic environment. His "North/White" composition (1973), which uses a snowmobile as an on-stage instrument, deals with the theme of the ravishing of Canadian space and purity.[65] Schafer's return to Ontario did not leave the region without adventurous composers. Barry Truax, Michael Conway Baker and Rudolf Komorous are only a few of the contemporary composers whose work has achieved eminence, with the province especially strong in electro-acoustical music.

Popular music also thrived. The Dal Richards and Mart Kenney dance bands had been prominent in the interwar and war-time years, and jazz found a real home, especially in Vancouver, where it included Chris Gage's piano at the Palomar and the Cave. Rock, too, put down roots, notably with the Chilliwack, the Bachman-Turner Overdrive, Mother Tucker's Yellow Duck and Bryan Adams.

The strongest postwar poetic voices remained Livesay and Birney, the latter now back in British Columbia, but preoccupied with teaching and encouraging others to create. Poetic British Columbia, like much of Canada, remained "in the doldrums in the 50's."[66] The same was not as true for the novel with the vividly contrasting voices of Ethel Wilson and Malcolm Lowry.

Wilson had grown up in British Columbia, arriving in Vancouver as a child. A 1921 subscription to *The New Statesman* was "the most valuable present" in her life. "What would have happened in my own mental life in a geographical area that was then still a periphery, not a centre, if this very fortuitous influence had not arrived and at that time, I don't quite know."[67] An elegant style, touched with a genius for irony and informed by a sense of the accidental, marked her writing. She was concerned with people, usually women, and their character and relationships. At the same time, she possessed "an inspired sense of place"—for Vancouver's West End, for the interior valleys of Lillooet and Lac Le Jeune, for the Gulf Islands—a regional sense that informed the atmosphere of *Hetty Dorval* (1947), *Swamp Angel* (1954) and her other works.[68] Her locale, she wrote, was British Columbia; there was no country "that I know and feel, and love in the same way." She, like Carr, had not chosen it; "it chose. It is very strong."[69]

In a different way, Lowry's fiction was about character and place. A Cambridge-trained Englishman, he arrived in British Columbia in 1937 and completed his masterpiece, *Under the Volcano* (1947), in a Burrard Inlet shack. The novel deals with Geoffrey Firmen and Mexico, but is more and less than that. Firmen is Lowry and the place is his own soul. The posthumous *Hear Us O Lord* (1961) and *October Ferry to Gabriola* (1970) derive from the more placid British Columbia landscape. *October Ferry* is "Lowry's Paradiso as compared to his Inferno" of *Under the Volcano*.[70] As significant in its way as *Under the Volcano* was Sheila Watson's *The Double Hook* (1959), a novel of rich texture and lyrical meaning set in Lillooet and resonating with the past of the Native people, the present of whites, and prophecies of their future.[71]

The great literary tumult that began at the University of British Columbia in 1961 owed little to any of these British Columbia writers. Livesay was in Africa and none of the UBC poets—Birney, Phyllis Webb, Roy Daniells—participated actively in the new poetry movement that exploded among graduate students at Point Grey. *Tish*, a mimeographed newsletter, was born with few local roots and even fewer Canadian ones. The poets who formed Tish (the name is a phonetic inversion) found their inspiration in the American modernist sensibility of Ezra Pound, William Carlos Williams, and the Black Mountain poets—Charles Olson, Robert Creeley and Robert Duncan. Concerned with writing "life" and with the "locus" of place, Frank Davey, George Bowering, Lionel Kearns, Gladys Hindmarsh and Fred Wah found Canadian poetry largely irrelevant. To a large degree, they hardly knew it. "We didn't get any Canadian writing at school in B.C." and only two knew of Raymond Souster, Louis Dudek and Irving Layton, the most appropriate Canadians. All, however, felt a great affinity with Williams and, after visits to Vancouver by Duncan and Creeley, with Black Mountain. The catalyst at UBC was Professor Warren Tallman, an American, not Birney, who was regarded by many students as connected to quite different sources and directed by quite different principles. To Birney, derisively (and unfairly) called "Mr. Canada," the Tish group was a jingoistic religion, worshipping saints and persecuting heretics.[72] American influences were deepened by Robin Blaser's move to Vancouver in 1966, but the poets soon moved into a modernism of their own. The American interest "began to fade as the energy centre shifted to what was happening in their own home town."[73] Although the Tish poets came under attack as being colonial continentalists,[74] the emphasis of their poetry was on the local, on a "sense of *belonging*." As *Tish* editor Davey later wrote, the concern was with the sense of a specific geography, "of being *at home* in place, community, and language." With *Tish* began a renewed localism of taste that was "virtually unconnected with Toronto-based CanLit, with presses, magazines, and major writers mostly unknown east of the Rockies," a community that "constituted its own traditions and genealogies, again largely unknown outside the province."[75]

The Tish group helped launch a ten-year explosion of poetry in Vancouver—by Bowering, Davey, Wah, Hindmarsh, Blaser, Gerry Gilbert, Daphne Marlatt, bill bissett and with secondary influences upon b. p. Nichol, Livesay, and even Birney. The explosion was not all Tish: Robin Skelton, Susan Musgrave, Patrick Lane, Tom Wayman, Pat Lowther, John Newlove, P. K. Page and Stanley Cooperman were removed, even opposed. It was an exciting decade. "I'd come back," wrote Livesay about her return to the province in

1963, "to a new world where suddenly everybody was talking poetry and it was very exciting; not just one or two poets reading but coffee house readings . . . three times a week." Much was "accessible": with Milton Acorn and Red Lane around, Livesay no longer felt isolated as a people's poet.[76]

From the 1960s the trajectory has been ever upward, with new writers continually emerging and older ones continuing their productivity. With government assistance available to help publish their work and more possibilities for publication including various literary journals, such as *Capilano Review* and *West Coast Line*, and regional presses such as Sono Nis and Talon Books, and increased employment opportunities once colleges and universities started employing writers as teachers, few good writers need go hungry and none unpublished. Among the most notable of prose writers was Jack Hodgins, whose 1976 *Spit Delaney's Island*, a collection of short stories, propelled him to the forefront of Canadian writing. His subsequent novels, including *The Invention of the World* (1977), *The Resurrection of Joseph Bourne* (1970) and *Innocent Cities* (1990), have maintained his reputation as a postmodernist writer whose mythic structures nevertheless allow his prose to capture the look and mood of the Vancouver Island setting and his burlesque characters the local idiom and mannerisms.

The visual arts went through equally vital and exciting times. Painters had returned to a postwar province to embrace a new modernism that emerged fully by the mid-1950s. Before the war abstraction had been an isolated exploration; after 1948, it became a conscious and co-operative movement, influenced from both New York and London. Painters like Jack Shadbolt, Don Jarvis, Bruno Bobak and John Korner retained, in explorations of their subjective reactions to the nature around them, earlier, more local roots, but they were following the London and New York mainstreams. The early emphasis was on natural forms without attempting to portray them at all realistically. Smith, after study in San Francisco, learned the mainstream tendency to treat painting as a personal expression independent of image or illusion. "We got into the act of painting. That was our subject matter and that's what we did."[77] The image disappeared entirely in the non-objective work of Smith, B. C. Binning, Toni Onley and others. By 1955, Alan Jarvis of the National Gallery could claim that there were "more good artists per square mile in B.C. than in all the rest of the country."[78] Although Vancouver might well have, as R. H. Hubbard put it in 1955, assumed artistic leadership in Canada, the lyric abstraction of the 1950s was tame and conventional compared to "the bizarre or the slightly wonky" that seized the art scene of the 1960s.[79]

Everything came together in that decade. Alvin Balkind, who in 1956 had opened the New Design Gallery with Abraham Rogatnick, was running the UBC gallery to which he brought an imaginative series of local and international exhibitions. The Vancouver Art Gallery, under Richard Simmins, Tony Emery and Doris Shadbolt, became "the most progressive," the swingingest gallery in Canada."[80] In 1966 Douglas Christmas opened the Douglas Gallery, which became an active promoter of the contemporary and the avant-garde. Between the UBC gallery, the Vancouver Art Gallery, and the Douglas Gallery art lovers could see much of the best from New York, London and Los Angeles. Christmas brought in New York luminaries Robert Rauschenburg and Frank Stella; the new art school at UBC under Binning staged an annual Festival of the Contemporary Arts, with visits by the headiest gurus of the decade, Buckminster Fuller and Marshall McLuhan.

The vitality rested in part upon external influences and a desire to "become more cosmopolitan."[81] The artists of the fifties had been closely in touch with developments in New York or London, but remained limited "by the condition of relative isolation."[82] Artists of the sixties lost that limitation. There "was a lot of contact between Los Angeles and Vancouver" and "a lot of to and fro between New York and Vancouver."[83] Some were new arrivals who brought with them international experience: Onley from England and Mexico, Roy Kiyooka from Saskatchewan's Emma Lake, Jack Wise from the United States and Japan, Iain Baxter from the United States. Native British Columbians, by travel, by reading art periodicals, or by exposure to exhibitions and international figures who visited Vancouver, knew where "art is at."[84]

As the "isms" whirled in the sixties, British Columbia's artists whirled with them. Op, hard edge, conceptual, performance, neo-Dadaism, minimal, and funk all enjoyed moments of success. Everything was possible, everything could be here and now. To Vancouver's artists in the sixties, marginality was dispensable. Iain Baxter, who arrived in Vancouver in 1964, was part of that mood. Inspired by a mixture of historical, Zen, and McLuhanesque influences, he began working in plastic. Declaring that the plastic bottle was "the common pottery of today," he reworked that banal item into objects of wit, parody and paradox, even an ambiguous beauty. Vacuum-formed plastic landscapes, then plastic-bagged landscapes, followed. A four-room apartment, with all its contents enveloped in plastic bags, formed a "Bagged Place" exhibit for the 1966 Festival of the Contemporary Arts. The same year he incorporated, with wife Ingrid, as N.E. Thing Co. and moved into conceptual art, a move from the physical to the mental, from the perceived to the conceived. In step with the mainstream, sometimes ahead of it, Baxter's achievements were noted in New York by Lucy Lippard, the Museum of Modern Art, and other avant-garde galleries. "Because of living so far away, I really forced myself into dealing with the problem of information and sending it."[85] As Lippard noted, "the original artist in isolated areas often comes out looking derivative," but Baxter succeeded in integrating "a regional and an international sensibility."[86]

Vancouver's Intermedia, an informal group of literary, visual and performance artists who created multi-media events, epitomized the experimental mood of the sixties. Visual artists moved into video and film, poets and audio artists collaborated with dancers as everyone became involved in live performances and multi-sensory installations. "We sort of fed off each other" in soundtrack, electronics and readings. The Vancouver Art Gallery, under Tony Emery, gave them lots of room: he "pretty much just opened the Gallery up to us and let us do what we wanted. . . . If we failed it didn't matter. It was a matter of trying to do something new."[87] By 1970 or so, Intermedia had burned itself out, but much of the élan went on to Western Front, an artists' co-operative that gave members exhibition space for innovative and frequently unmarketable work. Through Western Front, the hokey, the bizarre and the experimental "twinkled with dada irony and absurdity" and continued to thrive. Associated with all this was the new Simon Fraser University's arts program, where John Juliani produced his "Savage God" theatre, Iain Baxter ran his N.E. Thing Co., and Murray Schafer worked his sound magic.

The experimental mood of the sixties affected drama and dance as well as literature and the visual arts. Juliani's theatre was only the most dramatic. "Savage God" ended when he and the university parted uncomfortably. By then, however, drama was well represented in all major centres, especially by professional companies in Victoria and Vancouver. It had been a little tardy in its indigenous development. Into the theatre vacuum created by Hollywood, Depression and war had come Sydney Risk, a British Columbian recently returned from the British stage. Determined in 1946 to establish a repertory company, he assembled a dozen actors who, as Everyman Theatre, operated on a shoestring. Working first as a touring company (in their second season, 1947, they made a fifty-seven-stop Vancouver-to-Winnipeg tour by truck, bus and train), then as a Vancouver-based group (in three theatres in five years), Risk's company survived until 1953. Its end was hastened by police prosecution for the "lewd and filthy" *Tobacco Road*.

The Everyman troupe produced playwright Joy Coghill, actor Bruno Gerussi, and Peter Mannering, who did the pioneer work with Bastion Theatre in Victoria.[88] By the time Everyman folded, the Playhouse had begun, to be complemented by the Arts Club and, in the 1980s, an abundance of strong and varied professional theatre. Playwriting blossomed, with Birney's *Damnation* staged in 1966, Beverley Simons's *Crabdance* in 1969, and George Ryga's smash *The Ecstasy of Rita Joe*, a sombre drama of the death of an Native girl in the big city. Sharon Pollock followed, notably with her *Komagata Maru Incident* (1978), as did a younger generation of good drama writers.

Professional modern dance appeared only late in the sixties with the arrival of Anna Wyman, Paula Ross's innovative "visual poetry," Norbert Vesak's abortive Western Dance Theatre, and the establishment of academic programs under Helen Goodwin at the University of British Columbia and Iris Garland at Simon Fraser University. Dance companies proliferated in the seventies, with SFU spin-offs (Mountain Dance Theatre and Terminal City Dance), the Anna Wyman Dance Theatre, and Judith Marcuse among the most significant. All these were choreographically creative, though the single best-known work was Vesak's adaptation of *The Ecstasy of Rita Joe* for the Royal Winnipeg Ballet, one of the "biggest money-spinners" in its history.[89]

The visual arts, like the literary, grew immensely in the following decades. Toni Onley, after establishing a notable reputation as among the best of Canada's abstract expressionists, reintroduced a landscape imagery into his painting. Other painters followed the tendency, but no single trend characterized the diverse directions taken by a multitude of artists who made their way to recognition. One theme was the movement among younger artists away from pure form and abstraction towards interest in and involvement with subject matter. A second theme was a return to painting, notably by Gathie Falk, who abandoned her "funk" (found junk) art and performances for easel painting. New faces, such as Jeffrey Wall with his magical photographic images and Attila Richard Lukacs with his brutal neo-expressionism, captured the imagination of gallery curators if not always their audiences. Commercial galleries, notably Bau-Xi, Pitt, Buschlen-Mowatt and Diane Farris, allowed outlets for artists both new and established.

Elsewhere in the province there were strong echoes of the vibrant sixties. Victoria had established its art gallery in 1951 and in the following decade the University of Victoria opened its faculty of Fine Arts. Elza Mayhew, Pat Martin Bates, and Herbert Siebner were among the modernists of international sensibility working on Vancouver Island. The civic gallery encouraged local artists, though it was never, even under Richard Simmins in the 1970s, as avant-garde as Vancouver's gallery. A fine balance of traditional and contemporary, of regional and international (including Asian) made it the provincial favourite of benefactors who were often alienated by the vanguard élan of Vancouver. Thus Victoria's permanent collection tends to be rich in its diversity, whereas Vancouver's concentrates on the late twentieth century. Art galleries were established in many regional centres during the decade and provided a focus for art and artists. The rapidity of communications and transportation has, moreover, allowed artists to survive and prosper outside the metropolitan areas.

The fifties' generation of artists had been closely linked to a dramatic new wave of innovative architecture that represented "a release from the stale European nostalgias."[90] Binning pioneered new domestic forms in 1942 by building his West Vancouver house using post-and-beam construction to support a flat roof, a structural innovation that freed the floor plan and allowed adaptations to sloping sites. Window walls allowed openness and an indoor-outdoor mood. This set the precedent for the view-hungry, hill-clinging homes of the province. American wood technology, California and Oregon architects, and Oriental forms gave inspiration to a new generation of architects, including Ron Thom and Arthur Erickson. The sprawling ranch style, introduced to British Columbia by Robert Berwick and C. B. K. van Norman, became the prototype for extensive suburban development. These sprawling, single-storeyed, picture-windowed, shake-roofed, stone-chimneyed, patio palaces represented the most influential house style of the fifties and sixties.[91] They marked a major shift in design. Interwar domestic architecture had shown little in the way of innovation, continuing with modified revival forms, especially the California bungalow, and only occasionally adding a modernist gesture. The largest alteration had been the popularity of stucco, especially in renovating older wood-clad homes. This gave a dubious distinction to the province's neighbourhoods: the ubiquity of stuccoed-over clapboard or shingle, a style that abruptly disappears at the Blaine or Oroville border crossings.

The sixties saw another dubious innovation, the "Vancouver Special." A two-storey structure on a concrete slab, the Special was designed to optimize inexpensively the use of the standard 33-foot city lot, though it was soon adapted to larger sites. With a living-sleeping area on the upper floor, utilities and often a rental suite on the lower, and finished externally in stucco and brick with a second-floor balcony on the front, the Special was by far the most popular new style of family home design, not only in Vancouver but throughout the province. It dominated new construction on Vancouver's East Side, where it was particularly popular with Chinese and other ethnic groups.[92] Often accompanying the Special was a front landscape design (a sundeck/carport took up the rear garden) based on an enclosed courtyard of formal symmetry using gravel, ornaments, and small plantings that harkened back to Mediterranean models.[93]

The single most significant architectural achievement of the sixties was the construction of Simon Fraser University by Arthur Erickson and Geoffrey Massey. It marked the emergence of Erickson as the most innovative architect in the province, perhaps in Canada. He was to go on to design Vancouver's MacMillan Bloedel building, Robson Square, the UBC Museum of Anthropology, and stunning buildings elsewhere in Canada and the world. Extensive foreign travel gave him cosmopolitan sources for his imagination that led to widespread recognition. Even that was not enough. Erickson might, acknowledged New York's Philip Johnson, be the greatest architect on the continent, but he is "a Western architect and what's worse, he's in British Columbia, which is a province of a province to us."[94]

Erickson was just one of a new group of architects who made their mark: Ron Thom, Barry Downs, Bruno Freschi, and Randle Iredale, to single out a few. Behind their achievements lay the development of an indigenous training centre. UBC's school of architecture opened in 1947 under the Swiss-trained Fred Lasserre and Binning, an artist long interested in design. The fifties had seen the beginning of a transformation of the province's town centres. Vancouver led with its B.C. Hydro building, designed by Thompson, Berwick and Pratt, then with office and apartment blocks, both frame low-rises and high-rises of glass-wall and concrete column or steel construction. The style was International Modern and the best high-rises were often by local architects. By the mid-eighties, Postmodernism became the vogue, with columns, pediments, arches and domes as eclectic historical touches.

The rapid postwar urban redevelopment raised concerns about the destruction of older buildings of historical and architectural merit. The heritage movement had only limited successes against the development steamroller that naturally placed economic ahead of nostalgic values, but it did save some choice structures around the province, notably Vancouver's Christ Church Cathedral. In Victoria, the Hallmark Society and other groups were more successful in retaining vestiges of an older Victoria.

Although science maintained, perhaps even increased, its prestige in the war and postwar years, few individuals or even institutions achieved the fame or notoriety of cultural leaders. Biologist Ian McTaggart Cowan of UBC had a high profile as a public lecturer, but unless scientists entered other fields—Gordon Shrum in university and public administration and David Suzuki as a media figure—they remained known only to their professional peers. Even institutions, such as TRIUMF (the tri-university meson facility), though widely known among the public, retained an anonymity clothed in the mysteries of high-acceleration particles. Such apparent obscurity masked a maturation of both research and training. The major developments centred at UBC, which benefitted from association with the B.C. Research Council (created in 1944 by Shrum), forestry research institutions, and TRIUMF. Significant advances were achieved in virtually all areas, with notable expansion into nuclear physics, oceanography and medicine. Among the most significant achievements were UBC chemist Neil Bartlett's 1962 demonstration that "inert" gases were in fact capable of forming stable chemical compounds and the work by Gobind Khorana of the B.C. Research Council on the genetic code that led to his 1968 Nobel Prize. Recruited by Shrum in 1952, Khorana moved to a better position in the United States in 1960. George Volkoff worked with John Warren in establishing nuclear physics at UBC before going on the National Research Council and the Chalk River project. In the life sciences, Vladimir Krajina's work on biogeoclimatic zones made a significant contribution to an understanding of the ecology of the province while establishing Krajina's high international reputation. The apparent anonymity of the individual scientist was contradicted by the publicity that accompanied the awarding to UBC biochemist Michael Smith, along with a California colleague, of the 1994 Nobel Prize for biochemistry.

British Columbia's diversity has given its residents a wide choice of recreations, from bird watching to windsurfing, as their leisure time increased. The five-day week, which became standard in the 1950s, left most working people "waiting for the weekend." Sport remained, even intensified, as an outlet. The professional sports menu grew from 1954, when the new B.C. Lions were the principal attraction, to 1995, when they competed for attention with the Canucks of the National Hockey League, the new Grizzlies of the National Basketball Association, and professional baseball and soccer teams. As participants in sports and recreation, British Columbians reflected Canadian and continental trends. Downhill skiing grew, with runs in every area of the province and the establishment of major new facilities in the Whistler area. Cross-country skiing developed from almost nothing. The spread of the automobile and then the recreational vehicle turned almost the entire province into a touring park, a development with which the expanding provincial campgrounds could scarcely keep pace. Cottage ownership intensified in areas within reach of urban centres.

Most ubiquitous of all leisure pursuits, even for the apartment dweller with a balcony, was gardening. British Columbia, as a province of gardeners, remains "British" at least in this regard. Nowhere else in Canada is so much time and money spent on lawns, trees, shrubs and flowers, nowhere else does the nursery industry thrive as well, and nowhere else can boast of so many diverse and lovely gardens and parks. The appreciation of native plants declined after the First World War and thoughtless plantings of exotics on inappropriate sites mars many a streetscape and development. Paradoxically, native plants are usually more expensive and more difficult to obtain and to grow than introduced plants. A revival of interest in native plants is evident in the mid-1990s.

Despite the profusion of outdoor activities, the arrival of television made unquestionably the most significant alteration to leisure hours for postwar British Columbians. Initial reception came from American stations, then from the CBC in 1952, with colour introduced fifteen years later. TV replaced the golden age of radio's mass communication, but it also revolutionized evening and weekend hours, especially for children. Even more than radio, it eroded the province's isolation. Most programming originated outside the province, either in Toronto or the United States. Cable TV, exceptionally widely subscribed to in British Columbia, meant a high exposure to external programming, especially American.

ISOLATION AND MARGINALITY

Isolation has been a firm and constant factor in the intellectual and imaginative world of British Columbia. Remoteness from the centres and mainstreams of its common English-language culture has threatened a drift into the backwaters of provincialism, into the marginalization of the mind from a text being written elsewhere. Countering this factor has been the consciousness of belonging to that larger British, Canadian and American world. British Columbia's culture has always existed within this tension, within the fine balance between province, the *genius loci*, and the wider linguistic and cultural community of the continent and—until recently—the British empire. British Columbia's historians, those "who concerned themselves with the past and the character" of the province, have similarly demonstrated "a strong and consistent commitment to the idea that British Columbia could not be understood without taking full account of its relationship to the world around it."[95] Its provincialism remained "rooted in a large cosmopolitan civilization, sometimes conceived as Canadian, sometimes as continental, sometimes as British and Imperial."[96]

Emily Carr's career demonstrates the tension born of isolation and marginality. Acutely conscious of the limitations of her home province, she sought contact with the larger culture by study in San Francisco, London and Paris. Only the last provided what she needed, but even its Fauvist modernism proved inappropriate to her British Columbia subject matter. Outside contacts—Harris and the Group of Seven, along with Seattle artists and a study of contemporary trends—were necessary to liberate her genius. Yet it was British Columbia's own nature that provided the inspiration. A "little old lady on the edge of nowhere,"[97] she nevertheless needed her provincial "nowhere" as much as the inspiration that came from outside it. She would never have succeeded as an expatriate. "I stopped grieving about the isolation of the West," she wrote of the time when she began to set her own course. "I was glad we were cut off."[98]

The development of cosmopolitan centres within the province has made the problem of isolation seem less acute. Culture tends to be a metropolitan phenomenon: the arts, the imagination and the intellect flourish in urban settings. Athens, Rome, Florence, Paris, London and New York generate culture that they export to their hinterlands. They are the scene of publishing, exhibition and performance, the venue of cultural production and distribution. British Columbia's culture, aside from its Native component, has been shaped by London, San Francisco, Toronto, New York and Los Angeles. With the growth of cities such as Victoria and particularly Vancouver, it is now shaped as well by metropolitan centres within the province. British Columbia's major cities, though still subordinate to the greater cultural centres of the English-speaking world, are now large enough to provide focus for cultural activity. Because cultural events and institutions are concentrated in the cities, however, it is still possible to feel acutely "cut off" in smaller communities.

The threat of marginalizing isolation has also been countered by willful acts of cosmopolitanism. Aiding these has been a constant infusion by immigration. While some of the greatest creators have, like Carr, Hodgins and Erickson, been native-born, most have come from elsewhere. Even in recent years, the list is a long one, from Haig-Brown through Lowry, Onley and Woodcock to Daphne Marlatt, Edith Iglauer and Jane Rule. George Bowering, who is himself a native of the Okanagan, has observed that, "Nearly all our novelists have come here from other provinces and countries and have written about people who have done likewise." This, says Bowering, creates, as the unifying and informing symbol for the culture of the province, "the attempt to find or make a home."[99] To Bowering, this "home vs. isolation" is the tension of personal loneliness suffered by those without a traditional and settled home life. For many, however, the difficulty was not simply personal loneliness, but existence in a province that was so new it had no traditions or associations of its own and so remote that its connection to its cultural roots was weak.

Europeans did have difficulty finding a home in the province (and non-Europeans more so), even if it was, in many of its regions, climatically akin to their original home. The place, whatever attractive, even Edenic, qualities it may have had, was vacant of memory, a wilderness of nature, a desert of meaning. Rupert Brooke had noted the absence of ghosts, Haig-Brown that there was more for a writer to know and use in tiny Dorset than in all of British Columbia.[100] British gardens, Tudoresque homes, Alpine chalets or imported skylarks were all attempts to domesticate the wilderness. Even Carr tried to bring English song birds to the silent forests of her province. This sense of longing for a missing piece of Home, this aching for absent tradition, this nostalgia for a heritage, has never quite been overcome.

THE NATIVE TRADITION

British Columbia's Native people, on the other hand, were always at home, even when dispossessed of land and resources. They, both as culturally creative societies and as subjects for intellectual study, compensate for the marginality of many immigrant endeavours. The paradox is that Europeans, both willfully and unintentionally, alienated them from their own culture, an alienation only recently being undone.

Culturally and imaginatively, the Native peoples have been British Columbia's largest contributors to the world's culture. They may well, as Haig-Brown wrote, have "produced more creative development for the human spirit than has been produced in the hundred years of white civilization that have followed upon the time of their greatest flowering."[101] The art of British Columbia's coastal peoples, whether in textiles, sculpture or dance, possesses "an unmistakable stamp and genius" that "has shown evidence of a superior diversity and has demonstrated apparently inexhaustible talents for renewal."[102]

By the time of European contact, the art already had a long history of change and development. Simple life-forms initially appeared some 4,500 years ago. Between 3,500 and 1,500 years ago, the people of the northwest coast, "in an impressive flurry of creative achievement," expanded and elaborated their cultural themes and, in the process, diverged into regional styles that mutually influenced each other.[103] Moreover, their music was sophisticated, their dance ceremonialism elaborate, and their oral literature rich and complex.

The Native people of the coast exploited the forest, especially the cedar, for their houses, implements and art. They created a wealth of objects, almost all, whether fishing hooks or dance masks, decorated by paint or carving. Their style was distinguished for its precise attention to form, its subject matter depicting humanized animals or mythic creatures. The less sedentary Interior groups produced largely utilitarian objects, working with quill on tanned hide or in basketry.

Contact with European technology and trade led to a remarkable florescence of northwest coast art. Monumental sculpture, restricted to a relatively few examples before contact, blossomed into forests of totem poles such as those standing before Haida villages on the Queen Charlotte Islands by the 1870s. Like the artists of ancient Greece or medieval Europe, individual artists of the pre-contact and most of the contact period are unknown. The great artists of the early twentieth century, such as Charlie Edenshaw, Charlie James, Mungo Martin and Willie Seaweed, maintained a thread of continuity through the social and cultural decline of Native communities in the first half of the twentieth century. By the 1960s, however, a marked revival was underway. This was most apparent in art as new generations picked up the brushes and tools to create masks, boxes, poles and weavings that rival the best of the past.

Joe David of the Nootka (Nu-chau-nulth), Beau Dick and Tony Hunt of the Kwakiutl, Norman Tait of the Nishga (Nisga'a), Roy Vickers of the Gitksan, and Robert Davidson of the Haida, to name only a striking few, emerged as important artists deriving their inspiration from their Native heritage. Standing apart was Bill Reid, by blood only a quarter Haida and raised as a white. Reid was in his early teens before he "even became conscious of the fact that I was anything other than an average Caucasian North American."[104] Professionally a radio broadcaster, he learned jewellery making at Ryerson in Toronto and, back in British Columbia, began "becoming Haida." Apprenticing to Mungo Martin at the University of British Columbia's totem replication program, Reid became a full-time and fully fledged artist in the Haida style. After a period of "willing submission to the great original models" found in museums,[105] Reid began to stretch the style without breaking it. From this experimentation emerged his monumental "The Raven and the First Men at UBC's Museum of Anthropology, the "Killer Whale" bronze at the Vancouver Aquarium, and the "Black Canoe" at the Canadian Embassy in Washington. Reid, more than any other artist, symbolizes the bridging of cultures and cultural appreciation between Native and non-Native societies. A gulf remains, one that can only be closed through mutual appropriation.

The revival of Native art and culture was followed with deep interest by a growing audience of non-Natives, both within the province and beyond it. European concern with Native art dates back to Franz Boas's 1897 "The Decorative Art of the Indians of the North Pacific Coast" and elaborated in his *Primitive Art*.[106] The most significant contribution since Boas has been by Seattle's Bill Holm. His *Northwest Coast Indian Art: An Analysis of Form*[107] rediscovered the rules of form and quickly became a classic of the explication of the northern style, fundamental to practising artists as well as to art historians and connoisseurs. More audacious was the speculative brilliance of Wilson Duff's essays into the meaning underlying the function, form and style. His *Images Stone B.C.* and other essays set an imaginative example. Seeking systems of inner logic based on dualism, paradox, ambiguity and transformation, and with provocative attention to sexual symbolism, Duff's investigations were stunning.

Duff's work drew inspiration from the insights of France's Claude Lévi-Strauss, who had already provoked a realization of the complexity of the northwest coast mind with his examination of its mythology.[108] This most sagacious and influential of twentieth-century anthropologists brought a wide-ranging and poetic explication of the Salish Swaihwé and Kwakiutl Xwéxwé and Dzonokwa mask complexes. These were intellectual *tours de force*.[109] Similar contributions have come from others.[110]

The influence of European upon Native culture has been overwhelming. Languages were all but lost, cosmologies obliterated, mythologies forgotten, and art and music neglected. Much of this was the result of forced acculturation by government, school and church, though a great deal resulted from the desire of the Native people themselves to convert to Christianity and the white way.

But the adaptation was very imperfect. Tradition remained deep and in the later twentieth century re-emerged. Much that seemed lost had merely been altered, much that seemed passé became again relevant. Infused with a reborn pride in their identity, desiring to recapture what had been lost or "appropriated," rechristened as "First Nations" and reverting to old names and ways, British Columbia's Natives asserted their culture, their traditions, their heritage, and their right to their home. Although inextricably part of British Columbia's broader culture, they claim their own distinctive and dynamic culture within it. At home and yet not, they have their own version of modern British Columbia's central cultural ambiguity.

NOTES

1. Allan Pritchard, "West of the Great Divide: A View of the Literature of British Columbia," *Canadian Literature* 94 (Autumn 1982): 96-112; "West of the Great Divide: Man and Nature in the Literature of British Columbia," *Canadian Literature* 102 (Autumn 1984): 36-53; George Bowering, "Home Away: A Thematic Study of Some British Columbia Novels," *B.C. Studies* 62 (Summer 1984): 9-28; Maria Tippett and Douglas Cole, *From Desolation to Splendour: Changing Perceptions of the British Columbia Landscape* (Toronto: Clarke Irwin, 1977).

2. George Vancouver, *Voyage of Discovery to the North Pacific Ocean and Round the World . . . , 1790-95* (London: G. G. and J. Robinson, 1798) I: 305.

3. Alexander Mackenzie, *Voyages from Montreal* (London: Cadell, Jun. and W. Davies, 1801): 378.

4. William T. Stearn, "The Botanical Results of Captain Cook's Three Voyages and their Later Influence." (Paper presented to Captain James Cook and His Times Conference, Simon Fraser University, 1978): 4; "Ornithological History," in R. Wayne Campbell, *et al.*, *The Birds of British Columbia* (Victoria: Royal British Columbia Museum, 1990) I: 15-16. Fifteen bird species, including the bald eagle, the rufous hummingbird, the northern flicker, Steller's jay, and the junco, were recorded in Thomas Pennant's 1785 *Arctic Zoology*.

5. Michael Weber, "Malaspina Explores the Northwest Coast," *The Malaspina Expedition: In the Pursuit of Knowledge . . .* (Santa Fe: Museum of New Mexico Press, 1977): 7.

6. *Noticias de Nutka: An Account of Nootka Sound in 1792*, Iris Higbie (Engstrand),

ed. and trans. (rev. ed., Vancouver: Douglas & McIntyre; Seattle: University of Washington Press, 1991).

7. Eric W. Groves, "Archibald Menzies: An Early Botanist on the West Coast of North America." (Paper presented at the Vancouver Conference on Exploration and Discovery, 1992).

8. Susan Delano McKelvey, *Botanical Exploration of the Trans-Mississippi West, 1790-1850* (Jamaica Plains, N.Y.: Arnold Arboretum of Harvard University, 1955): 13.

9. The editors in collaboration with M. L. Tyrwhitt-Drake, "David Douglas," *Dictionary of Canadian Biography*, Francess G. Halpenny, gen. ed., vol. VI (Toronto: University of Toronto Press, 1987): 218-220.

10. McKelvey. *Botanical Exploration*, 242.

11. John Richardson, *Fauna Boreali Americana* (London: Murray, 1829-1837); W. J. Hooker, *Flora Boreali Americana* (London, H. G. Bohm, 1840).

12. Douglas to James Hargrave, 5 February 1843, in G. P. de T. Glazebrook, ed., *The Hargrave Correspondence, 1821-1843* (Toronto: The Champlain Society, 1938): 420-421.

13. John Hayman, ed., *Robert Brown and the Vancouver Island Exploring Expedition* (Vancouver: University of British Columbia Press, 1989). Brown (1842-1895) was unrelated to the more illustrious British natural scientist Robert Brown (1773-1858).

14. John Emmerson, *British Columbia and Vancouver Island: Voyages, Travels & Adventures* (Durham: by the author, 1865): 37; Duncan George Forbes Macdonald, *British Columbia and Vancouver's Island* (London: Longman, Green, Longman, Roberts, & Green, 1862): 29.

15. *Ibid.*, 172.

16. Margaret A. Ormsby, "Canada and the New British Columbia," Canadian Historical Association, *Annual Report* (1948): 78-79.

17. Dorothy Blakey Smith, "Music in the Furthest West a Hundred Years Ago," *Canadian Music Journal* 2 (Summer 1958): 14.

18. Jean Barman, *Growing up British in British Columbia: Boys in Private School* (Vancouver: University of British Columbia Press, 1984): 10.

19. J. G. Cooper and George Suckley, *The Natural History of Washington Territory* (Washington: U.S. Government Printing Office, 1859).

20. Morris Zaslow, *Reading the Rocks: The Story of the Geological Survey of Canada, 1842-1972* (Toronto: Macmillan Company of Canada, 1975): 114.

21. See Stephen Jay Gould, *Wonderful Life: The Burgess Shale and the Nature of History* (New York: W. W. Norton, 1989).

22. W. A. Waiser, *The Field Naturalist: John Macoun, the Geological Survey, and Natural Science* (Toronto: University of Toronto Press, 1989): 114.

23. *Ibid.*, 195.

24. John Fannin, *Check List of British Columbia Birds* (Victoria: Richard Wolfenden, 1891); Richard Mackie, *Hamilton Mack Laing, Hunter-Naturalist* (Victoria: Sono Nis, 1985); Campbell, *et al.*, *Birds of British Columbia* I: 16-32.

25. Allan Brooks and Harry S. Swarth, *A Distributional List of the Birds of British Columbia* (Berkeley: Cooper Ornithological Club, 1925). See also Hamilton Mack Laing, *Allan Brooks: Artist-Naturalist* (Victoria: B.C. Provincial Museum, 1979).

26. Joseph Kaye Henry, *Flora of Southern British Columbia and Vancouver Island* (Toronto: W. J. Gage, 1915): iii.

27. James R. Anderson, *Trees and Shrubs, Food, Medical and Poisonous Plants of British*

Columbia (Victoria: Department of Education, 1925); J. A. Munro, *Introduction to Bird Study in British Columbia* (Victoria: Department of Education, 1931).

28. Barman, *Growing Up British*, 10.

29. Rupert Brooke, *Letters from America* (London: Sidgewick & Jackson, 1923; orig, 1916): 147-156.

30. H. Glynn Ward, *The Glamour of British Columbia* (New York: The Century Co., 1926): 164.

31. P. H. Morris, "Sport," in *British Columbia* (London: Gresham Press, 1912): 463, 467.

32. *Ibid.*, 467.

33. Alan Metcalfe, *Canada Learns to Play* (Toronto: McClelland & Stewart, 1987): 44-45.

34. See Dale McIntosh, *History of Music in British Columbia, 1850-1950* (Victoria: Sono Nis Press, 1989).

35. Helmut Kallman, *A History of Music in Canada, 1534-1914* (Toronto: University of Toronto Press, 1960): 3.

36. Gordon Roper, Rupert Schneider, and S. Ross Beharriel, "The Kinds of Fiction, 1880-1920," in Carl F. Klink, ed., *The Literary History of Canada* (Toronto: University of Toronto Press, 1957): 300.

37. See Nicholas Tuele, *Thomas W. Fripp* (Victoria: Art Gallery of Greater Victoria, 1983).

38. Anon., "Vancouver, a City of Beautiful Homes," *British Columbia Magazine* (December 1911): 1313.

39. "A House in Vancouver," *The Craftsman* (March 1908): 675, quoted in Janet Bingham, *Samuel Maclure: Architect* (Ganges: Horsdal & Schubert, 1985): 1.

40. Barman, *Growing Up British*, 10.

41. Quoted in William C. Gibson, *Wesbrook and His University* (Vancouver: Library of the University of British Columbia, 1973): 85.

42. Russell A. Jarrell, *The Cold Light of Dawn: A History of Canadian Astronomy* (Toronto: University of Toronto Press, 1988): 87-125, 137.

43. Emily Carr, *Hundreds and Thousands: The Journals of Emily Carr* (Toronto: Clarke, Irwin, 1966): 3-18.

44. *Ibid.*, 148.

45. Weston, taped interview, Glenbow Institute Archives, Calgary.

46. Varley to A. Lismer, February 1928, quoted in Christopher Varley, *F. H. Varley: A Centennial Exhibition* (Edmonton: Edmonton Art Gallery, 1981): 78.

47. Shadbolt, "A Personal Recollection," in *Vancouver: Art and Artists, 1931-1983* (Vancouver: Vancouver Art Gallery, 1983): 39.

48. Jock Macdonald to John Varley, 8 December 1936, NGC, quoted in Joyce Zemans, *Jock Macdonald: The Inner Landscape, A Retrospective Exhibition* (Toronto: Art Gallery of Ontario, 1981): 96.

49. Shadbolt, *Vancouver*, 36.

50. *Ibid.*, 39.

51. Michael Ondaatje, "Howard O'Hagan and 'the Rough-Edged Chronicle'," in George Woodcock, ed., *The Canadian Novel in the Twentieth Century: Essays from Canadian Literature* (Toronto: McClelland & Stewart, 1975): 277; Margaret Fee, "Howard O'Hagan's 'Tay John': Making New World Myths," *Canadian Literature* 110 (Fall 1986): 24.

52. See Roger Leslie Hyman, "Wasted Heritage and *Waste Heritage*: The Critical

Disregard of an Important Canadian Novel," *Journal of Canadian Studies* 17 (Winter 1982-1983): 74-87.

53. Joan McCullagh, *Allen Crawley and Contemporary Verse* (Vancouver: University of British Columbia Press, 1976): 14.

54. *Ibid.*, 12; Ken Norris, *The Little Magazine in Canada, 1925-1980: Its Role in the Development of Modernism and Post-Modernism in Canadian Poetry* (Toronto: ECW Press, 1984): 22-27.

55. John Becker, *Discord: The Story of the Vancouver Symphony Orchestra* (Vancouver: Brighouse Press, 1989): 4-5.

56. "The Stage," *British Columbia Magazine* (April 1914): 203.

57. Andrew Parkin, "The New Frontier: Toward an Indigenous Theatre in British Columbia," in L. W. Conolly, ed., *The Theatrical Touring and Founding in North America* (Westport, Conn.: Greenwood Press, 1982): 101-112.

58. George Woodcock, *Ravens and Prophets* (London: Allan Wingate, 1952): 15.

59. Gerald Newman, interview, February 1991; Howard Fink, "Earle Birney's Radio Dramas," *Essays on Canadian Writing* 21 (Spring 1981): 53-72.

60. Becker, *Discord*, 20.

61. David Watmough, *The Unlikely Pioneer: Building Opera from the Pacific through the Prairies* (Oakville, Ont.: Mosaic Press, 1986).

62. Laurence Cluderay, "Jean Coulthard," *Music Scene* 240 (March-April 1968): 5.

63. Robert Turner, "Barbara Pentland," *Canadian Music Journal* 2 (Summer 1958): 24.

64. Peter Huse, "Barbara Pentland," *Music Scene* 240 (July-August 1968): 9. See also Sheila Eastman and Timothy J. McGee, *Barbara Pentland* (Toronto: University of Toronto Press, 1983).

65. Rick MacMillan, ed., "Schafer Sees Music Reflecting Country's Characteristics," *Music Scene* 293 (January-February 1977): 7; Alan M. Gilmor, "Murray Schafer," *Encyclopedia of Music in Canada*, Helmut Kallman, Gilles Potvin, and Kenneth Winters, eds. (Toronto: University of Toronto Press, 1981): 849-851; Stephen Adams, *R. Murray Schafer* (Toronto: University of Toronto Press, 1983).

66. Livesay, quoted in Lionel Kearns, ed., *Western Windows: A Comparative Anthology of Poetry in British Columbia* (Vancouver: CommCept Publications, 1977): 184.

67. Wilson, "A Cat Among the Falcons," in David Stouck, ed., *Ethel Wilson: Stories, Essays, and Letters* (Vancouver: University of British Columbia Press, 1987): 100-101.

68. Desmond Pacey, "Ethel Wilson's First Novel," *Canadian Literature* 29 (Summer 1966): 46.

69. Stouck, ed., *Ethel Wilson*, 103-107.

70. George Woodcock, "Lowry," in William Toye, gen. ed., *The Oxford Companion to Canadian Literature* (Toronto: Oxford University Press, 1983): 473.

71. Steven Putzel, "Under Coyote's Eye," *Canadian Literature* 102 (Autumn 1984): 7-16.

72. Bowering and Birney, in Caroline Bayard and Jack David, eds., *Outposts* (Toronto: Press Porcepic, 1978): 79-81, 113-114.

73. Warren Tallman, "Wonder Merchants: Modernist Poetry in Vancouver during the 1960s," in C. H. Gervais, ed., *The Writing Life: Historical & Cultural Views of the Tish Movement* (Coatsworth, Ont.: Black Moss Press, 1976): 40.

74. Keith Richardson, *Poetry and the Colonialized Mind* (Oakville: Mosaic Press, 1976).

75. Frank Davey, "Introduction," and "Tish, British Columbia and After," in C. H. Gervais, ed., *The Writing Life: Historical & Cultural Views of the Tish Movement* (Coatsworth, Ont.: Black Moss Press, 1976): 19, 160-161.

76. Doug Beardsley and Rosemary Sullivan, "An Interview with Dorothy Livesay," *Canadian Poetry* 3 (Fall/Winter 1978): 95-96.

77. Vancouver Art Gallery, *Gordon Smith, recent works: November 20, 1987 to January 10, 1988* (Vancouver: Vancouver Art Gallery, 1987).

78. In Anthony Emery, "British Columbia's Progressive Art," *The Studio* (June 1957): 168, in *Vancouver: Art and Artists, 1931-1983* (Vancouver: Vancouver Art Gallery, 1983): 72.

79. David P. Silcox, "An Outside View," *ibid.*, 158.

80. Joan Lowndes, "Simmons inspired a flowering of the visual arts," *The Province* (25 November 1966): Lowndes, "The Spirit of the Sixties by a Witness," *Vancouver: Art and Artists*, 142.

81. Scott Watson, "Art in the Fifties," *ibid.*, 97.

82. Doris Shadbolt, "The Vancouver Scene," in William Townsend, ed., *Canadian Art Today* (Greenwich, Conn.: New York Graphic Society, 1970): 61.

83. Glenn Lewis and Helen Goodwin quoted in Marguerite Pinney, "Voices," in *Vancouver: Art and Artists*, 180.

84. Doris Shadbolt, *Canadian Art Today*, 62.

85. Quoted in Marie L. Fleming, *Baxter SUPERSCRIPT 2: Any Choice Works* (Toronto: Art Gallery of Ontario, 1982): 90.

86. Ian Wallace in Alvin Balkind, "Vancouver Scene and Unscene," *Art in America* 58 (1970): 124.

87. David Rimmer, quoted in Marguerite Pinney, "Voices," *Vancouver: Art and Artists*, 183, 185.

88. James Hoffman, "Sydney Risk and the Everyman Theatre," *B.C. Studies* 76 (Winter 1987-1988): 33-57.

89. Max Wyman, *Dance Canada: An Illustrated History* (Vancouver: Douglas & McIntyre, 1989): 147.

90. Ron Thom, "Modern Architecture on the West Coast," in Leon Whiteson, *Modern Canadian Architecture* (Edmonton: Hurtig, 1983): 22.

91. Douglas Shadbolt, "Postwar Architecture in Vancouver," *Vancouver: Art and Artists*, 108-112; Vera Orufrychuk, "A West Coast Style to Modern Architecture." (Unpublished paper, B.C. Studies Conference, 1988.)

92. Vancouver City Planning Department, *The Vancouver Special* (Vancouver, June 1981).

93. Rodney A. Fowler, "Courtyard Gardens of Vancouver: A Study of the Contemporary Urban Landscape." (M.A. thesis, Simon Fraser University, 1990).

94. Quoted in Edith Iglauer, *Seven Stones: A Portrait of Arthur Erickson, Architect* (Madeira Park, B.C.: Harbour Publishing; Seattle: University of Washington Press, 1981): 12.

95. Allan Smith, "The Writing of British Columbia History," *B.C. Studies* 45 (Spring 1980): 101-102.

96. John Norris, "Margaret Ormsby," in John Norris and Margaret Prang, eds., *Personality and History in British Columbia: Essays in Honour of Margaret Ormsby* (Victoria, 1977): 15.

97. "Emily Carr: Little Lady on the Edge of Nowhere" (video, Toronto: CBC, 1978).

98. Emily Carr, *Growing Pains: The Autobiography of Emily Carr* (Toronto: Clarke, Irwin, 1946): 239.

99. George Bowering, "Home Away," *B.C. Studies* 62 (Summer 1984): 9, 10.

100. Roderick Haig-Brown, "Hardy's Dorset," *Tamarack Review* 2 (Winter 1957): 52, in W. J. Keith, "Roderick Haig-Brown," *Canadian Literature* 71 (Winter 1976): 19.

101. Roderick Haig-Brown, *The Living Land: An Account of the Natural Resources of British Columbia* (Toronto: Macmillan, 1961): 237.

102. Claude Lévi-Strauss, *The Way of the Masks*, trans. Sylvia Modelski (Seattle: University of Washington Press, 1982): 3-4, 8.

103. Roy L. Carlson, "Prehistory of the Northwest Coast," in Carlson, ed., *Indian Art Traditions of the Northwest Coast* (Burnaby: Simon Fraser University, nd): 203; Knut R. Fladmark, *British Columbia Prehistory* (Ottawa: National Museum of Canada, 1986): 81-84.

104. Quoted in Doris Shadbolt, *Bill Reid* (Vancouver: Douglas & McIntyre, 1986): 25.

105. *Ibid.*, 99.

106. *Bulletin of the American Museum of Natural History* 9 (1897): 123-176; Franz Boas, *Primitive Art* (Oslo: H. Aschehoug, 1927).

107. Bill Holm, *Northwest Coast Indian Art: An Analysis of Form* (Seattle: University of Washington Press, 1965).

108. "The Story of Asdiwal," in Edmond Leach, ed., *The Structural Study of Myth and Totemism* (London: Tavistock, 1967): 1-47.

109. Lévi-Strauss, *The Way of the Masks*.

110. For example, Marjorie Halpin's "The Structure of Tsimshian Totemism," in Jay Miller and Carol Eastman, eds., *The Tsimshian and their Neighbors* (Seattle: University of Washington Press, 1984): 16-35; Stanley Walens, *Feasting with Cannibals: An Essay on Kwakiutl Cosmology* (Princeton: Princeton University Press, 1981): George Macdonald, "Cosmic Equations in Northwest Coast Art," in Donald Abbott, ed., *The World is as Sharp as a Knife*; and John Cove, *Shattered Images: Dialogues and Meditations on Tsimshian Narratives* (Ottawa: Carlton University Press, 1987).

111. Allan Pritchard, "West of the Great Divide," *Canadian Literature* (1984): 100.

CONTRIBUTORS

HUGH J. M. JOHNSTON, General Editor for *The Pacific Province*, is professor of history at Simon Fraser University and the author of *The Voyage of the Komagata Maru: The Sikh Challenge to Canada's Colour Bar* (Oxford New Delhi, 1979, 1989, and University of British Columbia Press) and (with Tara Singh Bains) *The Four Quarters of the Night: The Life Journey of an Emigrant Sikh* (McGill-Queens, 1995).

JOHN BELSHAW, who teaches at the University College of the Cariboo, has published political, social and demographic studies in British Columbia history.

ROY CARLSON is the founding chairman of Simon Fraser University's archaeology department and a leading authority on archaeological sites in British Columbia. His many publications include *Indian Art Traditions of the Northwest Coast* (Archaeology Press, 1983).

DOUGLAS COLE teaches Canadian cultural, intellectual and political history at Simon Fraser University. Among his publications are *Captured Heritage: The Scramble for Northwest Coast Artifacts* (Douglas & McIntyre, 1985) and (with Ira Chaikin) *An Iron Hand upon the People: The Law against the Potlatch on the Northwest Coast* (Douglas & McIntyre, 1990).

ROBIN FISHER chairs the department of history and is Acting Dean of Arts and Science at the University of Northern British Columbia. His books include *Contact and Conflict: Indian-European Relations in British Columbia, 1774-1880* (University of British Columbia Press, 1979) and *Duff Pattullo of British Columbia* (University of Toronto Press, 1991).

J. I. LITTLE is well known for his local studies of the society of nineteenth-century Canada. His books include *Nationalism, Capitalism and Colonization in Nineteenth Century Quebec: The Upper St. Francis District* (McGill-Queens, 1989) and *Crofters and Habitants: Settler Society, Economy and Culture in a Quebec Township, 1848-1991* (McGill-Queens, 1991).

DAVID MITCHELL is a member of the B.C. Legislative Assembly and author of *W. A. C. Bennett and the Rise of British Columbia* (Douglas & McIntyre, 1983) and *Succession: The Political Reshaping of British Columbia* (Douglas & McIntyre, 1987) .

SHARON MEEN is the Director of Academic Studies at British Columbia's Open Learning Agency with extensive experience as a university teacher and researcher in Canadian social history.

ALLEN SEAGER is a specialist in labour history at Simon Fraser University and co-author with John Herd Thompson of *Canada 1922-1930: Decades of Discovery* (McClelland & Stewart, 1985).

VERONICA STRONG-BOAG is Director of the Centre for Research in Women's Studies and Gender Relations at the University of British Columbia. Her many publications include *The New Day Recalled: Lives of Girls and Women in English Canada, 1919-1939* (Penguin, 1988) and *Rethinking Canada: The Promise of Women's History* (Copp-Clark, 1986).

INDEX